First Edition 2017

ISBN 9781983890628

FinPolNomics (Green Finance Concept)
www.finpolnomics.org
Lagos, Nigeria

Author,
Adebayo Olumuyiwa

All rights reserved. No part of this publication may be reproduced, stored in a retrieval system or transmitted, in any form or by any means, electronic, mechanical, photocopying, recording or otherwise, without the prior written permission of the Author.

The contents of this book are intended as a guide and not professional advice. Although every effort has been made to ensure that the contents of this book are correct at the time of going to press, The Author makes no warranty that the information in this book is accurate or complete and accept no liability for any loss or damage suffered by any person acting or refraining from acting as a result of the material in this book.

I am grateful to the Professional Institutes (ICAN, ACCA, CIMA, CFA and others) for the use of contents and past examination questions.

The suggested solutions in this book is the view of the Author.

© 2017 Adebayo Olumuyiwa, CFA, FRM, FICA
+234(0)802 6937 304
olumuyiwa.adebayo2017@gmail.com

Dedication

I hereby dedicate this maiden edition of my book to ALMIGHTY GOD ("The Creator of Heaven and Earth").

Also, I am using this opportunity to further dedicate this book to the following people who in one way or the other affect my life positively:

- My Wife (Gbemisola) and my Daughters (FARAmade, FARAmola and FARAsimi);
- My Parents (Mr. & Mrs. Adebayo);
- Former President Olusegun Aremu Okikiola Obasanjo, GCFR
- Former (Late) President Umaru Musa Yar'Adua, GCFR; and
- Former President Goodluck Ebele Azikiwe Jonathan, GCFR

Acknowledgment

I would like to express my deepest appreciation to all those who provided me with the possibility to complete this book. A special gratitude I give to my professional colleagues (both senior, co-ordinate and junior) for their supports (moral, intellectual and technical), especially the following: Albert Folorunsho (Omowe), Uwadiae Oduware, Taiwo Oyedele (Prof.), Adeniyi Adeniji (Oluaye), Mr T.J. Tijani, Femi Abegunde (F-ab), Toba Amoo, Olushola Olanrewaju, Seyi Olanrewaju (Mass Attack), BalaZakka, Olufemi Adekoya, Dr. Kriz David, Aro Taiwo, Robert Igben (Roy), Tope Awe, Samuel Alonge, Reverend Emmanuel Alagbe, Rasheed Adam (Layowe) AbdhakeemBashorun (Bash), KareemKamilu, Abiodun Olugbenga (Abbey Wonder), Muritala Okunade, Ayo Oni (MoG), Mr Olawin (JAO Global), Mr. AbdullahiRasaq (De Gynaecologist), OdekunleMusibau (Prof.), Michael Ogunmuko, CharlesAkharayi, Dr. Waidi Gbadamosi, Festus Izevbizua, Bode Ashogbon, Tony Clever, SighanMustapha, Tosin Sanni, Olubukola Ogunleye, Steve Nwokocha, Idris Onibudo, Adesoji Adebayo, Tobi Sonowo, Owoyomi Abayomi, Paul Durosaro, Israel Nnanna, Oluseyi Simon Akinjobi, Osasere Collins Eguakun, UyiIzekor, Abisoye Adekoya, Seun Onanuga, Bolanle Onawunmi, Bolanle Rufa, Chinedu Okpareke, Ayodeji Adegbite, Obafemi Abidoye, Elder Ojo, LayiAdekanola, Mr Omojola (Omoje), Mr Adeosun (Pally), Snr. John Nwafa, KolawoleAbass, Femi Longe, JideOnabajo, BiodunAyinde, DejiOriola, FunmiNetufo-Oriola, Mariam Biliaminu, Uade Ahimie, GbengaAdepetu, GbengaAdekola, GbengaFarinde, Alex Ezurum, Kola Motajo, Moses Okunola, Folashade Ojikutu-Opokiti, Ita Onofiok, Nomnso Dike, Seqinah Akinwunmi, Bukola Salako, Folasade Akinoso, Abisola Akinsola, Amaka Chijioke-Osueze, ChinenyeChijioke-Osueze; Ademola Johnson, Ayobami Oyewole, Adenike Adeyemi, Kayode Agunbiade, Rekiyat Edinbus, Olabanke Olaleye, Odunayo Olasanmi, Boladale Bakare, Ohiseme Ozoya, Hyelhara Sajou, Olayinka Olusoga, Oluseyi Fasoro, Sasaenia Omilabu, Manuela Bamgbose-Martins, Seyi Williams, Omolola Osotimehin, Martin Orogun, Bunmi Olukoju, Bunmi Fafiyebi, Gbemileke Iledare, Dare Adekoya, Adedamola Oyeneyin, Emmanuel Oriade, Dairo Damilola, Ruth Olatunbosun, Olaoluwa Oyelade, Kingsley Agwu, Taiwo Yusuf, Oluwamese Dare, Emmanuel Udu, Omobowale Odofin, Adeshina Shojupe and Johnson Sanya.

Furthermore, I would also like to acknowledge with much appreciation the crucial role of my spiritual father (Reverend, Dr. TunjiBamgbose), my siblings Folashade Adebayo, Adetola Ajibola, Leye Adebayo and DapoAgoro; the WySE Associate's Registrar (Mr AkinpeluOluyemi)and the entire staff of WySE Associates Limited, who at all times provide necessary support and guidance.

Special thanks to my bosses and professional advisors at various times including Dr Erastus Akingbola, HettyDambo (Mrs.), OyekunleOyesola, Joseph Dauda, LekanOlofinlade, Shola Akinnukawe, Ade Odunsi, Kola Adesina, Tope Shonubi, Tonye Cole, Engr. James Ogungbemi, Mallam BubaLawan, Aigbe Olotu, Dr Anthony Youdeowei, Wale Ajibade, Moroti Adedoyin-Adeyinka (Mrs.), Dr George Oluwande, Mr DuroBabjide, Dr (Mrs)H.N.Akubuiro, Mrs Eniola, DrAdebakin, Oluyemi Adekunle (Mrs), Adeoye (Mrs), Ifeanyi Ogbonna, Aina Oluleke, O.S. Busari, C.A.Taiwo, FadipeAdeniyi Olubunmi (Major), Prof. Rufus Olowe, Prof. Rasheed Kola Ojikutu, Prof. AmoduDala, Prof. Ade Ibiwoye, ShiroAbass, Prof. Ayorinde, Dr Timmy Obiwuru, Dr. Adeleke, Peter Mbah (CEO, Pinnacle Oil & Gas), I.T.T. Jimoh, Michael Adeniyi (Murphy), ObatoshoObarinde (OBA), Adeoye Adebayo, Adekunle Adebayo, AderogbaAdeshakin, Adeyemi Ademola-Adeshakin, Adegbenro Adeshakin, Mrs. Idowu Oluwamese, and my in-laws (Mr. OlumideOsire, Mrs. BosedeOsire, LoluOsre, and WunmiOsire).

Last but not least, many thanks go to my friends and other colleagues who have provided different supports to me at all times. They include DapoAdebambi, Femi Sonowo,Tunji Afolabi, Adewale Obarinde, Israel Nnanna, Malik Mohammed, Diana Smart-Nwajiaku, Kemi Shobowale (K-show), Bode Afolayan, GbemisolaAisida, Femi Adeniran, Tunji Adeniran, LekanOlawore, MosunmolaObarinde, Doyin Obarinde, SemiuAnjorin, Joel Tella, SakiruFashola, Shola Adewunmi, Dupe, Omobolanle Oguntimehin, Anthony Kuforiji, Nkemdilim Oguchi, Anthony Odumuyiwa, Babatunde Osadare, Amani Emeson, Abiola Ogunleye, Ibukun Konu, Emmanuel Gbahabo, Bethel Obioma, Emmanuel Magani, Akinkunmi Akinnola, Ogochukwu Onyelucheya, Omolola Jaiyesimi, Aliyu Buba, Bunmi Isijola, Cordilia Aigbomian, Idakwo Shaibu, Osarieme Oke-Ifidon, Awoyemi Awoyokun, Nunayon Samuel, Kelechi Emenike, Bolanle Balogun, David Nwokoro, Samuel Whenu, Kingsley Alabi, Ayuba Gadzama, Jessical Obot, Tomi Daramola, Ejiro Gray, Ibienne Okeleke, Ifeoma Okoruen, Olaoluwa Orekha, Kelechi Johnson, Tunji Kuforiji, Ehimai Louis-Domeih, Owolabi Dawodu, Pearl Uzokwe, Victoria Loko, Efuru Nwakuche, Abibat Sunbola, Oluwabukola Mafe, Adebayo Adeniran, Dare Ogunrinde, Tayo Orisadare, Monday Salifu, Damilola Jibunoh, Edmund Carl Eduah, Oluwawemimo Adetayo, Emeka Kachikwu, Olasoji Fagbola, Babatomiwa Adesida, Oluseyi Ojurongbe, Henry Nwobodo, Henry Anozie, Oyekanmi Odujinrin, Adekanmi Adeshola, Sandra Iyoha, Olayinka Aliu, AdelaniAdeniyi, Rafiu Kazeem, ElemoshoAbidemi Oluseyi, Adeniran Olaleye, Kingsley Oguike, Trust Ojeiwa, Debo, KolawoleSakiru, Late Tunde Gbajabiamila, UgochukwuNwanuguo, OyebuchiIzuagwu, EchikaObianuju, Funmi Balogun, JolaoluFakoya, Abayomi Fakoya, Felicia Oyewunmi, and Bolaji Ajayi-Adesina.

Forward

The health of any business can be measured using different parameters; one of which is the financial statements of the company.

Contemporaneous Accounting for Business Combinations and Group Accounts encapsulates the body of knowledge in the principles and practices of assessing the critical variables in a diversified portfolio of business which exemplifies focused, intense and accurate reflection of the reality of the businesses for decision makers, investors, regulatory authorities, academicians, professionals in the field of accounting and finance, students of accounting and finance, auditors, and preparer of group accounts.

Reading through and digesting plus applying the methodologies adopted in this book will add value to the improvement and dynamics of international financial reporting and global best practices in accounting for business combinations and group accounts.

Let's measure, account and report well.

Kola Adesina
Chairman, EGBIN Power Plc

Chapter Listing

CHAPTER 1
Introduction to Intercorporate Investments and Basic Concepts of Business Combinations (Including Regulatory – Local and International Requirements)

CHAPTER 2
Basic Principles of Group Accounts

CHAPTER 3
Accounting for Investment in Parent's [Separate] Statement of Financial Position

CHAPTER 4
Introduction to Basic Consolidation Mechanics and Principles

CHAPTER 5
Accounting for Goodwill and Gain on Bargain Purchase

CHAPTER 6
Accounting for Mid-Year Acquisition and Preference Share Capital

CHAPTER 7
Fair Value Measurement in Business Combinations and Group Accounts

CHAPTER 8
Other Principles in Business Combinations Accounting and Group Accounts

CHAPTER 9
Adjustments in Group Accounts

CHAPTER 10
Extension of Basic Consolidation Mechanics and Principles in the Preparation of Statement of Profit or Loss and Other Comprehensive Income; and Statement of Changes in Equity

CHAPTER 11
Accounting for Investment in Associates and Joint Ventures

CHAPTER 12
Introduction to Accounting for Fellow Subsidiaries in a Group Structure

CHAPTER 13
Disclosure of Interests in Other Entities

CHAPTER 14
Guidance on End-of-Chapter Exercises

CHAPTER 15
Comprehensive Exercises

Table Of Content

Introduction to Intercorporate Investments and Basic Concepts of Business Combinations (Including Regulatory – Local and International Requirements)	7
Basic Principles of Group Accounts	40
Accounting for Investment in Parent's (Separate) Statement of Financial Position	65
Basic Principles of Group Accounts	77
Accounting for Goodwill and Gain on Bargain Purchase	94
Accounting for Mid-Year Acquisition and Preference Share Capital	132
Fair Value of Subsidiary's Net Assets on Acquisition	148
Other Principles in Business Combination Accounting and Group Accounts	178
Adjustments in Group Accounts	198
Extension of Basic Consolidation Mechanics and Principles in the Preparation of Statement of Profit or Loss and Other Comprehensive Income; and Statement of Changes in Equity	304
Investment in Associates and Joint Ventures	375
Introduction to Accounting for Fellow Subsidiaries in a Group Structure	393
Disclosure of Interests in Other Entities	402
Guidance on End-of-Chapter Exercises	407
Comprehensive Exercises	427
Bibliography	460
INDEX	461

Chapter 1

Introduction to Intercorporate Investments and Basic Concepts of Business Combinations
(including Regulatory - Local and International Requirements)

INTRODUCTION

This chapter will make the readers have fundamental understanding of the genesis of most of the business combinations in the most recent times; and also to have a clear picture of the forms of investments made by some entities in other entities and how these investments are being accounted for in the financial statements of the investing entities.

In this chapter, a consideration of the regulatory framework and legal requirements regarding accounting for acquisitions, mergers, and enlarge "Business Combinations", and which are to be reviewed within the context of International Financial Reporting Standards (IFRS) and Companies and Allied Matters Act (CAMA) CAP C20, LFN (2004 as amended).

Intercorporate Investments represent an important component of management strategy, which involves a company investing in other companies to achieve diversification, growth, and competitive advantage, but the structure and scope of these investments create comparability challenges for the potential investors', analysts, and the investing public at large. [1]Inter-corporate investments can have a significant impact on the investing entity's financial performance and position. Companies invest in the *debt* and *equity securities* of other companies to diversify their *asset base, enter new markets, obtain competitive advantages, and achieve additional profitability.*

Debt securities include commercial papers, corporate and government bonds and notes, redeemable preferred stocks, and asset-backed securities. **Equity securities** include common stocks (otherwise known as ordinary or equity shares) and irredeemable preferred stocks. The percentage of equity ownership a company acquires in an investee depends on the resources available, the ability to acquire the shares, and the desired level of influence or control.

Intercorporate Investments can substantially be categorised as *Minority Passive, Minority Active and Controlling Interest Investments*, while the fourth category is *Joint Venture/Arrangement* which involves *common and joint control*.

Percentage of ownership (*or voting rights*) is typically used to determine the appropriate category for financial reporting purposes, except in some extreme identifiable situations. *However, the ownership percentage is only a guide (which is based on a rebuttable presumption) and may not necessarily be the benchmark (as it will be discussed later in this text)*. Ultimately, the category of investment is based on the investor's ability to exert *significant influence, joint control or control* the investee.

DEFINITION of 'intercorporate Investment'
Securities that are purchased by corporations rather than individual investors. Intercorporate investments allow a company to achieve higher growth rates compared to keeping all of its funds in cash. These investments can also be used for strategic purposes like forming a joint ventures or making acquisitions. Companies purchase securities from other companies, banks and governments in order to take advantage of the returns from these securities. Marketable securities that can readily be exchanged for cash, such as notes and stocks, are usually preferred fro this type of investment.

BREAKING DOWN 'Intercorporate Investment'
Intercorporate investments are accounted for differently than other funds held by a company. Short-term investments that are expected to be turned into cash are considered current assets, while other investments are considered non-current assets. When companies buy intercorporate investments, divided and interest revenue is reported on the income statement.

- By Investopedia

---
1 An excerpt from Level II Volume 2 Financial Reporting and Analysis, 5th Edition. Pearson Learning Solutions.

Minority Passive:
A company's ownership interest of less than 20% in the equity of another company can be considered a passive investment. In this case, the investor cannot *significantly influence or control the investee*. Minority passive investments are classified in accordance with *IAS 39 (Financial Instruments- recognition and measurement of financial assets)* or *IFRS 9 (where it has early adopted the standard)* in the statement of financial position; when and only when the entity becomes a party to the contractual provisions of the instrument. The *Equity Instruments* can be classified as *financial assets* in the *individual statement of the financial position* of the investor. Equity financial assets will now to be measured at fair value at initial recognition (*IAS 39/IFRS 9*), while subsequent measurement at *"fair value through profit or loss (FVTPL), and fair value through other comprehensive income (FVOCI)"*, will depend on the objective evidence to which the financial asset is held vis-à-vis other fundamentals (including Business Models).

Minority Active:
An ownership interest between 20% and 50% is technically regarded as non-controlling investment for consolidation purposes. However, the investor is considered to have *significant influence* in the investee's business operations and decisions. *Significantly influence* can be evidenced by the following:

- *Board of Directors representation.*
- *Involvement in policy making.*
- *Material inter-corporate transactions.*
- *Interchange of managerial personnel.*
- *Dependence on Technology.*

It is possible to have significant influence with less than 20% ownership, but much more in an extreme case as considered in *IAS 28 (Interest in Associate and Joint Venture)*. In this case, the investment is considered *minority active (investment in associate)*. Conversely, without significant influence, an ownership interest between 20% and 50% is considered *minority passive (investment in financial assets)*. Interests in associates and joint entities will now to be accounted for using *Equity Method* (based on the revised position of *IAS 28* which became *effective January 1, 2013*), as opposed to the requirement of the withdrawn standard - *IAS 31 (Interests in joint ventures)* where the method of *proportionate consolidation* was permitted.

Controlling Interest:
An ownership interest of *more than 50%* in the voting rights of an entity (usually ascertained through shareholdings) is known as *controlling interest investment*. When the investor can control the investee, the *consolidation method (acquisition method)* is adopted. In accordance with the *"principle of substance over form"*, the relationship of the parent and subsidiary from the economic point of view is considered a single economic unit even when from the legal point of view; every company is a separate entity.

It is possible to own more than 50% of an investee and **control** *does not exist*. For example, control can be *temporary* or barriers may exist such as *bankruptcy, administration or government intervention*. In these identified scenarios, the investment may not be considered a **Controlling Interest**.

Conversely, it is possible to control with less than a 50% ownership interest in the equity of the subsidiary, and invariably the investment may be considered controlling interest as contained in *IFRS 3 (Revised in 2008) – Business Combinations,* and accounted for in the same way as required by *IFRS 10 (Consolidated Financial Statements).*

Joint Ventures/Entities:

A *joint venture/entity* is an entity where control is *shared* by *two or more investors*. Under *International Financial Reporting Standards (IFRS): IAS 28 (Revised in 2011) - Interests in Associates and Joint Ventures*, the only recommended method of accounting for such interests in joint entities is the **Equity Method**. The *proportionate consolidation* (as *contained in withdrawn IAS 31 – Interests in Joint Venture*) is no longer required *effective January 1, 2013*.

Accounting for Equity Investments

Ownership	Degree of Influence	Accounting Treatments
Less than 20% (Minority Passive/Investments in Financial Assets)	*No Significant Influence*	Equity Instruments – accounted for at, fair value through profit or loss, and fair value through other comprehensive income.
20% - 50% (Minority Active/Associate)	*Significant Influence*	Equity Method
More than 50% (Controlling Interests/Subsidiary)	*Control*	Consolidation through Acquisition Method
50/50 Interests (Joint Venture)	*Common/Joint Control*	Equity Method

REGULATORY REQUIREMENTS

International Financial Reporting Standards (IFRSs) as issued by the International Accounting Standard Board (IASB) provides detailed guidance on accounting for all forms of business combinations and similar intercorporate investments that are not considered a business combination.

The following standards give credence in the accounting for all forms of intercorporate investments and business combinations.

1. IAS 27 – Separate Financial Statements
2. IAS 28 – Accounting for Investment in Associates and Joint Ventures
3. IAS 32 – Financial Instruments (Presentation)
4. IAS 39 – Financial Instruments (Recognition and Measurement)
5. IFRS 3 – Business Combinations
6. IFRS 9 – Financial Instruments
7. IFRS 10 – Consolidated Financial Statements
8. IFRS 11 – Joint Arrangements
9. IFRS 12 – Disclosures of Interest in Other Entities
10. IFRS 13 – Fair Value Measurement

IAS 27 – Separate Financial Statements

IAS 27 contains accounting and disclosure requirements for investments in subsidiaries, joint ventures and associates when an entity prepares separate financial statements. The Standard requires an entity preparing separate financial statements to account for those investments either at cost, fair value in accordance with IAS 39/IFRS 9 Financial Instruments, or using the equity method under IAS 28.

IAS 27 applies to accounting for investments in subsidiaries, joint ventures and associates when an entity elects or is required by local regulations, to present separate financial statements. This Standard does not mandate which entities produce separate financial statements. It applies when an entity prepares separate financial statements that comply with International Financial Reporting Standards.

IAS 28 – Accounting for Investment in Associates and Joint Ventures

IAS 28 prescribes the accounting for investments in associates and sets out the requirements for the application of the equity method when accounting for investments in associates and joint ventures. The standard is to be applied by all entities that are investors with joint control of, or significant influence over, an investee.

The Standard defines significant influence as the power to participate in the financial and operating policy decisions of the investee but is not control or joint control of those policies.

IAS 32 – Financial Instruments (Presentation)

The objective of IAS 32 is to establish principles for presenting financial instruments as liabilities or equity and for offsetting financial assets and financial liabilities. It applies to the classification of financial instruments, from the perspective of the issuer, into financial assets, financial liabilities and equity instruments; the classification of related interest, dividends, losses and gains; and the circumstances in which financial assets and financial liabilities should be offset.

The principles in this Standard complement the principles for recognising and measuring financial assets and financial liabilities in IFRS 9 Financial Instruments, and for disclosing information about them in IFRS 7 Financial Instruments: Disclosures.

IAS 39 – Financial Instruments (Recognition and Measurement)

The objective of IAS 39 is to establish principles for recognising and measuring financial assets, financial liabilities and some contracts to buy or sell non-financial items. Requirements for presenting information about financial instruments are in IAS 32 Financial Instruments: Presentation. Requirements for disclosing information about financial instruments are in IFRS 7 Financial Instruments: Disclosures.

IFRS 3 – Business Combinations

The objective of IFRS 3 is to improve the relevance, reliability and comparability of the information that a reporting entity provides in its financial statements about a business combination and its effects. To accomplish that, IFRS 3 establishes principles and requirements for how the acquirer:

- Recognises and measures in its financial statements the identifiable assets acquired, the liabilities assumed and any non-controlling interest in the acquiree;
- Recognises and measures the goodwill acquired in the business combination or a gain from a bargain purchase; and
- Determines what information to disclose to enable users of the financial statements to evaluate the nature and financial effects of the business combination.

IFRS 9 – Financial Instruments

The objective of IFRS 9 is to establish principles for the financial reporting of financial assets and financial liabilities that will present relevant and useful information to users of financial statements for their assessment of the amounts, timing and uncertainty of an entity's future cash flows.

- Recognises and measures in its financial statements the identifiable assets acquired, the liabilities assumed and any non-controlling interest in the acquiree;
- Recognises and measures the goodwill acquired in the business combination or a gain from a bargain purchase; and
- Determines what information to disclose to enable users of the financial statements to evaluate the nature and financial effects of the business combination.

IFRS 10 – Consolidated Financial Statements

The objective of this IFRS is to establish principles for the presentation and preparation of consolidated financial statements when an entity controls one or more other entities.

To meet the objective stated above, IFRS 10:

- Requires an entity (the parent) that controls one or more other entities (subsidiaries) to present consolidated financial statements;
- Defines the principle of control, and establishes control as the basis for consolidation;
- Sets out how to apply the principle of control to identify whether an investor controls an investee and therefore must consolidate the investee;
- Sets out the accounting requirements for the preparation of consolidated financial statements; and
- Defines an investment entity and sets out an exception to consolidating particular subsidiaries of an investment entity.

IFRS 10 does not deal with the accounting requirements for business combinations and their effect on consolidation, including goodwill arising on a business combination.

IFRS 11 – Joint Arrangements

The objective of this IFRS is to establish principles for financial reporting by entities that have an interest in arrangements that are controlled jointly (i.e. joint arrangements).

To meet the objective stated above, IFRS 11 defines joint control and requires an entity that is a party to a joint arrangement to determine the type of joint arrangement in which it is involved by assessing its rights and obligations and to account for those rights and obligations in accordance with that type of joint arrangement.

IFRS 12 – Disclosures of Interest in Other Entities

The objective of this IFRS is to require an entity to disclose information that enables users of its financial statements to evaluate:
(a) The nature of and risks associated with, its interests in other entities; and
(b) The effects of those interests on its financial position, financial performance and cash flows.

Requirement of the Companies and Allied Matters Act (CAP C20, LFN 2004 as amended)

In Nigeria context, the foremost requirement to prepare Group Accounts is coined out of the provisions of the Companies and Allied Matters Act of 2004 (as amended). CAMA saddled the whole responsibilities of the preparation of Group Accounts with the Directors of the company as constituted by a Board (i.e. Board of Directors).

The underlying provisions of the Act (i.e. CAMA 2004 as amended) depict requirements that govern the preparation of Group Accounts.

Section 331 – Companies to keep accounting records

(1) Every company shall cause accounting records to be kept in accordance with this section.

(2) The accounting records shall be sufficient to show and explain the transactions of the company and shall be such as to-
(a) Disclose with reasonable accuracy, at any time, the financial position of the company; and
(b) Enable the directors to ensure that any financial statements prepared under this Part comply with the requirements of this Act as to the form and content of the company's financial statements.

(3) The accounting records shall, in particular, contain:
(a) Entries from day to day of all sums of money received and expended by the company, and the matters in respect of which the receipt and expenditure took place; and
(b) A record of the assets and liabilities of the company.

(4) If the business of the company involves dealing in goods, the accounting records shall contain:
(a) Statements of stocks held by the company at the end of each year of the company;
(b) All statements of stock-takings from which any such statement of stock as is mentioned in paragraph (a) of this subsection has been or is to be prepared; and
(c) Except in the case of goods sold by way of ordinary retail trade, statements of all goods sold and purchased, showing the goods and the buyers and sellers in sufficient detail to enable all these to be identified.

Section 334 – Directors' duty to prepare annual accounts

(1) In the case of every company, the directors shall in respect of each year of the company, prepare financial statements for the year.

(2) Subject to subsection (3) of this section, the financial statements required under subsection (1) of this section shall include-

(a) Statement of the accounting policies;
(b) The balance sheet as at the last day of the year;
(c) A profit and loss account or, in the case of a company not trading for profit, an income and expenditure account for the year;
(d) Notes on the accounts;
(e) The auditors' reports;
(f) The directors' report;
(g) A statement of the source and application of fund;
(h) A value-added statement for the year;
(i) A five-year financial summary; and
(j) In the case of a holding company, the group financial statements.

(3) The financial statements of a private company need not include the matters stated in paragraphs (a), (g), (h) and (i) of subsection (2) of this section.

(4) The directors shall at their first meeting after the incorporation of the company, determine what date in each year financial statements shall be made up, and they shall give notice of the date to the Commission within 14 days of the determination.

(5) In the case of a holding company, the directors shall ensure that, except where in their opinion there are good reasons against it, the year of each of its subsidiaries shall coincide with the year of the company.

Section 335 – Form and content of individual financial statements

(1) The financial statements of a company prepared under section 334 of this Act, shall comply with the requirements of the Second Schedule to this Act (so far as applicable) with respect to their form and content, and with the accounting standards laid down in the Statements of Accounting Standards issued from time to time by the Nigerian Accounting Standards Board to be constituted by the Minister after due consultation with such accounting bodies as he may deem fit in circumstances for this purposes: Provided that such accounting standards do not conflict with the provisions of this Act or the Second Schedule to this Act.

(2) The balance sheet shall give a true and fair view of the state of affairs of the company as at the end of the year, and the profit and loss account shall give a true and fair view of the profit or loss of the company for the year.

(3) The statement of the source and application of funds shall provide information on the generation and utilisation of funds by the company during the year.

(4) The value added statement shall report the wealth created by the company during the year and its distribution among various interest groups such as the employees, the government, creditors, proprietors and the company.

(5) The five-year financial summary shall provide a report for a comparison over a period of five years or more of vital financial information.

(6) Subsection (2) of this section shall override-

(a) The requirements of the Second Schedule to this Act; and
(b) All other requirements of this Act as to the matters to be included in the accounts of a company or in notes to those accounts, and accordingly, the provisions of subsections (7) and (8) of this section shall have an effect.

(7) If the balance sheet or profit and loss account is drawn up in accordance with those requirements would not provide sufficient information to comply with subsection (2) of this section, any necessary additional information shall be provided in that balance sheet or profit and loss account, or in a note to the accounts.

(8) If, owing to special circumstances in the case of any company, compliance with any such requirement in relation to the balance sheet or profit and loss account would prevent compliance with subsection (2) of this section, (even if additional information was provided in accordance with subsection (4) of this section), the directors shall depart from that requirement in preparing the balance sheet or profit and loss account (so far as necessary) in order to comply with subsection (2) of this section.

(9) If the directors depart from any such requirement, particulars of the departure, the reasons for it and its effects shall be given in a note to the accounts.

(10) Subsections (1) to (9) of this section shall not apply to group accounts prepared under section 336 of this Act and subsections (1) and (2) of this section shall apply to a company's profit and loss account (or require the notes otherwise required in relation to that account) if-

(a) The company has subsidiaries; and
(b) The profit and loss account is framed as a consolidated account dealing with all or any of the subsidiaries of the company as well as the company-
  (i) Complies with the requirements of this Act relating to consolidated profit and loss account; and
  (ii) Shows how much of the consolidated profit and loss for the year is dealt with in the individual financial statements of the company.

(11) If group financial statements are prepared and the advantage is taken of subsection (7) of this section, that fact shall be disclosed in a note to the group financial statements.

Section 336 – Group financial statements of holding company

(1) If at the end of a year a company has subsidiaries, the directors shall, as well as preparing individual accounts for that year, also prepare group financial statements being accounts or statements which deal with the state of affairs and profit or loss of the company and the subsidiaries.

(2) The provisions of subsection (1) of this section shall not apply if the company is a wholly owned subsidiary of another body corporate incorporated in Nigeria.

(3) A group financial statement may not deal with a subsidiary if the directors of the company are of the opinion that-

(a) It is impracticable, or would be of no real value to the members, in view of the insignificant amounts involved; or
(b) It would involve expense or delay out of proportion to its value to members of the company; or
(c) The result would be misleading, or harmful to the business of the company or any of its subsidiaries; or
(d) The business of the holding company and that of the subsidiary are so different that they cannot reasonably be treated as a single undertaking.

(4) The group financial statements of a company shall consist of a consolidated- (a) balance sheet dealing with the state of affairs of the company and all the subsidiaries of the company; and (b) profit and loss account of the company and its subsidiaries.

(5) If the directors are of the opinion that it is better for the purpose of presenting the same or equivalent information about the state of affairs and profit or loss of the company and its subsidiaries, and that to so present it may be readily appreciated by the members of the company, the group financial statements may be prepared in a form not consistent with subsection (1) of this section and in particular the group financial statement may consist of-

(a) More than one set of consolidated financial statements dealing respectively with the company and one group of subsidiaries and with other groups of subsidiaries; or
(b) Separate financial statements dealing with each of the subsidiaries; or

(c) Statements expanding the information about the subsidiaries in individual financial statements of the company, or in any other form.

(6) The group financial statements may be wholly or partly incorporated in the individual balance sheet and profit and loss account of the holding company.

Section 337 – Form and content of group financial statements

(1) The group financial statements of a holding company shall comply with the requirements of the Second Schedule to this Act, so far as applicable to group financial statements in the form in which those accounts are prepared with respect to the form and content of those statements and any additional information to be provided by way of notes to those accounts.

(2) Group financial statements together with any notes thereon shall give a true and fair view of the state of affairs and profit or loss of the company and the subsidiaries dealt with by those statements as a whole.

(3) Subsection (2) of this section shall override-

(a) The requirements of the Second Schedule to this Act; and
(b) All the requirements of this Act as to the matters to be included in group financial statements or in notes to those statements and accordingly subsections (4) and (5) of this section shall have an effect.

(4) If group financial statements are not in accordance with the requirements of this Act by not providing sufficient information in compliance with subsection (2) of this section, any necessary additional information shall be provided in, or in a note to, the group financial statements.

(5) If, owing to special circumstances in the case of any company, compliance with any such requirements in relation to its group financial statements would prevent the statements from complying with subsection (2) of this section, (even if additional information were provided in accordance with subsection (4) of this section, the directors may depart from that requirement in preparing the group financial statements).

Section 338 – Meaning of "holding company", "subsidiary" and "wholly-owned subsidiary"

(1) Subject to subsection (4) of this section, a company shall for the purposes of this Act be deemed to be a subsidiary of another company if-
(a) The company-
    (i) Are a member of it and controls the composition of its board of directors; or
    (ii) Holds more than half in nominal value of its equity share capital; or
(b) The first-mentioned company is a subsidiary of any company which is that other's subsidiary.

(2) For the purposes of subsection (1) of this section, the composition of the board of directors of a company shall be deemed to be controlled by another company if that other company by the exercise of some power, without the consent or concurrence of any other person, can appoint or remove the holders of all or majority of the directors.

(3) For purposes of subsection (2) of this section, the other company shall be deemed to have the power to appoint a director with respect to which any of the following conditions is satisfied that-

(a) A person cannot be appointed to it without the exercise in his favour by the other company of such power as is mentioned in this section; or

Introduction to Intercorporate Investments and Basic Concepts of Business Combinations

(b) The appointment of a person to the directorship follows necessarily from his appointment as director of the other company; or

(c) The directorship is held by the other company itself or by a subsidiary of it.

(4) In determining whether one company is a subsidiary of another-

(a) Any shares held or power exercisable by the other in a fiduciary capacity shall be treated as not held or exercisable by it;

(b) Subject to paragraphs (c) and (d) of this subsection, any shares held or power exercisable-
  (i) By any person as nominee for the other (except where the other is concerned only in a fiduciary capacity); or
  (ii) By, or by a nominee for, a subsidiary or the other (not being a subsidiary which is concerned only in a fiduciary capacity), shall be treated as held or exercisable by the other;

(c) Any shares held or power exercisable by any person by virtue of the provisions of any debentures of the first- mentioned company or of a trust deed for securing any issue of such debentures shall be disregarded;

(d) any shares held or power exercisable by, or by a nominee for, the other or its subsidiary (not being held or exercisable as mentioned in paragraph (c) of this subsection), shall be treated as not held or exercisable by the other, if the ordinary business of the other or its subsidiary (as the case may be) includes the lending of money and the shares are held or the power is exercisable as above mentioned by way of security only for the purposes of a transaction entered into in the ordinary course of that business.

(5) For the purposes of this Act-

(a) A company shall be deemed to be the holding company of another, if the other is its subsidiary; and

(b) A body corporate shall be deemed to be the wholly-owned subsidiary of another if it has no member except that other and that other's wholly owned subsidiaries are its or their nominees.

(6) In this section, "company" includes any body corporate.

Section 339 – Additional disclosure required in notes to financial statements

(1) The additional matters contained in the Third Schedule to this Act shall be disclosed in the company's financial statements for the year; and in that Schedule, where a thing is required to be stated or shown or information is required to be given, it shall be construed to mean that the thing shall be stated or shown, or the information is to be given in a note to those statements.

(2) In the Third Schedule to this Act-

(3) (a) Parts I and II deal respectively with the disclosure of particulars of the subsidiaries of the company and its shareholders;
(b) Part III deals with the disclosure of financial information relating to subsidiaries;
(c) Part IV requires a subsidiary company to disclose its ultimate holding company;
(d) Part V deals with the emoluments of directors, including emoluments waived, pensions of directors and compensation for loss of office to directors and past directors; and
(e) Part VI deals with disclosure of the number of the employees of the company who are remunerated at higher rates.

(4) Whenever it is stated in the Third Schedule to this Act that this subsection shall apply to certain particulars or information, the particulars or information shall be annexed to the annual return

first made by the company after copies of its financial statements have been laid before its shareholders in a general meeting and if a company fails to satisfy an obligation thus imposed, the company and every officer of it who is in default shall be guilty of an offence and liable to a fine of ₦50 and for continued contravention, to a daily default fine of ₦10.

(5) It shall be the duty of any director of a company to give notice to the company of such matters relating to himself as may be necessary for the purposes of Part V of the Third Schedule to this Act and this applies to persons who are or have at any time in the preceding three years been officers as it applies to directors.

(6) A person, who makes default in complying with the provisions of subsection (4) of this section, shall be guilty of an offence and liable to a fine of ₦10 for every day during which the default continues.

Technical Note:

Based on the enactment of the Financial Reporting Council (FRC) Act of 2011; International Financial Reporting Standards (IFRS) takes prominence over other existing legislations or Act that conflict with its requirement on all financial reporting matters. FRC Act 2011 establishes the formal and legislative adoption of IFRS with the first phase of its adoption being the period ended 31 December 2012.

In the situation of where there seems to be a conflict between the requirement of IFRSs (and its Interpretations, Conceptual Framework and Relevant Guidance as issued from time to time by the International Accounting Standard Board and the IFRS Interpretation Committee) and the provisions of CAMA 2004 (as amended; the requirement of IFRS supersedes the provision of CAMA 2004 (as amended).

Where there are no conflicts in the requirements and provisions of IFRSs and CAMA 2004 (as amended); IFRS requirements serves as "minimum requirement(s)"; and the additional provisions of CAMA should be complied with, and detail disclosure of the fact may be required in some instances such as those identified below.

Section 332, subsection 2 requires the disclosure of the listed items (as shown below) within the [consolidated] financial statements of a Company and a Group, which are in additions to the components of the financial statements as required by IAS 1 (Presentation of Financial Statements')

- The auditors' reports;
- The directors' report;
- A value-added statement for the year; and
- A five-year financial summary; and

*The requirement of CAMA 2004 (as amended) is far reaching as it requires beyond disclosures and presentation of financial statements, but equally, demands other reports that may be considered to entails a form of "**Integrated Reporting**[2]". Hence, the requirement is to prepare and present "Annual Accounts and Reports". Those statements or otherwise that are no IFRS requirement may be disclosed separately from IFRS Financial Statements within the same document, sometimes tagged "Annual Accounts and Reports".*

---

[2] **Integrated Reporting:** An integrated report is a concise communication about how an organization's strategy, governance, performance and prospects, in the context of its external environment, lead to the creation of value in the short, medium and long term.

BUSINESS COMBINATIONS

IFRS 3 Business Combinations outline the accounting when an acquirer obtains control of a business (*e.g. an acquisition or merger*). Such business combinations are accounted for using the *'acquisition method'*, which generally requires assets acquired and liabilities assumed to be measured at their fair value at the acquisition date.

Business Combination entails "a transaction or other event in which an **acquirer** obtains control of one or more **businesses**. Transactions sometimes referred to as '*true mergers*' or '*mergers of equals*' are also **business combinations** as that term is used in *IFRS 3*".

Definition of a Business

An integrated set of activities and assets that is capable of being conducted and managed for the purpose of providing a return in the form of dividends, lower costs or other economic benefits directly to investors or other owners, members or participants.

A business consists of inputs and processes applied to those inputs that have the ability to create outputs. Although businesses usually have outputs, outputs are not required for an integrated set to qualify as a business. The three elements of a business are defined as follows:

- **Input:** Any economic resource that creates, or has the ability to create, outputs when one or more processes are applied to it. Examples include non-current assets (including intangible assets or rights to use non-current assets), intellectual property, and the ability to obtain access to necessary materials or rights and employees.

- **Process:** Any system, standard, protocol, convention or rule that when applied to an input or inputs, creates or has the ability to create outputs. Examples include strategic management processes, operational processes and resource management processes. These processes typically are documented, but an organised workforce having the necessary skills and experience following rules and conventions may provide the necessary processes that are capable of being applied to inputs to create outputs. (Accounting, billing, payroll and other administrative systems typically are not processes used to create outputs.)

- **Output:** The result of inputs and processes applied to those inputs that provide or have the ability to provide a return in the form of dividends, lower costs or other economic benefits directly to investors or other owners, members or participants.

To be capable of being conducted and managed for the purposes defined, an integrated set of activities and assets requires two essential elements—inputs and processes applied to those inputs, which together are or will be used to create outputs. However, a business need not include all of the inputs or processes that the seller used in operating that business if market participants are capable of acquiring the business and continuing to produce outputs, for example, by integrating the business with their own inputs and processes.

The nature of the elements of a business varies by industry and by the structure of an entity's operations (activities), including the entity's stage of development.

Established businesses often have many different types of inputs, processes and outputs, whereas new businesses often have few inputs and processes and sometimes only a single output (product). Nearly all businesses also have liabilities, but a business need not have liabilities.

An integrated set of activities and assets in the development stage might not have outputs. If not, the acquirer should consider other factors to determine whether the set is a business. Those factors include, but are not limited to, whether the set:

- Has begun planned principal activities;
- Has employees, intellectual property and other inputs and processes that could be applied to those inputs;
- Is pursuing a plan to produce outputs; and
- Will be able to obtain access to customers that will purchase the outputs.

Technical Note:
Not all of those factors need to be present for a particular integrated set of activities and assets in the development stage to qualify as a business.

Determining whether a particular set of assets and activities is a business should be based on whether the integrated set is capable of being conducted and managed as a business by a market participant. Thus, in evaluating whether a particular set is a business, it is not relevant whether a seller operated the set as a business or whether the acquirer intends to operate the set as a business.

In the absence of evidence to the contrary, a particular set of assets and activities in which goodwill is present shall be presumed to be a business. However, a business need not have goodwill.

A TYPICAL DIAGRAM OF WHAT CONSTITUTES A BUSINESS

INPUT + PROCESS = OUTPUT

THESE ACTIVITIES REQUIRED @ ALL TIMES

THESE ACTIVITIES ARE NECESSARY FOR A BUSINESS

The requirement of IFRS3 and Accounting for business combination does not apply to:

(a) The accounting for the formation of a joint arrangement in the financial statements of the joint arrangement itself.

(b) The acquisition of an asset or a group of assets that does not constitute a *business*. In such cases, the acquirer shall identify and recognise the individual identifiable assets acquired (including those assets that meet the definition of, and recognition criteria for, *intangible assets* in IAS 38 *Intangible Assets*) and liabilities assumed. The cost of the group shall be allocated to

Introduction to Intercorporate Investments and Basic Concepts of Business Combinations

the individual identifiable assets and liabilities on the basis of their relative *fair value* at the date of purchase. Such a transaction or event does not give rise to goodwill.

(c) A combination of entities or businesses under common control

---

[3]Advantages and Disadvantages of Business Combination

The main objective of a business combination is to eliminate cut-throat competition and secure the advantages of large scale production.

Following are the advantages of business combination:
1. Competition between and among the companies will be eliminated.
2. The amount of capital can be increased by combining business.
3. Establishment and management cost can be reduced.
4. Benefits of large scale production can be secured.
5. Operating cost can be reduced by avoiding duplication.
6. Research and development facilities are increased.
7. Monopoly in the market can be achieved.
8. Economic of Scale. i.e. Bulk purchase of materials at a reduced price is possible.
9. Stability of the price of goods is maintained.

Following are the disadvantages of business combination:
1. The business combination brings monopoly in the market, which may be harmful to the society.
2. The identity of the old company finishes.
3. Goodwill of the old companies decrease.
4. Management of the company becomes difficult.
5. A business combination may result in over-capitalization.

---

[3] http://accountlearning.blogspot.com.ng/

FORTUNE

[4]**These Are the 12 Biggest Mergers and Acquisitions of 2016**
By Lucinda Shen @ShenLucinda JUNE 13, 2016

Microsoft's acquisition of Linkedin isn't even top.

In a move that no one saw coming, Microsoft announced it would acquire social network, LinkedIn, in what is the largest tech deal of 2016 Monday morning.

So where does it stand on the board among all sectors?

Many market watchers have predicted that 2016 will still be a robust year for mergers and acquisitions, largely boosted by a series of smaller deals. It's not expected to beat 2015's figures, when deal volumed skyrocketed above $5 trillion, buoyed by several mega-deals-some of which have since fallen through.

So far, numbers suggest the predictions are on track. In 2016, U.S. mergers and acquisitions value total about $642 billion, 18% lower from the same period in 2015-$786 billion, according to Dealogic, an analytics firm tracking mergers and acquisitions.

Deal value, courtesy of Dealogic, also includes the target's net debt.

---

[4] http://fortune.com/2016/06/13/12-biggest-mergers-and-acquisitions-of-2016/

1. The $32 billion deal between Shire and Baxalta

Industry: Pharmaceuticals

After a lengthy six month courtship, London-based drugmaker Shire announced plans to buy Baxalta in a $32 billion cash and stock offer, giving Shire a better foothold in treating rare

The year though, is just halfway through. One major deal that could supplement the crown is the back-and-forth between German pharmaceutical giant, Bayer, and its intended target, Monsanto. Bayer offered a whopping $62 billion to the latter in May. Monsanto then rejected the offer, calling the proposal "incomplete and financially inadequate. "Discussions for that deal are still ongoing.

2. The $30.6 billion bid for St Jude Medical by Abbott Laboratories

Industry: Medical Appliances and Equipment

In April, Abbot Labs announced plans to buy St. Jude Medical for $25 billion in a cash and stock deal, and assume or refinance St. Jude's net debt of about $5.7 billion.

One of the flurry of mergers and acquisitions in the healthcare space this year, the combined company will have a stronger medical-devices business in an increasingly competitive market. Increased scale will also give Abbot Labs more pricing power in the market.

3. The $28.1billion acquisition of LinkedIn by Microsoft

Sector: Tech

On Monday, Microsoft

On Monday, Microsoft announced it would buy social networking company, LinkedIn for a smooth $26.2 billion in an all-cash deal. That took LinkedIn's stock up 47% in trading. The deal, Microsoft's largest ever by a $20 billion long shot, will "accelerate the grwoth of LinkedIn, as well as Microsoft Office 365 and Dynamics," according to Microsoft CEO Satya Nadella.

The deal is also sixth largest tech merger and acquisition on record, according to Dealogic

4. The $16.6billion deal for Tyco International by Johnson Controls

Sector: Auto Parts

In January, car parks manufacturer, Johnson Controls and Ireland-based security systems maker, Tyco International agreed to merge in a deal that would help Johnson Controls dodge the high, about 35%, corporate tax rate in the U.S by moving headquarters to Ireland.

The deal will lead to at least $500 million in savings in the first three years, and at least $150 million in annual tax savings, the companies said.

5. The $13.6 billion bid to buy starwood by Marriot International

Sector: Service

Perhaps one of the most tense mergers and acquisitions of 2016 that ended with Starwood's top bidder, Anbang Insurance, calling it quits, the acquisition of Starwood by Marriott International takes number four on the list. After several months of bidding, the two companies agreed to merge in March, becoming the world's largest hotel chain in a cash and stock deal.

The merger would give the combined company scale to combat smaller, and rapidly growing competitors such as Airbnb. Its new size would also allow the company to negotiate better fees with online bookings sites including Expedia.

6. The $13.2 billion acquisition of Columbia Pipeline Group by TransCanada

Sector: Oil and Gas

The company behind the controversial Keystone XL oil pipeline, TransCanada, agreed to buy Columbia Pipeline Group for $10.2 billion in March, making the combined giant one of North America's largest regulated natural gas transmission businesses in an all cash deal.

For TransaCanada, the deal allows them to take Columbia off its list of rivals, and also access the cheaper gas from Marcellus and Utica shale regions. Competition from the latter had been eating away at TransCanada's revenue.

7. A $12.8 billion merger between IMS Health Holdings and Quintiles Transnational Holding

Sector: Biotech

Contract medical research provider, Quintiles, agreed to merge with healthcare information company. IMS Health to make a giant known as Quintiles IMS in an all-stock deal.

"This combination addresses life-science companies" most pressing needs: to transform the clinical development of innovative medicines, demonstrate the value of these medicines in the world, and drive commercial success," Art Bousbib, chairman and CEO of IMS Health said in a statement

8. The $12.4 billion acquisition of ADT by Protection 1

Sector: Security

In February, a security service for residential and small business properties, ADT, agreed to be acquired by an affiliate of Apollo Global Management, and merged with another home security firm. Protection 1. The merger would give the combined company greater reach throughout the U.S. and Canada, and also help ADT accelerate its expansion into the commercial sector.

9. Great Plains Energy's Bid for Westar Energy Worth $12.2 billion

Sector: Electrical Utilities

Great Plains Energy, based out of Kansas City, Mo., and Westar Energy, based out of Kansas, announced the deal late May in a cash and stock transaction.

"The utility industry is facing rising customer expectations, increasing environmental standards and emerging cyber security threats. These factors, coupled with slower demand growth for electricity, are driving our costs and customer rates higher," said Terry Bassham, chairman and chief executive officer of Great Plains Energy. By buying Westar however, the company hopes to reduce expenses and combine operations.

10. The $11.4 billion acquisition of Fortis by ITC Holdings announced in February

Sector: Electrical Utilities

Canadian utility operator Fortis announced plans to buy Novi-Mich-based ITC Holdings in February. For Fortis, the acquisition would give the company a foothold in the Midwest, and give the combined company a chance to expand.

11. The merger between NorthStar Asset Management Group, its former parent NorthStar Realty Finance, and Colony Capital for $11.3 billion in June

Sector: Finance

The three companies agreed to merge into a single real-estate investment in early June, according to the Wall Street Journal. The combined company, with roughly in asset, is to be named Colony NorthStar.

"We are confident that Colony NorthStar with its lower leverage, larger balance sheet and improved liquidity profile is poised for meaningful multiple expansion and substantially enhanced long term returns for shareholders." David Hamamoto, executive chairman of NorthStar Asset Management, which spun off from NorthStar Reality Finance in 2013, said in a statement.

12. Sherwin-Williams takeover of Valspar for $11.3 in March

Sector: Basic materials

Sherwin-Williams agreed to snap up its competitor, Valspar, in March. The deal would give Sherwin-Williams better access to big box retailers such as Home Depot and Lowes, where Valspar already has a strong presence. Sherwin though, has made its way mainly through its own stores.

The transaction would also accelerate Sherwin's growth into international markets in Asia. Europe, and the Middle East.

[5]Strategic Acquisition in 2016 in the Most Recent Time in Nigeria

NIPCO Acquires 60% Equity in Mobil Oil

The Nigerian Independent Petroleum Company (NIPCO) on Wednesday announced the acquisition of 60 per cent stake in the Mobil Oil Nigeria Plc (MON), a leading downstream player of high repute. The Managing Director, NIPCO Mr. Venkataraman Venkatapathy disclosed this in a statement after the completion of the signing of the deal.

Venkatapathy said that the acquisition was agreed with the execution of a Sales and Purchase Agreement with ExxonMobil. According to him, with the signing, we will start the transition period and initiate the process of obtaining regulatory approvals from the requisite federal agencies like Securities and Exchange Commission of Nigeria (SEC) and Nigerian Stock Exchange (NSE).

"The transition period will also enable NIPCO plc to effectively manage a smooth and successful completion of the transaction. NIPCO considers this acquisition an important synergy. It is part of our strategic move to support Nipco's continuous growth and expansion of its Nigerian retail footprint.

"We are confident of adding tremendous value to MON and likewise MON will add a huge value to Nipco," he said. The managing director said that NIPCO will continue to maintain the Mobil brand on its retail outlets as well as continue to blend and sell the Mobil brand of lubricants under Branding Licence(s) from ExxonMobil.

He, however, expressed the company's profound gratitude and appreciation to ExxonMobil for selecting us as the preferred bidder for the acquisition of MON. "We wish to give every assurance to ExxonMobil that having entrusted us with this invaluable asset.

"We will ensure full brand compliance with ExxonMobil's global standards as well as rigorously sustain and follow ExxonMobil's code of conduct/ethos and operational excellence, NAN quotes Venkatapathy saying. He said that NIPCO's expansion trend reinforces its implicit confidence in Nigeria's future.

He said that the Nigerian economy still provides a robust and premium return on investment and Nipco plc is privileged to have been given this opportunity by ExxonMobil on its home ground. Venkatapathy lauded the company's shareholders support, adding that it's a welcome development to a new dawn.

He said that NIPCO indigenous Nigerian downstream oil and gas company would ensure stability, prosperity, sustainability and growth of the company and the shareholders.

---

[5] http://www.nipcoplc.com/nipco-acquires-60-equity-mobil-oil.html

Sahara Group has acquired assets in Nigeria's power sector In keeping with its desire to "be the provider of choice wherever energy is consumed."

The acquisition was realised under the privatisation programme of the Federal Government of Nigeria which led to the transfer of former PHCN assets to private investors.

Working through a number of Special Purpose Vehicles (SPV), Sahara successfully acquired majority shareholding stakes in two (2) of the PHCN assets that were sold by the Nigerian Government, namely Egbin Power station – the largest Power Generation Plant in Nigeria – and Ikeja Electricity Distribution Company – the largest power distribution network in Nigeria.

The NEDC/KEPCO Consortium emerged as the majority shareholders of the former Ikeja Distribution Company and Egbin Power Plant respectively. The consortium which has the Korean Electric Power Corporation (KEPCO) as technical partners is committed to delivering efficient, affordable and sustainable power supply in the nearest future through investments in new technology, infrastructure upgrade and human capital development.

KEPCO, the largest electricity utility company in Asia in terms of Transmission and Distribution, is amongst the largest nuclear power exporting companies and is also involved in every form of generation from wind, thermal, coal, solar, mass, hydro and renewable energy. The corporation generates about 84,000MW in capacity and has a global efficiency record of a maximum down time period of slightly above three minutes annually.

The Sahara Group restates its commitment to creating and sustaining value for all stakeholders in the energy value chain through innovation, strategic investments and alliances.

Source:http://www.sahara-group.com/test-news-1.html

HVI acquires 60% stake in Downstream Oando

Consortium comprising Helios and Vitol to acquire equity stake in Oando's downstream businesses

A consortium comprising Helios Investment Partners ("Helios", acting on behalf of funds it advises) and The Vitol Group ("Vitol") (together, the "Consortium") today announced it has reached an agreement to acquire 60 per cent of the economic rights and 51 per cent of the voting rights in the West African downstream business of Oando Plc, an integrated oil and gas company headquartered in Nigeria, for a sum of circa US$276 million, subject to the receipt of regulatory approvals and customary purchase price adjustments, including working capital.

The new downstream and retail business will be established as a standalone, independent company, led by a local management team. Its assets will comprise over 400 service stations in Nigeria with supporting infrastructure, including 84,000 tonnes of storage and a newly built inbound logistics jetty; as well as complementary businesses, chiefly LPG filling and distribution, lubricants and an interest in a supply and bulk distribution company in Ghana. The new business will be the second largest downstream fuels company in Nigeria, with a market share of 12 per cent. The Consortium is committed to investing for growth, and working with the experienced and highly skilled local management team to enable the business to capitalise on the 3-5 per cent per annum growth in Nigerian demand for oil products. It is anticipated that the service stations will retain the Oando brand.

Ian Taylor, President and CEO, Vitol said; "Vitol has a long history of working in Nigeria and is proud to have served our customers here over many years. This investment is a further reflection of our confidence in the Nigerian economy and will be independent of the services we provide to our long standing Nigerian customers. We are looking forward to building this new downstream business, alongside our many other business activities in Nigeria."

Tope Lawani, co-founder and Managing Partner of Helios Investment Partners, said; "This is a market leading downstream energy business with a strong brand and exciting growth potential. Given our successful partnership with Vitol to create Vivo Energy, a leading downstream business which distributes and markets Shell-branded fuels and lubricants in 16 countries across Africa, we are confident that our expertise and regional presence will support the management team in capitalising on its strong market position and the compelling growth opportunities in Nigeria."

Source:http://www.vitol.com/consortium-comprising-helios-and-vitol-to-acquire-an-equity-stake-in-oandos-downstream-businesses/

The following types of transactions generally meet the definition of business combinations

1. The purchase of equity of another entity.
2. The purchase of all assets, liabilities and rights to the activities of an entity.
3. The purchase of some of the assets, liabilities and rights to activities of an entity that together meet the definition of a business.
4. The establishment of a new legal entity in which the assets, liabilities and activities of combined businesses will be held.

> The third transaction requires that the combined activity meet the definition of a business which effectively means 'an integrated set of activities and assets conducted and managed for the purposes of providing a return to investors or lower costs or other economic benefits...'. If the entity acquires a group of assets that does not constitute a business, it must allocate the cost of the acquisition of the acquired assets. It is also noteworthy that the standard considers that all transactions generating goodwill are considered to be business combinations (assuming all fair values of assets have been applied).

Types of Business Combinations

Various literature have proposed different forms or types of Strategic Business Acquisitions based on the modern-day acquisitions which included the following (but may not be exhaustive):

Horizontal Combination:

It is also known as parallel or trade unit integration. It is affected by units engaged in manufacturing similar products or rendering similar services. It involves the bringing together of competing firms under single ownership and management. For instance, if two or more sugar mills are combined under the same management, it will be a case of a horizontal combination. Tata Iron and Steel Ltd and associated cement company are the illustrations of the horizontal combination.

The benefit of the horizontal combination is as follows:
   i.   It eliminates wasteful inter-firm completion in the same line of industry
   ii. It helps in achieving economies of large-scale production and distribution.
   iii. It can control the supply of the product and market prices.

The horizontal combination may lead to the point of view of following evils:
   i.   It creates a monopoly which is harmful from the point of view of the customers.
   ii. There may be a restriction of output and exploitation of customers.
   iii. It gives rise to a concentration of economic power.

Vertical Combination:

It is also known as sequence or industry or process integration. It arises as a result of the integration of those business enterprises which are engaged in a different stage of production of a product. In other words, it implies combination under single control of enterprises in different stages of manufacturing the product. The aim of vertical integration is to gain self-sufficiency as regards raw materials and distribution of finished products.

Two or more business units engaged in successive stages of production, or producing articles leading to the same final product, may combine together and manage all stages of production and the distribution of the final product. For example, in the cotton textile industry, there may be a combination of units engaged in successive stages of cloth manufacturing. Such as spinning, weaving, bleaching and finishing of cloth. The vertical combination may result from backwards or forward integration. Manufacturers at successive stages in production may integrate backwards up to the sources of raw materials or they may expand through forwards integration to the retail selling of the finished product. Thus, the basic objective of the vertical combination is either to secure an assured supply of raw materials and other requirements or to create a steady market for the products manufactured. The former objective is fulfilled by backwards integration and the latter is realised by forward integration.

The advantages of vertical integration are as follows:
   i. *It reduces the dependence on other enterprises in the industry and helps in achieving self-sufficiency.*
   ii. *It eliminates the intermediate profits and thus reduces the cost of production.*
   iii. *There is steady production as a result of regular supply of raw materials and regular sales.*
   iv. *Products of higher quality can be obtained because of the control be achieved.*
   v. *Economies in storage, transport and handling of materials may be achieved.*

Vertical integration may lead to the following evils:
   i. *It does not eliminate competition as in the case of horizontal integrations.*
   ii. *The size of the business may grow and it may bring grow and it may bring inflexibility of operations.*
   iii. *Since its processes are interdependent, a slight interruption in one process may dislocate the entire production system.*
   iv. *It gives rise to a concentration of economic power.*

Lateral Combination:

It refers to the integration of business units producing and selling different but allied products. The lateral combination may be either convergent or divergent. Convergent lateral combination arises when firms producing different products but supplying to a common user join with him. For example, brick manufacturer, stone supplier, cement supplier, and the wood supplier may integrate with a construction company; Divergent lateral combination represents a combination of one supplier of a common raw material with different users. The example of divergent lateral integration is provided by a flourmill supplying flour to a number of units like a bakery, confectionary, and hotel. The main benefit of lateral integration is that both the supply of raw materials and availability and the existence of demand are ensured to the new combination. Benefits of centralised control of various units are achieved. Under divergent integration, markets are diversified and risks are scattered.

Diagonal Combination:

It means integration of a main activity or process with ancillary activities and services. For instance, a newspaper company may integrate with a transport company to ensure quick delivery of the newspaper to different parts of the country or an automobile plant may combine with a power generating unit. Thus, diversification of activities is diagonal. The purpose of diagonal integration is to ensure smooth and timely availability of ancillary services which are essential for the continuous working of the main units.

Circular Combination:

When there is the integration of business units which remotely connoted with one another in their production and sales, furculum integration is achieved. The remote connection may be found between products requiring similar manufacturing processes or using the same marketing or trade channels. Circular combination or created to build up big industrial empires. Business house of Tata's, Birla's and D.C.M. are the illustrations in this regard. For instance, the D.C.M. group controls the units engaged in textiles, chemicals, fertilisers, sugar, electronic goods, business machines, etc.

Source: https://www.classle.net/#!/classle/book/types-business-combinations/

Principle of Business Combinations & Group Accounts

Business combination involves the combination of two or more entities into a larger economic entity. Business combinations are typically motivated by expectations of added value through synergies, including the elimination of duplicate costs, tax advantages, coordination of the production process, and efficiency gains in the management of assets.

The principle of group accounts is the need to reflect the economic status and substance of the relationship between the investor company (parent) and the investee company (subsidiary), even when the dual companies stand as separate legal entities. The principle furthers that since parent controls subsidiary, therefore they form a *single economic unit/entity*[6] *("The Group")*. The companies included in group accounts are those as defined by *IFRS 10* (consolidated financial statement) to constitute a group.

An acquirer of a business recognises the assets acquired and liabilities assumed at their acquisition-date fair value and discloses information that enables users to evaluate the nature and financial effects of the acquisition.

Techniques Adopted for Structuring Business Combinations

The investor or acquirer can structure a business combination in series of ways that possibly satisfy the acquirer's strategic, operational, legal, tax, and risk management objectives. Some of the more frequently used structures are:

1. One or more businesses become subsidiaries of the acquirer. As subsidiaries, they continue to operate as separate legal entities.
2. The net assets of one or more businesses are legally merged into that if the acquirer. In this case, the acquiree entity ceases to exist (in legal vernacular, this is referred to as a statutory merger and normally the transaction is subject to approval by a majority of the outstanding voting shares of the acquiree).
3. The owners of the acquiree transfer their equity interests to the acquirer entity or the owners of the acquirer entity in exchange for equity interests in the acquirer.
4. All of the combining entities transfer their net assets or their owners transfer their equity interests into a new entity formed for the purpose of the transaction. This is sometimes referred to as a roll-up or put-together transaction.
5. A former owner or group of former owners of one of the combining entities obtains control of the combined entities collectively.
6. An acquirer might hold a non-controlling equity interest in an entity and subsequently purchase additional equity interests sufficient to give it control over the investee. These transactions are referred to as a step acquisitions (otherwise known as piecemeal acquisitions) or business combinations achieved in stages.
7. A business owner organises a partnership (such as AVA Corporation, or FTC to hold real estate). The real estate is the principal location of the commonly owned business and that business entity leases the real estate from the separate entity.

---

[6] The *single economic unit concept* focuses on the existence of the group as an economic unit rather than looking at it only through the eyes of the dominant shareholder group. It concentrates on the resources controlled by the entity.

Introduction to Intercorporate Investments and Basic Concepts of Business Combinations

What does *Acquisition Structure* mean?

An acquisition structure refers to the overall framework upon which the purchase/sale of a company will be structured. Fundamentally, the acquisition structure breaks down the company's enterprise value into the cash component and the non-cash consideration components. Non-cash consideration may include rolled equity, vendor take backs, earn-outs, etc.

In addition, the acquisition structure will also specify if the transaction is a share or asset deal; what assets are being included and excluded; and sets any other material terms, conditions, stock options (if any) and other post-acquisition arrangements that would affect the buyer and the seller.

Divestopedia explains *Acquisition Structure*

An acquisition arrangement can be structured in different ways depending on the buying or selling objectives, immediate deliverables and long-term goals of the parties involved. Share transactions involve buying the complete business entity, inclusive of future liabilities, loans and receivables. A solid entity may remain as a subsidiary or the wholly owned subsidiary of an acquiring company or may be amalgamated at the closing date.

Alternatively, asset acquisitions normally involve purchasing only the valuable assets, whereas the legal entity of the selling company may be kept intact. Valuable business assets include buying only the ongoing/running business which can be the physical inventory, any equipment, customer lists, brands, patents, trademarks, product/trade names, property and intangible assets.

Certain acquisition structures can provide tax advantages. When completing asset transactions, the buyer is typically entitled to future tax deductions through higher tax depreciation and possibly tax losses carried forward which can offset future taxable income.

Source:

https://www.divestopedia.com/definition/1276/acquisition-structure

---

Top Merger & Acquisition Considerations

Deal Structure   Author: John Fatteross

Choosing the best structure for a merger or acquisition is critical to the deal's success for both parties. These transactions are, after all, usually quite complex, and one type of structure may favour one party more than the other. For these reasons, both parties (and their attorneys, of course) must consider the respective legal, tax and business issues and craft a mutually beneficial transaction structure.

There are generally *three options* for structuring a merger or acquisition deal:

Stock purchase: The buyer purchases the target company's stock from its stockholders. The target company remains intact, but with new ownership. The buyer must negotiate representations and warranties concerning the business's assets and liabilities, to ensure a complete and accurate understanding of the target company.

Asset sale/purchase. The buyer purchases only assets and assumes liabilities that are specifically indicated in the purchase agreement. (Buyers often favour this structure because they can choose only the assets they wish to acquire and the liabilities they wish to assume. Sellers may not prefer this sale method because it can have adverse tax consequences due to the allocation of the purchase price to the various assets.) This structure is often used when the buyer wishes to acquire a single division or business unit within a company. It can be time-intensive and complex, because of the extra effort involved in identifying and transferring only the specified assets.

Merger. Two companies combine to form one legal entity, and the target company's stockholders receive cash, buyer company stock, or a combination. A key advantage of a merger is that it generally requires the consent of only a majority of the target company's stockholders—it could be a good choice when the target company has multiple stockholders.

Source: **The Hartford**
http://www.thehartford.com/business-playbook/in-depth/mergers-acquisitions-deal-structure

SUMMARY OF CHAPTER 1

1. Inter-corporate investments are debt and equity investments that corporate entities have in other entities, majorly when there are surplus funds in the coffers or reserves of the entities at different times.
2. In a more strategic situation, inter-corporate investments are necessitated by a need to maximise value to shareholders by way of synergy through acquisitions, mergers and another form of business combinations.
3. Business combinations within the context of International Financial Reporting Standards (IFRS) encompass all form of strategic decisions through acquisitions, mergers, amalgamation and absorption of other businesses in the aim to maximising shareholders' wealth.
4. Only some forms of equity inter-corporate investments that may result in a business combination, while inter-corporate investments through debt instruments will not give rise to a business combination.
5. Equity inter-corporate investments can be sub-grouped into *minority passive*, *minority active*, *controlling interest* and *joint venture investments*.
6. Minority passive investments are a combination of debt and equity investments, which are usually classified as: *"Held-to-Maturity Investments, Loans and Receivables, Held-for-Trading Securities, and Available-for-Sale financial assets"*.
7. Minority active investments are mostly equity-type financial assets investment that gives *significant influence* to the investors over the financial and operating policies of the investee.
8. Controlling interest investments are strictly equity investment of the investor or the acquirer in the net assets of the acquiree (or the acquired), and of which the acquirer obtains *control* of the acquiree in a business combination.
9. Joint venture investments are those of equity participation in the jointly controlled entities (or simply put, *"Joint Ventures"*), where joint and shared control of the financial and operating policies of the investee have been commonly and mutually agreed by the venturers (i.e. the investors) in the joint arrangement.
10. An equity inter-corporate investment with a sub-group of *"controlling interest"* is what *result* into business combination.
11. Business combinations are a common way for companies to grow in size, rather than growing through organic (internal) activities.
12. A business is an integrated set of activities and assets that can provide a return to investors in the form of dividends, reduced costs, or other economic benefits.
13. Business combinations sometimes come into being by way of the formation of a new (larger) entity through the coming together of two or more existing businesses.
14. Business combinations most times can take the form of lateral integration, backwards integration, forward integration, conglomeration and lots more.
15. International Financial Reporting Standards provide guidance in accounting for all form of inter-corporate investments vis-à-vis all form of business combinations.

16. Companies and Allied Matters Act (CAMA CAP C20, LFN 2004 – as amended) further provided local regulatory guidance on the reporting requirements for business combinations and the need to prepare group accounts.
17. The requirements of IFRSs take preeminence over the provisions of CAMA, in areas of conflict based on the adoption of IFRS by the Financial Reporting (FRC) Act of 2011.
18. By local regulatory requirement (i.e. CAMA), the Directors of the Group are solely responsible for the preparation of Group Accounts.

END OF CHAPTER 1 EXERCISES

1. What form of investment(s) can be considered inter-corporate investments?
2. Distinguish between Intercorporate Investments and Business Combinations.
3. Inter-corporate investments can be grouped into four categories. Kindly list and describe the categories.
4. Can debt investments by a body corporate in another entity result in a business combination?
5. _____ represent an important component of management strategy, which involves a company investing in other companies to achieve diversification, growth, and competitive advantage, but the structure and scope of these investments create comparability challenges for the potential investors', analysts, and the investing public at large.
6. Which standard addresses the Accounting for Business Combinations?
7. Which standard provides guidance in accounting for acquirer's investment in another entity in its separate financial statements?
8. Describe the objectives of IFRS 10; and how it differs from that of IFRS 3.
9. What constitutes a Business?
10. _____ entails transaction or other event in which an **acquirer** obtains control of one or more **businesses.**
11. Can Business Combinations have a negative side? Discuss
12. Itemise the techniques adopted for structuring business combinations.

Chapter 2

Basic Principles of Group Accounts

INTRODUCTION

This chapter will introduce the readers to what constitutes a group and the concept of group accounts. It will also allow the readers to appreciate the need to prepare group accounts because not all business combinations will require the preparation of group accounts.

Readers will subsequently be exposed to basic terminologies required for the purpose of preparing group accounts. Furthermore, the rationale for the preparation of group accounts will be discussed alongside other basic accounting issues in business combinations and the objectives of IFRS3.

The chapter will further explore issues regarding investment in subsidiaries, rights that give an investor power over an investee, exemptions from preparing group accounts, and exclusion of subsidiary from consolidation where it may be necessary.

Contemporary issues that bother on group accounts are equally discussed within this chapter and the basic process of consolidation of the accounts of the parent and that of it s subsidiaries are itemised and discussed. Also, the basic principle regarding *'Acquisition Method'* of accounting for a business combination will be discussed within the context of this chapter. The steps within the acquisition method of accounting will be discussed in full details.

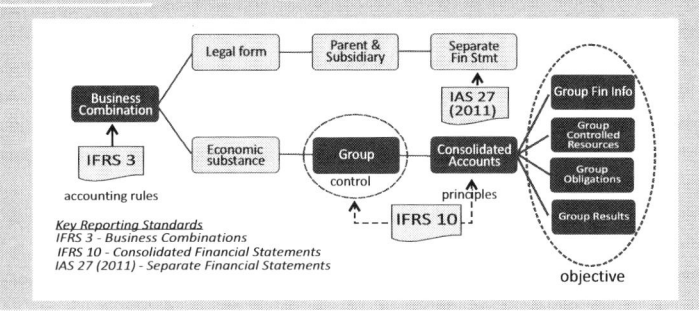

Key Reporting Standards
IFRS 3 - Business Combinations
IFRS 10 - Consolidated Financial Statements
IAS 27 (2011) - Separate Financial Statements

Basic Principles of Group Accounts

INTRODUCTION TO GROUP ACCOUNTS

A group[7] exists where one company (considered the parent) controls, either directly or indirectly, another company (the subsidiary) – *IFRS 10 (Consolidated Financial Statements)*. To identify a group, we need to identify the parent entity and subsidiary entities. Basically, subsidiary entities are those that are controlled by the parent.

Accounting for Business Combination precedes the preparation of Group Accounts. Group Accounts are only prepared under two conditions and on a continuous (or ongoing) basis as stated below:

1. Group Accounts are prepared only when the result of the Business Combination give rise to a **parent-subsidiary** relationship. That is, the acquirer eventually becomes the parent company, while the acquiree (or the acquired) becomes the subsidiary. The implication is that a Business Combination that entails *"**Two or more companies combine to form one legal entity**"* will not give rise to the preparation of Group Accounts.

2. Group Accounts are continuously prepared only when it is established that at every reporting date, **CONTROL** is still established. That is, it must be evident that the parent still *controls* the financial and operating policies of the subsidiary.

We will be looking at these *International Financial Reporting Standards (IFRSs)* in the context of preparing and diagnosing *Group Accounts* in its entirety.

- IAS 1 (Revised): Presentation of Financial Statements
- IAS 7: Statement of Cash Flows
- IAS 8: Accounting Policies, Changes in Accounting Estimates and Errors
- IAS 10: Events after the End of the Reporting Period
- IAS 12: Income taxes
- IAS 21: The Effects of Changes in Exchange Rates
- IAS 24: Related Party Disclosures
- IAS 27: (Revised June 2011): Separate Financial Statements (effective January 1, 2013)
- IAS 28: (Revised June 2011): Investments in Associates and Joint Ventures (effective January 1, 2013)
- IAS 32: Financial Instruments – Presentation
- IAS 36: Impairment of Assets
- IAS 37: Provisions, Contingent Assets and Contingent Liabilities
- IAS 39: Financial Instruments – Recognition & Measurement (to be totally replaced by IFRS 9 when IFRS 9 becomes effective by January 1, 2018).
- IFRS 3 (Revised): Business Combinations
- IFRS 7: Financial Instruments – Disclosure
- IFRS 9: Financial Instruments (which becomes effective on January 1, 2018).
- IFRS 10: Consolidated Financial Statements (effective January 1, 2013)
- IFRS 11: Joint Arrangements (effective January 1, 2013)
- IFRS 12: Disclosure of Interests in Other Entities (effective January 1, 2013)
- IFRS 13: Fair Value Measurement (effective January 1, 2013)

---

[7] **Group:** A **parent** and its **subsidiaries**.

Contemporaneous Accounting for Business Combinations and Group Accounts

These standards are all connected with different aspects of separate and consolidated financial statements of the controlling entity or simply put '**the Group**'; but there are some overlaps between them, particularly between *IFRS 3 (Revised) and IFRS 10*.

Definition of Terms

The following definitions apply to *business combinations* and *group accounts* as defined by the relevant **IFRSs**.

- *Group:* A parent and its subsidiaries.
- *Parent:* An entity that controls one or more entities.
- *Subsidiary:* An entity that is controlled by another entity (known as the parent).
- *Business Combination:* A transaction or other event in which an acquirer obtains control of one or more businesses. Transactions sometimes referred to as '*true mergers*' *or* '*mergers of equals*' are also business combinations as that term is used in this IFRS.
- *Consolidated Financial Statements (Group Accounts):* The financial statements of a group in which the assets, liabilities, equity, income, expenses and cash flows of the parent and its subsidiaries are presented as those of a single economic entity.
- *Control of an Investee[8]:* An investor controls an investee when the investor is exposed, or has rights, to variable returns from its involvement with the investee and has the ability to affect those returns through its power over the investee. **Control** was earlier defined by the old IAS 27 (as revised in 2008) as "the power to govern the financial and operating policies of an entity so as to obtain benefits from its activities".
- *Significant Influence:* The power o participate in the financial and operating policy decisions of an investee or an economic activity but is not control or joint control over those policies.
- *Power:* Existing rights that give the current ability to direct the relevant activities.
- *Associate[9]:* An entity, including an unincorporated entity such as partnership, in which an investor has significant influence and which is neither a subsidiary nor a joint venture of the investor.
- *Non-controlling interest[10]:* The equity in a subsidiary not attributable, directly or indirectly, to a parent. Also as a proportion of the net assets of a subsidiary entity that belongs to investors outside the group.
- *Acquisition Date:* The date on which the **acquirer** obtains control of the **acquiree**.
- *Identifiable*: An asset is identifiable if it either: is separable,(.i.e. capable of being separated or divided from the entity and sold, transferred, licensed, rented or exchanged, either individually or together with a related contract, identifiable asset or liability, regardless of whether the entity

---

[8] **Control of an investee:** Do not only represents the power to govern the financial and operating policies of an entity so as to obtain benefits from its activities, but also addresses exposure, or rights, to variable returns from its involvement with the investee and the ability to use its power over the investee to affect the amount of the investor's returns.

[9] An *associate* is an entity over which the investor has significant influence.

[10] **Non-controlling interest**: Equity in a **subsidiary** not attributable, directly or indirectly, to a **parent**.

intends to do so) or arises from contractual or other legal rights, regardless of whether those rights are transferable or separable from the entity or from other rights and obligations.

- **Intangible Asset:** An **identifiable** non-monetary asset without physical substance.
- **Goodwill:** An asset representing the future economic benefits arising from other assets acquired in a **business combination** that is not individually identified and separately recognised. It is measured primarily as the excess of the cost of consideration over the fair value of the net assets acquired
- **Cost of Combination:** This represents the consideration transferred or transferable to the investee upon acquisition by the investor. This includes: cash consideration; shares consideration; a combination of cash and shares consideration. Also, included in the cost of consideration is the present value (discounted value) of contingent consideration.

    The consideration transferrable is measured at the acquisition-date fair value of the total consideration transferred and the acquisition-date fair value of each major class of consideration, such as:
    a) Cash;
    b) Other tangible or intangible assets, including a business or subsidiary of the acquirer;
    c) Liabilities incurred, for example, a liability for contingent consideration; and
    d) Equity interests of the acquirer, including the number of instruments or interests, issued or issuable and the method of determining the fair value of those instruments or interests.

- **Contingent Consideration:** Usually, an obligation of the acquirer to transfer additional assets or equity interests to the former owners of an acquiree as part of the exchange for control of the acquiree if specified future events occur or conditions are met. This otherwise is a consideration transferrable to the investee in the future by the parent (investor) upon the occurrence of future events.
- **Fair Values:** The price that would be received to sell an asset or paid to transfer a liability in an orderly transaction between market participants at the measurement date. Fair value was earlier defined in IFRS 3 (before the introduction of IFRS 13) as the amount for which an asset can be exchanged or a liability settled between knowledgeable, willing parties in an arm's length transaction.
- **Net Assets:** This refers to the Share Capital and Reserves of the subsidiary at any point in time.
- **Pre-Acquisition Reserve:** This is the reserve of the subsidiary existing at the date of acquisition of controlling interest by the holding (parent) company.
- **Post-Acquisition Reserve:** This is the reserve of the subsidiary generated by it subsequent to the date of acquisition of controlling interest by the holding (parent) company.
- **Acquiree:** The business or businesses that the acquirer obtains control of in a business combination.
- **Acquirer:** The entity that obtains control of the acquiree.
- **Equity Interest:** Broadly used in IFRS to mean "Ownership Interests".
- **Bargain Purchase:** This occurs when the cost of consideration is less than the fair value of the subsidiary net assets acquired.

- ❖ **Decision Maker:** An entity with decision-making rights that is either a principal or an agent for other parties.
- ❖ **Protective Rights:** Rights designed to protect the interest of the party holding those rights without giving that party power over the entity to which those rights relate.
- ❖ **Relevant Activities**: For the purpose of this IFRS, relevant activities are activities of the investee that significantly affect the investee's returns.
- ❖ **Removal Rights:** Rights to deprive the decision maker of its decision-making authority.
- ❖ **Equity Method** is a method of accounting whereby the investment is initially recognised at cost and adjusted thereafter for the post-acquisition change in the investor's share of the investee's net assets.
- ❖ **The Investor's profit or loss:** includes its share of the investee's profit or loss and the investor's other comprehensive income includes its share of the investee's other comprehensive income.
- ❖ **A Joint Arrangement** is an arrangement of which two or more parties have joint control.
- ❖ **Joint Control:** is the contractually agreed sharing of control of an arrangement, which exists only when decisions about the relevant activities require the unanimous consent of the parties sharing control.
- ❖ **A Joint Venture** is a joint arrangement whereby the parties that have joint control of the arrangement have rights to the net assets of the arrangement.
- ❖ **A Joint Venturer:** is a party to a joint venture that has joint control of that joint venture.
- ❖ **Joint Control:** The contractually agreed sharing of control of an arrangement, which exists only when decisions about the relevant activities require the unanimous consent of the parties sharing control.
- ❖ **Joint Operation:** A joint arrangement whereby the parties that have joint control of the arrangement have rights to the assets, and obligations for the liabilities, relating to the arrangement.
- ❖ **Joint Operator:** A party to a joint operation that has joint control of that joint operation.
- ❖ **Party to a Joint Arrangement:** An entity that participates in a joint arrangement, regardless of whether that entity has joint control of the arrangement.
- ❖ **Separate Vehicle:** A separately identifiable financial structure, including separate legal entities or entities recognised by statute, regardless of whether those entities have a legal personality.
- ❖ **Mutual Entity:** An entity, other than an investor-owned entity, that provides dividends, lower costs or other economic benefits directly to its **owners**, members or participants. For example, a mutual insurance company, a credit union and a co-operative entity are all mutual entities.
- ❖ **Owners:** For the purposes **of IFRS 3(R) - business combination**, owners is used broadly to include holders of **equity interests** of investor-owned entities and owners or members of, or participants in, **mutual entities**.

Rationale for Consolidated Financial Statements

Over time there have been benefits attributed to the preparation of group accounts, which is not limited to those highlighted below:

1. It presents financial information about parent undertakings and its subsidiary undertakings as a single economic unit.
2. It shows the economic resources controlled by the group.
3. It shows the obligations of the group (as separate from the individual obligations of the individual legal entities).
4. It shows the results of the group as achieved by the group resources employed.
5. To prevent the preparation of misleading accounts by such means of as inflating sales (revenue) through selling (or consummating other fictitious transactions) with another member of a group.
6. To provide a better measurement of performance of a parent company.
7. To provide a more meaningful EPS figure and its analysis, as consolidated accounts show the full earnings of a parent company's investment while the parent separate financial statements only account for the dividend received (or receivable) from the subsidiary.

Basic Accounting Issues in Business Combinations

Major accounting issues affecting business combinations and the preparation of consolidated financial statements pertain to the following:

1. The proper recognition and measurement of the assets and liabilities of the combined entities.
2. The accounting for goodwill or gain from a bargain purchase (otherwise known as negative goodwill).
3. The elimination of intercompany/intergroup balances and transactions in the preparation and presentation of consolidated financial statements.
4. The manner of accounting and reporting of the non-controlling interests.

Objectives of IFRS 3 to Business Combinations

The overriding objective of the new standards is to improve the relevance, representational faithfulness, transparency, and comparability of information provided in a financial statement about business combinations and their effects on the reporting entity by establishing principles and requirements with respect to how an acquirer, in its consolidated financial statements:

1. Recognises and measure identifiable assets acquired, liabilities assumed, and the non-controlling interest in the acquiree, if any.
2. Recognises and measures acquired goodwill or a gain from a bargain purchase.
3. Determine the nature and extent of disclosures sufficient to enable the reader (and users of financial statements) to evaluate the nature of the business combination and its financial effects on the consolidated reporting entity.
4. Accounts for and reports non-controlling interests in subsidiaries, and
5. Deconsolidates a subsidiary when it ceases to hold controlling interest in it.

Investment in Subsidiaries

The important point in investment in subsidiary entities is "**Control**[11]". *IFRS 10* states that *control* can usually be assumed to exist when the *parent owns more than half (i.e. over 50%)* of the *voting power* of an entity unless it can be clearly shown that such ownership does not constitute control (*which is rare*). Thus, an investor controls an investee if and only if the investor has all of the following:

- Power over the investee.
- Exposure, or rights, to variable returns from its involvement with the investee; and
- The ability to use its power over the investee to affect the amount of the investor's returns.

OLD VIEW OF "CONTROL"

IAS 27 (revised 2008) states that control can usually be assumed to exist when the parent owns more than half (i.e. over 50%) of the voting power of an entity unless it can be clearly shown that such ownership does not constitute control (these situations are rare).

IAS 27 (revised 2008) lists the following situations where control exists, even when the parent owns only 50% or less of the voting power of an entity.

a) The parent has power over more than 50% of the voting rights by virtue of an agreement with other investors (e.g. voting trust arrangements or other contractual provisions).

b) The parent has the power to govern the financial and operating policies of the entity by statute or under an agreement.

c) The parent has the power to appoint or remove the majority of members of the board of directors (or equivalent governing body).

d) The parent has the power to cast a majority of votes at meetings of the board of directors.

IAS 27 (revised 2008) states that in ascertaining whether control is present or whether the reporting entity is to be regarded as the parent company and should therefore prepare and present a consolidated financial statements, the parent's *potential voting rights* in the subsidiary should also be considered alongside the *actual voting right*, if the *existence* and *effect* of the potential voting rights are *currently* exercisable or *currently* convertible.

The existence of potential voting rights or interest may exist due to the existence of *options, warrants, convertible securities (debts or shares), or a contractual agreement to acquire additional shares, including shares that the investor or parent entity may have sold to another shareholder in the subsidiary or to another party, with a right or contractual arrangement to reacquire the shares transferred at a later date*. But, the potential voting rights should not be taken into consideration when determining what fraction of the subsidiary's profit or loss (income and expenses) is allocated to the parent company.

IAS 27 (revised 2008) also states that a parent loses control when it loses the power to govern the financial and operating policies of an investee. Loss of control can occur without a change in ownership levels. This may happen if a subsidiary becomes subject to the control of the government, court administration or regulator (e.g. in Bankruptcy).

---

[11] An investor shall consider all facts and circumstances when assessing whether it controls an investee. The investor shall reassess whether it controls an investee if facts and circumstances indicate that there are changes to one or more of the three elements of control listed in paragraph 7 (IFRS 10).

Rights that give an investor power over an investee

Power arises from rights. To have power over an investee, an investor must have existing rights that give the investor the current ability to direct the relevant activities. The rights that may give an investor power can differ between investees.

Examples of rights that, either individually or in combination, can give an investor power include but are not limited to:
- Rights in the form of voting rights (or potential voting rights) of an investee;
- Rights to appoint, reassign or remove members of an investee's key management personnel who have the ability to direct the relevant activities;
- Rights to appoint or remove another entity that directs the relevant activities;
- Rights to direct the investee to enter into, or veto any changes to, transactions for the benefit of the investor; and
- Other rights (such as decision-making rights specified in a management contract) that give the holder the ability to direct the relevant activities.

Technical Note:
IFRS 10 technically no longer use the basis of voting right as a pre-condition for ascertaining existence of control, which depicts that mere holding more than 50% of the voting rights may or may not provide control over the investee, and holding less than 50% of the voting rights (minority active interest) in an investee may provide control, once the conditions established above are met.

IFRS 10 also states that an investor does not have power over an investee, even though the investor holds the majority of the voting rights in the investee when those voting rights are not substantive. For example, an investor that has more than half of the voting rights in an investee cannot have power if the relevant activities are subject to direction by a government, court, administrator, receiver, liquidator or regulator.

Consolidated Financial Statements

This is the financial statements of a group (*parent and its subsidiaries*) presented as those of a *single economic entity*. It is expected that a parent company prepares and presents consolidated financial statements that incorporate the financial statements of all its subsidiaries, both foreign and domestic.

The basic consolidation procedures to be followed in other to prepare and present the consolidated financial statements of a group *entail to*:
a) Combine like items of assets, liabilities, *equity[12] (i.e. those attributable to post-combination transactions and events), income, expenses and cash flows of the parent with those of its subsidiaries.
b) Offset (eliminate) the carrying amount of the parent's investment in each subsidiary and the parent's portion of the equity of each subsidiary (IFRS 3 explains how to account for any related goodwill, which will be discussed in the context of this text) as at acquisition-date.
c) Eliminate in full intra-group assets and liabilities, equity, income, expenses and cash flows relating to transactions between entities of the group (profits or losses resulting from intragroup transactions that are recognised in assets, such as inventory and components of [depreciable]

---
[12] ***equity:** The applicable components of equity to be consolidated are increase or decrease in reserves attributed to post-combination activities and performances.

non-current assets, are eliminated in full). Intra-group losses may indicate an impairment that requires recognition in the consolidated financial statements. IAS 12 Income Taxes applies to temporary differences that arise from the elimination of profits and losses resulting from intra-group transactions.

Exemption from Preparing Group Accounts

IFRS 10[13] outlines the circumstances in which a consolidated financial statement should be prepared for a group considered a single economic unit, which is stated as thus:

An entity that is a parent shall present consolidated financial statements. *IFRS 10* applies to all entities, except *(A parent need not present consolidated financial statements if it meets all the following conditions)*:

- It is a wholly-owned subsidiary or is a partially-owned subsidiary of another entity and all its other owners, including those not otherwise entitled to vote, have been informed about, and do not object to, the parent not presenting consolidated financial statements;
- Its debt or equity instruments are not traded in a public market (a domestic or foreign stock exchange or an over-the-counter market, including local and regional markets);
- It did not file, nor is it in the process of filing, its financial statements with a securities commission or other regulatory organisation for the purpose of issuing any class of instruments in a public market; and
- Its ultimate or any intermediate parent produces consolidated financial statements that are available for public use and comply with IFRSs.

Technical Note:
A parent that does not present consolidated financial statements must comply with the IAS 27 (Revised) rules on separate financial statements.

Investment entities consolidation exemption[14]

IFRS 10 contains special accounting requirements for investment entities. Where an entity meets the definition of an 'investment entity' (see above), it does not consolidate its subsidiaries or apply IFRS 3 Business Combinations when it obtains control of another entity.

Technical Note:
The investment entity consolidation exemption was introduced by Investment Entities, issued on 31 October 2012 and effective for annual periods beginning on or after 1 January 2014.]

An entity is required to consider all facts and circumstances when assessing whether it is an investment entity, including its purpose and design. IFRS 10 provides that an investment entity should have the following typical characteristics:
- *It has more than one investment*
- *It has more than one investor*
- *It has investors that are not related parties of the entity*
- *It has ownership interests in the form of equity or similar interests.*

---

[13] **IFRS 10 Consolidated Financial Statements** establishes principles for the presentation and preparation of consolidated financial statements when an entity controls one or more other entities.
14 IASplus webpage ... http://www.iasplus.com/en/standards/ifrs/ifrs10#investment_entities

Basic Principles of Group Accounts

The absence of any of these typical characteristics does not necessarily disqualify an entity from being classified as an investment entity.

An investment entity is required to measure an investment in a subsidiary at fair value through profit or loss in accordance with IFRS 9 Financial Instruments or IAS 39 Financial Instruments: Recognition and Measurement. However, an investment entity is still required to consolidate a subsidiary where that subsidiary provides services that relate to the investment entity's investment activities.

Because an investment entity is not required to consolidate its subsidiaries, intra-group related party transactions and outstanding balances are not eliminated.

Special requirements apply where an entity becomes, or ceases to be, an investment entity.

The exemption from consolidation only applies to the investment entity itself. Accordingly, a parent of an investment entity is required to consolidate all entities that it controls, including those controlled through an investment entity subsidiary, unless the parent itself is an investment entity.

Exclusion of a Subsidiary from Consolidation

The rules on exclusion from consolidation have been very strict. Based on *IFRS 10*, the subsidiary can only be excluded from consolidation only on the basis of ***actual loss of control***.

The standard does not consider other basis as contained in the *previous IAS 27 (before its revision in 2008 and ultimate replacement by IFRS 10)*, which include:

- *Where Control is intended to be temporary:* A subsidiary acquired exclusively with a view to its disposal within 12 months will probably meet the conditions in *IFRS 5* (Non-current assets held for sale and discontinued operations) for classification as held for sale. The implication is that such investment will not be accounted for under *IFRS 10* but rather under IFRS 5, which implies that all of its assets are presented as a single line item below current assets and all its liabilities are presented as a single line item below current liabilities. By so doing, the subsidiary is still consolidated, but in a different way.

- *On the grounds of dissimilar activities:* in the past, argument has been made that subsidiaries should be excluded from consolidation on the grounds of dissimilar activities (i.e. where the activities of the subsidiary are so different to the activities of the other companies within the group) that to include its results in the consolidated financial statement would be misleading. The exclusion on this ground is no longer acceptable and justifiable, as a group should consolidate the subsidiary results and then this will be explained by the segment information required by *IFRS 8 (Segment reporting)*.

- *Under a severe long-term restriction which significantly impair subsidiary inability to transfer funds to the parent:* The standard further posits that mere severe long-term restriction on the ability of the parent to manage a subsidiary does not require outright exclusion, rather such exclusion will only be permissible when such severe long-term restriction results in actual loss of control (i.e. control must actually be lost for exclusion to occur).

Technical Note:
Invariably subsidiary will be excluded from consolidation only when control is lost, and/or if its consideration will be deemed to be immaterial to the entire group operations and accounts.

Contemporary Issues in Group Accounts

A. Potential Voting Right:

The existence and effect of potential voting rights, including potential voting rights held by another entity, should be considered when assessing whether an entity has control over another entity (and therefore has a subsidiary). In assessing whether potential voting rights give rise to control, the entity examines all facts and circumstances that affect the rights (e.g. terms and conditions), except the intention of management and the financial ability to exercise the rights or convert them into equity shares.

When assessing control, an investor considers its potential voting rights as well as potential voting rights held by other parties, to determine whether it has power. Potential voting rights are rights to obtain voting rights of an investee, such as those arising from convertible instruments or options, including forward contracts. Those potential voting rights are considered only if the rights are substantive.

When considering potential voting rights, an investor shall consider the purpose and design of the instrument, as well as the purpose and design of any other involvement the investor has with the investee. This includes an assessment of the various terms and conditions of the instrument as well as the investor's apparent expectations, motives and reasons for agreeing to those terms and conditions.

If the investor also has voting or other decision-making rights relating to the investee's activities, the investor assesses whether those rights, in combination with potential voting rights, give the investor power.

B. Acquisition-Related Costs[15]:

The original *IFRS 3* (in 2003) required fees (legal, accounting, valuation etc.) paid in relation to a business acquisition to be included in the cost of investment, which meant that they were measured as part of goodwill. Under the revised *IFRS 3* (in 2011) costs relating to the acquisition must be recognised as an expense at the time of the acquisition. They are not regarded as an asset. *Costs of issuing debt or equity are to be accounted for under the rules of IAS 39 or IFRS 9 (where early adopted) and IAS 32 respectively*

Acquisition-related costs are costs the acquirer incurs to effect a business combination. Those costs include *finder's fees; advisory, legal, accounting, valuation and other professional or consulting fees; general administrative costs, including the costs of maintaining an internal acquisitions department; and costs of registering and issuing debt and equity securities*. The acquirer shall account for acquisition-related costs as expenses in the periods in which the costs are incurred and the services are received, with one exception which is the costs to issue debt or equity securities shall be recognised in accordance with *IAS 39 or IFRS 9 (where early adopted) and IAS 32 respectively*.

Technical Note:
All expenses including that of a professional accountant and solicitor to the business combination are to be written off as incurred. However, IFRS 3 and IAS 32 require the costs of issuing equity to be treated as a deduction from the proceeds of the equity issue. Share issue costs will to be debited to share premium account. Issue costs of financial instruments are generally deducted from the proceeds of the financial instruments.

---

[15] Acquisition cost include accounting fees, advisory fees, consulting fees, finder's fees, internal acquisition departmental cost, legal/solicitor's fees, other professional fees, valuation fees, etc.

C. Assets held for sale:
The acquirer shall measure an acquired non-current asset (or disposal group) that is classified as held for sale at the acquisition date in accordance with *IFRS 5* (Non-current Assets Held for Sale and Discontinued Operations) at fair value less cost of disposal.

D. Different Reporting Dates:
It is expected that the subsidiary and parent entity have the same *reporting date*, but in the instance where the reporting dates are different, the parent can still consolidate the results of its subsidiaries by adjusting the results to effect necessary adjustments provided the difference in reporting dates is not more than *three (3) months*.

The financial statements of the parent and its subsidiaries used in the preparation of the consolidated financial statements shall have the same reporting date. When the end of the reporting period of the parent is different from that of a subsidiary, the subsidiary prepares, for consolidation purposes, additional financial information as of the same date as the financial statements of the parent to enable the parent to consolidate the financial information of the subsidiary, unless it is impracticable to do so.

If it is impracticable to do so, the parent shall consolidate the financial information of the subsidiary using the most recent financial statements of the subsidiary adjusted for the effects of significant transactions or events that occur between the date of those financial statements and the date of the consolidated financial statements. In any case, the difference between the date of the subsidiary's financial statements and that of the consolidated financial statements shall be no more than three months, and the length of the reporting periods and any difference between the dates of the financial statements shall be the same from period to period.

E. Uniform Accounting Policies:
A parent shall prepare consolidated financial statements using *uniform accounting policies* for like transactions and other events in similar circumstances. The parent and subsidiaries are expected to have the same accounting policies, and in the absence of uniform accounting policies, it is expected that upon consolidation the financial statements of the subsidiaries are adjusted appropriately to adjust the accounting policies of the parent before consolidation.

Invariably, if a member of the group uses accounting policies other than those adopted in the consolidated financial statements for like transactions and events in similar circumstances, appropriate adjustments are made to that subsidiary's financial statements in preparing the consolidated financial statements to ensure conformity with the group's accounting policies.

F. Date of Inclusion/Exclusion:
Consolidation of a subsidiary shall begin from the date the investor obtains control of the investee and ceases when the investor loses control of the investee. The results of subsidiary undertakings are included in the consolidated financial statements from:
  i. *The date of 'acquisition'*, i.e. the date control passes to the parent, to
  ii. The date of 'disposal', i.e. the date control passes from the parent.

Technical Note:
Once an investment is no longer a subsidiary, it should be treated as an associate under IAS 28 (if applicable) or as a Financial Asset under IFRS 9/IAS 39 (as applicable).

G. Attribution of Losses:

Based on the provision of *IFRS 10*, *non-controlling interests* can be negative by absorbing losses in excess of its share of the net assets in the subsidiary. This is consistent with the idea that non-controlling interests are considered investors' of a separate class in the Group. Whereas, in the previous IAS 27 (*before its revision in 2008 and subsequent replacement by IFRS 10*), non-controlling interest could not be negative, as losses exceeding non-controlling interest were attributed to the parent and absorbed accordingly.

An entity shall attribute the *profit* or *loss* and each component of other comprehensive income to the owners of the parent and to the non-controlling interest. The entity shall also attribute total comprehensive income to the owners of the parent and to the non-controlling interests even if this results in the non-controlling interest having a deficit balance.

H. Accounting for Subsidiaries, Joint Controlled Entities and Associates in the Parent's Separated Financial Statements:

The parent is expected to show in its *separate/individual financial statement* the investments in subsidiaries, jointly controlled entities and associates at fair value at *initial measurement* (*first acquisition*) and subsequently *re-measured* based on *IFRS 9* (which include at *amortised cost, fair value through profit or loss, and fair value through other comprehensive income*) or *IAS 39* (*as applicable*).

I. Non-Controlling Interests:

IFRS 10 allows two alternative ways of accounting for non-controlling interest in the consolidated statement of the financial position upon acquisition. Non-controlling interest can be measured upon acquisition at:

a) Its proportion share of the fair value of the subsidiary's net assets.
b) Full (or fair) value (usually based on the market value of the shares held by non-controlling interest).

A parent shall present non-controlling interest in the consolidated statement of financial position within equity, separately from the equity of the owners of the parent. Non-controlling interest is no allowed to be presented as a **mezzanine finance** (*i.e. presented between equity line and liabilities, due to the fact that the group is now viewed as an economic unit, in which non-controlling interest is an investor in the group*). Changes in a parent's ownership interest in a subsidiary that do not result in the parent losing control of the subsidiary are considered equity transactions (*i.e. transactions with equity holders in their capacity as owners*).

Technical Note:
The option to value non-controlling interest at fair value is introduced by the revised IFRS 3 (2011), but it is just an option, which the company can choose to adopt it or continue to value non-controlling interest at a share of net assets. The option is applicable to different business combinations.

Basic Principles of Group Accounts

J. Gain on a Bargain Purchase:

Initially, goodwill arising from consolidation is the difference between the cost of combination (cost of acquisition) and the fair value of the subsidiary's net assets acquired, which is positive. But, sometimes the difference can be negative, which simply shows that the cost of combination may be less than the fair value of the subsidiary's net assets acquired (i.e. the aggregate of the fair value of the separable net assets acquired exceed what the parent company paid for them. *IFRS 3* refers to this as a "Bargain Purchase").

IFRS 3 recommended the following upon recognition of *Gain from Bargain Purchase*:

a) An entity (parent) should first re-assess the amounts at which it has re-measured both the cost of combination and the acquiree's (investee's) identifiable net assets. This exercise is expected to identify any error.
b) Any excess remaining should be recognised immediately as a gain in Group Profit or Loss.

K. Contingent Consideration:

The revised *IFRS 3* requires the acquisition-date fair value of contingent consideration to be recognised as part of the consideration for the acquiree once it can be measured reliably (i.e. The acquirer shall recognise the acquisition-date fair value of contingent consideration as part of the consideration transferred in exchange for the acquiree). The acquirer may be required to pay contingent consideration in form of equity or of a debt instrument or cash. An equity instrument should be presented as under *IAS 32* (Financial Instruments – Presentation). Contingent consideration can also be an asset if the consideration has already been transferred and the acquirer has the right to receiving returns of some of it, if certain situations or conditions *do* or *do not* exist.

Some changes in the fair value of contingent consideration that the acquirer recognises after the acquisition date may be as a result of additional information that the acquirer obtained after that date about facts and circumstances that existed at the acquisition date. Such changes are measurement period adjustments in accordance with *IFRS 3 (Revised)*.

However, changes resulting from events after the acquisition date, such as meeting an earnings target, reaching a specified share price or reaching a milestone on a research and development project, are not measurement period adjustments.

The acquirer shall account for changes in the fair value of contingent consideration that are not measurement period adjustments as follows:

(a) Contingent consideration classified as equity shall not be re-measured and its subsequent settlement shall be accounted for within equity.

(b) Other contingent consideration that:

i. Is within the scope of *IFRS 9* (or *IAS 39*); shall be measured at fair value at each reporting date and changes in fair value shall be recognised in profit or loss in accordance with the standard.
ii. Is not within the scope of *IFRS 9* (or *IAS 39*); shall be measured in accordance with the requirement of *IAS 37* (Provisions and Contingencies).

Technical Note:
The previous version of IFRS 3 only required contingent consideration to be recognised if it was probable that it would become payable and the consideration can be measured reliably. IFRS 3 revised dispenses

with this requirement – all contingent considerations are now recognised. It is possible that the fair value of the contingent consideration may change after the acquisition date. If this is due to additional information obtained that affects the position at the acquisition date, goodwill should be re-measured. If the change is due to events after the acquisition date (such as a higher earnings target has been met, so more is payable) it should be accounted for under IFRS 9 (or IAS 39) where the consideration is in form of a financial instrument (such as loan notes) or under IAS 37 as an increase in a provision if it is cash. Any equity instrument is not re-measured.

Post-Acquisition Changes in the Fair Value of the Contingent Consideration

The treatment depends on the circumstances as thus:

a) If the change in the fair value is due to additional information obtained that affects the position at the acquisition date, goodwill should be re-measured.

b) If the change is due to events which took place after the acquisition date, for example, meeting earnings targets:
   i. Account for under IFRS 9 or IAS 39 (Financial Instruments – Recognition and Measurement) if the consideration is in form of a financial instrument, for example, loan notes.
   ii. Account for under IAS 37 (Provisions, Contingent Liabilities and Contingent Assets) if the consideration is in the form of cash.
   iii. An equity instrument is not re-measured.

L. **IFRS 3 and Fair Value of Subsidiary's Net Assets:**
The acquirer should recognise the acquiree's identifiable assets, liabilities and contingent liabilities at the acquisition date only if they satisfy the following criteria:

a) In the case of an asset other than an intangible asset, it is probable that any associated future economic benefits will flow to the acquirer, and its fair value can be measured reliably.

b) In the case of a liability other than a contingent liability, it is probable that an outflow of resources embodying economic benefits will be required to settle the obligation, and its fair value can be measured reliably.

c) In the case of intangible assets or a contingent liability, its fair value can be measured reliably.

The acquiree's identifiable assets and liabilities might include assets and liabilities not previously recognised in the acquiree's financial statements. The fair value shall be regarded as the fair value on initial recognition of a financial asset in accordance with *IFRS 9* or, when appropriate, the cost on initial recognition of an investment in an associate or joint venture.

M. **Restructuring and Future Costs:**
Liabilities for future losses or other costs expected to be incurred as a result of business combination should not be recognised by the acquirer. *IFRS 3* explains that plan to restructure a subsidiary subsequent to its acquisition is not a present obligation of the acquiree at the acquisition date, neither does it meet the definition of a contingent liability. Invariably, an acquirer should not recognise a liability for such a restructuring plan as part of allocating the cost of the combination unless the subsidiary was already committed to the plan before the acquisition.

N. Indemnification assets:

The seller in a business combination may contractually indemnify the acquirer for the outcome of a contingency or uncertainty related to all or part of a specific asset or liability. For example, the seller may indemnify the acquirer against losses above a specified amount on a liability arising from a particular contingency; in other words, the seller will guarantee that the acquirer's liability will not exceed a specified amount.

As a result, the acquirer obtains an indemnification asset. The acquirer shall recognise an indemnification asset at the same time that it recognises the indemnified item measured on the same basis as the indemnified item, subject to the need for a valuation allowance for uncollectible amounts. Therefore, if the indemnification relates to an asset or a liability that is recognised at the acquisition date and measured at its acquisition-date fair value, the acquirer shall recognise the indemnification asset at the acquisition date measured at its acquisition-date fair value.

For an indemnification asset measured at fair value, the effects of uncertainty about future cash flows because of collectibility considerations are included in the fair value measurement and a separate valuation allowance may not be necessary.

Technical Note:

At the end of each subsequent reporting period, the acquirer shall measure an indemnification asset that was recognised at the acquisition date on the same basis as the indemnified liability or asset, subject to any contractual limitations on its amount and, for an indemnification asset that is not subsequently measured at its fair value, management's assessment of the collectability of the indemnification asset. The acquirer shall derecognise the indemnification asset only when it collects the asset, sells it or otherwise loses the right to it.

O. Intangible Assets:

The acquiree in some instances may have intangible assets, such as development cost of software, and other development expenditures. These can be recognised separately from goodwill only if they are identifiable. An intangible asset is identifiable only if it meets:

a) *Separability Criterion*[16]: The intangible asset is capable of being separated or divided from the entity that holds it, and sold, transferred, licensed, rented, or exchanged, regardless of the acquirer's intent to do so. An intangible asset meets this criterion even if its transfer would not be alone, but instead would be accompanied or bundled with a related contract, other identifiable asset, or a liability.

b) *Legal/Contractual Criterion*[17]: The intangible asset results from contractual or other legal rights. An intangible asset meets this criterion even if the rights are not transferable or separable from other rights and obligations of the acquiree.

IFRS 3(R) organises groups of identifiable intangibles into categories related to or based on *Marketing-related, Customers or Client-related, Artistic Works-related, Contractual-related, and Technological-related intangible assets.*

---

[16] Is separable, i.e. capable of being separated or divided from the entity and sold, transferred, or exchanged, either individually or together with a related contract, asset or liability

[17] Arises from contractual or other legal rights

P. Goodwill and Impairment:

Goodwill arising on consolidation is subjected to an annual impairment review and impairment may be expressed as an amount or a percentage. Goodwill should be carried in the statement of financial position at cost less any accumulated impairment losses.

Adjustments after the Initial Accounting Is Complete

In some situations, the fair value of the acquiree's identifiable assets, liabilities and contingent liabilities or the cost of the combination can only be determined provisionally by the end of the period in which the combination takes place. In this situation, the acquirer should account for the combination using those provisional values. The acquirer should recognise any adjustments to those provisional values as a result of completing the initial accounting:

a) Within twelve (12) months of the acquisition date, and
b) From the acquisition date (i.e. retrospectively).

This means that:

a) The carrying amount of an item that is recognised or adjusted as a result of completing the initial accounting shall be calculated as if its' fair value at the acquisition date had been recognised from that date.

b) Goodwill should be adjusted from the acquisition date by an amount equal to the adjustment to the fair value of the item being recognised or adjusted.

Any further adjustments after the initial accounting are complete should be recognised only to correct an error in accordance with *IAS 8 (Accounting Policies, Changes in Accounting Estimates and Errors)*. Any subsequent changes in estimates are dealt with in accordance with *IAS 8* (i.e. the effect is recognised in the current and future periods). *IAS 8* requires an entity to account an error correction retrospectively and to present financial statements as if the error had never occurred by restating the comparative information for the prior period(s) in which the error occurred.

Technical Note:

IAS 36 (Impairment of Assets) requires a subsidiary's full goodwill impairment to be allocated between the parent and the non-controlling interest on the same basis as the subsidiary's profits and losses are allocated. Although, it could be argued that this requirement depicts anomaly, but in this context, the impairment of goodwill on consolidation is to be allocated proportionately, even if the contribution to full goodwill by the non-controlling interest is not itself proportionate.

Q. Measurement period

If the initial accounting for a business combination is incomplete by the end of the reporting period in which the combination occurs, the acquirer shall report in its financial statements provisional amounts for the items for which the accounting is incomplete. During the measurement period, the acquirer shall retrospectively adjust the provisional amounts recognised at the acquisition date to reflect new information obtained about facts and circumstances that existed as of the acquisition date and, if known, would have affected the measurement of the amounts recognised as of that date.

During the measurement period, the acquirer shall also recognise additional assets or liabilities if new information is obtained about facts and circumstances that existed as of the acquisition date and, if known, would have resulted in the recognition of those assets and liabilities as of that date. The measurement period ends as soon as the acquirer receives the information it was seeking from facts and circumstances that existed as of the acquisition date or learns that more information is not obtainable. However, the measurement period shall not exceed one year from the acquisition date.

Technical Note:

The measurement period is the period after the acquisition date during which the acquirer may adjust the provisional amounts recognised for a business combination. The measurement period provides the acquirer with a reasonable time to obtain the information necessary to identify and measure the following as of the acquisition date in accordance with the requirements of IFRS 3:

- *The identifiable assets acquired, liabilities assumed and any non-controlling interest in the acquiree;*
- *The consideration transferred for the acquiree (or the other amount used in measuring goodwill);*
- *In a business combination achieved in stages, the equity interest in the acquiree previously held by the acquirer; and*
- *The resulting goodwill or gain on a bargain purchase.*

R. Reacquired rights:

The acquirer shall measure the value of a reacquired right recognised as an intangible asset on the basis of the remaining contractual term of the related contract regardless of whether market participants would consider potential contractual renewals when measuring its fair value.

Technical Note:

A reacquired right recognised as an intangible asset shall be amortised over the remaining contractual period of the contract in which the right was granted. An acquirer that subsequently sells a reacquired right to a third party shall include the carrying amount of the intangible asset in determining the gain or loss on the sale.

S. Reverse Acquisitions

IFRS 3 also addresses a certain type of acquisition, known as a *reverse acquisition or takeover*. This occurs when a company (*hypothetically called Success Plc*) acquires ownership of another company (*hypothetically called Dynamic Limited*) through a share exchange. (For example, a private entity may arrange to have itself 'acquired' by a smaller public entity as a means of obtaining a stock exchange listing). The number of shares issued by *Success Plc* as consideration to the shareholders of *Dynamic Limited* is so great that *control* of the combined entity after the transaction is with the shareholders of *Dynamic Limited*.

In legal terms, *Success Plc* may be regarded as the parent or controlling entity, but IFRS 3 states that, as it is *Dynamic Limited* shareholders who control the combined entity, *Dynamic Limited* should be treated as the acquirer. *Dynamic Limited* should apply the acquisition (or full consolidation) method to the assets and liabilities of *Success Plc*.

Furthermore, reverse acquisitions sometimes occur when a private operating entity wants to become a public entity but do not want to register its equity shares. To accomplish that, the private entity will arrange for a public entity to acquire its equity interests in exchange for the equity interests of the public entity. In this example, the public entity is the *legal acquirer* because it issued its equity interests, and the private entity is the *legal acquiree* because its equity interests were acquired. However, application of the guidance in the standard (*IFRS 3*) results in identifying:

a) The public entity as the acquiree for accounting purposes (the accounting acquiree); and
b) The private entity as the acquirer for accounting purposes (the accounting acquirer).

Technical Note:
The accounting acquiree must meet the definition of a business for the transaction to be accounted for as a reverse acquisition, and all of the recognition and measurement principles in IFRS 3, including the requirement to recognise goodwill, apply.

T. Contingent Liabilities:
IAS 37 (Provisions, Contingent Liabilities and Contingent Assets) defines a contingent liability as:

- ✓ A possible obligation that arises from past events and whose existence will be confirmed only by the occurrence or non-occurrence of one or more uncertain future events not wholly within the control of the entity; or

- ✓ A present obligation that arises from past events but is not recognised because:
  - It is not probable that an outflow of resources embodying economic benefits will be required to settle the obligation; or
  - The amount of the obligation cannot be measured with sufficient reliability.

The requirements in *IAS 37* do not apply in determining which contingent liabilities to recognise as of the acquisition date. Instead, the acquirer shall recognise as of the acquisition date a contingent liability assumed in a business combination if it is a present obligation that arises from past events and its fair value can be measured reliably. Therefore, contrary to *IAS 37*, the acquirer recognises a contingent liability assumed in a business combination at the acquisition date even if it is not probable that an outflow of resources embodying economic benefits will be required to settle the obligation.

After initial recognition and until the liability is settled, cancelled or expires, the acquirer shall measure a contingent liability recognised in a business combination at the higher of:

- The amount that would be recognised in accordance with *IAS 37*; and
- The amount initially recognised less, if appropriate, cumulative amortisation recognised in accordance with *IAS 18* Revenue (or IFRS 15 if early adopted).

Technical Note:
This requirement does not apply to contracts accounted for in accordance with IFRS 9/IAS 39.

U. Spin-off:
This entails the creation of an independent entity through the sale or distribution of new shares of an existing business/division of a parent company. This occurs occasionally when an entity disposes a wholly or partly owned subsidiary, or of an investee, by transferring it unilaterally to the entity's shareholders.

V. Special-Purpose Entity (SPE):
Is an entity created to accomplish a narrow and well-defined objective (e.g. to lease, research and development activities, or a securitization of financial assets), which can be a *corporation, trust, partnership or unincorporated entity*.

W. Reverse Spin-off:
It entails a spin-off transaction in which the *nominal or legal spinnor* is to be accounted for as the spine, in order to reflect the economic reality of the spin-off transaction.

Accounting for Business Combination (Acquisition Method)

IFRS 3(R) requires the accounting for the business combination to be based on *"Acquisition Method"* (*formerly termed the "Purchase Method"*) by the acquirer/investor. The change in terminology (i.e. *nomenclature*) emanated from the emphasis made by *IFRS 3(R)* that a business combination can occur even when a purchase transaction is not involved.

Acquisition method involves applying the following steps:

1. Identification of the acquirer.
2. Determination of the acquisition date (or so, the date of inclusion).
3. Recognition and measurement of identifiable tangible and intangible assets acquired and liabilities assumed.
4. Identification of assets and liabilities requiring a separate accounting.
5. Classification or designation of identifiable assets acquired and liabilities assumed.
6. Recognition and measurement of any non-controlling interest in the acquiree (subsidiary).
7. Measurement of the consideration transferred.
8. Recognition and measurement of goodwill or gain on bargain purchase (negative goodwill).

STEPS IN ACQUISITION METHOD ACCOUNTING OF BUSINESS COMBINATION

STEP 1: Identifying the acquirer

For each business combination, one of the combining entities shall be identified as the acquirer. The acquirer is the entity that obtains control of another entity, i.e. the acquiree.

STEP 2: Determining the acquisition date

The acquirer shall identify the acquisition date, which is the date on which it obtains control of the acquiree. The date on which the acquirer obtains control of the acquiree is generally the date on which the acquirer legally transfers the consideration, acquires the assets and assumes the liabilities of the acquiree—the closing date. However, the acquirer might obtain control on a date that is either earlier or later than the closing date. For example, the acquisition date precedes the closing date if a written agreement provides that the acquirer obtains control of the acquiree on a date before the closing date. An acquirer shall consider all pertinent facts and circumstances in identifying the acquisition date.

STEP 3: Recognition and measurement of identifiable tangible and intangible assets acquired and liabilities assumed

As of the acquisition date, the acquirer shall recognise, separately from goodwill, the identifiable assets acquired, the liabilities assumed and any non-controlling interest in the acquiree.

To qualify for recognition as part of applying the acquisition method, the identifiable assets acquired and liabilities assumed must meet the definitions of assets and liabilities in the *Framework for the Preparation and Presentation of Financial Statements* at the acquisition date. For example, costs the acquirer expects but is not obliged to incur in the future to effect its plan to exit an activity of an acquiree or to terminate the employment of or relocate an acquiree's employees are not liabilities at the acquisition date. Therefore, the acquirer does not recognise those costs as part of applying the acquisition method. Instead, the acquirer recognises those costs in its post-combination financial statements in accordance with other IFRSs.

STEP 4: The acquirer shall measure the identifiable assets acquired and the liabilities assumed at their acquisition-date fair value

For each business combination, the acquirer shall measure at the acquisition date components of non-controlling interests in the acquiree that are present ownership interests and entitle their holders to a proportionate share of the entity's net assets in the event of liquidation at either:
  i. Fair value; or
  ii. The present ownership instruments' proportionate share in the recognised amounts of the acquiree's identifiable net assets.

All other components of non-controlling interests shall be measured at their acquisition-date fair value unless another measurement basis is required by IFRSs.

Technical Note:
In addition, to qualify for recognition as part of applying the acquisition method, the identifiable assets acquired and liabilities assumed must be part of what the acquirer and the acquiree (or its former *owners*) exchanged in the business combination transaction rather than the result of separate transactions.

STEP 5: Identification of assets and liabilities requiring separate accounting

The acquirer's application of the recognition principle and conditions may result in recognising some assets and liabilities that the acquiree had not previously recognised as assets and liabilities in its financial statements. For example, the acquirer recognises the acquired identifiable intangible assets, such as a brand name, a patent or a customer relationship, that the acquiree did not recognise as assets in its financial statements because it developed them internally and charged the related costs to expense.

STEP 6: Classification or designation of identifiable assets acquired and liabilities assumed

The acquirer shall make those classifications or designations on the basis of the contractual terms, economic conditions, its operating or accounting policies and other pertinent conditions as they exist at the acquisition date.

In some situations, *IFRSs* provide for different accounting depending on how an entity classifies or designates a particular asset or liability. Examples of classifications or designations that the acquirer shall make on the basis of the pertinent conditions as they exist at the acquisition date include but are not limited to:

- Classification of particular financial assets and liabilities as a financial asset or liability at fair value through profit or loss, or as a financial asset available for sale or held to maturity, in accordance with IAS 39 *Financial Instruments: Recognition and Measurement*;
- Designation of a derivative instrument as a hedging instrument in accordance with IAS 39; and
- Assessment of whether an embedded derivative should be separated from the host contract in accordance with IAS 39 (which is a matter of 'classification' as this IFRS uses that term).

Exceptions to the aforementioned principles include:
- Classification of a lease contract as either an operating lease or a finance lease in

accordance with IAS 17 *Leases*; and
- Classification of a contract as an insurance contract in accordance with *IFRS 4 - Insurance Contracts*.

The acquirer shall classify those contracts on the basis of the contractual terms and other factors at the inception of the contract (or if the terms of the contract have been modified in a manner that would change its classification, at the date of that modification, which might be the acquisition date).

STEP 7: Recognition and measurement of any non-controlling interest in the acquiree (investee)

The acquirer is required to measure any non-controlling interest in the acquiree at either of:
i. Acquisition-date fair value, or
ii. The proportionate share of the identifiable assets acquired and liabilities assumed at of the acquisition-date (i.e. measure at the share of acquisition-date net assets).

Technical Note:
A parent shall present non-controlling interests in the consolidated statement of financial position within equity, separately from the equity of the owners of the parent.

STEP 8: Measurement of the consideration transferred

The acquirer shall measure consideration as of the acquisition date as the aggregate of:
i. The consideration transferred measured in accordance with *IFRS 3*, which generally requires acquisition-date fair value;
ii. The amount of any non-controlling interest in the acquire measured in accordance with this *IFRS*; and
iii. In a business combination achieved in stages, the acquisition-date fair value of the acquirer's previously held equity interest in the acquiree.

STEP 9: Recognising and measuring goodwill or a gain from a bargain purchase

The acquirer shall recognise goodwill as of the acquisition date measured as the excess of Consideration Transferred (and/or transferable); and the net of the acquisition-date amounts of the identifiable assets acquired and the liabilities assumed measured in accordance with *IFRS 3*. Otherwise, where the goodwill is negative, gain on **Bargain Purchase Transaction** is recognised in profit or loss of the group upon acquisition.

SUMMARY OF CHAPTER 2

1. A group is considered to comprise of the parent and its subsidiaries. A parent is the business entity that controls the financial and operating policies of the other entity (i.e. the subsidiary). The subsidiary is seen as the business entity that is susceptible to the control of the parent entity.
2. Whenever a group exists, there is a responsibility saddled with the parent to prepare group accounts.
3. Group accounts are the accounts of the parent and its subsidiaries "*as if*" they are accounts of a single economic entity.
4. The starting point of preparing group accounts is the first date the parent obtains control of the subsidiary.
5. The parent ceases to prepare group accounts only when it no longer has control over the financial and operating policies of the subsidiary. Invariably, when control of the subsidiary is lost or deemed to be lost.
6. Acquisition date is the date on which the acquirer obtains control of the acquiree.
7. Non-controlling interest represents the stake in the subsidiary other than that of the parent.
8. Control represents the power over the investee; the exposure, or rights, to variable returns from its involvement with the investee; and the ability to use its power over the investee to affect the amount of the investor's returns.
9. Potential voting rights may be considered where it is likely other than not that it will be exercised in the immediate future period in assessing the existence of control in an acquisition.
10. Acquisition-related costs are either expensed in profit or loss if they do not relate to issues of shares or debt instruments, and where acquisition related costs are attributable to issue of shares and/or the issue of debt instrument, such costs are used to reduce the proceeds on equity instruments and debt instruments in accordance with the requirement of IAS 32 and IAS 39/IFRS 9 respectively.
11. The acquisition method of accounting in a business combination may result in either a positive goodwill (i.e. partial or full goodwill) or negative goodwill (which results in a gain on bargain purchase).
12. The allowance is provided for the acquirer in a business combination to adopt provisional values in the accounting for business combination within the first twelve months of acquisition (termed, the "*Measurement Period*"); while subsequent adjustment within that period is permitted to restate the acquisition date accounting which may affect goodwill or gain on bargain purchase.
13. Where fair value is obtained after the elapse of the measurement period (i.e. grace period), the requirement of IAS 8 (Accounting Policies, Estimates and Errors) may apply.
14. Provisional values are either the carrying amount or other equivalent measures other than the fair value which is adopted as a surrogate for the acquisition-date fair value.
15. Non-controlling interest can either be accounted for at proportionate share of the identifiable net assets of the subsidiary at acquisition-date, or at the acquisition-date fair value of the equity instruments of the subsidiary.

16. Losses of the subsidiary can no longer be absorbed wholly by the acquirer or the parent, but such losses attributable to the non-controlling interest should be recognised in full, even when it results in a negative amount. Invariably, non-controlling interest can be negative and accounted for within equity.

17. It is preferable that the parent and the subsidiary have the same accounting period (i.e. year-end) to facilitates seamless process of consolidation, but situations are recognised that may warrant different reporting dates, but the consideration by the standard is such that the difference should not exceed 3 months; and material transactions within the 3 months should be adjusted for in the consolidation process. Where the difference in the reporting date is more than 3 months, a reconstruction of the accounts of the subsidiary to align with the reporting period of the parent will be necessary in order to conform to the requirement of IFRS 10.

18. Before consolidation of the subsidiary accounts with that of the parent, efforts should be made to adjust the financial statements of the subsidiary to reflect the accounting policies of the parent (which invariably is the accounting policies of the group).

19. The reverse acquisition may take place in a situation where the statutory acquirer (based on the legal structuring of the acquisition) later becomes the substantive acquiree; and the statutory acquiree now becomes the substantive acquirer. This is much more a strategy adopted by non-quoted companies to get listing status in the capital market.

20. There is an exception to the principle of IAS 37 on the recognition of contingent liabilities. Contingent liabilities are not to be accounted for; rather contingent liabilities are to be disclosed on the basis of materiality. The exception is the case in a business combination, as IFRS 3 requires the recognition of contingent liabilities that arose from a present obligation and of which the fair value can be reasonably and reliably measured or ascertained as at the acquisition date. Invariably, such recognition and accounting for contingent liabilities upon business combination will have effects in the measurement of goodwill or gain on bargain purchase transaction.

21. IFRS 10 contains special accounting requirements for investment entities. Where an entity meets the definition of an 'investment entity' (see above), it does not consolidate its subsidiaries or apply IFRS 3 Business Combinations when it obtains control of another entity.

END OF CHAPTER 2 EXERCISES

1. _____ exists where one company (considered the parent) controls, either directly or indirectly, another company (the subsidiary).
2. What constitutes group accounts?
3. Can a parent company with at least a subsidiary be exempted from preparing group accounts? If YES, kindly illustrate such instance(s).
4. What basis provides an avenue for the exclusion of a subsidiary from consolidation in group accounts?
5. What is non-controlling interest?
6. Are there options to accounting for non-controlling interest upon business combination? Describe, and which option is much preferable?
7. Is it arguable that non-controlling interest cannot reflect a negative amount in the consolidated financial position?
8. How are the following acquisition-related costs in business combination treated?
    a) Issue of shares
    b) Raising of debt instrument(s)
    c) Those relating to legal, professional, valuation and accounting services
9. Is it compulsory that the accounting policies and reporting date of the parent and the subsidiary be the same? Elucidate
10. Describe a reverse acquisition with the practical scenario.

Chapter 3

Accounting for Investment in Parent's (Separate) Statement of Financial Position

INTRODUCTION

This chapter will introduce the readers to different forms of purchase considerations available in a business combination.

Within the chapter, the cash consideration, shares exchange or considerations, assets transfers, issue of the debt instrument(s), deferred and contingent considerations will all be evaluated and their accounting implications considered.

The readers will further be introduced to the need to first recognise investment of the investor in the investee in its separate financial statements prior to any consideration for the consolidation of the subsidiary final results with that of the parent.

In conclusion, the subsequent effects of the accounting for changes in the fair value vis-à-vis the unwinding of discount inherent or embedded in the present value of the deferred and contingent considerations (other than those related to equity consideration) will all be considered in their details

ACCOUNTING FOR INVESTMENT IN PARENT'S [SEPARATE] STATEMENT OF FINANCIAL POSITION

IAS 27 ([18]*Separate financial statements*) requires an entity preparing separate financial statements to account for those investments at *cost*, equity method as described in *IAS 28*, or in accordance with *IAS 39/IFRS 9 Financial Instruments*. IAS 27 - *Separate financial statements* contains accounting and disclosure requirements for investments in subsidiaries, joint ventures and associates when an entity prepares separate financial statements.

Separate financial statements are those presented by a parent (i.e. an investor with control of a subsidiary) or an investor with joint control of, or significant influence over, an investee, in which the investments are accounted for at cost, equity method as described in *IAS 28*, or at fair value in accordance with *IAS 39/IFRS 9- Financial Instruments*.

Technical Note:
Financial statements in which the equity method is applied are not separate financial statements. Similarly, the financial statements of an entity that does not have a subsidiary, associate or joint venturer's interest in a joint venture are not separate financial statements.

Transactions and Events Accounted for as Business Combinations

A business combination results from the occurrence of a transaction or other event that results in an acquirer obtaining control of one or more businesses. This can occur in many different ways that include the following examples individually or in some cases, in combination:

1. Transfer of cash, cash equivalents, or other assets, including the transfer of assets of another business of the acquirer;
2. Incurring of liabilities;
3. Issuance of equity instruments;
4. Providing more than one type of consideration; or
5. By contract alone without transfer of consideration, such as when:
    a) An acquire business repurchases enough of its own ordinary shares to cause one of its existing investors (now the acquirer) to obtain control over it.
    b) There is a lapse of minority veto rights that had previously prevented the acquirer from controlling the acquiree in which it held majority voting interest.
    c) An acquirer and acquire contractually agree to combine their businesses without a transfer of consideration between them.

ILLUSTRATIVE SCENARIOS

SCENARIO A – CASH CONSIDERATION

Given the statement of financial position of **PARENT Plc** immediately prior to the company investing in the entire shares of **SUBSIDIARY Limited** on 31 December 2015 at a cost of ₦50 million, and this investment is yet to be accounted for in the financial statements of the investor as shown below.

---

[18] Separate financial statements are those presented in addition to consolidated financial statements or in addition to the financial statements of an investor that does not have investments in subsidiaries but has investments in associates or joint ventures in which the investments in associates or joint ventures are required by IAS 28 to be accounted for using the equity method, other than in the circumstances given exemption such as an Investment Entities.

Accounting for Investment in Parent's (Separate) Statement of Financial Position

Statement of Financial Position as at 31st December 2015

	₦' million
Property, plant and equipment	300
Current assets	120
	420
Share Capital & Reserves:	
Equity share capital (@ ₦1 per share)	250
Reserves (Retained Earnings)	90
Current liabilities	80
	420

Suppose the consideration of ₦50 million offered is a *cash consideration* to the equity holders of **SUBSIDIARY Limited**, which is made upon acquisition. The investment should be recognised in the separate financial statements of the parent as at the date of acquisition based on the provision of *IAS 39/IFRS 9*. The fair value of the cash consideration of ₦50 million should be recognised as a *financial asset* in the separate statement of financial position of the parent, based on the following accounting entries:

    Debit: Investment in subsidiary
    Credit: Bank (a component of current assets)   ₦50 million

The separate statement of financial position of the parent after recognition of the investment in the financial assets of the subsidiary will be depicted as follows:

Parent Plc
Statement of Financial Position as at 31st December 2015

	₦' million
Property, plant and equipment	300
Investment – **Subsidiary**	50
Current assets (120-50)	70
Total Assets	**420**
Share Capital & Reserves:	
Equity share capital (@ ₦1 per share)	250
Reserves	90
Total Equity	340
Current liabilities	80
Total Equity and liabilities	**420**

SCENARIO B – SHARES CONSIDERATION (OR SHARES EXCHANGE)

In some instances, consideration can be offered in form of *shares exchange or transfer* between the shareholders of the parent (acquirer) and that of the subsidiary (acquiree), as opposed to cash consideration, which was earlier considered in the illustration above. The recognition of the shares consideration will be measured at *fair value* based on the proposition of *IAS 39/IFRS 9*. The fair value of the shares consideration of ₦50 million (**HYPOTHETICAL:** being 40 million shares @ the market price of ₦1.25) should be recognised as a financial asset in the statement of financial position of the parent, based on the following accounting entries:

    Debit: Investment in subsidiary - ₦50 million
    Credit: Equity share capital (₦1 x 40 million shares) - ₦40 million
    Credit: Share Premium (₦0.25 x 40 million shares) - ₦10 million   ₦50 million

The separate financial statements of the parent after recognition of the investment in the financial assets (*through shares consideration*) in the subsidiary will be shown as follows:

Parent Plc
Statement of Financial Position as at 31st December 2015

	₦' million
Property, plant and equipment	300
Investment – **Subsidiary**	50
Current assets	120
Total Assets	**470**
Share Capital & Reserves:	
Equity share capital (@ ₦1 per share) (250 + 40)	290
Share premium	10
Reserves	90
Total Equity	390
Current liabilities	80
Total Equity and liabilities	**470**

SCENARIO C – COMBINATION OF CASH AND SHARES CONSIDERATIONS

Furthermore, the combination of *cash and shares considerations* can take a position in the acquisition of a subsidiary. The combination will be treated in consonance with earlier treatments above as it relates to cash consideration and shares consideration. Assuming partly cash of ₦20 million was made, while the remaining as shares (equity) consideration. The fair value of the cash consideration of ₦20 million and shares consideration of ₦30 million (**HYPOTHETICAL:** being 30 million shares @ the market price of ₦1) should be recognised as a financial asset in the separate statement of financial position of the parent, based on the following accounting entries:

Debit: Investment in subsidiary - ₦50 million
Credit: Equity share capital – ₦30 million
Credit: Bank (current assets) – ₦20 million   ₦50 million

The separate financial statements of the parent after recognition of the investment in the financial assets (*through shares and cash considerations*) in the subsidiary will be depicted as follows:

Parent Plc
Statement of Financial Position as at 31st December 2015

	₦' million
Property, plant and equipment	300
Investment – **Subsidiary**	50
Current assets (120 - 20)	100
Total Assets	**450**
Share Capital & Reserves:	
Equity share capital (@ ₦1 per share) (250 + 30)	280
Reserves	90
Total Equity	370
Current liabilities	80
Total Equity and liabilities	**450**

Accounting for Investment in Parent's (Separate) Statement of Financial Position

SCENARIO D – DEBT CONSIDERATION

The investor (or acquirer) can also explore the opportunity of *issuing debt securities* towards raising cash for the acquisition or investments in the *investee company*. The debt can either be issued out-rightly to the interested public/investors or issued in exchange for shares in the investee company (*but the latter is rarely common*). The *debt* will be recognised as a *financial liability* in line with the requirement of *IAS 39IFRS 9*, and simultaneously recognise the investment (made with this cash proceeds from the issuance of debt securities) in the subsidiary in its separate financial statements as a *financial asset*.

Given that a 10% convertible debt was issued to finance the cash consideration to the equity holders of the acquired company. The fair value of the financial liability (debt securities issued) and the financial asset (cash consideration of ₦50 million) will be recognised in accordance with the provisions of *IAS 39/IFRS 9* in the separate statement of financial position of the parent, based on the following accounting entries:

Financial Liability (Issuance of 10% convertible security)
  Debit: Bank
  Credit: 10% convertible debt   ₦50 million

Financial Asset (Cash consideration for shares acquired in the subsidiary)
  Debit: Investment in subsidiary
  Credit: Bank   ₦50 million

The effect of the above entries is based on the assumptions that ₦50 million was raised through debt securities and that same amount of ₦50 million used in the acquisition and that there exists *zero (Nil)* consequence on the company's cash and bank position (assuming no transaction and issue or floating costs). The separate financial statements of the parent after recognition of a financial liability (through debt issuance) and investment in the financial assets (through cash considerations) in the subsidiary will be depicted as follows:

Parent Plc
Statement of Financial Position as at 31st December 2015

	₦' million
Property, plant and equipment	300
Investment – **Subsidiary**	50
Current assets (120 + 50 - 50)	120
Total Assets	**470**
Share Capital & Reserves:	
Equity share capital (@ ₦1 per share)	250
Reserves	90
Total Equity	340
Non-current liabilities: (10% convertible debt)	50
Current liabilities	80
Total Equity and liabilities	**470**

SCENARIO E – DEFERRED OR CONTINGENT CONSIDERATION

The concept of *contingent consideration and deferred consideration* can also be evaluated as a consideration offered by the investor to the investee, which requires further considerations been made at a future date.

Deferred consideration involves an agreement made that requires part of the consideration for the business combination be paid in the future without any condition being attached (*i.e. it is a consideration that will be made in the future with certainty*). While **Contingent consideration** is the future consideration which is based on the *occurrence or non-occurrence* of *future uncertain events* that possibly exist based on attainment of some level of performance or targets by the acquired company sometimes into the future. A special case may involve contingent consideration that requires the parent after the payment of the sum of ₦10 million cash to acquire the shares of the subsidiary, but the contract may be subject to a clause relating to contingent consideration which stipulates that if certain criteria are met in the second year of ownership (relating perhaps to performance in terms of profitability), a further ₦2 million will be payable to the former shareholders of the subsidiary.

IFRS 3 (R) requires where an element of consideration is contingent on future events, that element should be included in the overall cost of acquisition without considering further whether it is probable (*unlike in the previous IFRS 3 that requires the adjustments or inclusion of contingent consideration only if the condition is probable – i.e. chance of more than 50% of its occurrence*), but must be able to be *measured reliably* based on its *fair value*. The fair value of contingent consideration should be measured based on the present value of future consideration payable (which is determined based on the investor's *hurdle rate i.e. cost of capital*) or acquisition-date fair value of the equity instrument transferrable.

Some changes in the fair value of *contingent consideration/deferred consideration* that the acquirer recognises after the acquisition date may be the result of additional information that the acquirer obtained after that date about facts and circumstances that existed at the acquisition date. Such changes are considered measurement period adjustments in ascertaining the real amount of goodwill. However, changes resulting from events after the acquisition date, such as meeting an earnings target, reaching a specified share price or reaching a milestone on a research and development project, are not measurement period adjustments. The acquirer shall account for changes in the fair value of *contingent consideration/deferred consideration* that is not measurement period adjustments as follows:

a) *Contingent consideration/deferred consideration* classified as equity shall not be re-measured and its subsequent settlement shall be accounted for within equity.

b) *Contingent consideration/deferred consideration* classified as an asset or a liability that:
   i. Is a financial instrument and is within the scope of *IFRS 9 (or IAS 39)* shall be measured at fair value, with any resulting gain or loss recognised either in profit or loss or in other comprehensive income in accordance with *IFRS 9*.
   ii. Is not within the scope of *IFRS 9/IAS 39* shall be accounted for in accordance with *IAS 37* or other *IFRSs* as appropriate.

Technical Note:
The accounting treatment of deferred consideration and contingent consideration is the same based on the revised IFRS 3, which no longer require the payment of contingent consideration to be probable before it can be recognised as part of the fair value of the consideration upon acquisition. The technical difference in the treatment of deferred consideration and contingent consideration is not at the point of initial or subsequent recognition but at the due date of the payment, which requires the de-recognition of the liability for contingent consideration if the condition of its payment no longer exist as at the date of payment.

Where contingent consideration involves the issue of ordinary shares, there is no liability (obligation to transfer economic benefits). Recognise this as part of the equity under a separate caption representing shares to be issued.

Accounting for Investment in Parent's (Separate) Statement of Financial Position

Cash consideration of ₦50 million offered the shareholders of the acquired company and also agrees to pay a further ₦10 million on 30 July, 2016, upon attainment of certain performance in the next two years. As shown below, and given information that the investment in the financial asset is yet to be accounted for in the separate financial statements of the investor. (*Assume the parent's hurdle rate or cost of capital is 12%*).

Parent Plc
Statement of Financial Position as at 30th June 2014

	₦' million
Property, plant and equipment	300
Current assets	120
	420
Share Capital & Reserves:	
Equity share capital (@ ₦1 per share)	250
Reserves (Retained Earnings)	90
Current liabilities	80
	420

The fair of the entire consideration upon the acquisition will have to be recognised in the separate financial statements of the investor (parent) which includes the fair value of cash consideration of ₦50 million offered/paid, and the fair value of the contingent consideration of ₦10 million payable in 2 years' time. The fair value of the entire consideration transferable upon acquisition is the sum of ₦57.97 million as shown below:

	₦' million
Cash	50.00
Contingent consolidation: $[10 (1.12)^{-2}]$	7.97
	57.97

The fair value of the cash consideration of ₦50 million and the present value of the fair value of the contingent consideration of ₦10 million (which is ₦7.97 million based on discount rate of 12%) should be recognised as a financial asset in the separate statement of financial position of the parent, based on the following accounting entries:

Debit: Investment in subsidiary - ₦57.97 million
Credit: Bank (current assets) –   ₦50 million
Credit: Contingent consideration – ₦7.97 million   ₦57.97 million

Parent Plc
Statement of Financial Position as at 30th June 2014

	₦' million
Property, plant and equipment	300.00
Investment – **Subsidiary**	57.97
Current assets (120 – 50)	70.00
Total Assets	**427.97**
Share Capital & Reserves:	
Equity share capital (@ ₦1 per share)	250.00
Reserves	90.00
Total Equity	**340.00**
Non-current liabilities (*contingent consideration*)	7.97
Current liabilities	80.00
Total Equity and liabilities	**427.97**

Technical Note:
The contingent consideration is treated in accordance with the provision of IFRS 3 (R), which requires the present value of the consideration to be considered as part of the cost of investment, and equally the corresponding credit (liability) is treated in line with the position of IAS 37, which is regarded as a provision for non-current liability as the consideration is payable (in cash) in two years' time, but would have been recognised as current liability if the consideration is payable within one year. Kindly note that if the contingent consideration is payable in equity shares, IAS 39/IFRS 9 will be applied and such equity value is not to be re-measured.

Assuming one year after the acquisition of the subsidiary, the further implication of the acquisition-date recognition principle will be the unwinding of the discount inherent in the contingent to profit or loss (i.e. income statement) of the group, and simultaneously recognised an increase in the liability (for contingent consideration) as shown below:

The unwinding of discounts on contingent consideration:

    Debit: Consolidated Income Statement
    Credit: Liability – Contingent consideration   ₦0.96 million

The *discount unwound* is determined based on the increase to the present value of the contingent consideration measured one year after the acquisition, as calculated below:

Unwinding of discounts (12% x ₦7.97 million)	=	₦0.96 million	or alternatively,
			₦' million
Contingent consolidation (measured a year after): $10(1.12)^{-1}$			8.93
Contingent consolidation (as measured at acquisition-date)			(7.97)
Discount unwound			**0.96**

The implication of the unwinding of discounts of the approximate sum of ₦0.96 million is that group profit is charged with a finance cost (being the discounts unwound) and the group liability towards contingent consideration increases to ₦8.93 million (i.e. ₦7.97 million plus ₦0.96 million).

Furthermore, at the end of the second year, there are two possible outcomes which include:
- The condition attached to the contingent consideration is being attained.
- The condition attached to the contingent consideration is not being attained.

If the performance which is the condition attached to the contingent consideration is met, the discounts unwound in the sum of ₦1.07 million as determined below will be availed the same treatment as earlier displayed and as shown below:

The unwinding of discounts on contingent consideration:

    Debit: Consolidated Income Statement
    Credit: Liability – Contingent consideration   ₦1.07 million

The *discount unwound* is determined based on the increase in the present value of the contingent consideration measured two years after the acquisition, as calculated below:

Unwinding of discounts (12% x ₦8.93 million) = ₦1.07 million

or alternatively,	₦' million
Contingent consolidation (measured 2 years after): $10(1.12)^{0}$	10.00
Contingent consolidation (measured a year after)	(8.93)
Discount unwound	**1.07**

The implication of the unwinding of discounts of the approximate sum of ₦1.07 million is that group profit is charged with a finance cost (being the discount unwound) and the group liability towards contingent consideration increased to ₦10 million (i.e. ₦8.93 million plus ₦1.07 million). The balance of ₦10 million outstanding as at end of year 2 (30 June 2016) will be payable in cash for such liability to be extinguished, and accounting entry will be:

      Debit: Liability – Contingent consideration
      Credit: Cash and Bank (Cash and Cash Equivalents)   ₦0.96 million

Where the performance is not achieved as being set upon acquisition of the subsidiary, the amount of the contingent consideration may be reversed in total or partly based on the proportion of the condition met (and as may be agreed in the contract) and will be treated as a change in accounting estimate (based on *IAS 8 - Accounting Policies, Changes in Accounting Estimates and Errors*), which requires a reversal to the income statement of the group at the date the contingent consideration becomes no longer payable in full or in part (which implies relevant portion being *de-recognised as a liability of the group*) as at 30 June 2016. In this case, and where the full amount is de-recognised, the following accounting entry is required:

      Debit: Liability – Contingent consideration
      Credit: Group Profit   ₦10 million

Technical Note:
The fair value of the contingent consideration at acquisition could be different to the consideration transferred, and any differences are normally treated as a change in accounting estimate and adjusted prospectively (and not retrospective) in accordance with IAS 8.

TABULAR APPRAISAL OF INVESTMENT ACCOUNTING IN SEPARATE FINANCIAL STATEMENTS

Mode of Consideration	Fair Value Measurement	Accounting Entries in Separate Financial Statements of the Investor
Cash Consideration	Amount of cash	Debit: Investment in subsidiary Credit: Cash and cash equivalents
Shares Exchange (Transfers)	Current market value (or its equivalent measurement of fair value for unquoted equity)	Debit: Investment in subsidiary Credit: Ordinary Share Capital Credit: Share Premium
Deferred Cash Consideration	Present value of the amount of cash based on Time-Value of Money (TVM)	Debit: Investment in subsidiary Credit: Liability
Deferred Shares Transfer	Current market value (or its equivalent measurement of fair value for unquoted equity)	Debit: Investment in subsidiary Credit: Other Components of Equity (Deferred Shares Reserve)
Contingent Deferred Cash Consideration	Nevertheless on how probably the occurrence of the uncertain events, the considerations are required to be measured at its fair value at acquisition date	Debit: Investment in subsidiary Credit: Liability
Contingent Deferred Shares Transfer		Debit: Investment in subsidiary Credit: Other Components of Equity (Deferred Shares Reserve)

Tangible Assets Transfer	Fair value of the assets transferred, such as raw land or properties	Debit: Investment in subsidiary Credit: Disposal of Assets *With the fair value of the assets transferred* Debit: Disposal of Assets Credit: Assets (e.g. Properties) *With the carrying value of the assets transferred*
Debt Consideration	Proceeds on Issue of Debt (if issued to 3rd Parties) or agreed exchanged value of issuing debt to existing shareholders of the investee (or subsidiary)	Debit: Investment in subsidiary Credit: Financial Liability (Debt Obligation)

SUMMARY OF CHAPTER 3

1. A parent company that prepares group accounts may have separate financial statements.
2. CAMA requires a company that prepares group accounts to also prepare and present separate financial statements.
3. Separate financial statements are those presented by a parent (i.e. an investor with control of a subsidiary) or an investor with joint control of, or significant influence over, an investee, in which the investments are accounted for at cost, equity method as described in *IAS 28*, or at fair value in accordance with *IAS 39/IFRS 9- Financial Instruments*.
4. There are different forms of the consideration that could be exchanged in a business combination, which may include cash, shares, assets transfer, debt instrument, deferred and contingent considerations.
5. All considerations arising from business combination should be measured and recognised at acquisition-date fair value.
6. Deferred and contingent considerations (other than those attributable to the subsequent issue of shares) should be measured at present value.
7. Deferred and contingent considerations regarding the subsequent issue of shares should be measured at acquisition-date fair value, which is synonymous to the fair market price.
8. Contingent consideration should be recognised at the acquisition date, whether or not it is probable to be settled in the future or delivery of shares will be made upon occurrence or non-occurrence of future uncertain events.
9. Movements or changes in the fair value or present value of the deferred and contingent considerations should be recognised in profit or loss of the parent.
10. Whereupon settlement or at due date, the contingent consideration is no longer required as the condition(s) precedent to its settlement is not met, the amount so accrued or provided for and till date should be derecognized as a liability and reported as an income in the books of the parent.

END OF CHAPTER 3 EXERCISES

1. _____ are those presented by a parent (i.e. an investor with control of a subsidiary) or an investor with joint control of, or significant influence over, an investee, in which the investments are accounted for at cost, equity method as described in *IAS 28*, or at fair value in accordance with *IAS 39/IFRS 9- Financial Instruments*.

2. What is the requirement of CAMA (2004 as amended) with respect to the preparation of separate financial statements?

3. How is purchase consideration measured at the acquisition of a subsidiary?

4. Distinguish between deferred and contingent consideration? And illustrate how their accounting differs.

5. How are movements in deferred consideration or contingent consideration recognised?

6. Can the liability initially recognised with respect to contingent consideration be de-recognised? And if so, illuminate on such instances and the implication(s).

7. An investor who agrees to pay cash consideration of ₦80 million immediately and subsequent consideration of ₦20 million in 2 years' time. What amount should be recognised as the cost of investment in its separate financial statements at acquisition-date, when its cost of capital is 10%.

8. An investor who agrees to pay cash consideration of ₦80 million immediately and additional consideration in shares of 10 million units of which the current market price is ₦2 per share (i.e. market value of ₦20 million); and the shares are deliverable in 2 years' time. What amount should be recognised as the cost of investment in its separate financial statements at acquisition-date, when its cost of capital is 10%.

9. An investor who agrees to pay cash consideration of ₦80 million immediately and subsequent consideration of ₦20 million in 2 years' time if the subsidiary is able to attain the optimal capacity level of production of 80%. What amount should be recognised as the cost of investment in its separate financial statements a year after acquisition; and what amount of movement or changes in the present value of the deferred consideration should be recognised in the profit or loss of the parent at the end of year 1 after the acquisition. The cost of capital is 10%.

Chapter 4

Basic Principles of Group Accounts

INTRODUCTION

This chapter will introduce the reader s to the basic mechanics and accounting for business combinations at acquisition date; and also on the principles required for consolidation of the accounts of members of a group. A consideration will be given to readers to have a basic idea of various group structures.

Within the chapter, the basic concept of cancellation of investment made by the investor and the net assets of the investee will be considered; and likewise the fundamental principle of consolidation of assets and liabilities of the subsidiary in totality without recourse to the percentage ownership by the acquirer in the acquired entity (or acquiree). The concept of splitting the reserves (or retained earnings) of the subsidiary into pre-acquisition reserves (i.e. reserves held by the acquiree before acquisition by the acquirer) and post-acquisition reserves (i.e. change in reserves held by the acquiree subsequent/after the acquisition by the acquirer).

The readers will further be introduced to the concept of identifying non-controlling interest in a business combination, where the acquirer owns less than 100% stake in the ordinary shares of the acquired; and also an understanding of the accounting models for measuring non-controlling interest upon acquisition of the subsidiary will be taking into consideration. The models entail either an accounting policy option of the acquisition-date fair value of the equity instruments in the subsidiary as held by the non-controlling interest or the proportionate share of the non-controlling interest in the identifiable net assets at the acquisition of the subsidiary.

Consolidated Statement of Financial Position

The *statement of financial position* (*formerly* called the *balance sheet*) presents an entity's assets, liabilities and equity as of a specific date—the end of the **reporting period**. This is equally extended to group entities, which is often called a *consolidated statement of financial position*.

Consolidated statement of financial position is the statement of financial position of the group (parent and its subsidiaries) as if it is a single entity. This involves combining the assets and liabilities of the parent and the subsidiary on a *line-by-line* basis.

Information to be presented in the statement of financial position

As a minimum, the statement of financial position shall include line items that present the following amounts:

1. Cash and cash equivalents*
2. Trade and other receivables*
3. Financial assets (excluding amounts shown under *)
4. Inventories
5. Property, plant and equipment
6. Investment property carried at fair value through profit or loss
7. Intangible assets
8. Biological assets carried at cost less accumulated depreciation and impairment
9. Biological assets carried at fair value through profit or loss
10. Investments in associates*
11. Investments in jointly controlled entities*
12. Trade and other payables**
13. Financial liabilities (excluding amounts shown under **)
14. Liabilities and assets for current tax
15. Deferred tax liabilities and deferred tax assets (these shall always be classified as non-current)
16. Provisions**
17. Non-controlling interest, presented within equity separately from the equity attributable to the owners of the parent
18. Equity attributable to the owners of the parent

An entity shall present additional line items, headings and subtotals in the statement of financial position of the group when such presentation is relevant to an understanding of the entity's financial position.

BASIC PRINCIPLES OF CONSOLIDATION AND CONSOLIDATION MECHANICS

Let us recall what a **Group** is in the context of financial reporting. A "**Group**" consists of a *Parent and its Subsidiaries.* To understand the mechanics of consolidation of group accounts, we will first explore the form of structures a *Group* can take, which includes the following:

a) **A Simple Group Structure**
   This is a group structure depicted either as consisting of the Parent and;
   i. **A Single Subsidiary**, or
   ii. **Fellow Subsidiaries** (in which none of the subsidiaries has equity interests or stake in another subsidiary)

Basic Principles of Group Accounts

b) A Complex Group Structure
In this form of Group Structure, the parent has subsidiaries layered in phases/stages such as:
  i. **Holding Indirect Subsidiary or Subsidiaries** (otherwise called, *Sub-subsidiary – A situation where a Parent has subsidiary, and the subsidiary equally has a subsidiary in which the parent has no direct interest*), or
  ii. **Mixed Group:** This entails a Parent and its Subsidiary having a common interest that gives *Control* in another entity. This is other known as Group Structure with a "*D-SHAPE*".

PICTORIAL REPRESENTATION OF GROUP STRUCTURES

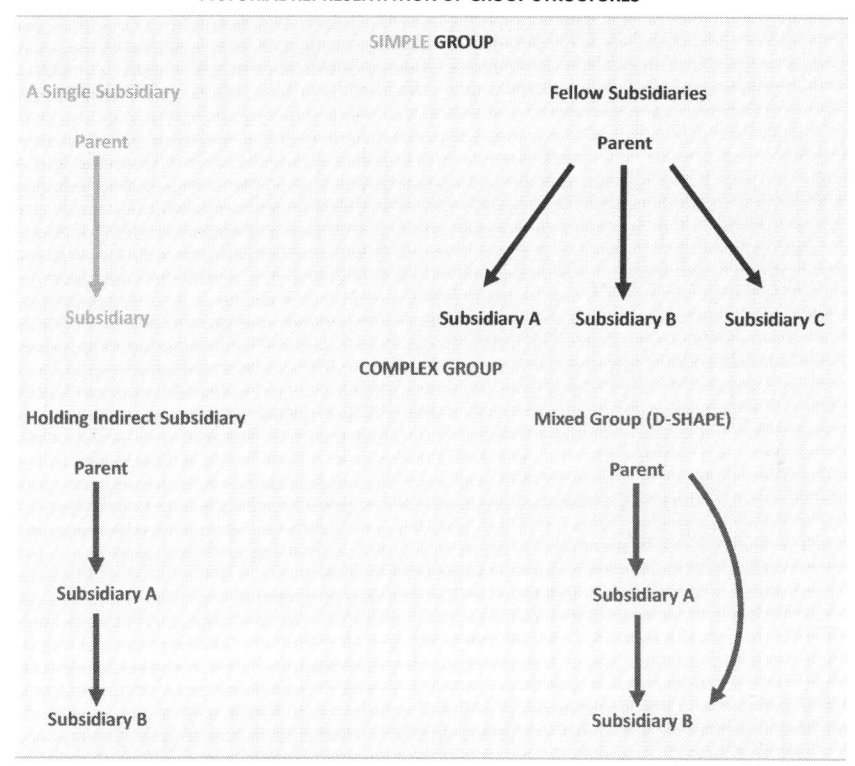

SIMPLE GROUP

A Single Subsidiary

Parent
↓
Subsidiary

Fellow Subsidiaries

Parent
↓ ↓ ↓
Subsidiary A   Subsidiary B   Subsidiary C

COMPLEX GROUP

Holding Indirect Subsidiary

Parent
↓
Subsidiary A
↓
Subsidiary B

Mixed Group (D-SHAPE)

Parent
↓ ↘
Subsidiary A
↓
Subsidiary B

Based on the understanding of Group Structures, we can now proceed to learn most of the basic principles and mechanics of consolidation by adopting a Simple Group Structure with a Single Subsidiary. Once we are able to grasp the required principles, we then apply same to other forms of Group Structures later in this text.

The General principle of consolidation is that "The financial statements of a parent and its subsidiaries are **combined on a line-by-line basis** by adding together like items of assets, liabilities, *equity*, income and expenses" subject to necessary adjustments termed "***Group Adjustments***".

79

Technical Note:
*Equity is being asterisked because most part of the equity (i.e. equity of the subsidiary at acquisition are not consolidated, but rather cancelled out upon consolidation). This principle alongside other principles will be learnt in the course of this study.

The principles to be learnt will be useful in ensuring the preparation of Group Accounts which entails the following statements:

1. Consolidated statement of financial position
2. Consolidated statement of profit or loss and other comprehensive income
3. Consolidated statement of changes in equity
4. Consolidated statement of cash flows

In this phase, we will start our understanding of the principles from the perspective of presenting the "**Consolidated Statement of Financial Position**".

FIRST PRINCIPLE:

100% OWNERSHIP OF THE SUBSIDIARY BY THE PARENT

There are situations where an investor company owns all of the voting rights in an investee company through ownership of the entire shares of the latter. In this situation, the subsidiary is said to be *wholly-owned* by the parent company. 100% ownership of a company (by the parent) in another company (in the subsidiary) will not give rise to *non-controlling interest* (*formerly known as minority interest*).

We can explore the principle of consolidating a wholly-owned subsidiary by adopting this illustration.

ILLUSTRATION 1:
The consolidation of the statement of financial position of the dual companies (parent and subsidiary) with 100% ownership of the shares of the subsidiary by the parent can be illustrated with the hypothetical scenario as shown below.

Company **P** acquired 100% of the equity shares of company **S** on the 31 December 2015 which is the reporting date for the dual companies. The statement of financial position of the two companies on this date stood as follows:

Statement of Financial Position as at 31st December 2015

	P	S
	₦' million	₦' million
Property, plant and equipment	300	130
Investment in S	180	-
Current assets	120	70
Total Assets	**600**	**200**
Share Capital & Reserves:		
Equity share capital (@ ₦1 per share)	400	120
Reserves (Retained Earnings)	120	60
	520	180
Current liabilities	80	20
Total Equity and Liabilities	**600**	**200**

Basic Principles of Group Accounts

In order to consolidate the statement of financial position of the parent (**P**) and the subsidiary (**S**), the following steps have to be observed:

- ✓ **Step 1**: *Determine the percentage holdings of investment of P in S as at the acquisition date (31 December 2015), which represents the date of inclusion (or first date of consolidation).* In this case, the percentage holding is already determined and ascertained to be 100%, otherwise, the percentage holdings can be obtained based on the proportion of shareholdings of the parent to the number of shares outstanding in the books of the subsidiary as at the date of acquisition.

- ✓ **Step 2**: *Ascertain the form of group structure in this parent-subsidiary relationship.* Since the subsidiary (**S**) is *wholly-owned* by the parent (**P**), the group structure is a simple structure as shown below:

    ```
    P
     \ 100%
      ↘
       S
    ```

- ✓ **Step 3**: *Determine the existence of goodwill or gain from a bargain purchase as at the date of acquisition based on the fair value or provisional values of subsidiary's identifiable assets and liabilities.* In this case, there exists no goodwill or gain on bargain purchase as it is shown below.

    To ascertain and determine the amount of goodwill or gain from a bargain purchase, the amount of investment of the parent (**P**) in the subsidiary (**S**) will be compared with the parent's share of identifiable assets and liabilities of the subsidiary that were acquired.

	₦' million	₦' million
Cost of business combination (i.e. the cost of investment of **P** in **S**)		180
P's share of Identifiable net assets of **S** acquired:		
• Share capital (100% of ₦120 million)	120	
• Pre-acquisition reserves (100% of ₦60 million)	60	(180)
		—

Technical Note:
For the purpose of consolidation of the statement of financial position, the subsidiary's net assets are represented by the equity at the acquisition of the subsidiary (i.e. ordinary share capital and pre-acquisition reserves of the subsidiary).

- ✓ **Step 4**: *Determine the amount of non-controlling interest as will be shown in the consolidated statement of financial position of the group.* In this case, there is no non-controlling interest as all equity interests are held by parent "**P**".

- ✓ **Step 5**: *Determine the amount to be included in the consolidated statement of financial position as consolidated reserves (otherwise known as consolidated retained earnings).* The consolidated retained earnings to be included in the consolidated statement of financial position of **P-Group** is only that of the parent, as the subsidiary retained earnings at the point of acquisition is entirely classified as *Pre-acquisition Retained Earnings*[19], which already has been considered as part of the net assets of the subsidiary upon acquisition. Invariably, it implies that only the *Post-acquisition Retained Earnings*[20] of the subsidiary that ought to be considered in ascertaining the group retained earnings. The consolidated retained earnings are usually determined as follows:

	₦' million
Parent's (**P**) retained earnings	120
Share of subsidiary's (**S**) post-acquisition retained earnings (100% of Nil)	--
	120

Technical Note:
Since the consolidation is at the date of acquisition, there exist no post-acquisition profits in the subsidiary.

- ✓ **Step 6:** Combine the assets and liabilities of the parent **(P)** and subsidiary **(S)** on an item-by-item basis (or Line-by-Line basis) excluding the initial investment of **P** in **S** as earlier shown in the separate financial statements of **P**, and also the exclusion of the equity share capital of **S**, as it has already been considered alongside with the pre-acquisition Retained Earnings in ascertaining the amount of goodwill or gain from bargain purchase inherent/embedded in the acquisition. The consolidated statement of financial position of the group will now be shown as thus:

P Group
Consolidated Statement of Financial Position as at 31 December 2015

Assets:	₦' million
Property, plant and equipment (300 + 130)	430
Current assets (120 + 70)	190
Total Assets	**620**
Share Capital & Reserves:	
Equity share capital (@ ₦1 per share)	400
Reserve (*Step 5 above*)	120
Total Equity	**520**
Current liabilities (80 + 20)	100
Total Equity & Liabilities	**620**

The above process depicts the simplest group model that we can ever come across, but the steps serve as a *stepping-stone* towards understanding the dynamics and mechanics of consolidation regardless of the group structure.

The above steps starting from *step 3 to step 5* can be replicated with a *Consolidation Schedule,* which in the long-run may make the mechanics of consolidation much easier to accommodate various adjustments required and equally for the consolidation of complex group structures such as fellow subsidiaries, indirect/sub-subsidiaries and joints subsidiaries (i.e. mixed group structure). In this case, as

---

[19] Pre-acquisition retained earnings represent retained earnings or reserves held by the subsidiary prior to acquisition or as at the acquisition-date.
[20] Post-acquisition retained earnings represent retained earnings or reserves generated (either positive or negative) after/subsequent to acquisition-date.

non-controlling interest is not involved, only two columns (i.e. *cost of control* [21] and consolidated reserves columns) are required instead of basic three columns (i.e. cost of control, non-controlling interest and consolidated reserves columns) as we will consider later in this text.

Consolidation Schedule

Subsidiary - S		Cost of control (P in S) as at 31 Dec. 2015 – 100%		Consolidated Reserves
Equity Share Capital	120	(100% x 120)	120	
Reserves (Pre-acquisition)	60	(100% x 60)	60	
Net asset on acquisition			180	
Cost of combination (cost of investment)			(180)	
			–	
P's Reserves				120
Consolidated Reserves				**120**

SECOND PRINCIPLE:

LESS THAN 100% OWNERSHIP OF THE SUBSIDIARY BY THE PARENT

In most of the cases in the group, the ownership interest of the parent company is sometimes and usually less than 100%, which means *wholly-owned* subsidiaries are less common to *partly-owned* subsidiaries, where part of the ownership interest in such subsidiaries is attributable to *non-controlling interest*. Non-controlling interest exists only where a subsidiary is partly owned by the parent company and the value of the non-controlling interest should be ascertained and shown as part of the total equity of the group, but classified under separate head (which is known as *equity attributable to non-controlling interest*) in the consolidated statement of financial position.

IFRS 3(R) establishes the principle for recognising and measuring the identifiable assets acquired, the liabilities assumed and any non-controlling interest in the acquiree. Any classifications or designations made in recognising these items must be made in accordance with the contractual terms, economic conditions; acquirer's operating or accounting policies and other factors that exist at the acquisition date.

Each identifiable asset and/or liability is measured at its acquisition-date fair value. Non-controlling interest in an acquiree that has present ownership interest and entitles their holders to a proportionate share of the entity's net assets in the event of liquidation are measured at either *fair value*[22] or the present ownership instruments' [23]*proportionate share in the recognised amounts of the acquiree's net identifiable assets*. All other components of non-controlling interests shall be measured at their acquisition-date fair value unless another measurement basis is required by *IFRSs*.

---

[21] Cost of control relates to transactions that occurred as at the date of acquisition, which entails the consideration transferred and identifiable net assets acquired.

22 The fair value is measured based on the market value of the acquiree (Subsidiary) shares prior to acquisition, and where the subsidiary is not quoted or market price cannot be obtained, other verifiable and valid valuation model can be adopted for the measurement. The fair value model is an optional model, and most be sued consistently after been adopted. The implication is that the model cannot be jettison once adopted.

23 Proportionate share in the recognised amounts of the acquiree's net identifiable assets has been the usual metric adopted in ascertaining the value of non-controlling interest prior to revision of IFRS 3.

Contemporaneous Accounting for Business Combinations and Group Accounts

Technical Note:
In a business combination achieved by contract alone, the acquirer shall attribute to the owners of the acquiree the amount of the acquiree's net assets recognised in accordance with this IFRS. In other words, the equity interests in the acquiree held by parties other than the acquirer are a non-controlling interest in the acquirer's post-combination financial statements even if the result is that all of the equity interests in the acquiree are attributed to the non-controlling interest.

We can explore the principle of consolidating a partly-owned subsidiary by adopting this illustration.

ILLUSTRATION 2:

Pally acquired 80% of the equity share capital of **Sussy** on the reporting date 31 December 2015. The statement of financial position of the two companies on this date is as shown below:

Statement of Financial Position as at 31st December 2015

	Pally ₦' million	Sussy ₦' million
Property, plant and equipment	300	130
Investment in **Sussy**	144	-
Current Assets	120	70
Total Assets	**564**	**200**
Share Capital & Reserves:		
Equity share capital (@ ₦1 per share)	400	120
Reserves (Retained Earnings)	84	60
Total Equity	**484**	**180**
Current Liabilities	80	20
Total Equity and Liabilities	**564**	**200**

In order to consolidate the statement of financial position of the parent (**Pally**) and the subsidiary (**Sussy**), the following steps have to be followed:

- ✓ **Step 1**: Determine the percentage holdings of investment of **Pally** in **Sussy** as at the acquisition date, which represents the date of inclusion (first date of consolidation). In this case, the percentage holding is already determined and ascertained to be 80%.

- ✓ **Step 2**: Ascertain the form of group structure in this parent-subsidiary relationship. Since the subsidiary (**Sussy**) is *partly-owned* by the parent (**Pally**), the group structure is still a simple structure as shown below:

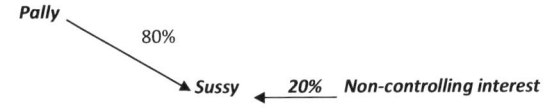

```
Pally
     \ 80%
      ↘
       Sussy ← 20%  Non-controlling interest
```

- ✓ **Step 3**: Determine the existence of goodwill or gain from a bargain purchase as at the date of acquisition based on the fair value or provisional values of subsidiary's identifiable assets and liabilities. In this case, there exists no goodwill or gain on bargain purchase as shown below.

Basic Principles of Group Accounts

To ascertain and determine the amount of goodwill or gain from a bargain purchase, the value of an investment of the parent (**Pally**) in the subsidiary (**Sussy**) will be compared with the parent's share of identifiable assets and liabilities of the subsidiary that were acquired.

	₦' million	₦' million
PARTIAL METHODOLOGY		
Cost of combination (i.e. the cost of investment of **Pally** in **Sussy**)		144
Pally's share of Identifiable net assets of **Sussy** acquired:		
• Share capital (80% of ₦120 million)	96	
• Pre-acquisition reserves (80% of ₦60 million)	48	(144)
		--

	₦' million	₦' million
FULL METHODOLOGY		
Cost of combination:		
• Cost of investment of **Pally** in **Sussy**		144
• Non-controlling interest in **Sussy** (*Step 4*)		36
		180
Identifiable net assets of **Sussy** acquired (@ 31 December 2015):		
• Share capital	120	
• Pre-acquisition reserves	60	(180)
		--

Technical Note
For the purpose of consolidation of the statement of financial position, the subsidiary's net assets are represented by the equity at the acquisition of the subsidiary (i.e. ordinary share capital and pre-acquisition reserves of the subsidiary).

✓ **Step 4:** Determine the amount of non-controlling interest as will be shown in the consolidated statement of financial position of the group. In this case, non-controlling interest will be measured at the proportionate share of subsidiary's identifiable assets and liabilities, which could be depicted as thus:

Non-controlling interest's share of Identifiable net assets of **Sussy** upon acquisition:	₦' million
• Share capital (20% of ₦120 million)	24
• Pre-acquisition reserves (20% of ₦60 million)	12
	36

✓ **Step 5:** Determine the amount to be included in the consolidated statement of financial position as consolidated reserves (otherwise known as consolidated retained earnings). The consolidated retained earnings to be included in the consolidated statement of financial position of **Pally-Group** is only that of the parent, as the subsidiary retained earnings at the point of acquisition is entirely classified as pre-acquisition retained earnings, which already has been considered as part of the net assets of the subsidiary upon acquisition. Invariably, it implies that only the post-acquisition retained earnings of the subsidiary that ought to be considered in ascertaining the group retained earnings. The consolidated retained earnings are usually determined as follows:

	₦' million
Parent's (**Pally**) retained earnings	84
Share of subsidiary's (**Sussy**) post-acquisition retained earnings (80% of Nil)	--
	84

Technical Note:
Since the consolidation is at the date of acquisition, there exist no post-acquisition profits in the subsidiary.

✓ **Step 6:** Combine the assets and liabilities of the parent (*Pally*) and subsidiary (*Sussy*) on an item-by-item basis excluding the initial investment of *Pally* in *Sussy* as earlier shown in the separate financial statements of *Pally*, and also the exclusion of the equity share capital of *Sussy*, as it has already been considered alongside with the pre-acquisition Retained Earnings in ascertaining the amount of goodwill or gain from bargain purchase inherent/embedded in the acquisition. The consolidated statement of financial position of the group will now be shown as thus:

Pally Group
Consolidated Statement of Financial Position as at 31 December 2015

Assets:	₦' million
Property, plant and equipment (300 + 130)	430
Current assets (120 + 70)	190
Total Assets	**620**
Share Capital & Reserves:	
Equity share capital (@ ₦1 per share)	400
Reserves	84
Equity attributable to *Pally's* shareholders	**484**
Non-controlling interest	36
Total Equity	**520**
Current liabilities (80 + 20)	100
Total Equity and Liabilities	**620**

Furthermore, the above process and group model can be replicated from *step 3 to step 5* with the use of consolidation schedule which in the long-run may make the mechanics of consolidation much easier to accommodate various adjustments required and equally for the consolidation of complex group structures such as *fellow subsidiaries, indirect/sub-subsidiaries and joints subsidiaries (i.e. mixed group structure)*. In this case, as non-controlling interest is now involved in this simple group, the three basic columns (i.e. cost of control, non-controlling interest and consolidated reserves columns) will be required unlike the illustration earlier considered that do requires the use of the two-column schedule (i.e. cost of control and consolidated reserves columns).

Consolidation Schedule

Subsidiary - Sussy		Cost of control (Pally in Sussy) as at 31 Dec. 2015 – 80%		Non-controlling interest – 20%		Consolidated Reserves
Equity Share Capital	120	(80% x 120)	96	(20% x 120)	24	
Reserve (Pre-acquisition)	60	(80% x 60)	48	(20% x 60)	12	
Net asset acquired			144			
Cost of combination			(144)			
			—			
Non-controlling interest					36	
Pally reserves						84
Consolidated Reserves						**84**

Fair Value of Non-Controlling Interest at Acquisition-Date

The position of the group's statement of financial position could change given that the *optional model* (*fair value measurement of the amount of non-controlling interest in the subsidiary*) is adopted. In which case the market value of the subsidiary's shares will serve as the predominant basis of ascertaining the fair value of non-controlling interest as at the date of acquisition as depicted as follows:

- ✓ **Step 4:** *Determine the amount of non-controlling interest as will be shown in the consolidated statement of financial position of the group.* In this case, non-controlling interest will then be valued at fair value, which will be assumed at this instance to equal the sum of ₦36 million based on market indicators (and simultaneously equals the amount obtained earlier as the proportionate share of the subsidiary's identifiable assets and liabilities acquired).

The consolidation schedule will slightly be modified (which will be considered later) to capture the possible effects of measurement of the amount of non-controlling interest at fair value, but in this case, there exist no such effects (because the fair value approximates the proportionate share of identifiable net assets at acquisition date) as neither do our solution result in goodwill nor gain from a bargain purchase.

In this scenario, the consolidated statement of financial position of the group remains the same, as coincidentally the fair value model and the proportionate share of net asset model produces the same amount of non-controlling interest to be included in the consolidated statement of financial position.

THIRD PRINCIPLE:

CONSOLIDATION SUBSEQUENT TO ACQUISITION AND ACCOUNTING FOR PRE & POST ACQUISITION RESERVES IN GROUP ACCOUNTS

In calculating goodwill upon acquisition or gains from a bargain purchase, pre-acquisition reserves in taken into consideration in determining the fair value of the subsidiary net assets acquired, while post-acquisition reserves will be added on to the parent's retained earnings (reserves) in ascertaining the consolidated reserves (consolidated retained earnings).

Pre-acquisition profits are profits or losses of a subsidiary made and undistributed (*i.e. retained*) before the date of acquisition and these profits/losses are a component of the net assets that exist in the subsidiary as at the date of acquisition. *Example*: If a subsidiary called "**AVA Plc**" is acquired on January 1, 2015, when its profits/reserves stood at ₦20 million, then the sum represents its pre-acquisition profits which already is part of its net asset as at the acquisition date.

Post-acquisition profits are profits or losses made subsequent to (*or after*) the date of acquisition. These profits or losses will have arisen whilst the subsidiary was under the control of the parent company, and these profits or losses will be reported through the *consolidated statement of profit or loss and other comprehensive income*, which end up in the *consolidated retained earnings* in the *consolidated statement of financial position*. *Example:* Given that the reserves of **LILLY Plc** stood at ₦20 million upon acquisition (on January 1, 2015) and as at the reporting date subsequent to acquisition (on December 31, 2015) the reserves stood at ₦30 million, hence the post –acquisition profits will stand as ₦10 million (being an increase in reserves to ₦30 million from ₦20 million). In another case, if the reserves as at

December 31, 2015, had been the sum of ₦15 million, the post-acquisition reserves would have been a loss of ₦5 million (being a decrease to ₦15 million from ₦20 million).

We can explore the principle of consolidating a partly-owned subsidiary subsequent to acquisition by adopting this illustration.

ILLUSTRATION 3:

Arsenal acquired 70% of the ordinary shares of **Manchester United** on 30 June 2015 when the balance in the latter retained earnings stood at ₦30,000.

Statement of Financial Position as at 30th June 2016

	Arsenal	Man United
	₦' 000	₦' 000
Non-current assets	500	240
Investment in **Manchester United**	196	
Current assets	140	180
	836	**420**
Share Capital & Reserves:		
Equity share capital (@ ₦1 per share)	600	250
Reserves (Retained Earnings)	186	50
	786	300
Current liabilities	50	120
	836	**420**

In order to consolidate the statement of financial position of the parent (**Arsenal**) and the subsidiary (**Manchester United**) as at 30 June 2016, the following steps have to be followed:

- ✓ **Step 1**: Determine the percentage holdings of investment of **Arsenal** in **Manchester United** as at the acquisition date (30 June 2015), which represents the date of inclusion (first date of consolidation). In this case, the percentage holding is already determined and ascertained to be 70%.

- ✓ **Step 2**: Ascertain the form of group structure in this parent-subsidiary relationship. Since the subsidiary (**Manchester United**) is *partly-owned* by the parent (**Arsenal**), the group structure is a simple structure as shown below:

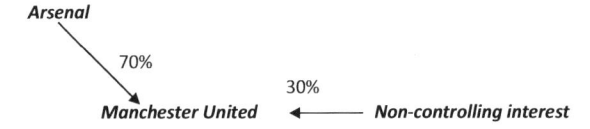

Arsenal
70%
30%
Manchester United ←———— **Non-controlling interest**

- ✓ **Step 3**: Determine the existence of goodwill or gain from a bargain purchase as the date of acquisition based on the fair value of subsidiary's identifiable assets and liabilities. In this case, there exists no goodwill or gain on bargain purchase as shown below.

To ascertain and determine the amount of goodwill or gain from a bargain purchase, the fair value of the total considerations in the subsidiary (**Manchester United**) will be compared with the identifiable assets and liabilities of the subsidiary that were acquired.

Basic Principles of Group Accounts

FULL METHODOLOGY	₦' 000	₦' 000
Cost of combination:		
• Cost of investment of **Pally** in **Sussy**		196
• Non-controlling interest in **Sussy** (*Step 4*)		84
		280
Identifiable net assets of **Sussy** acquired (@ 30 June 2015):		
• Share capital	250	
• Pre-acquisition reserves	30	(280)
		--

PARTIAL METHODOLOGY	₦'000	₦'000
Cost of combination (i.e. the cost of investment of **Arsenal** in **Manchester United**)		196
Arsenal's share of Identifiable net assets of **Manchester United** acquired:		
• Share capital (70% of ₦250,000)	175	
• Pre-acquisition reserves (70% of ₦30 million)	21	(196)
		--

Technical Note
For the purpose of consolidation of the statement of financial position, the subsidiary's net assets are represented by the equity at the acquisition of the subsidiary (i.e. ordinary share capital and pre-acquisition reserves of the subsidiary).

- ✓ **Step 4:** *Determine the amount of non-controlling interest as it will be shown in the consolidated statement of financial position of the group.* In this case, non-controlling interest will only be measured or accounted for at the proportionate share of subsidiary's identifiable assets and liabilities, which could be depicted as thus:

Non-controlling interest's share of Identifiable net assets of **Manchester United** as at 30 June 2016 is ascertained as thus:

	₦'000
• Share capital (30% of ₦250 million)	75
• Pre-acquisition reserves (30% of ₦30 million)	9
Non-controlling interest investment on acquisition (30 June 2015)	**84**
• Post-acquisition reserves (30% of ₦20 million)	6
Non-controlling interest investment as at reporting date (30 June 2016)	**90**

- ✓ **Step 5:** *Determine the amount to be included in the consolidated statement of financial position as consolidated reserves (otherwise known as consolidated retained earnings).* The consolidated retained earnings to be included in the consolidated statement of financial position of **Arsenal-Group** are that of the parent and of the parent's share of the post-acquisition profits of the subsidiary. Invariably, it implies that the share of post-acquisition Retained Earnings (which is the sum of ₦20,000 being the increase from ₦30,000 profits upon acquisition to ₦50,000 at the reporting date 30 June 2016 - a year after) of the subsidiary (**Manchester United**) will now be combined with the retained earnings (profits) of the parent (**Arsenal**) in ascertaining the group retained earnings. The consolidated retained earnings will be determined as follows:

	₦'000
Parent's (**Arsenal**) retained earnings	186
Share of subsidiary's (**Man U**) post-acquisition retained earnings (70% of ₦ 20,000)	14
	200

✓ **Step 6:** Combine the assets and liabilities of the parent (**Arsenal**) and subsidiary (**Manchester United**) on an item-by-item basis excluding the initial investment of **Arsenal** in **Manchester United** as earlier shown in the separate financial statements of **Arsenal**, and also the exclusion of the equity share capital of **Manchester United**, as it has already been considered alongside with the pre-acquisition Retained Earnings in ascertaining the amount of goodwill or gain from bargain purchase inherent/embedded in the acquisition. The consolidated statement of financial position of the group will now be shown as thus:

Arsenal Group
Consolidated Statement of Financial Position as at 30 June 2016

	₦'000
Assets:	
Non-current assets	
Property, plant and equipment (500 + 240)	740
Current asset (140 + 180)	320
Total Assets	**1,060**
Share Capital & Reserves:	
Equity share capital (@ ₦1 per share)	600
Reserves	200
Equity attributable to Arsenal's shareholders	**800**
Non-controlling interest	90
Total Equity	**890**
Current liability (50 + 120)	170
Total Equity and Liabilities	**1,060**

The consolidation schedule can equally be adopted for solving this group problem as scheduled below, adopting same mechanics as earlier carried out except for a modification to capture the effects of post-acquisition reserves on the consolidated reserves.

Consolidation Schedule

Subsidiary -Manchester United		Cost of control (Arsenal in Manchester United) as at 30 June 2015– 70%		Non-controlling interest – 30%		Consolidated Reserves
Equity Share Capital	250	(70% x 250)	175	(30% x 250)	75	
Reserves : Pre-acquisition	30	(70% x 30)	21	(30% x 30)	9	
Post-acquisition	20	-		(30% x 20)	6	(70% x 20) 14
Net assets acquired			196			
Cost of combination			(196)			
			-			
Non-controlling interest					90	
Arsenal reserves						186
Consolidated Reserves						**200**

The position of the group's statement of financial position could change given that the *optional model (fair value measurement of the amount of non-controlling interest in the subsidiary)* is adopted. In which case the market value of the subsidiary's shares will serve as the predominant basis of ascertaining the fair value of non-controlling interest as at the date of acquisition as depicted as follows:

- ✓ **Step 4:** *Determine the amount of non-controlling interest as will be shown in the consolidated statement of financial position of the group.* In this case, non-controlling interest will then be valued at fair value, which will be assumed at this instance to equal the sum of ₦84 million based on market indicators (and simultaneously equals the amount obtained earlier as the proportionate share of the subsidiary's identifiable assets and liabilities acquired).

The consolidation schedule will slightly be modified (which will be considered later) to capture the possible effects of measurement of the amount of non-controlling interest at fair value, but in this case, there exist no such effects (because the fair value approximates the proportionate share of identifiable net assets at acquisition date) as neither do our solution result in goodwill nor gain from a bargain purchase.

In this scenario, the consolidated statement of financial position of the group remains the same, as coincidentally the fair value model and the proportionate share of net asset model produces the same amount of non-controlling interest to be included in the consolidated statement of financial position.

SUMMARY OF CHAPTER 4

1. A wholly-owned subsidiary is that with 100% of its equity stake held by the parent, and which has no non-controlling interest.
2. Where a parent has less than 100% ownership of the equity of a subsidiary, the portion of the subsidiary equity held by other investors are termed "Non-controlling Interest"; and such subsidiary is considered a partly-owned subsidiary.
3. A non-controlling interest is considered the equity interest in a subsidiary other than those attributable to the parent.
4. Non-controlling interest may be accounted for within equity but as a separate class of equity.
5. Measurement and accounting for non-controlling interest at acquisition-date can either be at the acquisition-date fair value or at the proportionate share of the subsidiary's identifiable net assets at acquisition.
6. The first principle of consolidation (which may be termed first mechanics of consolidation) is the process of *netting-off* or *cancellation* of the equity investment(s) in the subsidiary and the identifiable net assets of the subsidiary at the acquisition date (both measured at acquisition-date fair value).
7. Upon acquisition, all reserves (either positive or negative) are considered pre-acquisition reserves and are deemed a component of the equity which represents the net assets.
8. Subsequent to the acquisition, there is a need to separate the reserves into pre-acquisition and post-acquisition. Pre-acquisition reserves are those reserves already aggregated and are a component of the subsidiary's net assets at acquisition, while post-acquisition reserves are the increase or decrease in the reserves since acquisition.
9. In the process of consolidation, the pre-acquisition reserves are part of the acquisition-date net assets of the subsidiary that will *cancel –out*, while the post-acquisition reserves will be consolidated (i.e. added to or subtracted from) with the reserves of the parent, in order to ascertain the consolidated reserves.
10. Consolidation requires the 100% summation of the assets and liabilities; income and expenses of the parent and the subsidiary, subject to necessary adjustments, so as to reflect the economic substance of the financial position and financial performance of the group.

END OF CHAPTER 4 EXERCISES

1. What does *'consolidation'* entails in the context of group accounts?
2. How can a non-controlling interest be recognised in a wholly-owned acquisition of a subsidiary?
3. How can a non-controlling interest be described?
4. Why the cancellation of the fair value amount of both the equity investment(s) in the subsidiary and the subsidiary's acquisition-date net assets?
5. Distinguish between pre-acquisition reserves and post-acquisition reserves and their accounting implications at the acquisition date.
6. IFRS 3 does require the *net-off* or *cancellation* of both the equity investment(s) in the subsidiary and the subsidiary's acquisition-date net assets. What is the essence?
7. Can a conclusion be reached that "the cancellation of both the equity investment(s) in the subsidiary and the subsidiary's acquisition-date net assets" perfectly offset (or net-off)?
8. What options hold for a parent that has to account for non-controlling interest within its group accounts?
9. Why will subsidiary's assets and liabilities be consolidated 100% with that of the parent assets and liabilities, without recourse (i.e. without giving consideration) to the percentage ownership or holdings in the subsidiary?
10. What constitutes a partly-owned subsidiary, and of what implication is it in acquisition-date accounting?

Chapter 5

Accounting for Goodwill and Gain on Bargain Purchase

INTRODUCTION

This chapter will introduce the readers to the concept of goodwill and gain arising from a bargain purchase transaction. In the context of this chapter, the difference between positive and negative goodwill will be considered and of their accounting implications.

Within the chapter, partial and full goodwill will be discussed in a dynamic fashion, so as to allow the readers to better appreciate the choice of accounting policies in the measurement of non-controlling interest that can result in the recognition of partial or full goodwill. Also, in this chapter readers will better appreciate the subsequent implication of making a choice towards recognition of partial or full goodwill.

The concept of impairment of goodwill will be introduced , reference will also be made to IAS 36 on how goodwill as a special form of intangible assets should be reviewed and tested for impairment vis-à-vis the basis to which the impairment losses are recognised and whether or not subsequent reversals of impairment loss es on goodwill is permitted.
The treatment of gain on bargain purchase transaction will carefully be considered and what is expected of the preparer of the group accounts to considered before such gains can be recognised; since it has been considered to have arisen from a negative goodwill.

ACCOUNTING FOR GOODWILL ON CONSOLIDATION

Goodwill represents the *excess* of the fair value of consideration (*i.e. the acquisition-date fair value of the consideration transferred plus the amount of any non-controlling interest in the acquiree plus the acquisition-date fair value of the acquirer's previously held equity interest in the acquiree*) *above* the acquisition-date fair value of the identifiable assets acquired and liabilities assumed. Presumably, if an investor company pays a premium price for the investment in the investee company, it has seen values that transcend the worth of the tangible assets and intangible assets, or else the deal would not have been consummated on such terms. Empirical evidence have shown that goodwill arising from acquisitions often traceable or consist largely of the synergies and economies of scale expected from combining the operations of the acquirer and the acquiree. IFRS 3(R) requires that all goodwill arising from business combinations or purchase of a business(es) should be recognised upon such acquisition as an *asset*.

In a *business combination* in which the acquirer and the acquiree (*or its former owners*) exchange only equity interests, the acquisition-date fair value of the acquiree's equity interests may be more reliably measurable than the acquisition-date fair value of the acquirer's equity interests. If so, the acquirer shall determine the amount of goodwill by using the acquisition-date fair value of the acquiree's equity interests instead of the acquisition-date fair value of the equity interests transferred. To determine the amount of goodwill in a business combination in which no consideration is transferred, the acquirer shall use the acquisition-date fair value of the acquirer's interest in the acquiree determined using a valuation technique in place of the acquisition-date fair value of the consideration transferred.

Technical Note:
*IFRS 3(R) requires the acquirer to recognise an increase (decrease) in the provisional amount recognised for an identifiable asset (liability) by means of a decrease (increase) in goodwill. However, new information obtained during the **measurement period** [24] may sometimes result in an adjustment to the provisional amount of more than one asset or liability. For example, the acquirer might have assumed a liability to pay damages related to an accident in one of the acquiree's facilities, part or all of which are covered by the acquiree's liability insurance policy. If the acquirer obtains new information during the measurement period about the acquisition-date fair value of that liability, the adjustment to goodwill resulting from a change to the provisional amount recognised for the liability would be offset (in whole or in part) by a corresponding adjustment to goodwill resulting from a change to the provisional amount recognised for the claim receivable from the insurer.*

The calculation of the goodwill on the acquisition can be summarized below:

	₦' million
PARTIAL METHODOLOGY	
Cost of combination (i.e. cost of acquisition) to the parent	100
Less: Parent's 80% share of the fair value of subsidiary's identifiable net assets	(88)
Positive goodwill (partial goodwill) attributable to the parent (i)	**12**
Amount of Investment in subsidiary to non-controlling interest*	30
Less: Non-controlling interest 20% share of the fair value of subsidiary's net assets	(22)
Positive goodwill attributable to non-controlling interest (ii)	**8**
Full Goodwill – positive (i) + (ii)	**20**

---

[24] Measurement Period is the period after the acquisition date during which the acquirer may adjust the provisional amounts recognised for a business combination. This period is not more than 12 months from the acquisition of the subsidiary (or acquiree).

Alternatively, the positive goodwill arising from acquisition of a subsidiary can be ascertained as thus:

FULL METHODOLOGY

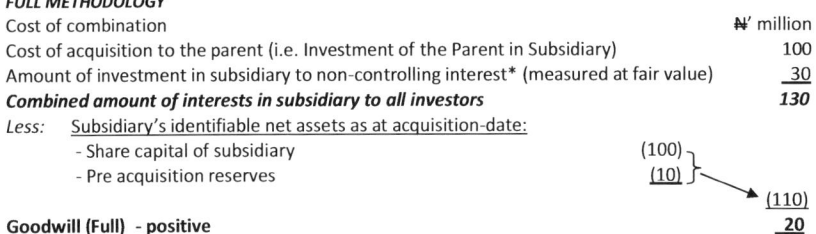

	₦' million
Cost of combination	
Cost of acquisition to the parent (i.e. Investment of the Parent in Subsidiary)	100
Amount of investment in subsidiary to non-controlling interest* (measured at fair value)	30
Combined amount of interests in subsidiary to all investors	**130**
Less: Subsidiary's identifiable net assets as at acquisition-date:	
- Share capital of subsidiary (100)	
- Pre acquisition reserves (10)	(110)
Goodwill (Full) - positive	**20**

Technical Note:
* The amount of non-controlling interest investment in the subsidiary as at acquisition can either be measured (based on revised position of IFRS 3) as follows:

- *Fair value; or*
- *The present ownership instruments' proportionate share in the recognised amounts of the acquiree's identifiable net assets.*

In accordance with *IFRS 3(R)-Business Combinations*, if the initial accounting for a business combination can be determined only provisionally by the end of the period in which the combination is effected; the acquirer:

a) Accounts for the combination using those provisional values; and
b) Recognises any adjustments to those provisional values as a result of completing the initial accounting within the measurement period, which will not exceed twelve months from the acquisition date.

Based on the *IFRS 3(R)*, the group is viewed as an *economic entity*. This means that it treats all providers of equity (including non-controlling interest) as shareholders of the group, even when they are not shareholders of the parent. Thus goodwill attributable to non-controlling interest needs to be recognised. The previous *IFRS 3* method considers goodwill calculation from the point of view of the parent *only*. It only recognises the goodwill *acquired* by the parent, and it is based on the parent's ownership interest rather than the goodwill *controlled* by the parent. Goodwill attributed to the non-controlling interest is not recognised under the former method (*old method*).

Furthermore, it is implied and taken as a benchmark treatment in measuring goodwill on acquisition that the amount of non-controlling interest upon acquisition of the subsidiary (by the parent) be measured at the proportionate share of the recognised amounts of the acquiree's (subsidiary's) identifiable net assets, but an acquirer can *elect* otherwise by adopting the fair value measurement, and this must be applied consistently from the date of such adoption (usually at acquisition) which can no longer be reversed. The election is not generic, as it can be adopted on a one-on-one basis for the purchase of businesses that may have occurred (i.e. if there are two or more business combinations that have taking place, the first business combination may have the choice of accounting for non-controlling interest different from the second business combination).

The above scenario of goodwill calculation depicts that goodwill to the group on the acquisition of the subsidiary amounts to ₦20 million, of which ₦12 million is attributable to the parent and ₦8 million attributable to the non-controlling interest. The goodwill attributable to the non-controlling interest is possible based on the fact that non-controlling interest investment was measured at the acquisition-date fair value of ₦30 million, otherwise no goodwill would have been attributable to non-controlling interest if the amount of non-controlling interest is measured at the proportionate share of the recognised amounts of the acquiree's identifiable net assets at acquisition. Whenever the investment of non-controlling interest is measured at proportionate share in the recognised amounts of the acquiree's identifiable net assets at subsidiary's acquisition by the parent, the amount of non-controlling interest stakes equate the non-controlling interest's share of the identifiable assets and liabilities of the subsidiary used in determining the goodwill, hence *no amount of goodwill* is arrived at *with respect to* non-controlling interest investments, as it is shown below:

		₦' million
Cost of combination (i.e. cost of acquisition) to the parent		100
Amount of investment in subsidiary to non-controlling interest* (20% of ₦110 million)		22
Combined amount of interests in subsidiary to all investors		**122**
Less: Subsidiary's identifiable net assets as at acquisition-date:		
- Share capital of subsidiary	(100)	
- Pre acquisition reserves	(10)	(110)
Goodwill (Partial) – Positive		**12**

Alternatively, the positive goodwill arising from acquisition of a subsidiary can be ascertained as thus:

		₦' million
Cost of combination (i.e. cost of acquisition) to the parent		100
Amount of investment in subsidiary to non-controlling interest*		22
Combined amount of interests in subsidiary to all investors		**122**
Less: Parent's 80% share of the fair value of subsidiary's identifiable net assets	(85)	
Non-controlling interest 20% share of the fair value of subsidiary's net assets	(25)	(110)
Goodwill (Partial) - Positive		**12**

We consider a simple illustration below to display the recognition and measurement of goodwill on consolidation of the financial statements of the subsidiary.

ILLUSTRATION 1:

Pally acquired 100% of the equity share capital of **Sussy** at the reporting date 31 December 2015. The statement of financial position of the dual companies on this date is as shown below:

Statement of Financial Position as at 31st December 2015

	Pally	Sussy
	₦' million	₦' million
Property, plant and equipment	300	130
Investment in **Sussy**	220	-
Current Assets	120	70
Total Assets	**640**	**200**
Share Capital & Reserves:		
Equity Share Capital (@ ₦1 per share)	400	120
Reserves (Retained Earnings)	160	60
	560	180
Current Liabilities	80	20
Total Equity and Liabilities	**640**	**200**

Based on the information presented above, the following *iterative* steps will be adopted:

- ✓ **Step 1**: *Determine the percentage holdings of investment of Pally in Sussy as at the acquisition date, which represents the date of inclusion (first date of consolidation).* In this case, the percentage holding is already determined and ascertained to be 100%.

- ✓ **Step 2**: *Ascertain the form of group structure in this parent-subsidiary relationship.* Since the subsidiary (**Sussy**) is *wholly-owned* by the parent (**Pally**), the group structure is a simple structure as shown below:

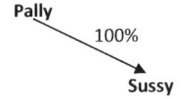

```
Pally
     \ 100%
      ↓
    Sussy
```

- ✓ **Step 3**: *Determine the existence of goodwill or gain from a bargain purchase as the date of acquisition based on the fair value or provisional values of subsidiary's identifiable assets and liabilities.* In this case, there exists goodwill as shown below.

  To ascertain and determine the amount of goodwill, the amount of investment of the parent (**Pally**) in the subsidiary (**Sussy**) will be compared with the parent's share of identifiable assets and liabilities of the subsidiary that were acquired.

	₦' million	₦' million
Cost of combination (i.e. the cost of investment of **Pally** in **Sussy**)		220
Pally's share of Identifiable net assets of **Sussy** acquired:		
• Share capital (100% of ₦120 million)	120	
• Pre-acquisition reserves (100% of ₦60 million)	60	(180)
Positive goodwill		**40**

  Technical Note:
  For the purpose of consolidation of the statement of financial position, the subsidiary's net assets are represented by the equity/ordinary share capital and pre-acquisition reserves of the subsidiary.

- ✓ **Step 4**: *Determine the amount of non-controlling interest as will be shown in the consolidated statement of financial position of the group.* In this case, there is *no non-controlling interest* and there is not value to be ascertained.

- ✓ **Step 5**: *Determine the amount to be included in the consolidated statement of financial position as consolidated reserves (otherwise known as consolidated retained earnings).* The consolidated retained earnings to be included in the consolidated statement of financial position of **Pally-Group** is only that of the parent, as the subsidiary retained earnings at the point of acquisition is entirely classified as pre-acquisition retained earnings, which already has been considered as part of the net assets of the subsidiary upon acquisition. Invariably, it implies that only the post-acquisition retained earnings of the subsidiary that ought to be considered in ascertaining the group retained earnings. The consolidated retained earnings are usually determined as follows:

	₦' million
Parent's (**Pally**) retained earnings	160
Share of subsidiary's (**Sussy**) post-acquisition retained earnings (100% of Nil)	--
	160

Technical Note:
In this illustration, there is no amount of post-acquisition reserves, as the consolidation is upon acquisition.

✓ **Step 6:** Combine the assets and liabilities of the parent **(Pally)** and subsidiary **(Sussy)** on an item-by-item basis excluding the initial investment of **Pally** in **Sussy** as earlier shown in the separate financial statements of **Pally**, and also the exclusion of the equity share capital of **Sussy**, as it has already been considered alongside with the pre-acquisition retained earnings in ascertaining the amount of goodwill or gain from bargain purchase inherent/embedded in the acquisition. The consolidated statement of financial position of the group will now be shown as thus:

Pally Group
Consolidated Statement of Financial Position as at 31 December 2015

Assets:	₦' million
Non-current assets:	
Property, plant and equipment (300 + 130)	430
Goodwill	40
Current asset (120 + 70)	190
Total Assets	**660**
Share Capital & Reserves:	
Equity share capital (@ ₦1 per share)	400
Reserves (*Step 5 above*)	160
Total Equity	**560**
Current liability (80 + 20)	100
Total Equity & Liabilities	**660**

The above steps starting from *step 3 to step 5* can be replicated with a form of consolidation schedule which in the long-run makes the mechanics of consolidation much easier to accommodate various adjustments required and equally for the consolidation of complex group structures such as fellow subsidiaries, indirect/sub-subsidiaries and joints subsidiaries (i.e. mixed group structure). In this case, as non-controlling interest is not involved in this simple group, only two columns (i.e. cost of control and consolidated reserves columns) are required instead of basic three columns (i.e. cost of control, non-controlling interest and consolidated reserves columns).

Consolidation Schedule

Subsidiary – Sussy		Cost of control (Pally in Sussy) as at 31 Dec. 2015 – 100%		Consolidated Reserves
Equity Share Capital	120	(100% x 120)	120	
Reserves (Pre-acquisition)	60	(100% x 60)	60	
Net asset on acquisition			180	
Cost of combination (cost of investment)			(220)	
Goodwill (positive)			**(40)**	
Pally Reserves				160
Consolidated Reserves				**160**

Accounting for Goodwill and Gain on Bargain Purchase

We can further explore an illustration that involves non-controlling interest in the group, and then consider the effects of the difference in the two methods permitted by IFRS 3(R) for determining the amount of non-controlling interest's investments in the subsidiary.

Pally acquired 80% of the equity share capital of **Sussy** as at the reporting date 31 December 2015. The statement of financial position of the two companies on this date stood as follows:

Statement of Financial Position as at 31st December 2015

	Pally	Sussy
	₦' million	₦' million
Property, plant and equipment	300	130
Investment in *Sussy*	160	-
Current assets	120	70
Total Assets	**580**	**200**
Share Capital & Reserves:		
Equity share capital (@ ₦1 per share)	400	120
Reserves (Retained Earnings)	100	60
	500	180
Current liabilities	80	20
Total Equity and Liabilities	**580**	**200**

(*Assuming the prevailing market price of **Sussy's** shares prior to the date of acquisition is ₦2 per share*).

Based on the information presented above, the possible two scenarios will be considered as it relates to the measurement of the *amount of investment of non-controlling interest in the subsidiary as at the date of acquisition.*

First, we assumed that the parent at the point of acquisition (when control was obtained), measured the amount of non-controlling interest at the proportionate share of the subsidiary's identifiable net assets (assets and liabilities). In this case, the consolidation process will be as follows:

- ✓ **Step 1**: Determine the percentage holdings of investment of **Pally** in **Sussy** as at the acquisition date (31 December 2015), which represents the date of inclusion (first date of consolidation). In this case, the percentage holding is already determined and ascertained to be 80%.

- ✓ **Step 2**: Ascertain the form of group structure in this parent-subsidiary relationship. Since the subsidiary (**Sussy**) is *partly-owned* by the parent (**Pally**), the group structure is a simple structure as shown below:

```
        Pally
          \
       80% \
            \         20%
             Sussy ←——————— Non-controlling interest
```

- ✓ **Step 3**: Determine the existence of goodwill or gain from a bargain purchase as the date of acquisition based on the fair value of subsidiary's identifiable assets and liabilities. In this case, there exists goodwill as shown below.

To ascertain and determine the amount of goodwill or gain from a bargain purchase, the value of an investment of the parent (**Pally**) in the subsidiary (**Sussy**) will be compared with the identifiable assets and liabilities of the subsidiary as at acquisition.

PARTIAL METHODOLOGY

	₦' million	₦' million
Cost of combination (i.e. the cost of investment of **Pally** in **Sussy**)		160
Less: **Pally's** share of Identifiable net assets of **Sussy** acquired:		
• Share capital (80% of ₦120 million)	96	
• Pre-acquisition reserves (80% of ₦60 million)	48	(144)
Goodwill attributable to **Pally's** (a)		16
Amount of investments of non-controlling interest in **Sussy**		36
Less: Non-controlling interest share of the fair value of subsidiary's net assets:		
• Share capital (20% of ₦120 million)	24	
• Pre-acquisition reserves (20% of ₦60 million)	12	(36)
Goodwill attributable to **non-controlling interests** (b)		---
PARTIAL Goodwill (a + b)		**16**

Alternatively, to ascertain and determine the amount of goodwill or gain from a bargain purchase, the fair value of the total considerations in the subsidiary (**Sussy**) will be compared with the identifiable assets and liabilities of the subsidiary that were acquired.

FULL METHODOLOGY

		₦' million
Cost of combination:		
• Cost of investment of **Pally** in **Sussy**		160
• Non-controlling interest in **Sussy** (*Step 4*)		36
		196
Identifiable net assets of **Sussy** acquired (@ 31 December 2015):		
• Share capital	120	
• Pre-acquisition reserves	60	(180)
PARTIAL Goodwill - positive		**16**

Technical Note:
The goodwill attributable to non-controlling should be zero since the investment to non-controlling interest is valued at the proportionate share of subsidiary's identifiable net assets as shown by the arrow.

✓ **Step 4:** Determine the amount of non-controlling interest as will be shown in the consolidated statement of financial position of the group. In this case, non-controlling interest will only be measured at the proportionate share of subsidiary's identifiable assets and liabilities, which could be depicted as thus:

Non-controlling interest's share of Identifiable net assets of **Sussy** upon acquisition:

	₦' million
• Share capital (20% of ₦120 million)	24
• Pre-acquisition reserves (20% of ₦60 million)	12
NCI's investment on 31 December 2015 (based on proportionate share of net assets)	**36**

✓ **Step 5:** Determine the amount to be included in the consolidated statement of financial position as consolidated reserves (otherwise known as consolidated retained earnings). The consolidated retained earnings to be included in the consolidated statement of financial position of **Pally-**

Accounting for Goodwill and Gain on Bargain Purchase

Group is that of the parent, as there exist no post-acquisition profits in the subsidiary as at acquisition. There will be post-acquisition profits in the subsidiary only when change is experienced in the reserves of the subsidiary subsequent to acquisition. The consolidated retained earnings will be determined as follows:

	₦' million
Parent's (*Pally*) retained earnings	100
Share of subsidiary's (*Sussy*) post-acquisition retained earnings (80% of Nil)	---
	100

✓ **Step 6:** Combine the assets and liabilities of the parent (*Pally*) and subsidiary (*Sussy*) on an item-by-item basis excluding the initial investment of *Pally* in *Sussy* as earlier shown in the separate financial statements of *Pally*, and also the exclusion of the equity share capital of *Sussy*, as it has already been considered alongside with the pre-acquisition retained earnings in ascertaining the amount of goodwill or gain from bargain purchase inherent/embedded in the acquisition. The consolidated statement of financial position of the group will now be shown as thus:

Pally Group
Consolidated Statement of Financial Position as at 31 December 2015

Assets:	₦' million
Non-current assets	
Property, plant and equipment (300 + 130)	430
Goodwill	16
Current asset (120 + 70)	190
Total Assets	**636**
Share Capital & Reserves:	
Equity share capital (@ ₦1 per share)	400
Reserves	100
Equity attributable to Pally's shareholders	**500**
Non-controlling interest	36
Total Equity	**536**
Current liability (80 + 20)	100
Total Equity and Liabilities	**636**

The consolidation schedule can equally be adopted for solving this group problem as scheduled below:

Consolidation Schedule

Subsidiary - Sussy		The cost of control (Pally in Sussy) as at 31 Dec. 2015 – 80%		Non-controlling Interests – 20%		Consolidated Reserves
Equity Share Capital	120	(80% x 120)	96	(20% x 120)	24	
Reserves (Pre-acquisition)	60	(80% x 60)	48	(20% x 60)	12	
Net asset on acquisition			144			
Cost of combination (cost of investment)			(160)			
Goodwill (positive)			**(16)**			
Non-controlling interests					**36**	
Pally Reserves						100
Consolidated Reserves						**100**

Second, we assumed that the parent at the point of acquisition (when control was obtained), measured the amount of non-controlling interest at fair value (which is predominantly based on market value of shares of the subsidiary). In this case, the consolidation process will be as follows:

- ✓ **Step 1**: *Determine the percentage holdings of investment of Pally in Sussy as at the acquisition date (31 December 2015), which represents the date of inclusion (first date of consolidation).* In this case, the percentage holding is already determined and ascertained to be 80%.

- ✓ **Step 2**: *Ascertain the form of group structure in this parent-subsidiary relationship.* Since the subsidiary (**Sussy**) is *partly-owned* by the parent (**Pally**), the group structure is a simple structure as shown below:

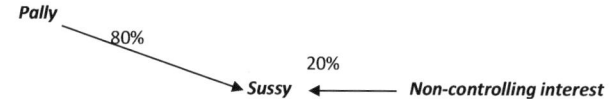

```
     Pally
        \ 80%
         \           20%
          → Sussy ←——— Non-controlling interest
```

- ✓ **Step 3**: *Determine the existence of goodwill or gain from a bargain purchase as the date of acquisition based on the fair value of subsidiary's identifiable assets and liabilities.* In this case, there exists goodwill as shown below.

To ascertain and determine the amount of goodwill or gain from a bargain purchase, the amount of investment of the parent (**Pally**) in the subsidiary (**Sussy**) will be compared with the parent's share of identifiable assets and liabilities of the subsidiary that were acquired, in additional to possible goodwill attributable to non-controlling interest.

PARTIAL METHODOLOGY

	₦' million	₦' million
Cost of combination (i.e. the cost of investment of **Pally** in **Sussy**)		160
Less: Pally's share of Identifiable net assets of **Sussy** acquired:		
• Share capital (80% of ₦120 million)	96	
• Pre-acquisition reserves (80% of ₦60 million)	48	(144)
Goodwill attributable to **Pally's** (a)		16
Amount of investments of non-controlling interest in **Sussy**		48
Less: Non-controlling interest share of the fair value of subsidiary's net assets:		
• Share capital (20% of ₦120 million)	24	
• Pre-acquisition reserves (20% of ₦60 million)	12	(36)
Goodwill attributable to **non-controlling interests** (b)		12
FULL Goodwill (a + b)		**28**

Technical Note:

*The goodwill attributable to non-controlling is ₦12 million since the investment to non-controlling interests is valued at fair value of ₦48 million (being the market price of shares prevailing prior to acquisition at ₦2.00 per share multiplied by the number of shares which is 20% of the shares existing in Sussy -120 million shares) as it different from the proportionate share of the identifiable net assets of the subsidiary upon acquisition.

Alternative, FULL METHODOLOGY

	₦' million
Cost of combination:	
• Cost of investment of **Pally** in **Sussy**	160
• Non-controlling interest in **Sussy** (₦2 per share * 24 million shares)	48
	208

Identifiable net assets of **Sussy** acquired (@ 31 December 2015):
- Share capital   120
- Pre-acquisition reserves   60   (180)

FULL Goodwill - positive   **28**

Technical Note:
* 24 million shares is arrived at by multiplying 20% of non-controlling interest by the number of sussy's shares in issue (which is 120 million shares by dividing share capital of ₦120 million by ₦1 nominal value of each share)

✓ **Step 4:** *Determine the amount of non-controlling interest as will be shown in the consolidated statement of financial position of the group.* In this case, non-controlling interest will only be valued at fair value, which could be depicted as thus:

The acquisition-date fair value of Non-controlling interest is ₦48 million, which resulted in an amount of goodwill of ₦12 million.

Fair value of non-controlling interest in **Sussy** upon acquisition can be further broken down as thus: ₦' million
- Share capital (20% of ₦120 million)   24
- Pre-acquisition reserves (20% of ₦60 million)   12

NCI's investment on 31 December 2015 (based on proportionate share of net assets)   **36**
Goodwill attributable to non-controlling interests on acquisition (Balancing Figure)   *12*
NCI's investment on 31 December 2015 (based on fair value)   **48**

✓ **Step 5:** *Determine the amount to be included in the consolidated statement of financial position as consolidated reserves (otherwise known as consolidated retained earnings).* The consolidated retained earnings to be included in the consolidated statement of financial position of **Pally-Group** is that of the parent, as there exist no post-acquisition profits in the subsidiary as at acquisition. There will be post-acquisition profits in the subsidiary only when change is experienced in the reserves of the subsidiary subsequent to acquisition. The consolidated retained earnings will be determined as follows: ₦' million

Parent's (**Pally**) retained earnings   100
Share of subsidiary's (**Sussy**) post-acquisition retained earnings (80% of Nil)   ---
    100

✓ **Step 6:** *Combine the assets and liabilities of the parent (Pally) and subsidiary (Sussy) on an item-by-item basis excluding the initial investment of Pally in Sussy as earlier shown in the separate financial statements of Pally, and also the exclusion of the equity share capital of Sussy, as it has already been considered alongside with the pre-acquisition retained earnings in ascertaining the amount of goodwill or gain from bargain purchase inherent/embedded in the acquisition.* The consolidated statement of financial position of the group will now be shown as thus:

Pally Group
Consolidated Statement of Financial Position as at 31 December 2015

	₦' million
Assets:	
Non-current assets	
Property, plant and equipment (300 + 130)	430
Goodwill	28
Current assets (120 + 70)	190
Total Assets	**648**

Share Capital & Reserves:

Equity share capital (@ ₦1 per share)	400
Reserves	100
Equity attributable to Pally's shareholders	**500**
Non-controlling interest	48
Total Equity	**548**
Current liabilities (80 + 20)	100
Total Equity and Liabilities	**648**

The consolidation schedule can equally be adopted for solving this group problem as scheduled below:

Consolidation Schedule

Subsidiary - Sussy		Cost of control (Pally in Sussy) as at 31 Dec. 2015 – 80%		Non-controlling Interests – 20%		Consolidated Reserves
Equity Share Capital	120	(80% x 120)	96	(20% x 120)	24	
Reserves (Pre-acquisition)	60	(80% x 60)	48	(20% x 60)	12	
Net asset on acquisition			144			
Cost of combination (cost of investment)			(160)			
Goodwill (positive)			(16)			
Goodwill attributable to NCI(see note)			(12)		12	
Full Goodwill (positive)			(28)			
Non-controlling interests					48	
Pally Reserves						100
Consolidated Reserves						**100**

Technical Note:
Goodwill attributable to non-controlling interest may be separately determined as thus;

	₦' million
Amount of investment of non-controlling interest in **Sussy**	48
Less: Non-controlling interest share of the fair value of subsidiary's net assets:	
• Share capital (20% of ₦120 million)	24
• Pre-acquisition reserves (20% of ₦60 million)	12 → (36)
Goodwill attributable to **non-controlling interests**	12

Accounting Entries:
Debit: Group Goodwill
Credit: Non-controlling interests' investment } ₦12 million

Do not be swayed by the negative sign on the amount of goodwill as shown in the schedule, as it is a mere consequence of the order. Rather, more emphasis should be placed on the principle that a "Positive Goodwill" arose from the excess of the cost of combination above the fair value of the identifiable net assets acquired.

Accounting for Goodwill and Gain on Bargain Purchase

In the context of the above illustration, we can explore the avenue of re-introducing the entire concept of goodwill by considering the effect of post-acquisition profits on goodwill (if any). The illustration below will show the treatments of post-acquisition profits and equally to confirm whether any possible effect exists on goodwill.

ILLUSTRATION 2:

Pally acquired 80% of the equity share capital of **Sussy** as at the reporting date 31 December 2013, when the retained earnings of **Sussy** was ₦40 million. The statement of financial position of the two companies as at reporting date 31 December 2015 is as follows:

Statement of Financial Position as at 31st December 2015

	Pally ₦' million	Sussy ₦' million
Property, plant and equipment	300	130
Investment in **Sussy**	160	-
Current assets	120	70
Total Assets	**580**	**200**
Share Capital & Reserves:		
Equity share capital (@ ₦1 per share)	400	120
Reserves (Retained Earnings)	100	60
	500	180
Current liabilities	80	20
Total Equity and Liabilities	**580**	**200**

(*Assuming the prevailing market price of **Sussy's** shares prior to the date of acquisition is ₦2 per share*).

In order to approach proffering solutions to this illustration, the processes adopted in the last illustration will be repeated, except for the introduction of *post-acquisition profits.*

First, we assumed that the parent at the point of acquisition (when control was obtained), measured the amount of non-controlling interests at the proportionate share of the subsidiary's identifiable net assets (assets and liabilities). In this case, the consolidation process will be as follows:

- ✓ **Step 1**: *Determine the percentage holdings of investment of **Pally** in **Sussy** as at the acquisition date (31 December 2013), which represents the date of inclusion (first date of consolidation).* In this case, the percentage holding is already determined and ascertained to be 80%.

- ✓ **Step 2**: *Ascertain the form of group structure in this parent-subsidiary relationship.* Since the subsidiary (**Sussy**) is *partly-owned* by the parent (**Pally**), the group structure is a simple structure as shown below:

```
         Pally
            \
          80% \
               \      20%
                Sussy ←────── Non-controlling interest
```

- ✓ **Step 3**: *Determine the existence of goodwill or gain from a bargain purchase as at the date of acquisition based on the fair value of subsidiary's identifiable assets and liabilities.* In this case, there exists goodwill as shown below.

To ascertain and determine the amount of goodwill or gain from a bargain purchase, the value of an investment of the parent (**Pally**) in the subsidiary (**Sussy**) will be compared with the parent's share of identifiable assets and liabilities of the subsidiary that were acquired.

PARTIAL METHODOLOGY	₦' million	₦' million
Cost of combination (i.e. the cost of investment of **Pally** in **Sussy**)		160
Less: **Pally**'s share of Identifiable net assets of **Sussy** acquired:		
• Share capital (80% of ₦120 million)	96	
• Pre-acquisition reserves (80% of ₦40 million)	32	(128)
Goodwill attributable to **Pally's** (a)		32
Amount of investments of non-controlling interest in **Sussy**		32
Less: Non-controlling interest share of the fair value of subsidiary's net assets:		
• Share capital (20% of ₦120 million)	24	
• Pre-acquisition reserves (20% of ₦40 million)	8	(32)
Goodwill attributable to **non-controlling interests** (b)		---
PARTIAL Goodwill (a + b)		**32**

Technical Note:
The goodwill attributable to non-controlling should be zero since the investment to non-controlling interests is valued at the proportionate share of subsidiary's identifiable net assets as shown by the arrow.

FULL METHODOLOGY		₦' million
Cost of combination (i.e. cost of acquisition) to the parent		160
Amount of Investment in subsidiary to non-controlling interest*		32
Combined amount of interests in subsidiary to all investors		**192**
Less: Identifiable net assets of **Sussy** acquired (@ 31 December 2013):		
• Share capital	120	
• Pre-acquisition reserves	40	(160)
PARTIAL Goodwill - positive		**32**

- ✓ **Step 4:** Determine the amount of non-controlling interest as will be shown in the consolidated statement of financial position of the group. In this case, non-controlling interest will only be measured at the proportionate share of subsidiary's identifiable assets and liabilities, which could be depicted as thus:

Non-controlling interest's share of Identifiable net assets of **Sussy**:

	₦' million
• Share capital (20% of ₦120 million)	24
• Pre-acquisition reserves (20% of ₦40 million)	8
NCI's investment on 31 December 2013 (*based on proportionate share of net assets*)	**32**
• Post-acquisition reserves (20% of ₦20 million)	4
NCI's investment on 31 December 2015 (*based on proportionate share of net assets*)	**36**

- ✓ **Step 5:** Determine the amount to be included in the consolidated statement of financial position as consolidated reserves (otherwise known as consolidated retained earnings). The consolidated retained earnings to be included in the consolidated statement of financial position of **Pally-Group** are that of the parent and of the post-acquisition profits of the subsidiary. Invariably, it implies that the post-acquisition retained earnings (which is the sum of ₦20 million being the increase from ₦40 million profits upon acquisition to ₦60 million as at the reporting date 31 December 2015 - *2 years after*) of the subsidiary (**Sussy**) will now be combined with the retained earnings (profits) of the parent (**Pally**) in ascertaining the group retained earnings. The consolidated retained earnings will be determined as follows:

	₦' million
Parent's (**Pally**) retained earnings	100
Share of subsidiary's (**Sussy**) post-acquisition profits (80% of ₦20 million)	<u>16</u>
	<u><u>116</u></u>

✓ **Step 6:** Combine the assets and liabilities of the parent (**Pally**) and subsidiary (**Sussy**) on an item-by-item basis excluding the initial investment of **Pally** in **Sussy** as earlier shown in the separate financial statements of **Pally**, and also the exclusion of the equity share capital of **Sussy**, as it has already been considered alongside with the pre-acquisition retained earnings in ascertaining the amount of goodwill or gain from bargain purchase inherent/embedded in the acquisition. The consolidated statement of financial position of the group will now be shown as thus:

Pally Group
Consolidated Statement of Financial Position as at 31 December 2015

Assets:	₦' million
Non-current assets	
Property, plant and equipment (300 + 130)	430
Goodwill	32
Current assets (120 + 70)	<u>190</u>
Total Assets	<u><u>652</u></u>
Share Capital & Reserves:	
Equity share capital (@ ₦1 per share)	400
Reserves	<u>116</u>
Equity attributable to Pally's shareholders	516
Non-controlling interest	<u>36</u>
Total Equity	552
Current liabilities (80 + 20)	<u>100</u>
Total Equity and Liabilities	<u><u>652</u></u>

The consolidation schedule can equally be adopted for solving this group problem as scheduled below:

Consolidation Schedule

Subsidiary - Sussy		Cost of control (Pally in Sussy) as at 31 Dec. 2013 – 80%		Non-controlling Interests – 20%		Consolidated Reserves	
Equity Share Capital	120	(80% x 120)	96	(20% x 120)	24		
Reserves (Pre-acquisition)	40	(80% x 40)	32	(20% x 40)	8		
Reserves (Post-acquisition)	20		-	(20% x 20)	4	(80% x 20)	16
Net asset on acquisition			128				
Cost of combination (cost of investment)			(160)				
Goodwill (positive)			(32)				
Non-controlling interests					36		
Pally Reserves							100
Consolidated Reserves							<u>116</u>

The conclusion in the above solution is that post-acquisition profits simply have no effect on goodwill, but it affects the consolidated retained earnings (reserves).

Second, we assumed that the parent at the point of acquisition (when control was obtained), measured the amount of non-controlling interest at fair value (which is predominantly based on market values of shares of the subsidiary). In this case, the consolidation process will be as follows:

- ✓ **Step 1**: Determine the percentage holdings of investment of **Pally** in **Sussy** as at the acquisition date (31 December 2013), which represents the date of inclusion (first date of consolidation). In this case, the percentage holding is already determined and ascertained to be 80%.

- ✓ **Step 2**: *Ascertain the form of group structure in this parent-subsidiary relationship.* Since the subsidiary (**Sussy**) is *partly-owned* by the parent (**Pally**), the group structure is a simple structure as shown below:

```
        Pally
         \ 80%
          \           20%
         Sussy ◄────── Non-controlling interest
```

- ✓ **Step 3**: *Determine the existence of goodwill or gain from a bargain purchase as at the date of acquisition based on the fair value of subsidiary's identifiable assets and liabilities.* In this case, there exists goodwill as shown below.

To ascertain and determine the amount of goodwill or gain from a bargain purchase, the amount of investment of the parent (**Pally**) in the subsidiary (**Sussy**) will be compared with the parent's share of identifiable assets and liabilities of the subsidiary that were acquired, in additional to possible goodwill attributable to non-controlling interest.

PARTIAL METHODOLOGY

	₦' million	₦' million
Cost of combination (i.e. the cost of investment of **Pally** in **Sussy**)		160
Less: **Pally's** share of Identifiable net assets of **Sussy** acquired:		
• Share capital (80% of ₦120 million)	96	
• Pre-acquisition reserves (80% of ₦40 million)	32	(128)
Goodwill attributable to **Pally's** (a)		32
Amount of investments of non-controlling interest in **Sussy**		48
Less: Non-controlling interest share of the fair value of subsidiary's net assets:		
• Share capital (20% of ₦120 million)	24	
• Pre-acquisition reserves (20% of ₦40 million)	8	(32)
Goodwill attributable to **non-controlling interests** (b)		16
FULL Goodwill (a + b)		**48**

Technical Note:
*The goodwill attributable to non-controlling is ₦16 million since the investment to non-controlling interests is valued at fair value of ₦48 million (being the market price of shares prevailing prior to acquisition at ₦2.00 per share multiplied by the number of shares which is 20% 0f the shares existing in **Sussy** -120 million shares).*

Alternative, FULL METHODOLOGY

		₦' million
Cost of combination:		
• Cost of investment of **Pally** in **Sussy**		160
• Non-controlling interest in **Sussy** (₦2 per share * 24 million shares)		48
		208
Less: Identifiable net assets of **Sussy** acquired (@ 31 December 2013):		
• Share capital	120	
• Pre-acquisition reserves	40	(160)
FULL Goodwill - positive		**48**

Technical Note:
* 24 million shares is arrived at by multiplying 20% of non-controlling interest by the number of Sussy's shares in issue (which is 120 million shares by dividing share capital of ₦120 million by ₦1 nominal value of each share)

✓ **Step 4:** Determine the amount of non-controlling interest as will be shown in the consolidated statement of financial position of the group. In this case, non-controlling interest will only be valued at fair value, which could be depicted as thus:

The fair value of non-controlling interests in **Sussy** upon is measured as thus:

	₦' million
NCI's investment on 31 December 2013 (*based on fair value*)	**48**
• Post-acquisition reserves (20% of ₦20 million)	4
NCI's investment on 31 December 2015	**52**

	₦' million
This can be further decomposed as thus:	
• Share capital (20% of ₦120 million)	24
• Pre-acquisition reserves (20% of ₦40 million)	8
NCI's investment on 31 December 2013 (*based on proportionate share of net assets*)	**32**
Goodwill attributable to non-controlling interests on acquisition (Balancing figure)	*16*
NCI's investment on 31 December 2013 (based on fair value)	**48**
• Post-acquisition reserves (20% of ₦20 million)	4
NCI's investment on 31 December 2015 (*based on fair value*)	**52**

✓ **Step 5:** Determine the amount to be included in the consolidated statement of financial position as consolidated reserves (otherwise known as consolidated retained earnings). The consolidated retained earnings to be included in the consolidated statement of financial position of **Pally-Group** are that of the parent and of the post-acquisition profits of the subsidiary. Invariably, it implies that the post-acquisition retained earnings (which is the sum of ₦20 million being the increase from ₦40 million profits upon acquisition to ₦60 million as at the reporting date 31 December 2015 - *2 years after*) of the subsidiary (**Sussy**) will now be combined with the retained earnings (profits) of the parent (**Pally**) in ascertaining the group retained earnings. The consolidated retained earnings will be determined as follows:

	₦' million
Parent's (**Pally**) retained earnings	100
Share of subsidiary's (**Sussy**) post-acquisition profits (80% of ₦20 million)	16
	116

✓ **Step 6:** Combine the assets and liabilities of the parent (**Pally**) and subsidiary (**Sussy**) on an item-by-item basis excluding the initial investment of **Pally** in **Sussy** as earlier shown in the separate financial statements of **Pally**, and also the exclusion of the equity share capital of **Sussy**, as it has already been considered alongside with the pre-acquisition retained earnings in ascertaining the amount of goodwill or gain from bargain purchase inherent/embedded in the acquisition. The consolidated statement of financial position of the group will now be shown as thus:

Pally Group
Consolidated Statement of Financial Position as at 31 December 2015

Assets:	₦' million
Non-current assets	
Property, plant and equipment (300 + 130)	430
Goodwill on consolidation	48
Current assets (120 + 70)	190
Total Assets	**668**
Share Capital & Reserves:	
Equity share capital (@ ₦1 per share)	400
Reserves	116
Equity attributable to Pally's shareholders	**516**
Non-controlling interest	52
Total Equity	**568**
Current liabilities (80 + 20)	100
Total Equity and Liabilities	**668**

The consolidation schedule can equally be adopted for solving this group problem as scheduled below:

Consolidation Schedule

Subsidiary - Sussy		Cost of control (Pally in Sussy) as at 31 Dec. 2013 – 80%		Non-controlling Interests – 20%		Consolidated Reserves	
Equity Share Capital	120	(80% x 120)	96	(20% x 120)	24		
Reserves (Pre-acquisition)	40	(80% x 40)	32	(20% x 40)	8		
Reserves (Pre-acquisition)	20	----		(20% x 20)	4	(80% x 20)	16
Net asset on acquisition			128				
Cost of combination (cost of investment)			(160)				
Goodwill (positive)			(32)				
Goodwill attributable to NCI(see note)			(16)		16		
Full Goodwill (positive)			**(48)**				
Non-controlling interests					**52**		
Pally Reserves							100
Consolidated Reserves							**116**

111

Technical Note:
Goodwill attributable to non-controlling interest may separately be determined as thus;

	₦' million
Value of investments of non-controlling interest in **Sussy**	48
Less: Non-controlling interest share of the fair value of subsidiary's net assets:	
• Share capital (20% of ₦120 million) — 24	
• Pre-acquisition reserves (20% of ₦40 million) — 8	(32)
Goodwill attributable to **non-controlling interests**	**16**

Accounting Entries:
Debit: Group Goodwill
Credit: Non-controlling interests' investment   ₦16 million

IMPAIRMENT OF GOODWILL

Impairment is a reduction in the recoverable amount of a non-current asset or goodwill below its carrying amount. The goodwill initially recognised upon acquisition would have been allocated to some or all of the *cash-generating units*[25] in the subsidiary. If goodwill recognised on acquisition is associated (or related) with only some of the cash-generating units of the subsidiary, the goodwill recognised in the statement of financial position should be allowed to only those assets or group of assets. Impairment tests will be *annual or more frequently* if circumstances indicate that the goodwill might be impaired.

IAS 36 recommends three steps for carrying out impairment test and review, which is stated as follows:

- *First*, the recoverable amount of a cash-generating unit which is the higher of the cash-generating unit's [26]*fair value less costs to sell (net selling price)* and its *value in use*[27] must be determined.
- *Second,* the recoverable amount of the cash-generating unit will be compared to its carrying value[28]. If the recoverable amount exceeds the carrying amount, then there is no goodwill impairment, and in this situation, the third testing step will not be required.
- *Third,* the excess of the carrying amount over the recoverable amount of the cash-generating unit as of the testing date is allocated to its assets (including intangible assets) and liabilities, with the remainder (if any) being assigned to goodwill. If the amount of goodwill resulting from this calculation is less than the carrying amount of goodwill, then the difference is *impaired goodwill* and must be charged to expense in the current period.

An *impairment loss* is first absorbed by goodwill, and only when goodwill has been eliminated entirely is any further impairment loss credited to other assets in the group (on a *pro-rata basis*, unless it is possible to measure the recoverable amounts of the individual assets). This has been considered arbitrary, but it is logical to the aforesaid since *excess earnings power (super profits)* represented by

---

[25] Cash generating unit is the smallest level of identifiable group of assets that generates cash inflows that are largely independent of the cash inflows from other assets or group of assets (not larger than an operating segment).
[26] *Fair value less costs to sell* is otherwise referred to as the *Net Realizable value*.
[27] *Value in use:* is otherwise referred to as the economic value. This is the present value of the estimated future cash flows expected to be derived from the cash-generating unit.
[28] *Carrying value:* The amount at which an asset is recognized after deducting any accumulated depreciation (amortization) and accumulated impairment losses (previous recognized). This is amount of asset and goodwill as measure at its book value.

goodwill must be deemed to have been lost if the recoverable amount of the cash-generating unit is less than its carrying amount.

A cash-generating unit to which goodwill is allocated for the purpose of impairment testing may not coincide with the level of which goodwill is allocated in accordance with *IAS 21 The Effects of Changes in Foreign Exchange Rates* for the purpose of measuring foreign currency gains and losses. For example, if an entity is required by *IAS 21* to allocate goodwill to relatively low levels for the purpose of measuring foreign currency gains and losses, it is not required to test the goodwill for impairment at that same level unless it also monitors the goodwill at that level for internal management purposes.

If goodwill has been allocated to a cash-generating unit and the entity *disposes of* an operation within that unit, the goodwill associated with the operation disposed of shall be:

- Included in the carrying amount of the operation when determining the gain or loss on disposal; and
- Measured on the basis of the relative values of the operation disposed of and the portion of the cash-generating unit retained unless the entity can demonstrate that some other method better reflects the goodwill associated with the operation disposed of.

Example: *An entity sells for ₦10 million an operation that was part of a cash-generating unit to which goodwill has been allocated. The goodwill allocated to the unit cannot be identified or associated with an asset group at a level lower than that unit, except arbitrarily. The recoverable amount of the portion of the cash-generating unit retained is ₦30 million.*

Because the goodwill allocated to the cash-generating unit cannot be non-arbitrarily identified or associated with an asset group at a level lower than that unit, the goodwill associated with the operation disposed of is measured on the basis of the relative values of the operation disposed of and the portion of the unit retained. Therefore, 25% of the goodwill allocated to the cash-generating unit is included in the carrying amount of the operation that is sold.

If an entity reorganises its reporting structure in a way that changes the composition of one or more cash-generating units to which goodwill has been allocated, the goodwill shall be reallocated to the units affected. This reallocation shall be performed using a relative value approach similar to that used when an entity disposes of an operation within a cash-generating unit unless the entity can demonstrate that some other method better reflects the goodwill associated with the reorganised units.

Example: *Goodwill had previously been allocated to cash-generating unit A. The goodwill allocated to A cannot be identified or associated with an asset group at a level lower than A, except arbitrarily. A is to be divided and integrated into three other cash-generating units, B, C and D. Because the goodwill allocated to A cannot be non-arbitrarily identified or associated with an asset group at a level lower than A, it is reallocated to units B, C and D on the basis of the relative values of the three portions of A before those portions are integrated with B, C and D.*

Once impairment loss on goodwill is recognised, it may not be reversed in a subsequent period, which helps in preventing the manipulation of period profits. *IAS 36* has imposed a requirement that reversals may not be recognised for previous write-downs in goodwill. Thus, a later recovery in the value of the cash-generating unit will be allocated to assets other than goodwill. The adjustments to those assets cannot be for amounts greater than would be needed to restore them to the carrying amounts of which they would be currently stated had the earlier impairment not been recognised (i.e. at the former carrying values less the depreciation that would have been recorded during the intervening period).

Technical Note:
Where impairment loss is recognised on goodwill, this should be allocated or apportioned to the parent and non-controlling interest (if the amount of non-controlling interest is measured at fair value) in the proportion profit or loss of the subsidiary is being shared, even when the goodwill may not be initially recognised in the same proportion. The impairment of goodwill will only be apportioned to the non-controlling interest if the amount of investment of the non-controlling interest is initially measured at fair value upon acquisition, otherwise the entire impairment loss on goodwill should only be absorbed by the parent if the amount of investment of non-controlling interest is measured at the proportionate share of the identifiable assets and liabilities of the subsidiary.

We can explore the principle of the treatment of impairment losses on goodwill (both PARTIAL and FULL Goodwill) by adopting this illustration.

ILLUSTRATION 3:

Pally acquired 80% of the equity share capital of **Sussy** as at the reporting date 31 December 2013, when the retained earnings of **Sussy** was ₦40 million. The statement of financial position of the two companies as at reporting date 31 December 2015 is as follows:

Statement of Financial Position as at 31st December 2015

	Pally ₦' million	Sussy ₦' million
Property, plant and equipment	300	130
Investment in *Sussy*	160	-
Current assets	120	70
Total Assets	**580**	**200**
Share Capital & Reserves:		
Equity share capital (@ ₦1 per share)	400	120
Reserves (Retained Earnings)	100	60
	500	180
Current liabilities	80	20
Total Equity and Liabilities	**580**	**200**

(*Assuming the prevailing market price of Sussy's shares prior to the date of acquisition is ₦2 per share*).

In order to understand the concept of the treatments of impairment losses on goodwill, we will approach the illustration earlier considered above where the treatment of goodwill is showcased, and we are to assume that the goodwill has since be impaired over time by ₦12 million.

First, we assumed that the parent at the point of acquisition (when control was obtained), a measured the amount of non-controlling interests at the proportionate share of the subsidiary's identifiable net assets (assets and liabilities). In this case, the consolidation process will be as follows:

- ✓ **Step 1**: Determine the percentage holdings of investment of **Pally** in **Sussy** as at the acquisition date (31 December 2013), which represents the date of inclusion (first date of consolidation). In this case, the percentage holding is already determined and ascertained to be 80%.

✓ **Step 2:** *Ascertain the form of group structure in this parent-subsidiary relationship.* Since the subsidiary (**Sussy**) is *partly-owned* by the parent (**Pally**), the group structure is a simple structure as shown below:

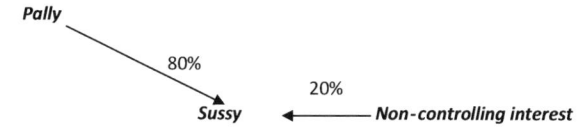

```
        Pally
          \
       80% \
            \         20%
            Sussy  ←———— Non-controlling interest
```

✓ **Step 3:** *Determine the existence of goodwill or gain from a bargain purchase as at the date of acquisition based on the fair value of subsidiary's identifiable assets and liabilities.* In this case, there exists goodwill as shown below.

To ascertain and determine the amount of goodwill or gain from a bargain purchase, the value of an investment of the parent (**Pally**) in the subsidiary (**Sussy**) will be compared with the parent's share of identifiable assets and liabilities of the subsidiary that were acquired.

	₦' million	₦' million
PARTIAL METHODOLOGY		
Cost of combination (i.e. the cost of investment of **Pally** in **Sussy**)		160
Less: **Pally**'s share of Identifiable net assets of **Sussy** acquired:		
• Share capital (80% of ₦120 million)	96	
• Pre-acquisition reserves (80% of ₦40 million)	32	(128)
*Goodwill attributable to **Pally's** (a)*		32
Amount of investments of non-controlling interest in **Sussy**		32
Less: Non-controlling interest share of the fair value of subsidiary's net assets:		
• Share capital (20% of ₦120 million)	24	
• Pre-acquisition reserves (20% of ₦40 million)	8	(32)
*Goodwill attributable to **non-controlling interests** (b)*		---
Partial Goodwill (a + b)		**32**
Less: Impairment loss		(12)
Goodwill on consolidation (@ 31 December 2015)		**20**

Technical Note:
*The goodwill attributable to non-controlling should be zero since the investment to non-controlling interests is valued at the proportionate share of subsidiary's identifiable net assets as shown by the arrow. The impairment loss of ₦12 million will only be absorbed by the parent company, as the non-controlling interest initially have zero amount contributed to the group goodwill upon acquisition.

		₦' million
Alternative, FULL METHODOLOGY		
Cost of combination (i.e. cost of acquisition) to the parent		160
Amount of Investment in subsidiary to non-controlling interest*		32
Combined amount of interests in subsidiary to all investors		**192**
Less: Identifiable net assets of **Sussy** acquired (@ 31 December 2013):		
• Share capital	120	
• Pre-acquisition reserves	40	(160)
PARTIAL Goodwill - positive		**32**
Less: Impairment loss		*(12)*
Goodwill on consolidation (@ 31 December 2015)		**20**

- **Step 4:** Determine the amount of non-controlling interest as will be shown in the consolidated statement of financial position of the group. In this case, non-controlling interest will only be measured at the proportionate share of subsidiary's identifiable assets and liabilities, which could be depicted as thus: ₦' million
    - Share capital (20% of ₦120 million) 24
    - Pre-acquisition reserves (20% of ₦40 million) 8

    NCI's investment on 31 December 2013 (*based on proportionate share of net assets*) 32
    - Post-acquisition reserves (20% of ₦20 million) 4

    NCI's investment on 31 December 2015 (*based on proportionate share of net assets*) 36

- **Step 5:** Determine the amount to be included in the consolidated statement of financial position as consolidated reserves (otherwise known as consolidated retained earnings). The consolidated retained earnings to be included in the consolidated statement of financial position of **Pally-Group** are that of the parent and of the post-acquisition profits of the subsidiary. Invariably, it implies that the post-acquisition retained earnings (which is the sum of ₦20 million being the increase from ₦40 million profits upon acquisition to ₦60 million as at the reporting date 31 December 2015 - *2 years after*) of the subsidiary (**Sussy**) will now be combined with the retained earnings (profits) of the parent (**Pally**) in ascertaining the group retained earnings, and the impairment loss of ₦12 million will be deducted as this is attributable only to the parent company. The consolidated retained earnings will be determined as follows: ₦' million

    Parent's (**Pally**) retained earnings 100
    Share of subsidiary's (**Sussy**) post-acquisition profits (80% of ₦20 million) 16
    Less: Impairment loss on goodwill *(12)*
    104

- **Step 6:** Combine the assets and liabilities of the parent (**Pally**) and subsidiary (**Sussy**) on an item-by-item basis excluding the initial investment of **Pally** in **Sussy** as earlier shown in the separate financial statements of **Pally**, and also the exclusion of the equity share capital of **Sussy**, as it has already been considered alongside with the pre-acquisition retained earnings in ascertaining the amount of goodwill or gain from bargain purchase inherent/embedded in the acquisition. The consolidated statement of financial position of the group will now be shown as thus:

Pally Group
Consolidated Statement of Financial Position as at 31 December 2015

Assets:	₦' million
Non-current assets	
Property, plant and equipment (300 + 130)	430
Goodwill	20
Current assets (120 + 70)	190
Total Assets	**640**
Share Capital & Reserves:	
Equity share capital (@ ₦1 per share)	400
Reserves	104
Equity attributable to Pally's shareholders	**504**
Non-controlling interest	36
Total Equity	**540**
Current liabilities (80 + 20)	100
Total Equity and Liabilities	**640**

The consolidation schedule can equally be adopted for solving this group problem as scheduled below:

Consolidation Schedule

Subsidiary - Sussy		Cost of control (Pally in Sussy) as at 31 Dec. 2013 – 80%		Non-controlling Interests – 20%		Consolidated Reserves	
Equity Share Capital	120	(80% x 120)	96	(20% x 120)	24		
Reserves (Pre-acquisition)	40	(80% x 40)	32	(20% x 40)	8		
Reserves (Post-acquisition)	20		-	(20% x 20)	4	(80% x 20)	16
Net asset on acquisition			128				
Cost of combination (cost of investment)			(160)				
Goodwill (positive)			(32)				
Less: Impairment loss			12				(12)
Goodwill on consolidation			(20)				
Non-controlling interests					36		
Pally Reserves							100
Consolidated Reserves							104

The conclusion in the above solution is that post-acquisition profits simply have no effect on goodwill, but it affects the consolidated retained earnings (reserves), and the impairment loss on goodwill reduces the carrying amount of goodwill to what is recoverable as at the reporting period (31 December 2015) and also impacts the consolidated retained earnings.

Second, we assumed that the parent at the point of acquisition (when control was obtained), measured the amount of non-controlling interest at fair value (which is predominantly based on market values of shares of the subsidiary). In this case, the consolidation process will be as follows:

- ✓ **Step 1**: *Determine the percentage holdings of investment of **Pally** in **Sussy** as at the acquisition date (31 December 2013), which represents the date of inclusion (first date of consolidation).* In this case, the percentage holding is already determined and ascertained to be 80%.

- ✓ **Step 2**: *Ascertain the form of group structure in this parent-subsidiary relationship.* Since the subsidiary (**Sussy**) is *partly-owned* by the parent (**Pally**), the group structure is a simple structure as shown below:

Pally
80%
20%
Sussy ⟵ Non-controlling interest

- ✓ **Step 3**: *Determine the existence of goodwill or gain from a bargain purchase as at the date of acquisition based on the fair value subsidiary's identifiable assets and liabilities.* In this case, there exists goodwill as shown below.

To ascertain and determine the amount of goodwill or gain from a bargain purchase, the amount of investment of the parent (**Pally**) in the subsidiary (**Sussy**) will be compared with the parent's share of identifiable assets and liabilities of the subsidiary that were acquired, in additional to possible goodwill attributable to non-controlling interest.

PARTIAL METHODOLOGY	₦' million	₦' million
Cost of combination (i.e. the cost of investment of **Pally** in **Sussy**)		160
Less: **Pally's** share of Identifiable net assets of **Sussy** acquired:		
• Share capital (80% of ₦120 million)	96	
• Pre-acquisition reserves (80% of ₦40 million)	32	(128)
Goodwill attributable to **Pally's** (a)		32
Amount of investments of non-controlling interest in **Sussy**		48
Less: Non-controlling interest share of the fair value of subsidiary's net assets:		
• Share capital (20% of ₦120 million)	24	
• Pre-acquisition reserves (20% of ₦40 million)	8	(32)
Goodwill attributable to **non-controlling interests** (b)		16
Full Goodwill (a + b)		48
Less: **Impairment loss**		(12)
Goodwill on consolidation (@ 31 December 2015)		36

Technical Note:

*The goodwill attributable to non-controlling is ₦16 million since the investment to non-controlling interests is valued at fair value of ₦48 million (being the market price of shares prevailing prior to acquisition at ₦2.00 per share multiplied by the number of shares which is 20% of the shares existing in **Sussy** -120 million shares). The impairment loss of ₦12 million will be apportioned between the parent and the non-controlling interest in the proportion profit or loss is being shared, which in this case it is 80% ratio 20%.*

Alternative, FULL METHODOLOGY		
Cost of combination:		₦' million
• Cost of investment of **Pally** in **Sussy**		160
• Non-controlling interest in **Sussy** (₦2 per share * 24 million shares)		48
		208
*Less: Identifiable net assets of **Sussy** acquired (@ 31 December 2013):*		
• Share capital	120	
• Pre-acquisition reserves	40	(160)
FULL Goodwill - positive		48
Less: *Impairment loss*		(12)
Goodwill on consolidation (@ 31 December 2015)		36

Technical Note:

* *24 million shares is arrived at by multiplying 20% of non-controlling interest by the number of Sussy's shares in issue (which is 120 million shares by dividing share capital of ₦120 million by ₦1 nominal value of each share)*

✓ **Step 4:** *Determine the amount of non-controlling interest as will be shown in the consolidated statement of financial position of the group. In this case, non-controlling interest will only be valued at fair value, which could be depicted as thus:*

The fair value of non-controlling interests in **Sussy** is measured as thus:

	₦' million
NCI's investment on 31 December 2013 (*based on fair value*)	**48.0**
• Post-acquisition reserves (20% of ₦20 million)	4.0
Less: Impairment loss (20% x ₦12 million)	*(2.4)*
NCI's investment on 31 December 2015	**49.6**

This can be further decomposed as thus	₦' million
• Share capital (20% of ₦120 million)	24.0
• Pre-acquisition reserves (20% of ₦40 million)	8.0
NCI's investment on 31 December 2013 (*based on proportionate share of net assets*)	**32.0**
Goodwill attributable to non-controlling interests on acquisition (Balancing figure)	*16.0*
NCI's investment on 31 December 2013 (*based on fair value*)	**48.0**
• Post-acquisition reserves (20% of ₦20 million)	4.0
Less: Impairment loss (20% x ₦12 million)	*(2.4)*
NCI's investment on 31 December 2015	**49.6**

✓ **Step 5:** Determine the amount to be included in the consolidated statement of financial position as consolidated reserves (otherwise known as consolidated retained earnings). The consolidated retained earnings to be included in the consolidated statement of financial position of **Pally-Group** are that of the parent and of the post-acquisition profits of the subsidiary. Invariably, it implies that the post-acquisition retained earnings (which is the sum of ₦20 million being the increase from ₦40 million profits upon acquisition to ₦60 million as at the reporting date 31 December 2015 - *2 years after*) of the subsidiary (**Sussy**) will now be combined with the retained earnings (profits) of the parent (**Pally**) in ascertaining the group retained earnings, and the impairment loss of ₦9.6 million (being 80% of ₦12 million) will be deducted as it represents the impairment loss on goodwill is attributable to the parent company. The consolidated retained earnings will be determined as follows:

	₦' million
Parent's (**Pally**) retained earnings	100.0
Share of subsidiary's (**Sussy**) post-acquisition profits (80% of ₦20 million)	16.0
Less: Impairment loss (80% x ₦12 million)	*(9.6)*
	106.4

✓ **Step 6:** Combine the assets and liabilities of the parent (**Pally**) and subsidiary (**Sussy**) on an item-by-item basis excluding the initial investment of **Pally** in **Sussy** as earlier shown in the separate financial statements of **Pally**, and also the exclusion of the equity share capital of **Sussy**, as it has already been considered alongside with the pre-acquisition retained earnings in ascertaining the amount of goodwill or gain from bargain purchase inherent/embedded in the acquisition. The consolidated statement of financial position of the group will now be shown as thus:

Pally Group
Consolidated Statement of Financial Position as at 31 December 2015

Assets:	₦' million
Non-current assets	
Property, plant and equipment (300 + 130)	430.0
Goodwill	36.0
Current assets (120 + 70)	190.0
Total Assets	**656.0**

Accounting for Goodwill and Gain on Bargain Purchase

Share Capital & Reserves:	
Equity share capital (@ ₦1 per share)	400.0
Reserves	106.4
Equity attributable to Pally's shareholders	**506.4**
Non-controlling interest	49.6
Total Equity	**556.0**
Current liabilities (80 + 20)	100.0
Total Equity and Liabilities	**656.0**

The consolidation schedule can equally be adopted for solving this group problem as scheduled below:

Consolidation Schedule

Subsidiary - Sussy		Cost of control (Pally in Sussy) as at 31 Dec. 2013 – 80%		Non-controlling Interests – 20%		Consolidated Reserves	
Equity Share Capital	120	(80% x 120)	96	(20% x 120)	24		
Reserves (Pre-acquisition)	40	(80% x 40)	32	(20% x 40)	8		
Reserves (Pre-acquisition)	20	----		(20% x 20)	4	(80% x 20)	16
Net asset on acquisition			128				
Cost of combination (cost of investment)			(160)				
Goodwill (positive)			**(32)**				
Goodwill attributable to NCI (see note)			(16)		16		
Full Goodwill (positive)			**(48)**				
Less: Impairment loss			*12*		*(2.4)*		*(9.6)*
Goodwill on consolidation			**(36)**				
Non-controlling interests					**49.6**		
Pally Reserves							100
Consolidated Reserves							**106.4**

Technical Note:
Goodwill attributable to non-controlling interest may separately be determined as thus; ₦' million

    Amount of investments of non-controlling interest in **Sussy**   48
    Less: Non-controlling interest share of the fair value of subsidiary's net assets:
- Share capital (20% of ₦120 million)   24
- Pre-acquisition reserves (20% of ₦40 million)   8   (32)

    Goodwill attributable to **non-controlling interests**   16
    Accounting Entries:
    Debit: Group Goodwill
    Credit: Non-controlling interests' investment   ₦16 million

The conclusion in the above solution is that post-acquisition profits simply have no effect on goodwill, but it affects the consolidated retained earnings (reserves), and the impairment loss on goodwill reduces the carrying amount of goodwill to what is recoverable as at the reporting period and also impacts the consolidated retained earnings and the amount of non-controlling interest in a proportion profit or loss is shared between the parent and the non-controlling interest.

Reversals of Previously Recognised Impairment of Goodwill

Although based on the general principle of IFRS, reversal of an impairment identified with a cash-generating unit is permitted, but due to special nature of goodwill, IAS 36 has imposed a requirement that reversals may not be recognised for previous write-downs in goodwill (i.e. impaired goodwill). Thus, a later recovery in the value of the cash-generating unit will be allocated to other class of assets other than goodwill subject to the requirement of IAS 36. Hence, the portion of the reversals to those other class of assets (within the assigned cash generating units) which serve as an adjustment cannot be for amounts greater than would be needed to restore (or restate) the to the carrying amounts of which they would be currently stated had the earlier impairment not been recognised (i.e. at the former carrying amount less the depreciation that would have been recorded during the intervening period).

ACCOUNTING FOR GAINS ON BARGAIN PURCHASE

In some business combination (but usually in an extreme case), the consideration transferred (and transferable) may be less that the fair value of the net assets acquired. This situation results in **"Negative Goodwill"** which is often identified and recognised as a **"Gain from a Bargain Purchase Transaction"**. IFRS 3(R) suggests that, since arm's length business acquisition transactions will usually favour neither party, the likelihood of the acquirer obtaining a bargain is considered remote. The standard *(IFRS 3-Revised)*, apparent instances of bargain purchase transactions giving rise to a gain from bargain purchase are more often the result of *measurement error(s)*, which include the measurement of the fair value of the consideration transferred (and those transferrable) and the fair value of the identifiable assets and liabilities of the subsidiary upon acquisition. Furthermore, gain from a bargain purchase can also be derived from the risk of future losses, recognised by both parties and incorporated into the transaction price.

IFRS 3(R) requires that the fair value of the consideration and the fair value of net assets acquired are reviewed (*including contingent liabilities that are probable at acquisition and of which the fair value can reliably be ascertained as of acquisition date*) and checked carefully to ensure that *errors* have not been made. After the review or assessment is completed, and indeed the fair value of identifiable assets acquired net of all liabilities assumed exceeds the fair value of total consideration transferred, then a gain from a bargain purchase will be acknowledged and immediately taken into profit (i.e. recognised directly into the income statement) of the group.

We can explore the principle of the treatment of Gains on Bargain Purchase Transaction in a Business Combination by adopting this illustration.

ILLUSTRATION 4:

Arsenal acquired 70% of the ordinary shares of Manchester United on 31 December 2012 when the balance in the latter retained earnings stood at ₦20 million.

Statement of Financial Position as at 31st December 2015

	Arsenal	Man United
	₦' million	₦' million
Property, plant and equipment	500	240
Investment in **Manchester United**	180	
Current assets	140	180
	820	420
Share Capital & Reserves		
Equity share capital (@ ₦1 per share)	580	250
Reserves (Retained Earnings)	200	50

Accounting for Goodwill and Gain on Bargain Purchase

	780	300
Current liabilities	40	120
	820	**420**

(*Assuming the prevailing market price of **Manchester United's** shares prior to the date of acquisition is ₦1.04 per share*).

First, we assumed that the parent at the point of acquisition (when control was obtained), valued investment of the non-controlling interests at the proportionate share of the subsidiary's identifiable net assets (assets and liabilities). In this case, the consolidation process will be as follows:

- ✓ **Step 1**: *Determine the percentage holdings of investment of **Arsenal** in **Manchester United** as at the acquisition date (31 December 2012), which represents the date of inclusion (first date of consolidation)*. In this case, the percentage holding is already determined and ascertained to be 70%.

- ✓ **Step 2**: *Ascertain the form of group structure in this parent-subsidiary relationship*. Since the subsidiary (**Manchester United**) is *partly-owned* by the parent (**Arsenal**), the group structure is a simple structure as shown below:

Arsenal

70%   30%

Manchester United ← **Non-controlling interest**

- ✓ **Step 3**: *Determine the existence of goodwill or gain from a bargain purchase as at the date of acquisition based on the fair value subsidiary's identifiable assets and liabilities.* In this case, there exists a gain on bargain purchase (negative goodwill) as shown below.

To ascertain and determine the amount of the gain from a bargain purchase due to the group, the fair value of investment of the parent (**Arsenal**) in the subsidiary (**Manchester United**) will be compared with the parent's share of identifiable assets and liabilities of the subsidiary that were acquired, plus any gain on bargain purchase attributable to non-controlling interest (if any).

PARTIAL METHODOLOGY

	₦' million	₦' million
Cost of combination (i.e. the cost of investment of **Arsenal** in **Manchester United**)		180
Less: Arsenal's share of Identifiable net assets of **Manchester United** acquired:		
• Share capital (70% of ₦250 million)	175	
• Pre-acquisition reserves (70% of ₦20 million)	14	(189)
*Gain on a bargain purchase attributable to **Arsenal's** (a)*		**9**
Amount of investments of non-controlling interest in **Manchester United**		81
Less: Non-controlling interest share of the fair value of subsidiary's net assets:		
• Share capital (30% of ₦250 million)	75	
• Pre-acquisition reserves (30% of ₦20 million)	6	(81)
*Gain on Bargain Purchase attributable to **non-controlling interests** (b)*		---
Gain on a Bargain Purchase (a + b)		**9**

Technical Note:
*The gain from a bargain purchase attributable to non-controlling will be zero since the investment to non-controlling interests is valued at the proportionate share of subsidiary's identifiable net assets as shown by the arrow.

Alternative, FULL METHODOLOGY

Cost of combination:	₦' million	₦' million
• Cost of investment of **Arsenal** in **Manchester United**		180
• Non-controlling interest in **Manchester United** (*Step 4*)		81
		261
Less: Identifiable net assets of **Manchester United** acquired (@ 31 December 2012):		
• Share capital	250	
• Pre-acquisition reserves	20	(270)
Gain on Bargain Purchase		**(9)**

✓ **Step 4:** *Determine the amount of non-controlling interest as will be shown in the consolidated statement of financial position of the group.* In this case, non-controlling interest will only be measured at the proportionate share of subsidiary's identifiable assets and liabilities, which could be depicted as thus:

Non-controlling interest's share of Identifiable net assets of **Manchester United**:

	₦' million
• Share capital (30% of ₦250 million)	75
• Pre-acquisition reserves (30% of ₦20 million)	6
NCI's investment on 31 December 2012 (*based on proportionate share of net assets*)	**81**
• Post-acquisition reserves (30% of ₦30 million)	9
NCI's investment on 31 December 2015 (*based on proportionate share of net assets*)	**90**

✓ **Step 5:** *Determine the amount to be included in the consolidated statement of financial position as consolidated reserves (otherwise known as consolidated retained earnings).* The consolidated retained earnings to be included in the consolidated statement of financial position of **Arsenal-Group** are that of the parent and of the post-acquisition profits of the subsidiary. Invariably, it implies that the post-acquisition retained earnings (which is the sum of ₦30 million being the increase from ₦20 million profits upon acquisition to ₦50 million as at the reporting date 31 December 2015 - *3 years after*) of the subsidiary (**Manchester United**) will now be combined with the retained earnings (profits) of the parent (**Arsenal**) in ascertaining the group retained earnings, plus the gain on bargain purchase due to the parent upon acquisition. The consolidated retained earnings will be determined as follows:

	₦' million
Parent's (**Arsenal**) retained earnings	200
Share of subsidiary's (**Manchester United**) post-acquisition profits (70% of ₦30 million)	21
Add: Gain from a bargain purchase	9
	230

✓ **Step 6:** Combine the assets and liabilities of the parent (**Arsenal**) and subsidiary (**Manchester United**) on an item-by-item basis excluding the initial investment of **Arsenal** in **Manchester United** as earlier shown in the separate financial statements of **Arsenal**, and also the exclusion of the equity share capital of **Manchester United**, as it has already been considered alongside with the pre-acquisition retained earnings in ascertaining the amount of goodwill or gain from *bargain purchase inherent/embedded in the acquisition.* The consolidated statement of financial position of the group will now be shown as thus:

Arsenal Group
Consolidated Statement of Financial Position as at 31 December 2015

Assets:	₦' million
Non-current assets	
Property, plant and equipment (500 + 240)	740
Current assets (140 + 180)	320
Total Assets	**1,060**
Share Capital & Reserves:	
Equity share capital (@ ₦1 per share)	580
Reserves	230
Equity attributable to Arsenal's shareholders	**810**
Non-controlling interest	90
Total Equity	**900**
Current liabilities (40 + 120)	160
Total Equity and Liabilities	**1,060**

The consolidation schedule can equally be adopted for solving this group problem as scheduled below:

Consolidation Schedule

Subsidiary - Manchester United		Cost of control (Arsenal in Manchester United) as at 31 Dec. 2012 – 70%	Non-controlling Interests – 30%	Consolidated Reserves
Equity Share Capital	250	(70% x 250) 175	(30% x 250) 75	
Reserves (Pre-acquisition)	20	(70% x 20) 14	(30% x 20) 6	
Reserves (Post-acquisition)	30		(30% x 30) 9	(70% x 30) 21
Net asset on acquisition		189		
Cost of combination (cost of investment)		(180)		
Gain on Bargain Purchase		9		
Transfer to profit		(9)		9
		(-)		
Non-controlling interests			**90**	
Arsenal Reserves				200
Consolidated Reserves				**230**

Second, we assumed that the parent at the point of acquisition (when control was obtained), measured investments of the non-controlling interest at fair value (which is predominantly based on market values of shares of the subsidiary). In this case, the consolidation process will be as follows:

- ✓ **Step 1**: Determine the percentage holdings of investment of **Arsenal** in **Manchester United** as at the acquisition date (31 December 2012), which represents the date of inclusion (first date of *consolidation)*. In this case, the percentage holding is already determined and ascertained to be 70%.

✓ **Step 2:** *Ascertain the form of group structure in this parent-subsidiary relationship.* Since the subsidiary (**Manchester United**) is *partly-owned* by the parent (**Arsenal**), the group structure is a simple structure as shown below:

```
        Arsenal
         70%                          30%
              ──────►  Manchester United  ◄──────  Non-controlling interest
```

✓ **Step 3:** *Determine the existence of goodwill or gain from a bargain purchase as at the date of acquisition based on the fair value subsidiary's identifiable assets and liabilities.* In this case, there exists a gain on bargain purchase (negative goodwill) as shown below.

To ascertain and determine the amount of the gain from a bargain purchase due to the group, the fair value of investment of the parent (**Arsenal**) in the subsidiary (**Manchester United**) will be compared with the parent's share of identifiable assets and liabilities of the subsidiary that were acquired, in additional to possible gain on bargain purchase attributable to non-controlling interest.

FULL METHODOLOGY

		₦' million
Cost of combination:		
• Cost of investment of **Arsenal** in **Manchester United**		180.0
• Non-controlling interest in **Manchester United** (*See Technical Note*)		78.0
		258.0
Less: Identifiable net assets of **Manchester United** acquired (@ 31 December 2012):		
• Share capital	250	
• Pre-acquisition reserves	20	(270)
Gain on Bargain Purchase		**(12.0)**

Alternative, PARTIAL METHODOLOGY

	₦' million	₦' million
Cost of combination (i.e. the cost of investment of **Arsenal** in **Manchester United**)		180
Less: Arsenal's share of Identifiable net assets of **Manchester United** acquired:		
• Share capital (70% of ₦250 million)	175	
• Pre-acquisition reserves (70% of ₦20 million)	14	(189)
*Gain on bargain purchase attributable to **Arsenal's** (a)*		*(9)*
Amount of investments of non-controlling interest in **Manchester United**		78.0
Less: Non-controlling interest share of the fair value of subsidiary's net assets:		
• Share capital (30% of ₦250 million)	75	
• Pre-acquisition reserves (30% of ₦20 million)	6	(81.0)
*Gain on bargain purchase attributable to **non-controlling interests** (b)*		*(3.0)*
Gain on Bargain Purchase (a + b)		**12.0**

Technical Note:

*The gain on bargain purchase attributable to the reduction in the value of non-controlling is ₦3 million. This is due to measurement of the investment of non-controlling interest in the subsidiary at the acquisition-date fair value of ₦78 million (being the market price of shares

Accounting for Goodwill and Gain on Bargain Purchase

prevailing prior to acquisition at ₦1.04 per share multiplied by the number of shares which is 30% of the shares existing in Manchester United – i.e. 250 million shares).

✓ **Step 4:** *Determine the amount of non-controlling interest as will be shown in the consolidated statement of financial position of the group.* In this case, non-controlling interest will only be valued at fair value, which could be depicted as thus:

Fair value of non-controlling interests in **Manchester United** is measured as thus:

	₦' million
NCI's investment on 31 December 2012 (*based on fair value*)	**78.0**
• Post-acquisition reserves (30% of ₦30 million)	9.0
NCI's investment on 31 December 2015	**87.0**

This can be further decomposed as thus :

Fair value of non-controlling interests in **Manchester United** upon acquisition is measured as thus: ₦' million

• Share capital (30% of ₦250 million)	75.0
• Pre-acquisition reserves (30% of ₦20 million)	6.0
NCI's investment on 31 December 2012 (*based on proportionate share of net assets*)	**81.0**
Less: Gain on bargain purchase to the parent	(3.0)
NCI's investment on 31 December 2012 (*based on fair value*)	**78.0**
• Post-acquisition reserves (30% of ₦30 million)	9.0
NCI's investment on 31 December 2015	**87.0**

✓ **Step 5:** *Determine the amount to be included in the consolidated statement of financial position as consolidated reserves (otherwise known as consolidated retained earnings).* The consolidated retained earnings to be included in the consolidated statement of financial position of **Arsenal-Group** are that of the parent and of the post-acquisition profits of the subsidiary. Invariably, it implies that the post-acquisition retained earnings (which is the sum of ₦30 million being the increase from ₦20 million profits upon acquisition to ₦50 million the reporting date 31 December 2015 - *3 years after*) of the subsidiary (**Manchester United**) will now be combined with the retained earnings (profits) of the parent (**Arsenal**) in ascertaining the group retained earnings, plus the entire gain from a bargain purchase transaction due to the parent from the acquisition. The consolidated retained earnings will be determined as follows:

	₦' million
Parent's (**Arsenal**) retained earnings	200.0
Share of subsidiary's (**Man U**) post-acquisition profits (70% of ₦30 million)	21.0
Add: Gain from a bargain purchase on the acquisition	*12.0*
	233.0

✓ **Step 6:** *Combine the assets and liabilities of the parent (**Arsenal**) and subsidiary (**Manchester United**) on an item-by-item basis excluding the initial investment of **Arsenal** in **Manchester United** as earlier shown in the separate financial statements of **Arsenal**, and also the exclusion of the equity share capital of **Manchester United**, as it has already been considered alongside with the pre-acquisition retained earnings in ascertaining the amount of goodwill or gain from bargain purchase inherent/embedded in the acquisition.* The consolidated statement of financial position of the group will now be shown as thus:

Arsenal Group
Consolidated Statement of Financial Position as at 31 December 2015

Assets:	₦' million
Non-current assets	
Property, plant and equipment (500 + 240)	740
Current assets (140 + 180)	320
Total Assets	**1,060**
Share Capital & Reserves:	
Equity share capital (@ ₦1 per share)	580
Reserves	233
Equity attributable to Arsenal's shareholders	**813**
Non-controlling interest	87
Total Equity	**900**
Current liabilities (40 + 120)	160
Total Equity and Liabilities	**1,060**

The consolidation schedule can equally be adopted for solving this group problem as scheduled below:

Consolidation Schedule

Subsidiary - Manchester United		Cost of control (Arsenal in Manchester United) as at 31 Dec. 2012 – 70%		Non-controlling Interests – 30%		Consolidated Reserves
Equity Share Capital	250	(70% x 250)	175	(30% x 250)	75	
Reserves (Pre-acquisition)	20	(70% x 20)	14	(30% x 20)	6	
Reserves (Post-acquisition)	30		–	(30% x 30)	9	(70% x 30) 21
Net asset on acquisition			189			
Cost of combination (cost of investment)			(180)			
Gain on Bargain Purchase			9			
Gain on bargain purchase attributable to NCI*			3		(3)	
Gain on Bargain Purchase due to the parent			12			
Transfer to profit			(12)			12
			(-)			
Non-controlling interests					**87**	
Arsenal Reserve						200
Consolidated Reserves						**233**

Technical Note*:
Gain from a bargain purchase transaction attributable to non-controlling interest may separately be determined as thus;

	₦' million
Fair value of investments of non-controlling interest in **Manchester United**	78
Less: Non-controlling interest share of the fair value of subsidiary's net assets:	
• Share capital (30% of ₦250 million) — 75	
• Pre-acquisition reserves (30% of ₦20 million) — 6	(81)
Gain on bargain purchase due to the parent as attributable from **non-controlling interest**	<u>(3)</u>

This will reduce the amount of non-controlling interest due to the fact that the parent elected to measure the amount of non-controlling interest at fair value, and in this instance, the fair value of the identifiable assets and liabilities of the subsidiary as at acquisition is higher that the fair value as perceived by the market and other market fundamentals.

Accounting Entries:
Debit: Non-controlling interests' investment
Credit: Consolidated retained earnings (profits) } ₦3 million

SUMMARY OF CHAPTER 5

1. Goodwill may be considered as the commercial advantage an entity or a business has over its competitors; and as such, every investor may be willing to pay for it.

2. In a business combination, goodwill may result from the fact that an investor may have offered purchase consideration of which its fair value may exceed the fair value of the identifiable net assets acquired (including assuming contingent liabilities that can be measured at fair value upon acquisition).

3. Only a purchased goodwill, which may have resulted from the acquisition of a business in a business combination that is required to be recognised under IFRS 3; as "Non-purchase or Inherent Goodwill" are not permitted to be recognised in IAS 38 (Intangible Assets).

4. Goodwill recognised on acquisition may be recognised in full (i.e. both portions attributable to the parent and non-controlling interest are recognised) or in part (i.e. partial goodwill, where only the goodwill attributable to the parent stake is required to be recognised).

5. Goodwill is not permitted for amortisation, based on the premise that it does not have a predetermined life (hence, it has an indefinite life); rather, goodwill should only be tested for impairment, at least once a year.

6. Impairment losses on a partial goodwill are only attributed to the parent, while the impairment losses on full goodwill are required to be attributed to the parent and non-controlling interest in the proportion the parent and the non-controlling interest share profit or loss.

7. Gain on bargain purchase is recognised when negative goodwill represents an outcome of the acquisition-date accounting of a business combination. The gain on bargain purchase is to be credited to the profit or loss upon acquisition, and is only to be attributed to the parent as non-controlling interest is not a party to the transaction that may have given rise to such "Day 1 Gain".

8. A negative goodwill is only recognised as a gain on bargain purchase, if and only if; a review or an assessment of the fair value of the consideration and the fair value of net assets acquired are (*including contingent liabilities that are probable at acquisition and of which the fair value can reliably be ascertained as of acquisition date*) are confirmed to have been appropriately measured and *errors* have not been made, otherwise necessary adjustments may be required.

END OF CHAPTER 5 EXERCISES

1. What is purchase goodwill?
2. How is goodwill measured in a business combination?
3. What influence does the choice of accounting policy in measuring non-controlling interest at acquisition have on the amount of goodwill to be recognised in a business combination?
4. Can goodwill be negative? Give your honest view
5. "*Impairment losses on full goodwill should be recognised in the proportion of goodwill attribution between the parent and the non-controlling interest*". Is this statement not of a contrarian?
6. Determine the amount of goodwill to be recognised based on the information provided below:
    - Cost of investment by the controlling interest ₦100 million
    - Subsidiary's share capital at acquisition ₦20 million
    - Subsidiary's share premium at acquisition ₦60 million
    - Retained earnings at acquisition ₦40 million
    - Non-controlling interest is to be accounted for at the share of subsidiary's net assets at acquisition
    - The controlling interest holds 16 million shares of the subsidiary shares in issue
    - The authorised share capital of the subsidiary at acquisition is ₦120 million
    - The issued share capital of the subsidiary at acquisition is ₦80 million
    - The nominal value of ₦1.00 per share
    - The market price is ₦6.40 per share
7. Determine the amount of goodwill to be recognised based on the information provided below:
    - Cost of investment by the controlling interest ₦100 million
    - Subsidiary's share capital at acquisition ₦20 million
    - Subsidiary's share premium at acquisition ₦60 million
    - Retained earnings at acquisition ₦40 million
    - Non-controlling interest is to be accounted for at the acquisition-date fair value of the subsidiary's equity instrument held
    - The controlling interest holds 16 million shares of the subsidiary shares in issue
    - The authorised share capital of the subsidiary at acquisition is ₦120 million
    - The issued share capital of the subsidiary at acquisition is ₦80 million
    - The nominal value of ₦1.00 per share
    - The market price is ₦6.40 per share
8. Determine the amount of goodwill to be recognised as at the reporting period 31 December 2016, and the amount of impairment losses to be attributed to the controlling and non-controlling interests based on the information provided below:
    - Cost of investment by the controlling interest ₦100 million
    - Subsidiary's share capital at acquisition ₦20 million
    - Subsidiary's share premium at acquisition ₦60 million
    - Retained earnings at acquisition ₦40 million
    - Non-controlling interest is to be accounted for at the share of subsidiary's net assets at acquisition
    - The controlling interest holds 16 million shares of the subsidiary shares in issue
    - The authorised share capital of the subsidiary at acquisition is ₦120 million

Contemporaneous Accounting for Business Combinations and Group Accounts

- The issued share capital of the subsidiary at acquisition is ₦80 million
- The nominal value of ₦1.00 per share
- The market price is ₦6.40 per share
- Impairment loss on the goodwill amounted to ₦1 million

9. Determine the amount of goodwill to be recognised as at the reporting period 31 December 2016, and the amount of impairment losses to be attributed to the controlling and non-controlling interests based on the information provided below:
   - Cost of investment by the controlling interest   ₦100 million
   - Subsidiary's share capital at acquisition   ₦20 million
   - Subsidiary's share premium at acquisition   ₦60 million
   - Retained earnings at acquisition   ₦40 million
   - Non-controlling interest is to be accounted for at the acquisition-date fair value of the subsidiary's equity instrument held
   - The controlling interest holds 16 million shares of the subsidiary shares in issue
   - The authorised share capital of the subsidiary at acquisition is ₦120 million
   - The issued share capital of the subsidiary at acquisition is ₦80 million
   - The nominal value of ₦1.00 per share
   - The market price is ₦6.40 per share
   - Impairment loss on the goodwill amounted to ₦1 million

10. Determine the amount of gain on bargain purchase to be recognised as at acquisition date based on the information provided below:
    - Cost of investment by the controlling interest   ₦95 million
    - Subsidiary's share capital at acquisition   ₦20 million
    - Subsidiary's share premium at acquisition   ₦60 million
    - Retained earnings at acquisition   ₦40 million
    - Non-controlling interest is to be accounted for at the share of subsidiary's net assets at acquisition
    - The controlling interest holds 16 million shares of the subsidiary shares in issue
    - The authorised share capital of the subsidiary at acquisition is ₦120 million
    - The issued share capital of the subsidiary at acquisition is ₦80 million
    - The nominal value of ₦1.00 per share
    - The market price is ₦6.40 per share

Chapter 6

Accounting for Mid-Year Acquisition and Preference Share Capital

INTRODUCTION

This chapter encompasses principles and fundamentals of accounting for a business combination in which acquisitions were made during the year, and most often mid-year. The principle of 'Date of Inclusion' will be demystified in this course of this chapter as consolidation of the final results of a subsidiary commences only from the date of acquisition, which is the first date in which the parent obtains control of the subsidiary. More emphasis will be placed on understanding the accounting system and the business cycle of the subsidiary, so as to aid the split of its retained earnings as at the end of the year in which the mid-year acquisition takes place into '*pre-acquisition reserves*' and '*post-acquisition reserves*'.

Furthermore within this chapter, a brief discussion on the implication of having preference share capital within the capital structure of the subsidiary will have in the consolidation process (*whether or not, preference share capital holdings can be used in whole or I part as a parameter to ascertaining the existence of control*); and ultimately how should the preference shares of the subsidiary be treated in group account under different situations which may include:

- When the parent holds 100% of the preference shares;
- When the parent owns less than 100% of the preference shares; and
- When the parent does not have stake or interest in the preference shares of the subsidiary.

ACCOUNTING FOR PREFERENCE SHARE CAPITAL IN GROUP ACCOUNT

It has become a common practice for a parent company in addition to the ordinary shares by which it obtained control of the subsidiary, may have acquired preference shares in the subsidiary. This implies in the separate financial statements of the parent, the amount paid by the parent company for its stake in the subsidiary's preference shares (*or preferred stock*) will be included in its investments in the subsidiary as would have been shown in the company's statement of financial position. Furthermore, as the ordinary shares represent part of the net assets acquired, so the parent's share of the preference shares in the subsidiary will represent part of the net assets acquired and should also be included in the calculation of goodwill as deemed appropriate and necessary. This proposition is acceptable on the premise that in accordance with the requirement of IAS 32 (Financial Instrument – Presentation), the preference shares are considered as an *Equity Instrument*.

The parent's investment in the preference shares of the subsidiary should not be used at any point to determine the *existence of control*, as the entire preference shares in the subsidiary do not at any point give rise to a residual interest in the subsidiary. This implies that preference shares held by one company in another are normally irrelevant in determining whether a *parent-subsidiary relationship* exists. This is because preference shares do not give voting rights and therefore could not result in control.

The treatment for any preference shares not held by the parent company, should be treated as part of the non-controlling interest, which implies that where the parent does not own 100% of the subsidiary's preference shares, the other equity interests not of the parent should still be treated as part of the non-controlling interest, because it is not necessary for the parent to hold 100% of the preference shares of the subsidiary.

In a situation where the preference shares are recognised as a liability of the subsidiary under *IAS 32 (Financial Instruments: Presentation)*, they should be accounted for in the same way as loan notes (which includes debt and/or bonds). Invariably upon consolidation, the preference shares acquired or purchased by the parent and included in the cost of investment (i.e. investment in the subsidiary as contained in the separate statement of financial position of the parent company) should be cancelled-out against the preference share capital in the subsidiary), while the portion that is not held by the parent will be treated as a liability to the group (*and not as a component of non-controlling interest*). This is because; non-controlling interest is a component of equity, whereas a preference share (usually redeemable and/or cumulative preference shares) may have been classified in accordance with *IAS 32* as a *Financial Liability*.

The implication of the investment made by the parent company in the preference shares considered an equity instrument (non-common shares) of the subsidiary is that the consolidation process of combining the parent and the subsidiary accounts should involve two stages, as stated below:

- ❑ *The calculation of the amount of investment of non-controlling interest will include:*
    - The non-controlling interest in the balance of the net assets that are financed solely by the ordinary (common) shares.
    - The non-controlling interest in the net assets financed by the preference shares.

- ❑ *The calculation of goodwill calculation will equally include:*
    - Goodwill attributable to the parent based on equity interest (via common/ordinary shares) or ownership in the subsidiary.

- Goodwill attributable to the parent based on preferred stocks (i.e. non-common shares) in the subsidiary – *if any*.

Where preference shares are recognised as a financial liability of the subsidiary under IAS 32 (Financial Instrument: Presentation) they are accounted for in a similar way as that of Loans held by the parent in the subsidiary (refer to other sections/chapters of this text). The conclusion on its accounting upon consolidation is that both the purchased preference shares by the parent (as included in the cost of investment) and the preference shares' liability in the subsidiary's books will be cancelled-out.

We can explore the principle of the treatment of Preference Shares in Group Accounts by adopting this illustration.

ILLUSTRATION 1:

Arsenal acquired 70% of the ordinary shares of **Manchester United** on 31 December 2012 when the balance in the latter retained earnings stood at ₦40 million at a consideration of ₦220 million and also invested the sum of ₦60 million in the 8% preferred stock of the company.

Statement of Financial Position as at 31st December 2015

	Arsenal	Man United
	₦' million	₦' million
Property, plant and equipment	500	260
Investment in **Manchester United**	280	
Current assets	260	280
	1,040	**540**
Share Capital & Reserves:		
Equity share capital (@ ₦1 per share)	600	250
8% Preferred share capital (@ ₦1 per share)	100	100
Reserves (Retained Earnings)	210	50
	910	400
Current liabilities	130	140
	1,040	**540**

In approaching the solution to this question, we assumed that the parent at the point of acquisition (when control was obtained), valued investments of the non-controlling interest at the proportionate share of the subsidiary's identifiable net assets (assets and liabilities). In this case, the consolidation process will be as follows:

- ✓ **Step 1**: *Determine the percentage holdings of investment of* **Arsenal** *in* **Manchester United** *as at the acquisition date (31 December 2012), which represents the date of inclusion (first date of consolidation).* In this case, the percentage holding is already determined and ascertained to be 70%.

- ✓ **Step 2:** *Ascertain the form of group structure in this parent-subsidiary relationship.* Since the subsidiary (**Manchester United**) is *partly-owned* by the parent (**Arsenal**), the group structure is a simple structure as shown below:

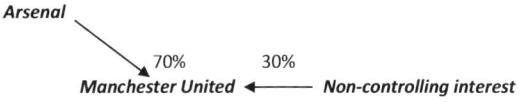

```
                    Arsenal
                   /       \
                70%         30%
                /             \
      Manchester United ← Non-controlling interest
```

Contemporaneous Accounting for Business Combinations and Group Accounts

✓ **Step 3(a):** Determine the existence of goodwill or gain from a bargain purchase as at the date of acquisition based on the fair value subsidiary's identifiable assets and liabilities. In this case, there exists goodwill as shown below.

To ascertain and determine the amount of goodwill to the group as it will be shown in the consolidated statement of financial position, the fair value of investment of the parent (**Arsenal**) in the subsidiary (**Manchester United**) will be compared with the fair value of the identifiable assets and liabilities of the subsidiary as at acquisition.

	₦' million	₦' million
Cost of combination (i.e. the cost of investment of **Arsenal** in **Manchester United**)		220
Less: **Arsenal's** share of Identifiable net assets of **Manchester United** acquired:		
• Share capital (70% of ₦250 million)	175	
• Pre-acquisition reserves (70% of ₦40 million)	28	(203)
Goodwill attributable to **Arsenal's** (a)		17
Amount of investments of non-controlling interest in **Manchester United**		87
Less: Non-controlling interest share of the fair value of subsidiary's net assets:		
• Share capital (30% of ₦250 million)	75	
• Pre-acquisition reserves (30% of ₦40 million)	12	(87)
Goodwill attributable to **non-controlling interests** (b)		---
Goodwill (a + b)		17

Technical Note:
*The goodwill attributable to non-controlling must be zero since the investment to non-controlling interests is valued at the proportionate share of subsidiary's identifiable net assets as shown by the arrow.

Alternative, FULL METHODOLOGY

Cost of combination:		₦' million
• Cost of investment of **Arsenal** in **Manchester United**		220
• Non-controlling interest in **Manchester United** (Step 4)		87
		307
Less: Identifiable net assets of **Manchester United** acquired (@ 31 December 2012):		
• Share capital	250	
• Pre-acquisition reserves	40	(290)
Goodwill		17

✓ **Step 3(b):** Determine the goodwill (if any) on the non-common equity interest (preference shares) acquired in the subsidiary as at acquisition.

	₦' million
Amount of investment in 8% preferred stock	60
Less: Parent's share of the 8% preferred stock of the subsidiary (60% x ₦100million)	(60)
Goodwill	---

✓ **Step 3(c):** The combined goodwill on equity interest and non-equity interest of the parent investment in the subsidiary is ₦17 million (which represents the sum of the ₦17 million and zero sum attributable to the equity and non-equity interests respectively), as shown below:

	₦' million
• Goodwill based on equity interest or ownership in the subsidiary	17
• Goodwill based on preferred stocks (i.e. non-common equity shares) in the subsidiary	_-_
	17

The entire Step 3 can be consolidated as thus (for simplicity):

Cost of combination:	₦' million	₦' million
- Cost of investment of *Arsenal* in *Manchester United* ordinary share capital		220
- Non-controlling interest in *Manchester United* (Step 4)		_87_
		307
- Investment of *Arsenal* in *Manchester United* preference share capital	60	
- Non-controlling interest in *Manchester United* (Step 4)	_40_	_100_
Total Investments		407
Less: *Identifiable net assets of Manchester United acquired (@ 31 December 2012):*		
• Ordinary share capital	250	
• Pre-acquisition reserves	_40_	
Net assets attributable to ordinary shareholders	290	
• Preference share capital	_100_	
Net assets attributable to all equity holders		(390)
Goodwill - PARTIAL		**_17_**

✓ **Step 4(a):** Determine the amount of non-controlling interest as will be shown in the consolidated statement of financial position of the group. In this case, non-controlling interest will only be measured at the proportionate share of subsidiary's identifiable assets and liabilities, which could be depicted as thus:

Non-controlling interest's share of Identifiable net assets of **Manchester United**:	₦' million
• Share capital (30% of ₦250 million)	75
• Pre-acquisition reserves (30% of ₦40 million)	_12_
NCI's investment on 31 December 2012 (based on proportionate share of net assets)	**87**
• Post-acquisition reserves (30% of ₦10 million)	_3_
NCI's investment on 31 December 2015 (based on proportionate share of net assets)	**90**

✓ **Step 4(b):** The part of the preference shares of the subsidiary not attributable to the parent, will now be treated as part of the non-controlling interest upon consolidation in the sum of ₦40 million (being 40% of the 8% preferred stock of ₦100 million).

✓ **Step 4(c):** The amount of non-controlling interest will be the combined amount as obtained on common equity interest and non-common equity interest of the non-controlling interest in the subsidiary which is ₦130 million as shown below:

	₦' million
• Non-controlling interest based on the ordinary (equity) shares	90
• Non-controlling interest based on the preference (non-equity) shares	_40_
	130

The entire Step 4 can be consolidated as thus (for simplicity):	₦' million
Ordinary Share capital (30% of ₦250 million)	75
Pre-acquisition reserves (30% of ₦40 million)	12
NCI's investment in ordinary shares as at 31 December 2012	**87**
Preference Share capital (40% of ₦100 million)	40
NCI's investment in equity of Manchester United as at 31 December 2012	**127**
Post-acquisition reserves (30% of ₦10 million)	3
NCI's investment on 31 December 2015 (@ proportionate share of net assets)	**130**

✓ **Step 5:** Determine the amount to be included in the consolidated statement of financial position as consolidated reserves (otherwise known as consolidated retained earnings). The consolidated retained earnings to be included in the consolidated statement of financial position of **Arsenal-Group** is that of the parent, as there are post-acquisition profits of ₦10 million in the subsidiary as at acquisition. There will be post-acquisition profits (being the increase in retained earnings from ₦40 million to ₦50 million after 3 years) in the subsidiary. The consolidated retained earnings will be determined as follows:

	₦' million
Parent's (**Arsenal**) retained earnings	210
Share of subsidiary's (**Man U**) post-acquisition reserves (70% of ₦10 million)	7
	217

✓ **Step 6:** Combine the assets and liabilities of the parent (**Arsenal**) and subsidiary (**Manchester United**) on an item-by-item basis excluding the initial investment of **Arsenal** in **Manchester United** as earlier shown in the separate financial statements of **Arsenal**, and also the exclusion of the equity and preference share capital of **Manchester United**, as it has already been considered alongside with the pre-acquisition retained earnings in ascertaining the amount of goodwill or gain from bargain purchase inherent/embedded in the acquisition. The consolidated statement of financial position of the group will now be shown as thus:

Arsenal Group
Consolidated Statement of Financial Position as at 31 December 2015

Assets:	₦' million
Non-current assets	
Property, plant and equipment (500 + 260)	760
Goodwill	17
Current assets (260 + 280)	540
Total Assets	**1,317**
Share Capital & Reserves:	
Equity share capital (@ ₦1 per share)	600
8% Preferred share capital (Arsenal)	100
Reserves	217
Equity attributable to Arsenal's shareholders	**917**
Non-controlling interest	130
Total Equity	**1,047**
Current liabilities (130 + 140)	270
Total Equity and Liabilities	**1,317**

The consolidation schedule can equally be adopted for solving this group problem as scheduled below:

Consolidation Schedule

Subsidiary - Manchester United		Cost of control (Arsenal in Manchester United) as at 31 Dec. 2012 – 70%	8% Preferred Stock – 60%	Non-controlling Interests – 30% & 40%	Consolidated Reserves
Equity Share Capital	250	(70% x 250) 175		(30% x 250) 75	
8% Preferred Stock	100	-	(60% x 100) 60	(40% x 100) 40	
Reserves (Pre-acquisition)	40	(70% x 40) 28		(30% x 40) 12	
(Post-acquisition)	10		–	(30% x 10) 3	(70% x 10) 7
Net asset on acquisition		203	60		
Cost of combination		(220)	(60)		
Goodwill (positive)		(17)	–		
Non-controlling interests				130	
Arsenal Reserves					210
Consolidated Reserves					217

ACQUISITION DURING THE YEAR (MID-YEAR ACQUISITION)

The extraordinary performance of a company probably in the first two quarters of the year may attract an investor, as the former is viewed to be a profitable subsidiary by the end of the year and in subsequent years. The profit or loss of a subsidiary acquired during the year will have to be taking into group profits only from the date of acquisition.

Hence, if a subsidiary is acquired during the year (or mid-year), it is necessary to ascertain the net assets at the date of acquisition in order to determine the amount goodwill or gain on bargain purchase and the amount of non-controlling interest and consolidated retained earnings as at the date of acquisition. This usually involves calculating the subsidiary's retained earnings at the date of acquisition. The profits of the subsidiary are assumed to accrue evenly over time unless there is information to the contrary.

This implies that when a subsidiary is acquired during the year, there exist challenges in separating *pre-acquisition profits and post-acquisition profits* in the subsidiary as the profit for the period may not have been easily ascertained and separately identified for the period before and after the acquisition. The implication is that profit for the year in the subsidiary's statement of profit or loss and other comprehensive income in the year of the acquisition will be *partly pre and partly post*. To ascertain the pre and post-acquisition profits, it could be assumed that profits accrue evenly except otherwise stated (which can be based on the *seasonal or cyclical trend* at which revenue is generated).

Technical Note:
If a parent company acquires a subsidiary during the year, the net assets at the date of acquisition equals the net assets at the beginning of the subsidiary's financial year plus the profits earned or losses suffered during the period up to the acquisition date (all things been equal, where there is no additional capital paid-in or introduced).

We can explore the principle of Mid-Year Acquisition in Group Accounts by adopting this illustration.

ILLUSTRATION 2:

Arsenal acquired 70% of the ordinary shares of Manchester United on 31 May 2015. The retained earnings of Manchester United was ₦26 million as at the beginning of the reporting period (1 January 2015).

Statement of Financial Position as at 31st December 2015

	Arsenal	Man United
	₦' million	₦' million
Property, plant and equipment	500	240
Investment in **Manchester United**	250	
Current assets	140	180
	890	**420**
Share Capital & Reserves:		
Equity share capital (@ ₦1 per share)	600	250
Reserves (Retained Earnings)	240	50
	840	300
Current liabilities	50	120
	890	**420**

Prepare the consolidated statement of financial position as at the reporting date, assuming:
a) Profit accrues evenly during the year.
b) Profit in the last quarter (i.e. 4th quarter) doubles that of the 1st, 2nd or 3rd quarter of the year.

First, we adopt the assumption that profit accrues evenly during the year and equally assumed that the parent company at the point of acquisition (when control was obtained), valued investment of the non-controlling interests at the proportionate share of the subsidiary's identifiable net assets (assets and liabilities). In this case, the consolidation process will be as follows:

- ✓ **Step 1**: Determine the percentage holdings of investment of **Arsenal** in **Manchester United** as at the acquisition date (31 May 2015), which represents the date of inclusion (first date of consolidation). In this case, the percentage holding is already determined and ascertained to be 70%.

- ✓ **Step 2**: Ascertain the form of group structure in this parent-subsidiary relationship. Since the subsidiary (**Manchester United**) is *partly-owned* by the parent (**Arsenal**), the group structure is a simple structure as shown below:

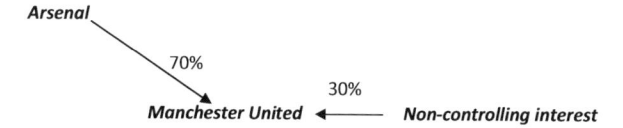

```
        Arsenal
           \
          70%
            \
             ↓         30%
      Manchester United ←——— Non-controlling interest
```

- ✓ **Step 3**: Determine the existence of goodwill or gain from a bargain purchase as at the date of acquisition based on the fair value subsidiary's identifiable assets and liabilities. In this case, there exists goodwill as shown below.

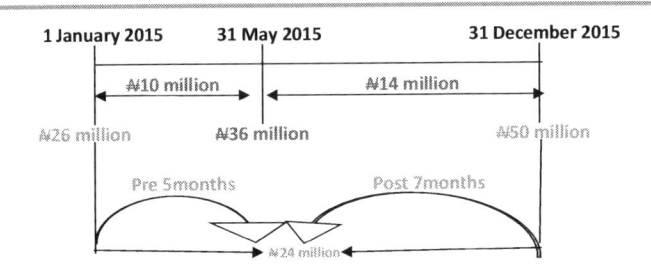

Accounting for Mid-Year Acquisition and Preference Share Capital

```
1 January 2015        31 May 2015           31 December 2015
      |←── ₦10 million ──→|←──── ₦14 million ────→|
   ₦26 million         ₦36 million              ₦50 million
         Pre 5months              Post 7months
                    ←── ₦24 million ──→
```

Since the profit for the year is ₦24 million (being the increase in reserves from ₦26 million to ₦50 million in the reporting period, it should be separated into pre and post-acquisition element as thus:

Pre-acquisition profits/reserves equals the retained earnings as at the beginning of the year ₦26 million plus the ₦10 million (being the portion attributable to 1st-5 months of the year i.e. 5/12 x ₦24 million) since profits accrue evenly.

Post-acquisition profits/reserves: equals the sum of ₦14 million (being the portion of the profit for the year that relates to the last 7 months of the year, i.e. 7/12 x ₦24 million) since profits accrue evenly, as shown below:

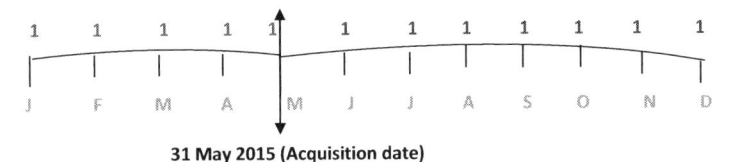

```
 1   1   1   1   1    1   1   1   1   1   1   1
 |   |   |   |   |    |   |   |   |   |   |   |
 J   F   M   A   M    J   J   A   S   O   N   D
                 ↓
      31 May 2015 (Acquisition date)
```

To ascertain and determine the amount of goodwill or gain from a bargain purchase, the value of investment of the parent (**Arsenal**) in the subsidiary (**Manchester United**) will be compared with the parent's share of identifiable assets and liabilities of the subsidiary that were acquired

FULL METHODOLOGY	₦ million	₦ million
Cost of combination (i.e. cost of acquisition) to **Arsenal**		250.0
Amount of Investment in subsidiary to non-controlling interest*		85.8
Combined amount of interests in subsidiary to all investors		**335.8**
Less: *Identifiable net assets acquired as at 31 May 2015*		
Ordinary share capital	250.0	
Pre-acquisition reserves	36.0	
		(286.0)
Goodwill - positive		**49.8**

Alternative, PARTIAL METHODOLOGY

	₦' million	₦' million
Cost of combination (i.e. the cost of investment of **Arsenal** in **Manchester United**)		250.0
Less: **Arsenal**'s share of Identifiable net assets of **Manchester United** acquired:		
• Share capital (70% of ₦250 million)	175.0	
• Pre-acquisition reserves (70% of ₦36 million)	25.2	(200.2)
*Goodwill attributable to **Arsenal's** (a)*		49.8
Amount of investments of non-controlling interest in **Manchester United**		85.8
Less: Non-controlling interest share of the fair value of subsidiary's net assets:		
• Share capital (30% of ₦250 million)	75.0	
• Pre-acquisition reserves (30% of ₦36 million)	10.8	(85.8)
*Goodwill attributable to **non-controlling interests** (b)*		---
Goodwill (a + b)		**49.8**

Technical Note:
The goodwill attributable to non-controlling must be zero since the investment to non-controlling interests is valued at the proportionate share of subsidiary's identifiable net assets as shown by the arrow.

✓ **Step 4:** Determine the amount of non-controlling interest as will be shown in the consolidated statement of financial position of the group. In this case, non-controlling interest will only be measured at the proportionate share of subsidiary's identifiable assets and liabilities, which could be depicted as thus:

Non-controlling interest's share of Identifiable net assets of **Manchester United**:

	₦' million
• Share capital (30% of ₦250 million)	75.0
• Pre-acquisition reserves (30% of ₦36 million)	10.8
NCI's investment on 31 May 2015 (*based on proportionate share of net assets*)	**85.8**
• Post-acquisition reserves (30% of ₦14 million)	4.2
NCI's investment on 31 December 2015 (*based on proportionate share of net assets*)	**90.0**

✓ **Step 5:** Determine the amount to be included in the consolidated statement of financial position as consolidated reserves (otherwise known as consolidated retained earnings). The consolidated retained earnings to be included in the consolidated statement of financial position of **Arsenal-Group** are that of the parent and of the post-acquisition profits of the subsidiary. Invariably, it implies a share of post-acquisition retained earnings (which is the sum of ₦14 million being the increase from ₦36 million profits upon acquisition to ₦50 million as at the reporting date 31 December 2015 - *7 months after*) of the subsidiary (**Manchester United**) will now be combined with the retained earnings (profits) of the parent (**Arsenal**) in ascertaining the group retained earnings. The consolidated retained earnings will be determined as follows:

	₦' million
Parent's (**Arsenal**) retained earnings	240.0
Share of subsidiary's (**Manchester United**) post-acquisition profits (70% of ₦14 million)	9.8
	249.8

✓ **Step 6:** Combine the assets and liabilities of the parent (**Arsenal**) and subsidiary (**Manchester United**) on an item-by-item basis excluding the initial investment of **Arsenal** in **Manchester United** as earlier shown in the separate financial statements of **Arsenal**, and also the exclusion of the equity share capital of **Manchester United**, as it has already been considered alongside with the pre-acquisition retained earnings in ascertaining the amount of goodwill or gain from bargain purchase inherent/embedded in the acquisition. The consolidated statement of financial position of the group will now be shown as thus:

Arsenal Group
Consolidated Statement of Financial Position as at 31 December 2015

Assets:	₦' million
Non-current assets	
Property, plant and equipment (500 + 240)	740.0
Goodwill on consolidation	49.8
Current assets (140 + 180)	320.0
Total Assets	**1,109.8**
Share Capital & Reserves:	
Equity share capital (@ ₦1 per share)	600.0
Reserves	249.8
Equity attributable to Arsenal's shareholders	**849.8**
Non-controlling interest	90.0
Total Equity	**939.8**
Current liabilities (50 + 120)	170.0
Total Equity and Liabilities	**1,109.8**

The consolidation schedule can equally be adopted for solving this group problem as scheduled below:

Consolidation Schedule

Subsidiary – Manchester United		Cost of control (Arsenal in Man U) as at 31 May 2015 – 70%		Non-controlling Interests – 30%		Consolidated Reserves
Equity Share Capital	250	(70% x 250)	175.0	(30% x 250)	75.0	
Reserves (Pre-acquisition)	36	(70% x 36)	25.2	(30% x 36)	10.8	
Reserves (Post-acquisition)	14			(30% x 14)	4.2	(70% x 14) 9.8
Net asset on acquisition			200.2			
Cost of combination (cost of investment)			(250.0)			
Goodwill (positive)			**(49.8)**			
Non-controlling interests					**90.0**	
Pally Reserves						240.0
Consolidated Reserves						**249.8**

Second, we considers the assumption that profit in the last quarter doubles that of the 1st, 2nd or 3rd quarter of the year and equally assumed that the parent at the point of acquisition (when control was obtained), valued investment of the non-controlling interests at the proportionate share of the subsidiary's identifiable net assets (assets and liabilities). In this case, the consolidation process will be as follows:

✓ **Step 1**: *Determine the percentage holdings of investment of **Arsenal** in **Manchester United** as at the acquisition date (31 May 2015), which represents the date of inclusion (first date of consolidation).* In this case, the percentage holding is already determined and ascertained to be 70%.

✓ **Step 2:** *Ascertain the form of group structure in this parent-subsidiary relationship.* Since the subsidiary (**Manchester United**) is *partly-owned* by the parent (**Arsenal**), the group structure is a simple structure as shown below:

Arsenal
↙ 70%   30%
Manchester United ← **Non-controlling interest**

✓ **Step 3:** *Determine the existence of goodwill or gain from a bargain purchase as at the date of acquisition based on the fair value or provisional values of subsidiary's identifiable assets and liabilities.* In this case, there exists goodwill as shown below.

To ascertain and determine the amount of goodwill or gain from a bargain purchase, the value of an investment of the parent (**Arsenal**) in the subsidiary (**Manchester United**) will be compared with the parent's share of identifiable assets and liabilities of the subsidiary that were acquired.

		₦' million
FULL METHODOLOGY		
Cost of combination (i.e. cost of acquisition) to the **Arsenal**		250.0
Amount of Investment in subsidiary to non-controlling interest*		85.2
Combined amount of interests in subsidiary to all investors		335.2
Less: <u>Identifiable net assets acquired as at 31 May 2015</u>		
Ordinary share capital	(250.0)	
Pre-acquisition reserves	(34.0)	(284.0)
Goodwill - positive		**51.2**

	₦' million	₦' million
Alternative, PARTIAL METHODOLOGY		
Cost of combination (i.e. the cost of investment of **Arsenal** in **Manchester United**)		250.0
Less: **Arsenal**'s share of Identifiable net assets of **Manchester United** acquired:		
• Share capital (70% of ₦250 million)	175.0	
• Pre-acquisition reserves (70% of ₦34 million)	23.8	(198.8)
Goodwill attributable to **Arsenal's** (a)		51.2
Amount of investments of non-controlling interest in **Manchester United**		85.2
Less: <u>Non-controlling interest share of the fair value of subsidiary's net assets:</u>		
• Share capital (30% of ₦250 million)	75.0	
• Pre-acquisition reserves (30% of ₦36 million)	10.2	(85.2)
Goodwill attributable to **non-controlling interests** (b)		---
Goodwill (a + b)		**51.2**

Technical Note:
*The goodwill attributable to non-controlling must be zero since the investment to non-controlling interests is valued at the proportionate share of subsidiary's identifiable net assets as shown by the arrow.

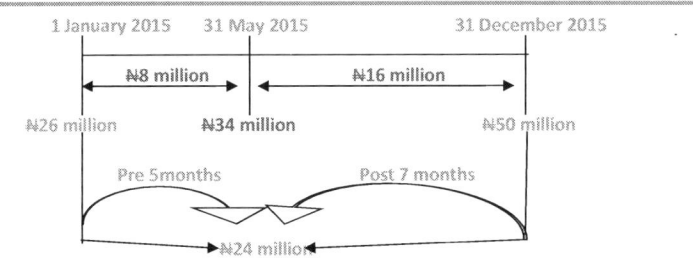

Accounting for Mid-Year Acquisition and Preference Share Capital

```
    1 January 2015      31 May 2015              31 December 2015
    |--------N8 million--------|--------N16 million--------|
    N26 million        N34 million                N50 million
              Pre 5months         Post 7 months
                    |----N24 million----|
```

Since the profit for the year is N24 million (being the increase in reserves from N26 million to N50 million in the reporting period, it should be separated from pre and post-acquisition element as thus:

Pre-acquisition profits/reserves equals the retained earnings as at the beginning of the year N26 million plus the N8 million (being the portion attributable to 1st-5 months of the year i.e. 5/15 x N24 million) since profits in a cyclical order and not accrue evenly.

Post-acquisition profits/reserves: equals the sum of N16 million (being the portion of the profit for the year that relates to the last 7 months of the year, i.e. 10/15 x N24 million) since profits in the last quarter doubles that of the 1st, 2nd or 3rd quarter of the year, as shown below:

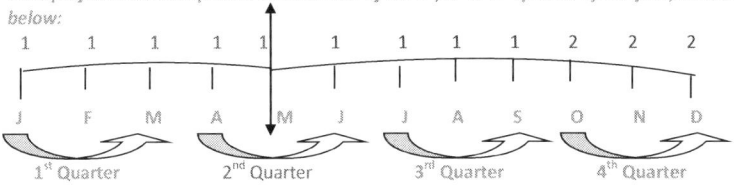

```
 1  1  1  1  1   1  1  1  1   2  2  2
 |--|--|--|--|---|--|--|--|---|--|--|
 J  F  M  A  M   J  J  A  S   O  N  D
   1st Quarter   2nd Quarter   3rd Quarter   4th Quarter
            31 May 2015 (Acquisition date)
```

- ✓ **Step 4:** *Determine the amount of non-controlling interest as will be shown in the consolidated statement of financial position of the group.* In this case, non-controlling interest will only be measured at the proportionate share of subsidiary's identifiable assets and liabilities, which could be depicted as thus:

  Non-controlling interest's share of Identifiable net assets of **Manchester United**:   N' million
  - Share capital (30% of N250 million)   75.0
  - Pre-acquisition reserves (30% of N34 million)   <u>10.2</u>

  NCI's investment on 31 May 2015 (*based on proportionate share of net assets*)   85.2
  - Post-acquisition reserves (30% of N16 million)   <u>4.8</u>

  NCI's investment on 31 December 2015 (*based on proportionate share of net assets*) <u>90.0</u>

- ✓ **Step 5:** *Determine the amount to be included in the consolidated statement of financial position as consolidated reserves (otherwise known as consolidated retained earnings).* The consolidated retained earnings to be included in the consolidated statement of financial position of **Arsenal-Group** are that of the parent and of the post-acquisition profits of the subsidiary. Invariably, it implies a share of post-acquisition retained earnings (which is the sum of N16 million being the increase from N34 million profits upon acquisition to N50 million as at the reporting date 31

December 2015 - *7 months after*) of the subsidiary (**Manchester United**) will now be combined with the retained earnings (profits) of the parent (**Arsenal**) in ascertaining the group retained earnings. The consolidated retained earnings will be determined as follows:

	₦' million
Parent's (**Arsenal**) retained earnings	240.0
Share of subsidiary's (**Manchester United**) post-acquisition profits (70% of ₦16 million)	11.2
	251.2

✓ **Step 6:** Combine the assets and liabilities of the parent (**Arsenal**) and subsidiary (**Manchester United**) on an item-by-item basis excluding the initial investment of **Arsenal** in **Manchester United** as earlier shown in the separate financial statements of **Arsenal**, and also the exclusion of the equity share capital of **Manchester United**, as it has already been considered alongside with the pre-acquisition retained earnings in ascertaining the amount of goodwill or gain from bargain purchase inherent/embedded in the acquisition. The consolidated statement of financial position of the group will now be shown as thus:

Arsenal Group
Consolidated Statement of Financial Position as at 31 December 2015

Assets:	₦' million
Non-current assets	
Property, plant and equipment (500 + 240)	740.0
Goodwill on consolidation	51.2
Current assets (140 + 180)	320.0
Total Assets	**1,111.2**
Share Capital & Reserves:	
Equity share capital (@ ₦1 per share)	600.0
Reserves	251.2
Equity attributable to Arsenal's shareholders	**851.2**
Non-controlling interest	90.0
Total Equity	**941.2**
Current liabilities (50 + 120)	170.0
Total Equity and Liabilities	**1,111.2**

The consolidation schedule can equally be adopted for solving this group problem as scheduled below:

Consolidation Schedule

Subsidiary – Manchester United		Cost of control (Arsenal in Man U) as at 31 May 2015 – 70%		Non-controlling Interests – 30%		Consolidated Reserves
Equity Share Capital	250	(70% x 250)	175.0	(30% x 250)	75.0	
Reserves (Pre-acquisition)	34	(70% x 34)	23.8	(30% x 34)	10.2	
Reserves (Post-acquisition)	16			(30% x 16)	4.8	(70% x 16) 11.2
Net asset on acquisition			198.8			
Cost of combination (cost of investment)			(250.0)			
Goodwill (positive)			**(51.2)**			
Non-controlling interests					90.0	
Pally Reserves						240.0
Consolidated Reserves						**251.2**

SUMMARY OF CHAPTER 6

1. Preference shares held by an investor in an investee cannot be adopted in ascertaining the existence or control in a business combination.

2. The amount of preference shares held by other parties other than the parent is accounted for within non-controlling interest, on the basis that the preference shares are classified as a equity instruments in accordance with the requirement of IAS 32

3. A subsidiary may be acquired at any time during the year, which may be termed mid-year acquisition or acquisition during the year.

4. Acquisition during the year requires the separation of reserves at the 1st year-end of the subsidiary's acquisition into pre-acquisition reserves and post-acquisition reserves.

5. If a parent company acquires a subsidiary during the year, the net assets at the date of acquisition equal the net assets at the beginning of the subsidiary's financial year plus or minus the profits/losses during the period up to the acquisition date

END OF CHAPTER 6 EXERCISES

1. Should consideration be given to preference shares holding of an investor in an investee in assessing the existence of control?

2. How should the preference shares held by other parties other than the parent be accounted for in the consolidated statement of financial position?

3. Where a subsidiary's preference shares are classified as a Financial Liability in accordance with IAS 32, how should the parent's stake be treated upon consolidation?

4. Given a subsidiary acquired on 1st of April 2016, when the company is at the start of four months into its financial year ending 31 December 2016. The reserves of the company as at beginning of the year 1 January 2016 was ₦20 million, while the companies reserves as at 31 December 2016 (being the year-end) now stood at ₦56 million. Determine the pre-acquisition reserves and post-acquisition reserves assuming revenue, cost and profit accrue evenly in 2016 financial year.

5. Given a subsidiary acquired on 1st of April 2016, when the company is at the start of four months into its financial year ending 31 December 2016. The reserves of the company as at beginning of the year 1 January 2016 was ₦20 million, while the companies reserves as at 31 December 2016 (being the year-end) now stood at ₦56 million. Determine the pre-acquisition reserves and post-acquisition reserves assuming a draft statement of profit or loss of the subsidiary up to the acquisition date amounted to ₦26 million.

6. Given a subsidiary acquired on 1st of April 2016, when the company is at the start of four months into its financial year ending 31 December 2016. The reserves of the company as at beginning of the year 1 January 2016 was ₦20 million, while the companies reserves as at 31 December 2016 (being the year-end) now stood at ₦56 million. Determine the pre-acquisition reserves and post-acquisition reserves assuming a draft statement of financial position of the subsidiary as at acquisition date amounted to ₦26 million.

Chapter 7

Fair Value of Subsidiary's Net Assets on Acquisition

INTRODUCTION

This chapter will expose the readers to the understanding of the requirement of IFRS 3 on the need to fair value both the consideration and identifiable net assets acquired in the acquire (or subsidiary) at the date of acquisition.

Furthermore, a practical application of the requirement of IFRS 3 on the implication of fair value of identifiable net assets (including contingent liabilities) at acquisition-date will be evaluated and a clear-cut understanding of how it may affect the resulting goodwill or gain on bargain purchase will be considered.

A later part of the chapter will expatiate on the subsequent effect(s) of the fair value of net assets at acquisition in the entire process of preparing and presenting group accounts.

FAIR VALUE AND BUSINESS COMBINATIONS

IFRS 3(R) requires the cost of investment and the identifiable assets and liabilities (net assets) of the subsidiary be measured at their fair value upon acquisition of the acquiree (or subsidiary). It has been observed over time, that the book value (carrying amount) of the subsidiary's net assets as at acquisition do vary from the fair value of the identifiable assets and liabilities as at acquisition date. The rationale for the net assets of the subsidiary to be revalued (re-measured at fair value) at the date of acquisition is to ensure current prices (including unrealized earnings – i.e. profit or losses) are reflected in the value of the net assets at the date of acquisition, and to prevent distortion of *Earnings per Share (EPS)* in periods subsequent to (or after) the acquisition. This makes it a necessity to revalue the identifiable assets and liabilities of the subsidiary prior to consolidation as at the date of acquisition. It is equally necessary to note, that the parent's assets and liabilities remain unchanged at book value (carrying amount as presented in its separate financial statements, and are not required to be fair valued at acquisition date), while it is only the subsidiary's position (assets and liabilities) that are to be fair value and adjusted for the purpose of the presenting consolidated accounts.

IFRS 3(R) sets out general principles for arriving at the fair value of subsidiary's identifiable assets and liabilities. The parent should recognise the subsidiary's identifiable assets, liabilities and contingent liabilities at the acquisition date if the following criteria exist:

a) In the case of an asset other than an intangible asset, it is probable that any associated future economic benefits will flow to the acquirer, and its fair value can be measured reliably.

b) In the case of a liability other than contingent liability, it is probable that an outflow of resources embodying economic benefits will be required to settle the obligation, and its fair value can be measured reliably.

c) In the case of an intangible asset or a contingent liability, its fair value can be measured reliably.

Technical Note:
The subsidiary's identifiable assets and liabilities might include assets and liabilities not previously recognised in the subsidiary's financial statements.

The fair value adjustment carried out upon acquisition of the subsidiary is considered as an adjustment to pre-acquisition reserves, which implies that prior to acquisition the value inherent in the subsidiary, and has surfaced and recaptured on the acquisition, should be considered in determining the amount of goodwill on acquisition or gain from a bargain purchase transaction. It is worthy to note, that fair value adjustment carried out subsequent to acquisition cannot be retrospectively applied or considered as an adjustment to pre-acquisition reserves, as such fair value adjustment was subsequent to economic and market effects (and fundamentals) of the subsidiary since acquisition; and in such case it is considered an adjustment to post-acquisition reserves, which should be included in the consolidated reserves.

In calculating goodwill arising on consolidation or gain from a bargain purchase, the net assets of the subsidiary should be re-stated at its fair value, and there exist two (2) possible ways of achieving this:

a) The subsidiary might have incorporated all necessary fair value adjustments in its financial statements, as its accounting policies may support measurement at fair value (such as financial instruments, biological assets, investment properties, some components of property, plant and equipment, etc.). In this case, we may consolidate directly as the assets and liabilities have been re-stated at fair value, and pre-requisite adjustments have been effected.

b) The fair value adjustments may be required as a consolidation adjustment without being incorporated in the subsidiary's financial statements. In this scenario, we need to make all necessary adjustments at the point of consolidation (i.e. upon preparing the group accounts).

Accounting Treatment of Fair Value in a Business Combination

The parent should recognise separately at the acquisition-date fair value the acquiree's (or subsidiary's) identifiable assets, liabilities and contingent liabilities only if they satisfy the following criteria at that date:

i. For an asset other than an intangible asset, it is probable that any associated future economic benefits will flow to the acquirer, and its fair value can be measured reliably.

ii. For a liability other than a contingent liability, it is probable that an outflow of resources embodying economic benefits will be required to settle the obligation, and its fair value can be measured reliably.

iii. In the case of an intangible asset or a contingent liability, its fair vale can be measured reliably.

Identifiable assets and liabilities recognised in the accounts are those of the acquired entity that existed at the acquisition date. The following specifically do not meet the criteria listed above and therefore must be dealt with as post-acquisition items:

i. Changes resulting from the acquirer's (or parent's) intentions or future actions.

ii. Changes resulting from post-acquisition events.

iii. Provisions for future operating losses or reorganisation costs incurred as a result of the acquisition.

Restructuring and future losses:

An acquirer should not recognise liabilities for future losses or other costs expected to be incurred as a result of the business combination.

IFRS 3 explains that a plan to restructure a subsidiary following an acquisition is not a present obligation of the acquiree at the acquisition date. Neither does it meet the definition of a contingent liability. Therefore an acquirer should not recognise a liability for such a restructuring plan as part of allocating the cost of the combination unless the subsidiary was already committed to the plan before the acquisition.

This prevents creative accounting. An acquirer cannot set up a provision for restructuring or future losses of a subsidiary and then release this to the profit or loss in subsequent periods in order to reduce losses or smooth profits.

Intangible assets:

The acquiree may have intangible assets, such as development expenditure. These can be recognised separately from goodwill only if they are identifiable. An intangible asset is identifiable only if it:

a) Is separable, i.e. capable of being separated or divided from the entity and sold, transferred, or exchanged, either individually or together with a related contract, asset or liability, or

b) Arises from contractual or other legal rights.

The acquiree may also have internally-generated assets such as brand names which have not been recognised as intangible assets. As the acquiring company is giving valuable consideration for these assets, they are now recognised as assets in the consolidated financial statements.

Contingent liabilities:

Contingent liabilities of the acquirer are recognised if their fair value can be measured reliably. This is a departure from the normal rules in IAS 37; contingent liabilities are not normally recognised but only disclosed. After their initial recognition, the acquirer should measure contingent liabilities that are recognised separately at the higher of:

a) The amount that would be recognised in accordance with IAS 37
b) The amount initially recognised

Determination of Fair Value upon Acquisition of a Subsidiary

IFRS 3(R) requires that the identifiable assets, liabilities and contingent liabilities acquired which will be recognised should be those of the acquiree (subsidiary) that existed at the date of acquisition. Liabilities that should be recognised should be that assumed (existing and absorbed upon acquisition) and not those resulting from the acquirer's (parent's) intentions or actions. This implies that liabilities for terminating or reducing the activities of the acquiree (subsidiary) should only be recognised where the acquiree (subsidiary) has, at the acquisition date; and existing liability for restructuring recognised in accordance with *IAS 37 (Provisions, Contingent Liabilities and Contingent Assets)*. Furthermore, liabilities should not be recognised for future losses or other costs expected to be incurred as a result of the acquisition, whether they relate to the acquirer or acquiree.

What is fair value?

IFRS 13 defines 'what a Fair value is' and also expatiate on the sources of obtaining fair value vis-à-vis the hierarchy of fair value measurement.

Fair value. The price that would be received to sell an asset or paid to transfer a liability in an orderly transaction between market participants at the measurement date.

IFRS 13 provides far-reaching guidance on how the fair value of assets and liabilities should be ascertained.

This standard requires that the following are considered in determining fair value.

a) The asset or liability being measured.
b) The principal market (i.e. that where the most activity takes place) or where there is no principal market, the most advantageous market (i.e. that in which the best price could be achieved) in which an orderly transaction would take place for the asset or liability.
c) The highest and best use of the asset or liability and whether it is used on a standalone basis or in conjunction with other assets or liabilities.
d) Assumptions that market participants would use when pricing the asset or liability.

IFRS 13 provides a hierarchy of inputs for arriving at fair value:

IFRS 13 - Fair Value Hierarchy

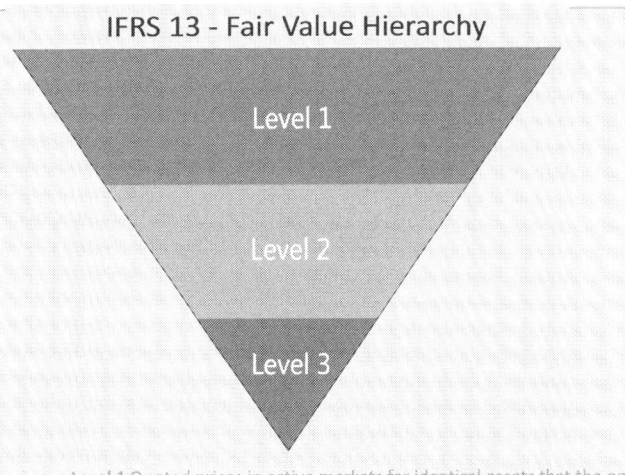

- **Level 1** Quoted prices in active markets for identical assets that the entity can access at the measurement date
- **Level 2** Inputs other than quoted prices that are directly or indirectly observable for the asset
- **Level 3** Unobservable inputs for the asset

Technical Note:
It requires that level 1 input is used where possible.

We are to consider the above-identified scenarios with simple illustrations as shown below:

Scenario A:
The fair value of the identifiable assets and liabilities of the subsidiary have been recognised upon acquisition in the financial statements of the subsidiary as stated below.

ILLUSTRATION 1:

Pally Plc acquired 80% of the equity share capital of Sussy Plc on the reporting date 31 December 2015. At the date of acquisition, the carrying amount (book value) of Sussy Plc Plant was ₦130 million, whereas the fair value of other assets and liabilities equal the carrying amount of acquisition. The fair value has already been recognised in the financial statements of the subsidiary as shown with the value of ₦150 million. The statement of financial position of the two companies on this date stood as follows:

Statement of Financial Position as at 31st December 2015

	Pally ₦' million	Sussy ₦' million
Plant	300	150
Investment in Sussy Plc	200	
Current assets	120	70
	620	**220**

Share Capital & Reserves:

Equity share capital (@ ₦1 per share)	400	120
Reserves (Retained Earnings)	140	60
Revaluation reserves	-	20
	540	200
Current liabilities	80	20
	620	**220**

(*Assuming the prevailing market price of Sussy's shares prior to the date of acquisition is ₦2 per share*).

Based on the information presented above, the possible two scenarios will be considered as it relates to the amount of investment of non-controlling interest in the subsidiary as at the date of acquisition.

First, we assumed that the parent at the point of acquisition (when control was obtained), valued investments of the non-controlling interest at the proportionate share of the subsidiary's identifiable net assets (assets and liabilities). In this case, the consolidation process will be as follows:

- ✓ **Step 1**: Determine the percentage holdings of investment of **Pally** in **Sussy** as at the acquisition date (31 December 2015), which represents the date of inclusion (first date of consolidation). In this case, the percentage holding is already determined and ascertained to be 80%.

- ✓ **Step 2**: Ascertain the form of group structure in this parent-subsidiary relationship. Since the subsidiary (**Sussy**) is *partly-owned* by the parent (**Pally**), the group structure is a simple structure as shown below:

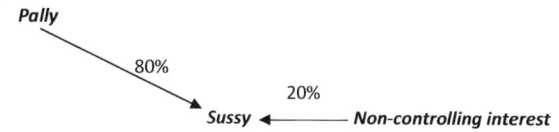

```
        Pally
         \
       80%\
           \          20%
            ↘ Sussy ←——— Non-controlling interest
```

- ✓ **Step 3**: Determine the existence of goodwill or gain from a bargain purchase as the date of acquisition based on the fair value or provisional values of subsidiary's identifiable assets and liabilities. In this case, there exists goodwill as shown below.

To ascertain and determine the amount of goodwill or gain from a bargain purchase, the value of an investment of the parent (**Pally**) in the subsidiary (**Sussy**) will be compared with the identifiable assets and liabilities of the subsidiary as at acquisition.

PARTIAL METHODOLOGY	₦'million	₦'million
Cost of combination (i.e. the cost of investment of **Pally** in **Sussy**)		200
Less: **Pally's** share of Identifiable net assets of **Sussy** acquired:		
• Share capital (80% of ₦120 million)	96	
• Pre-acquisition reserves (80% of ₦60 million)	48	
• Revaluation reserves (80% of ₦20 million)	16	
		(160)
Goodwill attributable to Pally's (a)		40
Amount of investments of non-controlling interest in **Sussy**		40
Less: Non-controlling interest share of the fair value of subsidiary's net assets:		
• Share capital (20% of ₦120 million)	24	
• Pre-acquisition reserves (20% of ₦60 million)	12	
• Revaluation reserves (20% of ₦20 million)	4	

Fair Value of Subsidiary's Net Assets on Acquisition

	(40)
*Goodwill attributable to **non-controlling interests** (b)*	---
Partial Goodwill (a + b)	**40**

The revaluation reserve upon acquisition has already been ascertained and incorporated in the financial statements of the subsidiary as determined as the difference between the fair value and the carrying amount of the subsidiary's plant as at acquisition date (31 December 2015), which is ₦20 million (being the excess of ₦150 million over ₦130 million).

Alternative, METHODOLOGY	₦' million	₦' million
Cost of combination (i.e. cost of acquisition) to the **Pally**		200
Amount of Investment in subsidiary to non-controlling interest*		40
Combined amount of interests in subsidiary to all investors		*240*
Less: Fair value of identifiable net assets aty acquisition-date (31 December 2015)		
Share capital	120	
Pre-acquisition reserve	60	
Revaluation reserve	20	(200)
Partial Goodwill - positive		**40**

Technical Note:
*The goodwill attributable to non-controlling must be zero since the investment to non-controlling interests is valued at the proportionate share of subsidiary's identifiable net assets as shown by the arrow.

✓ **Step 4:** *Determine the amount of non-controlling interest as will be shown in the consolidated statement of financial position of the group.* In this case, non-controlling interest will only be measured at the proportionate share of subsidiary's identifiable assets and liabilities, which could be depicted as thus:

Non-controlling interest's share of Identifiable net assets of **Sussy** upon acquisition:

	₦' million
• Share capital (20% of ₦120 million)	24
• Pre-acquisition reserves (20% of ₦60 million)	12
• Revaluation reserve (20% of ₦20 million)	16
NCI's investment on 31 December 2015 (based on proportionate share of net assets)	**40**

✓ **Step 5:** *Determine the amount to be included in the consolidated statement of financial position as consolidated reserves (otherwise known as consolidated retained earnings).* The consolidated retained earnings to be included in the consolidated statement of financial position of **Pally-Group** is that of the parent, as there exist no post-acquisition profits in the subsidiary as at acquisition. There will be post-acquisition profits in the subsidiary only when change is experienced in the reserves of the subsidiary subsequent to acquisition. The consolidated retained earnings will be determined as follows:

	₦' million
Parent's (**Pally**) retained earnings	140
Share of subsidiary's (**Sussy**) post-acquisition retained earnings (80% of Nil)	---
	140

✓ **Step 6:** Combine the assets and liabilities of the parent (**Pally**) and subsidiary (**Sussy**) on an item-by-item basis excluding the initial investment of **Pally** in **Sussy** as earlier shown in the separate financial statements of **Pally**, and also the exclusion of the equity share capital of **Sussy**, as it has already been considered alongside with the pre-acquisition retained earnings in ascertaining the amount of goodwill or gain from bargain purchase inherent/embedded in the acquisition. The consolidated statement of financial position of the group will now be shown as thus:

Pally Group
Consolidated Statement of Financial Position as at 31 December 2015

Assets:	₦' million
Non-current assets	
Plant (300 + 130 + 20)	450
Goodwill on acquisition	40
Current assets (120 + 70)	190
Total Assets	**680**
Share Capital & Reserves:	
Equity share capital (@ ₦1 per share)	400
Reserves	140
Equity attributable to Pally's shareholders	**540**
Non-controlling interest	40
Total Equity	**580**
Current liability (80 + 20)	100
Total Equity and Liabilities	**680**

The consolidation schedule can equally be adopted for solving this group problem as scheduled below:

Consolidation Schedule

Subsidiary – Sussy		Cost of control (Pally in Sussy) as at 31 Dec. 2015 – 80%		Non-controlling Interests – 20%		Consolidated Reserves
Equity Share Capital	120	(80% x 120)	96	(20% x 120)	24	
Reserves (Pre-acquisition)	60	(80% x 60)	48	(20% x 60)	12	
Revaluation reserves	20	(80% x 20)	16	(20% x 20)	4	
Net asset on acquisition			160			
Cost of combination (cost of investment)			(200)			
Goodwill (positive)			(40)			
Non-controlling interests					40	
Pally Reserve						140
Consolidated Reserves						**140**

Second, we assumed that the parent at the point of acquisition (when control was obtained), measured the amount of non-controlling interest at fair value (which is predominantly based on market values of shares of the subsidiary). In this case, the consolidation process will be as follows:

Fair Value of Subsidiary's Net Assets on Acquisition

✓ **Step 1**: Determine the percentage holdings of investment of **Pally** in **Sussy** as at the acquisition date (31 December 2015), which represents the date of inclusion (first date of consolidation). In this case, the percentage holding is already determined and ascertained to be 80%.

✓ **Step 2**: Ascertain the form of group structure in this parent-subsidiary relationship. Since the subsidiary (**Sussy**) is *partly-owned* by the parent (**Pally**), the group structure is a simple structure as shown below:

```
          Pally
            \
          80% \
               \      20%
                \
                 Sussy ◄──────── Non-controlling interest
```

✓ **Step 3**: Determine the existence of goodwill or gain from a bargain purchase as the date of acquisition based on the fair value or provisional values of subsidiary's identifiable assets and liabilities. In this case, there exists goodwill as shown below.

To ascertain and determine the amount of goodwill or gain from a bargain purchase, the amount of investment of the parent (**Pally**) in the subsidiary (**Sussy**) will be compared with the parent's share of identifiable assets and liabilities of the subsidiary that were acquired, in additional to possible goodwill attributable to non-controlling interest.

	₦' million	₦' million
PARTIAL METHODOLOGY:		
Cost of combination (i.e. the cost of investment of **Pally** in **Sussy**)		200
Less: **Pally's** share of Identifiable net assets of **Sussy** acquired:		
• Share capital (80% of ₦120 million)	96	
• Pre-acquisition reserves (80% of ₦60 million)	48	
• Revaluation reserve (80% of ₦20 million)	<u>16</u>	
		<u>(160)</u>
Goodwill attributable to **Pally's** *(a)*		<u>40</u>
Amount of investments of non-controlling interest in **Sussy** *(Technical Note)*		48
Less: Non-controlling interest share of the fair value of subsidiary's net assets:		
• Share capital (20% of ₦120 million)	24	
• Pre-acquisition reserves (20% of ₦60 million)	12	
• Revaluation reserve (20% of ₦20 million)	<u>4</u>	
		(40)
Goodwill attributable to **non-controlling interests** *(b)*		<u>8</u>
Full Goodwill (a + b)		<u>**48**</u>

The revaluation reserve upon acquisition has already been ascertained and incorporated in the financial statement of the subsidiary as determined as the difference between the fair value and the carrying amount of the subsidiary's plant as at acquisition date (31 December 2015), which is ₦20 million (being the excess of ₦150 million over ₦130 million).

	₦' million
Alternative, FULL METHODOLOGY	
Cost of combination (i.e. cost of acquisition) to the **Pally**	200
Amount of Investment in subsidiary to non-controlling interest*	<u>48</u>
Combined amount of interests in subsidiary to all investors	**248**

Contemporaneous Accounting for Business Combinations and Group Accounts

Less: Fair value of identifiable net assets at acquisition-date (31 December 2015)		
Share capital	120	
Pre-acquisition reserve	60	
Revaluation reserve	20	(200)
Full Goodwill		**48**

Technical Note:
The goodwill attributable to non-controlling is ₦8 million since the investment to non-controlling interest is measured at fair value of ₦48 million (being the market price of shares prevailing prior to acquisition at ₦2.00 per share multiplied by the number of shares which is 20% 0f the shares existing in **Sussy -120 million shares) as it different from the proportionate share of the identifiable net assets of the subsidiary upon acquisition.*

✓ **Step 4**: Determine the amount of non-controlling interest as will be shown in the consolidated statement of financial position of the group. In this case, non-controlling interest will only be valued at fair value, which could be depicted as thus:

The fair value of non-controlling interests in **Sussy** upon acquisition is measured as thus:

	₦' million
NCI's investment on 31 December 2015 (*based on fair value*)	**48**
This can be further decomposed as thus	₦' million
• Share capital (20% of ₦120 million)	24
• Pre-acquisition reserves (20% of ₦60 million)	12
• Revaluation reserve (20% of ₦20 million)	4
NCI's investment on 31 Dec. 2015 (based on proportionate share of net assets)	**40**
Goodwill attributable to non-controlling interest on acquisition (Balancing figure)	*8*
NCI's investment on 31 December 2015	**48**

✓ **Step 5**: Determine the amount to be included in the consolidated statement of financial position as consolidated reserves (otherwise known as consolidated retained earnings). The consolidated retained earnings to be included in the consolidated statement of financial position of **Pally-Group** is that of the parent, as there exist no post-acquisition profits in the subsidiary as at acquisition. There will be post-acquisition profits in the subsidiary only when change is experienced in the reserves of the subsidiary subsequent to acquisition. The consolidated retained earnings will be determined as follows:

	₦' million
Parent's (**Pally**) retained earnings	140
Share of subsidiary's (**Sussy**) post-acquisition retained earnings (80% of Nil)	---
	140

✓ **Step 6**: Combine the assets and liabilities of the parent (**Pally**) and subsidiary (**Sussy**) on an item-by-item basis excluding the initial investment of **Pally** in **Sussy** as earlier shown in the separate financial statements of **Pally**, and also the exclusion of the equity share capital of **Sussy**, as it has already been considered alongside with the pre-acquisition retained earnings in ascertaining the amount of goodwill or gain from bargain purchase inherent/embedded in the acquisition. The consolidated statement of financial position of the group will now be shown as thus:

Fair Value of Subsidiary's Net Assets on Acquisition

Pally Group
Consolidated Statement of Financial Position as at 31 December 2015

Assets:	₦' million
Non-current assets	
Plant (300 + 130 + 20)	450
Goodwill on acquisition	48
Current assets (120 + 70)	190
Total Assets	**688**
Share Capital & Reserves:	
Equity share capital (@ ₦1 per share)	400
Reserves	140
Equity attributable to Pally's shareholders	**540**
Non-controlling interest	48
Total Equity	**588**
Current liabilities (80 + 20)	100
Total Equity and Liabilities	**688**

The consolidation schedule can equally be adopted for solving this group problem as scheduled below:

Consolidation Schedule

Subsidiary - Sussy		Cost of control (Pally in Sussy) as at 31 Dec. 2015– 80%		Non-controlling Interests – 20%		Consolidated Reserves
Equity Share Capital	120	(80% x 120)	96	(20% x 120)	24	
Reserves (Pre-acquisition)	60	(80% x 60)	48	(20% x 60)	12	
Revaluation reserves	20	(80% x 60)	16	(20% x 20)	4	
Net asset on acquisition			160			
Cost of combination (cost of investment)			(200)			
Goodwill (positive)			(40)			
Goodwill attributable to NCI (see note)			(8)		8	
Full Goodwill (positive)			(48)			
Non-controlling interests					48	
Pally Reserves						140
Consolidated Reserves						**140**

Technical Note:

Goodwill attributable to non-controlling interest may be separately determined as thus;   ₦' million

    Amount of investment of non-controlling interest in **Sussy**   48

    Less: Non-controlling interest share of the fair value of subsidiary's net assets:
- Share capital (20% of ₦120 million)   24
- Pre-acquisition reserves (20% of ₦60 million)   12
- Fair value adjustments (20% of ₦20 million)   4

    (40)

*Goodwill attributable to **non-controlling interests***   8

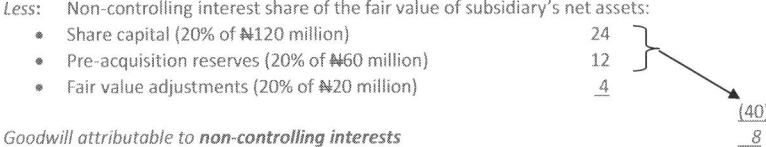

158

Contemporaneous Accounting for Business Combinations and Group Accounts

Accounting Entries:
Debit: Group Goodwill
Credit: Non-controlling interests' investment } ₦8 million

<u>Scenario B:</u>
The fair value of the identifiable assets and liabilities of the subsidiary have not been recognised upon acquisition in the financial statements of the subsidiary as stated below.

ILLUSTRATION 2:

Pally Plc acquired 80% of the equity share capital of **Sussy Plc** on the reporting date 31 December 2015. At the date of acquisition, the fair value of **Sussy Plc** *Plant* was ₦150 million, whereas the carrying amount (the book value) of other assets and liabilities equal the fair value upon acquisition. The statement of financial position of the two companies on this date stood as follows:

Statement of Financial Position as at 31st December 2015

	Pally ₦' million	Sussy ₦' million
Plant	300	130
Investment in *Sussy Plc*	200	
Current assets	120	70
	620	**200**
Share Capital & Reserves:		
Equity share capital (@ ₦1 per share)	400	120
Reserves (Retained Earnings)	140	60
	540	180
Current liabilities	80	20
	620	**200**

(Assuming the prevailing market price of **Sussy's** shares prior to the date of acquisition is ₦2 per share).

Based on the information presented above, the possible two scenarios will be considered as it relates to the amount of investment of non-controlling interest in the subsidiary as at the date of acquisition.

First, we assumed that the parent at the point of acquisition (when control was obtained), valued investments of the non-controlling interest at the proportionate share of the subsidiary's identifiable net assets (assets and liabilities). In this case, the consolidation process will be as follows:

- ✓ **Step 1**: Determine the percentage holdings of investment of **Pally** in **Sussy** as at the acquisition date (31 December 2015), which represents the date of inclusion (first date of consolidation). In this case, the percentage holding is already determined and ascertained to be 80%.

- ✓ **Step 2**: Ascertain the form of group structure in this parent-subsidiary relationship. Since the subsidiary (**Sussy**) is *partly-owned* by the parent (**Pally**), the group structure is a simple structure as shown below:

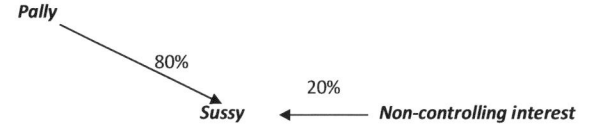

```
         Pally
        /
     80%
      ↓           20%
    Sussy  ←────────  Non-controlling interest
```

Fair Value of Subsidiary's Net Assets on Acquisition

✓ **Step 3:** Determine the existence of goodwill or gain from a bargain purchase as the date of acquisition based on the fair value or provisional values of subsidiary's identifiable assets and liabilities. In this case, there exists goodwill as shown below.

To ascertain and determine the amount of goodwill or gain from a bargain purchase, the value of an investment of the parent (**Pally**) in the subsidiary (**Sussy**) will be compared with the identifiable assets and liabilities of the subsidiary as at acquisition.

PARTIAL METHODOLOGY	₦' million	₦' million
Cost of combination (i.e. the cost of investment of **Pally** in **Sussy**)		200
Less: **Pally's** share of Identifiable net assets of **Sussy** acquired:		
• Share capital (80% of ₦120 million)	96	
• Pre-acquisition reserves (80% of ₦60 million)	48	
• Fair value adjustments (80% of ₦20 million)	16	
		(160)
Goodwill attributable to Pally's (a)		40
Amount of investments of non-controlling interest in **Sussy**		40
Less: Non-controlling interest share of the fair value of subsidiary's net assets:		
• Share capital (20% of ₦120 million)	24	
• Pre-acquisition reserves (20% of ₦60 million)	12	
• Fair value adjustments (20% of ₦20 million)	4	
		(40)
*Goodwill attributable to **non-controlling interests** (b)*		---
Goodwill (a + b)		**40**

The fair value adjustment upon acquisition is determined as the difference between the fair value and the carrying amount of the subsidiary's plant as at acquisition date (31 December 2015), which is ₦20 million (being the excess of ₦150 million over ₦130 million).

Accounting entries:
Debit: Plant
Credit: Revaluation reserves – subsidiary (Pre-acquisition) } ₦20 million

Alternative, FULL METHODOLOGY	₦' million	₦' million
Cost of combination (i.e. cost of acquisition) to the **Pally**		200
Amount of Investment in subsidiary to non-controlling interest*		40
Combined amount of interests in subsidiary to all investors		**240**
Less: Fair value of subsidiary's Identifiable net assets as acquisition-date (31 Dec. 2015)		
• Share capital (20% of ₦120 million)	120	
• Pre-acquisition reserves (20% of ₦60 million)	60	
• Fair value adjustments (20% of ₦20 million)	20	(200)
Goodwill - positive		**40**

Technical Note:
*The goodwill attributable to non-controlling must be zero since the investment to non-controlling interests is valued at the proportionate share of subsidiary's identifiable net assets as shown by the arrow.

✓ **Step 4:** Determine the amount of non-controlling interest as will be shown in the consolidated statement of financial position of the group. In this case, non-controlling interest will only be measured at proportionate share of subsidiary's identifiable assets and liabilities, which could be depicted as thus:

Non-controlling interest's share of Identifiable net assets of **Sussy** upon acquisition:

	₦' million
• Share capital (20% of ₦120 million)	24
• Pre-acquisition reserves (20% of ₦60 million)	12
• Fair value adjustments (20% of ₦20 million)	16
NCI's investment on 31 December 2015	**40**

✓ **Step 5:** Determine the amount to be included in the consolidated statement of financial position as consolidated reserves (otherwise known as consolidated retained earnings). The consolidated retained earnings to be included in the consolidated statement of financial position of **Pally-Group** is that of the parent, as there exist no post-acquisition profits in the subsidiary as at acquisition. There will be post-acquisition profits in the subsidiary only when change is experienced in the reserves of the subsidiary subsequent to acquisition. The consolidated retained earnings will be determined as follows:

	₦' million
Parent's (**Pally**) retained earnings	140
Share of subsidiary's (**Sussy**) post-acquisition retained earnings (80% of Nil)	---
	140

✓ **Step 6:** Combine the assets and liabilities of the parent (**Pally**) and subsidiary (**Sussy**) on an item-by-item basis excluding the initial investment of **Pally** in **Sussy** as earlier shown in the separate financial statements of **Pally**, and also the exclusion of the equity share capital of **Sussy**, as it has already been considered alongside with the pre-acquisition retained earnings in ascertaining the amount of goodwill or gain from bargain purchase inherent/embedded in the acquisition. The consolidated statement of financial position of the group will now be shown as thus:

Pally Group
Consolidated Statement of Financial Position as at 31 December 2015

Assets:	₦' million
Non-current assets	
Plant (300 + 130 + 20)	450
Goodwill	40
Current assets (120 + 70)	190
Total Assets	**680**
Share Capital & Reserves:	
Equity share capital (@ ₦1 per share)	400
Reserves	140
Equity attributable to Pally's shareholders	**540**
Non-controlling interest	40
Total Equity	**580**
Current liabilities (80 + 20)	100
Total Equity and Liabilities	**680**

Fair Value of Subsidiary's Net Assets on Acquisition

The consolidation schedule can equally be adopted for solving this group problem as scheduled below:

Consolidation Schedule

Subsidiary - Sussy		Cost of control (Pally in Sussy) as at 31 Dec. 2015– 80%		Non-controlling Interests – 20%		Consolidated Reserves
Equity Share Capital	120	(80% x 120)	96	(20% x 120)	24	
Reserves (Pre-acquisition)	60	(80% x 60)	48	(20% x 60)	12	
Fair value adjustments	*20*	*(80% x 20)*	*16*	*(20% x 20)*	*4*	
Net asset on acquisition			160			
Cost of combination (cost of investment)			(200)			
Goodwill (positive)			(40)			
Non-controlling interests					40	
Pally Reserve						140
Consolidated Reserves						140

Second, we assumed that the parent at the point of acquisition (when control was obtained), measured investments of the non-controlling interest at fair value (which is predominantly based on market values of shares of the subsidiary). In this case, the consolidation process will be as follows:

- ✓ **Step 1**: *Determine the percentage holdings of investment of **Pally** in **Sussy** as at the acquisition date (31 December 2015), which represents the date of inclusion (first date of consolidation).* In this case, the percentage holding is already determined and ascertained to be 80%.

- ✓ **Step 2**: *Ascertain the form of group structure in this parent-subsidiary relationship.* Since the subsidiary (**Sussy**) is *partly-owned* by the parent (**Pally**), the group structure is a simple structure as shown below:

```
        Pally
           \
          80%
             \
              20%
          Sussy  ←———— Non-controlling interest
```

- ✓ **Step 3**: *Determine the existence of goodwill or gain from a bargain purchase as the date of acquisition based on the fair value or provisional values of subsidiary's identifiable assets and liabilities.* In this case, there exists goodwill as shown below.

To ascertain and determine the amount of goodwill or gain from a bargain purchase, the amount of investment of the parent (**Pally**) in the subsidiary (**Sussy**) will be compared with the parent's share of identifiable assets and liabilities of the subsidiary that were acquired, in additional to possible goodwill attributable to non-controlling interest.

PARTIAL METHODOLOGY	₦' million	₦' million
Cost of combination (i.e. the cost of investment of **Pally** in **Sussy**)		200
Less: **Pally's** share of Identifiable net assets of **Sussy** acquired:		
• Share capital (80% of ₦120 million)	96	
• Pre-acquisition reserves (80% of ₦60 million)	48	
• Fair value adjustments (80% of ₦20 million)	16	
		(160)
*Goodwill attributable to **Pally's** (a)*		40
Amount of investments of non-controlling interest in **Sussy**		48
Less: Non-controlling interest share of the fair value of subsidiary's net assets:		
• Share capital (20% of ₦120 million)	24	
• Pre-acquisition reserves (20% of ₦60 million)	12	
• Fair value adjustments (20% of ₦20 million)	4	
		(40)
*Goodwill attributable to **non-controlling interests** (b)*		8
Full Goodwill (a + b)		**48**

The fair value adjustment upon acquisition is determined as the difference between the fair value and the carrying amount of the subsidiary's plant as at acquisition date (31 December 2015), which is ₦20 million (being the excess of ₦150 million over ₦130 million).

Accounting entries:
Debit: Plant
Credit: Revaluation reserves – subsidiary (Pre-acquisition) } ₦20 million

Alternatively, FULL METHODOLOGY	₦' million	₦' million
Cost of combination (i.e. cost of acquisition) to the parent		200
Amount of Investment in subsidiary to non-controlling interest*		48
Combined amount of interests in subsidiary to all investors		**248**
Less: Fair value of subsidiary's Identifiable net assets as acquisition-date (31 Dec. 2015)		
• Share capital (20% of ₦120 million)	120	
• Pre-acquisition reserves (20% of ₦60 million)	60	
• Fair value adjustments (20% of ₦20 million)	20	(200)
Goodwill - positive		**48**

Technical Note:

The goodwill attributable to non-controlling is ₦8 million since the investment to non-controlling interests is valued at fair value of ₦48 million (being the market price of shares prevailing prior to acquisition at ₦2.00 per share multiplied by the number of shares which is 20% Of the shares existing in **Sussy -120 million shares) as it different from the proportionate share of the identifiable net assets of the subsidiary upon acquisition.*

- ✓ **Step 4:** Determine the amount of non-controlling interest as will be shown in the consolidated statement of financial position of the group. In this case, non-controlling interest will only be valued at fair value, which could be depicted as thus:

Fair Value of Subsidiary's Net Assets on Acquisition

The fair value of non-controlling interests in **Sussy** upon acquisition is measured as thus:

	₦' million
NCI's investment on 31 December 2015 (*based on fair value*)	**48**

This can be further decomposed as thus	₦' million
• Share capital (20% of ₦120 million)	24
• Pre-acquisition reserves (20% of ₦60 million)	12
• Fair value adjustments (20% of ₦20 million)	4
NCI's investment on 31 December 2015 (based on proportionate share of net assets)	40
Goodwill attributable to non-controlling interests on acquisition (Balancing figure)	8
NCI's investment on 31 December 2015	**48**

✓ **Step 5:** *Determine the amount to be included in the consolidated statement of financial position as consolidated reserves (otherwise known as consolidated retained earnings).* The consolidated retained earnings to be included in the consolidated statement of financial position of **Pally-Group** is that of the parent, as there exist no post-acquisition profits in the subsidiary as at acquisition. There will be post-acquisition profits in the subsidiary only when change is experienced in the reserves of the subsidiary subsequent to acquisition. The consolidated retained earnings will be determined as follows:

	₦' million
Parent's (**Pally**) retained earnings	140
Share of subsidiary's (**Sussy**) post-acquisition retained earnings (80% of Nil)	---
	140

✓ **Step 6:** *Combine the assets and liabilities of the parent (**Pally**) and subsidiary (**Sussy**) on an item-by-item basis excluding the initial investment of **Pally** in **Sussy** as earlier shown in the separate financial statements of **Pally**, and also the exclusion of the equity share capital of **Sussy**, as it has already been considered alongside with the pre-acquisition retained earnings in ascertaining the amount of goodwill or gain from bargain purchase inherent/embedded in the acquisition.* The consolidated statement of financial position of the group will now be shown as thus:

Pally Group
Consolidated Statement of Financial Position as at 31 December 2015

	₦' million
Assets:	
Non-current assets	
Plant (300 + 130 + 20)	450
Goodwill	8
Current assets (120 + 70)	190
Total Assets	**688**
Share Capital & Reserves:	
Equity share capital (@ ₦1 per share)	400
Reserves	140
Equity attributable to Pally's shareholders	**540**
Non-controlling interest	48
Total Equity	**588**
Current liabilities (80 + 20)	100
Total Equity and Liabilities	**688**

The consolidation schedule can equally be adopted for solving this group problem as scheduled below:

Consolidation Schedule

Subsidiary - Sussy		Cost of control (Pally in Sussy) as at 31 Dec. 2015– 80%		Non-controlling Interests – 20%		Consolidated Reserves
Equity Share Capital	120	(80% x 120)	96	(20% x 120)	24	
Reserves (Pre-acquisition)	60	(80% x 60)	48	(20% x 60)	12	
Fair value adjustments	20	(80% x 20)	16	(20% x 20)	4	
Net asset on acquisition			160			
Cost of combination (cost of investment)			(200)			
Goodwill (positive)			(40)			
Goodwill attributable to NCI(see note)			(8)		8	
Full Goodwill (positive)			(48)			
Non-controlling interests					48	
Pally Reserve						140
Consolidated Reserves						140

Technical Note:
Goodwill attributable to non-controlling interest may be separately determined as thus;

₦' million

Amount of investment of non-controlling interest in **Sussy**   48
Less: Non-controlling interest share of the fair value of subsidiary's net assets:
- Share capital (20% of ₦120 million)   24
- Pre-acquisition reserves (20% of ₦60 million)   12
- Fair value adjustments (20% of ₦20 million)   4

                                                   (40)
Goodwill attributable to **non-controlling interests**   8

Accounting Entries:
Debit: Group Goodwill
Credit: Non-controlling interests' investment   ₦8 million

Scenario C:
The effect of fair value adjustment on the subsidiary's net assets acquired can be considered subsequent to acquisition where the subsidiary did not reflect fair value adjustment in its financial statement upon its acquisition by the parent company. The illustration(s) below will be adopted in showing the subsequent effect(s) of the fair value adjustments on the consolidated financial statements at a reporting date subsequent to the acquisition date.

ILLUSTRATION 3:
Pally Plc acquired 80% of the equity share capital of **Sussy Plc** on the reporting date 31 December 2013. At the date of acquisition, the fair value of **Sussy Plc** *Plant* was ₦170 million (when the remaining economic life of the Plant is 10 years), whereas the carrying amount (the book value) of other assets and liabilities equal the fair value upon acquisition. At the date of

Fair Value of Subsidiary's Net Assets on Acquisition

acquisition, the subsidiary's retained earnings were ₦40 million. The statement of financial position of the two companies on the reporting date 31 December 2015 stood as follows:

Statement of Financial Position as at 31ˢᵗ December 2015

	Pally	Sussy
	₦' million	₦' million
Plant	300	120
Investment in **Sussy Plc**	160	
Current assets	120	80
	580	**200**
Share Capital & Reserves:		
Equity share capital (@ ₦1 per share)	400	120
Reserves (Retained Earnings)	100	60
	500	180
Current liabilities	80	20
	580	**200**

(*Assuming the prevailing market price of **Sussy's** shares prior to the date of acquisition is ₦2 per share*).

Based on the information presented above, the possible two scenarios will be considered as it relates to the amount of investment of non-controlling interest in the subsidiary as at the date of acquisition.

First, we assumed that the parent at the point of acquisition (when control was obtained), valued investments of the non-controlling interest at the proportionate share of the subsidiary's identifiable net assets (assets and liabilities). In this case, the consolidation process will be as follows:

- ✓ **Step 1**: Determine the percentage holdings of investment of **Pally** in **Sussy** as at the acquisition date (31 December 2013), which represents the date of inclusion (first date of consolidation). In this case, the percentage holding is already determined and ascertained to be 80%.

- ✓ **Step 2**: Ascertain the form of group structure in this parent-subsidiary relationship. Since the subsidiary (**Sussy**) is *partly-owned* by the parent (**Pally**), the group structure is a simple structure as shown below:

```
        Pally
           \
         80% \
              \
               ↘
             Sussy  ←—— 20% ——  Non-controlling interest
```

- ✓ **Step 3**: Determine the existence of goodwill or gain from a bargain purchase as the date of acquisition based on the fair value of subsidiary's identifiable assets and liabilities. In this case, there exists goodwill as shown below.

To ascertain and determine the amount of goodwill or gain from a bargain purchase, the value of an investment of the parent (**Pally**) in the subsidiary (**Sussy**) will be compared with the identifiable assets and liabilities of the subsidiary as at acquisition.

PARTIAL METHODOLOGY	₦' million	₦' million
Cost of combination (i.e. the cost of investment of **Pally** in **Sussy**)		160
Less: **Pally's** share of Identifiable net assets of **Sussy** acquired:		
• Share capital (80% of ₦120 million)	96	
• Pre-acquisition reserves (80% of ₦40 million)	32	

• Fair value adjustments (80% of ₦20 million)	16	(144)
Goodwill attributable to Pally's (a)		16
Amount of investments of non-controlling interest in **Sussy**		36
Less: Non-controlling interest share of the fair value of subsidiary's net assets:		
• Share capital (20% of ₦120 million)	24	
• Pre-acquisition reserves (20% of ₦40 million)	8	
• Fair value adjustments (20% of ₦20 million)	4	(36)
Goodwill attributable to non-controlling interests (b)		---
Goodwill (a + b)		**16**

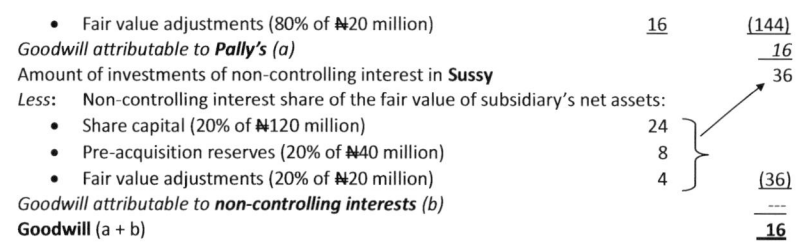

The fair value adjustment upon acquisition is determined as the difference between the fair value and the carrying amount of the subsidiary's plant as at acquisition date (31 December 2013), which is ₦20 million (being the excess of ₦170 million over ₦150 million) – *see Technical Note below for guidance*.

Accounting entries:
Debit: Plant
Credit: Revaluation reserves (Pre-acquisition) – subsidiary } ₦20 million

Alternative, FULL METHODOLOGY

Cost of Business Combination:		₦' million
Cost of acquisition of **Sussy** to **Pally**		160
Amount of Investment in subsidiary to non-controlling interest*		36
Combined amount of interests in subsidiary to all investors		**196**
Less: Fair value of subsidiary's Identifiable net assets as acquisition-date (31 Dec. 2013)		
• Share capital (20% of ₦120 million)	120	
• Pre-acquisition reserves (20% of ₦60 million)	40	
• Fair value adjustments (20% of ₦20 million)	20	(180)
Goodwill - positive		**16**

Technical Note:

1. The goodwill attributable to non-controlling must be zero since the investment to non-controlling interest is valued at the proportionate share of subsidiary's identifiable net assets as shown by the arrow.
2. The carrying amount of the Plant is arrived at (since it was not directly provided in the question) by adding the carrying amount of the Plant as at 31 December 2015 to the depreciation charged in 2014 and 2015 financial years (an approached known as **"Working Back"**). This can be shown in the **BOX** below.

Given the following information:
  i. The remaining useful life of the Plant as at **acquisition date** (31 December 2013) was **10 years**.
  ii. The remaining useful life of the Plant as at **reporting date** (31 December 2015) was **8 years**.
  iii. 2 years' depreciation charge has been recognised based on **initial carrying amount as at acquisition-date** (assumed on a straight-line basis, except otherwise stated).

Approach 1: Word Problems
Since ₦120 million represents the carrying amount of the Plant for the remaining 8 years as at 31 December 2015, and the method of depreciation is presumed straight-line

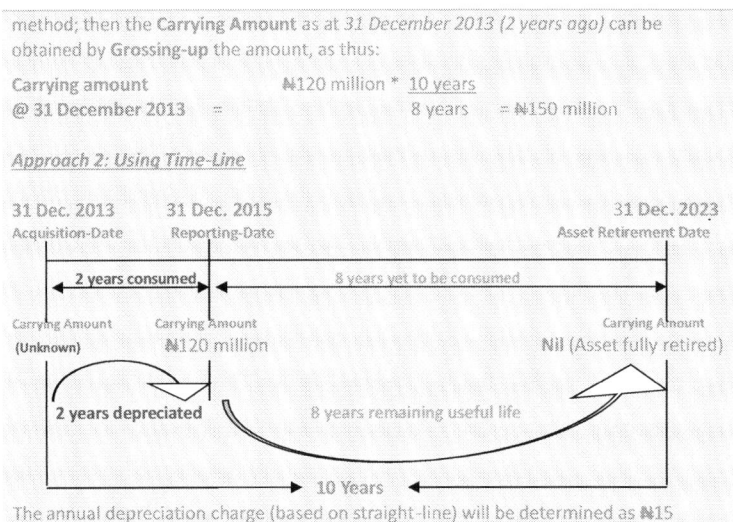

Fair Value of Subsidiary's Net Assets on Acquisition

> method; then the **Carrying Amount** as at *31 December 2013 (2 years ago)* can be obtained by **Grossing-up** the amount, as thus:
>
> Carrying amount   ₦120 million * 10 years
> @ 31 December 2013 =   8 years   = ₦150 million
>
> *Approach 2: Using Time-Line*
>
> | 31 Dec. 2013 | 31 Dec. 2015 | | 31 Dec. 2023 |
> |---|---|---|---|
> | Acquisition-Date | Reporting-Date | | Asset Retirement Date |
> | ← 2 years consumed → | ← 8 years yet to be consumed → | | |
> | Carrying Amount | Carrying Amount | | Carrying Amount |
> | (Unknown) | ₦120 million | | Nil (Asset fully retired) |
> | 2 years depreciated | | 8 years remaining useful life | |
> | | ← 10 Years → | | |
>
> The annual depreciation charge (based on straight-line) will be determined as ₦15 million (i.e. ₦120 million divided by 8 years remaining useful life till asset retirement in 2023).
>
> Therefore, 2 years' depreciation already charged between 2014 and 2015 would have amounted to ₦30 million (being ₦15 million annual depreciation charge multiplied by 2 years).
>
> Hence, to obtain the *Carrying Amount of the Plant as @ 31 December 2013*, which is ₦150 million, the carrying amount as @ 31 December 2015 of ₦120 million will be added back to ₦30 million '*depreciation charged*' for 2 years (2014 and 2015 respectively).

✓ **Step 4:** *Determine the amount of non-controlling interest as will be shown in the consolidated statement of financial position of the group.* In this case, non-controlling interest will only be measured at the proportionate share of subsidiary's identifiable assets and liabilities, which could be depicted as thus:

Non-controlling interest's share of Identifiable net assets of **Sussy**	₦' million
• Share capital (20% of ₦120 million)	24.0
• Pre-acquisition reserves (20% of ₦40 million)	8.0
• Fair value adjustments (20% of ₦20 million)	<u>16.0</u>
NCI's investment on 31 Dec. 2013 (based on proportionate share of net assets)	**36.0**
• Post-acquisition reserves (20% of ₦20 million)	4.0
• Less: *Extra depreciation due to fair value adjustment on Plant upon acquisition*	<u>(0.8)</u>
NCI's investment on 31 Dec. 2015 (based on proportionate share of net assets)	**<u>39.2</u>**

✓ **Step 5:** *Determine the amount to be included in the consolidated statement of financial position as consolidated reserves (otherwise known as consolidated retained earnings).* The consolidated retained earnings to be included in the consolidated statement of financial position of **Pally-Group** are that of the parent and of the post-acquisition profits of the subsidiary. Invariably, it implies a share of post-acquisition retained earnings (which is the sum of ₦20 million being the increase from ₦40 million profits upon acquisition to ₦60 million as at the reporting date 31 December 2015 - *2 years after*) of the subsidiary (**Sussy**) will now be combined with the retained earnings (profits) of the parent (**Pally**) in ascertaining the group retained earnings. The consolidated retained earnings will be determined as follows:

	₦' million
Parent's (**Pally**) retained earnings	100.0
Share of subsidiary's (**Sussy**) post-acquisition reserves (80% of ₦20 million)	16.0
Less: *Additional depreciation due to fair value adjustment on PPE upon acquisition	(3.2)
	112.8

*Basis of Determining Additional Depreciation:

The additional (extra) depreciation is as a result of the increase of ₦20 million created in the carrying amount of *Plant* emanating from fair value adjustment to the subsidiary's net assets. This will require us to recognise an increase in depreciation (being the allocation of additions to the carrying amount of the Plant) which was not recognised in the financial statements of the subsidiary because the fair value of the Plant was not reflected in the subsidiary's financial statements upon acquisition. The remaining economic life of the plant is 10 years, which implies that given a straight line depreciation, the asset would have been depreciated at an approximate amount of ₦15 million each year (i.e. ₦150 million carrying value divided by 10 years remaining), instead of being depreciated at an amount approximate to ₦17 million (being ₦170 million fair value divided by 10 years remaining). Hence, the extra (or additional) depreciation to be recognised as a charge to the group's profit or loss is ₦4 million (being the extra depreciation of ₦2 million per year for the two years – 2014 and 2015). The extra depreciation will be apportioned to the parent (Pally) and the non-controlling interest in the proportion profit or loss in the subsidiary is being shared. In this case, we shared the sum of ₦3.2 million to the parent (pally) via consolidated retained earnings (being 80% of ₦4 million), and the sum of ₦0.8 million attributed to non-controlling interest (being 20% of ₦4 million).

Accounting entries:
Debit: *Consolidated retained earnings* – ₦3.2 million ⎫
Debit: *Non-controlling interest*   – ₦0.8 million ⎬ ₦4.0 million
Credit: *Plant*   – ₦4.0 million ⎭

- ✓ **Step 6:** Combine the assets and liabilities of the parent (**Pally**) and subsidiary (**Sussy**) on an item-by-item basis excluding the initial investment of **Pally** in **Sussy** as earlier shown in the separate financial statements of **Pally**, and also the exclusion of the equity share capital of **Sussy**, as it has already been considered alongside with the pre-acquisition retained earnings in ascertaining the amount of goodwill or gain from bargain purchase inherent/embedded in the acquisition. The consolidated statement of financial position of the group will now be shown as thus:

Pally Group
Consolidated Statement of Financial Position as at 31 December 2015

Assets:	₦' million
Non-current assets	
Plant (300 + 120 + 20 - 4)	436
Goodwill	16
Current assets (120 + 80)	200
Total Assets	**652**

Fair Value of Subsidiary's Net Assets on Acquisition

Share Capital & Reserves:	
Equity share capital (@ ₦1 per share)	400
Reserves	112
Equity attributable to Pally's shareholders	**512**
Non-controlling interest	40
Total Equity	**552**
Current liabilities (80 + 20)	100
Total Equity and Liabilities	**652**

The consolidation schedule can equally be adopted for solving this group problem as scheduled below:

Consolidation Schedule

Subsidiary - Sussy		Cost of control (Pally in Sussy) as at 31 Dec. 2013 – 80%		Non-controlling Interests – 20%		Consolidated Reserves	
Equity Share Capital	120	(80% x 120)	96	(20% x 120)	24		
Reserves (Pre-acquisition)	40	(80% x 40)	32	(20% x 40)	8		
Reserves (Post-acquisition)	20			(20% x 20)	4	(80% x 20)	16
Fair value adjustments	20	(80% x 20)	16	(20% x 20)	4		
Net asset on acquisition			144				
Cost of combination			(160)				
Goodwill (positive)			(16)				
Extra (additional) depreciation					(0.8)		(3.2)
Non-controlling interests					**39.2**		
Pally Reserves							100
Consolidated Reserves							**112.8**

Second, we assumed that the parent at the point of acquisition (when control was obtained), measured investments of the non-controlling interest at fair value (which is predominantly based on market values of shares of the subsidiary). In this case, the consolidation process will be as follows:

✓ **Step 1**: Determine the percentage holdings of investment of **Pally** in **Sussy** as at the acquisition date (31 December 2013), which represents the date of inclusion (first date of consolidation). In this case, the percentage holding is already determined and ascertained to be 80%.

✓ **Step 2**: Ascertain the form of group structure in this parent-subsidiary relationship. Since the subsidiary (**Sussy**) is *partly-owned* by the parent (**Pally**), the group structure is a simple structure as shown below:

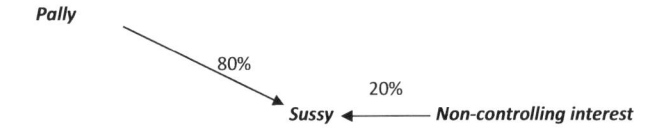

```
    Pally
       \
        80%
           \        20%
            Sussy ◀──── Non-controlling interest
```

✓ **Step 3:** *Determine the existence of goodwill or gain from a bargain purchase as the date of acquisition based on the fair value of subsidiary's identifiable assets and liabilities.* In this case, there exists goodwill as shown below.

To ascertain and determine the amount of goodwill or gain from a bargain purchase, the amount of investment of the parent (**Pally**) in the subsidiary (**Sussy**) will be compared with the parent's share of identifiable assets and liabilities of the subsidiary that were acquired, in additional to possible goodwill attributable to non-controlling interest.

PARTIAL METHODOLOGY	₦' million	₦' million
Cost of combination (i.e. the cost of investment of **Pally** in **Sussy**)		160
Less: **Pally's** share of Identifiable net assets of **Sussy** acquired:		
• Share capital (80% of ₦120 million)	96	
• Pre-acquisition reserves (80% of ₦40 million)	32	
• Fair value adjustments (80% of ₦20 million)	16	(144)
Goodwill attributable to **Pally's** (a)		16
Amount of investments of non-controlling interest in **Sussy**		48
Less: Non-controlling interest share of the fair value of subsidiary's net assets:		
• Share capital (20% of ₦120 million)	24	
• Pre-acquisition reserves (20% of ₦40 million)	8	
• Fair value adjustments (20% of ₦20 million)	4	(36)
Goodwill attributable to **non-controlling interests** (b)		12
Full Goodwill (a + b)		**28**

The fair value adjustment upon acquisition is determined as the difference between the fair value and the carrying amount of the subsidiary's plant as at acquisition date (31 December 2013), which is ₦20 million (being the excess of ₦170 million over ₦150 million) – *see Technical Note below for guidance*.

Accounting entries:
Debit: Plant
Credit: Revaluation reserves (Pre-acquisition) – subsidiary   } ₦20 million

Alternative, FULL METHODOLOGY

Cost of Business Combination:		₦' million
Cost of acquisition of **Sussy** to **Pally**		160
Amount of Investment in subsidiary to non-controlling interest*		48
Combined amount of interests in subsidiary to all investors		**196**
Less: Fair value of subsidiary's Identifiable net assets as acquisition-date (31 Dec. 2013)		
• Share capital (20% of ₦120 million)	120	
• Pre-acquisition reserves (20% of ₦60 million)	40	
• Fair value adjustments (20% of ₦20 million)	20	(180)
Goodwill - positive		**28**

Technical Note:

1. The goodwill attributable to non-controlling is ₦12 million since the investment to non-controlling interest is measured at fair value of ₦48 million (being the market price of shares prevailing prior to acquisition at ₦2.00 per share multiplied by the number of shares which is 20% 0f the shares existing in **Sussy** -120 million shares) as it different from the proportionate share of the identifiable net assets of the subsidiary upon acquisition.

171

2. The goodwill attributable to non-controlling must be zero since the investment to non-controlling interests is valued at the proportionate share of subsidiary's identifiable net assets as shown by the arrow.

3. The carrying amount of the Plant is arrived at (since it was not directly provided in the question) by adding the carrying amount of the Plant as at 31 December 2015 to the depreciation charged in 2014 and 2015 financial years (an approached known as *"Working Back"*). This can be shown in the **BOX** below.

> Given the following information:
>   i. The remaining useful life of the Plant as at **acquisition date** (31 December 2013) was **10 years**.
>   ii. The remaining useful life of the Plant as at **reporting date** (31 December 2015) was **8 years**.
>   iii. 2 years' depreciation charge has been recognised based on **initial carrying amount as at acquisition-date** (assumed on a straight-line basis, except otherwise stated).
>
> *Approach 1: Word Problems*
>
> Since ₦120 million represents the carrying amount of the Plant for the remaining 8 years as at 31 December 2015, and the method of depreciation is presumed a straight-line method; then the **Carrying Amount** as at *31 December 2013 (2 years ago)* can be obtained by **Grossing-up** the amount, as thus:
>
> Carrying amount   ₦120 million * 10 years
> @ 31 December 2013   =   ─────────   = ₦150 million
>   8 years
>
> *Approach 2: Using Time-Line*
>
> 31 Dec. 2013   31 Dec. 2015   31 Dec. 2023
> Acquisition-Date   Reporting-Date   Asset Retirement Date
>
> |◄── 2 years consumed ──►|◄────── 8 years yet to be consumed ──────►|
>
> Carrying Amount   Carrying Amount   Carrying Amount
> (Unknown)   ₦120 million   Nil (Asset fully retired)
>
> 2 years depreciated   8 years remaining useful life
>
>   ──► 10 Years ◄──
>
> The annual depreciation charge (based on straight-line) will be determined as ₦15 million (i.e. ₦120 million divided by 8 years remaining useful life till asset retirement in 2023). Therefore, 2 years' depreciation already charged between 2014 and 2015 would have amounted to ₦30 million (being ₦15 million annual depreciation charge multiplied by 2 years).
>
> Hence, to obtain the *Carrying Amount of the Plant as @ 31 December 2013*, which is **₦150 million**, the carrying amount as @ 31 December 2015 of ₦120 million will be added back to ₦30 million *'depreciation charged'* for 2 years (2014 and 2015 respectively).

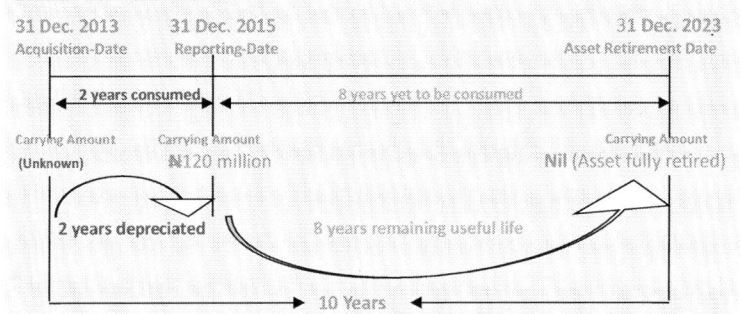

Contemporaneous Accounting for Business Combinations and Group Accounts

- **Step 4:** *Determine the amount of non-controlling interest as will be shown in the consolidated statement of financial position of the group.* In this case, non-controlling interest will only be valued at fair value, which could be depicted as thus:

The fair value of non-controlling interests in **Sussy** is measured as thus:

	₦' million
NCI's investment on 31 December 2013 (*based on fair value*)	**48.0**
• Post-acquisition reserves (20% of ₦20 million)	4.0
Less: *Extra depreciation on fair value adjustment on Plant upon acquisition	*(0.8)*
NCI's investment on 31 December 2015	**51.2**

This can be further decomposed as thus

	₦' million
• Share capital (20% of ₦120 million)	24.0
• Pre-acquisition reserves (20% of ₦40 million)	8.0
• Fair value adjustments (20% of ₦20 million)	4.0
NCI's investment on 31 December 2013 (based on proportionate share of net assets)	**36.0**
Goodwill attributable to non-controlling interests on acquisition (Balancing figure)	*12.0*
NCI's investment on 31 December 2013 (based on fair value)	**48.0**
• Post-acquisition reserves (20% of ₦20 million)	4.0
Less: *Extra depreciation on fair value adjustment on Plant upon acquisition	*(0.8)*
NCI's investment on 31 December 2015	**51.2**

- **Step 5:** *Determine the amount to be included in the consolidated statement of financial position as consolidated reserves (otherwise known as consolidated retained earnings).* The consolidated retained earnings to be included in the consolidated statement of financial position of **Pally-Group** are that of the parent and of the post-acquisition profits of the subsidiary. Invariably, it implies a share of post-acquisition retained earnings (which is the sum of ₦20 million being the increase from ₦40 million profits upon acquisition to ₦60 million as at the reporting date 31 December 2015 - *2 years after*) of the subsidiary (**Sussy**) will now be combined with the retained earnings (profits) of the parent (**Pally**) in ascertaining the group retained earnings. The consolidated retained earnings will be determined as follows:

	₦' million
Parent's (**Pally**) retained earnings	100.0
Share of subsidiary's (**Sussy**) post-acquisition reserves (80% of ₦20 million)	16.0
Less:* Extra (additional) depreciation on fair value adjustment on Plant upon acquisition	*(3.2)*
	112.8

*Basis of Determining Additional Depreciation:

The additional (extra) depreciation is as a result of the increase of ₦20 million created in the carrying amount of *Plant* emanating from fair value adjustment to the subsidiary's net assets. This will require us to recognise an increase in depreciation (being the allocation of additions to the carrying amount of the Plant) which was not recognised in the financial statements of the subsidiary because the fair value of the Plant was not reflected in the subsidiary's financial statements upon acquisition. The remaining economic life of the plant is 10 years, which implies that given a straight line depreciation, the asset would have been depreciated at an approximate amount of ₦15 million each year (i.e. ₦150 million carrying value divided by 10 years remaining), instead of being depreciated at an amount approximate to ₦17 million (being ₦170 million fair value divided by 10 years remaining). Hence, the extra (or additional) depreciation to be recognised as a charge to the group's profit or loss is ₦4 million (being the extra depreciation of ₦2 million per year for the two years – 2014 and 2015). The extra depreciation will be apportioned to the parent (Pally) and the non-controlling interest in the proportion profit or loss in the subsidiary is being shared. In this case, we shared the sum of ₦3.2 million to the parent (pally) via consolidated retained earnings (being 80% of ₦4 million), and the sum of ₦0.8 million attributed to non-controlling interest (being 20% of ₦4 million).

Accounting entries:
Debit: Consolidated retained earnings – ₦3.2 million
Debit: Non-controlling interest – ₦0.8 million } *₦4.0 million*
Credit: Plant – ₦4.0 million

- ✓ **Step 6:** *Combine the assets and liabilities of the parent (**Pally**) and subsidiary (**Sussy**) on an item-by-item basis excluding the initial investment of **Pally** in **Sussy** as earlier shown in the separate financial statements of **Pally**, and also the exclusion of the equity share capital of **Sussy**, as it has already been considered alongside with the pre-acquisition retained earnings in ascertaining the amount of goodwill or gain from bargain purchase inherent/embedded in the acquisition.* The consolidated statement of financial position of the group will now be shown as thus:

Pally Group
Consolidated Statement of Financial Position as at 31 December 2015

	₦' million
Assets:	
Non-current assets	
Plant (300 + 130 + 20 - 4)	446
Goodwill	28
Current assets (120 + 70)	190
Total Assets	**664**
Share Capital & Reserves:	
Equity share capital (@ ₦1 per share)	400
Reserves	112
Equity attributable to Pally's shareholders	**512**
Non-controlling interest	52
Total Equity	**564**
Current liabilities (80 + 20)	100
Total Equity and Liabilities	**664**

The consolidation schedule can equally be adopted for solving this group problem as scheduled below:

Consolidation Schedule

Subsidiary - Sussy		Cost of control (Pally in Sussy) as at 31 Dec. 2013 – 80%		Non-controlling Interests – 20%		Consolidated Reserves	
Equity Share Capital	120	(80% x 120)	96	(20% x 120)	24		
Reserves (Pre-acquisition)	40	(80% x 40)	32	(20% x 40)	8		
Reserves (Post-acquisition)	20			(20% x 20)	4	(80% x 20)	16
Fair value adjustments	20	(80% x 20)	16	(20% x 20)	4		
Net asset on acquisition			144				
Cost of combination (cost of investment)			(160)				
Goodwill (positive)			(16)				
Goodwill attributable to NCI (see note)			*(12)*		*12*		
Full Goodwill (positive)			**(28)**				
Extra (additional) depreciation					*(0.8)*		*(3.2)*
Non-controlling interests					**51.2**		
Pally Reserves							100
Consolidated Reserves							**112.8**

Technical Note:
Goodwill attributable to non-controlling interest may be separately determined as thus;   ₦' million
    Amount of investment of non-controlling interest in **Sussy**   48
    Less: Non-controlling interest share of the fair value of subsidiary's net assets:
- Share capital (20% of ₦120 million)   24
- Pre-acquisition reserves (20% of ₦40 million)   8
- Fair value adjustments (20% of ₦20 million)   4

                                                   (36)
Goodwill attributable to **non-controlling interests**   12

Accounting Entries:
Debit: Group Goodwill
Credit: Non-controlling interests' investment   } ₦12 million

SUMMARY OF CHAPTER 7

1. Fair value is the price that would be received to sell an asset or paid to transfer a liability in an orderly transaction between market participants at the measurement date.

2. Upon acquisition of a business, IFRS 3 requires both the consideration and the identifiable assets, liabilities, including contingent liabilities to be recognised at the acquisition-date fair value.

3. Fair value is obtained based on the principal market on which the assets and liabilities trade.

4. Fair value hierarchy entails Level 1; Level 2 and Level 3 respectively, with Level 1 most preferable.

5. The resulting adjustment arising from the fair value of the identifiable net assets of the acquired business should constitute part of the net assets acquired. Invariably, the adjustment is effected on pre-acquisition reserves.

6. Subsequent events such as depreciation, amortisation or otherwise that may subsequently arise from the acquisition-date fair value of subsidiary's net assets should be considered post-combination adjustments which may affect the post-acquisition profits of the subsidiary for consolidation purposes.

7. IFRS 3 states that the fair value of property, plant and equipment should be determined by market value or, if information on a market price is not available (as is the case here), then by reference to depreciated replacement cost, reflecting normal business practice.

8. Fair values are very important in calculating goodwill.

END OF CHAPTER 7 EXERCISES

1. _____ is the price that would be received to sell an asset or paid to transfer a liability in an orderly transaction between market participants at the measurement date.

2. What is the requirement of IFRS 3 as regards the fair value of acquired net assets at acquisition date?

3. How many levels existed within the IFRS 13 Hierarchy of Fair Value? Briefly Describe

4. Will the recognition of identifiable assets, liabilities, including contingent liabilities have any effect on the resulting amount of goodwill or gain on bargain purchase transaction as at acquisition-date?

5. Should fair value adjustments arising from the acquisition-date accounting of business combination be considered pre-acquisition adjustments or post-combination adjustments? Justify

6. Can the books of the subsidiary directly adjust for the fair value adjustments arising from acquisition-date fair value measurement? Elucidate.

7. Determine the amount of goodwill or gain on bargain purchase to be recognised based on the information provided below:
   - Cost of investment by the controlling interest   ₦100 million
   - Subsidiary's share capital   at acquisition   ₦20 million
   - Subsidiary's share premium at acquisition   ₦60 million
   - Retained earnings at acquisition   ₦40 million
   - Non-controlling interest is to be accounted for at the share of subsidiary's net assets at acquisition
   - The controlling interest holds 16 million shares of the subsidiary shares in issue
   - The authorised share capital of the subsidiary at acquisition is ₦120 million
   - The issued share capital of the subsidiary at acquisition is ₦80 million
   - The nominal value of ₦1.00 per share
   - The market price is ₦6.40 per share
   - Acquisition-date fair value of the identifiable net assets acquired was ₦130 million

Chapter 8

Other Principles in Business Combination Accounting and Group Accounts

INTRODUCTION

This chapter will expose the readers to the understanding of the requirement of IFRS 3 and IFRS 10 on accounting for contingent liabilities at acquisition-date, the requirement for uniform accounting policies and reporting date.

A practical consideration in preparing consolidated financial statements is to have information on all constituents' entities current as of the parent's year-end. Then, if a subsidiary has different financial year, it may be required that updated financial information is necessary as of the parent's year-end, in order to facilitate the preparation of the consolidated financial statements.

There is a presumption (except where reputable, which is very unlikely) that all members of the group should adopt the same accounting policies and standards in accounting for similar events and transactions. In practice, this may not be, but upon consolidation, it will be required to align the accounting policies of the subsidiaries' to that of the parent, which invariably may require some adjustments to be made before consolidation can be effected.

Even though the requirement of IAS 37 is extremely clear that a contingent liability should not be recognised but rather disclosed on the basis of its materiality, but with regards to business combinations and group accounts, a contingent liability that satisfies the basic requirement of a liability (as being probable as of the acquisition date) and can be measured reliably at the acquisition-date fair value may be recognised alongside the business combination accounting.

UNIFORM REPORTING DATE AND ACCOUNTING POLICIES

IFRS 10 requires a parent entity to prepare and present consolidated financial statements in any year the parent have control over another entity as at the reporting date. Since consolidated financial statements preparation is from a *"single –economic unit/entity"* perspective, it is paramount and important that each member of the group adopts the *same accounting policy* and *reporting dates*. It is worthy to know that *IFRS 3(R)* allows a parent to further consolidate a subsidiary and adjust the subsidiary's accounts as appropriate where the reporting dates are not the same (and that it is practicable and reliable to carry out significant adjustments for transactions outside the common period), but the difference between the reporting dates should not be more than *3 months*.

In most cases, all group companies will prepare accounts to the same reporting date. One or more subsidiaries may, however, prepare accounts to a different reporting date from the parent and the bulk of other subsidiaries in the group. In such cases, the subsidiary may prepare additional statements to the reporting date of the rest of the group, for consolidation purposes. If this is not possible, the subsidiary's accounts may still be used for the consolidation, *provided that* the gap between the reporting dates is **three months or less**. Where a subsidiary's accounts are drawn up to a different accounting date, **adjustments should be made** for the effects of significant transactions or other events that occur between that date and the parent's reporting date.

Consolidated financial statements should be prepared using **uniform accounting policies** for like transactions and other events in similar circumstances. **Adjustments** must be made where members of a group use different accounting policies so that their financial statements are suitable for consolidation.

Hence, consolidated financial statements should be prepared using *uniform accounting policies* (no alternatives is allowed to the contrary). IFRS 10 states that if accounting policies differ in the individual entities, adjustments need to be made on consolidation to achieve uniformity.

The following illustration will assist in establishing the principle as required by the standard as it relates to the adjustments on uniform accounting policies within the group.

ILLUSTRATION 1:

You are given the statement of financial position of **Pally** and its subsidiary **Sussy** at December 31, 2015.:

Statement of Financial Position as at 31st December 2015

	Pally	Sussy
	₦' million	₦' million
Property, plant & equipment	40	35
Investment in **Sussy Plc**	50	
Intangible asset	10	15
Current assets	20	40
	120	**90**
Share Capital & Reserves:		
Equity share capital (@ ₦1 per share)	60	50
Reserves (Retained Earnings)	50	20
	110	70
Current liabilities	10	20
	120	**90**

Additional information:

a) Pally acquired 40 million of the ₦1 shares of Sussy on 1 January, 2014 for ₦50 million when the reserves of the subsidiary (Sussy) showed a balance of ₦10 million. There has been no impairment of goodwill on consolidation since acquisition. The market price of the company's shares prior to acquisition is ₦1.10 *per share*.

b) Sussy has all its accounting policies to be the same with that of Pally except for that of intangible assets included in its books. A component of intangible assets of Sussy is of a type whose recognition would not be permitted under *IAS 38 (Intangible Assets)*. *IAS 38* is to be allowed in preparing the consolidated financial statements. When Pally made its investment in Sussy on 1 January, 2014 the intangible assets of Sussy included ₦8 million that would not qualify for recognition under *IAS 38*. The Intangible assets of Sussy are of *indefinite life*.

(**Assume:** Sussy operates under different accounting standards which are similar in all respect to IFRS except for some aspect relating to recognition of Intangible Assets).

The suggested solution to the above illustration can be carried out based on the underlying steps earlier adopted in the earlier approaches to consolidation:

First, we assumed that the parent at the point of acquisition (when control was obtained), a measured the amount of non-controlling interest at the proportionate share of the subsidiary's identifiable net assets (assets and liabilities). In this case, the consolidation process will be as follows:

- ✓ **Step 1**: *Determine the percentage holdings of investment of **Pally** in **Sussy** as at the acquisition date (1 January 2014), which represents the date of inclusion (first date of consolidation).* In this case, the percentage holding is ascertained to be 80% as thus:

  Expressing the 40 million shares acquired as a percentage of the outstanding number of shares in the subsidiary, which is 50 million shares (being the share capital of ₦50 million divided by the face/nominal value per share of ₦1).

- ✓ **Step 2:** *Ascertain the form of group structure in this parent-subsidiary relationship.* Since the subsidiary (**Sussy**) is *partly-owned* by the parent (**Pally**), the group structure is a simple structure as shown below:

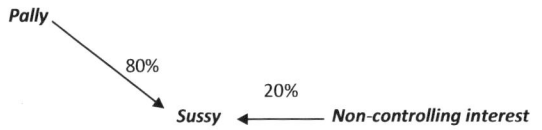

  Pally

  80%   20%

  Sussy ← **Non-controlling interest**

- ✓ **Step 3:** *Determine the existence of goodwill or gain from a bargain purchase as the date of acquisition based on the fair value of subsidiary's identifiable assets and liabilities.* In this case, there exists goodwill as shown below.

  To ascertain and determine the amount of goodwill or gain from a bargain purchase, the value of an investment of the parent (**Pally**) in the subsidiary (**Sussy**) will be compared with the identifiable assets and liabilities of the subsidiary as at acquisition.

PARTIAL METHODOLOGY

	₦' million	₦' million
Cost of combination (i.e. the cost of investment of **Pally** in **Sussy**)		50
Less: **Pally's** share of Identifiable net assets of **Sussy** acquired:		
• Share capital (80% of ₦50 million)	40.0	
• Pre-acquisition reserves (80% of ₦2 million*)	1.6	(41.6)
*Goodwill attributable to **Pally's** (a)*		*8.4*

Amount of investments of non-controlling interest in **Sussy**   10.4
Less: Non-controlling interest share of the fair value of subsidiary's net assets:
- Share capital (20% of ₦50 million)   10.0
- Pre-acquisition reserves (20% of ₦2 million)   0.4   (10.4)

*Goodwill attributable to **non-controlling interests** (b)*   ---
Goodwill (a + b)   **8.4**

*The adjustment required in respect of Sussy to reflect the accounting policy difference has the following effects:

- The net assets of the subsidiary as at the reporting date (1 January 2014) has been overstated by ₦8 million (being the amount of unqualified intangible assets recognised in its financial statements), and likewise its reserves as at that date. Hence, we have to restate the subsidiary's financial position (through its assets and reserves).

- The overstatement of ₦8 million in reserves as earlier identified above is attributable to pre-acquisition reserves because the value of ₦8 million was the carrying value of the intangible assets at acquisition that does not qualify as an Intangible Asset under IAS 38. The balance of ₦7 million qualify as an intangible asset as at acquisition.

Accounting entries:
     Debit: *Pre-acquisition reserves*
     Credit: *Intangible assets (Group)*
     With ₦8 million

The implication of the adjustments above will be as follows:

- The pre-acquisition reserves will be reduced to ₦2 million (being the reversal of ₦8 million from the initial ₦10 million recognised on acquisition).

- The post-acquisition reserves remain ₦10 million (being an increase from ₦10 million on 1 January 2014 to ₦20 million as at 31 December 2015) and unaffected by the de-recognition adjustment required at acquisition.

- A portion of the intangible assets of ₦8 million will no longer be consolidated (*as it has been de-recognised at acquisition based on the accounting entries stated above*) due to the accounting policy of the group which does not recognise such intangible asset as it does not conform to *IAS 38*.

FULL METHODOLOGY

Cost of combination	₦' million	₦' million
Investment of **Pally** in **Sussy**		50.0
Amount of Investment in subsidiary to non-controlling interest*		10.4
Combined amount of interests in subsidiary to all investors		**60.4**
Less: Fair value of identifiable assets and liabilities acquired @ 1 January 2014		
Share capital	50.0	
Pre-acquisition reserves	10.0	
Less: De-recognised intangible asset	(8.0) 2.0	(52.0)
Goodwill - positive		**8.4**

Other Principles in Business Combination Accounting and Group Accounts

Technical Note:
The goodwill attributable to non-controlling must be zero since the investment to non-controlling interests is valued at the proportionate share of subsidiary's identifiable net assets as shown by the arrow.

✓ **Step 4:** Determine the amount of non-controlling interest as will be shown in the consolidated statement of financial position of the group. In this case, non-controlling interest will only be measured at proportionate share of subsidiary's identifiable assets and liabilities, which could be depicted as thus:

Non-controlling interest's share of Identifiable net assets of **Sussy** upon acquisition:

	₦' million
• Share capital (20% of ₦50 million)	10.0
• Pre-acquisition reserves (20% of ₦2.0 million)	0.4
NCI's investment on 1 January 2014 (based on proportionate share of net assets)	**10.4**
• Post-acquisition reserves (20% of ₦10 million)	2.0
NCI's investment on 31 December 2015	**12.4**

✓ **Step 5:** Determine the amount to be included in the consolidated statement of financial position as consolidated reserves (otherwise known as consolidated retained earnings). The consolidated retained earnings to be included in the consolidated statement of financial position of **Pally-Group** are that of the parent and of the post-acquisition profits of the subsidiary. Invariably, it implies that the post-acquisition retained earnings (which is the sum of ₦10 million being the increase from ₦10 million profits upon acquisition to ₦20 million as at the reporting date 31 December 2015. The consolidated retained earnings will be determined as follows:

	₦' million
Parent's (**Pally**) retained earnings	50
Share of subsidiary's (**Sussy**) post-acquisition reserves (80% of ₦10 million)	8
	52

✓ **Step 6:** Combine the assets and liabilities of the parent (**Pally**) and subsidiary (**Sussy**) on an item-by-item basis excluding the initial investment of **Pally** in **Sussy** as earlier shown in the separate financial statements of **Pally**, and also the exclusion of the equity share capital of **Sussy**, as it has already been considered alongside with the pre-acquisition retained earnings in ascertaining the amount of goodwill or gain from bargain purchase inherent/embedded in the acquisition. The consolidated statement of financial position of the group will now be shown as thus:

Pally Group
Consolidated Statement of Financial Position as at 31 December 2015

Assets:	₦' million	₦' million
Non-current assets		
Property, plant & equipment (40 + 35)		75.0
Intangible assets – Goodwill	8.4	
– Others (10 + 7)	17.0	25.4
Current assets (20 + 40)		60.0
Total Assets		**160.4**
Share Capital & Reserves:		
Equity share capital		60.0
Reserves		58.0

Equity attributable to Pally's shareholders		118.0
Non-controlling interest		12.4
Total Equity		130.4
Current liabilities (10 + 20)		30.0
Total Equity and Liabilities		**160.4**

The consolidation schedule can equally be adopted for solving this group problem as scheduled below:

Consolidation Schedule

Subsidiary - Sussy		Cost of control (Pally in Sussy) as at 1 Jan. 2014 – 80%		Non-controlling Interests – 20%		Consolidated Reserves
Equity Share Capital	50.0	(80% x 50.0)	40.0	(20% x 50.0) 10.5		
Reserves (Pre-acquisition)	2.0	(80% x 2.0)	1.6	(20% x 2.0) 0.4		
Reserves (Post-acquisition)	10.0		-	(20% x 10.0) 2.0		(80% x 10.0) 8
Net asset on acquisition			41.6			
Cost of combination (cost of investment)			(50.0)			
Goodwill (positive)			**(8.4)**			
Non-controlling interests				12.4		
Pally Reserves						50
Consolidated Reserves						**58**

Second, we assumed that the parent at the point of acquisition (when control was obtained), measured investments of the non-controlling interest at fair value (which is predominantly based on market values of shares of the subsidiary). In this case, the consolidation process will be as follows:

✓ **Step 1**: Determine the percentage holdings of investment of **Pally** in **Sussy** as at the acquisition date (1 January 2014), which represents the date of inclusion (first date of consolidation). In this case, the percentage holding is ascertained to be 80% as thus:

Expressing the 40 million shares acquired as a percentage of the outstanding number of shares in the subsidiary, which is 50 million shares (being the share capital of ₦50 million divided by the face/nominal value per share of ₦1).

✓ **Step 2**: Ascertain the form of group structure in this parent-subsidiary relationship. Since the subsidiary (**Sussy**) is *partly-owned* by the parent (**Pally**), the group structure is a simple structure as shown below:

```
        Pally
          \
       80% \
            ↘         20%
             Sussy ←——— Non-controlling interest
```

✓ **Step 3**: Determine the existence of goodwill or gain from a bargain purchase as the date of acquisition based on the fair value of subsidiary's identifiable assets and liabilities. In this case, there exists goodwill as shown below.

To ascertain and determine the amount of goodwill or gain from a bargain purchase, the amount of investment of the parent (**Pally**) in the subsidiary (**Sussy**) will be compared with the parent's share of identifiable assets and liabilities of the subsidiary that were acquired, in additional to possible goodwill attributable to non-controlling interest.

	₦' million	₦' million
PARTIAL METHODOLOGY		
Cost of combination (i.e. the cost of investment of **Pally** in **Sussy**)		50
Less: **Pally's** share of Identifiable net assets of **Sussy** acquired:		
• Share capital (80% of ₦50 million)	40.0	
• Pre-acquisition reserves (80% of ₦2 million*)	1.6	(41.6)
*Goodwill attributable to **Pally's** (a)*		8.4
Amount of investments of non-controlling interest in **Sussy** (₦1.10 * 10 million shares)		11.0
Less: Non-controlling interest share of the fair value of subsidiary's net assets:		
• Share capital (20% of ₦50 million)	10.0 ⎤	
• Pre-acquisition reserves (20% of ₦2 million)	0.4 ⎦	(10.4)
*Goodwill attributable to **non-controlling interests** (b)*		0.6
Goodwill (a + b)		**9.0**

*The adjustment required in respect of Sussy to reflect the accounting policy difference has the following effects:

- The net assets of the subsidiary as at the reporting date (1 January 2014) has been overstated by ₦8 million (being the amount of unqualified intangible assets recognised in its financial statements), and likewise its reserves as at that date. Hence, we have to restate the subsidiary's financial position (through its assets and reserves).

- The overstatement of ₦8 million in reserves as earlier identified above is attributable to pre-acquisition reserves because the value of ₦8 million was the carrying value of the intangible assets at acquisition that does not qualify as an Intangible Asset under IAS 38. The balance of ₦7 million qualify as an intangible asset as at acquisition.

Accounting entries:
    Debit: Pre-acquisition reserves
    Credit: Intangible assets (Group)
    With ₦8 million

The implication of the adjustments above will be as follows:

- The pre-acquisition reserves will be reduced to ₦2 million (being the reversal of ₦8 million from the initial ₦10 million recognised on acquisition).

- The post-acquisition reserves remain ₦10 million (being an increase from ₦10 million on 1 January 2014 to ₦20 million as at 31 December 2015) and unaffected by the de-recognition adjustment required at acquisition.

- A portion of the intangible assets of ₦8 million will no longer be consolidated (*as it has been de-recognised at acquisition based on the accounting entries stated above*) due to the accounting policy of the group which does not recognise such intangible asset as it does not conform to *IAS 38*.

FULL METHODOLOGY

Cost of combination	₦' million	₦' million
Investment of **Pally** in **Sussy**		50.0
Amount of Investment in subsidiary to non-controlling interest*		11.0
Combined amount of interests in subsidiary to all investors		**61.0**
Less: Fair value of identifiable assets and liabilities acquired @ 1 January 2014		
Share capital	50.0	
Pre-acquisition reserves	10.0	
Less: De-recognised intangible asset	(8.0) 2.0	(52.0)
Goodwill - positive		**9.0**

Technical Note:

*The goodwill attributable to non-controlling is ₦0.6 million since the investment to non-controlling interests is valued at fair value of ₦11 million (being the market price of shares prevailing prior to acquisition at ₦1.10 per share multiplied by the number of shares which is 20% Of the shares existing in **Sussy** - 50 million shares) as it different from the proportionate share of the identifiable net assets of the subsidiary upon acquisition.*

✓ **Step 4:** Determine the amount of non-controlling interest as will be shown in the consolidated statement of financial position of the group. In this case, non-controlling interest will only be valued at fair value, which could be depicted as thus:

The fair value of non-controlling interests in **Sussy** is measured as thus:

	₦' million
NCI's investment on 1 January 2014 (*based on fair value*)	**11.0**
• Post-acquisition reserves (20% of ₦20 million)	2.0
NCI's investment on 31 December 2015	**51.2**

This can be further decomposed as thus	₦' million
• Share capital (20% of ₦50 million)	10.0
• Pre-acquisition reserves (20% of ₦2.0 million)	0.4
NCI's investment on 1 January 2014 (based on proportionate share of net assets)	**10.4**
Goodwill attributable to non-controlling interests on acquisition (Balancing figure)	*0.6*
NCI's investment on 1 January 2014 (based on fair value)	**11.0**
• Post-acquisition reserves (20% of ₦10 million)	2.0
NCI's investment on 31 December 2015	**13.0**

✓ **Step 5:** Determine the amount to be included in the consolidated statement of financial position as consolidated reserves (otherwise known as consolidated retained earnings). The consolidated retained earnings to be included in the consolidated statement of financial position of **Pally-Group** are that of the parent and of the post-acquisition profits of the subsidiary. Invariably, it implies that the post-acquisition retained earnings (which is the sum of ₦10 million being the increase from ₦10 million profits upon acquisition to ₦20 million as at the reporting date 31 December 2015. The consolidated retained earnings will be determined as follows:

	₦' million
Parent's (**Pally**) retained earnings	50
Share of subsidiary's (**Sussy**) post-acquisition reserves (80% of ₦10 million)	8
	52

Other Principles in Business Combination Accounting and Group Accounts

✓ **Step 6:** Combine the assets and liabilities of the parent (**Pally**) and subsidiary (**Sussy**) on an item-by-item basis excluding the initial investment of **Pally** in **Sussy** as earlier shown in the separate financial statements of **Pally**, and also the exclusion of the equity share capital of **Sussy**, as it has already been considered alongside with the pre-acquisition retained earnings in ascertaining the amount of goodwill or gain from bargain purchase inherent/embedded in the acquisition. The consolidated statement of financial position of the group will now be shown as thus:

Pally Group
Consolidated Statement of Financial Position as at 31 December 2015

	₦ million	₦ million
Assets:		
Non-current assets		
Property, plant & equipment (40 + 35)		75.0
Intangible assets – Goodwill	9.0	
- Others (10 + 7)	17.0	26.0
Current assets (20 + 40)		60.0
Total Assets		**161.0**
Share Capital & Reserves:		
Equity share capital		60.0
Reserves		58.0
Equity attributable to Pally's shareholders		118.0
Non-controlling interest		13.0
Total Equity		131.6
Current liabilities (10 + 20)		30.0
Total Equity and Liabilities		**161.0**

The consolidation schedule can equally be adopted for solving this group problem as scheduled below:

Consolidation Schedule

Subsidiary - Sussy		Cost of control (Pally in Sussy) as at 1 January 2014 – 80%		Non-controlling Interests – 20%		Consolidated Reserves	
Equity Share Capital	50.0	(80% x 50)	40.0	(20% x 50.0)	10.0		
Reserves (Pre-acquisition)	2.5	(80% x 2.5)	1.6	(20% x 2.0)	0.4		
Reserves (Post-acquisition)	2.5		–	(20% x 10.0)	2.0	(80% x 10.0)	8.0
Net asset on acquisition			41.6				
Cost of combination (cost of investment)			(50)				
Goodwill (positive)			(8.4)				
Goodwill attributable to NCI			(0.6)		0.6		
Full Goodwill (positive)			(9.0)				
Non-controlling interests					13.0		
Pally Reserves							50.0
Consolidated Reserves							**58.0**

186

Contemporaneous Accounting for Business Combinations and Group Accounts

Technical Note:
Goodwill attributable to non-controlling interest may be separately determined as thus;

		₦' million
Amount of investment of non-controlling interest in **Sussy**		11.0
Less: Non-controlling interest share of the fair value of subsidiary's net assets:		
• Share capital (20% of ₦50 million)	10.0	
• Pre-acquisition reserves (20% of ₦2.0 million)	0.4	(10.4)
Goodwill attributable to **non-controlling interests**		**0.6**

Accounting Entries:
Debit: Group Goodwill
Credit: Non-controlling interests' investment } ₦0.6 million

CONTINGENT LIABILITIES

Contingent liabilities usually give rise to material loss upon crystallisation which is expected to be incorporated in the financial statement of companies. Contingent liabilities of the acquiree (for consolidation purpose) are recognised if their fair value can be measured reliably. A contingent liability in this instance must be recognised even if the outflow of future economic benefit is not probable, provided there is a present obligation. This is as opposed to the criteria of *IAS 37 (Provisions, Contingent Liabilities and Contingent Assets)*; contingent liabilities are not normally recognised but only disclosed.

After their initial recognition, the acquirer should measure contingent liabilities that are recognised separately at the higher of:
   a) The amount that would be recognised in accordance with IAS 37; and
   b) The amount initially recognised.

Invariably it means that the recognition of contingent liabilities upon acquisition will reduce the pre-acquisition reserves of the acquiree (subsidiary).

Recognition of Contingent Liabilities on Acquisition
Debit: Reserves (Retained earnings) of Subsidiary
Credit: Contingent Liability (Accounts payables) } *with the contingent liability measured reliably*

There exist instances where the subsidiary has adjustments to the subsidiary's contingent liability subsequent to acquisition, the recognition of such we only affect the post-acquisition reserves in the subsidiary upon consolidation.

Excerpt from IFRS 3 (Revised) on Contingent Liabilities

Contingent liabilities:

IAS 37 Provisions, Contingent Liabilities and Contingent Assets defines a contingent liability as:

   (a) a possible obligation that arises from past events and whose existence will be confirmed only by the occurrence or non-occurrence of one or more uncertain future events not wholly within the control of the entity; or

   (b) a present obligation that arises from past events but is not recognised because:

Other Principles in Business Combination Accounting and Group Accounts

i. It is not probable that an outflow of resources embodying economic benefits will be required to settle the obligation; or
ii. The amount of the obligation cannot be measured with sufficient reliability.

The requirements in IAS 37 do not apply in determining which contingent liabilities to recognise as of the acquisition date. Instead, the acquirer shall recognise as of the acquisition date a contingent liability assumed in a business combination if it is a present obligation that arises from past events and its fair value can be measured reliably. Therefore, contrary to IAS 37, the acquirer recognises a contingent liability assumed in a business combination at the acquisition date even if it is not probable that an outflow of resources embodying economic benefits will be required to settle the obligation.

The following illustration will assist in establishing the principle as required by the standard as it relates to the recognition of contingent liabilities on the acquisition.

ILLUSTRATION 2:
Given the statement of financial position of **Pally** and its subsidiary **Sussy** at 31 December 2015 are as follows:

Statement of Financial Position as at 31ˢᵗ December 2015

	Pally ₦' million	Sussy ₦' million
Property, plant & equipment	40	50
Investment in *Sussy Plc*	60	
Current assets	20	40
	120	90
Share Capital & Reserves:		
Equity share capital (₦1 each)	60	50
Reserves (Retained Earnings)	50	20
	110	70
Current liabilities	10	20
	120	90

Additional information:
i. Pally acquired 40 million equity shares of Sussy on December 31, 2015.
ii. The market price of the company's shares prior to acquisition is ₦1.50 per share.
iii. There was a liability that is contingent upon unfavourable legal dispute to the right to intellectual property which is estimated reliably to cause the subsidiary award of damages of ₦5 million.

The suggested solution to the above illustration can be carried out based on the underlying steps earlier adopted in the earlier approaches to consolidation:

First, we assumed that the parent at the point of acquisition (when control was obtained), valued investments of the non-controlling interest at the proportionate share of the subsidiary's identifiable net assets (assets and liabilities). In this case, the consolidation process will be as follows:

✓ **Step 1**: *Determine the percentage holdings of investment of **Pally** in **Sussy** as at the acquisition date (31 December 2015), which represents the date of inclusion (first date of consolidation).* In this case, the percentage holding is ascertained to be 80% as thus:

Expressing the 40 million shares acquired as a percentage of the outstanding number of shares in the subsidiary, which is 50 million shares (being the share capital of ₦50 million divided by the face/nominal value per share of ₦1).

✓ **Step 2**: *Ascertain the form of group structure in this parent-subsidiary relationship.* Since the subsidiary (**Sussy**) is *partly-owned* by the parent (**Pally**), the group structure is a simple structure as shown below:

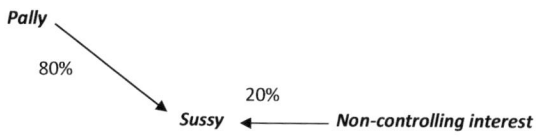

```
     Pally
      \
   80% \
        \
         ↘         20%
          Sussy ←——————— Non-controlling interest
```

✓ **Step 3**: *Determine the existence of goodwill or gain from a bargain purchase as the date of acquisition based on the fair value or provisional values of subsidiary's identifiable assets and liabilities.* In this case, there exists goodwill as shown below.

To ascertain and determine the amount of goodwill or gain from a bargain purchase, the value of an investment of the parent (**Pally**) in the subsidiary (**Sussy**) will be compared with the identifiable assets and liabilities of the subsidiary as at acquisition.

PARTIAL METHODOLOGY	₦' million	₦' million
Cost of combination (i.e. the cost of investment of **Pally** in **Sussy**)		60
Less: **Pally's** share of Identifiable net assets of **Sussy** acquired:		
• Share capital (80% of ₦50 million)	40	
• Pre-acquisition reserves (80% of ₦15 million*)	12	(52)
Goodwill attributable to **Pally's** (a)		8
Amount of investments of non-controlling interest in **Sussy**		13.0
Less: Non-controlling interest share of the fair value of subsidiary's net assets:		
• Share capital (20% of ₦50 million)	10	
• Pre-acquisition reserves (20% of ₦15 million*)	3	(13.0)
Goodwill attributable to **non-controlling interests** (b)		---
Goodwill (a + b)		**8**

*The adjustment required in respect of Sussy to reflect the contingent liability in the consolidated financial statements has the following effects:

- The net assets of the subsidiary as at the reporting date (31 December 2015) will be reduced by ₦5 million (being the estimated fair value of contingent liability to be recognised in the consolidated financial statements), and likewise its reserves as at acquisition-date. Hence, we have to restate the subsidiary's financial position (through its liabilities and reserves).

- The reduction of ₦5 million in reserves as earlier identified above, is attributable to pre-acquisition reserves because the estimated fair value of ₦5 million was the amount of contingent liabilities to be recognised upon acquisition (which will be adjusted against the pre-acquisition reserves at acquisition date) as thus:

Accounting entries:

Debit: Pre-acquisition reserves ⎫
Credit: Contingent liabilities (subsidiary) ⎬ ₦5 million

The implication of the adjustment above will be as follows:
- The pre-acquisition reserves will be reduced to ₦15 million (being the charge of ₦5 million from the initial ₦20 million recognised on acquisition).
- The contingent liability of ₦5 million will now be recognised in the consolidated statement of financial position in accordance with the *revised IFRS 3* which does recognise subsidiary's contingent liability at acquisition.

Alternative, FULL METHODOLOGY

Cost of Business Combination:		₦' million
Cost of combination (i.e. cost of acquisition) to the parent		60
Amount of Investment in subsidiary to non-controlling interest*		13
Combined amount of interests in subsidiary to all investors		**73**
Less: Fair value of identifiable assets and liabilities acquired @ 1 January 2016		
Share capital	50	
Pre-acquisition reserves	20	
Less: Recognised amount of Contingent Liability	(5)	(65)
Goodwill - positive		**8**

Technical Note:
*The goodwill attributable to non-controlling must be zero since the investment to non-controlling interests is valued at the proportionate share of subsidiary's identifiable net assets as shown by the arrow.

✓ **Step 4:** *Determine the amount of non-controlling interest as will be shown in the consolidated statement of financial position of the group.* In this case, non-controlling interest will only be measured at the proportionate share of subsidiary's identifiable assets and liabilities, which could be depicted as thus:

Non-controlling interest's share of Identifiable net assets of **Sussy** upon acquisition:

	₦' million
• Share capital (20% of ₦50 million)	10.0
• Pre-acquisition reserves (20% of ₦15 million)	3.0
NCI's investment on 31 December 2015 (based on proportionate share of net assets)	**13.0**

✓ **Step 5:** *Determine the amount to be included in the consolidated statement of financial position as consolidated reserves (otherwise known as consolidated retained earnings).* The consolidated retained earnings to be included in the consolidated statement of financial position of **Pally-Group** is that of the parent, as there exist no post-acquisition profits in the subsidiary as at acquisition. There will be post-acquisition profits in the subsidiary only when change is experienced in the reserves of the subsidiary subsequent to acquisition. The consolidated retained earnings will be determined as follows:

	₦' million
Parent's (**Pally**) retained earnings	50
Share of subsidiary's (**Sussy**) post-acquisition reserves (80% of Nil)	-
	50

✓ **Step 6:** Combine the assets and liabilities of the parent (**Pally**) and subsidiary (**Sussy**) on an item-by-item basis excluding the initial investment of **Pally** in **Sussy** as earlier shown in the separate financial statements of **Pally**, and also the exclusion of the equity share capital of **Sussy**, as it has already been considered alongside with the pre-acquisition retained earnings in ascertaining the amount of goodwill or gain from bargain purchase inherent/embedded in the acquisition. The consolidated statement of financial position of the group will now be shown as thus:

Pally Group
Consolidated Statement of Financial Position as at 31 December 2015

	₦' million
Assets:	
Non-current assets	
Property, plant & equipment (40 + 50)	90
Goodwill on acquisition	8
Current assets (20 + 40)	60
Total Assets	**158**
Share Capital & Reserves:	
Equity share capital	60
Reserves	50
Equity attributable to Pally's shareholders	**110**
Non-controlling interest	13
Total Equity	**123**
Current liabilities (10 + 20 + 5)	35
Total Equity and Liabilities	**158**

The consolidation schedule can equally be adopted for solving this group problem as scheduled below:

Consolidation Schedule

Subsidiary - Sussy		Cost of control (Pally in Sussy) as at 31 Dec. 2015 – 80%		Non-controlling Interests – 20%		Consolidated Reserves
Equity Share Capital	50	(80% x 50)	40	(20% x 50)	10.0	
Reserves (Pre-acquisition)	15	(80% x 15)	12	(20% x 15)	3.0	
Net asset on acquisition			52			
Cost of combination (cost of investment)			(60)			
Goodwill (positive)			**(8)**			
Non-controlling interests					**13**	
Pally Reserves						50
Consolidated Reserves						**50**

Second, we assumed that the parent at the point of acquisition (when control was obtained), measured investments of the non-controlling interest at fair value (which is predominantly based on market values of shares of the subsidiary). In this case, the consolidation process will be as follows:

Other Principles in Business Combination Accounting and Group Accounts

✓ **Step 1**: *Determine the percentage holdings of investment of **Pally** in **Sussy** as at the acquisition date (31 December 2015), which represents the date of inclusion (first date of consolidation).* In this case, the percentage holding is ascertained to be 80% as thus:

Expressing the 40 million shares acquired as a percentage of the outstanding number of shares in the subsidiary, which is 50 million shares (being the share capital of ₦50 million divided by the face/nominal value per share of ₦1).

✓ **Step 2**: *Ascertain the form of group structure in this parent-subsidiary relationship.* Since the subsidiary (**Sussy**) is *partly-owned* by the parent (**Pally**), the group structure is a simple structure as shown below:

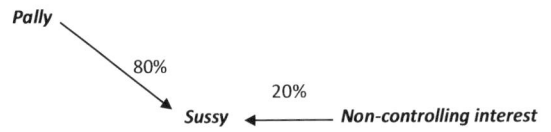

```
           Pally
             \
              \ 80%
               \       20%
              Sussy ←────── Non-controlling interest
```

✓ **Step 3**: *Determine the existence of goodwill or gain from a bargain purchase as the date of acquisition based on the fair value or provisional values of subsidiary's identifiable assets and liabilities.* In this case, there exists goodwill as shown below.

To ascertain and determine the amount of goodwill or gain from a bargain purchase, the value of an investment of the parent (**Pally**) in the subsidiary (**Sussy**) will be compared with the identifiable assets and liabilities of the subsidiary as at acquisition.

PARTIAL METHODOLOGY	₦' million	₦' million
Cost of combination (i.e. the cost of investment of **Pally** in **Sussy**)		60
Less: **Pally's** share of Identifiable net assets of **Sussy** acquired:		
• Share capital (80% of ₦50 million)	40	
• Pre-acquisition reserves (80% of ₦15 million)	12	(52)
*Goodwill attributable to **Pally's** (a)*		8
Amount of investments of non-controlling interest in **Sussy**		15
Less: Non-controlling interest share of the fair value of subsidiary's net assets:		
• Share capital (20% of ₦50 million)	10	
• Pre-acquisition reserves (20% of ₦15 million)	3	(13)
*Goodwill attributable to **non-controlling interests** (b)*		2
Full Goodwill (a + b)		**10**

*The adjustment required in respect of Sussy to reflect the contingent liability in the consolidated financial statements has the following effects:

➕ The net assets of the subsidiary as at the reporting date (31 December 2015) will be reduced by ₦5 million (being the estimated fair value of contingent liability to be recognised in the consolidated financial statements), and likewise its reserves as at acquisition-date. Hence, we have to restate the subsidiary's financial position (through its liabilities and reserves).

➕ The reduction of ₦5 million in reserves as earlier identified above is attributable to pre-acquisition reserves because the estimated fair value of ₦5 million was the value of contingent liabilities to be recognised upon acquisition (which will be adjusted against the pre-acquisition reserves at acquisition date) as thus:

Accounting entries:
Debit: Pre-acquisition reserves ⎫
Credit: Contingent liabilities (subsidiary) ⎬ ₦5 million

The implication of the adjustment above will be as follows:
- The pre-acquisition reserves will be reduced to ₦15 million (being the charge of ₦5 million from the initial ₦20 million recognised on acquisition).
- The contingent liability of ₦5 million will now be recognised in the consolidated statement of financial position in accordance with the *revised IFRS 3* which does recognise subsidiary's contingent liability at acquisition.

Alternative, FULL METHODOLOGY

Cost of Business Combination:		₦' million
Cost of combination (i.e. cost of acquisition) to the parent		60
Amount of Investment in subsidiary to non-controlling interest*		15
Combined amount of interests in subsidiary to all investors		**75**
Less: Fair value of identifiable assets and liabilities acquired @ 1 January 2016		
Share capital	50	
Pre-acquisition reserves	20	
Less: Recognised amount of Contingent Liability	(5)	(65)
Full Goodwill - positive		**10**

Technical Note:
*The goodwill attributable to non-controlling is ₦2 million since the investment to non-controlling interests is valued at fair value of ₦15 million (being the market price of shares prevailing prior to acquisition at ₦1.50 per share multiplied by the number of shares which is 20% Of the shares existing in **Sussy** -50 million shares) as it different from the proportionate share of the identifiable net assets of the subsidiary upon acquisition.

✓ **Step 4:** Determine the amount of non-controlling interest as will be shown in the consolidated statement of financial position of the group. In this case, non-controlling interest will only be valued at fair value, which could be depicted as thus:

	₦' million
NCI's investment on 31 December 2015 (*based on fair value*)	**15**
This can be further decomposed as thus:	₦' million
• Share capital (20% of ₦50 million)	10
• Pre-acquisition reserves (20% of ₦15 million)	3
NCI's investment on 31 December 2015 (based on proportionate share of net assets)	**13**
Goodwill attributable to non-controlling interests on acquisition (Balancing figure)	2
NCI's investment on 31 December 2015 (based on fair value)	**15**

✓ **Step 5:** Determine the amount to be included in the consolidated statement of financial position as consolidated reserves (otherwise known as consolidated retained earnings). The consolidated retained earnings to be included in the consolidated statement of financial position of **Pally-Group** is that of the parent, as there exist no post-acquisition profits in the subsidiary as at acquisition. There will be post-acquisition profits in the subsidiary only when change is experienced in the reserves of the subsidiary subsequent to acquisition. The consolidated retained earnings will be determined as follows:

Other Principles in Business Combination Accounting and Group Accounts

	₦' million
Parent's (*Pally*) retained earnings	50
Share of subsidiary's (*Sussy*) post-acquisition reserves (80% of Nil)	—
	50

✓ **Step 6:** Combine the assets and liabilities of the parent (*Pally*) and subsidiary (*Sussy*) on an item-by-item basis excluding the initial investment of *Pally* in *Sussy* as earlier shown in the separate financial statements of *Pally*, and also the exclusion of the equity share capital of *Sussy*, as it has already been considered alongside with the pre-acquisition retained earnings in ascertaining the amount of goodwill or gain from bargain purchase inherent/embedded in the acquisition. The consolidated statement of financial position of the group will now be shown as thus:

Pally Group
Consolidated Statement of Financial Position as at 31 December 2015

Assets:	₦' million
Non-current assets	
Property, plant & equipment (40 + 50)	90.0
Goodwill on acquisition	10.0
Current assets (20 + 40)	60.0
Total Assets	**160.0**
Share Capital & Reserves:	
Equity share capital	60.0
Reserves	50.0
Equity attributable to Pally's shareholders	**110.0**
Non-controlling interest	15.0
Total Equity	**125.0**
Current liabilities (10 + 20)	35.0
Total Equity and Liabilities	**160.0**

The consolidation schedule can equally be adopted for solving this group problem as scheduled below:

Consolidation Schedule

Subsidiary - Sussy		Cost of control (Pally in Sussy) as at 31 Dec. 2015 – 80%		Non-controlling Interests – 20%		Consolidated Reserves
Equity Share Capital	50.0	(80% x 50)	40	(20% x 50)	10	
Reserves (Pre-acquisition)	15.0	(80% x 15)	12	(20% x 15)	3	
Net asset on acquisition			52			
Cost of combination (cost of investment)			(60)			
Goodwill (positive)			(8)			
Goodwill attributable to NCI (see note)			(2)		2	
Full Goodwill (positive)			(10)			
Non-controlling interests					15	
Pally Reserves						50
Consolidated Reserves						**50**

194

Technical Note:
Goodwill attributable to non-controlling interest may be separately determined as thus;

	₦' million
Amount of investment of non-controlling interest in **Sussy**	15
Less: Non-controlling interest share of the fair value of subsidiary's net assets:	
• Share capital (20% of ₦50 million) 10.0	
• Pre-acquisition reserves (20% of ₦15 million) 3.0	(13)
*Goodwill attributable to **non-controlling interests***	**2**

Accounting Entries:
Debit: Group Goodwill
Credit: Non-controlling interests' investment   ₦2 million

SUMMARY OF CHAPTER 8

1. IFRS 10 requires the accounting policies and standards adopted by the members of the Group should be the same and uniform.

2. Where the subsidiaries' accounting policies are not necessarily the same with that of the parent, an adjustment is required to align the subsidiaries' financial statements to reflect the accounting policies of the group in order to prepare the consolidated financial statements.

3. IFRS 10 requires the accounting/reporting date of the subsidiaries to be the same with that of the parent.

4. Where the subsidiaries' accounting date is not the same with that of the parent, and the difference is within 3 months, the accounts of the subsidiary can be consolidated with that of the parent subject to material adjustment for transactions and events that may have occurred within that period, so as to prepare the consolidated financial statements.

5. Where the subsidiaries' accounting date is not the same with that of the parent, and the difference is more than 3 months, the financial statements of the subsidiaries' may be reconstructed in a manner that reflects the accounting period of the parent, so as to facilitate the preparation of the consolidated financial statements.

6. Contingent liabilities that are probable as at the acquisition of the subsidiary should be recognised in the business combination accounting at acquisition-date fair value.

7. After their initial recognition of contingent liabilities upon business combinations, the acquirer should measure contingent liabilities that are recognised separately at the higher of: the amount that would be recognised in accordance with IAS 37; and the amount initially recognised.

END OF CHAPTER 8 EXERCISES

1. The difference in accounting dates between the parent and the subsidiaries' should not exceed _____ months for the purpose of preparing the consolidated financial statements.

2. Must the accounting policies of the parent and the subsidiaries be uniform?

3. Should contingent liabilities be recognised in a business combination accounting?

4. How possible can consolidation of a parent and its subsidiary be affected given that they have different reporting dates?

5. What is the subsequent accounting treatment of a contingent liability recognised at acquisition-date fair value?

Chapter 9

Adjustments in Group Accounts

INTRODUCTION

This chapter will expose the readers to the understanding of the requirement of IFRS 10 for all intra-group trading (and the effects thereof) to be eliminated on consolidation. In addition, any intra-group balances must also be eliminated on consolidation so as to show the results of the group as a single economic entity.

The chapter will further consider the possible effect if intra-group trading (and the effects of intra-group trading) are not eliminated on consolidation, as this can seriously distort the figures by overstating income, expenses, assets and liabilities, thereby not reflecting the true financial position and performance of the group as a whole.

In the course of the chapter a consideration of the effect and treatment where intra-group balances do not cancel each other out and it is important that the differences are found in order that the balances can be eliminated on consolidation.

A consideration will finally be considered in a situation where the subsidiary has appropriately declared dividend prior to (or in extreme case as at the end of the year) the year-end and of which the amount of the dividend so appropriately declared remains outstanding as a liability at the reporting date. Also, the treatment of bonus shares issued by a subsidiary after the acquisition is treated within the group accounts.

ADJUSTMENTS TO GROUP ACCOUNTS

It is not an aberration subsequent to acquisition for the parent and the subsidiary to carry out series of transactions with one another, which is usually considered and referred to as a *related party transaction*. These transactions *may or may not* be *effectuated at arm's length*, and may distort the true financial position and performance of the individual entities and also consider the parent and the subsidiary from a single economic unit requires the need to eliminate such transactions (*intra-group transactions or intercompany transactions* must be *eliminated*). A situation might exist where the parent sells some items of inventory to the subsidiary at a *cost* or with *profit loading*, and this transaction might not reflect its economic status. It is required that upon consolidation of the accounts (of the parent and subsidiary), balances due to or from members of the group should also be eliminated (*i.e. cancelled out against each other*), alongside relevant adjustments for unrealized profit or losses.

The rationale for the elimination of intercompany transactions within the group is to avoid the possibility of grossing up the financial statements for transactions and/or balances that do not represent economic events with outside parties. The non-existence of the principle of elimination of intra-group transactions and balances in preparing consolidated financial statements might misrepresent its (the group) true financial position and performance, where the group entity would be seen to be larger than it is in reality, which is attributable to multiple transactions with itself (i.e. parent and the subsidiary).

The adjustments required on consolidation can be observed to be [29]*upstream transactions* or [30]*downstream transactions* which need to be eliminated from the consolidated financial statements in order to avoid duplications in the accounts. Some items may surface in the statement of financial position of the parent (or subsidiary) as an asset, while simultaneously as a liability in the financial statements of the subsidiary (or parent).

Invariably, for consolidation purposes, and to depict the "*economic power or substance*" of the consolidated financial statements; *intra-group or intercompany balances* are better-reported *net* (i.e. *netted-off/ cancelled-out*).

The intercompany transactions and requisite adjustments include and *not limited* to the following:
- Unrealized profits on the sale or transfer of goods within the group.
- Unrealized profits on the sale or transfer of assets (such as property, plant and equipment) within the group.
- Intra-group (intercompany) current accounts' balances.
- Intra-group (intercompany) accrued or prepaid expenses and income.
- Intra-group (intercompany) loans
- Intra-group (intercompany) accrued interest on loan
- Intra-group (intercompany) bills of exchange and discounted bills treatment.
- Increase in shares of the subsidiary as held by the parent with no additional cost incurred (i.e. bonus issues).
- Treatment of dividend received and/or receivable from the subsidiary

---

[29] Downstream transaction: For consolidation purposes, can be considered as a transaction emanating from the parent to the subsidiary (or associate/joint venture).

[30] Upstream transaction: For consolidation purposes, can be considered as a transaction emanating from the subsidiary (or associate/joint venture) to the parent.

Unrealized Profit on Inventory

The transaction between the parent and the subsidiary as regards sales of items of goods to each other are usually carried out with some element of profit embedded. It is initially assumed that the goods sold or transferred to the other entity within the group will eventually be sold before the year-end of the entities (or the parent entity, when the reporting dates differ), but this may not usually be the case as some of the goods may remain unsold by the other entity (the entity that made the purchases) to third parties as at the end of the reporting period for the group. The profit earned by the entity that sold the goods to the other within the group would have been recognised as *profit on the sales* in its individual financial statements. This profit will be considered on consolidation as *unrealized* within the group as those goods are not yet sold outside the group (sold to third parties). The inter-company sale of goods may take a form of *Upstream* or *Downstream Transactions*. This implies that if inventories of a group member contain goods purchased from another group member then the carrying value may include a profit element that is unrealized from the group perspective (i.e. from the group perspective, such profit cannot be recognised until the goods are sold outside the group).

Furthermore, sales within the group should only be regarded as a mere transfer rather than an outright sale of goods. But, there exist no problem upon consolidation if all the sales made at a profit within the group have been duly sold to other parties outside the group. There exist challenges on consolidation which require adjustments only if the sales within the group are made at *profit* (and not at *cost*) and a fraction or all remain unsold as at the reporting date.

Scenario Analysis to Justify Elimination of Unrealised Profit on Inventory Arising from Intra-Group Transactions

In this context, we will consider 4 scenarios (Scenarios A, B, C & D) as depicted below:

Scenario A:

- The parent and the subsidiary deal in the same line of trading business but separated by demographics (i.e. physical location). The parent operates in the Southern part of Nigeria, while the subsidiary operates within the Northern part of the country.
- As a result of economy of scale and on the basis of credit worthiness, it is much more profitable for the Group to centralise its purchasing/procurement, in which the parent company is saddled with.
- In the year, the parent purchased 10 million litres of Diesel (AGO) at a weighted average cost of ₦200 per litre. The parent sold 7 million litres to 3rd party customers in the year at average selling price of ₦220 per litre; and equally transferred (or sold) about 2 million litres at the cost price to its subsidiary during the year, while the unsold 1 million litres of Diesel constitute the amount of inventory in the books of the parent as at year-end.
- The subsidiary was unable to sell any of the litres of Diesel in the year due to the security situation in the Northern part of the country as a result of the Boko Haram Insurgency.

Hence, as at the year-end, we intend to ascertain the amount of the inventory to be reported in the Consolidated Financial Statements of the Group.

Individual Entities' Level:		₦'000
Inventory of Parent	(1 million litres of Diesel @ ₦200 per litre)	200,000
Inventory of Subsidiary	(2 million litres of Diesel @ ₦200 per litre)	400,000
Combined Inventory		**600,000** ✓

If we reconsider the situation and assume that the subsidiary only acts as an agent of the parent to sell the litres of Diesel in the northern part of the country for a commission. **Can the amount of the inventory from the parent perspectives remain the same?**

In this case, we reconsider the case and since the subsidiary has no ability to sell in the northern part of the country due to the security situation, then the goods in the first instance would not have been transferred to the subsidiary.

Then, the litres of Diesel unsold will increase in the custody of the parent to 3 million as only 7 million litres have since been sold as at the reporting date.

Parent Inventory Accounting:		₦'000
Inventory of Parent	(3 million litres of Diesel @ ₦200 per litre)	600,000 ✓

Scenario B:

- The parent and the subsidiary deal in the same line of trading business but separated by demographics (i.e. physical location). The parent operates in the Southern part of Nigeria, while the subsidiary operates within the Northern part of the country.
- As a result of economy of scale and on the basis of credit worthiness, it is much more profitable for the Group to centralise its purchasing/procurement, in which the parent company is saddled with.
- In the year, the parent purchased 10 million litres of Diesel (AGO) at a weighted average cost of ₦200 per litre. The parent sold 7 million litres to 3rd party customers in the year at average selling price of ₦220 per litre; and equally transferred (or sold) about 2 million litres (at an average price ₦210 per litre) to its subsidiary during the year, while the unsold 1 million litres of diesel constitute the amount of inventory in the books of the parent as at year-end.
- The subsidiary was able to sell all of the litres of Diesel in the year despite the security situation in the Northern part of the country as a result of the Boko Haram Insurgency.

Hence, as at the year-end, we intend to ascertain the amount of the inventory to be reported in the Consolidated Financial Statements of the Group.

Individual Entities' Level:		₦'000
Inventory of Parent	(1 million litres of Diesel @ ₦200 per litre)	200,000
Inventory of Subsidiary	(Zero litres of Diesel @ ₦200 per litre)	-
Combined Inventory		**200,000** ✓

If we reconsider the situation and assume that the subsidiary only acts as an agent of the parent to sell the litres of Diesel in the Northern part of the country for a commission. **Can the amount of the inventory from the parent perspectives remain the same?**

In this case, we reconsider the case and since the subsidiary is uncertain of selling the litres of Diesel based on the Boko Haram Insurgency in the Northern part of the country, then the goods in the first instance may be sold directly by the parent to the customers (haulage companies and industries in the Northern part of the country) as may be assigned by the subsidiary for commission.

Then, the litres of Diesel unsold will likely still remain the same as it is in the custody of the parent (*since on either case, the total of 9 million litres would have been sold as it comprises of 7 million litres sold by the parent to its customers and 2 million litres presumed sold on the basis of assigned sales by its agent, which simultaneously stands as its subsidiary*) as at the reporting date.

Parent Inventory Accounting:	₦'000
Inventory of Parent (1 million litres of Diesel @ ₦200 per litre)	200,000

Scenario C:

- The parent and the subsidiary deal in the same line of trading business but separated by demographics (i.e. physical location). The parent operates in the Southern Part of Nigeria, while the subsidiary operates within the Northern part of the country.
- As a result of economy of scale and on the basis of credit worthiness, it is much more profitable for the Group to centralise its purchasing/procurement, in which the parent company is saddled with.
- In the year, the parent purchased 10 million litres of Diesel (AGO) at a weighted average cost of ₦200 per litre. The parent sold 7 million litres to 3rd party customers in the year at average selling price of ₦220 per litre; and equally transferred (or sold) about 2 million litres at the cost price to its subsidiary during the year, while the unsold 1 million litres of diesel constitute the amount of inventory in the books of the parent as at year-end.
- The subsidiary was able to sell only 1 million litres of Diesel in the year as a result of the security situation in the Northern part of the country due to Boko Haram Insurgency.

Hence, as at the year-end, we intend to ascertain the amount of the inventory to be reported in the Consolidated Financial Statements of the Group.

Individual Entities' Level:	₦'000
Inventory of Parent (1 million litres of Diesel @ ₦200 per litre)	200,000
Inventory of Subsidiary (1 million litres of Diesel @ ₦200 per litre)	200,000
Combined Inventory	**400,000**

If we reconsider the situation and assume that the subsidiary only acts as an agent of the parent to sell the litres of Diesel in the northern part of the country for a commission. **Can the amount of the inventory from the parent perspectives remain the same?**

In this case, we reconsider the case and since the subsidiary is uncertain of selling the litres of Diesel based on the Boko Haram Insurgency in the Northern part of the country, then the goods in the first instance may be sold directly by the parent to the customers (haulage companies and industries in the Northern part of the country) as may be assigned by the subsidiary for commission.

Then, the litres of Diesel unsold will increase in the custody of the parent to 2 million (*since on either case, the total of 8 million litres would have been sold as it comprises of 7 million litres sold by the parent to its customers and 1 million litres presumed sold on the basis of assigned sales by its agent, which simultaneously stands as its subsidiary*) as at the reporting date.

Parent Inventory Accounting:	₦'000
Inventory of Parent (2 million litres of Diesel @ ₦200 per litre)	400,000 ✓

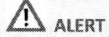

Scenario D:

- The parent and the subsidiary deal in the same line of trading business but separated by demographics (i.e. physical location). The parent operates in the Southern Part of Nigeria, while the subsidiary operates within the Northern part of the country.
- As a result of economy of scale and on the basis of credit worthiness, it is much more profitable for the Group to centralise its purchasing/procurement, in which the parent company is saddled with.
- In the year, the parent purchased 10 million litres of Diesel (AGO) at a weighted average cost of ₦200 per litre. The parent sold 7 million litres to 3rd party customers in the year at average selling price of ₦220 per litre; and equally transferred (or sold) about 2 million litres (at an average price ₦210 per litre) to its subsidiary during the year, while the unsold 1 million litres of diesel constitute the amount of inventory in the books of the parent as at year-end.
- The subsidiary was able to sell only 1 million litres of Diesel in the year as a result of the security situation in the Northern part of the country due to Boko Haram Insurgency.

Hence, as at the year-end, we intend to ascertain the amount of the inventory to be reported in the Consolidated Financial Statements of the Group.

Individual Entities' Level:		₦'000
Inventory of Parent	(1 million litres of Diesel @ ₦200 per litre)	200,000
Inventory of Subsidiary	(1 million litres of Diesel @ ₦210 per litre)	210,000
Combined Inventory		**410,000** ✗

If we reconsider the situation and assume that the subsidiary only acts as an agent of the parent to sell the litres of Diesel in the northern part of the country for a commission. **Can the amount of the inventory from the parent perspectives remain the same?**

In this case, we reconsider the case and since the subsidiary is uncertain of selling the litres of Diesel based on the Boko Haram Insurgency in the Northern part of the country, then the goods in the first instance may be sold directly by the parent to the customers (haulage companies and industries in the Northern part of the country) as may be assigned by the subsidiary for commission.

Then, the litres of Diesel unsold will increase in the custody of the parent to 2 million (*since on either case, the total of 8 million litres would have been sold as it comprises of 7 million litres sold by the parent to its customers and 1 million litres presumed sold on the basis of assigned sales by its agent, which simultaneously stands as its subsidiary*) as at the reporting date.

Parent Inventory Accounting:		₦'000
Inventory of Parent	(2 million litres of Diesel @ ₦200 per litre)	400,000 ✓

⚠ **ALERT**

There is a ***trigger*** in Scenario D, as the amount of inventory at the two portrayed instances do not result in the same amount of inventory to be recognised in the Group Accounts as signified by the two signs (✗ and ✓) in Scenario D above.

Hence, it then implies an adjustment to the amount of inventory is required at individual entities' level (based on which entity sold to the other; and as in this case, it is pictured that the parent sold to the subsidiary; then the adjustment impacts the overstated amount of inventory in the books of the subsidiary vis-à-vis an overstated profit position in the books of the parent) as depicted below:

Individual Entities' Level:	₦'000
Inventory of Parent (1 million litres of Diesel @ ₦200 per litre)	200,000
Inventory of Subsidiary (1 million litres of Diesel @ ₦210 per litre)	210,000
Less: Unrealised profit - URP (1 million litres of Unsold Diesel @ URP of ₦10 per litre)	(10,000)
Combined Inventory	400,000 ✓

The unrealized profit per litre is ₦10 (being the difference between the selling price of ₦210 per litre by the parent to its subsidiary and the average cost price to the parent of ₦200 per litre.

In conclusion, the above scenarios (A, B, C & D) would have laid a solid foundation to understanding the need to carry out some adjustments and eliminations in Group Accounts as a result of intra-group (or inter-company) transaction and balances.

We could further classify the transactions between the parent and the subsidiary as either of a *Downstream (i.e. down-the-stream)* or *Upstream (i.e. up-the-stream)* transactions. Downstream transactions are those transactions emanating from the parent to the subsidiary, e.g. goods worth ₦10 million transferred/sold to the subsidiary. Upstream transactions are those transactions emanating from the subsidiary to the parent, e.g. goods worth ₦10 million transferred/sold to the parent.

Downstream Transactions:

This involves the sale of goods by the investor (parent) to the investee (subsidiary). Since the profit is recognised by the parent upon sale to the subsidiary, the unrealized profit should be adjusted against the consolidated retained earnings, as thus:

Accounting entries:

    Debit: Consolidated retained earnings
    Credit: Group Inventories } With the total unrealized profit

ILLUSTRATION 1:

Pally Plc acquired 160 million of the shares of Sussy plc when the reserves were ₦20 million. During the year to 31 December 2015, Pally Plc sold goods costing ₦10 million @ a profit of 20% on the cost to Sussy Plc. As at the reporting date, only 40% of these goods were sold to external customers by Sussy. In the same period the statement of financial position of the dual companies as at 31st December 2015 is as follows:

Statement of Financial Position as at 31 December 2015

	Pally Plc	Sussy Plc
Assets:	₦' million	₦' million
Non-current assets		
Property, plant and equipment	110	120
Investment in Sussy Plc	100	
Current Assets:		
Inventories	40	45

Contemporaneous Accounting for Business Combinations and Group Accounts

Accounts receivables	15	12
Bank	5	7
Total Assets	**270**	**184**
Equities and Liabilities:		
Equity – Ordinary shares (₦0.50/share)	80	100
Retained earnings	140	60
Current liabilities	50	24
Total equity and liabilities	**270**	**184**

We are to approach the solution in the following steps:

✓ **Step 1**: *Determine the percentage holdings of investment of **Pally** in **Sussy** as at the acquisition date (some time ago), which represents the date of inclusion (first date of consolidation).* In this case, the percentage holding is determined and ascertained to be 80%.

The 80% interest of Pally is ascertained by expressing 160 million shares as a proportion of 200 million shares of Sussy in issue as at acquisition (this is obtained by dividing the share capital of ₦100 million by ₦0.50 nominal price per share).

✓ **Step 2**: *Ascertain the form of group structure in this parent-subsidiary relationship.* Since the subsidiary (**Sussy**) is *partly-owned* by the parent (**Pally**), the group structure is a simple structure as shown below:

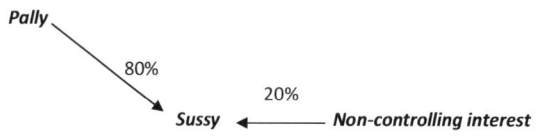

```
Pally
   \ 80%
    \         20%
     → Sussy ←——— Non-controlling interest
```

✓ **Step 3**: *Determine the existence of goodwill or gain from a bargain purchase as at the date of acquisition based on the fair value of subsidiary's identifiable assets and liabilities.* In this case, there exists goodwill as shown below.

To ascertain and determine the amount of goodwill or gain from a bargain purchase, the value of an investment of the parent (**Pally**) in the subsidiary (**Sussy**) will be compared with the parent's share of identifiable assets and liabilities of the subsidiary that were acquired.

	₦' million	₦' million
PARTIAL METHODOLOGY		
Cost of combination (i.e. the cost of investment of **Pally** in **Sussy**)		100
Less: **Pally**'s share of Identifiable net assets of **Sussy** acquired:		
• Share capital (80% of ₦100 million)	80	
• Pre-acquisition reserves (80% of ₦20 million)	16	(96)
*Goodwill attributable to **Pally's** (a)*		4
Amount of investments of non-controlling interest in **Sussy**		24
Less: Non-controlling interest share of the fair value of subsidiary's net assets:		
• Share capital (20% of ₦100 million)	20	
• Pre-acquisition reserves (20% of ₦20 million)	4	(24)
*Goodwill attributable to **non-controlling interests** (b)*		---
Goodwill (a + b)		**4**

Technical Note:
*The goodwill attributable to non-controlling must be zero since the investment to non-controlling interests is valued at the proportionate share of subsidiary's identifiable net assets as shown by the arrow.

Alternative, FULL METHODOLOGY		₦' million
Cost of Business Combination		
Cost of acquisition to Pally		100
Amount of Investment in subsidiary to non-controlling interest (Step 4)		_24_
Combined amount of interests in subsidiary to all investors		**124**
Less: Fair value of identified assets and liabilities acquired at acquisition-date		
Share capital	100	
Pre-acquisition reserves	_20_	(120)
Goodwill - positive		**_4_**

✓ **Step 4:** Determine the amount of non-controlling interest as will be shown in the consolidated statement of financial position of the group. In this case, non-controlling interest will only be measured at the proportionate share of subsidiary's identifiable assets and liabilities, which could be depicted as thus:

Non-controlling interest's share of Identifiable net assets of **Sussy**:	₦' million
• Share capital (20% of ₦100 million)	20
• Pre-acquisition reserves (20% of ₦20 million)	_4_
NCI's investment @ Acquisition-date (*based on proportionate share of net assets*)	**24**
• Post-acquisition reserves (20% of ₦40 million)	_8_
NCI's investment on 31 December 2015	**_32_**

✓ **Step 5:** Determine the amount to be included in the consolidated statement of financial position as consolidated reserves (otherwise known as consolidated retained earnings). The consolidated retained earnings to be included in the consolidated statement of financial position of **Pally-Group** are that of the parent and of the post-acquisition profits of the subsidiary. Invariably, it implies that the post-acquisition retained earnings (which is the sum of ₦40 million being the increase from ₦20 million profits upon acquisition to ₦60 million the reporting date 31 December 2015 - *some years after*) of the subsidiary (**Sussy**) will now be combined with the retained earnings (profits) of the parent (**Pally**) in ascertaining the group retained earnings. The consolidated retained earnings will be determined as follows:

	₦' million
Parent's (**Pally**) retained earnings	140.0
Share of subsidiary's (**Sussy**) post-acquisition profits (80% of ₦40 million)	32.0
Less: Unrealized profit of inventories*	_(1.2)_
	_170.8_

*The unrealized profits on sale of goods by the parent (Pally) is the sum of ₦1.2 million, being **60% (representing unsold inventories)** of the profit of sale of ₦2 million recognised immediately by Pally (20% of ₦10 million); or alternatively, unrealized profit of ₦1.2 million ascertained as the percentage of unsold stock (60%) on the amount of inventory of ₦10 million, multiply by the mark-up (profit on cost) of 20%.

Accounting entries:
Debit: Consolidated retained earnings ⎤
Credit: Group inventories   ⎦   ₦1.2 million

✓ **Step 6:** Combine the assets and liabilities of the parent (**Pally**) and subsidiary (**Sussy**) on an item-by-item basis excluding the initial investment of **Pally** in **Sussy** as earlier shown in the separate financial statements of **Pally**, and also the exclusion of the equity share capital of **Sussy**, as it has already been considered alongside with the pre-acquisition retained earnings in ascertaining the amount of goodwill or gain from bargain purchase inherent/embedded in the acquisition. The consolidated statement of financial position of the group will now be shown as thus:

Pally Group
Consolidated Statement of Financial Position as at 31 December 2015

Assets:	₦' million	₦' million
Non-current assets		
Property, plant and equipment (110 + 120)		230.0
Goodwill		4.0
Current assets:		
Inventories (40 + 45 – 1.2)	83.8	
Accounts receivables (15 + 12)	27.0	
Bank (5 + 7)	12.0	122.8
Total Assets		**356.8**
Share Capital & Reserves:		
Equity share capital		80.0
Reserves		170.8
Equity attributable to Pally's shareholders		**250.8**
Non-controlling interest		32.0
Total Equity		**282.8**
Current liabilities (50 + 24)		74.0
Total Equity and Liabilities		**356.8**

The consolidation schedule can equally be adopted for solving this group problem as scheduled below:

Consolidation Schedule

Subsidiary - Sussy		Cost of control (Pally in Sussy) as at Acquisition – 80%	Non-controlling Interests – 20%	Consolidated Reserves
Equity Share Capital	100	(80% x 100) 80.0	(20% x 100) 20.0	
Reserves (Pre-acquisition)	20	(80% x 20) 16.0	(20% x 10) 4.0	
Reserves (Post-acquisition)	40	—	(20% x 50) 8.0	(80% x 40) 32.0
Net asset on acquisition		96.0		
Cost of combination (cost of investment)		(100.0)		
Goodwill (positive)		**(4.0)**		
Non-controlling interests			**32.0**	
Unrealized profit on inventory				(1.2)
Pally Reserves				140.0
Consolidated Reserves				**170.8**

Upstream Transactions:

This involves the sale of goods by the investee (subsidiary) to the investor (parent). Since the profit is recognised by the subsidiary upon sales to the parent, the unrealized profit should be adjusted partly against the consolidated retained earnings (*with respect to those attributable to the parent*) and partly against the non-controlling interest (*with respect to those attributable to the parent and where the subsidiary is partly owned by the parent company*).

Accounting treatment and entries: Remove the whole profit loading, and charge the non-controlling interest with their proportion (Preferred Method).

Debit: Consolidated retained earnings - With the parent's share of the unrealized profit
Debit: Non-controlling interest - With the NCI's share of the unrealized profit
Credit: Group inventory (Statement of financial position) - With the total unrealized profit.

ILLUSTRATION 2:

Pally Plc acquired 160 million of the shares of Sussy plc when the reserves were ₦20 million. During the year to 31 December 2015, Sussy Plc sold goods costing ₦10 million @ a profit of 20% on the cost to Pally Plc. As at the reporting date, only 40% of these goods were sold to external customers by Pally. In the same period the statement of financial position of the dual companies as at 31st December 2015 is as follows:

Statement of Financial Position as at 31 December 2015

Assets:	Pally Plc ₦' million	Sussy Plc ₦' million
Non-current assets		
Property, plant and equipment	110	120
Investment in Sussy Plc	100	
Current Assets:		
Inventories	40	45
Accounts receivables	15	12
Bank	5	7
Total Assets	**270**	**184**
Equities and Liabilities:		
Equity – Ordinary shares (₦0.50/share)	80	100
Retained earnings	140	60
Current liabilities	50	24
Total equity and liabilities	**270**	**184**

We are to approach the solution in the following steps:

- ✓ **Step 1**: Determine the percentage holdings of investment of **Pally** in **Sussy** as at the acquisition date (some time ago), which represents the date of inclusion (first date of consolidation). In this case, the percentage holding is determined and ascertained to be 80%.

  The 80% interest of Pally is ascertained by expressing 160 million shares as a proportion of 200 million shares of Sussy in issue as at acquisition (this is obtained by dividing the share capital of ₦100 million by ₦0.50 nominal price per share).

✓ **Step 2:** Ascertain the form of group structure in this parent subsidiary relationship. Since the subsidiary (**Sussy**) is *partly-owned* by the parent (**Pally**), the group structure is a simple structure as shown below:

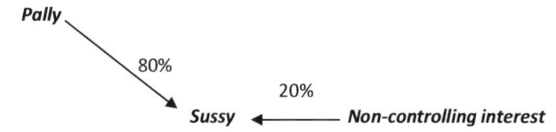

```
        Pally
           \
           80%
             \      20%
             Sussy ←────── Non-controlling interest
```

✓ **Step 3:** Determine the existence of goodwill or gain from a bargain purchase as at the date of acquisition based on the fair value of subsidiary's identifiable assets and liabilities. In this case, there exists goodwill as shown below.

To ascertain and determine the amount of goodwill or gain from a bargain purchase, the value of an investment of the parent (**Pally**) in the subsidiary (**Sussy**) will be compared with the parent's share of identifiable assets and liabilities of the subsidiary that were acquired.

PARTIAL METHODOLOGY	₦' million	₦' million
Cost of combination (i.e. the cost of investment of **Pally** in **Sussy**)		100
Less: **Pally**'s share of Identifiable net assets of **Sussy** acquired:		
• Share capital (80% of ₦100 million)	80	
• Pre-acquisition reserves (80% of ₦20 million)	16	(96)
Goodwill attributable to **Pally's** (a)		4
Amount of investments of non-controlling interest in **Sussy**		24
Less: Non-controlling interest share of the fair value of subsidiary's net assets:		
• Share capital (20% of ₦100 million)	20	
• Pre-acquisition reserves (20% of ₦20 million)	4	(24)
Goodwill attributable to **non-controlling interests** (b)		---
Goodwill (a + b)		**4**

Technical Note:
The goodwill attributable to non-controlling must be zero since the investment to non-controlling interests is valued at the proportionate share of subsidiary's identifiable net assets as shown by the arrow.

Alternative, FULL METHODOLOGY		₦' million
Cost of Business Combination		
Cost of acquisition to Pally		100
Amount of Investment in subsidiary to non-controlling interest (Step 4)		24
Combined amount of interests in subsidiary to all investors		**124**
Less: Fair value of identified assets and liabilities acquired at acquisition-date		
Share capital	100	
Pre-acquisition reserves	20	(120)
Goodwill - positive		**4**

✓ **Step 4:** Determine the amount of non-controlling interest as will be shown in the consolidated statement of financial position of the group. In this case, non-controlling interest will only be measured at proportionate share of subsidiary's identifiable assets and liabilities, which could be depicted as thus:

Non-controlling interest's share of Identifiable net assets of **Sussy** upon acquisition:

	₦' million
• Share capital (20% of ₦100 million)	20.00
• Pre-acquisition reserves (20% of ₦20 million)	4.00
NCI's investment @ Acquisition-date (*based on proportionate share of net assets*)	**24.00**
• Post-acquisition reserves (20% of ₦40 million)	8.00
Less: Unrealized profit of inventories*	(0.24)
NCI's investment on 31 December 2015	**31.76**

✓ **Step 5:** *Determine the amount to be included in the consolidated statement of financial position as consolidated reserves (otherwise known as consolidated retained earnings).* The consolidated retained earnings to be included in the consolidated statement of financial position of **Pally-Group** are that of the parent and of the post-acquisition profits of the subsidiary. Invariably, it implies that the post-acquisition retained earnings (which is the sum of ₦40 million being the increase from ₦20 million profits upon acquisition to ₦60 million the reporting date 31 December 2015 - *some years after*) of the subsidiary (**Sussy**) will now be combined with the retained earnings (profits) of the parent (**Pally**) in ascertaining the group retained earnings. The consolidated retained earnings will be determined as follows:

	₦' million
Parent's (**Pally**) retained earnings	140.00
Share of subsidiary's (**Sussy**) post-acquisition profits (80% of ₦40 million)	32.00
Less: Unrealized profit of inventories*	(0.96)
	171.04

*The unrealized profits on sale of goods by the subsidiary (Sussy) is the sum of ₦1.2 million, being **60% (representing unsold inventories)** of the profit of sale of ₦2 million recognised immediately by Sussy (20% of ₦10 million); or alternatively, unrealized profit of ₦1.2 million ascertained as the percentage of unsold stock (60%) on the amount of inventory of ₦10 million, multiply by the *mark-up (profit on cost) of 20%*. The unrealized profit on the inventories will be adjusted on a proportionate basis to the parent (through consolidated retained earnings) and to the non-controlling interest in the proportion profit or loss of the subsidiary is apportioned or shared.

Accounting entries:
  Debit: Consolidated retained earnings – ₦0.96 million (representing 80%) ⎤
  Debit: Non-controlling interest – ₦0.24 million (representing 20%)   ⎦ ₦1.2 million
  Credit: Group inventories - ₦1.2 million

✓ **Step 6:** *Combine the assets and liabilities of the parent (**Pally**) and subsidiary (**Sussy**) on an item-by-item basis excluding the initial investment of **Pally** in **Sussy** as earlier shown in the separate financial statements of **Pally**, and also the exclusion of the equity share capital of **Sussy**, as it has already been considered alongside with the pre-acquisition retained earnings in ascertaining the amount of goodwill or gain from bargain purchase inherent/embedded in the acquisition.* The consolidated statement of financial position of the group will now be shown as thus:

Pally Group
Consolidated Statement of Financial Position as at 31 December 2015

Assets:	₦' million	₦' million
Non-current assets		
Property, plant and equipment (110 + 120)		230.00
Goodwill		4.00
Current assets:		
Inventories (40 + 45 – 1.2)	83.80	
Accounts receivables (15 + 12)	27.00	
Bank (5 + 7)	12.00	122.80
Total Assets		**356.80**
Share Capital & Reserves:		
Equity share capital		80.00
Reserves		171.04
Equity attributable to Pally's shareholders		**251.04**
Non-controlling interest		31.76
Total Equity		**282.80**
Current liabilities (50 + 24)		74.00
Total Equity and Liabilities		**356.80**

The consolidation schedule can equally be adopted for solving this group problem as scheduled below:

Consolidation Schedule

Subsidiary - Sussy		Cost of control (Pally in Sussy) as at Acquisition – 80%	Non-controlling Interests – 20%	Consolidated Reserves
Equity Share Capital	100	(80% x 100) 80.00	(20% x 100) 20.00	
Reserves (Pre-acquisition)	20	(80% x 20) 16.00	(20% x 10) 4.00	
Reserves (Post-acquisition)	40	–	(20% x 50) 8.00	(80% x 40) 32.00
Net asset on acquisition		96.00		
Cost of combination (cost of investment)		(100.00)		
Goodwill (positive)		**(4.00)**		
Unrealized profit on inventory			(0.24)	(0.96)
Non-controlling interests			**31.76**	
Pally Reserves				140.00
Consolidated Reserves				**171.04**

Memory Recall

At elementary stage of accounting, certain relationships and equations were observed of which at this level may be germane to ascertaining the true amount of adjustments that may be required in order to eliminate unrealized profit on inventory as a result of inter-company sale of goods at a price above the cost price to the selling party within the group.

One of these relationships is that of "*Mark-up*" and "*Margin*". **Mark-up** is considered as a relative expression of profit to cost (i.e. *Profit/Cost Price* and expressed in percentages), while **Margin** is considered as a relative expression of profit to selling price (i.e. *Profit/Selling Price* and expressed in percentages). The selling price is considered a value (or worth) obtainable by a seller in a sales' transaction, and which comprises the *cost price* to *profit* desired by the seller.

Mark-up is applicable whenever the cost price is available to obtain the amount of gross profit (or profit) on sales transaction, while margin is relevant whenever the selling price is available to obtain the amount of gross profit (or profit) in a sales transaction.

Hence, situations exist when the margin is what is considered available when cost price is provided, and vice-versa (i.e. mark-up is what is considered available when the selling price is provided). In such situations, what is required is to explore the relationship between the two equations (or expression) as thus:

Scenario 1:

Given mark-up of 25% and a Selling Price of ₦100,000. This can be converted to the margin in order to obtain the amount of profit made on the transaction.

$$\text{Mark-up} = \frac{\text{Profit}}{\text{Cost Price}} = \frac{25}{100}$$

Then conversion to Margin entails:

$$\text{Margin} = \frac{\text{Profit}}{\text{Cost Price + Profit}} = \frac{25}{100 + 25} = \underline{\mathbf{20\%}}$$

Hence, profit on the sales' transaction is ₦20,000 (i.e. 20% Margin on ₦100,000 Selling Price).

Scenario 2:

Given Margin of 20% and a Cost Price of ₦80,000. This can be converted to mark-up in order to obtain the amount of profit made on the transaction.

$$\text{Margin} = \frac{\text{Profit}}{\text{Selling Price}} = \frac{20}{100}$$

Then conversion to Mark-up entails:

$$\text{Mark-up} = \frac{\text{Profit}}{\text{Selling Price - Profit}} = \frac{20}{100 - 20} = \underline{\mathbf{25\%}}$$

Hence, profit on the sales' transaction is ₦20,000 (i.e. 25% Mark-up on ₦80,000 Cost Price).

Intra-Group Transfer/Sale of Property, Plant & Equipment (Including Similar Assets)

It is a common practice for intra-group transfer (or sales) of property, plant and equipment (PPE), investment properties, intangible assets, etc. There is no problem upon consolidation if the non-current assets have been transferred at carrying values, otherwise, it poses a challenge upon consolidation to eliminate any profit or loss (resulting from differences between the carrying values and transferred prices).

The transaction is similar to that of the sale of goods only that there may be a need for additional adjustment resulting from the transfer of non-current assets at a value different from its carrying value which will ultimately result in over/(under) depreciation on the assets (provided the asset is depreciable). The adjustment may require the reversal of over-depreciation (excess depreciation), where the transfer price is greater than the carrying amount and charging of additional depreciation with respect to under-depreciation (depreciation shortfall), where the transfer price is less than the carrying amount. The adjustment requiring additional depreciation with respect to transfer (within the group) below carrying amount, may not be necessary if there is an evidence of possible impairment of the asset(s) transferred. This arose from the fact that prior to the transfer; there may be an impairment trigger that justified the reduction of the initial carrying amount of the asset to its recoverable amount. In such case, no adjustment will be required for the reversal of loss on transfer (since it is considered an impairment loss, which is consistent with the requirement of IAS 36) and charge of additional depreciation.

We could further classify the transactions between the parent and the subsidiary as either of a *Downstream (i.e. down-the-stream)* or *Upstream (i.e. up-the-stream)* transactions. Downstream transactions are those transactions emanating from the parent to the subsidiary, e.g. Plant transferred to the subsidiary by the parent. Upstream transactions are those transactions emanating from the subsidiary to the parent, e.g. Plant transferred to the parent by the subsidiary.

Downstream Transactions:
This involves the sale of a non-current asset by the investor (parent) to the investee (subsidiary). Since the profit is recognised by the parent upon transfer of the asset to the subsidiary, the unrealized profit should be adjusted against the consolidated retained earnings.

- *Unrealized profit on sale/transfer of Property, plant and equipment*
Debit: Consolidated retained earnings
Credit: Group property, plant and equipment } with the total unrealized profit on transfer of asset
(Technical Note: Reverse entries, if it is a loss on sale/transfer of Property, plant and equipment, other than an Impairment Loss)

- *Over-depreciation of Property, plant and equipment*
Debit: Group property, plant and equipment
Credit: Consolidated retained earnings } with the over-depreciation profit on transfer of asset
(Technical Note: Reverse entries, if it is a loss on sale/transfer of Property, plant and equipment, other than an Impairment Loss)

ILLUSTRATION 3:
Pally Plc acquired 160 million of the shares of Sussy plc since the incorporation of that company. Pally Plc transferred Plant to Sussy Plc for ₦40 million and has a carrying value of ₦36 million as at the transfer date 1 January 2014. The group has a uniform depreciation method for the same class of assets (which is a straight-line method). As at the transfer date, the remaining useful life

of the plant is 10 years. The statements of financial position of the dual companies as at 31 December 2015 were as follows:

Statement of Financial Position as at 31 December 2015

Assets:	Pally Plc ₦' million	Sussy Plc ₦' million
Non-current assets		
Property, plant and equipment	110	120
Investment in Sussy Plc	100	
Current Assets:		
Inventories	40	45
Accounts receivables	15	12
Bank	5	7
Total Assets	**270**	**184**
Equities and Liabilities:		
Equity – Ordinary shares (₦0.50/share)	80	100
Retained earnings	140	60
Current liabilities	50	24
Total equity and liabilities	**270**	**184**

We are to approach the solution in the following steps:

✓ **Step 1**: *Determine the percentage holdings of investment of Pally in Sussy as at the acquisition date (some time ago), which represents the date of inclusion (first date of consolidation).* In this case, the percentage holding is determined and ascertained to be 80%.

The 80% interest of Pally is ascertained by expressing 160 million shares as a proportion of 200 million shares of Sussy in issue as at acquisition (this is obtained by dividing the share capital of ₦100 million by ₦0.50 nominal price per share).

✓ **Step 2:** *Ascertain the form of group structure in this parent-subsidiary relationship.* Since the subsidiary (**Sussy**) is *partly-owned* by the parent (**Pally**), the group structure is a simple structure as shown below:

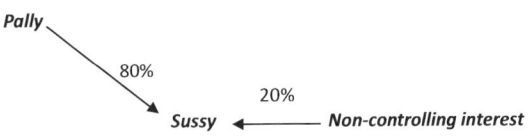

```
        Pally
          \
        80%\
            \      20%
           Sussy ←────── Non-controlling interest
```

✓ **Step 3:** *Determine the existence of goodwill or gain from a bargain purchase as at the date of acquisition based on the fair value of subsidiary's identifiable assets and liabilities.* In this case, there exists goodwill as shown below.

To ascertain and determine the amount of goodwill or gain from a bargain purchase, the value of an investment of the parent (**Pally**) in the subsidiary (**Sussy**) will be compared with the parent's share of identifiable assets and liabilities of the subsidiary that were acquired.

PARTIAL METHODOLOGY	₦' million	₦' million
Cost of combination (i.e. the cost of investment of **Pally** in **Sussy**)		100
Less: **Pally**'s share of Identifiable net assets of **Sussy** acquired:		
• Share capital (80% of ₦100 million)	80	
• Pre-acquisition reserves (80% of Nil*)	–	(80)
*Goodwill attributable to **Pally's** (a)*		20
Amount of investments of non-controlling interest in **Sussy**		20
Less: Non-controlling interest share of the fair value of subsidiary's net assets:		
• Share capital (20% of ₦100 million)	20	
• Pre-acquisition reserves (20% of Nil*)	–	(20)
*Goodwill attributable to **non-controlling interests*** (b)*		---
Goodwill (a + b)		**20**

Technical Note:

* Since the subsidiary was acquired at incorporation (that an equity stake of 80%), there exist no pre-acquisition profits, as all profits as at the reporting date (31 December 2015) are all considered post-acquisition.

**The goodwill attributable to non-controlling must be zero since the investment to non-controlling interests is valued at the proportionate share of subsidiary's identifiable net assets as shown by the arrow.

Alternative, FULL METHODOLOGY		₦' million
Cost of Business Combination		
Cost of acquisition to Pally		100
Amount of Investment in subsidiary to non-controlling interest*		20
Combined amount of interests in subsidiary to all investors		120
Less: Fair value of identified assets and liabilities acquired at acquisition-date		
Share capital	100	
Pre-acquisition reserves	0	(100)
Goodwill - positive		**20**

✓ **Step 4:** *Determine the amount of non-controlling interest as will be shown in the consolidated statement of financial position of the group.* In this case, non-controlling interest will only be measured at the proportionate share of subsidiary's identifiable assets and liabilities, which could be depicted as thus:

Non-controlling interest's share of Identifiable net assets of **Sussy**:

	₦' million
• Share capital (20% of ₦100 million)	20
• Pre-acquisition reserves (20% of Nil)	–
NCI's investment @ acquisition-date (*based on proportionate share of net assets*)	**20**
• Post-acquisition reserves (20% of ₦60 million)	12
NCI's investment on 31 December 2015 (*based on proportionate share of net assets*)	**32**

✓ **Step 5:** *Determine the amount to be included in the consolidated statement of financial position as consolidated reserves (otherwise known as consolidated retained earnings).* The consolidated retained earnings to be included in the consolidated statement of financial position of **Pally-Group** are that of the parent and of the post-acquisition profits of the subsidiary. Invariably, it implies that the post-acquisition retained earnings is ₦60 million (since there was no pre-acquisition profit, as the subsidiary was acquired at point of incorporation 80% equity interest in the subsidiary) will now be combined with the retained earnings (profits) of the parent (**Pally**) in ascertaining the group retained earnings. The consolidated retained earnings will be determined as follows:

	₦' million
Parent's (**Pally**) retained earnings	140.0
Share of subsidiary's (**Sussy**) post-acquisition profits (80% of ₦60 million)	48.0
Less: Unrealized profit of transfer of Plant*	(4.0)
Add: Adjustment for excess depreciation on Plant**	0.8
	184.8

* The unrealized profits on the transfer of Plant by the parent (Pally) is the sum of ₦4 million, being the excess of transfer price (₦40 million) over the carrying amount (₦36 million) at the point of transfer (1 January 2014).

> ***Accounting entries: Unrealized profit on transfer of PPE***
> *Debit: Consolidated retained earnings*
> *Credit: Group property, plant and equipment* ⎱ ₦4 million

** The excess depreciation can be ascertained as follows:

- Excess depreciation = $\dfrac{\text{Used Life since transfer}}{\text{Useful Life from Transfer Date}}$ × Unrealized profit on transfer of Plant
  = 2/10 years × ₦4 million
  = **₦800,000**

- Excess depreciation is the difference between the assumed depreciation based on consolidation process and the actual depreciation charged by the subsidiary.

	₦' million
Depreciation by subsidiary (depreciation rate × transfer price)	xx
Depreciation based on consolidation (depreciation based on carrying amount)	(xx)
Excess depreciation/Over-depreciation	**x**

	₦' million
Depreciation by subsidiary (2/10 years × ₦40 million)	8.0
Depreciation based on consolidation (2/10 years × ₦36 million)	(7.2)
Excess depreciation	**0.8**

> ***Accounting entries: Over-depreciation of Property, plant and equipment***
> *Debit: Group property, plant and equipment*
> *Credit: Consolidated retained earnings* ⎱ ₦0.8 million

✓ **Step 6:** Combine the assets and liabilities of the parent (**Pally**) and subsidiary (**Sussy**) on an item-by-item basis excluding the initial investment of **Pally** in **Sussy** as earlier shown in the separate financial statements of **Pally**, and also the exclusion of the equity share capital of **Sussy**, as it has already been considered alongside with the pre-acquisition retained earnings in ascertaining the amount of goodwill or gain from bargain purchase inherent/embedded in the acquisition. The consolidated statement of financial position of the group will now be shown as thus:

Pally Group
Consolidated Statement of Financial Position as at 31 December 2015

Assets:	₦' million	₦' million
Non-current assets		
Property, plant and equipment (110 + 120 – 4 + 0.8)		226.8
Goodwill		20.0
Current assets:		
Inventories (40 + 45)	85.0	
Accounts receivables (15 + 12)	27.0	
Bank (5 + 7)	12.0	124.0
Total Assets		**370.8**
Share Capital & Reserves:		
Equity share capital		80.0
Reserves		184.8
Equity attributable to Pally's shareholders		**264.8**
Non-controlling interest		32.0
Total Equity		**296.8**
Current liabilities (50 + 24)		74.0
Total Equity and Liabilities		**370.8**

The consolidation schedule can equally be adopted for solving this group problem as scheduled below:

Consolidation Schedule

Subsidiary - Sussy		Cost of control (Pally in Sussy) as at Acquisition – 80%	Non-controlling Interests – 20%	Consolidated Reserves
Equity Share Capital	100	(80% x 100) 80.0	(20% x 100) 20.0	
Reserves (Pre-acquisition)	Nil	(80% x Nil) -	(20% x Nil) -	
Reserves (Post-acquisition)	60	-	(20% x 60) 12.0	(80% x 60) 48.0
Net asset on acquisition		80.0		
Cost of combination (cost of investment)		100.0)		
Goodwill (positive)		**(20.0)**		
Non-controlling interests			**32.0**	
Unrealized profit on Plant				(4.0)
Excess depreciation on transferred Plant				0.4
Pally Reserves				140.0
Consolidated Reserves				**184.4**

Upstream Transactions:

This involves the sale of a non-current asset by the investee (subsidiary) to the investor (parent). Since the profit is recognised by the subsidiary upon transfer of the asset to the parent, the unrealized profit may be adjusted partly against the consolidated retained earnings (*with respect to those attributable to the parent*) and partly against the non-controlling interest (*with respect to those attributable to the parent and where the subsidiary is partly owned by the parent company*).

Accounting treatment and entries:

- **Remove the whole profit loading, charging the non-controlling interest with their proportion (Preferred Method).**

  Debit: Consolidated retained earnings- parent's share of unrealized profit
  Debit: Non-controlling interest – NCI's share of unrealized profit
  Credit: Group property, plant and equipment - with the total unrealized profit on transfer of Plant

  (Technical Note: Reverse entries, if it is a loss on sale/transfer of Property, plant and equipment, other than an Impairment Loss)

- **Excess-depreciation of Property, plant and equipment**

  Debit: Group property, plant and equipment - with the over-depreciation profit on transfer of Plant
  Credit: Consolidated retained earnings – parent's share of unrealized profit
  Credit: Non-controlling interest – NCI's share of unrealized profit

  (Technical Note: Reverse entries, if it is a loss on sale/transfer of Property, plant and equipment, other than an Impairment Loss)

ILLUSTRATION 4:

Pally Plc acquired 160 million of the shares of Sussy plc since the incorporation of that company. Sussy Plc transferred Plant to Pally Plc for ₦40 million and has a carrying value of ₦36 million as at the transfer date 1 January 2014. The group has a uniform depreciation method for the same class of assets (which is a straight-line method). As at the transfer date, the remaining useful life of the plant is 10 years. The statements of financial position of the dual companies as at 31 December 2015 were as follows:

Statement of Financial Position as at 31 December 2015

	Pally Plc ₦ million	Sussy Plc ₦' million
Assets:		
Non-current assets		
Property, plant and equipment	110	120
Investment in Sussy Plc	100	
Current Assets:		
Inventories	40	45
Accounts receivables	15	12
Bank	5	7
Total Assets	**270**	**184**
Equities and Liabilities:		
Equity – Ordinary shares (₦0.50/share)	80	100
Retained earnings	140	60
Current liabilities	50	24
Total equity and liabilities	**270**	**184**

We are to approach the solution in the following steps:

- ✓ **Step 1**: Determine the percentage holdings of investment of **Pally** in **Sussy** as at the acquisition date (some time ago), which represents the date of inclusion (first date of consolidation). In this case, the percentage holding is determined and ascertained to be 80%.

The 80% interest of Pally is ascertained by expressing 160 million shares as a proportion of 200 million shares of Sussy in issue as at acquisition (this is obtained by dividing the share capital of ₦100 million by ₦0.50 nominal price per share).

✓ **Step 2:** Ascertain the form of group structure in this parent-subsidiary relationship. Since the subsidiary (**Sussy**) is *partly-owned* by the parent (**Pally**), the group structure is a simple structure as shown below:

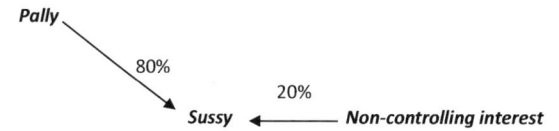

```
        Pally
           \
         80%\
             \      20%
              ↘ Sussy ← Non-controlling interest
```

✓ **Step 3:** Determine the existence of goodwill or gain from a bargain purchase as at the date of acquisition based on the fair value of subsidiary's identifiable assets and liabilities. In this case, there exists goodwill as shown below.

To ascertain and determine the amount of goodwill or gain from a bargain purchase, the value of an investment of the parent (**Pally**) in the subsidiary (**Sussy**) will be compared with the parent's share of identifiable assets and liabilities of the subsidiary that were acquired.

PARTIAL METHODOLOGY	₦' million	₦' million
Cost of combination (i.e. the cost of investment of **Pally** in **Sussy**)		100
Less: **Pally's** share of Identifiable net assets of **Sussy** acquired:		
• Share capital (80% of ₦100 million)	80	
• Pre-acquisition reserves (80% of Nil*)	–	(80)
*Goodwill attributable to **Pally's** (a)*		20
Amount of investments of non-controlling interest in **Sussy**		20
Less: Non-controlling interest share of the fair value of subsidiary's net assets:		
• Share capital (20% of ₦100 million)	20	
• Pre-acquisition reserves (20% of Nil*)	–	(20)
*Goodwill attributable to **non-controlling interests**** (b)*		---
Goodwill (a + b)		**20**

Technical Note:

* Since the subsidiary was acquired at incorporation (that an equity stake of 80%), there exist no pre-acquisition profits, as all profits as at the reporting date (31 December 2015) are all considered post-acquisition.

**The goodwill attributable to non-controlling must be zero since the investment to non-controlling interests is valued at the proportionate share of subsidiary's identifiable net assets as shown by the arrow.

Alternative, FULL METHODOLOGY	₦' million
Cost of Business Combination	
Cost of acquisition to Pally	100
Amount of Investment in subsidiary to non-controlling interest*	20
Combined amount of interests in subsidiary to all investors	*120*

Adjustments in Group Accounts

Less: *Fair value of identified assets and liabilities acquired at acquisition-date*		
Share capital	100	
Pre-acquisition reserves	0	(100)
Goodwill - positive		**20**

✓ **Step 4:** *Determine the amount of non-controlling interest as will be shown in the consolidated statement of financial position of the group.* In this case, non-controlling interest will only be measured at proportionate share of subsidiary's identifiable assets and liabilities, which could be depicted as thus:

Non-controlling interest's share of Identifiable net assets of **Sussy** upon acquisition:

	₦' million
• Share capital (20% of ₦100 million)	20.00
• Pre-acquisition reserves (20% of Nil)	—
NCI's investment acquisition-date @ (*based on proportionate share of net assets*)	**20.00**
• Post-acquisition reserves (20% of ₦60 million)	12.00
Less: Unrealized profit of transfer of Plant*	(0.80)
Add: Adjustment for excess depreciation on Plant	0.16
NCI's investment on 31 December 2015	**31.36**

✓ **Step 5:** *Determine the amount to be included in the consolidated statement of financial position as consolidated reserves (otherwise known as consolidated retained earnings).* The consolidated retained earnings to be included in the consolidated statement of financial position of **Pally-Group** are that of the parent and of the post-acquisition profits of the subsidiary. Invariably, it implies that the post-acquisition retained earnings is ₦60 million (since there was no pre-acquisition profit, as the subsidiary was acquired at point of incorporation 80% equity interest in the subsidiary) will now be combined with the retained earnings (profits) of the parent (**Pally**) in ascertaining the group retained earnings. The consolidated retained earnings will be determined as follows:

	₦' million
Parent's (**Pally**) retained earnings	140.00
Share of subsidiary's (**Sussy**) post-acquisition profits (80% of ₦60 million)	48.00
Less: Unrealized profit of transfer of Plant*	(3.20)
Add: Adjustment for excess depreciation on Plant**	0.64
	185.44

* The unrealized profits on the transfer of Plant by the subsidiary (Sussy) is the sum of ₦4 million, being the excess of transfer price (₦40 million) over carrying amount (₦36 million) at the point of transfer (1 January 2014). The unrealized profit on the sale of plant and adjustment for excess depreciation will be adjusted on a proportionate basis to the parent (through consolidated retained earnings) and to the non-controlling interest in the proportion profit or loss of the subsidiary is apportioned or shared.

> *Accounting entries: Unrealized profit on transfer of PPE*
> Debit: Consolidated retained earnings (80%)   – ₦3.2 million ⎤
> Debit: Non-controlling interest (20%)   – ₦0.8 million ⎦ - ₦4 million
> Credit: Group property, plant and equipment   - ₦4 million

** The excess depreciation can be ascertained as follows:

❖ Excess depreciation = $\frac{\text{Used Life since transfer}}{\text{Useful Life from Transfer Date}}$ x Unrealized profit on transfer of Plant

= 2/10 years x ₦4 million
= ₦800,000

❖ Excess depreciation is the difference between the assumed depreciation based on consolidation process and the actual depreciation charged by the subsidiary.

	₦' million
Depreciation by subsidiary (depreciation rate x transfer price)	xx
Depreciation based on consolidation (depreciation based on carrying amount)	(xx)
Excess depreciation/Over-depreciation	**x**

	₦' million
Depreciation by subsidiary (2/10 years x ₦40 million)	8.0
Depreciation based on consolidation (2/10 years x ₦36 million)	(7.2)
Excess depreciation	**0.8**

Accounting entries: Over-depreciation of Property, plant and equipment
Debit: Group property, plant and equipment — ₦0.80 million
Credit: Consolidated retained earnings (80%) — ₦0.64 million ⎤
Debit: Non-controlling interest (20%) — ₦0.16 million ⎦ — ₦0.8 million

✓ **Step 6:** Combine the assets and liabilities of the parent (**Pally**) and subsidiary (**Sussy**) on an item-by-item basis excluding the initial investment of **Pally** in **Sussy** as earlier shown in the separate financial statements of **Pally**, and also the exclusion of the equity share capital of **Sussy**, as it has already been considered alongside with the pre-acquisition retained earnings in ascertaining the amount of goodwill or gain from bargain purchase inherent/embedded in the acquisition. The consolidated statement of financial position of the group will now be shown as thus:

Pally Group
Consolidated Statement of Financial Position as at 31 December 2015

Assets:	₦' million	₦' million
Non-current assets		
Property, plant and equipment (110 + 120 – 4 + 0.8)		226.80
Goodwill		20.00
Current assets:		
Inventories (40 + 45)	85.00	
Accounts receivables (15 + 12)	27.00	
Bank (5 + 7)	12.00	124.00
Total Assets		**370.80**
Share Capital & Reserves:		
Equity share capital		80.00
Reserves		185.44
Equity attributable to Pally's shareholders		265.44
Non-controlling interest		31.36
Total Equity		296.80
Current liabilities (50 + 24)		74.00
Total Equity and Liabilities		**370.80**

Adjustments in Group Accounts

The consolidation schedule can equally be adopted for solving this group problem as scheduled below:

Consolidation Schedule

Subsidiary - Sussy		Cost of control (Pally in Sussy) as at Acquisition – 80%	Non-controlling Interests – 20%	Consolidated Reserves
Equity Share Capital	100	(80% x 100) 80.00	(20% x 100) 20.00	
Reserves (Pre-acquisition)	Nil	(80% x Nil) -	(20% x Nil) -	
Reserves (Post-acquisition)	60	-	(20% x 60) 12.00	(80% x 60) 48.00
Net asset on acquisition		80.00		
Cost of combination (cost of investment)		(100.00)		
Goodwill (positive)		(20.00)		
Unrealized profit on Plant			(0.80)	(3.20)
Excess depreciation on transferred Plant			0.16	0.64
Non-controlling interests			31.36	
Pally Reserves				140.00
Consolidated Reserves				185.44

> There is a *"School of Thought"* that explored alternative approach towards the treatment accorded to *Downstream* and *Upstream Transactions* regarding the requisite adjustment for excess depreciation (or over depreciation) of assets transferred within the group at a price above (or below – other than a recognition of impairment loss) the carrying amount. This thought can be attributed to the lacuna in *IFRS 10* without clear guidance on the treatment of depreciation adjustments on the intercompany transfer of depreciable assets. The treatments according to this "School of Thought" are as thus:

Downstream Transactions:
This involves the sale of a non-current asset by the investor (parent) to the investee (subsidiary). Since the profit is recognised by the parent upon transfer of the asset to the subsidiary, the unrealized profit should be adjusted against the consolidated retained earnings.

- *Unrealized profit on sale/transfer of Property, plant and equipment*
  Debit: Consolidated retained earnings
  Credit: Group property, plant and equipment   } with the total unrealized profit on transfer of asset
  (Technical Note: Reverse entries, if it is a loss on sale/transfer of Property, plant and equipment, other than an Impairment Loss)

- *Excess-depreciation of Property, plant and equipment*
  Debit: Group property, plant and equipment - with the over-depreciation profit on transfer of Plant
  Credit: Consolidated retained earnings – parent's share of unrealized profit
  Credit: Non-controlling interest – NCI's share of unrealized profit
  (Technical Note: Reverse entries, if it is a loss on sale/transfer of Property, plant and equipment, other than an Impairment Loss)

ILLUSTRATION 5:

Pally Plc acquired 160 million of the shares of Sussy plc since the incorporation of that company. Pally Plc transferred Plant to Sussy Plc for ₦40 million and has a carrying value of ₦36 million as at the transfer date 1 January 2014. The group has a uniform depreciation method for the same class of assets (which is a straight-line method). As at the transfer date, the remaining useful life of the plant is 10 years. The statements of financial position of the dual companies as at 31 December 2015 were as follows:

Statement of Financial Position as at 31 December 2015

	Pally Plc	Sussy Plc
Assets:	₦' million	₦' million
Non-current assets		
Property, plant and equipment	110	120
Investment in Sussy Plc	100	
Current Assets:		
Inventories	40	45
Accounts receivables	15	12
Bank	5	7
Total Assets	**270**	**184**
Equities and Liabilities:		
Equity – Ordinary shares (₦0.50/share)	80	100
Retained earnings	140	60
Current liabilities	50	24
Total equity and liabilities	**270**	**184**

We are to approach the solution in the following steps:

- ✓ **Step 1**: *Determine the percentage holdings of investment of **Pally** in **Sussy** as at the acquisition date (some time ago), which represents the date of inclusion (first date of consolidation).* In this case, the percentage holding is determined and ascertained to be 80%.

  The 80% interest of Pally is ascertained by expressing 160 million shares as a proportion of 200 million shares of Sussy in issue as at acquisition (this is obtained by dividing the share capital of ₦100 million by ₦0.50 nominal price per share).

- ✓ **Step 2**: *Ascertain the form of group structure in this parent-subsidiary relationship.* Since the subsidiary (**Sussy**) is *partly-owned* by the parent (**Pally**), the group structure is a simple structure as shown below:

  Pally
  ↘ 80%
     Sussy ← 20% — **Non-controlling interest**

- ✓ **Step 3**: *Determine the existence of goodwill or gain from a bargain purchase as at the date of acquisition based on the fair value of subsidiary's identifiable assets and liabilities.* In this case, there exists goodwill as shown below.

Adjustments in Group Accounts

To ascertain and determine the amount of goodwill or gain from a bargain purchase, the value of an investment of the parent (**Pally**) in the subsidiary (**Sussy**) will be compared with the parent's share of identifiable assets and liabilities of the subsidiary that were acquired.

PARTIAL METHODOLOGY	₦' million	₦' million
Cost of combination (i.e. the cost of investment of **Pally** in **Sussy**)		100
Less: **Pally**'s share of Identifiable net assets of **Sussy** acquired:		
• Share capital (80% of ₦100 million)	80	
• Pre-acquisition reserves (80% of Nil*)	–	(80)
*Goodwill attributable to **Pally's** (a)*		_20_
Amount of investments of non-controlling interest in **Sussy**		20
Less: Non-controlling interest share of the fair value of subsidiary's net assets:		
• Share capital (20% of ₦100 million)	20	
• Pre-acquisition reserves (20% of Nil*)	–	(20)
*Goodwill attributable to **non-controlling interests**** (b)*		---
Goodwill (a + b)		**_20_**

Technical Note:

* Since the subsidiary was acquired at incorporation (that an equity stake of 80%), there exist no pre-acquisition profits, as all profits as at the reporting date (31 December 2015) are all considered post-acquisition.

**The goodwill attributable to non-controlling must be zero since the investment to non-controlling interests is valued at the proportionate share of subsidiary's identifiable net assets as shown by the arrow.

Alternative, FULL METHODOLOGY		₦' million
Cost of Business Combination		
Cost of acquisition to Pally		100
Amount of Investment in subsidiary to non-controlling interest*		_20_
Combined amount of interests in subsidiary to all investors		*120*
Less: Fair value of identified assets and liabilities acquired at acquisition-date		
Share capital	100	
Pre-acquisition reserves	0	(100)
Goodwill - positive		**_20_**

✓ **Step 4:** *Determine the amount of non-controlling interest as will be shown in the consolidated statement of financial position of the group.* In this case, non-controlling interest will only be measured at proportionate share of subsidiary's identifiable assets and liabilities, which could be depicted as thus:

Non-controlling interest's share of Identifiable net assets of **Sussy** upon acquisition:

	₦' million
• Share capital (20% of ₦100 million)	20.00
• Pre-acquisition reserves (20% of Nil)	–
NCI's investment on @ acquisition-date (*based on proportionate share of net assets*)	**20.00**
• Post-acquisition reserves (20% of ₦60 million)	12.00
Add: Adjustment for excess depreciation on Plant	*0.16*
NCI's investment on 31 December 2015 (*based on proportionate share of net assets*)	**32.16**

✓ **Step 5:** *Determine the amount to be included in the consolidated statement of financial position as consolidated reserves (otherwise known as consolidated retained earnings).* The consolidated retained earnings to be included in the consolidated statement of financial position of **Pally-Group** are that of the parent and of the post-acquisition profits of the subsidiary. Invariably, it implies that the post-acquisition retained earnings is ₦60 million (since there was no pre-acquisition profit, as the subsidiary was acquired at point of incorporation 80% equity interest in the subsidiary) will now be combined with the retained earnings (profits) of the parent (**Pally**) in ascertaining the group retained earnings. The consolidated retained earnings will be determined as follows:

		₦' million
Parent's (**Pally**) retained earnings		140.00
Share of subsidiary's (**Sussy**) post-acquisition profits (80% of ₦60 million)		48.00
Less: Unrealized profit of transfer of Plant*		(4.00)
Add: Adjustment for excess depreciation on Plant		0.64
		184.64

* The unrealized profits on the transfer of Plant by the parent (Pally) is the sum of ₦4 million, being the excess of transfer price (₦40 million) over carrying amount (₦36 million) at the point of transfer (1 January 2014), and adjusted only to Consolidated retained earnings.

Accounting entries: Unrealized profit on transfer of PPE
  Debit: Consolidated retained earnings ⎤
  Credit: Group property, plant and equipment ⎦ ₦4 million

** The excess depreciation can be ascertained as follows:

❖ Excess depreciation = $\frac{\text{Used Life since transfer}}{\text{Useful Life from Transfer Date}}$ x Unrealized profit transfer of Plant
  = 2/10 years x ₦4 million
  = **₦800,000**

❖ Excess depreciation is the difference between the assumed depreciation based on consolidation process and the actual depreciation charged by the subsidiary.

	₦' million
Depreciation by subsidiary (depreciation rate x transfer price)	xx
Depreciation based on consolidation (depreciation based on carrying amount)	(xx)
Excess depreciation/Over-depreciation	**x**
	₦' million
Depreciation by subsidiary (2/10 years x ₦40 million)	8.0
Depreciation based on consolidation (2/10 years x ₦36 million)	(7.2)
Excess depreciation	**0.8**

* The unrealized adjustment for excess depreciation will be adjusted on a proportionate basis to the parent (through consolidated retained earnings) and to the non-controlling interest in the proportion profit or loss of the subsidiary is apportioned or shared.

Accounting entries: Over-depreciation of Property, plant and equipment
  Debit: Group property, plant and equipment – ₦4.00 million
  Credit: Consolidated retained earnings (80%) – ₦0.64 million ⎤
  Debit: Non-controlling interest (20%) – ₦0.16 million ⎦ – ₦4 million

Adjustments in Group Accounts

✓ **Step 6:** *Combine the assets and liabilities of the parent (**Pally**) and subsidiary (**Sussy**) on an item-by-item basis excluding the initial investment of **Pally** in **Sussy** as earlier shown in the separate financial statements of **Pally**, and also the exclusion of the equity share capital of **Sussy**, as it has already been considered alongside with the pre-acquisition retained earnings in ascertaining the amount of goodwill or gain from bargain purchase inherent/embedded in the acquisition.* The consolidated statement of financial position of the group will now be shown as thus:

Pally Group
Consolidated Statement of Financial Position as at 31 December 2015

Assets:	₦' million	₦' million
Non-current assets		
Property, plant and equipment (110 + 120 – 4 + 0.8)		226.80
Goodwill		20.00
Current assets:		
Inventories (40 + 45)	85.0	
Accounts receivables (15 + 12)	27.0	
Bank (5 + 7)	12.0	124.00
Total Assets		**370.80**
Share Capital & Reserves:		
Equity share capital		80.00
Reserves		184.64
Equity attributable to Pally's shareholders		**264.64**
Non-controlling interest		32.16
Total Equity		**296.80**
Current liabilities (50 + 24)		74.00
Total Equity and Liabilities		**370.80**

The consolidation schedule can equally be adopted for solving this group problem as scheduled below:

Consolidation Schedule

Subsidiary - Sussy		Cost of control (Pally in Sussy) as at Acquisition – 80%	Non-controlling Interests – 20%	Consolidated Reserves
Equity Share Capital	100	(80% x 100) 80.00	(20% x 100) 20.00	
Reserves (Pre-acquisition)	Nil	(80% x Nil) –	(20% x Nil) –	
Reserves (Post-acquisition)	60	–	(20% x 60) 12.00	(80% x 60) 48.00
Net asset on acquisition		80.00		
Cost of combination (cost of investment)		(100.00)		
Goodwill (positive)		**(20.00)**		
Unrealized profit on Plant				(4.00)
Excess depreciation on transferred Plant			0.16	0.64
Non-controlling interests			**32.16**	
Pally Reserves				140.00
Consolidated Reserves				**184.64**

Upstream Transactions:

This involves the sale of a non-current asset by the investee (subsidiary) to the investor (parent). Since the profit is recognised by the subsidiary upon transfer of the asset to the parent, the unrealized profit may be adjusted partly against the consolidated retained earnings (*with respect to those attributable to the parent*) and partly against the non-controlling interest (*with respect to those attributable to the parent and where the subsidiary is partly owned by the parent company*).

Accounting treatment and entries:
- Remove the whole profit loading, charging the non-controlling interest with their proportion (Preferred Method).

Debit: Consolidated retained earnings- parent's share of unrealized profit
Debit: Non-controlling interest – NCI's share of unrealized profit
Credit: Group property, plant and equipment - with the total unrealized profit on transfer of Plant

(Technical Note: Reverse entries, if it is a loss on sale/transfer of Property, plant and equipment, other than an Impairment Loss)

- Over-depreciation of Property, plant and equipment

Debit: Group property, plant and equipment
Credit: Consolidated retained earnings } with the over-depreciation profit on transfer of asset

(Technical Note: Reverse entries, if it is a loss on sale/transfer of Property, plant and equipment, other than an Impairment Loss)

ILLUSTRATION 6:

Pally Plc acquired 160 million of the shares of Sussy plc since the incorporation of that company. Sussy Plc transferred Plant to Pally Plc for ₦40 million and has a carrying value of ₦36 million as at the transfer date 1 January 2014. The group has a uniform depreciation method for the same class of assets (which is a straight-line method). As at the transfer date, the remaining useful life of the plant is 10 years. The statements of financial position of the dual companies as at 31 December 2015 were as follows:

Statement of Financial Position as at 31 December 2015

Assets:	Pally Plc ₦' million	Sussy Plc ₦' million
Non-current assets		
Property, plant and equipment	110	120
Investment in Sussy Plc	100	
Current Assets:		
Inventories	40	45
Accounts receivables	15	12
Bank	5	7
Total Assets	**270**	**184**
Equities and Liabilities:		
Equity – Ordinary shares (₦0.50/share)	80	100
Retained earnings	140	60
Current liabilities	50	24
Total equity and liabilities	**270**	**184**

We are to approach the solution in the following steps:

- ✓ **Step 1**: *Determine the percentage holdings of investment of **Pally** in **Sussy** as at the acquisition date (some time ago), which represents the date of inclusion (first date of consolidation).* In this case, the percentage holding is determined and ascertained to be 80%.

   The 80% interest of Pally is ascertained by expressing 160 million shares as a proportion of 200 million shares of Sussy in issue as at acquisition (this is obtained by dividing the share capital of ₦100 million by ₦0.50 nominal price per share).

- ✓ **Step 2**: *Ascertain the form of group structure in this parent-subsidiary relationship.* Since the subsidiary (**Sussy**) is *partly-owned* by the parent (**Pally**), the group structure is a simple structure as shown below:

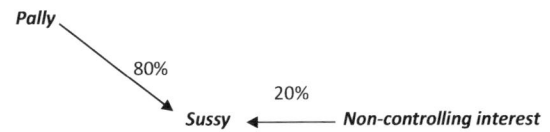

  ```
                Pally
                   \
                80% \
                     \         20%
                      → Sussy ←——— Non-controlling interest
  ```

- ✓ **Step 3**: *Determine the existence of goodwill or gain from a bargain purchase as at the date of acquisition based on the fair value of subsidiary's identifiable assets and liabilities.* In this case, there exists goodwill as shown below.

   To ascertain and determine the amount of goodwill or gain from a bargain purchase, the value of an investment of the parent (**Pally**) in the subsidiary (**Sussy**) will be compared with the parent's share of identifiable assets and liabilities of the subsidiary that were acquired.

PARTIAL METHODOLOGY	₦' million	₦' million
Cost of combination (i.e. the cost of investment of **Pally** in **Sussy**)		100
Less: **Pally**'s share of Identifiable net assets of **Sussy** acquired:		
• Share capital (80% of ₦100 million)	80	
• Pre-acquisition reserves (80% of Nil*)	—	(80)
*Goodwill attributable to **Pally's** (a)*		20
Amount of investments of non-controlling interest in **Sussy**		20
Less: Non-controlling interest share of the fair value of subsidiary's net assets:		
• Share capital (20% of ₦100 million)	20	
• Pre-acquisition reserves (20% of Nil*)	—	(20)
*Goodwill attributable to **non-controlling interests*** (b)*		---
Goodwill (a + b)		**20**

Technical Note:

* Since the subsidiary was acquired at incorporation (that an equity stake of 80%), there exist no pre-acquisition profits, as all profits as at the reporting date (31 December 2015) are all considered post-acquisition.

**The goodwill attributable to non-controlling must be zero since the investment to non-controlling interests is valued at the proportionate share of subsidiary's identifiable net assets as shown by the arrow.

Alternative, FULL METHODOLOGY		₦' million
Cost of Business Combination		
Cost of acquisition to Pally		100
Amount of Investment in subsidiary to non-controlling interest*		20
Combined amount of interests in subsidiary to all investors		120
Less: Fair value of identified assets and liabilities acquired at acquisition-date		
Share capital	100	
Pre-acquisition reserves	0	(100)
Goodwill - positive		**20**

✓ **Step 4:** Determine the amount of non-controlling interest as will be shown in the consolidated statement of financial position of the group. In this case, non-controlling interest will only be measured at the proportionate share of subsidiary's identifiable assets and liabilities, which could be depicted as thus:

Non-controlling interest's share of Identifiable net assets of **Sussy** upon acquisition:

	₦' million
• Share capital (20% of ₦100 million)	20.00
• Pre-acquisition reserves (20% of Nil)	-
NCI's investment on 1 January 2014 (*based on proportionate share of net assets*)	**20.00**
• Post-acquisition reserves (20% of ₦60 million)	12.00
Less: Unrealized profit of transfer of Plant*	(0.80)
NCI's investment on 31 December 2015	**31.20**

✓ **Step 5:** Determine the amount to be included in the consolidated statement of financial position as consolidated reserves (otherwise known as consolidated retained earnings). The consolidated retained earnings to be included in the consolidated statement of financial position of **Pally-Group** are that of the parent and of the post-acquisition profits of the subsidiary. Invariably, it implies that the post-acquisition retained earnings is ₦60 million (since there was no pre-acquisition profit, as the subsidiary was acquired at point of incorporation 80% equity interest in the subsidiary) will now be combined with the retained earnings (profits) of the parent (**Pally**) in ascertaining the group retained earnings. The consolidated retained earnings will be determined as follows:

	₦' million
Parent's (**Pally**) retained earnings	140.00
Share of subsidiary's (**Sussy**) post-acquisition profits (80% of ₦60 million)	48.00
Less: Unrealized profit of transfer of Plant*	(3.20)
Add: Adjustment for excess depreciation on Plant	0.80
	185.60

* The unrealized profits on the transfer of Plant by the parent (Pally) is the sum of ₦4 million, being the excess of transfer price (₦40 million) over carrying amount (₦36 million) at the point of transfer (1 January 2014). The unrealized profit on the sale of the plant will be adjusted on a proportionate basis to the parent (through consolidated retained earnings) and to the non-controlling interest in the proportion profit or loss of the subsidiary is apportioned or shared.

Accounting entries: Unrealized profit on transfer of PPE
Debit: Consolidated retained earnings (80%) – ₦3.2 million ⎫
Debit: Non-controlling interest (20%)   – ₦0.8 million ⎬ - ₦4 million
Credit: Group property, plant and equipment   - ₦4 million

Adjustments in Group Accounts

** The excess depreciation can be ascertained as follows:

- Excess depreciation = $\dfrac{\text{Used Life since transfer}}{\text{Useful Life from Transfer Date}}$ x Unrealized profit on transfer of Plant
  = 2/10 years x ₦4 million
  = **₦800,000**

- Excess depreciation is the difference between the assumed depreciation based on consolidation process and the actual depreciation charged by the subsidiary.

	₦' million
Depreciation by subsidiary (depreciation rate x transfer price)	xx
Depreciation based on consolidation (depreciation based on carrying amount)	(xx)
Excess depreciation/Over-depreciation	**x**

	₦' million
Depreciation by subsidiary (2/10 years x ₦40 million)	8.0
Depreciation based on consolidation (2/10 years x ₦36 million)	(7.2)
Excess depreciation	**0.8**

* The unrealized adjustment for excess depreciation will be adjusted in totality to the consolidated retained earnings.

Accounting entries: Over-depreciation of Property, plant and equipment
  Debit: Group property, plant and equipment ⎱ ₦0.8 million
  Credit: Consolidated retained earnings ⎰

✓ **Step 6:** *Combine the assets and liabilities of the parent (Pally) and subsidiary (Sussy) on an item-by-item basis excluding the initial investment of Pally in Sussy as earlier shown in the separate financial statements of Pally, and also the exclusion of the equity share capital of Sussy, as it has already been considered alongside with the pre-acquisition retained earnings in ascertaining the amount of goodwill or gain from bargain purchase inherent/embedded in the acquisition. The consolidated statement of financial position of the group will now be shown as thus:*

Pally Group
Consolidated Statement of Financial Position as at 31 December 2015

Assets:	₦' million	₦' million
Non-current assets		
Property, plant and equipment (110 + 120 – 4 + 0.8)		226.80
Goodwill		20.00
Current assets:		
Inventories (40 + 45)	85.00	
Accounts receivables (15 + 12)	27.00	
Bank (5 + 7)	12.00	124.00
Total Assets		**370.80**
Share Capital & Reserves:		
Equity share capital		80.00
Reserves		185.60
Equity attributable to Pally's shareholders		**265.60**
Non-controlling interest		31.20
Total Equity		**296.80**
Current liabilities (50 + 24)		74.00
Total Equity and Liabilities		**370.80**

The consolidation schedule can equally be adopted for solving this group problem as scheduled below:

Consolidation Schedule

Subsidiary - Sussy		Cost of control (Pally in Sussy) as at Acquisition – 80%	Non-controlling Interests – 20%	Consolidated Reserves
Equity Share Capital	100	(80% x 100) 80.00	(20% x 100) 20.00	
Reserves (Pre-acquisition)	Nil	(80% x Nil) -	(20% x Nil) -	
Reserves (Post-acquisition)	60	-	(20% x 60) 12.00	(80% x 60) 48.00
Net asset on acquisition		80.00		
Cost of combination (cost of investment)		100.00)		
Goodwill (positive)		(20.00)		
Unrealized profit on Plant			(0.80)	(3.20)
Excess depreciation on transferred Plant			-	0.80
Non-controlling interests			**31.20**	
Pally Reserves				140.00
Consolidated Reserves				**185.60**

Intra Group Current Accounts

There are situations where the parent and subsidiary maintain current accounts (intercompany receivables and payables) for tracking the intercompany balances and remittance of funds made on transactions between the duo (parent and subsidiary). It is always expected that since the current accounts maintained by the parent and subsidiary accommodate the remittance of funds between them, then the balances should agree at all times as the accounts *mirror* each other. If the current accounts do not agree, it means there may be some elements of accounting errors that must be corrected or some transactions considered to be *in-transit*, such as *cash-in-transit and goods-in-transit*. Prior to consolidation, the balances are required to be reconciled and necessary adjustments should be effected before consolidation. Upon consolidation, it is a requirement that intercompany balances should be *cancelled-out*; this is to ensure that the economic and financial position, performance and cash flows of the group as a single economic unit are reflected in the consolidated financial statements.

Where adjustments for cash-in-transit and/or goods-in-transit are required and for the purpose of the reconciliation of intercompany balance (i.e. current accounts), the following accounting entry is required:

Accounting entries for recognition of Cash/Inventories-in-Transit:
    Debit: Group Cash and Bank/Inventories
    Credit Current Account (either of the current account as they ultimately will cancel out)
    With the amount of cash and/or goods-in-transit

Adjustments in Group Accounts

We considered an illustration where the current accounts maintained by the dual companies agree as at the reporting date, as depicted below:

ILLUSTRATION 7:

Pally Plc acquired 160 million of the shares of Sussy plc since the incorporation of that company. The statements of financial position of the dual companies as at 31 December 2015 were as follows:

Statement of Financial Position as at 31 December 2015

	Pally Plc	Sussy Plc
Non-Current Assets:	₦' million	₦' million
Property, plant and equipment	110	120
Investment in **Sussy Plc**	100	
Current Assets:		
Inventories	30	45
Trade receivables	15	12
Current account – Sussy	10	
Bank	5	7
Total Assets	**270**	**184**
Equities and Liabilities:		
Equity – Ordinary shares (₦0.50/share)	80	100
Retained earnings	140	60
Current liabilities:		
Trade payables	50	14
Current account – Pally	—	10
Total equity and liabilities	**270**	**184**

We are to approach the solution in the following steps:

- ✓ **Step 1**: Determine the percentage holdings of investment of **Pally** in **Sussy** as at the acquisition date (some time ago), which represents the date of inclusion (first date of consolidation). In this case, the percentage holding is determined and ascertained to be 80%.

    The 80% interest of Pally is ascertained by expressing 160 million shares as a proportion of 200 million shares of Sussy in issue as at acquisition (this is obtained by dividing the share capital of ₦100 million by ₦0.50 nominal price per share).

- ✓ **Step 2:** Ascertain the form of group structure in this parent-subsidiary relationship. Since the subsidiary (**Sussy**) is *partly-owned* by the parent (**Pally**), the group structure is a simple structure as shown below:

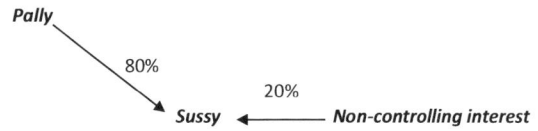

    Pally

    80% ↘

    Sussy ← 20% — Non-controlling interest

- ✓ **Step 3**: Determine the existence of goodwill or gain from a bargain purchase as at the date of acquisition based on the fair value of subsidiary's identifiable assets and liabilities. In this case, there exists goodwill as shown below.

To ascertain and determine the amount of goodwill or gain from a bargain purchase, the value of an investment of the parent (**Pally**) in the subsidiary (**Sussy**) will be compared with the parent's share of identifiable assets and liabilities of the subsidiary that were acquired.

PARTIAL METHODOLOGY	₦' million	₦' million
Cost of combination (i.e. the cost of investment of **Pally** in **Sussy**)		100
Less: Pally's share of Identifiable net assets of **Sussy** acquired:		
• Share capital (80% of ₦100 million)	80	
• Pre-acquisition reserves (80% of Nil*)	–	(80)
Goodwill attributable to **Pally's** (a)		20
Amount of investments of non-controlling interest in **Sussy**		20
Less: Non-controlling interest share of the fair value of subsidiary's net assets:		
• Share capital (20% of ₦100 million)	20	
• Pre-acquisition reserves (20% of Nil*)	–	(20)
Goodwill attributable to **non-controlling interests** ** (b)		--
Goodwill (a + b)		**20**

Technical Note:

* Since the subsidiary was acquired at incorporation (that an equity stake of 80%), there exist no pre-acquisition profits, as all profits as at the reporting date (31 December 2015) are all considered post-acquisition.

**The goodwill attributable to non-controlling must be zero since the investment to non-controlling interests is valued at the proportionate share of subsidiary's identifiable net assets as shown by the arrow.

Alternative, FULL METHODOLOGY	₦' million	₦' million
Cost of Business Combination		
Cost of acquisition to Pally		100
Amount of Investment in subsidiary to non-controlling interest*		20
Combined amount of interests in subsidiary to all investors		**120**
Less: Fair value of identifiable assets and liabilities at acquisition-date		
Share capital	100	
Pre-acquisition reserves	0	(100)
Goodwill - positive		**20**

✓ **Step 4:** *Determine the amount of non-controlling interest as will be shown in the consolidated statement of financial position of the group.* In this case, non-controlling interest will only be measured at proportionate share of subsidiary's identifiable assets and liabilities, which could be depicted as thus:

Non-controlling interest's share of Identifiable net assets of **Sussy**:

	₦' million
• Share capital (20% of ₦100 million)	20
• Pre-acquisition reserves (20% of Nil)	–
NCI's investment on acquisition (*based on proportionate share of net assets*)	**20**
• Post-acquisition reserves (20% of ₦60 million)	12
NCI's investment on 31 December 2015	**32**

✓ **Step 5:** *Determine the amount to be included in the consolidated statement of financial position as consolidated reserves (otherwise known as consolidated retained earnings).* The consolidated retained earnings to be included in the consolidated statement of financial position of **Pally-Group** are that of the parent and of the post-acquisition profits of the subsidiary. Invariably, it implies that the post-acquisition retained earnings is ₦60 million (since there was no pre-acquisition profit, as the subsidiary was acquired at point of incorporation 80% equity interest in the subsidiary) will now be combined with the retained earnings (profits) of the parent (**Pally**) in ascertaining the group retained earnings. The consolidated retained earnings will be determined as follows:

	₦' million
Parent's (**Pally**) retained earnings	140.00
Share of subsidiary's (**Sussy**) post-acquisition profits (80% of ₦60 million)	48.00
	188.00

- **Step 6**: Combine the assets and liabilities of the parent (**Pally**) and subsidiary (**Sussy**) on an item-by-item basis excluding the initial investment of **Pally** in **Sussy** as earlier shown in the separate financial statements of **Pally**, and also the exclusion of the equity share capital of **Sussy**, as it has already been considered alongside with the pre-acquisition retained earnings in ascertaining the amount of goodwill or gain from bargain purchase inherent/embedded in the acquisition.

- **Step 7**: In order to cancel out the intra-group current accounts, we first ensure that the *current accounts (intercompany balances)* of the parent and the subsidiary *agree*, and the balances will then be *cancelled-out*.

Accounting entries for cancellation of agreed intercompany balances:
Debit: Current account (payable) of Sussy
Credit: Current account (receivable) of Pally
With the amount of intercompany balance of ₦10 million

The consolidated statement of financial position of the group will now be shown (which will no longer fixture the current accounts as they have totally cancelled-out), as thus:

Pally Group
Consolidated Statement of Financial Position as at 31 December 2015

Assets:	₦' million	₦' million
Non-current assets		
Property, plant and equipment (110 + 120)		230.00
Goodwill		20.00
Current assets:		
Inventories (30 + 45)	75.00	
Trade receivables (15 + 12)	27.00	
~~Current account (10 – 10)~~	0.00	
Bank (5 + 7)	12.00	114.00
Total Assets		**364.00**
Share Capital & Reserves:		
Equity share capital		80.00
Reserves		188.00
Equity attributable to Pally's shareholders		**268.00**
Non-controlling interest		32.00
Total Equity		**300.00**

Current liabilities:
Trade payables (50 + 14)   64.00
~~Current account (10 – 10)~~   ~~0.00~~   64.00
Total Equity and Liabilities   **364.00**

The consolidation schedule can equally be adopted for solving this group problem as scheduled below:

Consolidation Schedule

Subsidiary - Sussy		Cost of control (Pally in Sussy) as at Acquisition – 80%		Non-controlling Interests – 20%		Consolidated Reserves	
Equity Share Capital	100	(80% x 100)	80	(20% x 100)	20		
Reserves (Pre-acquisition)	Nil	(80% x Nil)	-	(20% x Nil)	-		
Reserves (Post-acquisition)	60		-	(20% x 60)	12	(80% x 60)	48
Net asset on acquisition			80				
Cost of combination (cost of investment)			(100)				
Goodwill (positive)			**(20)**				
Non-controlling interests					**32**		
Pally Reserves							140
Consolidated Reserves							**188**

We can equally explore the situation where the current accounts of the parent and subsidiary do not agree (but attributed to "Cash In-transit" as at the reporting date), as illustrated below:

ILLUSTRATION 8:

Pally Plc acquired 160 million of the shares of Sussy plc since the incorporation of that company. The statements of financial position of the dual companies as at 31 December 2015 were as follows:

Statement of Financial Position as at 31 December 2015

	Pally Plc ₦' million	Sussy Plc ₦' million
Non-Current Assets:		
Property, plant and equipment	110	120
Investment in *Sussy Plc*	100	
Current Assets:		
Inventories	30	45
Accounts receivables	15	12
Current account – Sussy	10	
Bank	5	7
Total Assets	**270**	**184**
Equities and Liabilities:		
Equity – Ordinary shares (₦0.50/share)	80	100
Retained earnings	140	60
Current liabilities:		
Trade payables	50	16
Current account – Pally	—	8
Total equity and liabilities	**270**	**184**

Adjustments in Group Accounts

We are to approach the solution in the following steps:

✓ **Step 1**: Determine the percentage holdings of investment of **Pally** in **Sussy** as at the acquisition date (some time ago), which represents the date of inclusion (first date of consolidation). In this case, the percentage holding is determined and ascertained to be 80%.

The 80% interest of Pally is ascertained by expressing 160 million shares as a proportion of 200 million shares of Sussy in issue as at acquisition (this is obtained by dividing the share capital of ₦100 million by ₦0.50 nominal price per share).

✓ **Step 2**: Ascertain the form of group structure in this parent-subsidiary relationship. Since the subsidiary (**Sussy**) is *partly-owned* by the parent (**Pally**), the group structure is a simple structure as shown below:

```
        Pally
          \
        80% \
             \         20%
              ↘ Sussy ← ——— Non-controlling interest
```

✓ **Step 3**: Determine the existence of goodwill or gain from a bargain purchase as at the date of acquisition based on the fair value of subsidiary's identifiable assets and liabilities. In this case, there exists goodwill as shown below.

To ascertain and determine the amount of goodwill or gain from a bargain purchase, the value of an investment of the parent (**Pally**) in the subsidiary (**Sussy**) will be compared with the parent's share of identifiable assets and liabilities of the subsidiary that were acquired.

PARTIAL METHODOLOGY	₦' million	₦' million
Cost of combination (i.e. the cost of investment of **Pally** in **Sussy**)		100
Less: **Pally's** share of Identifiable net assets of **Sussy** acquired:		
• Share capital (80% of ₦100 million)	80	
• Pre-acquisition reserves (80% of Nil*)	–	(80)
Goodwill attributable to **Pally's** (a)		20
Amount of investments of non-controlling interest in **Sussy**		20
Less: Non-controlling interest share of the fair value of subsidiary's net assets:		
• Share capital (20% of ₦100 million)	20	
• Pre-acquisition reserves (20% of Nil*)	–	(20)
Goodwill attributable to **non-controlling interests** ** (b)		--
Goodwill (a + b)		**20**

Technical Note:

* Since the subsidiary was acquired at incorporation (that an equity stake of 80%), there exist no pre-acquisition profits, as all profits as at the reporting date (31 December 2015) are all considered post-acquisition.

**The goodwill attributable to non-controlling must be zero since the investment to non-controlling interests is valued at the proportionate share of subsidiary's identifiable net assets as shown by the arrow.

Alternative, FULL METHODOLOGY	₦' million	₦' million
Cost of Business Combination		
Cost of acquisition to Pally		100
Amount of Investment in subsidiary to non-controlling interest*		20
Combined amount of interests in subsidiary to all investors		**120**
Less: Fair value of identifiable assets and liabilities at acquisition-date		
Share capital	100	
Pre-acquisition reserves	0	(100)
Goodwill - positive		**20**

✓ **Step 4:** Determine the amount of non-controlling interest as will be shown in the consolidated statement of financial position of the group. In this case, non-controlling interest will only be measured at proportionate share of subsidiary's identifiable assets and liabilities, which could be depicted as thus:

Non-controlling interest's share of Identifiable net assets of **Sussy**:

	₦' million
• Share capital (20% of ₦100 million)	20
• Pre-acquisition reserves (20% of Nil)	-
NCI's investment on acquisition (*based on proportionate share of net assets*)	**20**
• Post-acquisition reserves (20% of ₦60 million)	12
NCI's investment on 31 December 2015	**32**

✓ **Step 5:** Determine the amount to be included in the consolidated statement of financial position as consolidated reserves (otherwise known as consolidated retained earnings). The consolidated retained earnings to be included in the consolidated statement of financial position of **Pally-Group** are that of the parent and of the post-acquisition profits of the subsidiary. Invariably, it implies that the post-acquisition retained earnings is ₦60 million (since there was no pre-acquisition profit, as the subsidiary was acquired at point of incorporation 80% equity interest in the subsidiary) will now be combined with the retained earnings (profits) of the parent (**Pally**) in ascertaining the group retained earnings. The consolidated retained earnings will be determined as follows:

	₦' million
Parent's (**Pally**) retained earnings	140
Share of subsidiary's (**Sussy**) post-acquisition profits (80% of ₦60 million)	48
	188

✓ **Step 6:** Combine the assets and liabilities of the parent (**Pally**) and subsidiary (**Sussy**) on an item-by-item basis excluding the initial investment of **Pally** in **Sussy** as earlier shown in the separate financial statements of **Pally**, and also the exclusion of the equity share capital of **Sussy**, as it has already been considered alongside with the pre-acquisition retained earnings in ascertaining the amount of goodwill or gain from bargain purchase inherent/embedded in the acquisition.

✓ **Step 7:** In order to cancel out the current account balances as maintained by the parent and subsidiary, we first ensure we reconcile the difference of ₦2 million (resulting from ₦10 million recognised as an asset by the parent and ₦8 million recognised as a liability by the subsidiary). We could assume cash-in-transit as the cause of the difference, but in an examination, it will expressly be stated the cause of the imbalance (either directly or indirectly) as at the reporting date.

Adjustments in Group Accounts

Accounting entries for recognition of Cash-in-Transit:
Debit: Group cash/bank
Credit: Current account (either of the parent or subsidiary) ⎤ ₦2 million

In order to *cancel-out* the intra-group current accounts, we reconciled the *current accounts (intercompany balances)* of the parent and the subsidiary, as thus:

Reconciled Intercompany Balances (current Accounts):

	Pally ₦' million	Sussy ₦' million
Balance as per accounts	10	8
Less: cash in-transit	(2)	–
Accounts reconciled	**8**	**8**

The balance ₦8 million can now be *cancelled-out*.

Accounting entries for cancellation of agreed intercompany balances:
Debit: Current account (payable) of Sussy
Credit: Current account (receivable) of Pally
With the amount of intercompany balance of ₦8 million

The consolidated statement of financial position of the group will now be shown (which will no longer fixture the current accounts as they have totally cancelled-out), as thus:

Pally Group
Consolidated Statement of Financial Position as at 31 December 2015

Assets:	₦' million	₦' million
Non-current assets		
Property, plant and equipment (110 + 120)		230
Goodwill		20
Current assets:		
Inventories (30 + 45)	75	
Trade receivables (15 + 12)	27	
~~Current account (8 – 8)~~	~~0~~	
Bank (5 + 7 + 2)	14	116
Total Assets		**366**
Share Capital & Reserves:		
Equity share capital		80
Reserves		188
Equity attributable to Pally's shareholders		**268**
Non-controlling interest		32
Total Equity		**300**
Current liabilities:		
Trade payables (50 + 14)	66	
~~Current account (10 – 2 – 8)~~	~~0~~	66
Total Equity and Liabilities		**366**

Contemporaneous Accounting for Business Combinations and Group Accounts

The consolidation schedule can equally be adopted for solving this group problem as scheduled below:

Consolidation Schedule

Subsidiary - Sussy		Cost of control (Pally in Sussy) as at Acquisition – 80%		Non-controlling Interests – 20%		Consolidated Reserves	
Equity Share Capital	100	(80% x 100)	80	(20% x 100)	20		
Reserves (Pre-acquisition)	Nil	(80% x Nil)	-	(20% x Nil)	-		
Reserves (Post-acquisition)	60		_-_	(20% x 60)	12	(80% x 60)	48
Net asset on acquisition			80				
Cost of combination (cost of investment)			(100)				
Goodwill (positive)			(20)				
Non-controlling interests					**32**		
Pally Reserves							140
Consolidated Reserves							**188**

We can equally explore the situation where the current accounts of the parent and subsidiary do not agree (but attributed to "Goods In-transit" as at the reporting date), as illustrated below:

ILLUSTRATION 9:

Pally Plc acquired 160 million of the shares of Sussy plc since the incorporation of that company. The statements of financial position of the dual companies as at 31 December 2015 were as follows:

Statement of Financial Position as at 31 December 2015

	Pally Plc ₦' million	Sussy Plc ₦' million
Non-Current Assets:		
Property, plant and equipment	110	120
Investment in *Sussy Plc*	100	
Current Assets:		
Inventories	30	45
Trade receivables	15	12
Current account – Sussy	10	
Bank	_5_	_7_
Total Assets	**270**	**184**
Equities and Liabilities:		
Equity – Ordinary shares (₦0.50/share)	80	100
Retained earnings	140	60
Current liabilities:		
Trade payables	50	16
Current account – Pally	___	_8_
Total equity and liabilities	**270**	**184**

Adjustments in Group Accounts

We are to approach the solution in the following steps:

- ✓ **Step 1**: Determine the percentage holdings of investment of **Pally** in **Sussy** as at the acquisition date (some time ago), which represents the date of inclusion (first date of consolidation). In this case, the percentage holding is determined and ascertained to be 80%.

  The 80% interest of Pally is ascertained by expressing 160 million shares as a proportion of 200 million shares of Sussy in issue as at acquisition (this is obtained by dividing the share capital of ₦100 million by ₦0.50 nominal price per share).

- ✓ **Step 2**: Ascertain the form of group structure in this parent-subsidiary relationship. Since the subsidiary (**Sussy**) is *partly-owned* by the parent (**Pally**), the group structure is a simple structure as shown below:

  ```
              Pally
                \
             80% \
                  \         20%
                   Sussy ←——— Non-controlling interest
  ```

- ✓ **Step 3**: Determine the existence of goodwill or gain from a bargain purchase as at the date of acquisition based on the fair value of subsidiary's identifiable assets and liabilities. In this case, there exists goodwill as shown below.

  To ascertain and determine the amount of goodwill or gain from a bargain purchase, the value of an investment of the parent (**Pally**) in the subsidiary (**Sussy**) will be compared with the parent's share of identifiable assets and liabilities of the subsidiary that were acquired.

PARTIAL METHODOLOGY	₦' million	₦' million
Cost of combination (i.e. the cost of investment of **Pally** in **Sussy**)		100
Less: **Pally**'s share of Identifiable net assets of **Sussy** acquired:		
• Share capital (80% of ₦100 million)	80	
• Pre-acquisition reserves (80% of Nil*)	–	(80)
Goodwill attributable to **Pally's** (a)		20
Amount of investments of non-controlling interest in **Sussy**		20
Less: Non-controlling interest share of the fair value of subsidiary's net assets:		
• Share capital (20% of ₦100 million)	20	
• Pre-acquisition reserves (20% of Nil*)	–	(20)
Goodwill attributable to **non-controlling interests** ** (b)		–
Goodwill (a + b)		**20**

Technical Note:

* Since the subsidiary was acquired at incorporation (that an equity stake of 80%), there exist no pre-acquisition profits, as all profits as at the reporting date (31 December 2015) are all considered post-acquisition.

**The goodwill attributable to non-controlling must be zero since the investment to non-controlling interests is valued at the proportionate share of subsidiary's identifiable net assets as shown by the arrow.

Alternative, FULL METHODOLOGY	₦' million	₦' million
Cost of Business Combination		
Cost of acquisition to Pally		100
Amount of Investment in subsidiary to non-controlling interest*		20
Combined amount of interests in subsidiary to all investors		**120**
Less: Fair value of identifiable assets and liabilities at acquisition-date		
Share capital	100	
Pre-acquisition reserves	0	(100)
Goodwill - positive		**20**

✓ **Step 4:** Determine the amount of non-controlling interest as will be shown in the consolidated statement of financial position of the group. In this case, non-controlling interest will only be measured at proportionate share of subsidiary's identifiable assets and liabilities, which could be depicted as thus:

Non-controlling interest's share of Identifiable net assets of **Sussy**:	₦' million
• Share capital (20% of ₦100 million)	20
• Pre-acquisition reserves (20% of Nil)	-
NCI's investment on acquisition (*based on proportionate share of net assets*)	**20**
• Post-acquisition reserves (20% of ₦60 million)	12
NCI's investment on 31 December 2015	**32**

✓ **Step 5:** Determine the amount to be included in the consolidated statement of financial position as consolidated reserves (otherwise known as consolidated retained earnings). The consolidated retained earnings to be included in the consolidated statement of financial position of **Pally-Group** are that of the parent and of the post-acquisition profits of the subsidiary. Invariably, it implies that the post-acquisition retained earnings is ₦60 million (since there was no pre-acquisition profit, as the subsidiary was acquired at point of incorporation 80% equity interest in the subsidiary) will now be combined with the retained earnings (profits) of the parent (**Pally**) in ascertaining the group retained earnings. The consolidated retained earnings will be determined as follows:

	₦' million
Parent's (**Pally**) retained earnings	140
Share of subsidiary's (**Sussy**) post-acquisition profits (80% of ₦60 million)	48
	188

✓ **Step 6:** Combine the assets and liabilities of the parent (**Pally**) and subsidiary (**Sussy**) on an item-by-item basis excluding the initial investment of **Pally** in **Sussy** as earlier shown in the separate financial statements of **Pally**, and also the exclusion of the equity share capital of **Sussy**, as it has already been considered alongside with the pre-acquisition retained earnings in ascertaining the amount of goodwill or gain from bargain purchase inherent/embedded in the acquisition.

✓ **Step 7:** In order to cancel out the current account balances as maintained by the parent and subsidiary, we first ensure we reconcile the difference of ₦2 million (resulting from ₦10 million recognised as an asset by the parent and ₦8 million recognised as a liability by the subsidiary). We could assume goods-in-transit as the cause of the difference, but in an examination, it will expressly be stated the cause of the imbalance (either directly or indirectly).

Accounting entries for recognition of Goods-in-Transit:
Debit: Group inventory
Credit: Current account (either of the parent or subsidiary) ⎱ ₦2 million

In order to *cancel-out* the intra-group current accounts, we reconciled the *current accounts (intercompany balances)* of the parent and the subsidiary, as thus:

Reconciled Intercompany Balances (current Accounts):	Pally ₦' million	Sussy ₦' million
Balance as per accounts	10	8
Less: goods in-transit	(2)	–
Accounts reconciled	**8**	**8**

The balance ₦8 million can now be *cancelled-out*.

Accounting entries for cancellation of agreed intercompany balances:
Debit: Current account (payable) of Sussy
Credit Current account (receivable) of Pally
With the amount of intercompany balance of ₦8 million

The consolidated statement of financial position of the group will now be shown (which will no longer fixture the current accounts as they have totally cancelled-out), as thus:

Pally Group
Consolidated Statement of Financial Position as at 31 December 2015

Assets:	₦' million	₦' million
*Non-*current assets		
Property, plant and equipment (110 + 120)		230
Goodwill		20
Current assets:		
Inventories (30 + 45 +2)	77	
Trade receivables (15 + 12)	27	
~~Current account (8 – 8)~~	0	
Bank (5 + 7)	12	116
Total Assets		**366**
Share Capital & Reserves:		
Equity share capital		80
Reserves		188
Equity attributable to Pally's shareholders		**268**
Non-controlling interest		32
Total Equity		**300**
Current liabilities:		
Trade payables (50 + 14)	66	
~~Current account (10 – 2 – 8)~~	0	66
Total Equity and Liabilities		**366**

The consolidation schedule can equally be adopted for solving this group problem as scheduled below:

Consolidation Schedule

Subsidiary - Sussy		Cost of control (Pally in Sussy) as at Acquisition – 80%		Non-controlling Interests – 20%		Consolidated Reserves	
Equity Share Capital	100	(80% x 100)	80	(20% x 100)	20		
Reserves (Pre-acquisition)	Nil	(80% x Nil)	-	(20% x Nil)	-		
Reserves (Post-acquisition)	60		—	(20% x 60)	12	(80% x 60)	48
Net asset on acquisition			80				
Cost of combination (cost of investment)			(100)				
Goodwill (positive)			(20)				
Non-controlling interests					**32**		
Pally Reserves							140
Consolidated Reserves							**188**

Accrued Intra Group Service Charges and Income

Companies within the group sometimes render a different form of services to one another. These services may include (*but not limited to those identified below*):

- ❖ Shared and Management services
- ❖ Training and development of personnel
- ❖ Intra-group hire of assets

In the individual financial statements of the entities (parent company and the subsidiary), the expenses incurred and income earned on these intra-group transactions (as stated above) will have to be accrued for as appropriate, especially prior to invoicing. In the process of consolidation, the accrued intra-group expenses and income will have to be cancelled out as this will make the financial statements of the group more fairly presented and depicts the group's true financial position as at the reporting date.

ILLUSTRATION 10:

Pally Plc acquired 160 million of the shares of Sussy plc since the incorporation of that company. The statements of financial position of the dual companies as at 31 December 2015 were as follows:

Statement of Financial Position as at 31 December 2015

	Pally Plc	Sussy Plc
Non-Current Assets:	₦' million	₦' million
Property, plant and equipment	110	120
Investment in *Sussy Plc*	100	
Current Assets:		
Inventories	30	45
Trade receivables	21	12
Accrued Income (due from Sussy)	4	
Bank	5	7
Total Assets	**270**	**184**

Adjustments in Group Accounts

Equities and Liabilities:		
Equity – Ordinary shares (₦0.50/share)	80	100
Retained earnings	140	60
Current liabilities:		
Trade payables	50	20
Accrued expenses (due to Pally)	__	_4_
Total equity and liabilities	**270**	**184**

We are to approach the solution in the following steps:

- ✓ **Step 1**: *Determine the percentage holdings of investment of* **Pally** *in* **Sussy** *as at the acquisition date (some time ago), which represents the date of inclusion (first date of consolidation).* In this case, the percentage holding is determined and ascertained to be 80%.

    The 80% interest of Pally is ascertained by expressing 160 million shares as a proportion of 200 million shares of Sussy in issue as at acquisition (this is obtained by dividing the share capital of ₦100 million by ₦0.50 nominal price per share).

- ✓ **Step 2:** *Ascertain the form of group structure in this parent-subsidiary relationship.* Since the subsidiary (**Sussy**) is *partly-owned* by the parent (**Pally**), the group structure is a simple structure as shown below:

    Pally
        ↘ 80%
            20%
        Sussy ← **Non-controlling interest**

- ✓ **Step 3:** *Determine the existence of goodwill or gain from a bargain purchase as at the date of acquisition based on the fair value of subsidiary's identifiable assets and liabilities.* In this case, there exists goodwill as shown below.

    To ascertain and determine the amount of goodwill or gain from a bargain purchase, the value of an investment of the parent (**Pally**) in the subsidiary (**Sussy**) will be compared with the parent's share of identifiable assets and liabilities of the subsidiary that were acquired.

	₦' million	₦' million
PARTIAL METHODOLOGY		
Cost of combination (i.e. the cost of investment of **Pally** in **Sussy**)		100
Less: **Pally**'s share of Identifiable net assets of **Sussy** acquired:		
• Share capital (80% of ₦100 million)	80	
• Pre-acquisition reserves (80% of Nil*)	_-_	(80)
*Goodwill attributable to **Pally's** (a)*		_20_
Amount of investments of non-controlling interest in **Sussy**		20
Less: Non-controlling interest share of the fair value of subsidiary's net assets:		
• Share capital (20% of ₦100 million)	20	
• Pre-acquisition reserves (20% of Nil*)	_-_	(20)
*Goodwill attributable to **non-controlling interests**** (b)*		_--_
Goodwill (a + b)		**20**

Technical Note:
* Since the subsidiary was acquired at incorporation (that an equity stake of 80%), there exist no pre-acquisition profits, as all profits as at the reporting date (31 December 2015) are all considered post-acquisition.

**The goodwill attributable to non-controlling must be zero since the investment to non-controlling interests is valued at the proportionate share of subsidiary's identifiable net assets as shown by the arrow.

Alternative, FULL METHODOLOGY	₦' million	₦' million
Cost of Business Combination		
Cost of acquisition to Pally		100
Amount of Investment in subsidiary to non-controlling interest*		20
Combined amount of interests in subsidiary to all investors		**120**
Less: Fair value of identifiable assets and liabilities at acquisition-date		
Share capital	100	
Pre-acquisition reserves	0	(100)
Goodwill - positive		**20**

✓ **Step 4: Determine the amount of non-controlling interest as will be shown in the consolidated statement of financial position of the group.** In this case, non-controlling interest will only be measured at proportionate share of subsidiary's identifiable assets and liabilities, which could be depicted as thus:

Non-controlling interest's share of Identifiable net assets of **Sussy**:

	₦' million
• Share capital (20% of ₦100 million)	20
• Pre-acquisition reserves (20% of Nil)	-
NCI's investment on acquisition (*based on proportionate share of net assets*)	**20**
• Post-acquisition reserves (20% of ₦60 million)	12
NCI's investment on 31 December 2015	**32**

✓ **Step 5: Determine the amount to be included in the consolidated statement of financial position as consolidated reserves (otherwise known as consolidated retained earnings).** The consolidated retained earnings to be included in the consolidated statement of financial position of **Pally-Group** are that of the parent and of the post-acquisition profits of the subsidiary. Invariably, it implies that the post-acquisition retained earnings is ₦60 million (since there was no pre-acquisition profit, as the subsidiary was acquired at point of incorporation 80% equity interest in the subsidiary) will now be combined with the retained earnings (profits) of the parent (**Pally**) in ascertaining the group retained earnings. The consolidated retained earnings will be determined as follows:

	₦' million
Parent's (**Pally**) retained earnings	140
Share of subsidiary's (**Sussy**) post-acquisition profits (80% of ₦60 million)	48
	188

✓ **Step 6:** Combine the assets and liabilities of the parent (**Pally**) and subsidiary (**Sussy**) on an item-by-item basis excluding the initial investment of **Pally** in **Sussy** as earlier shown in the separate financial statements of **Pally**, and also the exclusion of the equity share capital of **Sussy**, as it has

Adjustments in Group Accounts

already been considered alongside with the pre-acquisition retained earnings in ascertaining the amount of goodwill or gain from bargain purchase inherent/embedded in the acquisition.

✓ **Step 7:** In order to cancel out the intra-group current accounts, we first ensure that the *accrued expenses and income (intercompany balances)* of the parent and the subsidiary *agree*, and the balances will then be *cancelled-out*.

Accounting entries for cancellation of agreed intercompany balances:

Debit: *Accrued expenses by Sussy*
Credit   *Accrued income by Pally*
With the amount of intercompany balance of ₦4 million

The consolidated statement of financial position of the group will now be shown (*which will no longer fixture the inter-company accruals as they have totally cancelled out*), as thus:

Pally Group
Consolidated Statement of Financial Position as at 31 December 2015

Assets:	₦' million	₦' million
Non-current assets		
Property, plant and equipment (110 + 120)		230
Goodwill		20
Current assets:		
Inventories (30 + 45)	75	
Trade receivables (21 + 12)	33	
~~Accrued income (10 – 2 – 8)~~	0	
Bank (5 + 7)	12	120
Total Assets		**370**
Share Capital & Reserves:		
Equity share capital		80
Reserves		188
Equity attributable to Pally's shareholders		268
Non-controlling interest		32
Total Equity		300
Current liabilities:		
Trade payables (50 + 20)	70	
~~Accrued expenses (10 – 2 – 8)~~	0	70
Total Equity and Liabilities		**370**

The consolidation schedule can equally be adopted for solving this group problem as scheduled below:

Consolidation Schedule

Subsidiary - Sussy		Cost of control (Pally in Sussy) as at Acquisition – 80%		Non-controlling Interests – 20%		Consolidated Reserves	
Equity Share Capital	100	(80% x 100)	80	(20% x 100)	20		
Reserves (Pre-acquisition)	Nil	(80% x Nil)	-	(20% x Nil)	-		
Reserves (Post-acquisition)	60	-		(20% x 60)	12	(80% x 60)	48

Net asset on acquisition	80	
Cost of combination (cost of investment)	(100)	
Goodwill (positive)	**(20)**	
Non-controlling interests	**32**	
Pally Reserves		140
Consolidated Reserves		**188**

Bills of Exchange

There are instances where *bills* are exchanged as a means of acknowledging indebtedness and demonstration of willingness and ability of the indebted party within the group to pay the other in an *arms' length* manner. On one side is *Bills Receivable* and on the other side is the *Bills Payable*. These transactions sometimes involve two or more companies within the group.

There are two possible scenarios applicable or possible when bills of exchange surface in the statement of financial position of the parent and the subsidiary, which include:

a) Where there are no intra-group Bills: The Bills to be shown in the statement of financial position is that of the group (either by the parent or the subsidiary, or both).

b) Where there is an element of intra-group Bills: The Bills to be shown in the statement of financial position is that of the parent and the subsidiary less any intra-group bills.

ILLUSTRATION 11:

Pally Plc acquired 160 million of the shares of Sussy plc since the incorporation of that company. The statements of financial position of the dual companies as at 31 December 2015 were as follows:

Statement of Financial Position as at 31 December 2015

	Pally Plc	Sussy Plc
Non-Current Assets:	₦' million	₦' million
Property, plant and equipment	110	120
Investment in *Sussy Plc*	100	
Current Assets:		
Inventories	30	45
Accounts receivables	19	12
Bills receivable (₦2 million due from Sussy)	6	
Bank	5	7
Total Assets	**270**	**184**
Equities and Liabilities:		
Equity – Ordinary shares (₦0.50/share)	80	100
Retained earnings	140	60
Current liabilities:		
Accounts payables	50	19
Bills payable (₦2 million due to Pally)	—	5
Total equity and liabilities	**270**	**184**

We are to approach the solution in the following steps:

- ✓ **Step 1**: *Determine the percentage holdings of investment of **Pally** in **Sussy** as at the acquisition date (some time ago), which represents the date of inclusion (first date of consolidation).* In this case, the percentage holding is determined and ascertained to be 80%.

    The 80% interest of Pally is ascertained by expressing 160 million shares as a proportion of 200 million shares of Sussy in issue as at acquisition (this is obtained by dividing the share capital of ₦100 million by ₦0.50 nominal price per share).

- ✓ **Step 2**: *Ascertain the form of group structure in this parent-subsidiary relationship.* Since the subsidiary (**Sussy**) is *partly-owned* by the parent (**Pally**), the group structure is a simple structure as shown below:

    Pally

    80% 20%

    Sussy ← Non-controlling interest

- ✓ **Step 3**: *Determine the existence of goodwill or gain from a bargain purchase as at the date of acquisition based on the fair value of subsidiary's identifiable assets and liabilities.* In this case, there exists goodwill as shown below.

    To ascertain and determine the amount of goodwill or gain from a bargain purchase, the value of an investment of the parent (**Pally**) in the subsidiary (**Sussy**) will be compared with the parent's share of identifiable assets and liabilities of the subsidiary that were acquired.

PARTIAL METHODOLOGY	₦' million	₦' million
Cost of combination (i.e. the cost of investment of **Pally** in **Sussy**)		100
Less: **Pally**'s share of Identifiable net assets of **Sussy** acquired:		
• Share capital (80% of ₦100 million)	80	
• Pre-acquisition reserves (80% of Nil*)	–	(80)
Goodwill attributable to **Pally's** (a)		20
Amount of investments of non-controlling interest in **Sussy**		20
Less: Non-controlling interest share of the fair value of subsidiary's net assets:		
• Share capital (20% of ₦100 million)	20	
• Pre-acquisition reserves (20% of Nil*)	–	(20)
Goodwill attributable to **non-controlling interests**** (b)		--
Goodwill (a + b)		**20**

Technical Note:

* Since the subsidiary was acquired at incorporation (that an equity stake of 80%), there exist no pre-acquisition profits, as all profits as at the reporting date (31 December 2015) are all considered post-acquisition.

**The goodwill attributable to non-controlling must be zero since the investment to non-controlling interests is valued at the proportionate share of subsidiary's identifiable net assets as shown by the arrow.

Alternative, FULL METHODOLOGY	₦' million	₦' million
Cost of Business Combination		
Cost of acquisition to Pally		100
Amount of Investment in subsidiary to non-controlling interest*		20
Combined amount of interests in subsidiary to all investors		**120**
Less: Fair value of identifiable assets and liabilities at acquisition-date		
Share capital	100	
Pre-acquisition reserves	0	(100)
Goodwill - positive		**20**

✓ **Step 4:** *Determine the amount of non-controlling interest as will be shown in the consolidated statement of financial position of the group.* In this case, non-controlling interest will only be measured at the proportionate share of subsidiary's identifiable assets and liabilities, which could be depicted as thus:

Non-controlling interest's share of Identifiable net assets of **Sussy**:	₦' million
• Share capital (20% of ₦100 million)	20
• Pre-acquisition reserves (20% of Nil)	-
NCI's investment on acquisition (*based on proportionate share of net assets*)	**20**
• Post-acquisition reserves (20% of ₦60 million)	12
NCI's investment on 31 December 2015	**32**

✓ **Step 5:** *Determine the amount to be included in the consolidated statement of financial position as consolidated reserves (otherwise known as consolidated retained earnings).* The consolidated retained earnings to be included in the consolidated statement of financial position of **Pally-Group** are that of the parent and of the post-acquisition profits of the subsidiary. Invariably, it implies that the post-acquisition retained earnings is ₦60 million (since there was no pre-acquisition profit, as the subsidiary was acquired at point of incorporation 80% equity interest in the subsidiary) will now be combined with the retained earnings (profits) of the parent (**Pally**) in ascertaining the group retained earnings. The consolidated retained earnings will be determined as follows:

	₦' million
Parent's (**Pally**) retained earnings	140
Share of subsidiary's (**Sussy**) post-acquisition profits (80% of ₦60 million)	48
	188

✓ **Step 6:** *Combine the assets and liabilities of the parent (**Pally**) and subsidiary (**Sussy**) on an item-by-item basis excluding the initial investment of **Pally** in **Sussy** as earlier shown in the separate financial statements of **Pally**, and also the exclusion of the equity share capital of **Sussy**, as it has already been considered alongside with the pre-acquisition retained earnings in ascertaining the amount of goodwill or gain from bargain purchase inherent/embedded in the acquisition.*

✓ **Step 7:** In order to *cancel out* the Intra-group bills as maintained by the parent and subsidiary, we first ensure that the Intra-group bills of ₦2 million (receivable by the parent and payable by the subsidiary) agree, and the balances will then be cancelled out, while the bills due to or from third parties to the members of the group are those to be recognised in the statement of financial position of the group.

Adjustments in Group Accounts

Accounting entries for cancellation of agreed intercompany balances:
Debit: Bills payable by Sussy
Credit: Bills receivable by Pally — *With the amount of intercompany balance of ₦2 million*

The consolidated statement of financial position of the group will now be shown (which will no longer fixture the intra-group bills as they have totally cancelled out):

Pally Group
Consolidated Statement of Financial Position as at 31 December 2015

Assets:	₦' million	₦' million
Non-current assets		
Property, plant and equipment (110 + 120)		230
Goodwill on consolidation		20
Current assets:		
Inventories (30 + 45)	75.0	
Accounts receivables (19 + 12)	31.0	
Bills receivable (6 – 2*)	4.0	
Bank (5 + 7)	12.0	122
Total Assets		**372**
Share Capital & Reserves:		
Equity share capital		80
Reserves		188
Equity attributable to Pally's shareholders		**268**
Non-controlling interest		32
Total Equity		**300**
Current liabilities:		
Accounts payables (50 + 19)		69
Bills payable (5 – 2*)		3
Total Equity and Liabilities		**372**

The consolidation schedule can equally be adopted for solving this group problem as scheduled below:

Consolidation Schedule

Subsidiary - Sussy		Cost of control (Pally in Sussy) as at Acquisition – 80%		Non-controlling Interests – 20%		Consolidated Reserves	
Equity Share Capital	100	(80% x 100)	80	(20% x 100)	20		
Reserves (Pre-acquisition)	Nil	(80% x Nil)	-	(20% x Nil)	-		
Reserves (Post-acquisition)	60		-	(20% x 60)	12	(80% x 60)	48
Net asset on acquisition			80				
Cost of combination (cost of investment)			(100)				
Goodwill (positive)			**(20)**				
Non-controlling interests					**32**		
Pally Reserves							140
Consolidated Reserves							**188**

Bills of Exchange Discounted

As the bill of exchange is a negotiable instrument, it could be discounted. A Bill receivable by a company can be discounted as a negotiable instrument in order to raise immediate cash for liquidity purposes. Discounting of a bill involves the holder of a bill (bills receivable) who is the creditor could approach a discount house or a financial institution prior to its maturity for immediate access to funds or cash. The discount house then takes ownership of the bills which will be presented as the bearer at the due date to the debtor. Discounting of a bill implies that the original creditor (the writer of the bill) obtains an amount lower than the face value of the bill, while the balance represents the *discount* retained by the finance house as commission or interest on the discounting of the bill. An intercompany bill receivable by a company within the group can be discounted with a third party financial institution in order to raise short-term cash and/or liquidity. Hence, the portion of the bill(s) discounted will no longer constitute intercompany balance, rather it is a portion of the intercompany bill(s) now payable to a third party (in this case, it becomes a liability of the group).

ILLUSTRATION 12:

Barcelona Plc acquired 75% of the shares of Chelsea plc on 31 December 2013, when the profit of the latter stood at ₦40 million. The statements of financial position of the dual companies as at 31 December 2015 were as follows:

Statement of Financial Position as at 31 December 2015

	Barcelona ₦' million	Chelsea ₦' million
Non-Current Assets:		
Property, plant and equipment	130	120
Investment in *Chelsea Plc*	110	
Current assets:		
Inventories	45	25
Accounts receivables	15	28
Bills receivable (₦2 million is due from Chelsea)	7	
Cash/Bank	13	17
Total Assets	**320**	**190**
Equities and Liabilities:		
Equity – Ordinary Shares (₦0.50/share)	150	100
Retained earnings	130	60
Current liabilities:		
Accounts payables (including ₦5 million to Barcelona)	20	14
Bills payable (₦3 million is due to Barcelona)		10
Bank overdraft	20	6
Total equity and liabilities	**320**	**190**

Additional information:
Barcelona during the reporting period discounted ₦1 million *tranche* of the bill receivable from Chelsea, which makes the balance of ₦2 million bills receivable from Chelsea as at the reporting date.

We are to approach the solution in the following steps:

- ✓ **Step 1**: Determine the percentage holdings of investment of **Barcelona** in **Chelsea** as at the acquisition date (31 December 2013), which represents the date of inclusion (first date of consolidation). In this case, the percentage holding is already determined and ascertained to be 75%.

- ✓ **Step 2**: Ascertain the form of group structure in this parent-subsidiary relationship. Since the subsidiary (**Chelsea**) is *partly-owned* by the parent (**Barcelona**), the group structure is a simple structure as shown below:

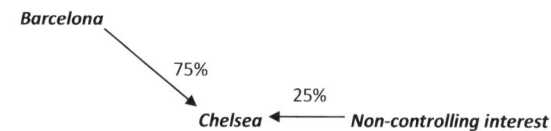

```
                Barcelona
              ↙ 75%
                      25%
          Chelsea ←――― Non-controlling interest
```

- ✓ **Step 3**: Determine the existence of goodwill or gain from a bargain purchase as at the date of acquisition based on the fair value or provisional values of subsidiary's identifiable assets and liabilities. In this case, there exists goodwill as shown below.

To ascertain and determine the amount of goodwill or gain from a bargain purchase, the value of an investment of the parent (**Barcelona**) in the subsidiary (**Chelsea**) will be compared with the parent's share of identifiable assets and liabilities of the subsidiary that were acquired.

PARTIAL METHODOLOGY	₦' million	₦' million
Cost of combination (i.e. the cost of investment of **Barcelona** in **Chelsea**)		110
Less: **Barcelona**'s share of Identifiable net assets of **Chelsea** acquired:		
• Share capital (75% of ₦100 million)	75	
• Pre-acquisition reserves (75% of ₦40 million)	30	(105)
*Goodwill attributable to **Barcelona's** (a)*		5
Amount of investments of non-controlling interest in **Chelsea**		35
Less: Non-controlling interest share of the fair value of subsidiary's net assets:		
• Share capital (25% of ₦100 million)	25	
• Pre-acquisition reserves (25% of ₦40 million)	10	(35)
*Goodwill attributable to **non-controlling interests*** (b)		--
Goodwill (a + b)		5

Technical Note:
The goodwill attributable to non-controlling must be zero since the investment to non-controlling interests is valued at the proportionate share of subsidiary's identifiable net assets as shown by the arrow.

Alternative, FULL METHODOLOGY		₦' million
Cost of Business Combination		
Cost of combination (i.e. cost of acquisition) to the Barcelona		110
Amount of Investment in subsidiary to non-controlling interest*		35
Combined amount of interests in subsidiary to all investors		**145**
Less: Fair value of Identifiable net assets acquired @ 31 December 2013		
• Share capital	100	
• Pre-acquisition reserves	40	(140)
Goodwill - positive		**5**

✓ **Step 4:** *Determine the amount of non-controlling interest as will be shown in the consolidated statement of financial position of the group.* In this case, non-controlling interest will only be measured at proportionate share of subsidiary's identifiable assets and liabilities, which could be depicted as thus:

Non-controlling interest's share of Identifiable net assets of **Chelsea**:

	₦' million
• Share capital (25% of ₦100 million)	25
• Pre-acquisition reserves (25% of ₦40 million)	10
NCI's investment on 31 December 2013 (*based on proportionate share of net assets*)	**35**
• Post-acquisition reserves (25% of ₦20 million)	5
NCI's investment on 31 December 2015	**40**

✓ **Step 5:** *Determine the amount to be included in the consolidated statement of financial position as consolidated reserves (otherwise known as consolidated retained earnings).* The consolidated retained earnings to be included in the consolidated statement of financial position of **Barcelona-Group** are that of the parent and of the post-acquisition profits of the subsidiary. Invariably, it implies that the post-acquisition retained earnings (which is the sum of ₦20 million being the increase from ₦40 million profits upon acquisition to ₦60 million the reporting date 31 December 2013 - *2 years after*) of the subsidiary (**Chelsea**) will now be combined with the retained earnings (profits) of the parent (**Barcelona**) in ascertaining the group retained earnings. The consolidated retained earnings will be determined as follows:

	₦' million
Parent's (**Barcelona**) retained earnings	130
Share of subsidiary's (**Chelsea**) post-acquisition profits (75% of ₦20 million)	15
	145

✓ **Step 6:** Combine the assets and liabilities of the parent (**Barcelona**) and subsidiary (**Chelsea**) on an item-by-item basis excluding the initial investment of **Barcelona** in **Chelsea** as earlier shown in the separate financial statements of **Barcelona**, and also the exclusion of the equity share capital of **Chelsea**, as it has already been considered alongside with the pre-acquisition retained earnings in ascertaining the amount of goodwill or gain from bargain purchase inherent/embedded in the acquisition.

✓ **Step 7:** In order to *cancel out* the Intra-group bills as maintained by the parent and subsidiary, we first ensure that the Intra-group bills of ₦2 million (receivable by the parent) are canceled out against the ₦3 million initially payable to the parent, and the difference or balance of ₦1 million is now owed and payable by the subsidiary to 3rd party (i.e. the discount or finance house), and invariably this constitute a liability to the group.

Accounting entries for cancellation of agreed intercompany balances (Bills):

Debit: Bills payable by Chelsea
Credit: Bills receivable by Barcelona
With the amount of intercompany balance of ₦2 million

Accounting entries for cancellation of agreed intercompany balances (receivable and payable):

Debit: Accounts payable by Chelsea
Credit: Accounts receivable by Barcelona
With the amount of intercompany balance of ₦5 million

The consolidated statement of financial position of the group will now be shown (which will no longer fixture the intra-group bills to the extent that is not discounted):

Barcelona Group
Consolidated Statement of Financial Position as at 31 December 2015

Assets:	₦' million	₦' million
Non-current assets		
Property, plant and equipment (130 + 120)		250
Goodwill		5
Current assets:		
Inventories (45 + 25)	70	
Accounts receivables (15 + 28 – 5*)	38	
Bills receivable (7 – 2*)	5	
Bank (13 + 17)	30	143
Total Assets		**398**
Share Capital & Reserves:		
Equity share capital		150
Reserves		145
Equity attributable to Barcelona's shareholders		295
Non-controlling interest		40
Total Equity		335
Current liabilities:		
Accounts payables (20 + 14 – 5*)	29	
Bills payable (10 – 2*)	8	
Bank overdraft (20 + 6)	26	63
Total Equity and Liabilities		**398**

The consolidation schedule can equally be adopted for solving this group problem as scheduled below:

Consolidation Schedule

Subsidiary - Chelsea		Cost of control (Barcelona in Chelsea) as at 31 Dec. 2013 – 75%		Non-controlling Interests – 25%		Consolidated Reserves	
Equity Share Capital	100	(75% x 100)	75	(25% x 100)	20		
Reserves (Pre-acquisition)	40	(75% x 40)	30	(25% x 40)	10		
Reserves (Post-acquisition)	20	-		(25% x 20)	5	(75% x 20)	15
Net asset on acquisition			105				
Cost of combination (cost of investment)			(110)				
Goodwill (positive)			(5)				
Non-controlling interests					40		
Barcelona Reserves							130
Consolidated Reserves							**145**

Intra Group Loans

There are situations where the parent extends borrowings to its subsidiary in order to boost further the operations, performance and position of the subsidiary. If the parent invests in the borrowings of the subsidiary, then effectively the parent has lent cash to the subsidiary. The parent's investment in the borrowings of the subsidiary is effectively a financial asset to the parent, and this should be *cancelled out* on consolidation against the relevant borrowings (financial liabilities) in the subsidiary's books. Loan or Debt instruments within the group should be cancelled out upon consolidation. Any accrued interests (accrued interest income by the parent and accrued interest expense by the subsidiary) should equally be aggregated with the principal portion (*either at amortised cost or fair value*) and thereafter cancelled-out upon consolidation.

However, the amount of bonds/loans not held by the parent will not be part of the non-controlling interest as they do not bestow any rights of ownership by the shareholders. They are effectively considered a form of a long-term loan (a financial liability) and will be shown as such in the consolidated statement of financial position.

Furthermore, in a situation where the preference shares are recognised as a liability of the subsidiary under *IAS 32 (Financial Instruments: Presentation)*, they should be accounted for in the same way as loan notes (*which includes debt and/or bonds*). Invariably upon consolidation, the preference shares acquired or purchased by the parent and included in the cost of investment (i.e. investment in the subsidiary as contained in the separate statement of financial position of the parent company) should be cancelled-out against the preference share capital in the subsidiary), while the portion that is not held by the parent will be treated as a liability to the group (*and not as a component of non-controlling interest*). This is because; non-controlling interest is a component of equity, whereas a preference share (usually redeemable and/or cumulative preference shares) may have been classified in accordance with *IAS 32* as a *Financial Liability*.

ILLUSTRATION 13:

Arsenal acquired 70% of the ordinary shares of **Manchester United** on 31 December 2013 when the balance in the latter retained earnings stood at ₦40 million at a consideration of ₦220 million and also invested the sum of ₦100 million in the 10% loan notes of the subsidiary.

Statement of Financial Position as at 31st December 2015

	Arsenal ₦' million	Man United ₦' million
Property, plant and equipment	560	260
Investment in **Manchester United**	320	
Current assets	260	280
	1,140	**540**
Share Capital & Reserves:		
Equity share capital	600	250
8% Preferred share capital	100	
Reserves (Retained Earnings)	290	50
	990	300
Non-current liabilities (Debentures)	-	120
Current liabilities	150	220
	1,140	**540**

Adjustments in Group Accounts

In approaching the solution to this illustration, we assumed that the amount of investment in subsidiary's loan notes recognised in the separate financial statements of the parent equals the parent's loan note outstanding with the subsidiary as shown in the subsidiary's statement of financial position, and equally that the parent at point of acquisition (when control was obtained), valued investments of the non-controlling interest at the proportionate share of the subsidiary's identifiable net assets (assets and liabilities). In this case, the consolidation process will be as follows:

- ✓ **Step 1**: *Determine the percentage holdings of investment of **Arsenal** in **Manchester United** as at the acquisition date (31 December 2013), which represents the date of inclusion (first date of consolidation).* In this case, the percentage holding is already determined and ascertained to be 70%.

- ✓ **Step 2:** *Ascertain the form of group structure in this parent-subsidiary relationship.* Since the subsidiary (**Manchester United**) is *partly-owned* by the parent (**Arsenal**), the group structure is a simple structure as shown below:

    Arsenal

    70%

    Manchester United ◄──── 30% **Non-controlling interest**

- ✓ **Step 3(a):** *Determine the existence of goodwill or gain from a bargain purchase as the date of acquisition based on the fair value or provisional values of subsidiary's identifiable assets and liabilities.* In this case, there exists goodwill as shown below.

To ascertain and determine the amount of goodwill to the group as it will be shown in the consolidated statement of financial position, the fair value of investment of the parent (**Arsenal**) in the subsidiary (**Manchester United**) and that of the Non-controlling interest will be compared with the fair value of the identifiable assets and liabilities of the subsidiary as at acquisition.

FULL METHODOLOGY	₦' million	₦' million
Cost of Business Combination		
Arsenal investment in Sussy		220
Non-controlling interest stake in Sussy (Step 3b		_87_
Combined amount of interests in subsidiary to all investors		**307**
Less: Fair value of Identifiable net assets acquired @ 31 December 2013		
• Ordinary share capital of Sussy	250	
• Pre-acquisition reserves	_40_	(290)
Goodwill - positive		**_17_**

Technical Note:
*The goodwill attributable to non-controlling must be zero since the investment to non-controlling interests is valued at the proportionate share of subsidiary's identifiable net assets as shown by the arrow.

- **Step 3(b): Alternative, PARTIAL METHODOLOGY**

		₦' million	₦' million
Cost of combination (i.e. the cost of investment of **Arsenal** in **Manchester United**)			220
Less: **Arsenal's** share of Identifiable net assets of **Manchester United** acquired:			
• Share capital (70% of ₦250 million)		175	
• Pre-acquisition reserves (70% of ₦40 million)		28	(203)
Goodwill attributable to **Arsenal's** (a)			**17**
Amount of investments of non-controlling interest in **Manchester United**			87
Less: Non-controlling interest share of the fair value of subsidiary's net assets:			
• Share capital (30% of ₦250 million)		75	
• Pre-acquisition reserves (30% of ₦40 million)		12	(87)
Goodwill attributable to **non-controlling interests** (b)			---
Goodwill (a + b)			**17**

- **Step 4:** Determine the amount of non-controlling interest as will be shown in the consolidated statement of financial position of the group. In this case, non-controlling interest will only be measured at proportionate share of subsidiary's identifiable assets and liabilities, which could be depicted as thus:

Non-controlling interest's share of Identifiable net assets of **Manchester**:

	₦' million
• Share capital (30% of ₦250 million)	75
• Pre-acquisition reserves (30% of ₦40 million)	12
NCI's investment on 31 December 2013 (based on proportionate share of net assets)	**87**
• Post-acquisition reserves (30% of ₦10 million)	3
NCI's investment on 31 December 2015	**90**

- **Step 5:** Determine the amount to be included in the consolidated statement of financial position as consolidated reserves (otherwise known as consolidated retained earnings). The consolidated retained earnings to be included in the consolidated statement of financial position of **Arsenal-Group** is that of the parent, as there are post-acquisition profits of ₦10 million in the subsidiary as at acquisition. There will be post-acquisition profits (being the increase in retained earnings from ₦40 million to ₦50 million after 2 years) in the subsidiary. The consolidated retained earnings will be determined as follows:

	₦' million
Parent's (**Arsenal**) retained earnings	290
Share of subsidiary's (**Manchester United**) post-acquisition reserves (70% of ₦10 million)	7
	297

- **Step 6:** Combine the assets and liabilities of the parent (**Arsenal**) and subsidiary (**Manchester United**) on an item-by-item basis excluding the initial investment of **Arsenal** in **Manchester United** as earlier shown in the separate financial statements of **Arsenal**, and also the exclusion of the equity and preference share capital of **Manchester United**, as it has already been considered alongside with the pre-acquisition retained earnings in ascertaining the amount of goodwill or gain from bargain purchase inherent/embedded in the acquisition.

- **Step 7:** In order to *cancel out* the Intra-group loans as maintained by the parent and subsidiary, we first ensure that the Intra-group loans of ₦100 million (receivable by the parent and payable by the subsidiary) agree, and the balances will then be cancelled out, while the loans due to

Adjustments in Group Accounts

third parties to the group are those to be recognised in the statement of financial position of the group.

Accounting entries for cancellation of agreed intercompany balances:
Debit: Loans (as a liability) by Manchester United
Credit: Loans (as an asset) by Arsenal
With the amount of intercompany balance of ₦100 million

The consolidated statement of financial position of the group will now be shown:

Arsenal Group
Consolidated Statement of Financial Position as at 31 December 2015

Assets:	₦' million
Non-current assets	
Property, plant and equipment (560 + 260)	820
~~Investment in Manchester United (320 – 220 – 100)~~	~~0~~
Goodwill	17
Current assets (260 + 280)	540
Total Assets	**1,377**
Share Capital & Reserves:	
Equity share capital	600
8% Preferred share capital (parent only)	100
Reserves	297
Equity attributable to Arsenal's shareholders	**997**
Non-controlling interest	90
Total Equity	**1,087**
Non-current liabilities:	
Debentures (120-100)	20*
Current liabilities (150 + 120)	270
Total Equity and Liabilities	**1,377**

Technical Note:
*The amount of loan notes of ₦20 million represents those owned by outsiders (i.e. loan notes not attributable to the parent's interest or investment in the subsidiary).

The consolidation schedule can equally be adopted for solving this group problem as scheduled below:

Consolidation Schedule

Subsidiary - Manchester United		Cost of control (Arsenal in Manchester United) as at 31 Dec. 2013 – 70%	Non-controlling Interests – 30%	Consolidated Reserves
Equity Share Capital	250	(70% x 250) 175	(30% x 250) 75	
Reserves (Pre-acquisition)	40	(70% x 40) 28	(30% x 40) 12	
(Post-acquisition)	10		(30% x 10) 3	(70% x 10) 7
Net asset on acquisition		203		
Cost of combination		(220)		

258

Goodwill (positive)	(17)	
Non-controlling interests		90
Arsenal Reserves		290
Consolidated Reserves		**297**

ILLUSTRATION 14:

Arsenal acquired 70% of the ordinary shares of **Manchester United** on 31 December 2013 when the balance in the latter retained earnings stood at ₦40 million at a consideration of ₦220 million and also invested the sum of ₦60 million and ₦100 million in the 8% preferred stock and loan notes respectively in the subsidiary.

Statement of Financial Position as at 31st December 2015

	Arsenal	Man United
	₦' million	₦' million
Property, plant and equipment	500	360
Investment in **Manchester United**	380	
Current assets	260	280
	1,140	640
Share Capital & Reserves:		
Equity share capital	600	250
8% Preferred share capital	100	100
Reserves (Retained Earnings)	290	50
	990	400
Non-current liabilities (Debentures)	-	120
Current liabilities	150	120
	1,140	540

In approaching the solution to this illustration, we assumed that the amount of investment in subsidiary's loan notes recognised in the separate financial statements of the parent equals the parent's loan note outstanding with the subsidiary as shown in the subsidiary's statement of financial position, and equally that the parent at point of acquisition (when control was obtained), valued investments of the non-controlling interest at the proportionate share of the subsidiary's identifiable net assets (assets and liabilities). In this case, the consolidation process will be as follows:

- ✓ **Step 1**: Determine the percentage holdings of investment of **Arsenal** in **Manchester United** as at the acquisition date (31 December 2013), which represents the date of inclusion (first date of consolidation). In this case, the percentage holding is already determined and ascertained to be 70%.

- ✓ **Step 2**: Ascertain the form of group structure in this parent-subsidiary relationship. Since the subsidiary (**Manchester United**) is *partly-owned* by the parent (**Arsenal**), the group structure is a simple structure as shown below:

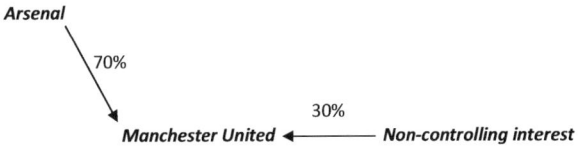

```
        Arsenal
          |
          | 70%
          ↓         30%
   Manchester United ←——— Non-controlling interest
```

Adjustments in Group Accounts

✓ **Step 3(a):** Determine the existence of goodwill or gain from a bargain purchase as the date of acquisition based on the fair value or provisional values of subsidiary's identifiable assets and liabilities. In this case, there exists goodwill as shown below.

To ascertain and determine the amount of goodwill to the group as it will be shown in the consolidated statement of financial position, the fair value of investment of the parent (**Arsenal**) in the subsidiary (**Manchester United**) and that of the Non-controlling interest will be compared with the fair value of the identifiable assets and liabilities of the subsidiary as at acquisition.

FULL METHODOLOGY	₦' million	₦' million
Cost of Business Combination		
Arsenal investment in ordinary share capital of Sussy		220
Arsenal investment in preference share capital of Sussy		60
		280
Non-controlling interest in ordinary share capital of Sussy (Step 3b)	87	
Non-controlling interest in preference share capital of Sussy (Step 3c)	40	127
Combined amount of interests in subsidiary to all investors		407
Less: Fair value of Identifiable net assets acquired @ 31 December 2013		
• Ordinary share capital of Sussy	250	
• Pre-acquisition reserves	40	
Net assets attributable to ordinary shareholders	**290**	
• Preference share capital of Sussy	100	(390)
Goodwill - positive		**17**

Technical Note:
The goodwill attributable to non-controlling must be zero since the investment to non-controlling interests is valued at the proportionate share of subsidiary's identifiable net assets as shown by the arrow.

✓ **Step 3(b):** Alternative, PARTIAL METHODOLOGY

	₦' million	₦' million
Cost of combination (i.e. the cost of investment of **Arsenal** in **Manchester United**)		220
Less: **Arsenal's** share of Identifiable net assets of **Manchester United** acquired:		
• Share capital (70% of ₦250 million)	175	
• Pre-acquisition reserves (70% of ₦40 million)	28	(203)
Goodwill attributable to **Arsenal's** (a)		**17**
Amount of investments of non-controlling interest in **Manchester United**		87
Less: Non-controlling interest share of the fair value of subsidiary's net assets:		
• Share capital (30% of ₦250 million)	75	
• Pre-acquisition reserves (30% of ₦40 million)	12	(87)
Goodwill attributable to **non-controlling interests** (b)		---
Goodwill (a + b)		**17**

✓ **Step 3(c):** Determine the goodwill (if any) on the non-equity interest (preference shares) acquired in the subsidiary as at acquisition.

	₦' million
Amount of investment in 8% preferred stock	60
Less: Parent's share of the 8% preferred stock of the subsidiary (60% x ₦100million)	(60)
Goodwill	---

260

✓ **Step 3(d):** The combined goodwill on common equity interest and non-common equity interest of the parent in the subsidiary is ₦17 million (which represents the sum of the *₦17 million* and *zero sum* attributable to the equity and non-equity interests respectively), as shown below:

	₦' million
• Goodwill based on common equity interest or ownership in the subsidiary	17
• Goodwill based on preferred stocks (i.e. non-equity shares) in the subsidiary	-
	17

✓ **Step 4:** *Determine the amount of non-controlling interest as will be shown in the consolidated statement of financial position of the group.* In this case, non-controlling interest will only be measured at proportionate share of subsidiary's identifiable assets and liabilities, which could be depicted as thus:

	₦ ' million
• Ordinary share capital (30% of ₦250 million)	75
• Preference share capital (40% of ₦100 million)	40
• Pre-acquisition reserves (30% of ₦40 million)	12
NCI's investment on 31 December 2013 (based on proportionate share of net assets)	**127**
• Post-acquisition reserves (30% of ₦10 million)	3
NCI's investment on 31 December 2015	**130**

✓ **Step 4(a):** Non-controlling interest's share of Identifiable net assets attributable to ordinary shareholders of **Manchester United**:

	₦' million
• Share capital (30% of ₦250 million)	75
• Pre-acquisition reserves (30% of ₦40 million)	12
NCI's investment on 31 December 2013 (based on proportionate share of net assets)	**87**
• Post-acquisition reserves (30% of ₦10 million)	3
NCI's investment on 31 December 2015	**90**

✓ **Step 4(b):** The part of the preference shares of the subsidiary not attributable to the parent, will now be treated as part of the non-controlling interest upon consolidation with ₦40 million (being 40% of the 8% preferred stock of ₦100 million).

✓ **Step 4(c):** The amount of non-controlling interest will be the combined amount as obtained on common equity interest and non-common equity interest of the non-controlling interest in the subsidiary which is ₦130 million as shown below:

	₦' million
• Non-controlling interest based on the ordinary (equity) shares	90
• Non-controlling interest based on the preference (non-equity) shares	40
	130

✓ **Step 5:** *Determine the amount to be included in the consolidated statement of financial position as consolidated reserves (otherwise known as consolidated retained earnings).* The consolidated retained earnings to be included in the consolidated statement of financial position of **Arsenal-Group** is that of the parent and the share of post-acquisition profits of ₦10 million in the subsidiary as at acquisition. There is post-acquisition profits ₦10 million (being the increase in retained earnings from ₦40 million to ₦50 million after 2 years) in the subsidiary. The consolidated retained earnings will be determined as follows:

	₦' million
Parent's (**Arsenal**) retained earnings	290
Share of subsidiary's (**Manchester United**) post-acquisition reserves (70% of ₦10 million)	7
	297

Adjustments in Group Accounts

- ✓ **Step 6:** Combine the assets and liabilities of the parent (**Arsenal**) and subsidiary (**Manchester United**) on an item-by-item basis excluding the initial investment of **Arsenal** in **Manchester United** as earlier shown in the separate financial statements of **Arsenal**, and also the exclusion of the equity and preference share capital of **Manchester United**, as it has already been considered alongside with the pre-acquisition retained earnings in ascertaining the amount of goodwill or gain from bargain purchase inherent/embedded in the acquisition.

- ✓ **Step 7:** In order to *cancel out* the Intra-group loans as maintained by the parent and subsidiary, we first ensure that the Intra-group loans of ₦100 million (receivable by the parent and payable by the subsidiary) agree, and the balances will then be cancelled out, while the loans due to third parties to members of the group are those to be recognised in the statement of financial position of the group.

    Accounting entries for cancellation of agreed intercompany balances:
    Debit: Loans (as a liability) by Manchester United
    Credit: Loans (as an asset) by Arsenal
    With the amount of intercompany balance of ₦100 million

The consolidated statement of financial position of the group will now be shown:

Arsenal Group
Consolidated Statement of Financial Position as at 31 December 2015

	₦' million
Assets:	
Non-current assets	
Property, plant and equipment (500 + 360)	860
~~Investment in Manchester United (380 – 220 – 60 – 100)~~	~~0~~
Goodwill	17
Current assets (260 + 280)	540
Total Assets	**1,417**
Share Capital & Reserves:	
Equity share capital	600
8% Preferred share capital (parent only)	100
Reserves	297
Equity attributable to Arsenal's shareholders	997
Non-controlling interest	130
Total Equity	**1,127**
Non-current liabilities:	
Debentures (120-100)	20*
Current liabilities (150 + 120)	270
Total Equity and Liabilities	**1,417**

Technical Note:
*The amount of loan notes of ₦20 million represents those owned by outsiders (i.e. loan notes not attributable to the parent's interest or investment in the subsidiary).

The consolidation schedule can equally be adopted for solving this group problem as scheduled below:

Consolidation Schedule

Subsidiary - Manchester United		Cost of control (Arsenal in Manchester United) as at 31 Dec. 2013 – 70%	8% Preferred Stock – 60%	Non-controlling Interests – 30% & 40%	Consolidated Reserves
Equity Share Capital	250	(70% x 250) 175		(30% x 250) 75	
8% Preferred Stock	100	-	(60% x 100) 60	(40% x 100) 40	
Reserves (Pre-acquisition)	40	(70% x 40) 28		(30% x 40) 12	
(Post-acquisition)	10		–	(30% x 10) 3	(70% x 10) 7
Net asset on acquisition		203	60		
Cost of combination		(220)	(60)		
Goodwill (positive)		(17)	–		
Non-controlling interests				**130**	
Arsenal Reserves					290
Consolidated Reserves					**297**

BONUS ISSUE

Bonus shares are shares given to the existing shareholders of an entity at *no explicit cost to the shareholders*, which requires the shareholders to be given shares that do no change their initial percentage holdings. The bonus shares are a mere recapitalization of undistributed profits or reserves and are classified as a *script* or *capitalization issue*. There are instances subsequent to acquisition where the subsidiary makes bonus issue in which the parent company is a beneficiary in the proportion of its interests outstanding in the subsidiary as at the date of the bonus issue. There are three identified implications when bonus shares are made by a subsidiary after its acquisition by the parent company.

- ☐ The bonus may have been issued out of pre-acquisition profits
- ☐ The bonus issued may have been issued out of post-acquisition profits
- ☐ The bonus issued partly out of pre and post-acquisition profits.

In a situation where the bonus is considered to be issued out of pre-acquisition profits, this will be considered a mere transfer from pre-acquisition profits (*an amount equivalent of the bonus*) to the share capital of the subsidiary. The implication is that any form of bonus issue subsequently to the acquisition of a subsidiary should not affect the goodwill or gain from a bargain purchase as initially ascertained and recognised at acquisition-date.

If the bonus shares result from the recapitalization of a portion of the post-acquisition profits, it implies that this fact should also be considered in ascertaining the appropriate post-acquisition profits on subsequent consolidations, as this should not in any way affects goodwill or gain on bargain purchase as initially ascertained and recognised at acquisition. There exists the need to adjust the share capital of the subsidiary to separate the share capital as at the reporting date to two (i.e. to share capital at acquisition which constituted part of the net assets upon acquisition of the subsidiary and increase in share capital resulting from the bonus issue). The portion of the share capital as at reporting date but attributed to the increase due to bonus issue should be considered as part of consolidated reserves for consolidation purpose and in the group accounts, as it constitutes a post-acquisition element of net assets through reserves.

In order to understand the dynamics of the aforementioned positions, we need to first establish whether the bonus issued prior to the reporting date or as at reporting date has been included in the financial statements of the subsidiary, as stated below:

- ✓ Ascertain if the accounting entries as regard the bonus issue have been passed.
- ✓ Ascertain from which portion of the reserves (*pre or post*) the bonus shares were issued.

We are to consider the following position in exploring the effect of bonus issue on consolidation.

a) **Where accounting entries have not been passed to record the bonus issue, and the bonus shares were:**

❑ *Issued out of Pre-Acquisition Reserves*

When bonus issue is made out of pre-acquisition reserve and accounting entries have not been passed, it will be best to ignore the capitalization issue as it will not affect the consolidation process likewise will it affect the computation of goodwill or gain on bargain purchase. This is because; it will only result in a mere reclassification of pre-acquisition reserves to equity share capital (of which both are components of net assets acquired).

❑ *Issued out of Post-Acquisition Reserves*

Where capitalization issue is made from post-acquisition reserves, accounting entries need not be passed as it does not affect the consolidation process, rather you ignore the bonus issue, as passing the accounting entries is tantamount to bringing a post-acquisition element into the consolidation process (schedule), which will require additional process on consolidation in separating the share capital of the subsidiary at acquisition into share capital at acquisition which constituted part of the net assets upon acquisition of the subsidiary, and increase in share capital resulting from the bonus issue.

b) **Where accounting entries have been passed to record the bonus issue; and the bonus shares were:**

❑ *Issued out of Pre-Acquisition Reserves*

In this instance, the bonus issue made has been reflected in the net assets (Share Capital and Reserves) of the subsidiary and the amount of reserves recapitalized as a result of capitalization issue should be used to reduce the pre-acquisition reserves of the subsidiary and simultaneously increase the post-acquisition reserves (invariably, the entire reserves do not change but merely a reclassification of the relevant portion or amount of *pre-acquisition reserves* to *post-acquisition reserves*). This process entails separating the net assets of the subsidiary as at reporting date into two (i.e. to share capital at acquisition which constituted part of the net assets upon acquisition of the subsidiary, and increase in share capital resulting from the bonus issue made subsequent to acquisition). The portion of the share capital as at reporting date but attributed to the increase due to bonus issue subsequent to acquisition should be considered as part of consolidated reserves for consolidation purpose and group accounts, as it still constitutes a post-acquisition element of net assets through reserves.

ILLUSTRATION 15:

AVA acquired 60% of the equity shares of ZOE on 31 December 2013 at cost of ₦320 million when the balance on the reserve account stood at ₦180 million. On 31 December 2015, ZOE made a bonus of 2 for 5 out of pre-acquisition reserve which has been accounted for in the books of ZOE.

Statements of Financial Position as at 31 December 2015

	AVA	ZOE
	₦' million	₦' million
Non-Current Assets		
Property, plant and equipment	2,100	250
Investments	400	
Current assets	2,000	500
	4,500	**750**
Equities and Liabilities:		
Ordinary share capital (₦1 each)	1,000	420
Reserves	2,400	200
Current liabilities	1,100	130
	4,500	**750**

We are to approach the solution in the following steps:

- ✓ **Step 1**: Determine the percentage holdings of investment of **AVA** in **ZOE** as at the acquisition date (31 December 2013), which represents the date of inclusion (first date of consolidation). In this case, the percentage holding is already determined and ascertained to be 60%.

- ✓ **Step 2**: Ascertain the form of group structure in this parent-subsidiary relationship. Since the subsidiary (**ZOE**) is *partly-owned* by the parent (**AVA**), the group structure is a simple structure as shown below:

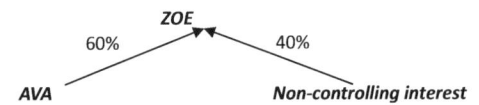

```
                    ZOE
            60%  ↗     ↖  40%
          AVA              Non-controlling interest
```

- ✓ **Step 3**: Determine the existence of goodwill or gain from a bargain purchase as at the date of acquisition based on the fair value or provisional values of subsidiary's identifiable assets and liabilities. In this case, there exists goodwill as shown below.

- ✓ To ascertain and determine the amount of goodwill or gain from a bargain purchase, the value of an investment of the parent (**AVA**) in the subsidiary (**ZOE**) will be compared with the parent's share of identifiable assets and liabilities of the subsidiary that were acquired.

SCENARIO A: Involves reducing the increase in share capital of the subsidiary resulting from bonus issue from the pre-acquisition reserve, as this implies that the subsidiary's net assets as at acquisition still remain the same.

- ✓ **Step 3(a):** Determine the existence of goodwill or gain from a bargain purchase as the date of acquisition based on the fair value or provisional values of subsidiary's identifiable assets and liabilities. In this case, there exists goodwill as shown below.

To ascertain and determine the amount of goodwill to the group as it will be shown in the consolidated statement of financial position, the fair value of investment of the parent (**AVA**) in the subsidiary (**ZOE**) and that of the Non-controlling interest will be compared with the fair value of the identifiable assets and liabilities of the subsidiary as at acquisition.

FULL METHODOLOGY	₦' million	₦' million
Cost of Business Combination		
Arsenal investment in ordinary share capital of Sussy		320
Non-controlling interest in ordinary share capital of Sussy (40% of ₦480 million)		192
Combined amount of interests in subsidiary to all investors		**512**
Less: Fair value of Identifiable net assets acquired @ 31 December 2012		
• Ordinary share capital of Sussy	420	
• Pre-acquisition reserves	60	
Net assets attributable to ordinary shareholders		(480)
Goodwill - positive		**32**

	₦' million
Cost of combination (i.e. cost of acquisition) to the parent	320
Amount of Investment in subsidiary to non-controlling interest*	192
Combined amount of interests in subsidiary to all investors	**512**
Less: Parent's share of the fair value of subsidiary's identifiable net assets (288)	
Non-controlling interest share of the fair value of subsidiary's net assets (192)	
	(480)
Goodwill - positive	**32**

Technical Note:
The goodwill attributable to non-controlling must be zero since the investment to non-controlling interests is valued at the proportionate share of subsidiary's identifiable net assets as shown by the arrow.

In order to ascertain the pre and post-acquisition profits on consolidation, will have to determine the bonus amount that was recapitalized to share capital from reserves, as shown below: Let: "A" represents existing share capital before bonus issue
"B" represents Bonus
"C" represents share capital after bonus issue
$C = A + B$
$B = 2/5$ of A (which represents 2 bonus shares for every 5 existing shares)
$C = A + 2A/5$
$C = 7A/5 = 420$
$7A = 5 \times 420$
$A = \underline{2,100}$
            7   = ₦300 million

$B = 2A/5 = 2 \times 300/5 = $ ₦120 million

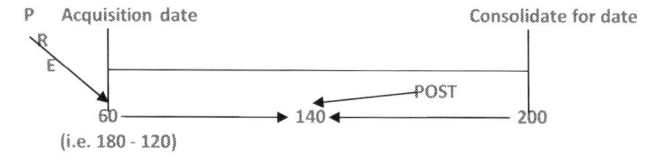

P   Acquisition date   Consolidate for date
R
E
                                     POST
        60 ─────────→ 140 ←───────── 200
     (i.e. 180 - 120)

Contemporaneous Accounting for Business Combinations and Group Accounts

		₦' million	₦' million
✓ **Step 3(b):** Alternative, PARTIAL METHODOLOGY			
Cost of combination (i.e. the cost of investment of **AVA** in **ZOE**)			320
Less: **AVA's** share of Identifiable net assets of **ZOE** acquired:			
• Share capital (60% of ₦420 million)		252	
• Pre-acquisition reserves (60% of ₦60 million)		36	(288)
Goodwill attributable to **AVA**(a)			**32**
Amount of investments of non-controlling interest in **ZOE**			192
Less: Non-controlling interest share of the fair value of subsidiary's net assets:			
• Share capital (40% of ₦420 million)		168	
• Pre-acquisition reserves (40% of ₦60 million)		24	(192)
Goodwill attributable to **non-controlling interests** (b)			---
Goodwill (a + b)			**32**

SCENARIO B: Involves separating the increase in the share capital of the subsidiary resulting from bonus issue, and add back to the reserves as at the reporting date (31 December 2015).

		₦' million	₦' million
FULL METHODOLOGY			
Cost of Business Combination			
Arsenal investment in ordinary share capital of Sussy			320
Non-controlling interest in ordinary share capital of Sussy (40% of ₦480 million)			192
Combined amount of interests in subsidiary to all investors			512
Less: Fair value of Identifiable net assets acquired @ 31 December 2012			
• Ordinary share capital of Sussy (420 – 120)		300	
• Pre-acquisition reserves		180	
Net assets attributable to ordinary shareholders			**(480)**
Goodwill - positive			**32**
✓ **Step 3(b):** Alternative, PARTIAL METHODOLOGY		₦' million	₦' million
Cost of combination (i.e. the cost of investment of **AVA** in **ZOE**)			320
Less: **AVA's** share of Identifiable net assets of **ZOE** acquired:			
• Share capital (60% of ₦300 million)		180	
• Pre-acquisition reserves (60% of ₦180 million)		108	(288)
Goodwill attributable to **AVA**(a)			**32**
Amount of investments of non-controlling interest in **ZOE**			192
Less: Non-controlling interest share of the fair value of subsidiary's net assets:			
• Share capital (40% of ₦300 million)		120	
• Pre-acquisition reserves (40% of ₦180 million)		72	(192)
Goodwill attributable to **non-controlling interests** (b)			---
Goodwill (a + b)			**32**

Technical Note:
The goodwill attributable to non-controlling must be zero since the investment to non-controlling interests is valued at the proportionate share of subsidiary's identifiable net assets as shown by the arrow.

✓ **Step 4:** Determine the amount of non-controlling interest as will be shown in the consolidated statement of financial position of the group. In this case, non-controlling interest will only be measured at the proportionate share of subsidiary's identifiable assets and liabilities, which could be depicted as thus:

Adjustments in Group Accounts

Non-controlling interest's share of Identifiable net assets of **ZOE**:

	₦' million
• Share capital (40% of ₦420 million)	168
• Pre-acquisition reserves (40% of ₦60 million)	24
NCI's investment on 31 December 2012 (*based on proportionate share of net assets*)	**192**
• Post-acquisition reserves (40% of ₦140 million)	56
NCI's investment on 31 December 2015 (*based on proportionate share of net assets*)	**248**

OR

Non-controlling interest's share of Identifiable net assets of **ZOE**:

	₦' million
• Share capital (40% of ₦300 million)	120
• Pre-acquisition reserves (40% of ₦180 million)	72
NCI's investment on 31 December 2012 (*based on proportionate share of net assets*)	**192**
• Post-acquisition reserves (40% of ₦140 million)	56
NCI's investment on 31 December 2015 (*based on proportionate share of net assets*)	**248**

✓ **Step 5**: *Determine the amount to be included in the consolidated statement of financial position as consolidated reserves (otherwise known as consolidated retained earnings).* The consolidated retained earnings to be included in the consolidated statement of financial position of **AVA-Group** are that of the parent and of the share of the post-acquisition profits of the subsidiary. Invariably, it implies that the post-acquisition retained earnings (which is the sum of ₦140 million being the increased from ₦180 million profits upon acquisition to ₦320 million or increase from ₦60 million to ₦200 million as at the reporting date 31 December 2015 - *3 years after*) of the subsidiary (**ZOE**) will now be combined with the retained earnings (profits) of the parent (**AVA**) in ascertaining the group retained earnings. The consolidated retained earnings will be determined as follows:

	₦' million
Parent's (**AVA**) retained earnings	2,400
Share of subsidiary's (**ZOE**) post-acquisition profits (60% of ₦140 million)	84
	2,484

✓ **Step 6**: *Combine the assets and liabilities of the parent (**AVA**) and subsidiary (**ZOE**) on an item-by-item basis excluding the initial investment of **AVA** in **ZOE** as earlier shown in the separate financial statements of **AVA**, and also the exclusion of the equity share capital of **ZOE**, as it has already been considered alongside with the pre-acquisition retained earnings in ascertaining the amount of goodwill or gain from bargain purchase inherent/embedded in the acquisition.* The consolidated statement of financial position of the group will now be shown as thus:

AVA Group
Consolidated Statement of Financial Position as at 31 December 2015

	₦' million	₦' million
Property, plant and equipment (2,100 + 250)		2,350
Investments* (400 – 320)		80
Goodwill on consolidation		32
Current assets (2,000 + 500)		2,500
Total Assets		**4,962**

Share Capital & Reserves:

Equity share capital	1,000
Reserves	2,484
Equity attributable to AVA's shareholders	3,484
Non-controlling interest	248
Total Equity	**3,732**
Current liabilities (1,100 + 130)	1,230
Total Equity and Liabilities	**4,962**

Technical Note:
Investment to be shown in the consolidated statement of financial position should be investments not attributable to control of another entity, but rather other investments in financial instruments, associates and joint venture. In this case, the investment to be reported in the consolidated statement of financial position is ₦80 million, being the excess of the investments of ₦400 million of AVA over the investment in the subsidiary (of which the initial investment in subsidiary of ₦320 million has been used in ascertaining the goodwill of ₦20 million in ZOE) of ₦320 million.

The consolidation schedule can equally be adopted for solving this group problem as scheduled below:

Consolidation Schedule

Company ZOE		Cost of control (AVA in ZOE) as at 31 December 2012 – 60%		Non-controlling Interests – 40%		Consolidated Reserves	
Equity Share Capital	420	(60% x 420)	252	(40% x 420)	168		
Reserves (Pre-acquisition)	60	(60% x 80)	36	(40% x 60)	24		
Reserves (Post-acquisition)	140			(40% x 140)	56	(60% x 140)	84
Net assets on acquisition			288				
Cost of combination (cost of investment)			(320)				
Goodwill (positive)			(32)				
Non-controlling interests					248		
AVA Reserves							2,400
Consolidated Reserves							2,484

OR

Consolidation Schedule

Company ZOE		Cost of control (AVA in ZOE) as at 31 December 2012 – 60%		Non-controlling Interests – 40%		Consolidated Reserves	
Equity Share Capital	300	(60% x 300)	180	(40% x 300)	120		
Reserves (Pre-acquisition)	180	(60% x 180)	108	(40% x 180)	72		
Reserves (Post-acquisition)	140			(40% x 140)	56	(60% x 140)	84
Net assets on acquisition			288				
Cost of combination (cost of investment)			(320)				

Goodwill (positive)	(32)	
Non-controlling interests	248	
AVA Reserves		2,400
Consolidated Reserves		2,484

- **Issued out of Post-Acquisition Reserves**

   In this instance, the bonus shares made have been reflected in the net assets (Share Capital and Reserves) of the subsidiary. The process involves the reverse of the entries passed as the share capital of the subsidiary contains the bonus elements (attributable to a post –acquisition profits) which do not constitute part of the net assets of the subsidiary at the acquisition date.

   Reversal of Bonus Issue Accounting Entry:

   Debit: Share Capital (Subsidiary)
   Credit: Reserves (Subsidiary)

ILLUSTRATION 16:

AVA acquired 60% of the equity shares of ZOE on 31 December 2012 at cost of ₦320 million when the balance on the reserve account stood at ₦180 million. On 31 December 2015, ZOE made a bonus of 1 for 4 out of post-acquisition reserve which has been accounted for in the books of ZOE.

Statements of Financial Position as at 31 December 2015

	AVA	ZOE
	₦' million	₦' million
Non-Current Assets:		
Property, plant and equipment	2,100	250
Investments	400	
Current assets	2,000	500
	4,500	750
Equities and Liabilities:		
Ordinary share capital (₦1 each)	1,000	400
Reserves	2,400	200
Current liabilities	1,100	150
	4,500	750

We are to approach the solution in the following steps:

- ✓ **Step 1**: Determine the percentage holdings of investment of **AVA** in **ZOE** as at the acquisition date (31 December 2012), which represents the date of inclusion (first date of consolidation). In this case, the percentage holding is already determined and ascertained to be 60%.

- ✓ **Step 2**: Ascertain the form of group structure in this parent-subsidiary relationship. Since the subsidiary (**ZOE**) is *partly-owned* by the parent (**AVA**), the group structure is a simple structure as shown below:

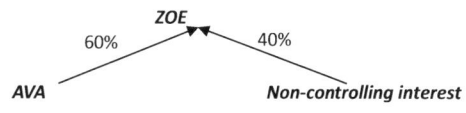

```
              ZOE
         60%   ▼    40%
        ╱            ╲
      AVA         Non-controlling interest
```

✓ **Step 3(a): Determine the existence of goodwill or gain from a bargain purchase as the date of acquisition based on the fair value or provisional values of subsidiary's identifiable assets and liabilities.** In this case, there exists goodwill as shown below.

To ascertain and determine the amount of goodwill to the group as it will be shown in the consolidated statement of financial position, the fair value of investment of the parent (**AVA**) in the subsidiary (**ZOE**) and that of the Non-controlling interest will be compared with the fair value of the identifiable assets and liabilities of the subsidiary as at acquisition.

FULL METHODOLOGY	₦' million	₦' million
Cost of Business Combination		
Arsenal investment in ordinary share capital of Sussy		320
Non-controlling interest in ordinary share capital of Sussy (40% of ₦500 million)		200
Combined amount of interests in subsidiary to all investors		**520**
Less: Fair value of Identifiable net assets acquired @ 31 December 2012		
• Ordinary share capital of Sussy	320	
• Pre-acquisition reserves	180	
Net assets attributable to ordinary shareholders		**(500)**
Goodwill - positive		**20**

	₦' million
Cost of combination (i.e. cost of acquisition) to the parent	320
Amount of Investment in subsidiary to non-controlling interest*	200
Combined amount of interests in subsidiary to all investors	**520**
Less: 60% Parent's share of the fair value of subsidiary's identifiable net assets (300)	
40% Non-controlling interest share of the fair value of subsidiary's net assets (200)	
	(500)
Goodwill - positive	**20**

Technical Note:

In order to ascertain the pre and post-acquisition profits on consolidation, will have to determine the bonus amount that was recapitalized to share capital from reserves, as shown below:

Let: "A" represents existing share capital before bonus issue
"B" represents Bonus
"C" represents share capital after bonus issue
$C = A + B$
$B = ¼$ of A (which represents 1 bonus share for every 5 existing shares)
$C = A + A/4$
$C = 5A/4 = 400$
$7A = 4 \times 400$
$A = \underline{1,600}$
     $5 = ₦320$ million

$B = A/4 = 320/4 = ₦80$ million

Accounting Entry: Debit: Share capital ⎤
                  Credit: Reserves   ⎦ ₦80 million

Share capital (before bonus issue) is ₦320 million
Reserves = ₦280 million (being the ₦200 million plus ₦80 million)

Adjustments in Group Accounts

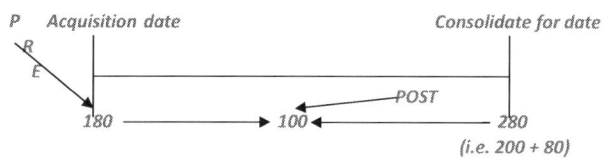

```
P   Acquisition date              Consolidate for date
R
E                         POST
    180 ──────────► 100 ◄──────── 280
                          (i.e. 200 + 80)
```

✓ **Step 3(b):** Alternative, **PARTIAL METHODOLOGY**   ₦' million   ₦' million
Cost of combination (i.e. the cost of investment of **AVA** in **ZOE**)   320
Less: AVA's share of Identifiable net assets of ZOE acquired:
- Share capital (60% of ₦320 million)   192
- Pre-acquisition reserves (60% of ₦180 million)   <u>108</u>   <u>(300)</u>

Goodwill attributable to **AVA** (a)   **<u>20</u>**
Amount of investments of non-controlling interest in **ZOE**   200
Less: Non-controlling interest share of the fair value of subsidiary's net assets:
- Share capital (40% of ₦320 million)   128
- Pre-acquisition reserves (40% of ₦180 million)   <u>72</u>   (200)

Goodwill attributable to **non-controlling interests** (b)   ---
Goodwill (a + b)   **<u>20</u>**

Technical Note:
The goodwill attributable to non-controlling must be zero since the investment to non-controlling interests is valued at the proportionate share of subsidiary's identifiable net assets as shown by the arrow.

✓ **Step 4:** Determine the amount of non-controlling interest as will be shown in the consolidated statement of financial position of the group. In this case, non-controlling interest will only be measured at the proportionate share of subsidiary's identifiable assets and liabilities, which could be depicted as thus:

Non-controlling interest's share of Identifiable net assets of **ZOE**:   ₦' million
- Share capital (40% of ₦320 million)   128
- Pre-acquisition reserves (40% of ₦180 million)   <u>72</u>

NCI's investment on 31 December 2012 (*based on proportionate share of net assets*)   **200**
- Post-acquisition reserves (40% of ₦100 million)   <u>40</u>

NCI's investment on 31 December 2015 (*based on proportionate share of net assets*)   **240**

✓ **Step 5:** Determine the amount to be included in the consolidated statement of financial position as consolidated reserves (otherwise known as consolidated retained earnings). The consolidated retained earnings to be included in the consolidated statement of financial position of **AVA-Group** are that of the parent and of the share of post-acquisition profits of the subsidiary. Invariably, it implies that the post-acquisition retained earnings (which is the sum of ₦100 million being the increased from ₦180 million profits upon acquisition to ₦280 million the reporting date 31 December 2015 - *3 years after*) of the subsidiary (**ZOE**) will now be combined with the retained earnings (profits) of the parent (**AVA**) in ascertaining the group retained earnings. The consolidated retained earnings will be determined as follows: ₦' million
Parent's (**AVA**) retained earnings   2,400
Share of subsidiary's (**ZOE**) post-acquisition profits (60% of ₦100 million)   <u>60</u>
    2,460

✓ **Step 6:** Combine the assets and liabilities of the parent (**AVA**) and subsidiary (**ZOE**) on an item-by-item basis excluding the initial investment of **AVA** in **ZOE** as earlier shown in the separate financial statements of **AVA**, and also the exclusion of the equity share capital of **ZOE**, as it has already been considered alongside with the pre-acquisition retained earnings in ascertaining the amount of goodwill or gain from bargain purchase inherent/embedded in the acquisition. The consolidated statement of financial position of the group will now be shown as thus:

AVA Group
Consolidated Statement of Financial Position as at 31 December 2015

	₦' million	₦' million
Property, plant and equipment (2,100 + 250)		2,350
Investments* (400 – 320)		80
Goodwill on consolidation		20
Current assets (2,000 + 500)		2,500
Total Assets		**4,950**
Share Capital & Reserves:		
Equity share capital		1,000
Reserves		2,460
Equity attributable to AVA's shareholders		3,460
Non-controlling interest		240
Total Equity		**3,700**
Current liabilities (1,100 + 150)		1,250
Total Equity and Liabilities		**4,950**

Technical Note:
Investment to be shown in the consolidated should be investments not attributable to control of another entity, but rather other investments in financial instruments, associate and joint venture (where the joint venture is accounted under equity method). In this case, the investment to be reported in the consolidated statement of financial position is ₦80 million, being the excess of the investments of ₦400 million of AVA over the investment in the subsidiary (of which the investment in subsidiary of ₦320 million has been used in ascertaining the goodwill of ₦20 million in ZOE) of ₦320 million.

The consolidation schedule can equally be adopted for solving this group problem as scheduled below:

Consolidation Schedule

Company ZOE		Cost of control (AVA in ZOE) as at 31 December 2012 – 60%		Non-controlling Interests – 40%		Consolidated Reserves
Equity Share Capital	320	(60% x 320)	192	(40% x 320)	128	
Reserves (Pre-acquisition)	180	(60% x 180)	108	(40% x 180)	72	
Reserves (Post-acquisition)	100			(40% x 100)	40	(60% x 100) 60
Net asset on acquisition			300			
Cost of combination (cost of investment)			(320)			
Goodwill (positive)			(20)			
Non-controlling interests					240	
AVA Reserve						2,400
Consolidated Reserves						2,460

DIVIDEND ANALYSIS

It parent is expected to earn returns from its investments in the subsidiary, and part of the returns earned in a subsidiary is the dividend received from the subsidiary. Dividends paid by a company is due and payable to all shareholders of the company, it then implies that where the subsidiary is partly acquired/owned the parent, the dividend declared, paid or payable is due to both the parent and the non-controlling interests. That is, if the subsidiary has a proposed divided at the reporting date, then some of this is payable to the parent and also to the non-controlling interests based on the proportion of shares held as at the reporting date.

Technical Note:
IAS 10 (revised) – Events after the Reporting Period, proposed dividends declared after the reporting period (balance sheet date) are not to be recognised as a liability, and dividends are to be debited against retained earnings when they are paid. It implies that if dividends have been declared prior to the reporting or balance sheet date, such constitute a liability as at the reporting/balance sheet date in line with the provisions of IAS 37 – Provisions, Contingent Liabilities and Contingent Assets.

When dividends are declared by the subsidiary, both the parent and the non-controlling interest are entitled to their own share, which is derived based on the percentage holdings in the subsidiary. Some situations exist where dividends are paid either from pre-acquisition profits or post-acquisition profits, but the current position of IFRS requires the same treatment as "Dividend is only considered as a Return on Investment", as against the prior distinction between Dividend being either a "Return of Investment" or a "Return on Investment". Further, in this text, the old position will be considered immediately after the consideration of the current requirement in a bid to appreciate the dynamism and the paradigm-shift by the IASB in its consideration as first evidenced in the revision made to IAS 27 in 2008.

The new position of IAS 27 (REVISED IN 2008), which further flows into IFRS 10 now requires the treatment of dividend received or receivable from a subsidiary as a return on the parent's investment regardless of the whether it is paid/ declared from pre-acquisition profits or post-acquisition profits. The implication is that goodwill is no longer affected with the old principle of reduction of cost of investments with the dividends paid out of pre-acquisition profits (considered a pre-acquisition dividend).

If the parent has not recognized the dividend received or receivable from the subsidiary in its separate financial statement, it is more preferable to adjust the financial statement of the parent before proceeding with the consolidation, or alternatively, we adjust for the dividends on consolidation based on the principles of consolidation as it relates to dividends paid whether from pre-acquisition profits or post-acquisition profits (*the same treatments is accorded*).

Debit: Bank – *If received/ Dividend Receivable – if it is outstanding*
Credit: *Statement of Profit or Loss of the Parent (or Income Statement)*
With the (parent share of) dividend payable (declared) or paid by the subsidiary

ILLUSTRATION 17:

FARAMADE Plc acquired 80% of the shares of ADEBOLA Plc as at 30 December 2016. FARAMADE Plc was included in the register of shareholders in of ADEBOLA Plc before the register was closed and before the declaration date (31 December 2016) of dividend by ADEBOLA Plc which coincide with the reporting date, and this makes FARAMADE Plc entitled to dividend of ADEBOLA Plc as at the year ended 31st December 2015 has the amount of the dividend is still outstanding.

Statement of Financial Position as at 31 December 2016

	FARAMADE Plc	ADEBOLA Plc
	₦' million	₦' million
Non-Current Assets:		
Property, plant and equipment	90	120
Investment in **ADEBOLA Plc**	140	
Current Assets:		
Inventories	25	45
Account Receivables	12	12
Dividend Receivable	8	
Bank	5	7
Total Assets	**280**	**184**
Equity and Liabilities:		
Equity – Ordinary Shares (₦0.50/share)	80	100
Retained Earnings	140	60
Current Liabilities:		
Account Payables	40	14
Dividend Payable	20	10
Total equity and liabilities	**280**	**184**

Required:
Prepare the consolidated statement of financial position as at 31 December 2010.

We are to approach the solution in the following steps:

- ✓ **Step 1:** Determine the percentage holdings of investment of **FARAMADE Plc** in **ADEBOLA Plc** as at the acquisition date (30 December 2016), which represents the date of inclusion (first date of consolidation). In this case, the percentage holding is already determined and ascertained to be 80%.

- ✓ **Step 2:** Ascertain the form of group structure in this parent-subsidiary relationship. Since the subsidiary (**ADEBOLA Plc**) is *partly-owned* by the parent (**FARAMADE Plc**), the group structure is a simple structure as shown below:

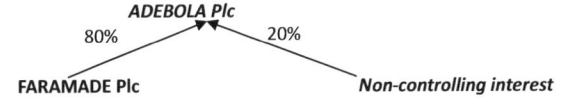

```
              ADEBOLA Plc
           80%  ↑↑  20%
    FARAMADE Plc      Non-controlling interest
```

- ✓ **Step 3:** Determine the existence and calculate goodwill or gain from a bargain purchase as at the date of acquisition based on the fair value or provisional values of subsidiary's identifiable assets and liabilities. In this case, there exists goodwill as shown below.

Adjustments in Group Accounts

To ascertain and determine the value of goodwill or gain from a bargain purchase, the value of an investment of the parent (**FARAMADE Plc**) in the subsidiary (**ADEBOLA Plc**) will be compared with the parent's share of identifiable assets and liabilities of the subsidiary that were acquired.

	₦' million	₦' million
Cost of combination (i.e. the cost of investment of **FARAMADE** in **ADEBOLA**)		140
Less: **FARAMADE**'s share of Identifiable net assets of **ADEBOLA** acquired:		
• Share capital (80% of ₦100 million)	80	
• Pre-acquisition reserves (80% of ₦60 million)	48	(128)
Goodwill attributable to **FARAMADE Plc** *(a)*		4
Amount of investments of non-controlling interest in **ADEBOLA Plc**		32
Less: Non-controlling interest share of the fair value of subsidiary's net assets:		
• Share capital (20% of ₦100 million)	20	
• Pre-acquisition reserves (20% of ₦60 million)	12	(32)
Goodwill attributable to **non-controlling interests** *(b)*		---
Goodwill (a + b)		**12**

Technical Note:
*The goodwill attributable to non-controlling must be zero since the investment to non-controlling interests is valued at the proportionate share of subsidiary's identifiable net assets as shown by the arrow.

		₦' million
Cost of combination (i.e. cost of acquisition) to the parent		140
Amount of Investment in subsidiary to non-controlling interest*		32
Combined amount of interests in subsidiary to all investors		**172**
Less: Fair value of Identifiable net assets acquired @ 30 December 2016		
• Ordinary share capital of Sussy	100	
• Pre-acquisition reserves	60	
Net assets attributable to ordinary shareholders		(160)
Goodwill - positive		**12**

✓ **Step 4**: *Determine the value of non-controlling interest as will be shown in the consolidated statement of financial position of the group.* In this case, non-controlling interest will only be valued at the proportionate share of subsidiary's identifiable assets and liabilities, which could be ascertained as thus:

Non-controlling interest's share of Identifiable net assets of **ADEBOLA** upon acquisition:

	₦' million
• Share capital (20% of ₦100 million)	20
• Pre-acquisition reserves (20% of ₦60 million)	12
NCI's investment on 31 December 2016 *(based on proportionate share of net assets)*	**32**

✓ **Step 5**: *Determine the amount to be included in the consolidated statement of financial position as consolidated reserves (otherwise known as consolidated retained earnings).* The consolidated retained earnings to be included in the group statement of financial position of **FARAMADE-Group** is only that of the parent, as the subsidiary retained earnings at the point of acquisition is entirely classified as pre-acquisition retained profit, which already as for is considered as part of the net asset of the subsidiary upon acquisition. Invariably, it implies that only the post-acquisition retained profit of the subsidiary that ought to be considered in ascertaining the group retained earnings. The consolidated retained earnings are usually determined as follows:

	₦' million
Parent's (**FARAMADE Plc**) retained earnings	140
Less: Share of post-acquisition reserves (80% of Zero)	--
	140

- ✓ **Step 6:** Combine the assets and liabilities of the parent (**FARAMADE Plc**) and subsidiary (**ADEBOLA Plc**) on an item-by-item basis excluding the initial investment of **FARAMADE Plc** in **ADEBOLA Plc** as earlier shown in the separate financial statement of **FARAMADE Plc**, and also the exclusion of the equity share capital of **ADEBOLA Plc**, as it has already been considered alongside with the pre-acquisition retained profits in ascertaining the value of goodwill or gain from bargain purchase inherent/embedded in the acquisition.

- ✓ **Step 7:** The Dividend receivable in the statement of financial position of FARAMADE Plc will have to be cancelled out against the dividend payable (accruable or due to the parent-FARAMADE) as outstanding in the statement of financial position of ADEBOLA. In this case, the sum of ₦8 million is due to FARAMADE (80% of dividend payable of the subsidiary - ₦10 million), will be cancelled out between dividend receivable by the parent and dividend payable by the subsidiary. Any balance due on both the dividend receivable of the parent and dividend payable by the subsidiary will be attributed to third parties (i.e. outside the group), and primarily should constitute group assets and liabilities respectively. In this case, the dividend receivable is zero after the adjustment which signifies no dividend receivable outside the group by the parent, whereas, there exist the balance of ₦2 million on dividend payable (being ₦10 million – ₦8 million due to the parent or equivalent of 20% of ₦10 million), which is due to third parties (in this case, it is due to non-controlling interest) and will be considered part of *other liabilities*. The consolidated statement of financial position of the group will now be shown as thus:

FARAMADE Group
Consolidated Statement of Financial Position as at 31 December 2016

Non-current assets:	₦' million
Property, plant and equipment (90 + 120)	210
Goodwill	12
Current assets:	
Inventories (25 + 45)	70
Account receivables (12 + 12)	24
Bank (5 + 7)	12
Total Assets	**328**
Share Capital & Reserves:	
Equity share capital	80
Reserves	140
Equity attributable to FARAMADE's shareholders	**220**
Non-controlling interest	32
Total Equity	**252**
Current liabilities:	
Account payables (40 + 14)	54
Dividend payables (parent only)	20
Other liabilities (Dividend payable to non-controlling interest)	2
Total Equity and Liabilities	**328**

Adjustments in Group Accounts

The consolidation schedule can equally be adopted for solving this group problem as scheduled below:

Consolidation Schedule

ADEBOLA Plc		Cost of control (FARAMADE in ADEBOLA) as at 31 December 2016 – 80%		Non-controlling Interests – 20%		Consolidated Reserves
Equity Share Capital	100	(80% x 100)	80	(20% x 100)	20	
Reserves (Pre-acquisition)	60	(80% x 60)	48	(20% x 60)	12	
Net asset on acquisition			128			
Cost of combination (cost of investment)			(140)			
Goodwill (positive)			(12)			
Non-controlling interests					32	
FARAMADE Plc Reserves						140
Consolidated Reserves						140

ILLUSTRATION 18:

FARAMADE Plc acquired 80% of the shares of ADEBOLA Plc as at 31 December 2015 when the retained profits of the later stood at ₦40 million. The statements of financial positions of the dual entities are as shown below:

Statement of Financial Position as at 31 December 2016

	FARAMADE Plc	ADEBOLA Plc
Non-Current Assets:	₦' million	₦' million
Property, plant and equipment	130	120
Investment in **ADEBOLA Plc**	100	
Current Assets:		
Inventories	25	45
Account Receivables	12	12
Dividend Receivable	8	
Bank	5	7
Total Assets	**280**	**184**
Equity and Liabilities:		
Equity – Ordinary Shares (₦0.50/share)	80	100
Retained Earnings	140	60
Current Liabilities:		
Account Payables	40	14
Dividend Payable	20	10
Total equity and liabilities	**280**	**184**

We are to approach the solution in the following steps:

- ✓ *Step 1*: Determine the percentage holdings of investment of **FARAMADE Plc** in **ADEBOLA Plc** as at the acquisition date (31 December 2015), which represents the date of inclusion (first date of *consolidation).* In this case, the percentage holding is already determined and ascertained to be 80%.

✓ **Step 2:** *Ascertain the form of group structure in this parent-subsidiary relationship.* Since the subsidiary (**ADEBOLA Plc**) is *partly-owned* by the parent (**FARAMADE Plc**), the group structure is a simple structure as shown below:

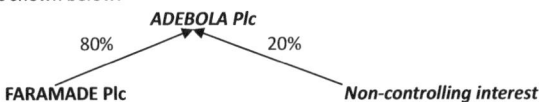

```
                    ADEBOLA Plc
              80%   ↗↖   20%
      FARAMADE Plc      Non-controlling interest
```

✓ **Step 3:** *Determine the existence and calculate goodwill or gain from a bargain purchase as at the date of acquisition based on the fair value or provisional values of subsidiary's identifiable assets and liabilities.* In this case, there exists goodwill as shown below.

To ascertain and determine the value of goodwill or gain from a bargain purchase, the value of an investment of the parent (**FARAMADE Plc**) in the subsidiary (**ADEBOLA Plc**) will be compared with the parent's share of identifiable assets and liabilities of the subsidiary that were acquired.

	₦' million	₦' million
Cost of combination (i.e. the cost of investment of **FARAMADE** in **ADEBOLA**)		100
Less: **FARAMADE**'s share of Identifiable net assets of **ADEBOLA** acquired:		
• Share capital (80% of ₦100 million)	80	
• Pre-acquisition reserves (80% of ₦20 million)	16	(96)
Goodwill attributable to **FARAMADE Plc** *(a)*		4
Amount of investments of non-controlling interest in **ADEBOLA Plc**		24
Less: Non-controlling interest share of the fair value of subsidiary's net assets:		
• Share capital (20% of ₦100 million)	20	
• Pre-acquisition reserves (20% of ₦20 million)	4	(24)
Goodwill attributable to **non-controlling interests*** *(b)*		---
Goodwill (a + b)		**4**

Technical Note:
The goodwill attributable to non-controlling must be zero since the investment to non-controlling interests is valued at the proportionate share of subsidiary's identifiable net assets as shown by the arrow.

	₦' million
Cost of combination (i.e. cost of acquisition) to the parent	100
Amount of Investment in subsidiary to non-controlling interest*	24
Combined amount of interests in subsidiary to all investors	**124**
Less: Fair value of Identifiable net assets acquired @ 31 December 2015	
• Ordinary share capital of Sussy	100
• Pre-acquisition reserves	20
Net assets attributable to ordinary shareholders	(120)
Goodwill - positive	**4**

✓ **Step 4:** *Determine the value of non-controlling interest as will be shown in the consolidated statement of financial position of the group.* In this case, non-controlling interest will only be valued at the proportionate share of subsidiary's identifiable assets and liabilities, which could be ascertained as thus:

Non-controlling interest's share of Identifiable net assets of **ADEBOLA**:

	₦' million
• Share capital (20% of ₦100 million)	20
• Pre-acquisition reserves (20% of ₦20 million)	4
NCI's investment on 31 December 2015 (*based on proportionate share of net assets*)	**24**
• Post-acquisition reserves (20% of ₦40 million)	8
NCI's investment on 31 December 2016 (*based on proportionate share of net assets*)	**32**

✓ **Step 5:** *Determine the amount to be included in the consolidated statement of financial position as consolidated reserves (otherwise known as consolidated retained earnings).* The consolidated retained earnings to be included in the group statement of financial position of **FARAMADE-Group** is only that of the parent, as the subsidiary retained earnings at the point of acquisition is entirely classified as pre-acquisition retained profit, which already as for is considered as part of the net asset of the subsidiary upon acquisition. Invariably, it implies that only the post-acquisition retained profit of the subsidiary that ought to be considered in ascertaining the group retained earnings. The consolidated retained earnings are usually determined as follows:

	₦' million
Parent's (**FARAMADE Plc**) retained earnings	140
Post-acquisition reserves (80% of ₦40 million)	32
	172

✓ **Step 6:** *Combine the assets and liabilities of the parent (**FARAMADE Plc**) and subsidiary (**ADEBOLA Plc**) on an item-by-item basis excluding the initial investment of **FARAMADE Plc** in **ADEBOLA Plc** as earlier shown in the separate financial statement of **FARAMADE Plc**, and also the exclusion of the equity share capital of **ADEBOLA Plc**, as it has already been considered alongside with the pre-acquisition retained profits in ascertaining the value of goodwill or gain from bargain purchase inherent/embedded in the acquisition.*

✓ **Step 7:** *The Dividend receivable in the statement of financial position of FARAMADE Plc will have to be cancelled out against the dividend payable (accruable or due to the parent-FARAMADE) as outstanding in the statement of financial position of ADEBOLA.* In this case, the sum of ₦8 million is due to FARAMADE (80% of dividend payable of the subsidiary - ₦10 million), will be cancelled out between dividend receivable by the parent and dividend payable by the subsidiary. Any balance due on both the dividend receivable of the parent and dividend payable by the subsidiary will be attributed to third parties (i.e. outside the group), and primarily should constitute group assets and liabilities respectively. In this case, the dividend receivable is zero after the adjustment which signifies no dividend receivable outside the group by the parent, whereas, there exist the balance of ₦2 million on dividend payable (being ₦10 million – ₦8 million due to the parent or equivalent of 20% of ₦10 million), which is due to third parties (non-controlling interest) and will be considered part of *other liabilities*. The consolidated statement of financial position of the group will now be shown as thus:

FARAMADE Group
Consolidated Statement of Financial Position as at 31 December 2016

	₦ million
Non-current assets:	
Property, plant and equipment (130 + 120)	250
Goodwill	4
Current assets:	
Inventories (25 + 45)	70
Account receivables (12 + 12)	24
Bank (5 + 7)	12
Total Assets	**350**
Share Capital & Reserves:	
Equity share capital	80
Reserves	172
Equity attributable to FARAMADE's shareholders	**252**
Non-controlling interest	32
Total Equity	**284**
Current liabilities:	
Account payables (40 + 14)	54
Dividend payables (parent only)	20
Other liabilities (Dividend payable to non-controlling interest)	2
Total Equity and Liabilities	**350**

The consolidation schedule can equally be adopted for solving this group problem as scheduled below:

Consolidation Schedule

ADEBOLA Plc		Cost of control (FARAMADE in ADEBOLA) as at 31 December 2015 – 80%		Non-controlling Interests – 20%		Consolidated Reserves	
Equity Share Capital	100	(80% x 100)	80	(20% x 100)	20		
Reserves (Pre-acquisition)	20	(80% x 20)	48	(20% x 20)	4		
Reserves (Post-acquisition)	40			(20% x 40)	8	(80% x 40)	32
Net asset on acquisition			96				
Cost of combination (cost of investment)			(100)				
Goodwill (positive)			(4)				
Non-controlling interest					32		
FARAMADE Plc Reserves							140
Consolidated Reserves							172

Adjustments in Group Accounts

ILLUSTRATION 19:

POPSY acquired 70% of the ordinary shares of **LILLY** on May 31, 2016. The retained earnings of **LILLY** was ₦26 million as at the beginning of the reporting period December 31, 2016.

Statement of Financial Position as at 31ˢᵗ December 2016

	POPSY	LILLY
Non-current assets:	₦' million	₦' million
Property, plant and equipment	500	240
Investment in **LILLY**	250	
Current assets:		
Inventories	63	120
Account receivables	50	40
Dividend receivable	7	
Bank	20	20
	890	**420**
Share Capital & Reserves:		
Equity share capital	600	250
Reserves (Retained profit)	240	50
	840	300
Current liabilities:		
Account payables	30	110
Dividend payable	20	10
	890	**420**

Assume: Profit accrues evenly during the year

As we adopt the assumption that profit accrues evenly during the year and equally assumed that the dividend declared immediately prior to the reporting date (year-end) mimics the profit for the year. Also, we assume the parent at the point of acquisition (when control was obtained), investment of the non-controlling interests is measured at the proportionate share of the subsidiary's identifiable net assets (assets and liabilities). In this case, the consolidation process will be as follows:

- ✓ **Step 1**: *Determine the percentage holdings of investment of POPSY in LILLY as at the acquisition date (31 May 2016), which represents the date of inclusion (first date of consolidation).* In this case, the percentage holding is already determined and ascertained to be 70%.

- ✓ **Step 2**: *Ascertain the form of group structure in this parent-subsidiary relationship.* Since the subsidiary (**LILLY**) is *partly-owned* by the parent (**POPSY**), the group structure is a simple structure as shown below:

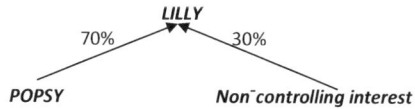

```
              LILLY
          70% ↗ ↖ 30%
        POPSY      Non-controlling interest
```

- ✓ **Step 3**: *Determine the existence and calculate goodwill or gain from a bargain purchase as at the date of acquisition based on the fair value or provisional values of subsidiary's identifiable assets and liabilities.* In this case, there exists goodwill as shown below.

To ascertain and determine the value of goodwill or gain from a bargain purchase, the value of an investment of the parent (**POPSY**) in the subsidiary (**LILLY**) will be compared with the parent's share of identifiable assets and liabilities of the subsidiary that were acquired.

	₦' million	₦' million
Cost of combination (i.e. the cost of investment of **POPSY** in **LILLY**)		250.0
Less: POPSY's share of Identifiable net assets of LILLY acquired:		
• Share capital (70% of ₦250 million)	175.0	
• Pre-acquisition reserves (70% of ₦36 million)	25.2	(200.2)
Goodwill attributable to POPSY's (a)		49.8
Amount of investments of non-controlling interest in **LILLY**		85.8
Less: Non-controlling interest share of the fair value of subsidiary's net assets:		
• Share capital (30% of ₦250 million)	75.0	
• Pre-acquisition reserves (30% of ₦36 million)	10.8	(85.8)
*Goodwill attributable to **non-controlling interests** (b)*		---
Goodwill (a + b)		**49.8**

Technical Note:
The goodwill attributable to non-controlling must be zero since the investment to non-controlling interests is valued at the proportionate share of subsidiary's identifiable net assets as shown by the arrow.

	₦' million
Cost of combination (i.e. cost of acquisition) to the parent	250.0
Amount of Investment in subsidiary to non-controlling interest*	85.8
Combined amount of interests in subsidiary to all investors	335.8
Less: Fair value of Identifiable net assets acquired @ 31 May 2016	
• Ordinary share capital of Sussy	250
• Pre-acquisition reserves	36 (286)
Goodwill - positive	**49.8**

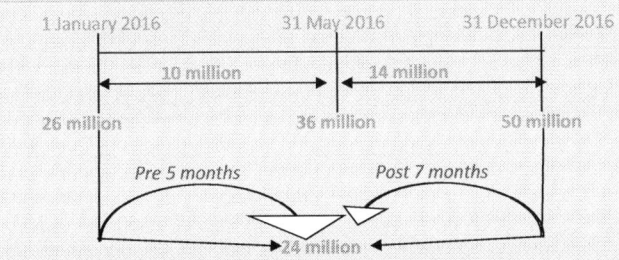

```
1 January 2016        31 May 2016        31 December 2016
         10 million              14 million
   26 million          36 million          50 million
              Pre 5 months      Post 7 months
                          24 million
```

Since the profit for the year is ₦24 million (being the increase in reserves from ₦26 million to ₦50 million in the reporting period, it should be separated into pre and post-acquisition element as thus:

Pre-acquisition profits/reserves equal the retained profits as at the beginning of the year ₦26 million plus the ₦10 million (being the portion attributable to 1st-5 months of the year i.e. 5/12 x ₦24 million) since profits accrue evenly.

Post-acquisition profits/reserves: equals the sum of ₦14 million (being the portion of the profit for the year that relates to the last 7 months of the year, i.e. 7/12 x ₦24 million) since profits accrue evenly, as shown below:

Adjustments in Group Accounts

✓ **Step 4:** Determine the value of non-controlling interest as will be shown in the consolidated statement of financial position of the group. In this case, non-controlling interest will only be measured at the proportionate share of subsidiary's identifiable assets and liabilities, which could be ascertained as thus:

Non-controlling interest's share of Identifiable net assets of **LILLY**:   ₦' million
- Share capital (30% of ₦250 million)   75.0
- Pre-acquisition reserves (30% of ₦36 million)   10.8

NCI's investment on 31 May 2016 (*based on proportionate share of net assets*)   85.8
- Post-acquisition reserves (30% of ₦14 million)   4.2

NCI's investment on 31 December 2016 (*based on proportionate share of net assets*)   **90.0**

✓ **Step 5:** Determine the amount to be included in the consolidated statement of financial position as consolidated reserves (otherwise known as consolidated retained earnings). The consolidated retained earnings to be included in the group statement of financial position of **POPSY-Group** are that of the parent and of the post-acquisition profits of the subsidiary. Invariably, it implies that the post-acquisition retained profit (which is the sum of ₦14 million being the increase from ₦36 million profits upon acquisition to ₦50 million the reporting date 31 December 2016 - *7 months after*) of the subsidiary (**LILLY**) will now be combined with the retained earnings (profits) of the parent (**POPSY**) in ascertaining the group retained earnings. The consolidated retained earnings will be determined as follows:

                                                                                                                  ₦' million
Parent's (**POPSY**) retained earnings   240.0
Share of subsidiary's (**LILLY**) post-acquisition profits (70% of ₦14 million)   9.8
                                                                                                                  249.8

✓ **Step 6:** Combine the assets and liabilities of the parent (**POPSY**) and subsidiary (**LILLY**) on an item-by-item basis excluding the initial investment of **POPSY** in **LILLY** as earlier shown in the separate financial statement of **POPSY**, and also the exclusion of the equity share capital of **LILLY**, as it has already been considered alongside with the pre-acquisition retained profits in ascertaining the value of goodwill or gain from bargain purchase inherent/embedded in the acquisition

✓ **Step 7:** The Dividend receivable in the statement of financial position of POPSY Plc will have to be cancelled out against the dividend payable (accruable or due to the parent-POPSY) as outstanding in the statement of financial position of LILLY. In this case, the sum of ₦7 million is due to POPSY (70% of dividend payable of the subsidiary - ₦10 million), will be cancelled out between dividend receivable by the parent and dividend payable by the subsidiary. Any balance due on both the dividend receivable of the parent and dividend payable by the subsidiary will be attributed to third parties (i.e. outside the group), and primarily should constitute group assets and liabilities respectively. In this case, the dividend receivable is zero after the adjustment which signifies no dividend receivable outside the group by the parent, whereas, there exist the balance of ₦3 million on dividend payable (being ₦10 million – ₦7 million due to the parent or equivalent of 30% of ₦10 million), which is due to third parties (non-controlling interest) and will be considered part of *other liabilities*. The consolidated statement of financial position of the group will now be shown as thus:

POPSY Group
Consolidated Statement of Financial Position as at 31 December 2016

Non-current assets:	₦' million	₦' million
Non-current asset (500 + 240)		740.0
Goodwill		49.8
Current asset:		
Inventories (63 + 120)	183.0	
Account receivables (50 + 40)	90.0	
Bank (20 + 20)	40.0	313.0
Total Assets		**1,102.8**
Share Capital & Reserves:		
Equity share capital		600.0
Reserves		249.8
Equity attributable to POPSY's shareholders		**849.8**
Non-controlling interest		90.0
Total Equity		**939.8**
Current liabilities:		
Account payables (30 + 110)	140.0	
Dividend payable (parent only)	20.0	
Other liabilities*	3.0	
		163.0
Total Equity and Liabilities		**1,102.8**

The consolidation schedule can equally be adopted for solving this group problem as scheduled below:

Consolidation Schedule

	LILLY	Cost of control (POPSY in LILLY) as at 31 May 2016 – 70%		Non-controlling Interests – 30%		Consolidated Reserves
Equity Share Capital	250	(70% x 250)	175.0	(30% x 250)	75.0	
Reserves (Pre-acquisition)	36	(70% x 36)	25.2	(30% x 36)	10.8	
Reserves (Post-acquisition)	14			(30% x 14)	4.2	(70% x 14) 9.8
Net asset on acquisition			200.2			
Cost of combination (cost of investment)			(247.1)			
Goodwill (positive)			(46.9)			
Non-controlling interests					90.0	
Pally Reserve						240.0
Consolidated Reserves						249.8

OLD POSITION OF IAS 27 (BEFORE THE REVISED POSITION IN 2008)

When dividends are declared by the subsidiary, both the parent and the non-controlling interest are entitled to their own share, which is derived based on the percentage holdings in the subsidiary. Some situations exist where dividends are paid either from pre-acquisition profits or post-acquisition profits.

If dividends are paid out of post-acquisition reserves there is no problem, because the dividends would have been recognised as appropriate directly into the income statement of the parent (i.e. The parent simply credits the relevant amount to its own statement of comprehensive income, as with any other dividend income), as shown below.

Debit: Bank / (Dividend Receivable)
Credit: Statement of Comprehensive Income of the Parent (or Income Statement)
With the (parent share of) dividend payable (declared) or paid by the subsidiary

The dividends received by the parent and paid by the subsidiary are then cancelled upon consolidation. This will totally cancel out only if the subsidiary is wholly owned by the parent, otherwise it will not cancel out in full, and the non-cancelled amount of the dividend payable in the subsidiary's statement of financial position will be the amount payable to the non-controlling interest and will be reported in the consolidated statement of financial position as dividend payable to non-controlling interest (i.e. as payable by the group to third parties) and normally shown separately from any dividend payable by the parent.

When dividends are paid out of pre-acquisition reserves, we are faced with certain challenges, which simply is what treatment should be accorded the dividends. Where a dividend is paid from pre-acquisition reserves, it eventually reduces the cost of the parent's investment (cost of combination), as for being treated *more-or-less* as a discount or rebate (refund of part of the cost of investments) obtained in the course of acquisition. The necessarily accounting entry to be passed when the dividend is paid out of pre-acquisition profits and recognised in the income statement of the parent is to reverse such and consider it as a reduction of the cost of investment for consolidation purpose, as shown below:

Debit: Statement of Comprehensive Income of the Parent (or Income Statement)
Credit: Investment in Subsidiary
With the (parent share of) dividend payable (declared) or paid by the subsidiary

The dividend is said to be paid from pre-acquisition reserves if dividends paid to the parent company in respect of previous accounting period upon the first day of the accounting period the parent acquires the subsidiary. Otherwise, if the shares of the subsidiary are acquired during the subsidiary's accounting period (reporting period), it will be best to adopt a *time-apportionment* in determining the portion of the dividend paid from pre-acquisition profits and that of post-acquisition profits. The time-apportionment can be considered on an *even basis* or *uneven basis* (especially when the business activities of the subsidiary are considered seasonal or cyclical in nature.

When dividends are declared by the subsidiary, both the parent and the non-controlling interest are entitled to their own share, which is derived based on the percentage holdings in the subsidiary. The situation exists where dividends are paid either from pre-acquisition profits or post-acquisition profits.

If dividends are paid out of post acquisition reserves there is no problem, because the dividends would have been recognised as appropriate directly into the income statement of the parent (i.e. The parent simply credits the relevant amount to its own statement of comprehensive income, as with any other dividend income), as shown below.

Debit: Bank / (Dividend Receivable)
Credit: Statement of Comprehensive Income of the Parent (or Income Statement)
With the (parent share of) dividend payable (declared) or paid by the subsidiary

The dividends received by the parent and paid by the subsidiary are then cancelled upon consolidation. This will totally cancel out only if the subsidiary is wholly owned by the parent, otherwise it will not cancel out in full, and the non-cancelled amount of the dividend payable in the subsidiary's statement of financial position will be the amount payable to the non-controlling interest and will be reported in the consolidated statement of financial position as dividend payable to non-controlling interest (i.e. as payable by the group to third parties) and normally shown separately from any dividend payable by the parent.

When dividends are paid out of pre-acquisition reserves, we are faced with certain challenges, which simply is what treatment should be accorded the dividends. Where a dividend is paid from pre-acquisition reserves, it eventually reduces the cost of the parent's investment (cost of combination), as for being treated *more-or-less* as a discount or rebate (refund of part of the cost of investments) obtained in the course of acquisition. The necessarily accounting entry to be passed when the dividend is paid out of pre-acquisition profits and recognised in the income statement of the parent is to reverse such and consider it as a reduction of the cost of investment for consolidation purpose, as shown below:

Debit: Statement of Comprehensive Income of the Parent (or Income Statement)
Credit: Investment in Subsidiary
With the (parent share of) dividend payable (declared) or paid by the subsidiary

The dividend is said to be paid from pre-acquisition reserves if dividends paid to the parent company in respect of previous accounting period upon the first day of the accounting period, the parent acquires the subsidiary. Otherwise, if the shares of the subsidiary are acquired during the subsidiary's accounting period (reporting period), it will be best to adopt a *time-apportionment* in determining the portion of the dividend paid from pre-acquisition profits and that of post-acquisition profits. The time-apportionment can be considered on an *even basis or uneven basis (especially when the business activities of the subsidiary are considered seasonal or cyclical in nature.*

If the parent has not recognised the dividend received or receivable from the subsidiary in its separate financial statements, it is more preferred to adjust the financial statement of the parent before proceeding with the consolidation, or alternatively, we adjust for the dividends on consolidation based on the principles of consolidation as it relates to dividends paid either from pre-acquisition profits or post-acquisition profits.

ILLUSTRATION A:

FARAMADE Plc acquired 80% of the shares of ADEBOLA Plc as at 30 December 2016. FARAMADE Plc was included in the register of shareholders in of ADEBOLA Plc before the register was closed and before the declaration date (31 December 2016) of dividend by ADEBOLA Plc which coincide with the reporting date, and this makes FARAMADE Plc entitled to dividend of ADEBOLA Plc as at the year ended 31 December 2016 has the amount of the dividend is still outstanding.

Adjustments in Group Accounts

	Statement of Financial Position as at 31 December 2016	
	FARAMADE Plc	ADEBOLA Plc
	₦' million	₦' million
Non-Current Assets:		
Property, plant and equipment	90	120
Investment in *ADEBOLA Plc*	140	
Current Assets:		
Inventories	25	45
Accounts receivables	12	12
Dividend Receivable	8	
Bank	5	7
Total Assets	280	184
Equity and Liabilities:		
Equity – Ordinary Shares (₦0.50/share)	80	100
Retained Earnings	140	60
Current Liabilities:		
Accounts payables	40	14
Dividend Payable	20	10
Total equity and liabilities	280	184

We are to approach the solution in the following steps:

✓ **Step 1:** *Determine the percentage holdings of investment of* FARAMADE Plc *in* ADEBOLA Plc *as at the acquisition date (31 December 2016), which represents the date of inclusion (first date of consolidation).* In this case, the percentage holding is already determined and ascertained to be 80%.

✓ **Step 2:** *Ascertain the form of group structure in this parent-subsidiary relationship.* Since the subsidiary (*ADEBOLA Plc*) is *partly-owned* by the parent (FARAMADE Plc), the group structure is a simple structure as shown below:

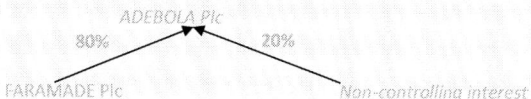

```
                    ADEBOLA Plc
                   ↗          ↖
              80%              20%
             ↙                    ↘
       FARAMADE Plc          Non-controlling interest
```

✓ **Step 3:** *Determine the existence of goodwill or gain from a bargain purchase as at the date of acquisition based on the fair value or provisional values of subsidiary's identifiable assets and liabilities.* In this case, there exists goodwill as shown below.

To ascertain and determine the amount of goodwill or gain from a bargain purchase, the value of an investment of the parent (FARAMADE Plc) in the subsidiary (*ADEBOLA Plc*) will be compared with the parent's share of identifiable assets and liabilities of the subsidiary that were acquired.

	₦' million	₦' million
Cost of combination (i.e. the cost of investment of FARAMADE in *ADEBOLA*)		132*
Less: FARAMADE's share of Identifiable net assets of *ADEBOLA* acquired:		

- Share capital (80% of ₦100 million)   80
- Pre-acquisition reserves (80% of ₦60 million)   48   (128)

Goodwill attributable to FARAMADE Plc (a)   4
Amount of investments of non-controlling interest in ADEBOLA Plc   32
Less: Non-controlling interest share of the fair value of subsidiary's net assets:
- Share capital (20% of ₦100 million)   20
- Pre-acquisition reserves (20% of ₦60 million)   12   (32)

Goodwill attributable to non-controlling interests*(b)   —
Goodwill (a + b)   4

Technical Note:
The goodwill attributable to non-controlling must be zero since the investment to non-controlling interests is valued at the proportionate share of subsidiary's identifiable net assets as shown by the arrow.

	₦' million
Cost of combination (i.e. cost of acquisition) to the parent	132*
Amount of Investment in subsidiary to non-controlling interest*	32
Combined amount of interests in subsidiary to all investors	164
Less: Fair value of Identifiable net assets acquired @ 31 December 2016	
• Ordinary share capital of Sussy 100	
• Pre-acquisition reserves 60	
Net assets attributable to ordinary shareholders	(160)
Goodwill - positive	4

* The dividend income recognised in the income statement of FARAMADE Plc should be reversed as a credit against the cost of investments in ADEBOLA Plc, as dividend due on acquisition is considered a reduction of the cost of investment on the acquisition of the subsidiary (ADEBOLA Plc), as shown below:

Debit: Consolidated retained earnings (or retained earnings of FARAMADE Plc)
Credit: Investments in ADEBOLA Plc   } ₦8 million

The dividend recognised as income upon acquisition is the sum of ₦8 million is 80% of the dividend of ₦10 million declared as at the reporting date (31 December 2016) by the subsidiary.

Hence, the cost of investment in the subsidiary will be reduced to ₦132 million (being the reduction from the sum of ₦140 million resulting from ₦8 million dividend receivable at acquisition).

✓ *Step 4: Determine the amount of non-controlling interest as will be shown in the consolidated statement of financial position of the group.* In this case, non-controlling interest will only be measured at the proportionate share of subsidiary's identifiable assets and liabilities, which could be depicted as thus:

Non-controlling interest's share of Identifiable net assets of ADEBOLA:

	₦' million
• Share capital (20% of ₦100 million)	20
• Pre-acquisition reserves (20% of ₦60 million)	12
NCI's investment on 31 December 2016 (based on proportionate share of net assets)	32

Adjustments in Group Accounts

- ✓ *Step 5: Determine the amount to be included in the consolidated statement of financial position as consolidated reserves (otherwise known as consolidated retained earnings).* The consolidated retained earnings to be included in the consolidated statement of financial position of FARAMADE-Group is only that of the parent, as the subsidiary retained earnings at the point of acquisition is entirely classified as pre-acquisition retained earnings, which already has been considered as part of the net assets of the subsidiary upon acquisition. Invariably, it implies that only the post-acquisition retained earnings of the subsidiary that ought to be considered in ascertaining the group retained earnings. The consolidated retained earnings are usually determined as follows:

	₦' million
Parent's (FARAMADE Plc) retained earnings	140
Less: Dividend from the subsidiary initially recognised as income on acquisition	(8)
	132

* Furthermore, the retained earnings of the Parent (FARAMADE Plc) or the consolidated retained earnings will be reduced by the reversal of the dividend from the subsidiary of ₦8 million earlier recognised on acquisition as income in the statement of comprehensive income (or Income statement) of the parent for the reporting period ending December 31, 2010.

- ✓ *Step 6: Combine the assets and liabilities of the parent (FARAMADE Plc) and subsidiary (ADEBOLA Plc) on an item-by-item basis excluding the initial investment of FARAMADE Plc in ADEBOLA Plc as earlier shown in the separate financial statements of FARAMADE Plc, and also the exclusion of the equity share capital of ADEBOLA Plc, as it has already been considered alongside with the pre-acquisition retained earnings in ascertaining the amount of goodwill or gain from bargain purchase inherent/embedded in the acquisition.*

- ✓ *Step 7: The Dividend receivable in the statement of financial position of FARAMADE Plc will have to be cancelled out against the dividend payable (accruable or due to the parent- FARAMADE) as outstanding in the statement of financial position of ADEBOLA.* In this case, the sum of ₦8 million is due to FARAMADE (80% of dividend payable of the subsidiary - ₦10 million), will be cancelled out between dividend receivable by the parent and dividend payable by the subsidiary. Any balance due on both the dividend receivable of the parent and dividend payable by the subsidiary will be attributed to third parties (i.e. outside the group), and primarily should constitute group assets and liabilities respectively. In this case, the dividend receivable is zero after the adjustment which signifies no dividend receivable outside the group by the parent, whereas, there exist the balance of ₦2 million on dividend payable (being ₦10 million – ₦8 million due to the parent or equivalent of 20% of ₦10 million), which is due to third parties (non-controlling interest) and will be considered part of *other liabilities*. The consolidated statement of financial position of the group will now be shown as thus:

FARAMADE Group
Consolidated Statement of Financial Position as at 31 December 2016

Non-current assets:	₦' million
Property, plant and equipment (90 + 120)	210
Goodwill on consolidation	4
Current assets:	
Inventories (25 + 45)	70
Accounts receivables (12 + 12)	24
Bank (5 + 7)	12
Total Assets	320

Share Capital & Reserves:	
Equity share capital	80
Reserves	132
Equity attributable to FARAMADE's shareholders	212
Non-controlling interest	32
Total Equity	244
Current liabilities:	
Accounts payables (40 + 14)	54
Dividend payables (parent only)	20
Other liabilities	2
Total Equity and Liabilities	320

The consolidation schedule can equally be adopted for solving this group problem as scheduled below:

Consolidation Schedule

ADEBOLA Plc		Cost of control (FARAMADE in ADEBOLA) as at 31 December 2016 – 80%		Non-controlling Interests – 20%		Consolidated Reserves
Equity Share Capital	100	(80% x 100)	80	(20% x 100)	20	
Reserves (Pre-acquisition)	60	(80% x 60)	48	(20% x 60)	12	
Net asset on acquisition			128			
Cost of combination (cost of investment)			(132)			
Goodwill (positive)			(4)			
Non-controlling interests					32	
Dividend from the subsidiary						(8)
FARAMADE Plc Reserves						140
Consolidated Reserves						132

ILLUSTRATION B:

FARAMADE Plc acquired 80% of the shares of ADEBOLA Plc as at 31 December 2015 when the retained earnings of the later stood at ₦40 million. The statements of financial positions of the dual entities are as shown below:

Statement of Financial Position as at 31 December 2016

	FARAMADE Plc ₦' million	ADEBOLA Plc ₦' million
Non-Current Assets:		
Property, plant and equipment	130	120
Investment in ADEBOLA Plc	100	
Current Assets:		
Inventories	25	45
Accounts receivables	12	12
Dividend Receivable	8	
Bank	5	7
Total Assets	280	184

Adjustments in Group Accounts

Equity and Liabilities:		
Equity – Ordinary Shares (₦0.50/share)	80	100
Retained Earnings	140	60
Current Liabilities:		
Accounts payables	40	14
Dividend Payable	20	10
Total equity and liabilities	280	184

We are to approach the solution in the following steps:

- ✓ *Step 1: Determine the percentage holdings of investment of* FARAMADE Plc *in* ADEBOLA Plc *as at the acquisition date (31 December 2015), which represents the date of inclusion (first date of consolidation).* In this case, the percentage holding is already determined and ascertained to be 80%.

- ✓ *Step 2: Ascertain the form of group structure in this parent-subsidiary relationship.* Since the subsidiary (ADEBOLA Plc) is *partly-owned* by the parent (FARAMADE Plc), the group structure is a simple structure as shown below:

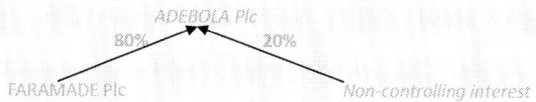

```
              ADEBOLA Plc
          80%↗       ↖20%
      FARAMADE Plc        Non-controlling interest
```

- ✓ *Step 3: Determine the existence of goodwill or gain from a bargain purchase as at the date of acquisition based on the fair value or provisional values of subsidiary's identifiable assets and liabilities.* In this case, there exists goodwill as shown below.

To ascertain and determine the amount of goodwill or gain from a bargain purchase, the value of an investment of the parent (FARAMADE Plc) in the subsidiary (ADEBOLA Plc) will be compared with the parent's share of identifiable assets and liabilities of the subsidiary that were acquired.

	₦' million	₦' million
Cost of combination (i.e. the cost of investment of FARAMADE in ADEBOLA)		100
Less: FARAMADE's share of Identifiable net assets of ADEBOLA acquired:		
• Share capital (80% of ₦100 million)	80	
• Pre-acquisition reserves (80% of ₦20 million)	16	(96)
Goodwill attributable to FARAMADE Plc *(a)*		4
Amount of investments of non-controlling interest in ADEBOLA Plc		24
Less: Non-controlling interest share of the fair value of subsidiary's net assets:		
• Share capital (20% of ₦100 million)	20	
• Pre-acquisition reserves (20% of ₦20 million)	4	(24)
Goodwill attributable to non-controlling interests*(b)		–
Goodwill (a + b)		4

Technical Note:
*The goodwill attributable to non-controlling must be zero since the investment to non-controlling interests is valued at the proportionate share of subsidiary's identifiable net assets as shown by the arrow.

	₦' million
Cost of combination (i.e. cost of acquisition) to the parent	100
Amount of Investment in subsidiary to non-controlling interest*	24
Combined amount of interests in subsidiary to all investors	124
Less: Fair value of Identifiable net assets acquired @ 30 December 2016	
• Ordinary share capital of Sussy 100	
• Pre-acquisition reserves 20	
Net assets attributable to ordinary shareholders	(120)
Goodwill - positive	4

✓ Step 4: Determine the amount of non-controlling interest as will be shown in the consolidated statement of financial position of the group. In this case, non-controlling interest will only be measured at the proportionate share of subsidiary's identifiable assets and liabilities, which could be depicted as thus:

Non-controlling interest's share of Identifiable net assets of ADEBOLA upon acquisition:

	₦' million
• Share capital (20% of ₦100 million)	20
• Pre-acquisition reserves (20% of ₦20 million)	4
NCI's investment on 31 December 2015 (based on proportionate share of net assets)	24
• Post-acquisition reserves (20% of ₦40 million)	8
NCI's investment on 31 December 2016 (based on proportionate share of net assets)	32

✓ Step 5: Determine the amount to be included in the consolidated statement of financial position as consolidated reserves (otherwise known as consolidated retained earnings). The consolidated retained earnings to be included in the consolidated statement of financial position of FARAMADE-Group is only that of the parent, as the subsidiary retained earnings at the point of acquisition is entirely classified as pre-acquisition retained earnings, which already has been considered as part of the net assets of the subsidiary upon acquisition. Invariably, it implies that only the post-acquisition retained earnings of the subsidiary that ought to be considered in ascertaining the group retained earnings. The consolidated retained earnings are usually determined as follows:

	₦' million
Parent's (FARAMADE Plc) retained earnings	140
Post-acquisition reserves (80% of ₦40 million)	32
	172

Technical Note:
There is no reversal of dividend income recognised by the parent into the income statement because it is considered to have been issued out of post-acquisition profits.

✓ Step 6: Combine the assets and liabilities of the parent (FARAMADE Plc) and subsidiary (ADEBOLA Plc) on an item-by-item basis excluding the initial investment of FARAMADE Plc in ADEBOLA Plc as earlier shown in the separate financial statements of FARAMADE Plc, and also the exclusion of the equity share capital of ADEBOLA Plc, as it has already been considered alongside with the pre-acquisition retained earnings in ascertaining the amount of goodwill or gain from bargain purchase inherent/embedded in the acquisition.

✓ Step 7: The Dividend receivable in the statement of financial position of FARAMADE Plc will have to be cancelled out against the dividend payable (accruable or due to the parent-

FARAMADE) as outstanding in the statement of financial position of *ADEBOLA*. In this case, the sum of ₦8 million is due to FARAMADE (80% of dividend payable of the subsidiary - ₦10 million), will be cancelled out between dividend receivable by the parent and dividend payable by the subsidiary. Any balance due on both the dividend receivable of the parent and dividend payable by the subsidiary will be attributed to third parties (i.e. outside the group), and primarily should constitute group assets and liabilities respectively. In this case, the dividend receivable is zero after the adjustment which signifies no dividend receivable outside the group by the parent, whereas, there exist the balance of ₦2 million on dividend payable (being ₦10 million – ₦8 million due to the parent or equivalent of 20% of ₦10 million), which is due to third parties (non-controlling interest) and will be considered part of *other liabilities*. The consolidated statement of financial position of the group will now be shown as thus:

FARAMADE Group
Consolidated Statement of Financial Position as at 31 December 2016

	₦' million
Non-current assets:	
Property, plant and equipment (130 + 120)	250
Goodwill on consolidation	4
Current assets:	
Inventories (25 + 45)	70
Accounts receivables (12 + 12)	24
Bank (5 + 7)	12
Total Assets	350
Share Capital & Reserves:	
Equity share capital	80
Reserves	172
Equity attributable to FARAMADE's shareholders	252
Non-controlling interest	32
Total Equity	284
Current liabilities:	
Accounts payables (40 + 14)	54
Dividend payables (parent only)	20
Other liabilities	2
Total Equity and Liabilities	350

The consolidation schedule can equally be adopted for solving this group problem as scheduled below:

Consolidation Schedule

ADEBOLA Plc		Cost of control (FARAMADE in ADEBOLA) as at 31 December 2015 – 80%		Non-controlling Interests – 20%		Consolidated Reserves
Equity Share Capital	100	(80% x 100)	80	(20% x 100)	20	
Reserves (Pre-acquisition)	20	(80% x 20)	48	(20% x 20)	4	
Reserves (Post-acquisition)	40			(20% x 40)	8	(80% x 40) 32
Net asset on acquisition			96			
Cost of combination (cost of investment)			(100)			

Goodwill (positive)		(4)	
Non-controlling interests			32
FARAMADE Plc Reserves			140
Consolidated Reserves			172

ILLUSTRATION C:

POPSY acquired 70% of the ordinary shares of LILLY on May 31, 2016. The retained earnings of LILLY was ₦26 million as at the beginning of the reporting period December 31, 2016.

Statement of Financial Position as at 31st December 2016

	POPSY	LILLY
	₦' million	₦' million
Non-current assets:		
Property, plant and equipment	500	240
Investment in LILLY	250	
Current assets:		
Inventories	63	120
Accounts receivables	50	40
Dividend receivable	7	
Bank	20	20
	890	420
Share Capital & Reserves:		
Equity share capital	600	250
Reserves (Retained Earnings)	240	50
	840	300
Current liabilities:		
Accounts payables	30	110
Dividend payable	20	10
	890	420

Assume: *Profit accrues evenly during the year*

As we adopt the assumption that profit accrues evenly during the year and equally assumed that the dividend declared immediately prior to the reporting date (year-end) mimics the profit for the year. Also, we assume the parent at the point of acquisition (when control was obtained), valued investment of the non-controlling interests at the proportionate share of the subsidiary's identifiable net assets (assets and liabilities). In this case, the consolidation process will be as follows:

- ✓ *Step 1: Determine the percentage holdings of investment of POPSY in LILLY as at the acquisition date (31 May 2016), which represents the date of inclusion (first date of consolidation).* In this case, the percentage holding is already determined and ascertained to be 70%.

- ✓ *Step 2: Ascertain the form of group structure in this parent-subsidiary relationship.* Since the subsidiary (LILLY) is *partly-owned* by the parent (POPSY), the group structure is a simple structure as shown below:

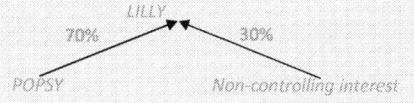

```
              LILLY
          70%↗    ↖30%
        POPSY      Non-controlling interest
```

Adjustments in Group Accounts

✓ **Step 3:** Determine the existence of goodwill or gain from a bargain purchase as at the date of acquisition based on the fair value or provisional values of subsidiary's identifiable assets and liabilities. In this case, there exists goodwill as shown below.

To ascertain and determine the amount of goodwill or gain from a bargain purchase, the value of an investment of the parent (POPSY) in the subsidiary (LILLY) will be compared with the parent's share of identifiable assets and liabilities of the subsidiary that were acquired.

	N' million	N' million
Cost of combination (i.e. the cost of investment of POPSY in LILLY)		247.1
Less: POPSY's share of Identifiable net assets of LILLY acquired:		
• Share capital (70% of N250 million)	175.0	
• Pre-acquisition reserves (70% of N36 million)	25.2	(200.2)
Goodwill attributable to POPSY's (a)		46.9
Amount of investments of non-controlling interest in LILLY		85.8
Less: Non-controlling interest share of the fair value of subsidiary's net assets:		
• Share capital (30% of N250 million)	75.0	
• Pre-acquisition reserves (30% of N36 million)	10.8	(85.8)
Goodwill attributable to non-controlling interests (b)		---
Goodwill (a + b)		46.9

Technical Note:
*The goodwill attributable to non-controlling must be zero since the investment to non-controlling interests is valued at the proportionate share of subsidiary's identifiable net assets as shown by the arrow.

	N' million
Cost of combination (i.e. cost of acquisition) to the parent	247.1
Amount of Investment in subsidiary to non-controlling interest*	85.8
Combined amount of interests in subsidiary to all investors	332.9
Less: Fair value of identifiable net assets of LILLY acquired:	
• Share capital	250.0
• Pre-acquisition reserves	36.0 (286.0)
Goodwill - positive	46.9

```
1 January 2016        31 May 2016          31 December 2016
     |--------10 million--------|---------14 million---------|
   N26 million          N36 million              N50 million

              Pre (5 months)      Post (7 months)
                        →N24 million←
```

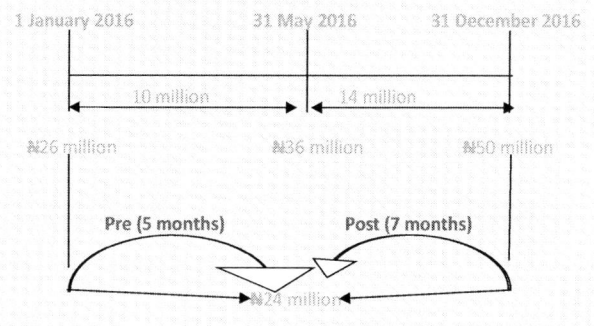

Since the profit for the year is N24 million (being the increase in reserves from N26 million to N50

million in the reporting period, it should be separated into pre and post-acquisition element as thus:

Pre-acquisition profits/reserves equal the Retained Earnings as at the beginning of the year ₦26 million plus the ₦10 million (being the portion attributable to 1st-5 months of the year i.e. 5/12 x ₦24 million) since profits accrue evenly.

Post-acquisition profits/reserves: equals the sum of ₦14 million (being the portion of the profit for the year that relates to the last 7 months of the year, i.e. 7/12 x ₦24 million) since profits accrue evenly, as shown below:

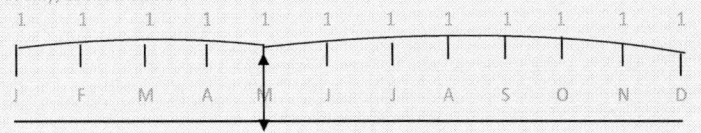

```
  1   1   1   1   1   1   1   1   1   1   1   1
  |   |   |   |   |   |   |   |   |   |   |   |
  J   F   M   A   M   J   J   A   S   O   N   D
              31 May 2016 (Acquisition date)
```

- The dividend income recognised in the income statement of **POPSY Plc** should be reversed as a credit against the cost of investments in **LILLY Plc**, as dividend due on acquisition is considered a reduction of the cost of investment on the acquisition of the subsidiary (**LILLY Plc**), as shown below:

    Debit: Consolidated retained earnings (or retained earnings of POPSY Plc)
    Credit: Investments in LILLY Plc ₦2.1 million

- The dividend recognised as income upon acquisition is the sum of ₦7 million is 70% of the dividend of ₦10 million declared as at the reporting date (31 December 2016) by the subsidiary. The dividend was partly from pre-acquisition profits and partly from post-acquisition profits. The dividend considered made out of pre-acquisition profits is ₦2.9 million, and out of post-acquisition profits is ₦4.1 million, as shown below:

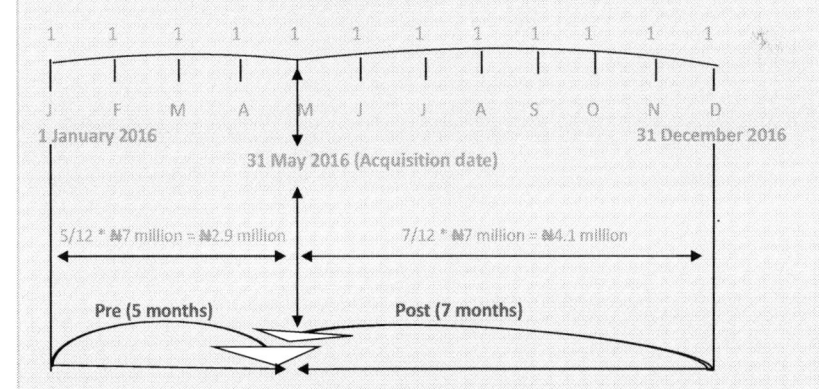

```
  1   1   1   1   1   1   1   1   1   1   1   1
  |   |   |   |   |   |   |   |   |   |   |   |
  J   F   M   A   M   J   J   A   S   O   N   D
1 January 2016                              31 December 2016
              31 May 2016 (Acquisition date)

  5/12 * ₦7 million = ₦2.9 million    7/12 * ₦7 million = ₦4.1 million

         Pre (5 months)                   Post (7 months)
```

Hence, the cost of investment in the subsidiary will be reduced to ₦247.1 million (being the reduction from the sum of ₦250 million resulting from ₦2.9 million dividends made from pre-acquisition profits (for the year).

Adjustments in Group Accounts

✓ *Step 4: Determine the amount of non-controlling interest as will be shown in the consolidated statement of financial position of the group.* In this case, non-controlling interest will only be measured at the proportionate share of subsidiary's identifiable assets and liabilities, which could be depicted as thus:

	₦' million
Non-controlling interest's share of Identifiable net assets of LILLY:	
• Share capital (30% of ₦250 million)	75.0
• Pre-acquisition reserves (30% of ₦36 million)	10.8
NCI's investment on 31/05/2016 *(based on proportionate share of net assets)*	85.8
• Post-acquisition reserves (30% of ₦14 million)	4.2
NCI's investment on 31/12/2016 *(based on proportionate share of net assets)*	90.0

✓ *Step 5: Determine the amount to be included in the consolidated statement of financial position as consolidated reserves (otherwise known as consolidated retained earnings).* The consolidated retained earnings to be included in the consolidated statement of financial position of POPSY-Group are that of the parent and of the post-acquisition profits of the subsidiary. Invariably, it implies that the post-acquisition retained earnings (which is the sum of ₦14 million being the increase from ₦36 million profits upon acquisition to ₦50 million the reporting date 31/12/2010 - 7 months after) of the subsidiary (LILLY) will now be combined with the retained earnings (profits) of the parent (POPSY) in ascertaining the group retained earnings. The consolidated retained earnings will be determined as follows:

	₦' million
Parent's (POPSY) retained earnings	240.0
Share of subsidiary's (LILLY) post-acquisition profits (70% of ₦14 million)	9.8
Less: Dividend from the subsidiary initially recognised as income on acquisition	(2.9)
	246.9

* Furthermore, the retained earnings of the Parent (POPSY Plc) or the consolidated retained earnings will be reduced by the reversal of the dividend from the subsidiary of ₦2.9 million earlier recognised on acquisition as income in the statement of comprehensive income (or Income statement) of the parent for the reporting period ending December 31, 2010.

✓ *Step 6: Combine the assets and liabilities of the parent (POPSY) and subsidiary (LILLY) on an item-by-item basis excluding the initial investment of POPSY in LILLY as earlier shown in the separate financial statements of POPSY, and also the exclusion of the equity share capital of LILLY, as it has already been considered alongside with the pre-acquisition retained earnings in ascertaining the amount of goodwill or gain from bargain purchase inherent/embedded in the acquisition*

✓ *Step 7: The Dividend receivable in the statement of financial position of POPSY Plc will have to be cancelled out against the dividend payable (accruable or due to the parent POPSY) as outstanding in the statement of financial position of LILLY.* In this case, the sum of ₦7 million is due to POPSY (70% of dividend payable of the subsidiary - ₦10 million), will be cancelled out between dividend receivable by the parent and dividend payable by the subsidiary. Any balance due on both the dividend receivable of the parent and dividend payable by the subsidiary will be attributed to third parties (i.e. outside the group), and primarily should constitute group assets and liabilities respectively. In this case, the dividend receivable is zero after the adjustment which signifies no dividend receivable outside the group by the parent, whereas, there exist the balance of ₦3 million on dividend payable (being ₦10 million – ₦7 million due to the parent or equivalent of 30% of ₦10 million), which is due to third parties (non-controlling interest) and will be considered part of *other liabilities*. The consolidated statement of financial position of the group will now be shown as thus:

POPSY Group
Consolidated Statement of Financial Position as at 31 December 2016

Non-current asset	₦' million	₦' million
Property, plant and equipment (500 + 240)		740.0
Goodwill		46.9
Current assets:		
Inventories (63 + 120)	183.0	
Accounts receivables (50 + 40)	90.0	
Bank (20 + 20)	40.0	313.0
Total Assets		1,099.9
Share Capital & Reserves:		
Equity share capital		600.0
Reserves		246.9
Equity attributable to POPSY's shareholders		846.9
Non-controlling interest		90.0
Total Equity		936.9
Current liabilities:		
Accounts payables (30 + 110)	140.0	
Dividend payable (parent only)	20.0	
Other liabilities*	3.0	163.0
Total Equity and Liabilities		1,099.9

The consolidation schedule can equally be adopted for solving this group problem as scheduled below:

Consolidation Schedule

LILLY		Cost of control (POPSY in LILLY) as at 31 May 2016 – 70%		Non-controlling Interests – 30%		Consolidated Reserves
Equity Share Capital	250	(70% x 250)	175.0	(30% x 250)	75.0	
Reserves (Pre-acquisition)	36	(70% x 36)	25.2	(30% x 36)	10.8	
Reserves (Post-acquisition)	14		–	(30% x 14)	4.2	(70% x 14) 9.8
Net asset on acquisition			200.2			
Cost of combination (cost of investment)			(247.1)			
Goodwill (positive)			(46.9)			
Non-controlling interest					90.0	
Dividend received from the subsidiary						(2.9)
Pally Reserves						240.0
Consolidated Reserves						**246.9**

Technical Note:
The new position of IAS 27 (REVISED IN 2008) now requires the treatment of dividend received or receivable from a subsidiary as a return on the parent's investment regardless of the whether it is paid/ declared from pre-acquisition profits or post-acquisition profits. The implication is that goodwill is no longer affected with the old principle of reduction of cost of investments with the dividends paid out of pre-acquisition profits (considered a pre-acquisition dividend).

SUMMARY OF CHAPTER 9

1. Group adjustments are necessary when consolidating the accounts of the parent and that of its subsidiaries, which invariably tends to allow the group present a financial position, financial performance and cash flows that vividly depicts that of a presumed single economic entity.

2. Most of the required group adjustments are necessitated on the intercompany transactions and balances held within the group in the reporting period.

3. The requirement of IFRS 10 is that inter-company transactions should be eliminated in totality.

4. Also, inter-company balances are required to be eliminated, so as not only to avoid overstatement of the amount of assets and liabilities (in their equivalent amount) but to equally reflect the true financial and economic position and performance of the group.

5. Where inventory of either the parent or the subsidiary included a portion of purchases made from a member of the group, such inventory is required to be adjusted for unrealized profit inherent in the value of the inventory as at the reporting date.

6. The effect of unrealized profit is adjusted against the parent only (i.e. adjusted within the consolidated retained earnings) if the inter-company sales were initiated by the parent and sales made to the subsidiary.

7. The effect of unrealized profit is adjusted against the parent and the non-controlling interest in the proportion profit or loss is shared (i.e. adjusted within the consolidated retained earnings and amount of non-controlling interest), if the inter-company sales were initiated by the subsidiary, and sales made to the parent.

8. Unrealised profit on inventory is required only when inter-company sales (by either party) involves profit-loading by the selling party and a portion or whole of the goods purchased by the other party remain unsold as at the reporting date.

9. Where depreciable or non-depreciable assets are transferred within the group, such should not at the point of transfer give rise to profit in the books of the transferor (or the seller, as the case may be), otherwise such profit arising from the inter-company transfer or sale of assets would be eliminated in similar like to that of unrealized profit on inventory.

10. Where the transfer of assets within the group gives rise to a loss, such loss will have to be evaluated on the premise that an impairment of the asset may have occurred. Hence, impairment assessment will have to be carried out in line with the requirement of IAS 36 (Impairment of Assets). The fact is that the sale of the asset below it carrying value may have signalled a trigger of possible impairment of the asset. Invariably, if the loss is solely attributed to the impairment of the asset, no adjustment is required; otherwise, an opposite adjustment of a profit on inter-company transfer/sale of the asset will be required.

11. The effect of unrealized profit on intercompany sale/transfer of an asset is adjusted against the parent only (i.e. adjusted within the consolidated retained earnings) if the inter-company sale/transfer was initiated by the parent and sale/transfer made to the subsidiary.

12. The effect of unrealized profit on intercompany sale/transfer of asset is adjusted against the parent and the non-controlling interest in the proportion profit or loss is shared (i.e. adjusted

within the consolidated retained earnings and amount of non-controlling interest), if the inter-company sale/transfer was initiated by the subsidiary, and sale/transfer made to the parent.

13. Since the adjustment for unrealized profit is not made directly to the books of the buying entity, the depreciation charged by the buying entity on the asset purchased would have been understated. Hence, an adjustment for excess depreciation will be required, so as to reflect what the carrying amount of the asset would have been if the initial carrying amount was recognised.

14. The effect of excess depreciation is adjusted against the parent only (i.e. adjusted within the consolidated retained earnings) if the inter-company sale/transfer was initiated by the parent and sale/transfer made to the subsidiary. Although, another school of thought requires an intuitive adjustment which states as thus "The effect of excess depreciation is adjusted against the parent and the non-controlling interest in the proportion profit or loss is shared (i.e. adjusted within the consolidated retained earnings and amount of non-controlling interest), if the inter-company sale/transfer was initiated by the parent and sale/transfer made to the subsidiary".

15. The effect of excess depreciation is adjusted against the parent and the non-controlling interest in the proportion profit or loss is shared (i.e. adjusted within the consolidated retained earnings and amount of non-controlling interest), if the inter-company sale/transfer was initiated by the subsidiary, and sale/transfer made to the parent. Although, another school of thought requires an intuitive adjustment which states as thus "The effect of excess depreciation is adjusted against the parent only (i.e. adjusted within the consolidated retained earnings) if the inter-company sale/transfer was initiated by the subsidiary and sale/transfer made to the parent.

16. The inter-company transaction is likely to give rise to inter-company balances where there is outstanding settlement/indebtedness as at the reporting date, as a result of the inter-company transactions. The requirement of IFRS 10 is to eliminate the inter-company balances (including accounts payables and account receivables; current account balances, etc.) as maintained by the parent and the subsidiary in their individual books.

17. It is worthy of note that before inter-company receivable and intercompany payable can be eliminated, the two balances in either book (i.e. the parent and the subsidiary) must agree, but where the books are not in agreement, a reconciliation is required to identify if errors or in-transit items (such as *cash-in-transit* and *goods-in-transit*) are to be adjusted for.

18. Inter-company bills of exchange (i.e. inter-company bills receivable and intercompany bills payable) may exist in the books of the parent and the subsidiary as at the reporting date; the treatment will be *in tandem* with that of a conventional inter-company account receivable and intercompany account payable.

19. Where an inter-company bill receivable has been discounted by the inter-company creditor (which may be either party and based on the situation in concern), such discounted portion is no longer an inter-company balance in the books of the debtors (other party within the group), as the acknowledgment of the indebtedness is no longer within the group, rather it is no longer within the group as it is now owed to the finance/discount house (or other institutions) that may have discounted and honoured the premature bill of exchange.

20. Where there is loan within the group, such amount that constitutes inter-company balance should be eliminated in similar terms with that of inter-company bills receivable and

intercompany bills payable. Same goes for preference shares considered as a financial liability in accordance with IAS 32 (Financial Instrument – Presentation).

21. Where share bonus is issued subsequent to acquisition (regardless of the time), the summary of the requirement is that such capitalization of reserve to permanent capital should not in any way affect the initial pre-acquisition reserves of the acquired entity (i.e. the subsidiary); and likewise the amount of post-acquisition reserve will also not be influenced by such events from the group perspective.

22. Dividend received or receivable from a subsidiary by the parent should always be considered as a return on investment (and not a return of investment), regardless of when and how it is being paid.

23. Dividend payable and receivable within the group should be eliminated. The portion of subsidiary dividend payable that is not to be eliminated should be those related to the non-controlling interest as at the reporting date.

END OF CHAPTER 9 EXERCISES

1. On what basis is an adjustment for unrealized profit on inventory is required.

2. How should an unrealized profit arising from the inter-company sale of goods by the subsidiary to the parent be treated in group accounts?

3. How should an unrealized profit arising from the inter-company sale of the motor vehicle by the parent to the subsidiary be treated in group accounts?

4. A parent sold goods worth ₦20 million to its subsidiary in a financial year. The profit on cost is approximately 25%. Of the goods purchased by the subsidiary from the parent, only ₦12 million has since been sold as at the reporting date. What is the amount of unrealized profit to be eliminated?

5. A subsidiary sold goods which worth ₦20 million to its parent in a financial year. The profit-loaded is 20% margin. Of the goods purchased by the parent from the subsidiary, only ₦12 million has since been sold as at the reporting date. What is the amount of unrealized profit to be eliminated, and what treatment should be accorded the adjustment?

6. A parent transferred its motor vehicle with a carrying amount of ₦100 million to its subsidiary for a transfer price of ₦120 million as at 31 December 2016. What is the implication of this transaction in the course of preparing group accounts as at 31 December 2016?

7. A parent transferred its motor vehicle with a carrying amount of ₦100 million to its subsidiary for a transfer price of ₦120 million as at 31 December 2014, when the remaining useful life of the asset is 10 years. What is the implication of this transaction in the course of preparing group accounts as at 31 December 2016, assuming the group depreciation method is straight-line? What alternative treatment holds for the same transaction – if any?

8. A parent transferred its motor vehicle with a carrying amount of ₦100 million to its subsidiary for a transfer price of ₦90 million as at 31 December 2016. What is the implication of this transaction in the course of preparing group accounts as at 31 December 2016, assuming an event triggers possible impairment of the asset so transferred by the parent below its carrying amount?

9. What are the relevant accounting entries required in a situation where the parent has a balance of ₦20 million in its current account maintained on behalf of its subsidiary, while the subsidiary equally maintain a current account with a balance of ₦24 million in favour of the parent, given that a reconciliation as at the reporting date (31 December 2016) revealed the different attributable solely to cash-in-transit as at same date.

10. A subsidiary appropriately declared a dividend of ₦10 million and remained payable as at the reporting date (31 December 2016). The parent holds 60% of the ordinary shares of the subsidiary. What treatment should be accorded this event as at the reporting date (31 December 2016)?

Chapter 10

Extension of Basic Consolidation Mechanics and Principles in the Preparation of Statement of Profit or Loss and Other Comprehensive Income; and Statement of Changes in Equity

INTRODUCTION

This chapter will further provide the readers with the opportunity to understand and appreciate the mechanics and principles required to prepare the consolidated statement of profit or loss and other comprehensive income; and the consolidated statement of changes in equity.

The earlier mechanics and principles adopted in the course of preparing the consolidated statement of financial position are equally applicable to a large extent in this chapter.

This chapter will consider in details the attribution of profit and total comprehensive income to the parent and the non-controlling interest in the proportion to which they are expected to share profit or loss, which may be subjected to some adjustments.

In this chapter, guidance will be provided in ascertaining the amount of opening consolidated retained earnings (or opening consolidated reserves) and the amount of non-controlling interest as at the beginning of a reporting period.

Extension of Basic Consolidation Mechanics and Principles in the Preparation of Statement of Profit or Loss and Other Comprehensive Income; and Statement of Changes in Equity

As in the *statement of profit or loss and other comprehensive income and statement of changes in equity* of a single entity which show the results of the year operations, so does *consolidated statement of profit or loss and other comprehensive income and consolidated statement of changes in equity* show the results of trading in the year by the parent with its subsidiaries.

Mechanics of consolidation

Consolidated statement of profit or loss and other comprehensive income and consolidated statement of changes in equity is the combination of the *statement of profit or loss and other comprehensive income and statement of changes in equity* of the parent and its subsidiaries, after making adjustments as it relates to intra-group transactions (i.e. elimination of inter-company items, unrealized profits and so on) and other related adjustments.

The basic idea is to present one set of financial statements for all entities under common control. In the context of the statement of profit or loss and other comprehensive income, this implies presenting the results of all members of the group (i.e. the parent and all of its subsidiaries) in a single (but considered) consolidated statement of profit or loss and other comprehensive income. As far as the consolidated statement of changes in equity is concerned, this means just one statement dealing with all entities in the group.

The entire financial performances (within the statement of profit or loss and other comprehensive income) are a simple aggregation of the results of the parent entity and all the subsidiaries. Non-controlling interest is ignored in the aggregations, as with the consolidated statement of financial position already considered within the context of this text.

Non-controlling Interest

In consolidating the results of a partly-owned subsidiary, it is essential to note that the profits or losses of the subsidiary belong to both the parent and non-controlling interest, which have to be shared in the proportion of percentage holdings or investment in the subsidiary. IAS 1 (Presentation of Financial Statements) states that profit for the period must be analysed between the profit attributable to non-controlling interest and profit attributable to equity holders (ordinary shareholders) of the parent.

Reserves Brought Forward

It is essential to calculate or determine the amount of reserves (*which included the retained profits or accumulated losses*) brought forward (*at the beginning of the period/year*) from the previous year. For the purpose of consolidated financial statements, the consolidated retained earnings brought forward consist of:

- Parent's retained earnings brought forward, plus
- Parent's share of the post-acquisition retained earnings of the subsidiary.

Basic consolidation techniques

As earlier considered in the early chapter of this text, it is significant to primarily identify the group structure, as once again we only consolidate the parent and subsidiary results (*in this case financial performance*) from the date of inclusion (*which is the first date the parent obtains the **CONTROL** of the subsidiary – i.e. Acquisition-date*). Again we will be applying the single entity concept.

Recall, consolidation entails:

Parent results + subsidiaries' results +/- any adjustments

Step one:
Identify the group structure, i.e. which company is the subsidiary?

Step two:
Eliminate any intra-group sales between the parent and subsidiary, ***NOT the associate or joint venture (this will be discussed later in one of the chapters)***.

This will result in:

⇓ (Decrease) Revenue
⇓ (Decrease) Cost of sales

Step three:
Eliminate any unrealised profit in closing inventory from intra-group sales.

This will result in:
⇑ (Increase) Cost of sales

Technical Note:
Remember: Closing inventory is reducing, hence causing the cost of sales to increase.

Step four:
Make any other adjustments for *current year* additional depreciation due to any fair value adjustments or *current year* impairment.

⇑ (Increase) Expenses (could be cost of sales/administration/distribution – follow examiners instructions or use the most appropriate)

Step five:
Remove any intra-group interest relating to intra-group loans between the parent and subsidiary.

⇓ (Decrease) Investment/Interest income
⇓ (Decrease) Finance costs

Step six:
Remove any intra-group dividends

⇓ (Decrease) Investment income

Step seven:
Calculate the share of associate/joint venture's profit and add to the group profit.

FIRST PRINCIPLE:

100% OWNERSHIP OF THE SUBSIDIARY BY THE PARENT

There are situations where an investor company owns all of the voting rights in an investee company through ownership of the entire ordinary shares of the latter. In this situation, the subsidiary is said to be *wholly-owned* by the parent company. 100% ownership of a company (by the parent) in another company (in the subsidiary) will not give rise to *non-controlling interest (formerly known as minority interest)*.

We can explore the principle of consolidating a wholly-owned subsidiary by adopting this illustration.

ILLUSTRATION 1:

Arsenal acquired 100% interests in the equity of Chelsea as January 1, 2014, when it was incorporated. The Board of Arsenal strictly wants to comply with the requirement of IFRS regarding consolidation of the financial statements of the subsidiary with that of the parent as at December 31, 2016.

Income Statement for the year ended December 31, 2016

	Arsenal	Chelsea
	₦'000	₦'000
Revenue	600,000	390,000
Cost of sales	(345,000)	(201,000)
Gross profit	**255,000**	**189,000**
Distribution costs	(75,000)	(45,000)
Administrative expenses	(105,000)	(90,000)
Profit on before tax	**75,000**	**54,000**
Income tax	(25,000)	(29,000)
Profit for the year	**50,000**	**25,000**
Movement in Reserves:		
Retained profits brought forward	120,000	65,000
Profit for the year	50,000	25,000
Retained profit carried forward	**170,000**	**90,000**

Required:

Prepare the consolidated of profit or loss and the consolidated statement of changes in equity, given that the share capital of Arsenal stood at ₦200 million and that of Chelsea amounted to ₦100 million.

In this context of this text, we will approach a step-by-step approach to explaining the requirement of **IFRS 10** with regards to consolidating the financial results of the parent and the subsidiary as depicted below.

Arsenal Group
Consolidated Statement of Profit or Loss for the year ended 31 December 2016

	₦'000
Revenue (600,000 + 390,000)	990,000
Cost of sales (345,000 + 201,000)	(546,000)
Gross profit	**444,000**
Distribution costs (75,000 + 45,000)	(120,000)
Administrative expenses (105,000 + 90,000)	(195,000)
Profit on before tax	**129,000**

Consolidated Statement of Profit or Loss and Other Comprehensive Income; and Statement of Changes in Equity

Income tax (25,000 + 29,000)	(54,000)
Profit for the year	**75,000**

Profit, attributable to:

* Owners' of Arsenal (Note 1)	75,000
** Non-controlling interest (Note 1)	-
	75,000

Arsenal Group
Consolidated Statement of Changes in Equity for the year ended 31 December 2016

	Share Capital	Retained Earnings	Equity – of the Parent	Non-controlling Interest	Total Equity
	₦'000	₦'000	₦'000	₦'000	₦'000
As at 1 January 2016	200,000	185,000 (Note 2)	385,000	- (Note 3)	385,000
Profit for the year		75,000	75,000	-	75,000
As at 31 December, 2016	200,000	260,000	460,000	-	460,000

Or Better Depicted As Thus:

Arsenal Group
Consolidated Statement of Changes in Equity for the year ended 31 December 2016

	Share Capital	Retained Earnings	Total Equity
	₦'000	₦'000	₦'000
As at 1 January 2016	200,000	185,000 (Note 2)	385,000
Profit for the year		75,000	75,000
As at 31 December, 2016	200,000	260,000	460,000

Working Notes:

1. **Profit attributable to:**

	Arsenal	Non-controlling interest
	₦'000	₦'000
Arsenal's profit after tax	50,000	-
Chelsea' profit after tax (100:0)	25,000	-
	75,000	**-**

Chelsea' profit after tax is shared between the parent and the non-controlling interest in the ratio of 100% to 0% in which profit or loss is required to be allocated based on the stake held in the ordinary shares of the subsidiary. The implication is that since the subsidiary is owned 100% or wholly by the parent (Arsenal) no portion of the profit of the subsidiary is attributable to Noncontrolling interest (as no Non-controlling interest exists in the ownership structure of Chelsea as at the reporting date).

2. **Consolidated Retained Earnings as at 1 January 2016**

	₦'000
Arsenal's retained earnings as at 1 January 2016	120,000
100% of Chelsea's post acquisition retained earnings as at 1 January 2016 {100% x (₦65 million – Pre acquisition profit)}	65,000
	185,000

In this case, there is no pre-acquisition profit as the subsidiary was acquired upon its incorporation, which signifies that no profit or loss would have been accumulated.

3. **Non-controlling interest as at 1 January 2016**   ₦'000
   Amount of NCI as at acquisition (1 January 2014)   -
   0% of Chelsea's post acquisition retained earnings as at 1 January 2016
   {0% x (₦65 million – Pre acquisition profit)}   -
            -

In this case, there is no non-controlling interest and also the no pre-acquisition profit because the subsidiary was acquired upon its incorporation, which signifies that no profit or loss would have been accumulated.

SECOND PRINCIPLE:

LESS THAN 100% OWNERSHIP OF THE SUBSIDIARY BY THE PARENT

In most of the cases in the group, the ownership interest of the parent company is sometimes and usually less than 100%, which means *wholly-owned* subsidiaries are less common to *partly-owned* subsidiaries, where part of the ownership interest in such subsidiaries is attributable to *non-controlling interest*. Non-controlling interest exists only where a subsidiary is partly owned by the parent company and the profit or loss of the subsidiary will be attributable to the parent and non-controlling interest in the proportion to which subsidiary's profit or loss is required to be distributed, which usually is in tandem with the stake (or percentage of ordinary shares) held in the subsidiary by the parent and the subsidiary as at the reporting date.

Each identifiable asset and/or liability is measured at its acquisition-date fair value. Non-controlling interest in an acquiree that has a present ownership interest and entitles their holders to a proportionate share of the entity's net assets in the event of liquidation are measured at either *fair value*[31] or the present ownership instruments' [32]*proportionate share in the recognised amounts of the acquiree's net identifiable assets*. All other components of non-controlling interests shall be measured at their acquisition-date fair value unless another measurement basis is required by *IFRSs*.

We can explore the principle of consolidating a partly-owned subsidiary by adopting this illustration.

ILLUSTRATION 2:

Arsenal acquired 80% interests in the equity of Chelsea as January 1, 2014, when it was incorporated. The Board of Arsenal strictly wants to comply with the requirement of IFRS regarding consolidation of the financial statements of the subsidiary with that of the parent as at December 31, 2016.

Income Statement for the year ended December 31, 2016

	Arsenal	Chelsea
	₦'000	₦'000
Revenue	600,000	390,000
Cost of sales	(345,000)	(201,000)
Gross profit	**255,000**	**189,000**

---

[31] The fair value is measured based on the market value of the acquiree (Subsidiary) shares prior to acquisition, and where the subsidiary is not quoted or market price cannot be obtained, other verifiable and valid valuation model can be adopted for the measurement. The fair value model is an optional model, and most be sued consistently after been adopted. The implication is that the model cannot be jettison once adopted.

[32] Proportionate share in the recognised amounts of the acquiree's net identifiable assets has been the usual metric adopted in ascertaining the value of non-controlling interest prior to revision of IFRS 3.

Consolidated Statement of Profit or Loss and Other Comprehensive Income; and Statement of Changes in Equity

Distribution costs	(75,000)	(45,000)
Administrative expenses	(105,000)	(90,000)
Profit on before tax	**75,000**	**54,000**
Income tax	(25,000)	(29,000)
Profit for the year	**50,000**	**25,000**
Movement in Reserves:		
Retained profits brought forward	120,000	65,000
Profit for the year	50,000	25,000
Retained profit carried forward	**170,000**	**90,000**

Required:

Prepare the consolidated of profit or loss and the consolidated statement of changes in equity, given that the share capital of Arsenal stood at ₦200 million and that of Chelsea amounted to ₦100 million, and the amount of Non-controlling interest at acquisition as measured at fair value stood at ₦20 million.

In this context of this text, we will approach a step-by-step approach to explaining the requirement of **IFRS 10** with regards to consolidating the financial results of the parent and the subsidiary as depicted below.

Arsenal Group
Consolidated Statement of Profit or Loss for the year ended 31 December 2016

	₦'000
Revenue (600,000 + 390,000)	990,000
Cost of sales (345,000 + 201,000)	(546,000)
Gross profit	**444,000**
Distribution costs (75,000 + 45,000)	(120,000)
Administrative expenses (105,000 + 90,000)	(195,000)
Profit on before tax	**129,000**
Income tax (25,000 + 29,000)	(54,000)
Profit for the year	**75,000**
Profit, attributable to:	
* Owners' of Arsenal (Note 1)	70,000
** Non-controlling interest (Note 1)	5,000
	75,000

Arsenal Group
Consolidated Statement of Changes in Equity for the year ended 31 December 2016

	Share Capital	Retained Earnings	Equity – of the Parent	Non-controlling Interest	Total Equity
	₦'000	₦'000	₦'000	₦'000	₦'000
As at 1 January 2016	200,000	172,000	372,000	33,000	405,000
		(Note 2)		(Note 3)	
Profit for the year		70,000	70,000	5,000	75,000
As at 31 December, 2016	200,000	242,000	442,000	38,000	480,000

310

Working Notes:

1. Profit attributable to:

	Arsenal	Non-controlling interest
	₦'000	₦'000
Arsenal's profit after tax	50,000	-
Chelsea' profit after tax (80:20)	20,000	5,000
	70,000	**5,000**

Chelsea' profit after tax is shared between the parent and the non-controlling interest in the ratio of 80% to 20% in which profit or loss is required to be allocated based on the stake held in the ordinary shares of the subsidiary.

2. Consolidated Retained Earnings as at 1 January 2016

	₦'000
Arsenal's retained earnings as at 1 January 2016	120,000
80% of Chelsea's post acquisition retained earnings as at 1 January 2016 {80% x (₦65 million – Pre acquisition profit)}	52,000
	172,000

In this case, there is no pre-acquisition profit as the subsidiary was acquired upon its incorporation, which signifies that no profit or loss would have been accumulated.

3. Non-controlling interest as at 1 January 2016

	₦'000
Amount of NCI as at acquisition (1 January 2014)	20,000
20% of Chelsea's post acquisition retained earnings as at 1 January 2016 {20% x (₦65 million – Pre acquisition profit)}	13,000
	33,000

In this case, there is no pre-acquisition profit as the subsidiary was acquired upon its incorporation, which signifies that no profit or loss would have been accumulated.

THIRD PRINCIPLE:

CONSOLIDATION SUBSEQUENT TO ACQUISITION IN GROUP ACCOUNTS

In the process of obtaining the consolidated retained earnings as at the beginning of the financial year in the current reporting period, consideration regarding the adjustment to opening retained earnings on the elimination (by subtraction) of the pre-acquisition reserves (or earnings) will be material towards obtaining the consolidated retained earnings brought forward which will invariably serve as input to completing the consolidated statement of changes in equity as at the reporting date.

Pre-acquisition profits are profits or losses of a subsidiary made and undistributed (*i.e. retained*) before the date of acquisition and these profits/losses are a component of the net assets that exist in the subsidiary as at the date of acquisition. *Example*: If a subsidiary called "ZOE Plc" is acquired on January 1, 2016, when its profits/reserves stood at ₦50 million, then the sum represents its pre-acquisition profits which already is part of its net assets as at the acquisition date, which also have been taking into consideration in obtaining the amount of *goodwill or gain on bargain purchase – if any*.

Post-acquisition profits are profits or losses made subsequent to (*or after*) the date of acquisition. These profits or losses will have arisen whilst the subsidiary was under the control of the parent company, and these profits or losses will be reported through the *consolidated statement of profit or loss and other*

Consolidated Statement of Profit or Loss and Other Comprehensive Income; and Statement of Changes in Equity

comprehensive income, which end up in the consolidated retained earnings in the *consolidated statement of financial position*. *Example:* Given that the reserves of **ZOE Plc** stood at ₦50 million upon acquisition (on January 1, 2016) and as at the reporting date subsequent to acquisition (on December 31, 2016) the reserves stood at ₦60 million, hence the post –acquisition profits will stand as ₦10 million (being an increase in reserves to ₦60 million from ₦50 million). In another case, if the reserves as at December 31, 2016, had been the sum of ₦45 million, the post-acquisition reserves would have been a loss of ₦5 million (being a decrease to ₦45 million from ₦50 million).

We can explore the principle of consolidating a partly-owned subsidiary subsequent to acquisition by adopting this illustration.

ILLUSTRATION 3:

Arsenal acquired 80% interests in the equity of Chelsea as January 1, 2014, when the retained earnings stood at ₦20 million. The Board of Arsenal strictly wants to comply with the requirement of IFRS regarding consolidation of the financial statements of the subsidiary with that of the parent as at December 31, 2016.

Income Statement for the year ended December 31, 2016

	Arsenal	Chelsea
	₦'000	₦'000
Revenue	600,000	390,000
Cost of sales	(345,000)	(201,000)
Gross profit	**255,000**	**189,000**
Distribution costs	(75,000)	(45,000)
Administrative expenses	(105,000)	(90,000)
Profit on before tax	**75,000**	**54,000**
Income tax	(25,000)	(29,000)
Profit for the year	**50,000**	**25,000**
Movement in Reserves:		
Retained profits brought forward	120,000	65,000
Profit for the year	50,000	25,000
Retained profit carried forward	**170,000**	**90,000**

Required:

Prepare the consolidated of profit or loss and the consolidated statement of changes in equity, given that the share capital of Arsenal stood at ₦200 million and that of Chelsea amounted to ₦100 million, and the amount of non-controlling interest at acquisition as measured at fair value stood at ₦24 million.

In this context of this text, we will approach a step-by-step approach to explaining the requirement of **IFRS 10** with regards to consolidating the financial results of the parent and the subsidiary as depicted below.

Arsenal Group
Consolidated Statement of Profit or Loss for the year ended 31 December 2016

	₦'000
Revenue (600,000 + 390,000)	990,000
Cost of sales (345,000 + 201,000)	(546,000)
Gross profit	**444,000**

Distribution costs (75,000 + 45,000)		(120,000)
Administrative expenses (105,000 + 90,000)		(195,000)
Profit on before tax		**129,000**
Income tax (25,000 + 29,000)		(54,000)
Profit for the year		**75,000**

Profit, attributable to:
* Owners' of Arsenal (Note 1)	70,000
** Non-controlling interest (Note 1)	5,000
	75,000

Arsenal Group
Consolidated Statement of Changes in Equity for the year ended 31 December 2016

	Share Capital	Retained Earnings	Equity – of the Parent	Non-controlling Interest	Total Equity
	₦'000	₦'000	₦'000	₦'000	₦'000
As at 1 January 2016	200,000	156,000 (Note 2)	356,000	33,000 (Note 3)	389,000
Profit for the year		70,000	70,000	5,000	75,000
As at 31 December, 2016	200,000	226,000	426,000	38,000	464,000

Working Notes:

1. **Profit attributable to:**

	Arsenal	Non-controlling interest
	₦'000	₦'000
Arsenal's profit after tax	50,000	-
Chelsea' profit after tax (80:20)	20,000	5,000
	70,000	**5,000**

Chelsea' profit after tax is shared between the parent and the non-controlling interest in the ratio of 80% to 20% in which profit or loss is required to be allocated based on the stake held in the ordinary shares of the subsidiary.

2. **Consolidated Retained Earnings as at 1 January 2016**

	₦'000
Arsenal's retained earnings as at 1 January 2016	120,000
80% of Chelsea's post acquisition retained earnings as at 1 January 2016	
{80% x (₦65 million – ₦20 million)}	36,000
	156,000

In this case, there was a pre-acquisition profit of ₦20 million which was the opening retained earnings.

3. **Non-controlling interest as at 1 January 2016**

	₦'000
Amount of NCI as at acquisition (1 January 2014)	24,000
20% of Chelsea's post acquisition retained earnings as at 1 January 2016	
{20% x (₦65 million – ₦20 million)}	9,000
	33,000

In this case, there was a pre-acquisition profit of ₦20 million which was the opening retained earnings.

Consolidated Statement of Profit or Loss and Other Comprehensive Income; and Statement of Changes in Equity

FOURTH PRINCIPLE:

CONSOLIDATION SUBSEQUENT TO ACQUISITION IN GROUP ACCOUNTS AND ELIMINATION OF INTERCOMPANY DIVIDEND INCOME

Inter-company Dividends – Ordinary Shares

Complications do exist in preparing a consolidated statement of profit or loss when the dividend is paid by the subsidiary during the reporting period and to which the amount of dividend received by the parent from the subsidiary is reported within the investment income in the parent's profit or loss.

Investment income of the parent may include:

- Ordinary dividends received from subsidiaries
- Income from other investments.

Upon consolidation, only the income from other investments is shown separately as income in the consolidated statement of profit or loss, while inter-company dividends are eliminated on consolidation. The elimination of inter-company dividend income is necessary because the principle of "Single Entity Concept" signifies that the dividend considered as an income earned and received (or sometimes receivable) from the subsidiary is already a component of the final results (financial performance with respect to subsidiary's profits) that have been consolidated into that of the parent; and which invariably will be tantamount to double-counting and duplication of the group earnings for the reporting period.

Technical Note:
Group retained earnings are adjusted for dividends paid to the parent company shareholders. Dividends paid by the subsidiary to the parent are cancelled on consolidation and dividends paid to non-controlling interest are replaced by the allocation to the non-controlling interest of their share of the profit for the year of the subsidiary.

ILLUSTRATION 4:

Arsenal acquired 80% interests in the equity of Chelsea as January 1, 2014, when the retained earnings stood at ₦20 million. The Board of Arsenal strictly wants to comply with the requirement of IFRS regarding consolidation of the financial statements of the subsidiary with that of the parent as at December 31, 2016.

Income Statement for the year ended December 31, 2016

	Arsenal	Chelsea
	₦'000	₦'000
Revenue	600,000	390,000
Cost of sales	(345,000)	(201,000)
Gross profit	**255,000**	**189,000**
Distribution costs	(75,000)	(45,000)
Administrative expenses	(107,000)	(90,000)
Dividend Income	2,000	–
Profit on before tax	**75,000**	**54,000**
Income tax	(25,000)	(29,000)
Profit for the year	**50,000**	**25,000**
Movement in Reserves:		
Retained profits brought forward	120,000	67,500
Profit for the year	50,000	25,000
Dividend Paid – Interim	(10,000)	(2,500)
Retained profit carried forward	**160,000**	**90,000**

Required:

Prepare the consolidated of profit or loss and the consolidated statement of changes in equity, given that the share capital of Arsenal stood at ₦200 million and that of Chelsea amounted to ₦100 million, and the amount of non-controlling interest at acquisition as measured at fair value stood at ₦24 million.

In this context of this text, we will approach a step-by-step approach to explaining the requirement of **IFRS 10** with regards to consolidating the financial results of the parent and the subsidiary as depicted

Arsenal Group
Consolidated Statement of Profit or Loss for the year ended 31 December 2016

	₦'000
Revenue (600,000 + 390,000)	990,000
Cost of sales (345,000 + 201,000)	(546,000)
Gross profit	**444,000**
Distribution costs (75,000 + 45,000)	(120,000)
Administrative expenses (107,000 + 90,000)	(197,000)
~~Dividend Income (2,000 + 0 – 2,000 Intercompany)~~	0
Profit on before tax	**127,000**
Income tax (25,000 + 29,000)	(54,000)
Profit for the year	**73,000**

Profit, attributable to:
* Owners' of Arsenal (Note 1)	68,000
** Non-controlling interest (Note 1)	5,000
	73,000

Arsenal Group
Consolidated Statement of Changes in Equity for the year ended 31 December 2016

	Share Capital	Retained Earnings	Equity – of the Parent	Non-controlling Interest	Total Equity
	₦'000	₦'000	₦'000	₦'000	₦'000
As at 1 January 2016	200,000	158,000 (Note 2)	358,000	33,500 (Note 3)	391,500
Profit for the year		68,000	68,000	5,000	73,000
Dividend		(10,000)	(10,000)	(500)	(10,500)
As at 31 December, 2016	200,000	216,000	416,000	38,000	454,000

Working Notes:

1. **Profit attributable to:**

	Arsenal	Non-controlling interest
	₦'000	₦'000
Arsenal's profit after tax	50,000	-
Chelsea' profit after tax (80:20)	20,000	5,000
Less: Elimination of inter-company dividend income	(2,000)	-
	68,000	**5,000**

Consolidated Statement of Profit or Loss and Other Comprehensive Income; and Statement of Changes in Equity

The amount of dividend income to be eliminated is the portion traceable to have been earned and received from other entities' within the group during the reporting period. In this context, the amount of dividend paid by the subsidiary was ₦2.5 million of which 80% is received by the parent in the sum of ₦2 million. Hence, the amount reported in the parent's profit or loss also amounted to ₦2 million, which implies that that amount represents the dividend income solely received by the parent from the subsidiary in the reporting period. Likewise, the sum of ₦500,000 (being the portion of 20% of ₦2.5 million)of the subsidiary's dividend paid to non-controlling interest has to be deducted from the amount of non-controlling interest, so as to be reduced from the amount of subsidiary's profit already attributed to the non-controlling interest.

Also, Chelsea' profit after tax is shared between the parent and the non-controlling interest in the ratio of 80% to 20% in which profit or loss is required to be allocated based on the stake held in the ordinary shares of the subsidiary.

2. **Consolidated Retained Earnings as at 1 January 2016**

	₦'000
Arsenal's retained earnings as at 1 January 2016	120,000
80% of Chelsea's post acquisition retained earnings as at 1 January 2016 {80% x (₦67.5 million – ₦20 million)}	38,000
	158,000

In this case, there was a pre-acquisition profit of ₦20 million which was the opening retained earnings.

3. **Non-controlling interest as at 1 January 2016**

	₦'000
Amount of NCI as at acquisition (1 January 2014)	24,000
20% of Chelsea's post acquisition retained earnings as at 1 January 2016 {20% x (₦67.5 million – ₦20 million)}	9,500
	33,500

In this case, there was a pre-acquisition profit of ₦20 million which was the opening retained earnings.

ILLUSTRATION 5:

Arsenal acquired 80% interests in the equity of Chelsea as January 1, 2014, when the retained earnings stood at ₦20 million. The Board of Arsenal strictly wants to comply with the requirement of IFRS regarding consolidation of the financial statements of the subsidiary with that of the parent as at December 31, 2016.

Income Statement for the year ended December 31, 2016

	Arsenal	Chelsea
	₦'000	₦'000
Revenue	600,000	390,000
Cost of sales	(345,000)	(201,000)
Gross profit	**255,000**	**189,000**
Distribution costs	(75,000)	(45,000)
Administrative expenses	(108,000)	(90,000)
Dividend Income	3,000	-
Profit on before tax	**75,000**	**54,000**

Contemporaneous Accounting for Business Combinations and Group Accounts

Income tax	(25,000)	(29,000)
Profit for the year	**50,000**	**25,000**
Movement in Reserves:		
Retained profits brought forward	120,000	67,500
Profit for the year	50,000	25,000
Dividend Paid – Interim	(10,000)	(2,500)
Retained profit carried forward	**160,000**	**90,000**

Required:

Prepare the consolidated of profit or loss and the consolidated statement of changes in equity, given that the share capital of Arsenal stood at ₦200 million and that of Chelsea amounted to ₦100 million, and the amount of non-controlling interest at acquisition as measured at fair value stood at ₦24 million.

In this context of this text, we will approach a step-by-step approach to explaining the requirement of **IFRS 10** with regards to consolidating the financial results of the parent and the subsidiary as depicted

Arsenal Group
Consolidated Statement of Profit or Loss for the year ended 31 December 2016

	₦'000
Revenue (600,000 + 390,000)	990,000
Cost of sales (345,000 + 201,000)	(546,000)
Gross profit	**444,000**
Distribution costs (75,000 + 45,000)	(120,000)
Administrative expenses (107,000 + 90,000)	(198,000)
Dividend Income (3,000 + 0 – *2,000 {Note 1} Intercompany*)	1,000
Profit on before tax	**127,000**
Income tax (25,000 + 29,000)	(54,000)
Profit for the year	**73,000**
Profit, attributable to:	
* Owners' of Arsenal (Note 1)	68,000
** Non-controlling interest (Note 1)	5,000
	73,000

Arsenal Group
Consolidated Statement of Changes in Equity for the year ended 31 December 2016

	Share Capital	Retained Earnings	Equity – of the Parent	Non-controlling Interest	Total Equity
	₦'000	₦'000	₦'000	₦'000	₦'000
As at 1 January 2016	200,000	158,000 (Note 2)	358,000	33,500 (Note 3)	391,500
Profit for the year		68,000	68,000	5,000	73,000
Dividend		(10,000)	(10,000)	(500) {Note 1}	(10,500)
As at 31 December, 2016	200,000	216,000	416,000	38,000	454,000

Consolidated Statement of Profit or Loss and Other Comprehensive Income; and Statement of Changes in Equity

Working Notes:

1. **Profit attributable to:**

	Arsenal	Non-controlling interest
	₦'000	₦'000
Arsenal's profit after tax	50,000	-
Chelsea' profit after tax (80:20)	20,000	5,000
Less: Elimination of inter-company dividend income	(2,000)	-
	68,000	**5,000**

The amount of dividend income to be eliminated is the portion traceable to have been earned and received from other entities' within the group during the reporting period. In this context, the amount of dividend paid by the subsidiary was ₦2.5 million of which 80% is received by the parent in the sum of ₦2 million. Hence, the amount reported in the parent's profit or loss showed ₦3 million, which implies that that amount represents the dividend income received by the parent from the subsidiary and other investment outside the group in the reporting period. The implication is that only the sum of ₦2 million attributable to the intercompany dividend is considered what to be eliminated, leaving the sum of ₦1 million reported in the consolidated statement of profit or loss as an income to the group. Likewise, the sum of ₦500,000 (being the portion of 20% of ₦2.5 million)of the subsidiary's dividend paid to non-controlling interest has to be deducted from the amount of non-controlling interest, so as to be reduced from the amount of subsidiary's profit already attributed to the non-controlling interest.

Also, Chelsea' profit after tax is shared between the parent and the non-controlling interest in the ratio of 80% to 20% in which profit or loss is required to be allocated based on the stake held in the ordinary shares of the subsidiary.

2. **Consolidated Retained Earnings as at 1 January 2016**

	₦'000
Arsenal's retained earnings as at 1 January 2016	120,000
80% of Chelsea's post acquisition retained earnings as at 1 January 2016 {80% x (₦67.5 million – ₦20 million)}	38,000
	158,000

In this case, there was a pre-acquisition profit of ₦20 million which was the opening retained earnings.

3. **Non-controlling interest as at 1 January 2016**

	₦'000
Amount of NCI as at acquisition (1 January 2014)	24,000
20% of Chelsea's post acquisition retained earnings as at 1 January 2016 {20% x (₦67.5 million – ₦20 million)}	9,500
	33,500

In this case, there was a pre-acquisition profit of ₦20 million which was the opening retained earnings.

OLD POSITION OF IAS 27 (BEFORE THE REVISED POSITION IN 2008)

Pre-acquisition Dividends

This represents dividends paid to a parent company by its subsidiary out of pre-acquisition profits. This does occur as a result of the following:

- *When a parent company acquires a subsidiary at the subsidiary's year-end, and of which the register of the subsidiary has not been closed, which eventually make the parent company be entitled to the dividends.*
- *When a parent company acquires a subsidiary during the year, which depicts that the profit for the year is partly pre and partly post, of which the dividend is paid.*

Exclusively, there are two (2) possible ways of accounting for pre-acquisition dividends in the accounts of the parent and in Consolidated Financial Statements.

- *Treat the dividend as a return to the parent company of part of the cost of its investment (i.e. reduction in the carrying value of the parent's investment in the subsidiary). This is the traditional view of pre-acquisition dividends. The reason is that only post-acquisition profits can be treated as profits of the group and therefore only dividends paid out of post-acquisition profits can be treated as income. A further argument for this treatment is that a dividend paid out of pre-acquisition profits reduces the value of the parent's investment in the subsidiary to less than cost.*
- *Treat the dividend as a realised profit in the hands of the parent (i.e. as investment income). The rationale for this treatment is that the payment of a pre-acquisition dividend does not cause a permanent diminution in the value of the parent's investment in the subsidiary. Therefore no write-down is necessary.*

Accounting standards do not provide a definitive answer to the problem. The cost of an investment should be reduced by dividends received only if they clearly represent a recovery of part of the cost, but this is unlikely to be obvious in practice.

The concluding position is that in the individual income statement of the parent company, the dividends received (whether paid out of pre-acquisition profits or out of post-acquisition profits) will be recognized as investment income, while adjustment reversing the entry (i.e. as a reduction of cost of investment in subsidiary) will be required on consolidation, if the dividends are paid out of pre-acquisition profits.

Technical Note:

The revised IAS 27 (as revised in 2008), now requires the dividend received from a subsidiary to be treated as an investment income in the separate financial statement of the parent regardless of whether it was paid or declared out of pre-acquisition profits or post-acquisition profits.

Consolidated Statement of Profit or Loss and Other Comprehensive Income; and Statement of Changes in Equity

FIFTH PRINCIPLE:

CONSOLIDATION SUBSEQUENT TO ACQUISITION IN GROUP ACCOUNTS AND ELIMINATION OF INTERCOMPANY INTEREST INCOME & EXPENSE

Intra-group Interests

Where a parent company makes a loan to its subsidiary (or vice versa, but in an extreme situation), the resulting interest represents an expense in the subsidiary's financial statements as may be shown under the heading of finance cost (or interest expense). The parent would have included the same amount being interest in the financial statements line of investment income (or finance income or other income).

Upon consolidation, these amounts (interest expense and interest income) must be eliminated by making an appropriate entry as an adjustment to the expense and income lines within the consolidated statement of profit or loss.

The elimination of intercompany interest income and expense is necessitated on the premise of the principle of "Single Entity Concept", which signifies that the non-elimination of the intercompany interest expense and interest income will be tantamount to a mere summation of amount attributable to items within the financial statements that tend to reflect the financial performance but not really the true and economic position of the group financial performance. In a simple sense, a group cannot be seen to have made income out of itself and simultaneously such income taking out via recognition of expense for the same amount. Hence, the only amount of interest income and interest expense to be recognised in the group accounts are those attributable to what was earned and incurred during the reporting period.

ILLUSTRATION 6:

Arsenal acquired 80% interests in the equity of Chelsea as January 1, 2014, when the retained earnings stood at ₦20 million. The Board of Arsenal strictly wants to comply with the requirement of IFRS regarding consolidation of the financial statements of the subsidiary with that of the parent as at December 31, 2016.

Income Statement for the year ended December 31, 2016

	Arsenal	Chelsea
	₦'000	₦'000
Revenue	600,000	390,000
Cost of sales	(345,000)	(201,000)
Gross profit	**255,000**	**189,000**
Distribution costs	(75,000)	(45,000)
Administrative expenses	(95,000)	(80,000)
Investment Income	10,000	-
Operating profit	**95,000**	**64,000**
Finance cost	(20,000)	(10,000)
Profit on before tax	**75,000**	**54,000**
Income tax	(25,000)	(29,000)
Profit for the year	**50,000**	**25,000**
Movement in Reserves:		
Retained profits brought forward	120,000	65,000
Profit for the year	50,000	25,000
Retained profit carried forward	**170,000**	**90,000**

Required:

Prepare the consolidated of profit or loss and the consolidated statement of changes in equity, given that the share capital of Arsenal stood at ₦200 million and that of Chelsea amounted to ₦100 million, and the amount of non-controlling interest at acquisition as measured at fair value stood at ₦24 million. As at 1 January 2016, the parent provided a loan facility of ₦100 million to the subsidiary at an interest rate of 10% p.a. The loan remains outstanding as at the reporting date. The interest income is reported as an investment income in the books of the parent as shown in the financial statements for the year ended 31 December 2016.

In this context of this text, we will approach a step-by-step approach to explaining the requirement of **IFRS 10** with regards to consolidating the financial results of the parent and the subsidiary as depicted

Arsenal Group
Consolidated Statement of Profit or Loss for the year ended 31 December 2016

	₦'000
Revenue (600,000 + 390,000)	990,000
Cost of sales (345,000 + 201,000)	(546,000)
Gross profit	**444,000**
Distribution costs (75,000 + 45,000)	(120,000)
Administrative expenses (95,000 + 80,000)	(175,000)
Investment Income (10,000 + 0 – *10,000 Intercompany*)	-
Operating profit	**149,000**
Finance cost (20,000 + 10,000 – *10,000 Intercompany*)	(20,000)
Profit on before tax	**129,000**
Income tax (25,000 + 29,000)	(54,000)
Profit for the year	**75,000**

Profit, attributable to:
* Owners' of Arsenal (Note 1)	70,000
** Non-controlling interest (Note 1)	5,000
	75,000

Arsenal Group
Consolidated Statement of Changes in Equity for the year ended 31 December 2016

	Share Capital	Retained Earnings	Equity – of the Parent	Non-controlling Interest	Total Equity
	₦'000	₦'000	₦'000	₦'000	₦'000
As at 1 January 2016	200,000	156,000 (Note 2)	356,000	33,000 (Note 3)	389,000
Profit for the year		70,000	70,000	5,000	77,000
As at 31 December, 2016	200,000	226,000	426,000	38,000	464,000

Consolidated Statement of Profit or Loss and Other Comprehensive Income; and Statement of Changes in Equity

Working Notes:

1. **Profit attributable to:**

	Arsenal	Non-controlling interest
	₦'000	₦'000
Arsenal's profit after tax	50,000	-
Chelsea' profit after tax (80:20)	20,000	5,000
Less: Elimination of inter-company interest income	(10,000)	-
Add: Elimination of inter-company interest income	10,000	-
	70,000	**5,000**

The amount of interest income and interest expense to be eliminated is the portion traceable to have been earned and received from other entities' within the group during the reporting period. In this context, the amount of interest expense to the subsidiary was ₦10 million (being 10% of ₦10 million for a period of 12 months full calendar year). Hence, the amount reported in the parent's profit or loss as interest income also amounted to ₦10 million, which implies that that amount represents the interest income solely received by the parent from the subsidiary in the reporting period.

Also, Chelsea' profit after tax is shared between the parent and the non-controlling interest in the ratio of 80% to 20% in which profit or loss is required to be allocated based on the stake held in the ordinary shares of the subsidiary.

2. **Consolidated Retained Earnings as at 1 January 2016**

	₦'000
Arsenal's retained earnings as at 1 January 2016	120,000
80% of Chelsea's post acquisition retained earnings as at 1 January 2016 {80% x (₦65 million – ₦20 million)}	36,000
	156,000

In this case, there was a pre-acquisition profit of ₦20 million which was the opening retained earnings.

3. **Non-controlling interest as at 1 January 2016**

	₦'000
Amount of NCI as at acquisition (1 January 2014)	24,000
20% of Chelsea's post acquisition retained earnings as at 1 January 2016 {20% x (₦65 million – ₦20 million)}	9,000
	33,000

In this case, there was a pre-acquisition profit of ₦20 million which was the opening retained earnings.

SIXTH PRINCIPLE:

CANCELLATION OF INTRA-GROUP TRANSACTIONS: INTRA-GROUP SALES

Cancellation of intra-group transactions

All intra-group trading, items, unrealized profits on inventory, unrealized profits on transfer of property, plant and equipment (tangible non-current assets or long-lived assets) and excess depreciation must be eliminated in order to produce a consolidated statement of profit or loss that will reflect the true financial performance of the group as at the reporting date.

Intra-group Sales

The consolidated figures for sales revenue and cost of sales should represent *'sales to'* and *'purchases from'* outsiders (i.e. parties outside the group). Adjustment is, therefore, necessary to reduce the sales revenue and cost of sales figures by the amount of intra-group sales made during the reporting period. Furthermore, the adjustment becomes more complex if there is unrealized profit resulting from the sale of goods by either party when such sales value includes *add-on* (or *loaded*) profit of which part or the entire inventory is yet to be sold. In this case, there exists the need to calculate the unrealized profit on intra-group unsold goods (or closing inventories) at the year end and reduce consolidated gross profits by this amount. By implication, the adjustment to cost of sales will be the *balancing figure* (*i.e. intercompany revenue less unrealised profit*).

ILLUSTRATION 7: A Downstream Transaction (Sale of Goods by the Parent to the Subsidiary)

Arsenal acquired 80% interests in the equity of Chelsea as January 1, 2014, when the retained earnings stood at ₦20 million. The Board of Arsenal strictly wants to comply with the requirement of IFRS regarding consolidation of the financial statements of the subsidiary with that of the parent as at December 31, 2016.

Income Statement for the year ended December 31, 2016

	Arsenal ₦'000	Chelsea ₦'000
Revenue	600,000	390,000
Cost of sales	(345,000)	(201,000)
Gross profit	**255,000**	**189,000**
Distribution costs	(75,000)	(45,000)
Administrative expenses	(105,000)	(90,000)
Profit on before tax	**75,000**	**54,000**
Income tax	(25,000)	(29,000)
Profit for the year	**50,000**	**25,000**
Movement in Reserves:		
Retained profits brought forward	120,000	65,000
Profit for the year	50,000	25,000
Retained profit carried forward	**170,000**	**90,000**

Additional Information:

Arsenal sold goods to Chelsea for ₦50 million, when it actually cost the parent company ₦40 million. Unfortunate as at the year-end, included in the inventory of Chelsea Plc is the whole inventory sold by Arsenal Plc.

Required:

Prepare the consolidated of profit or loss and the consolidated statement of changes in equity, given that the share capital of Arsenal stood at ₦200 million and that of Chelsea amounted to ₦100 million, and the amount of non-controlling interest at acquisition as measured at fair value stood at ₦24 million.

In this context of this text, we will approach a step-by-step approach to explaining the requirement of **IFRS 10** with regards to consolidating the financial results of the parent and the subsidiary as depicted below.

Consolidated Statement of Profit or Loss and Other Comprehensive Income; and Statement of Changes in Equity

Arsenal Group
Consolidated Statement of Profit or Loss for the year ended 31 December 2016

	₦'000
Revenue (600,000 + 390,000 – 50,000 {Note 1})	940,000
Cost of sales (345,000 + 201,000 – 40,000 {Note 1})	(506,000)
Gross profit	**434,000**
Distribution costs (75,000 + 45,000)	(120,000)
Administrative expenses (105,000 + 90,000)	(195,000)
Profit on before tax	**119,000**
Income tax (25,000 + 29,000)	(54,000)
Profit for the year	**65,000**

Profit, attributable to:

* Owners' of Arsenal (Note 1)	60,000
** Non-controlling interest (Note 1)	5,000
	65,000

Arsenal Group
Consolidated Statement of Changes in Equity for the year ended 31 December 2016

	Share Capital	Retained Earnings	Equity – of the Parent	Non-controlling Interest	Total Equity
	₦'000	₦'000	₦'000	₦'000	₦'000
As at 1 January 2016	200,000	156,000 (Note 2)	356,000	33,000 (Note 3)	389,000
Profit for the year		60,000	60,000	5,000	65,000
As at 31 December, 2016	200,000	216,000	416,000	38,000	454,000

Working Notes:

1. Profit attributable to:

	Arsenal	Non-controlling interest
	₦'000	₦'000
Arsenal's profit after tax	50,000	-
Chelsea' profit after tax (80:20)	20,000	5,000
Less: Unrealised profit on inventories	(10,000)	-
	60,000	**5,000**

The intercompany sales of ₦50 million will have to be eliminated alongside the intra-group cost of sales (which is arrived at by deducting the amount of unrealised profit from the intercompany sales)

The unrealised profit is determined by multiply the percentage of unsold goods (which in this case is 100%) by the profit on sales as made from the intercompany sales of goods during the reporting period.

The profit on sales amounted to ₦10 million (being the difference between the proceeds of ₦50 million earned on the intercompany sales and cost price of ₦40 million to the seller, which in this case is the parent).

Hence, the amount of unrealized profit stood at ₦10 million (being 100% unsold inventories multiplied by ₦10 million profit on sales made during the reporting period).

Then, the amount of inter-company cost of sales will amount to ₦40 million (being amount of intercompany sales of ₦50 million less the ₦10 million unrealised profit as at the reporting date).

The unrealised profit being eliminated is solely attributable to the parent, as the sales transaction was made by the parent being a downstream transaction.

Chelsea' profit after tax is shared between the parent and the non-controlling interest in the ratio of 80% to 20% in which profit or loss is required to be allocated based on the stake held in the ordinary shares of the subsidiary.

2. **Consolidated Retained Earnings as at 1 January 2016**

	₦'000
Arsenal's retained earnings as at 1 January 2016	120,000
80% of Chelsea's post acquisition retained earnings as at 1 January 2016 {80% x (₦65 million – ₦20 million)}	36,000
	156,000

In this case, there was a pre-acquisition profit of ₦20 million which was the opening retained earnings.

3. **Non-controlling interest as at 1 January 2016**

	₦'000
Amount of NCI as at acquisition (1 January 2014)	24,000
20% of Chelsea's post acquisition retained earnings as at 1 January 2016 {20% x (₦65 million – ₦20 million)}	9,000
	33,000

In this case, there was a pre-acquisition profit of ₦20 million which was the opening retained earnings.

ILLUSTRATION 8: A Downstream Transaction (Sale of Goods by the Parent to the Subsidiary)

Arsenal acquired 80% interests in the equity of Chelsea as January 1, 2014, when the retained earnings stood at ₦20 million. The Board of Arsenal strictly wants to comply with the requirement of IFRS regarding consolidation of the financial statements of the subsidiary with that of the parent as at December 31, 2016.

Income Statement for the year ended December 31, 2016

	Arsenal	Chelsea
	₦'000	₦'000
Revenue	600,000	390,000
Cost of sales	(345,000)	(201,000)
Gross profit	**255,000**	**189,000**
Distribution costs	(75,000)	(45,000)
Administrative expenses	(105,000)	(90,000)
Profit on before tax	**75,000**	**54,000**
Income tax	(25,000)	(29,000)
Profit for the year	**50,000**	**25,000**
Movement in Reserves:		
Retained profits brought forward	120,000	65,000
Profit for the year	50,000	25,000
Retained profit carried forward	**170,000**	**90,000**

Consolidated Statement of Profit or Loss and Other Comprehensive Income; and Statement of Changes in Equity

Additional Information:

Arsenal sold goods to Chelsea for ₦50 million, when it actually cost the parent company ₦40 million. As at the year-end, included in the inventory of Chelsea Plc is 40% of the inventory sold by Arsenal Plc.

Required:

Prepare the consolidated of profit or loss and the consolidated statement of changes in equity, given that the share capital of Arsenal stood at ₦200 million and that of Chelsea amounted to ₦100 million, and the amount of non-controlling interest at acquisition as measured at fair value stood at ₦24 million.

In this context of this text, we will approach a step-by-step approach to explaining the requirement of **IFRS 10** with regards to consolidating the financial results of the parent and the subsidiary as depicted below.

Arsenal Group
Consolidated Statement of Profit or Loss for the year ended 31 December 2016

	₦'000
Revenue (600,000 + 390,000 − 50,000 {Note 1})	940,000
Cost of sales (345,000 + 201,000 − 46,000 {Note 1})	(500,000)
Gross profit	**440,000**
Distribution costs (75,000 + 45,000)	(120,000)
Administrative expenses (105,000 + 90,000)	(195,000)
Profit on before tax	**125,000**
Income tax (25,000 + 29,000)	(54,000)
Profit for the year	**71,000**
Profit, attributable to:	
* Owners' of Arsenal (Note 1)	66,000
** Non-controlling interest (Note 1)	5,000
	71,000

Arsenal Group
Consolidated Statement of Changes in Equity for the year ended 31 December 2016

	Share Capital	Retained Earnings	Equity – of the Parent	Non-controlling Interest	Total Equity
	₦'000	₦'000	₦'000	₦'000	₦'000
As at 1 January 2016	200,000	156,000 (Note 2)	356,000	33,000 (Note 3)	389,000
Profit for the year		66,000	66,000	5,000	71,000
As at 31 December, 2016	200,000	222,000	422,000	38,000	460,000

Working Notes:

1. **Profit attributable to:**

	Arsenal	Non-controlling interest
	₦'000	₦'000
Arsenal's profit after tax	50,000	-
Chelsea' profit after tax (80:20)	20,000	5,000
Less: Unrealised profit on inventories	(4,000)	-
	66,000	**5,000**

326

The intercompany sales of ₦50 million will have to be eliminated alongside the intra-group cost of sales (which is arrived at by deducting the amount of unrealised profit from the intercompany sales)

The unrealised profit is determined by multiply the percentage of unsold goods (which in this case is 40%) by the profit on sales as made from the intercompany sales of goods during the reporting period.

The profit on sales amounted to ₦10 million (being the difference between the proceeds of ₦50 million earned on the intercompany sales and cost price of ₦40 million to the seller, which in this case is the parent).

Hence, the amount of unrealized profit stood at ₦4 million (being 40% unsold inventories multiplied by ₦10 million profit on sales made during the reporting period).

Then, the amount of inter-company cost of sales will amount to ₦46 million (being amount of intercompany sales of ₦50 million less the ₦4 million unrealised profit as at the reporting date).

The unrealised profit being eliminated is solely attributable to the parent, as the sales transaction was made by the parent being a downstream transaction.

Chelsea' profit after tax is shared between the parent and the non-controlling interest in the ratio of 80% to 20% in which profit or loss is required to be allocated based on the stake held in the ordinary shares of the subsidiary.

2. **Consolidated Retained Earnings as at 1 January 2016**

	₦'000
Arsenal's retained earnings as at 1 January 2016	120,000
80% of Chelsea's post acquisition retained earnings as at 1 January 2016 {80% x (₦65 million – ₦20 million)}	36,000
	156,000

In this case, there was a pre-acquisition profit of ₦20 million which was the opening retained earnings.

3. **Non-controlling interest as at 1 January 2016**

	₦'000
Amount of NCI as at acquisition (1 January 2014)	24,000
20% of Chelsea's post acquisition retained earnings as at 1 January 2016 {20% x (₦65 million – ₦20 million)}	9,000
	33,000

In this case, there was a pre-acquisition profit of ₦20 million which was the opening retained earnings.

Effect of Elimination of Unrealized Profit on Non-controlling Interest

Where the unrealized profit originally recognised in the subsidiary (as a result of **upstream sales transaction**), the non-controlling interest must be adjusted for its share of the unrealized profit. By at large, this is an adjustment made in calculating the non-controlling interest's share of post-tax profits; while in the first instance all the unrealized profit must be eliminated to determine the correct amount of gross profit earned by the group trading as if it were a single [economic] entity.

Consolidated Statement of Profit or Loss and Other Comprehensive Income; and Statement of Changes in Equity

ILLUSTRATION 9: An Upstream Transaction (Sale of Goods by the Subsidiary to the Parent)

Arsenal acquired 80% interests in the equity of Chelsea as January 1, 2014, when the retained earnings stood at ₦20 million. The Board of Arsenal strictly wants to comply with the requirement of IFRS regarding consolidation of the financial statements of the subsidiary with that of the parent as at December 31, 2016.

Income Statement for the year ended December 31, 2016

	Arsenal	Chelsea
	₦'000	₦'000
Revenue	600,000	390,000
Cost of sales	(345,000)	(201,000)
Gross profit	**255,000**	**189,000**
Distribution costs	(75,000)	(45,000)
Administrative expenses	(105,000)	(90,000)
Profit on before tax	**75,000**	**54,000**
Income tax	(25,000)	(29,000)
Profit for the year	**50,000**	**25,000**
Movement in Reserves:		
Retained profits brought forward	120,000	65,000
Profit for the year	50,000	25,000
Retained profit carried forward	**170,000**	**90,000**

Additional Information:

Chelsea sold goods to Arsenal for ₦50 million, when it actually cost the parent company ₦40 million. As at the year-end, included in the inventory of Arsenal Plc is 40% of the inventory sold by Chelsea Plc.

Required:

Prepare the consolidated of profit or loss and the consolidated statement of changes in equity, given that the share capital of Arsenal stood at ₦200 million and that of Chelsea amounted to ₦100 million, and the amount of non-controlling interest at acquisition as measured at fair value stood at ₦24 million.

In this context of this text, we will approach a step-by-step approach to explaining the requirement of **IFRS 10** with regards to consolidating the financial results of the parent and the subsidiary as depicted below.

Arsenal Group
Consolidated Statement of Profit or Loss for the year ended 31 December 2016

	₦'000
Revenue (600,000 + 390,000 – 50,000 {Note 1})	940,000
Cost of sales (345,000 + 201,000 – 46,000 {Note 1})	(500,000)
Gross profit	**440,000**
Distribution costs (75,000 + 45,000)	(120,000)
Administrative expenses (105,000 + 90,000)	(195,000)
Profit on before tax	**125,000**
Income tax (25,000 + 29,000)	(54,000)
Profit for the year	**71,000**
Profit, attributable to:	
* Owners' of Arsenal (Note 1)	66,000
** Non-controlling interest (Note 1)	5,000
	71,000

Arsenal Group
Consolidated Statement of Changes in Equity for the year ended 31 December 2016

	Share Capital	Retained Earnings	Equity – of the Parent	Non-controlling Interest	Total Equity
	N'000	N'000	N'000	N'000	N'000
As at 1 January 2016	200,000	156,000 (Note 2)	356,000	33,000 (Note 3)	389,000
Profit for the year		66,80	66,800	4,200	71,000
As at 31 December, 2016	200,000	222,800	422,800	37,200	460,000

Working Notes:

1. **Profit attributable to:**

	Arsenal	Non-controlling interest
	N'000	N'000
Arsenal's profit after tax	50,000	-
Chelsea' profit after tax (80:20)	20,000	5,000
Less: Unrealised profit on inventories (80:20)	(3,200)	(800)
	66,800	**4,200**

The intercompany sales of ₦50 million will have to be eliminated alongside the intra-group cost of sales (which is arrived at by deducting the amount of unrealised profit from the intercompany sales)

The unrealised profit is determined by multiply the percentage of unsold goods (which in this case is 40%) by the profit on sales as made from the intercompany sales of goods during the reporting period.

The profit on sales amounted to ₦10 million (being the difference between the proceeds of ₦50 million earned on the intercompany sales and cost price of ₦40 million to the seller, which in this case is the subsidiary).

Hence, the amount of unrealized profit stood at ₦4 million (being 40% unsold inventories multiplied by ₦10 million profit on sales made during the reporting period).

Then, the amount of inter-company cost of sales will amount to ₦46 million (being amount of intercompany sales of ₦50 million less the ₦4 million unrealised profit as at the reporting date).

The unrealised profit being eliminated is attributable to the parent and the non-controlling interest in the proportion to which profit or loss is being shared. This treatment is required because the unrealised profit sits within the enlarge profit of the subsidiary as at the reporting date (as the sales transaction was made by the subsidiary being an upstream transaction).

Chelsea' profit after tax is shared between the parent and the non-controlling interest in the ratio of 80% to 20% in which profit or loss is required to be allocated based on the stake held in the ordinary shares of the subsidiary.

Consolidated Statement of Profit or Loss and Other Comprehensive Income; and Statement of Changes in Equity

2. **Consolidated Retained Earnings as at 1 January 2016**

	₦'000
Arsenal's retained earnings as at 1 January 2016	120,000
80% of Chelsea's post acquisition retained earnings as at 1 January 2016 {80% x (₦65 million – ₦20 million)}	36,000
	156,000

In this case, there was a pre-acquisition profit of ₦20 million which was the opening retained earnings.

3. **Non-controlling interest as at 1 January 2016**

	₦'000
Amount of NCI as at acquisition (1 January 2014)	24,000
20% of Chelsea's post acquisition retained earnings as at 1 January 2016 {20% x (₦65 million – ₦20 million)}	9,000
	33,000

In this case, there was a pre-acquisition profit of ₦20 million which was the opening retained earnings.

Unrealized Profit and Excess Depreciation on Transfer/Sale of Property, Plant and Equipment (PPE)

Adjustments for unrealised profit and subsequent adjustment for excess depreciation are necessitated as a result sale or transfer of items of Property, Plant and Equipment (PPE) or its equivalent depreciable long-lived assets made by either party at a transfer price that may be above their carrying amount (i.e. book value), which equally will bring about excess depreciation as a result of subjecting the higher value (transfer price) of the sold assets to depreciation policy of the group.

In this case, there exists the need to institute two (2) complimentary adjustments as thus:

- Elimination of unrealized profits on the asset(s) transfer by reducing group profit by the amount of the unrealized profit.
- Adjustment reversing the excess depreciation arising from the transfer price rather than the carrying value of the asset(s) to the group depreciation policy.

Effect on Non-controlling Interest

This will have an effect on the non-controlling interest share of post-tax profit of the subsidiary if the transaction is a "***Downstream Transaction***" (i.e. the transfer originates or arose from the subsidiary), which is similar to that observed in the elimination of unrealized profits on unsold inventory as at year-end".

ILLUSTRATION 10: A Downstream Transaction (Sale of Plant by the Parent to the Subsidiary)

Arsenal acquired 80% interests in the equity of Chelsea as January 1, 2014, when the retained earnings stood at ₦20 million. The Board of Arsenal strictly wants to comply with the requirement of IFRS regarding consolidation of the financial statements of the subsidiary with that of the parent as at December 31, 2016.

Income Statement for the year ended December 31, 2016

	Arsenal	Chelsea
	₦'000	₦'000
Revenue	600,000	390,000
Cost of sales	(345,000)	(201,000)
Gross profit	**255,000**	**189,000**

Distribution costs	(75,000)	(45,000)
Administrative expenses	(115,000)	(90,000)
Other income (*profit on disposal of plant*)	10,000	-
Profit on before tax	**75,000**	**54,000**
Income tax	(25,000)	(29,000)
Profit for the year	**50,000**	**25,000**
Movement in Reserves:		
Retained profits brought forward	120,000	65,000
Profit for the year	50,000	25,000
Retained profit carried forward	**170,000**	**90,000**

Additional Information:

Arsenal sold a plant to Chelsea for ₦50 million, when it's carrying amount stood at ₦40 million as at the transfer date (being 1 January 2016). As at the transfer date, the plant has a remaining useful life of 5 years and the pattern of consumption has since not changed. It is the company's depreciation policy to adopt a straight-line method of depreciation.

Required:

Prepare the consolidated of profit or loss and the consolidated statement of changes in equity, given that the share capital of Arsenal stood at ₦200 million and that of Chelsea amounted to ₦100 million, and the amount of non-controlling interest at acquisition as measured at fair value stood at ₦24 million.

In this context of this text, we will approach a step-by-step approach to explaining the requirement of **IFRS 10** with regards to consolidating the financial results of the parent and the subsidiary as depicted below.

Arsenal Group
Consolidated Statement of Profit or Loss for the year ended 31 December 2016

	₦'000
Revenue (600,000 + 390,000)	990,000
Cost of sales (345,000 + 201,000)	(546,000)
Gross profit	**444,000**
Distribution costs (75,000 + 45,000)	(120,000)
Administrative expenses (115,000 + 90,000 – 2,000 {Note 1})	(203,000)
~~Other income (*profit on disposal of plant*) (10,000 + 0 – 10,000 {Note 1})~~	0
Profit on before tax	**121,000**
Income tax (25,000 + 29,000)	(54,000)
Profit for the year	**67,000**
Profit, attributable to:	
* Owners' of Arsenal (Note 1)	62,000
** Non-controlling interest (Note 1)	5,000
	67,000

Consolidated Statement of Profit or Loss and Other Comprehensive Income; and Statement of Changes in Equity

Arsenal Group
Consolidated Statement of Changes in Equity for the year ended 31 December 2016

	Share Capital	Retained Earnings	Equity – of the Parent	Non-controlling Interest	Total Equity
	₦'000	₦'000	₦'000	₦'000	₦'000
As at 1 January 2016	200,000	156,000 (Note 2)	356,000	33,000 (Note 3)	389,000
Profit for the year		62,000	62,000	5,000	67,000
As at 31 December, 2016	200,000	218,000	418,000	38,000	456,000

Working Notes:

1. **Profit attributable to:**

	Arsenal	Non-controlling interest
	₦'000	₦'000
Arsenal's profit after tax	50,000	-
Chelsea' profit after tax (80:20)	20,000	5,000
Less: Unrealised profit on sale of plant	(10,000)	-
Add: Excess depreciation adjustment	2,000	-
	62,000	**5,000**

The intercompany sale of plant amounted to ₦50 million and of which the carrying amount of the plant as at the transfer date (1 January 2016) was ₦40 million, which signifies the need to carrying-out an elimination of the perceived unrealised profit of ₦10 million as already included in other income of the parent in its separate statement of profit or loss.

The unrealised profit of ₦10 million is determined as the difference between the proceeds of ₦50 million earned on the intercompany sale of plant and the carrying amount of ₦40 million to the seller, which in this case is the parent during the reporting period.

Hence, the amount of unrealized profit will further necessitate an excess depreciation adjustment on the premise that the buyer (which in this case is the subsidiary) would have depreciated the asset since its purchase and at least for one year as at the reporting date. The depreciation amount would have been higher than if the transfer was made at its carrying amount. The principle of single economic entity depicts that mere intra-group transfers and/or transactions should not crystallise in a profit or loss nor trigger any unnecessary movement in profit or loss during the reporting period.

Hence, the amount so depreciated as based on the transfer price was ₦10 million (i.e. ₦50 million divided by 5 years being the adoption of straight-line depreciation method); whereas, the amount that would have reflected the status quo should have been ₦8 million (i.e. ₦40 million divided by 5 years being the adoption of straight-line depreciation method). Invariably, there exists an excess depreciation amount of ₦2 million (i.e. ₦10 million less ₦8 million) that is required to be eliminated in order to abide by the group principle of single entity concept.

The unrealised profit and excess depreciation adjustments are solely attributable to the parent. This treatment is required because the unrealised profit sits within the enlarge profit of the parent as at the reporting date (as the sales transaction was made by the parent being a downstream transaction).

Chelsea' profit after tax is shared between the parent and the non-controlling interest in the ratio of 80% to 20% in which profit or loss is required to be allocated based on the stake held in the ordinary shares of the subsidiary.

2. **Consolidated Retained Earnings as at 1 January 2016**

	₦'000
Arsenal's retained earnings as at 1 January 2016	120,000
80% of Chelsea's post acquisition retained earnings as at 1 January 2016	
{80% x (₦65 million – ₦20 million)}	36,000
	156,000

In this case, there was a pre-acquisition profit of ₦20 million which was the opening retained earnings.

3. **Non-controlling interest as at 1 January 2016**

	₦'000
Amount of NCI as at acquisition (1 January 2014)	24,000
20% of Chelsea's post acquisition retained earnings as at 1 January 2016	
{20% x (₦65 million – ₦20 million)}	9,000
	33,000

In this case, there was a pre-acquisition profit of ₦20 million which was the opening retained earnings.

ILLUSTRATION 11: An Upstream Transaction (Sale of Plant by the Subsidiary to the Parent)

Arsenal acquired 80% interests in the equity of Chelsea as January 1, 2014, when the retained earnings stood at ₦20 million. The Board of Arsenal strictly wants to comply with the requirement of IFRS regarding consolidation of the financial statements of the subsidiary with that of the parent as at December 31, 2016.

Income Statement for the year ended December 31, 2016

	Arsenal	Chelsea
	₦'000	₦'000
Revenue	600,000	390,000
Cost of sales	(345,000)	(201,000)
Gross profit	**255,000**	**189,000**
Distribution costs	(75,000)	(45,000)
Administrative expenses	(105,000)	(100,000)
Other income (*profit on disposal of plant*)	-	10,000
Profit on before tax	**75,000**	**54,000**
Income tax	(25,000)	(29,000)
Profit for the year	**50,000**	**25,000**
Movement in Reserves:		
Retained profits brought forward	120,000	65,000
Profit for the year	50,000	25,000
Retained profit carried forward	**170,000**	**90,000**

Consolidated Statement of Profit or Loss and Other Comprehensive Income; and Statement of Changes in Equity

Additional Information:

Chelsea sold a plant to Arsenal for ₦50 million, when it's carrying amount stood at ₦40 million as at the transfer date (being 1 January 2016). As at the transfer date, the plant has a remaining useful life of 5 years and the pattern of consumption has since not changed. It is the company's depreciation policy to adopt a straight-line method of depreciation.

Required:

Prepare the consolidated of profit or loss and the consolidated statement of changes in equity, given that the share capital of Arsenal stood at ₦200 million and that of Chelsea amounted to ₦100 million, and the amount of non-controlling interest at acquisition as measured at fair value stood at ₦24 million.

In this context of this text, we will approach a step-by-step approach to explaining the requirement of **IFRS 10** with regards to consolidating the financial results of the parent and the subsidiary as depicted below.

Arsenal Group
Consolidated Statement of Profit or Loss for the year ended 31 December 2016

	₦'000
Revenue (600,000 + 390,000)	990,000
Cost of sales (345,000 + 201,000)	(546,000)
Gross profit	**444,000**
Distribution costs (75,000 + 45,000)	(120,000)
Administrative expenses (105,000 + 100,000 – 2,000 {Note 1})	(203,000)
~~Other income (profit on disposal of plant) (0 + 10,000 – 10,000 {Note 1})~~	~~0~~
Profit on before tax	**121,000**
Income tax (25,000 + 29,000)	(54,000)
Profit for the year	**67,000**
Profit, attributable to:	
* Owners' of Arsenal (Note 1)	63,600
** Non-controlling interest (Note 1)	3,400
	67,000

Arsenal Group
Consolidated Statement of Changes in Equity for the year ended 31 December 2016

	Share Capital	Retained Earnings	Equity – of the Parent	Non-controlling Interest	Total Equity
	₦'000	₦'000	₦'000	₦'000	₦'000
As at 1 January 2016	200,000	156,000 (Note 2)	356,000	33,000 (Note 3)	389,000
Profit for the year		63,600	63,600	3,400	67,000
As at 31 December, 2016	200,000	219,600	419,600	36,400	456,000

Working Notes:

1. **Profit attributable to:**

	Arsenal	Non-controlling interest
	₦'000	₦'000
Arsenal's profit after tax	50,000	-
Chelsea' profit after tax (80:20)	20,000	5,000
Less: Unrealised profit on sale of plant (80:20)	*(8,000)*	*(2,000)*
Add: Excess depreciation adjustment (80:20)	*1,600*	*400*
	63,600	**3,400**

The intercompany sale of plant amounted to ₦50 million and of which the carrying amount of the plant as at the transfer date (1 January 2016) was ₦40 million, which signifies the need to carrying-out an elimination of the perceived unrealised profit of ₦10 million as already included in other income of the subsidiary in its individual statement of profit or loss.

The unrealised profit of ₦10 million is determined as the difference between the proceeds of ₦50 million earned on the intercompany sale of plant and the carrying amount of ₦40 million to the seller, which in this case is the subsidiary during the reporting period.

Hence, the amount of unrealized profit will further necessitate an excess depreciation adjustment on the premise that the buyer (which in this case is the parent) would have depreciated the asset since its purchase and at least for one year as at the reporting date. The depreciation amount would have been higher than if the transfer was made at its carrying amount. The principle of single economic entity depicts that mere intra-group transfers and/or transactions should not crystallise in a profit or loss nor trigger any unnecessary movement in profit or loss during the reporting period.

Hence, the amount so depreciated as based on the transfer price was ₦10 million (i.e. ₦50 million divided by 5 years being the adoption of straight-line depreciation method); whereas, the amount that would have reflected the status quo should have been ₦8 million (i.e. ₦40 million divided by 5 years being the adoption of straight-line depreciation method). Invariably, there exists an excess depreciation amount of ₦2 million (i.e. ₦10 million less ₦8 million) that is required to be eliminated in order to abide by the group principle of single entity concept.

The unrealised profit and excess depreciation adjustments are attributable to the parent and the non-controlling interest in the proportion to which profit or loss is being shared. This treatment is required because the unrealised profit sits within the enlarge profit of the subsidiary as at the reporting date (as the sales transaction was made by the subsidiary being an upstream transaction).

Chelsea' profit after tax is shared between the parent and the non-controlling interest in the ratio of 80% to 20% in which profit or loss is required to be allocated based on the stake held in the ordinary shares of the subsidiary.

2. **Consolidated Retained Earnings as at 1 January 2016**

	₦'000
Arsenal's retained earnings as at 1 January 2016	120,000
80% of Chelsea's post acquisition retained earnings as at 1 January 2016	
{80% x (₦65 million – ₦20 million)}	36,000
	156,000

In this case, there was a pre-acquisition profit of ₦20 million which was the opening retained earnings.

Consolidated Statement of Profit or Loss and Other Comprehensive Income; and Statement of Changes in Equity

3. **Non-controlling interest as at 1 January 2016**

	₦'000
Amount of NCI as at acquisition (1 January 2014)	24,000
20% of Chelsea's post acquisition retained earnings as at 1 January 2016 {20% x (₦65 million – ₦20 million)}	9,000
	33,000

In this case, there was a pre-acquisition profit of ₦20 million which was the opening retained earnings.

There is a *"School of Thought"* that explored alternative approach towards the treatment accorded to *Downstream* and *Upstream Transactions* regarding the requisite adjustment for excess depreciation (or over depreciation) of assets transferred within the group at a price above (or below – other than a recognition of impairment loss) the carrying amount. This thought can be attributed to the lacuna in *IFRS 10* without clear guidance on the treatment of depreciation adjustments on the intercompany transfer of depreciable assets. The treatments according to this "School of Thought" are as thus:

Downstream Transactions:

This involves the sale of a non-current asset by the investor (parent) to the investee (subsidiary). Since the profit is recognised by the parent upon transfer of the asset to the subsidiary, the unrealized profit should be adjusted solely against the parent's profit as attributable from the group position; while the adjustment for excess depreciation should be made against both the parent and the non-controlling interest I the proportion to which they share profit or loss of the subsidiary.

The argument of this approach or methodology lies in the fact that the asset so affected by the transfer price and of the depreciation effect, stands in the books of the buyer (which in this case is the subsidiary). Which invariably depicts that the necessary adjustment will ultimately impact the subsidiary's profit and subsequently the consequence will be felt by both the parent and the subsidiary in the proportion of which the subsidiary's profit or loss is distributed.

ILLUSTRATION 12: A Downstream Transaction (Sale of Plant by the Parent to the Subsidiary)

Arsenal acquired 80% interests in the equity of Chelsea as January 1, 2014, when the retained earnings stood at ₦20 million. The Board of Arsenal strictly wants to comply with the requirement of IFRS regarding consolidation of the financial statements of the subsidiary with that of the parent as at December 31, 2016.

Income Statement for the year ended December 31, 2016

	Arsenal	Chelsea
	₦'000	₦'000
Revenue	600,000	390,000
Cost of sales	(345,000)	(201,000)
Gross profit	**255,000**	**189,000**
Distribution costs	(75,000)	(45,000)
Administrative expenses	(115,000)	(90,000)
Other income (*profit on disposal of plant*)	10,000	-
Profit on before tax	**75,000**	**54,000**
Income tax	(25,000)	(29,000)
Profit for the year	**50,000**	**25,000**

Movement in Reserves:

Retained profits brought forward	120,000	65,000
Profit for the year	50,000	25,000
Retained profit carried forward	**170,000**	**90,000**

Additional Information:

Arsenal sold a plant to Chelsea for ₦50 million, when it's carrying amount stood at ₦40 million as at the transfer date (being 1 January 2016). As at the transfer date, the plant has a remaining useful life of 5 years and the pattern of consumption has since not changed. It is the company's depreciation policy to adopt a straight-line method of depreciation.

Required:

Prepare the consolidated of profit or loss and the consolidated statement of changes in equity, given that the share capital of Arsenal stood at ₦200 million and that of Chelsea amounted to ₦100 million, and the amount of non-controlling interest at acquisition as measured at fair value stood at ₦24 million.

In this context of this text, we will approach a step-by-step approach to explaining the requirement of **IFRS 10** with regards to consolidating the financial results of the parent and the subsidiary as depicted below.

Arsenal Group
Consolidated Statement of Profit or Loss for the year ended 31 December 2016

	₦'000
Revenue (600,000 + 390,000)	990,000
Cost of sales (345,000 + 201,000)	(546,000)
Gross profit	**444,000**
Distribution costs (75,000 + 45,000)	(120,000)
Administrative expenses (115,000 + 90,000 – 2,000 {Note 1})	(203,000)
~~Other income (profit on disposal of plant) (10,000 + 0 – 10,000 {Note 1})~~	0
Profit on before tax	**121,000**
Income tax (25,000 + 29,000)	(54,000)
Profit for the year	**67,000**
Profit, attributable to:	
* Owners' of Arsenal (Note 1)	61,600
** Non-controlling interest (Note 1)	5,400
	67,000

Arsenal Group
Consolidated Statement of Changes in Equity for the year ended 31 December 2016

	Share Capital	Retained Earnings	Equity – of the Parent	Non-controlling Interest	Total Equity
	₦'000	₦'000	₦'000	₦'000	₦'000
As at 1 January 2016	200,000	156,000 (Note 2)	356,000	33,000 (Note 3)	389,000
Profit for the year		61,600	61,600	5,400	67,000
As at 31 December, 2016	200,000	217,600	417,600	38,400	456,000

337

Consolidated Statement of Profit or Loss and Other Comprehensive Income; and Statement of Changes in Equity

Working Notes:

1. **Profit attributable to:**

	Arsenal	Non-controlling interest
	₦'000	₦'000
Arsenal's profit after tax	50,000	-
Chelsea' profit after tax (80:20)	20,000	5,000
Less: Unrealised profit on sale of plant	*(10,000)*	*-*
Add: Excess depreciation adjustment (80:20)	*1,600*	*400*
	61,600	**5,400**

The intercompany sale of plant amounted to ₦50 million and of which the carrying amount of the plant as at the transfer date (1 January 2016) was ₦40 million, which signifies the need to carrying-out an elimination of the perceived unrealised profit of ₦10 million as already included in other income of the parent in its separate statement of profit or loss.

The unrealised profit of ₦10 million is determined as the difference between the proceeds of ₦50 million earned on the intercompany sale of plant and the carrying amount of ₦40 million to the seller, which in this case is the parent during the reporting period.

Hence, the amount of unrealized profit will further necessitate an excess depreciation adjustment on the premise that the buyer (which in this case is the subsidiary) would have depreciated the asset since its purchase and at least for one year as at the reporting date. The depreciation amount would have been higher than if the transfer was made at its carrying amount. The principle of single economic entity depicts that mere intra-group transfers and/or transactions should not crystallise in a profit or loss nor trigger any unnecessary movement in profit or loss during the reporting period.

Hence, the amount so depreciated as based on the transfer price was ₦10 million (i.e. ₦50 million divided by 5 years being the adoption of straight-line depreciation method); whereas, the amount that would have reflected the status quo should have been ₦8 million (i.e. ₦40 million divided by 5 years being the adoption of straight-line depreciation method). Invariably, there exists an excess depreciation amount of ₦2 million (i.e. ₦10 million less ₦8 million) that is required to be eliminated in order to abide by the group principle of single entity concept.

The unrealised profit is solely attributable to the parent, while the excess depreciation adjustments will be attributable to the parent and the non-controlling interest in the proportion to which subsidiary's profit is shared. This treatment is required because the unrealised profit sits within the enlarge profit of the parent, while the excess depreciation primarily affects the profit of the subsidiary as at the reporting date (as the sales transaction was made by the parent being a downstream transaction).

Chelsea' profit after tax is shared between the parent and the non-controlling interest in the ratio of 80% to 20% in which profit or loss is required to be allocated based on the stake held in the ordinary shares of the subsidiary.

2. **Consolidated Retained Earnings as at 1 January 2016**

	₦'000
Arsenal's retained earnings as at 1 January 2016	120,000
80% of Chelsea's post acquisition retained earnings as at 1 January 2016 {80% x (₦65 million – ₦20 million)}	36,000
	156,000

In this case, there was a pre-acquisition profit of ₦20 million which was the opening retained earnings.

3. **Non-controlling interest as at 1 January 2016**

	N'000
Amount of NCI as at acquisition (1 January 2014)	24,000
20% of Chelsea's post acquisition retained earnings as at 1 January 2016	
{20% x (N65 million – N20 million)}	9,000
	33,000

In this case, there was a pre-acquisition profit of N20 million which was the opening retained earnings.

Upstream Transactions:

This involves the sale of a non-current asset by the investee (subsidiary) to the investor (parent). Since the profit is recognised by the subsidiary upon transfer of the asset to the parent, the unrealized profit may be adjusted partly against the consolidated retained earnings (*with respect to those attributable to the parent*) and partly against the non-controlling interest (*with respect to those attributable to the non-controlling interest and where the subsidiary is partly owned by the parent company*).

The argument of this approach or methodology lies in the fact that the asset so affected by the transfer price and of the depreciation effect, stands in the books of the buyer (which in this case is the parent). Which invariably depicts that the necessary adjustment will ultimately impact the parent's profit and subsequently the consequence will be felt by only by the parent.

ILLUSTRATION 13: An Upstream Transaction (Sale of Plant by the Subsidiary to the Parent)

Arsenal acquired 80% interests in the equity of Chelsea as January 1, 2014, when the retained earnings stood at N20 million. The Board of Arsenal strictly wants to comply with the requirement of IFRS regarding consolidation of the financial statements of the subsidiary with that of the parent as at December 31, 2016.

Income Statement for the year ended December 31, 2016

	Arsenal	Chelsea
	N'000	N'000
Revenue	600,000	390,000
Cost of sales	(345,000)	(201,000)
Gross profit	**255,000**	**189,000**
Distribution costs	(75,000)	(45,000)
Administrative expenses	(105,000)	(100,000)
Other income (*profit on disposal of plant*)	-	10,000
Profit on before tax	**75,000**	**54,000**
Income tax	(25,000)	(29,000)
Profit for the year	**50,000**	**25,000**
Movement in Reserves:		
Retained profits brought forward	120,000	65,000
Profit for the year	50,000	25,000
Retained profit carried forward	**170,000**	**90,000**

Additional Information:

Chelsea sold a plant to Arsenal for N50 million, when it's carrying amount stood at N40 million as at the transfer date (being 1 January 2016). As at the transfer date, the plant has a remaining useful life of 5 years and the pattern of consumption has since not changed. It is the company's depreciation policy to adopt a straight-line method of depreciation.

Required:

Prepare the consolidated of profit or loss and the consolidated statement of changes in equity, given that the share capital of Arsenal stood at ₦200 million and that of Chelsea amounted to ₦100 million, and the amount of non-controlling interest at acquisition as measured at fair value stood at ₦24 million.

In this context of this text, we will approach a step-by-step approach to explaining the requirement of **IFRS 10** with regards to consolidating the financial results of the parent and the subsidiary as depicted below.

Arsenal Group
Consolidated Statement of Profit or Loss for the year ended 31 December 2016

	₦'000
Revenue (600,000 + 390,000)	990,000
Cost of sales (345,000 + 201,000)	(546,000)
Gross profit	**444,000**
Distribution costs (75,000 + 45,000)	(120,000)
Administrative expenses (105,000 + 100,000 – 2,000 {Note 1})	(203,000)
~~Other income (profit on disposal of plant) (0 + 10,000 – 10,000 {Note 1})~~	0
Profit on before tax	**121,000**
Income tax (25,000 + 29,000)	(54,000)
Profit for the year	**67,000**

Profit, attributable to:
* Owners' of Arsenal (Note 1)	64,000
** Non-controlling interest (Note 1)	3,000
	67,000

Arsenal Group
Consolidated Statement of Changes in Equity for the year ended 31 December 2016

	Share Capital	Retained Earnings	Equity – of the Parent	Non-controlling Interest	Total Equity
	₦'000	₦'000	₦'000	₦'000	₦'000
As at 1 January 2016	200,000	156,000 (Note 2)	356,000	33,000 (Note 3)	389,000
Profit for the year		64,000	64,000	3,000	67,000
As at 31 December, 2016	200,000	220,000	420,000	36,000	456,000

Working Notes:

1. **Profit attributable to:**

	Arsenal	Non-controlling interest
	₦'000	₦'000
Arsenal's profit after tax	50,000	–
Chelsea' profit after tax (80:20)	20,000	5,000
Less: Unrealised profit on sale of plant (80:20)	(8,000)	(2,000)
Add: Excess depreciation adjustment	2,000	–
	64,000	**3,000**

The intercompany sale of plant amounted to ₦50 million and of which the carrying amount of the plant as at the transfer date (1 January 2016) was ₦40 million, which signifies the need to carrying-out an elimination of the perceived unrealised profit of ₦10 million as already included in other income of the subsidiary in its individual statement of profit or loss.

The unrealised profit of ₦10 million is determined as the difference between the proceeds of ₦50 million earned on the intercompany sale of plant and the carrying amount of ₦40 million to the seller, which in this case is the subsidiary during the reporting period.

Hence, the amount of unrealized profit will further necessitate an excess depreciation adjustment on the premise that the buyer (which in this case is the parent) would have depreciated the asset since its purchase and at least for one year as at the reporting date. The depreciation amount would have been higher than if the transfer was made at its carrying amount. The principle of single economic entity depicts that mere intra-group transfers and/or transactions should not crystallise in a profit or loss nor trigger any unnecessary movement in profit or loss during the reporting period.

Hence, the amount so depreciated as based on the transfer price was ₦10 million (i.e. ₦50 million divided by 5 years being the adoption of straight-line depreciation method); whereas, the amount that would have reflected the status quo should have been ₦8 million (i.e. ₦40 million divided by 5 years being the adoption of straight-line depreciation method). Invariably, there exists an excess depreciation amount of ₦2 million (i.e. ₦10 million less ₦8 million) that is required to be eliminated in order to abide by the group principle of single entity concept.

The unrealised profit is attributable to the parent and the non-controlling interest in the proportion to which profit or loss is being shared, while the excess depreciation adjustment is solely attributable to the parent. This treatment is required because the unrealised profit sits within the enlarge profit of the subsidiary as at the reporting date (as the sales transaction was made by the subsidiary being an upstream transaction), while the excess depreciation primarily affects the profit of the parent as at the reporting date

Chelsea' profit after tax is shared between the parent and the non-controlling interest in the ratio of 80% to 20% in which profit or loss is required to be allocated based on the stake held in the ordinary shares of the subsidiary.

2. **Consolidated Retained Earnings as at 1 January 2016**　　　　　₦'000
   Arsenal's retained earnings as at 1 January 2016　　　　　　　　120,000
   80% of Chelsea's post acquisition retained earnings as at 1 January 2016
   {80% x (₦65 million – ₦20 million)}　　　　　　　　　　　　　　　36,000
   　　　　　　　　　　　　　　　　　　　　　　　　　　　　　　156,000

   In this case, there was a pre-acquisition profit of ₦20 million which was the opening retained earnings.

3. **Non-controlling interest as at 1 January 2016**　　　　　　　　₦'000
   Amount of NCI as at acquisition (1 January 2014)　　　　　　　　24,000
   20% of Chelsea's post acquisition retained earnings as at 1 January 2016
   {20% x (₦65 million – ₦20 million)}　　　　　　　　　　　　　　　9,000
   　　　　　　　　　　　　　　　　　　　　　　　　　　　　　　33,000

   In this case, there was a pre-acquisition profit of ₦20 million which was the opening retained earnings.

Consolidated Statement of Profit or Loss and Other Comprehensive Income; and Statement of Changes in Equity

SEVENTH PRINCIPLE:

ACQUISITION DURING THE YEAR

In some instances, it has been observed that subsidiaries are sometimes acquired during the year. The implication of such acquisition is that part of the profit for the year will be pre-acquisition profit/loss, while another part is considered post-acquisition profit/loss. Furthermore, it is necessary and essential to separate the subsidiary's items of profit or loss into the pre-acquisition items and post-acquisition items; as only the post-acquisition items are required to be consolidated with the financial results of the parent as at the first reporting date.

In summary, only the post-acquisition element of the subsidiary's profit for the year is consolidated.

ILLUSTRATION 14:

Arsenal acquired 80% interests in the equity of Chelsea as 1 April 2016. The Board of Arsenal strictly wants to comply with the requirement of IFRS regarding consolidation of the financial statements of the subsidiary with that of the parent as at December 31, 2016.

Income Statement for the year ended December 31, 2016

	Arsenal	Chelsea
	₦'000	₦'000
Revenue	600,000	390,000
Cost of sales	(345,000)	(201,000)
Gross profit	**255,000**	**189,000**
Distribution costs	(75,000)	(45,000)
Administrative expenses	(105,000)	(90,000)
Profit on before tax	**75,000**	**54,000**
Income tax	(25,000)	(29,000)
Profit for the year	**50,000**	**25,000**
Movement in Reserves:		
Retained profits brought forward	120,000	65,000
Profit for the year	50,000	25,000
Retained profit carried forward	**170,000**	**90,000**

Additional Information:

Given that the share capital of Arsenal stood at ₦200 million and that of Chelsea amounted to ₦100 million, and the amount of non-controlling interest at acquisition as measured at fair value stood at ₦24 million.

Required:

Prepare the consolidated of profit or loss and the consolidated statement of changes in equity

In this context of this text, we will approach a step-by-step approach to explaining the requirement of **IFRS 10** with regards to consolidating the financial results of the parent and the subsidiary as depicted below.

Arsenal Group
Consolidated Statement of Profit or Loss for the year ended 31 December 2016

	₦'000
Revenue (600,000 + {9/12 x 390,000})	892,500
Cost of sales (345,000 + {9/12 x 201,000})	(495,750)
Gross profit	**396,750**
Distribution costs (75,000 + {9/12 x 45,000})	(108,750)
Administrative expenses (105,000 + {9/12 x 90,000})	(172,500)
Profit on before tax	**115,500**
Income tax (25,000 + {9/12 x 29,000})	(46,750)
Profit for the year	**68,750**
Profit, attributable to:	
* Owners' of Arsenal (Note 1)	65,000
** Non-controlling interest (Note 1)	3,750
	68,750

Arsenal Group
Consolidated Statement of Changes in Equity for the year ended 31 December 2016

	Share Capital	Retained Earnings	Equity – of the Parent	Non-controlling Interest	Total Equity
	₦'000	₦'000	₦'000	₦'000	₦'000
As at 1 January 2016	200,000	120,000 (Note 2)	320,000	–	320,000
Profit for the year		65,000	65,000	3,750	68,750
Transactions within Equity:					
Added on Acquisition				24,000 (Note 3)	24,000
As at 31 December, 2016	200,000	185,000	385,000	27,750	412,750

Working Notes:

1. Profit attributable to:

	Arsenal	Non-controlling interest
	₦'000	₦'000
Arsenal's profit after tax	50,000	–
Chelsea' profit after tax (80:20)	15,000	3,750
	65,000	**3,750**

The income statement items are presumed to have accrued evenly, and on this premise, the individual items (expense and income) are apportioned into pre-acquisition and post-acquisition items on the basis of time proportion. In this scenario, since the acquisition took place sometimes during the year (specifically on 1st day of April 2016), then the portion of pre-acquisition was considered 3 months (i.e. between 1 January 2016 and 31 March 2016), while post-acquisition period stood at 9 months (1 April 2016 to 31 December 2016).

Consolidated Statement of Profit or Loss and Other Comprehensive Income; and Statement of Changes in Equity

The portion to be consolidated alongside that of a full calendar year (of 12 months) of the parent is the post-combination period of 9 months. This is what gave rise the prorated amount of income and expense consolidated (as shown above).

The attribution of subsidiary's profit in this illustration was based on the 9 months post-acquisition results of Chelsea, which stood at ₦18,750,000 (i.e. 9/12 of ₦25 million profit after tax for the whole year).

Chelsea' profit after tax is shared between the parent and the non-controlling interest in the ratio of 80% to 20% in which profit or loss is required to be allocated based on the stake held in the ordinary shares of the subsidiary.

2. **Consolidated Retained Earnings as at 1 January 2016**

	₦'000
Arsenal's retained earnings as at 1 January 2016	120,000
80% of Chelsea's post acquisition retained earnings as at 1 January 2016	- (Nil)
	120,000

In this case, there is no post-acquisition profit as the subsidiary was acquired during the reporting year. Same can be said of a subsidiary acquired on the first date of the reporting period.

3. **Non-controlling Interest (Added on Acquisition) as at 1 April 2016**

In this case, there is no opening balance for non-controlling interest as at 1 January 2016, as there was no Group and neither would a non-controlling interest in Chelsea would have been recognised as at 1 January 2016 (being the start of the reporting period of the presumed parent). Rather, the amount to be recognised with respect to non-controlling interest will be the amount added on the acquisition of Chelsea, which will be based on the accounting policy of the Group on the measurement of the amount of non-controlling interest upon acquisition. In this case, the amount of non-controlling interest is considered to have been measured at an acquisition-date fair value of ₦24 million.

ILLUSTRATION 15:

Arsenal acquired 80% interests in the equity of Chelsea as 1 April 2016. The Board of Arsenal strictly wants to comply with the requirement of IFRS regarding consolidation of the financial statements of the subsidiary with that of the parent as at December 31, 2016.

Income Statement for the year ended December 31, 2016

	Arsenal	Chelsea
	₦'000	₦'000
Revenue	600,000	390,000
Cost of sales	(345,000)	(201,000)
Gross profit	**255,000**	**189,000**
Distribution costs	(75,000)	(45,000)
Administrative expenses	(105,000)	(90,000)
Profit on before tax	**75,000**	**54,000**
Income tax	(25,000)	(29,000)
Profit for the year	**50,000**	**25,000**

Movement in Reserves:

Retained profits brought forward	120,000	65,000
Profit for the year	50,000	25,000
Retained profit carried forward	**170,000**	**90,000**

Additional Information:

It was obtained that on 15 March 2016, Arsenal already sold goods to Chelsea for ₦50 million, when it actually cost Arsenal ₦40 million. As at the year-end, included in the inventory of Chelsea Plc is 40% of the inventory sold by Arsenal Plc as of 15th March 2016.

Required:

Prepare the consolidated of profit or loss and the consolidated statement of changes in equity, given that the share capital of Arsenal stood at ₦200 million and that of Chelsea amounted to ₦100 million, and the amount of non-controlling interest at acquisition as measured at fair value stood at ₦24 million.

In this context of this text, we will approach a step-by-step approach to explaining the requirement of **IFRS 10** with regards to consolidating the financial results of the parent and the subsidiary as depicted below.

Arsenal Group
Consolidated Statement of Profit or Loss for the year ended 31 December 2016

	₦'000
Revenue (600,000 + {9/12 x 390,000})	892,500
Cost of sales (345,000 + {9/12 x 201,000})	(495,750)
Gross profit	**396,750**
Distribution costs (75,000 + {9/12 x 45,000})	(108,750)
Administrative expenses (105,000 + {9/12 x 90,000})	(172,500)
Profit on before tax	**115,500**
Income tax (25,000 + {9/12 x 29,000})	(46,750)
Profit for the year	**68,750**
Profit, attributable to:	
* Owners' of Arsenal (Note 1)	65,000
** Non-controlling interest (Note 1)	3,750
	68,750

Arsenal Group
Consolidated Statement of Changes in Equity for the year ended 31 December 2016

	Share Capital	Retained Earnings	Equity – of the Parent	Non-controlling Interest	Total Equity
	₦'000	₦'000	₦'000	₦'000	₦'000
As at 1 January 2016	200,000	120,000 (Note 2)	320,000	–	320,000
Profit for the year		65,000	65,000	3,750	68,750
Transactions within Equity:					
Added on Acquisition				24,000 (Note 3)	24,000
As at 31 December, 2016	**200,000**	**185,000**	**385,000**	**27,750**	**412,750**

345

Consolidated Statement of Profit or Loss and Other Comprehensive Income; and Statement of Changes in Equity

Working Notes:

1. **Profit attributable to interest**

	Arsenal	Non-controlling
	₦'000	₦'000
Arsenal's profit after tax	50,000	-
Chelsea' profit after tax (80:20)	15,000	3,750
	65,000	**3,750**

*No adjustment regarding the elimination of intercompany sales, the intercompany cost of sales and invariably elimination of unrealized profit is required in this context. This is as a result that, as of 15th day of March 2016 when the sales transaction was initiated between Arsenal and Chelsea, there was no established **parent-subsidiary relationship**, and such sales transaction cannot be termed an intercompany transaction that may have required such adjustment.*

Only post-combination transactions between the parent and subsidiary are required to be accorded strict treatment of elimination, so as to depict the true economic and financial performance of the Group.

The income statement items are presumed to have accrued evenly, and on this premise, the individual items (expense and income) are apportioned into pre-acquisition and post-acquisition items on the basis of time proportion. In this scenario, since the acquisition took place sometimes during the year (specifically on 1st day of April 2016), then the portion of pre-acquisition was considered 3 months (i.e. between 1 January 2016 and 31 March 2016), while post-acquisition period stood at 9 months (1 April 2016 to 31 December 2016).

The portion to be consolidated alongside that of a full calendar year (of 12 months) of the parent is the post-combination period of 9 months. This is what gave rise the prorated amount of income and expense consolidated (as shown above).

The attribution of subsidiary's profit in this illustration was based on the 9 months post-acquisition results of Chelsea, which stood at ₦18,750,000 (i.e. 9/12 of ₦25 million profit after tax for the whole year).

Chelsea' profit after tax is shared between the parent and the non-controlling interest in the ratio of 80% to 20% in which profit or loss is required to be allocated based on the stake held in the ordinary shares of the subsidiary.

2. **Consolidated Retained Earnings as at 1 January 2016**

	₦'000
Arsenal's retained earnings as at 1 January 2016	120,000
80% of Chelsea's post acquisition retained earnings as at 1 January 2016	- (Nil)
	120,000

In this case, there is no post-acquisition profit as the subsidiary was acquired during the reporting year. Same can be said of a subsidiary acquired on the first date of the reporting period.

3. **Non-controlling Interest (Added on Acquisition) as at 1 April 2016**

In this case, there is no opening balance for non-controlling interest as at 1 January 2016, as there was no Group and neither would a non-controlling interest in Chelsea would have been recognised as at 1 January 2016 (being the start of the reporting period of the presumed parent). Rather, the amount to be recognised with respect to non-controlling interest will be the amount added on the acquisition of Chelsea, which will be based on the accounting policy of the Group on the measurement of the amount of non-controlling interest upon acquisition. In this case, the amount of non-controlling interest is considered to have been measured at an acquisition-date fair value of ₦24 million.

ILLUSTRATION 16:

Arsenal acquired 80% interests in the equity of Chelsea as 1 April 2016. The Board of Arsenal strictly wants to comply with the requirement of IFRS regarding consolidation of the financial statements of the subsidiary with that of the parent as at December 31, 2016.

Income Statement for the year ended December 31, 2016

	Arsenal	Chelsea
	₦'000	₦'000
Revenue	600,000	390,000
Cost of sales	(345,000)	(201,000)
Gross profit	**255,000**	**189,000**
Distribution costs	(75,000)	(45,000)
Administrative expenses	(105,000)	(90,000)
Profit on before tax	**75,000**	**54,000**
Income tax	(25,000)	(29,000)
Profit for the year	**50,000**	**25,000**
Movement in Reserves:		
Retained profits brought forward	120,000	65,000
Profit for the year	50,000	25,000
Retained profit carried forward	**170,000**	**90,000**

Additional Information:

It was obtained that on 19 May 2016, Arsenal already sold goods to Chelsea for ₦50 million, when it actually cost Arsenal ₦40 million. As at the year-end, included in the inventory of Chelsea Plc is 40% of the inventory sold by Arsenal Plc as of 19th May 2016.

Required:

Prepare the consolidated of profit or loss and the consolidated statement of changes in equity, given that the share capital of Arsenal stood at ₦200 million and that of Chelsea amounted to ₦100 million, and the amount of non-controlling interest at acquisition as measured at fair value stood at ₦24 million.

In this context of this text, we will approach a step-by-step approach to explaining the requirement of **IFRS 10** with regards to consolidating the financial results of the parent and the subsidiary as depicted below.

Arsenal Group
Consolidated Statement of Profit or Loss for the year ended 31 December 2016

	₦'000
Revenue (600,000 + {9/12 x 390,000} – 50,000 {Note 1})	842,500
Cost of sales (345,000 + {9/12 x 201,000} – 46,000 {Note 1})	(449,750)
Gross profit	**392,750**
Distribution costs (75,000 + {9/12 x 45,000})	(108,750)
Administrative expenses (105,000 + {9/12 x 90,000})	(172,500)

Consolidated Statement of Profit or Loss and Other Comprehensive Income; and Statement of Changes in Equity

Profit on before tax	111,500
Income tax (25,000 + {9/12 x 29,000})	(46,750)
Profit for the year	**64,750**
Profit, attributable to:	
* Owners' of Arsenal (Note 1)	61,000
** Non-controlling interest (Note 1)	3,750
	64,750

Arsenal Group
Consolidated Statement of Changes in Equity for the year ended 31 December 2016

	Share Capital	Retained Earnings	Equity – of the Parent	Non-controlling Interest	Total Equity
	N'000	N'000	N'000	N'000	N'000
As at 1 January 2016	200,000	120,000 (Note 2)	320,000	–	320,000
Profit for the year		61,000	61,000	3,750	64,750
Transactions within Equity:					
Added on Acquisition				24,000 (Note 3)	24,000
As at 31 December, 2016	200,000	181,000	381,000	27,750	408,750

Working Notes:

1. **Profit attributable to: interest**

	Arsenal	Non-controlling
	N'000	N'000
Arsenal's profit after tax	50,000	-
Chelsea' profit after tax (80:20)	15,000	3,750
Less: Unrealised profit on inventories	(4,000)	--
	61,000	**3,750**

Adjustments regarding the elimination of intercompany sales, the intercompany cost of sales and invariably elimination of unrealized profit are required in this context. This is as a result that, as of 19th day of May 2016 when the sales transaction was initiated between Arsenal and Chelsea, a *parent-subsidiary relationship* has since been established, and such sales transaction can be termed an intercompany transaction that requires such an adjustment.

Only post-combination transactions between the parent and subsidiary are required to be accorded strict treatment of elimination, so as to depict the true economic and financial performance of the Group.

The intercompany sales of N50 million will have to be eliminated alongside the intra-group cost of sales (which is arrived at by deducting the amount of unrealised profit from the intercompany sales)

The unrealised profit is determined by multiply the percentage of unsold goods (which in this case is 40%) by the profit on sales as made from the intercompany sales of goods during the reporting period.

The profit on sales amounted to ₦10 million (being the difference between the proceeds of ₦50 million earned on the intercompany sales and cost price of ₦40 million to the seller, which in this case is the parent).

Hence, the amount of unrealized profit stood at ₦4 million (being 40% unsold inventories multiplied by ₦10 million profit on sales made during the reporting period).

Then, the amount of inter-company cost of sales will amount to ₦46 million (being amount of intercompany sales of ₦50 million less the ₦4 million unrealised profit as at the reporting date).

The unrealised profit being eliminated is solely attributable to the parent, as the sales transaction was made by the parent being a downstream transaction.

The income statement items are presumed to have accrued evenly, and on this premise, the individual items (expense and income) are apportioned into pre-acquisition and post-acquisition items on the basis of time proportion. In this scenario, since the acquisition took place sometimes during the year (specifically on 1st day of April 2016), then the portion of pre-acquisition was considered 3 months (i.e. between 1 January 2016 and 31 March 2016), while post-acquisition period stood at 9 months (1 April 2016 to 31 December 2016).

The portion to be consolidated alongside that of a full calendar year (of 12 months) of the parent is the post-combination period of 9 months. This is what gave rise the prorated amount of income and expense consolidated (as shown above).

The attribution of subsidiary's profit in this illustration was based on the 9 months post-acquisition results of Chelsea, which stood at ₦18,750,000 (i.e. 9/12 of ₦25 million profit after tax for the whole year).

Chelsea' profit after tax is shared between the parent and the non-controlling interest in the ratio of 80% to 20% in which profit or loss is required to be allocated based on the stake held in the ordinary shares of the subsidiary.

2. **Consolidated Retained Earnings as at 1 January 2016**

	₦'000
Arsenal's retained earnings as at 1 January 2016	120,000
80% of Chelsea's post acquisition retained earnings as at 1 January 2016	- (Nil)
	120,000

In this case, there is no post-acquisition profit as the subsidiary was acquired during the reporting year. Same can be said of a subsidiary acquired on the first date of the reporting period.

3. **Non-controlling Interest (Added on Acquisition) as at 1 April 2016**

In this case, there is no opening balance for non-controlling interest as at 1 January 2016, as there was no Group and neither would a non-controlling interest in Chelsea would have been recognised as at 1 January 2016 (being the start of the reporting period of the presumed parent). Rather, the amount to be recognised with respect to non-controlling interest will be the amount added on the acquisition of Chelsea, which will be based on the accounting policy of the Group on the measurement of the amount of non-controlling interest upon acquisition. In this case, the amount of non-controlling interest is considered to have been measured at an acquisition-date fair value of ₦24 million.

Consolidated Statement of Profit or Loss and Other Comprehensive Income; and Statement of Changes in Equity

EIGHTH PRINCIPLE:

MID-YEAR ACQUISITION AND RECOGNITION OF GAIN ON BARGAIN PURCHASE

ILLUSTRATION 17:

Arsenal acquired 80% interests in the equity of Chelsea as 1 April 2016. The Board of Arsenal strictly wants to comply with the requirement of IFRS regarding consolidation of the financial statements of the subsidiary with that of the parent as at December 31, 2016.

Income Statement for the year ended December 31, 2016

	Arsenal	Chelsea
	₦'000	₦'000
Revenue	600,000	390,000
Cost of sales	(345,000)	(201,000)
Gross profit	**255,000**	**189,000**
Distribution costs	(75,000)	(45,000)
Administrative expenses	(105,000)	(90,000)
Profit on before tax	**75,000**	**54,000**
Income tax	(25,000)	(29,000)
Profit for the year	**50,000**	**25,000**
Movement in Reserves:		
Retained profits brought forward	120,000	65,000
Profit for the year	50,000	25,000
Retained profit carried forward	**170,000**	**90,000**

Additional Information:

Required:

Prepare the consolidated of profit or loss and the consolidated statement of changes in equity, given that the share capital of Arsenal stood at ₦200 million and that of Chelsea amounted to ₦100 million, and the amount of non-controlling interest at acquisition as measured at fair value stood at ₦24 million. On acquisition of the subsidiary, there was a gain on bargain purchase of ₦3 million which is yet to be recognised.

In this context of this text, we will approach a step-by-step approach to explaining the requirement of **IFRS 10** with regards to consolidating the financial results of the parent and the subsidiary as depicted below.

Arsenal Group
Consolidated Statement of Profit or Loss for the year ended 31 December 2016

	₦'000
Revenue (600,000 + {9/12 x 390,000})	892,500
Cost of sales (345,000 + {9/12 x 201,000})	(495,750)
Gross profit	**396,750**
Distribution costs (75,000 + {9/12 x 45,000})	(108,750)
Administrative expenses (105,000 + {9/12 x 90,000})	(172,500)
Other income (Gain on Bargain Purchase Transaction – Note 4)	3,000
Profit on before tax	**118,500**
Income tax (25,000 + {9/12 x 29,000})	(46,750)
Profit for the year	**71,750**
Profit, attributable to:	
* Owners' of Arsenal (Note 1)	68,000
** Non-controlling interest (Note 1)	3,750
	71,750

350

Arsenal Group
Consolidated Statement of Changes in Equity for the year ended 31 December 2016

	Share Capital	Retained Earnings	Equity – of the Parent	Non-controlling Interest	Total Equity
	₦'000	₦'000	₦'000	₦'000	₦'000
As at 1 January 2016	200,000	120,000 (Note 2)	320,000	-	320,000
Profit for the year		68,000	68,000	3,750	71,750
Transactions within Equity:					
Added on Acquisition				24,000 (Note 3)	24,000
As at 31 December, 2016	200,000	188,000	388,000	27,750	415,750

Working Notes:

1. **Profit attributable to:**

	Arsenal	Non-controlling interest
	₦'000	₦'000
Arsenal's profit after tax	50,000	-
Chelsea' profit after tax (80:20)	15,000	3,750
	65,000	**3,750**

The income statement items are presumed to have accrued evenly, and on this premise, the individual items (expense and income) are apportioned into pre-acquisition and post-acquisition items on the basis of time proportion. In this scenario, since the acquisition took place sometimes during the year (specifically on 1st day of April 2016), then the portion of pre-acquisition was considered 3 months (i.e. between 1 January 2016 and 31 March 2016), while post-acquisition period stood at 9 months (1 April 2016 to 31 December 2016).

The portion to be consolidated alongside that of a full calendar year (of 12 months) of the parent is the post-combination period of 9 months. This is what gave rise the prorated amount of income and expense consolidated (as shown above).

The attribution of subsidiary's profit in this illustration was based on the 9 months post-acquisition results of Chelsea, which stood at ₦18,750,000 (i.e. 9/12 of ₦25 million profit after tax for the whole year).

Chelsea' profit after tax is shared between the parent and the non-controlling interest in the ratio of 80% to 20% in which profit or loss is required to be allocated based on the stake held in the ordinary shares of the subsidiary.

2. **Consolidated Retained Earnings as at 1 January 2016**

	₦'000
Arsenal's retained earnings as at 1 January 2016	120,000
80% of Chelsea's post acquisition retained earnings as at 1 January 2016	- (Nil)
	120,000

In this case, there is no post-acquisition profit as the subsidiary was acquired during the reporting year. Same can be said of a subsidiary acquired on the first date of the reporting period.

Consolidated Statement of Profit or Loss and Other Comprehensive Income; and Statement of Changes in Equity

3. **Non-controlling Interest (Added on Acquisition) as at 1 April 2016**

   In this case, there is no opening balance for non-controlling interest as at 1 January 2016, as there was no Group and neither would a non-controlling interest in Chelsea would have been recognised as at 1 January 2016 (being the start of the reporting period of the presumed parent). Rather, the amount to be recognised with respect to non-controlling interest will be the amount added on the acquisition of Chelsea, which will be based on the accounting policy of the Group on the measurement of the amount of non-controlling interest upon acquisition. In this case, the amount of non-controlling interest is considered to have been measured at an acquisition-date fair value of ₦24 million.

4. **Gain on Bargain Purchase Transaction as at Acquisition-Date (1 April 2016)**

   In accordance with the requirement of IFRS 3, the gain on bargain purchase of ₦3 million should be recognised immediately upon acquisition as an income to the parent. No portion of the gain can be considered a credit to the non-controlling interest because non-controlling interest is not a party to the transaction. Hence, the gain is solely that of the parent in any form of business combination.

NINTH PRINCIPLE:

OTHER COMPREHENSIVE INCOME

ILLUSTRATION 18:

Arsenal acquired 80% interests in the equity of Chelsea as January 1, 2014, when it was incorporated. The Board of Arsenal strictly wants to comply with the requirement of IFRS regarding consolidation of the financial statements of the subsidiary with that of the parent as at December 31, 2016.

Income Statement for the year ended December 31, 2016

	Arsenal	Chelsea
	₦'000	₦'000
Revenue	600,000	390,000
Cost of sales	(345,000)	(201,000)
Gross profit	**255,000**	**189,000**
Distribution costs	(75,000)	(45,000)
Administrative expenses	(105,000)	(90,000)
Profit on before tax	**75,000**	**54,000**
Income tax	(25,000)	(29,000)
Profit for the year	**50,000**	**25,000**
Other Comprehensive Income:		
Fair value gains/ (loss) on financial assets @ FVOCI	(10,000)	3,000
Revaluation surplus on property, plant and equipment	4,000	2,000
Total Comprehensive Income	**44,000**	**30,000**
Movement in Retained Earnings:		
Retained profits brought forward	120,000	65,000
Profit for the year	50,000	25,000
Retained profit carried forward	**170,000**	**90,000**
Movement in Other Component of Equity:		
Other Reserves brought forward	38,000	4,000
Other comprehensive income for the year	(6,000)	5,000
Other Reserves carried forward	**32,000**	**9,000**

Required:

Prepare the consolidated of profit or loss and the consolidated statement of changes in equity, given that the share capital of Arsenal stood at ₦200 million and that of Chelsea amounted to ₦100 million, and the amount of Non-controlling interest at acquisition as measured at proportionate of net assets share stood at ₦20 million.

In this context of this text, we will approach a step-by-step approach to explaining the requirement of **IFRS 10** with regards to consolidating the financial results of the parent and the subsidiary as depicted below.

Arsenal Group
Consolidated Statement of Profit or Loss for the year ended 31 December 2016

		₦'000
Revenue (600,000 + 390,000)		990,000
Cost of sales (345,000 + 201,000)		(546,000)
Gross profit		**444,000**
Distribution costs (75,000 + 45,000)		(120,000)
Administrative expenses (105,000 + 90,000)		(195,000)
Profit on before tax		**129,000**
Income tax (25,000 + 29,000)		(54,000)
Profit for the year		**75,000**

Total Comprehensive Income:	₦'000	₦'000
Profit for the year		75,000
Other comprehensive income:		
Fair value gains/ (loss) on AFS financial assets (-10,000 + 3,000)	(7,000)	
Revaluation surplus on property, plant and equipment (4,000 + 2,000)	6,000	(1,000)
Total Comprehensive Income for the year		**74,000**

Profit, attributable to:	
* Owners' of Arsenal (Note 1)	70,000
** Non-controlling interest (Note 1)	5,000
	75,000
Total comprehensive income, attributable to:	
* Owners' of Arsenal (Note 4)	68,000
** Non-controlling interest (Note 4)	6,000
	74,000

Arsenal Group
Consolidated Statement of Changes in Equity for the year ended 31 December 2016

	Share Capital	Retained Earnings	Other Component of Equity	Equity – of the Parent	Non-controlling Interest	Total Equity
	₦'000	₦'000	₦'000	₦'000	₦'000	₦'000
As at 1 January 2016	200,000	172,000 (Note 2a)	41,200 (Note 2b)	413,200	33,800 (Note 3)	447,000
Profit for the year		70,000		70,000	5,000	75,000
Other Comprehensive Income			(2,000)	(2,000)	1,000	(1,000)
As at 31 December, 2016	200,000	242,000	39,200	481,200	39,800	521,000

Consolidated Statement of Profit or Loss and Other Comprehensive Income; and Statement of Changes in Equity

Working Notes:

1. **Profit attributable to:**

	Arsenal	Non-controlling interest
	₦'000	₦'000
Arsenal's profit after tax	50,000	-
Chelsea' profit after tax (80:20)	20,000	5,000
	70,000	**5,000**

Chelsea' profit after tax is shared between the parent and the non-controlling interest in the ratio of 80% to 20% in which profit or loss is required to be allocated based on the stake held in the ordinary shares of the subsidiary.

2a). Consolidated Retained Earnings as at 1 January 2016

	₦'000
Arsenal's retained earnings as at 1 January 2016	120,000
80% of Chelsea's post acquisition retained earnings as at 1 January 2016	
{80% x (₦65 million – Pre acquisition profit)}	52,000
	172,000

2b). Consolidated Other Components of Equity (OCE) as at 1 January 2016

	₦'000
Arsenal's OCE as at 1 January 2016	38,000
80% of Chelsea's post acquisition OCE as at 1 January 2016	
{80% x (₦4 million – Pre acquisition OCE of zero)}	3,200
	41,200

In this case, there is no pre-acquisition profit as the subsidiary was acquired upon its incorporation, which signifies that no profit or loss would have been accumulated.

3. **Non-controlling interest as at 1 January 2016**

	₦'000
Amount of NCI as at acquisition (1 January 2014)	20,000
20% of Chelsea's post acquisition retained earnings as at 1 January 2016	
{20% x (₦65 million – Pre-acquisition profit of zero)}	13,000
20% of Chelsea's post acquisition OCE as at 1 January 2016	
{20% x (₦4 million – Pre-acquisition OCE of zero)}	800
	33,800

In this case, there is no pre-acquisition profit as the subsidiary was acquired upon its incorporation, which signifies that no profit or loss would have been accumulated.

4. **Total Comprehensive Income Attribution**

*In this instance, the amount of total comprehensive income is the summation of the profit for the year with the other comprehensive income. This is tends attributed to the portion of the parent and that of the non-controlling interest. The parent will have to recognise its entire amount of total comprehensive income for the year and its portion (or share) of total comprehensive income of the subsidiary for the same year. While the non-controlling interest only recognises its share of the subsidiary's total comprehensive income. Below are the alternatives to ascertaining the "**Total Comprehensive Income Attribution**".*

Scenario A:	Arsenal	Non-controlling Interest
	₦'000	₦'000
Profit for the year {working note 1} (i)	**70,000**	**5,000**
Other comprehensive income:		
Fair value gains on AFS financial assets		
→ Arsenal	(10,000)	–
→ Chelsea (80:20)	2,400	600
Revaluation surplus on PPE (80:20)		
→ Arsenal	4,000	–
→ Chelsea (80:20)	1,600	400
Other Comprehensive Income for the year (ii)	**(2,000)**	**1,000**
Total Comprehensive Income for the year (i + ii)	**68,000**	**6,000**

Scenario B:	Arsenal	Non-controlling Interest
	₦'000	₦'000
Total comprehensive income:		
Arsenal (50,000 – 10,000 + 4,000)	44,000	-
Chelsea (25,000 + 3,000 + 2,000) @ 80:20	24,000	6,000
Total Comprehensive Income for the year	**68,000**	**6,000**

TENTH PRINCIPLE:
IMPAIRMENT LOSS ON GOODWILL

ILLUSTRATION 19:

Arsenal acquired 80% interests in the equity of Chelsea as January 1, 2010, when the retained earnings stood at ₦20 million. The Board of Arsenal strictly wants to comply with the requirement of IFRS regarding consolidation of the financial statements of the subsidiary with that of the parent as at December 31, 2016.

Income Statement for the year ended December 31, 2016

	Arsenal	Chelsea
	₦'000	₦'000
Revenue	600,000	390,000
Cost of sales	(345,000)	(201,000)
Gross profit	255,000	189,000
Distribution costs	(75,000)	(45,000)
Administrative expenses	(105,000)	(90,000)
Profit on before tax	75,000	54,000
Income tax	(25,000)	(29,000)
Profit for the year	**50,000**	**25,000**
Movement in Reserves:		
Retained profits brought forward	120,000	65,000
Profit for the year	50,000	25,000
Retained profit carried forward	**170,000**	**90,000**

Required:

Prepare the consolidated of profit or loss and the consolidated statement of changes in equity, given that the share capital of Arsenal stood at ₦200 million and that of Chelsea amounted to ₦100 million, and the amount of non-controlling interest at acquisition as measured at fair value stood at ₦24 million. As at the reporting date (31 December 2016), the goodwill has been impaired to the tune of ₦12 million, and of which only ₦5 million represents the impairment loss attributable to 2016 financial year.

Consolidated Statement of Profit or Loss and Other Comprehensive Income; and Statement of Changes in Equity

In this context of this text, we will approach a step-by-step approach to explaining the requirement of **IFRS 10** with regards to consolidating the financial results of the parent and the subsidiary as depicted below.

Arsenal Group
Consolidated Statement of Profit or Loss for the year ended 31 December 2016

	₦'000
Revenue (600,000 + 390,000)	990,000
Cost of sales (345,000 + 201,000)	(546,000)
Gross profit	**444,000**
Distribution costs (75,000 + 45,000)	(120,000)
Administrative expenses (105,000 + 90,000 + 5,000 Impairment loss on goodwill)	(200,000)
Profit on before tax	**124,000**
Income tax (25,000 + 29,000)	(54,000)
Profit for the year	**70,000**

Profit, attributable to:
* Owners' of Arsenal (Note 1)	66,000
** Non-controlling interest (Note 1)	4,000
	70,000

Arsenal Group
Consolidated Statement of Changes in Equity for the year ended 31 December 2016

	Share Capital	Retained Earnings	Equity – of the Parent	Non-controlling Interest	Total Equity
	₦'000	₦'000	₦'000	₦'000	₦'000
As at 1 January 2016	200,000	150,400 (Note 2)	350,400	31,600 (Note 3)	382,000
Profit for the year		66,000	66,000	4,000	70,000
As at 31 December, 2016	200,000	216,400	416,400	35,600	452,000

Working Notes:

1. **Profit attributable to:**

	Arsenal	Non-controlling interest
	₦'000	₦'000
Arsenal's profit after tax	50,000	–
Chelsea' profit after tax (80:20)	20,000	5,000
Less: Impairment loss on goodwill (80:20)	(4,000)	(1,000)
	66,000	**4,000**

Chelsea' profit after tax is shared between the parent and the non-controlling interest in the ratio of 80% to 20% in which profit or loss is required to be allocated based on the stake held in the ordinary shares of the subsidiary.

The impairment loss to be recognised in group profit or loss is the ₦5 million resulting from the current period assessment, while the earlier ₦7 million impairment loss (i.e. the difference between ₦12 million and ₦5 million) should have been earlier recognised in the period to which it relates and its effect should have been reflected in the opening retained earnings.

The effect of the impairment loss of ₦5 million will be charged to the parent and non-controlling interest in the proportion (i.e. 80%:20%) the subsidiary's profit or loss is charged. This is so because the goodwill that has been impaired is considered a Full Goodwill. That is, a full goodwill is a goodwill that is attributable to both the parent and the non-controlling interest at the acquisition of the subsidiary, which usually exists on the accounting policy choice of measuring non-controlling interest at acquisition-date fair value.

2. **Consolidated Retained Earnings as at 1 January 2016**

	₦'000
Arsenal's retained earnings as at 1 January 2016	120,000
80% of Chelsea's post acquisition retained earnings as at 1 January 2016	
{80% x (₦65 million – ₦20 million - goodwill impairment loss of ₦7 million)}	30,400
	150,400

In this case, there was a pre-acquisition profit of ₦20 million which was the opening retained earnings.

3. **Non-controlling interest as at 1 January 2016**

	₦'000
Amount of NCI as at acquisition (1 January 2010)	24,000
20% of Chelsea's post acquisition retained earnings as at 1 January 2016	
{20% x (₦65 million – ₦20 million - goodwill impairment loss of ₦7 million)}	7,600
	31,600

In this case, there was a pre-acquisition profit of ₦20 million which was the opening retained earnings.

ILLUSTRATION 20:

Arsenal acquired 80% interests in the equity of Chelsea as January 1, 2010, when the retained earnings stood at ₦20 million. The Board of Arsenal strictly wants to comply with the requirement of IFRS regarding consolidation of the financial statements of the subsidiary with that of the parent as at December 31, 2016.

Income Statement for the year ended December 31, 2016

	Arsenal	Chelsea
	₦'000	₦'000
Revenue	600,000	390,000
Cost of sales	(345,000)	(201,000)
Gross profit	**255,000**	**189,000**
Distribution costs	(75,000)	(45,000)
Administrative expenses	(105,000)	(90,000)
Profit on before tax	**75,000**	**54,000**
Income tax	(25,000)	(29,000)
Profit for the year	**50,000**	**25,000**
Movement in Reserves:		
Retained profits brought forward	120,000	65,000
Profit for the year	50,000	25,000
Retained profit carried forward	**170,000**	**90,000**

Required:

Consolidated Statement of Profit or Loss and Other Comprehensive Income; and Statement of Changes in Equity

Prepare the consolidated of profit or loss and the consolidated statement of changes in equity, given that the share capital of Arsenal stood at ₦200 million and that of Chelsea amounted to ₦130 million; and the amount of non-controlling interest at acquisition was measured at the proportionate share of the subsidiary's identifiable net assets, which amounted to ₦30 million. As at the reporting date (31 December 2016), the goodwill has been impaired to the tune of ₦12 million, and of which only ₦5 million represents the impairment loss attributable to 2016 financial year.

In this context of this text, we will approach a step-by-step approach to explaining the requirement of **IFRS 10** with regards to consolidating the financial results of the parent and the subsidiary as depicted below.

Arsenal Group
Consolidated Statement of Profit or Loss for the year ended 31 December 2016

	₦'000
Revenue (600,000 + 390,000)	990,000
Cost of sales (345,000 + 201,000)	(546,000)
Gross profit	**444,000**
Distribution costs (75,000 + 45,000)	(120,000)
Administrative expenses (105,000 + 90,000 + 5,000 Impairment loss on goodwill)	(200,000)
Profit on before tax	**124,000**
Income tax (25,000 + 29,000)	(54,000)
Profit for the year	**70,000**

Profit, attributable to:
* Owners' of Arsenal (Note 1)	65,000
** Non-controlling interest (Note 1)	5,000
	70,000

Arsenal Group
Consolidated Statement of Changes in Equity for the year ended 31 December 2016

	Share Capital	Retained Earnings	Equity – of the Parent	Non-controlling Interest	Total Equity
	₦'000	₦'000	₦'000	₦'000	₦'000
As at 1 January 2016	200,000	149,000	349,000	39,000	388,000
		(Note 2)		(Note 3)	
Profit for the year		65,000	65,000	5,000	70,000
As at 31 December, 2016	200,000	214,000	414,000	44,000	458,000

Working Notes:

1. Profit attributable to:

	Arsenal	Non-controlling interest
	₦'000	₦'000
Arsenal's profit after tax	50,000	–
Chelsea' profit after tax (80:20)	20,000	5,000
<u>Less:</u> Impairment loss on goodwill (100:0)	(5,000)	–
	65,000	**5,000**

Chelsea' profit after tax is shared between the parent and the non-controlling interest in the ratio of 80% to 20% in which profit or loss is required to be allocated based on the stake held in the ordinary shares of the subsidiary.

The impairment loss to be recognised in group profit or loss is the ₦5 million resulting from the current period assessment, while the earlier ₦7 million impairment loss (i.e. the difference between ₦12 million and ₦5 million) should have been earlier recognised in the period to which it relates and its effect should have been reflected in the opening retained earnings.

The effect of the impairment loss of ₦5 million will be charged to the parent only. This is so because the goodwill that has been impaired is considered a Partial Goodwill. That is, a partial goodwill is a goodwill that is attributable to only to the parent at the acquisition of the subsidiary, which only exists on the accounting policy choice of measuring non-controlling interest at the proportionate share of subsidiary's identifiable assets and liabilities at acquisition-date.

2. **Consolidated Retained Earnings as at 1 January 2016**

	₦'000
Arsenal's retained earnings as at 1 January 2016	120,000
80% of Chelsea's post acquisition retained earnings as at 1 January 2016	
[{80% x ₦65 million – ₦20 million)} - goodwill impairment loss of ₦7 million]	**29,000**
	149,000

In this case, there was a pre-acquisition profit of ₦20 million which was the opening retained earnings.

3. **Non-controlling interest as at 1 January 2016**

	₦'000
Amount of NCI as at acquisition (1 January 2010)	30,000
20% of Chelsea's post acquisition retained earnings as at 1 January 2016	
{20% x (₦65 million – ₦20 million)}	**9,000**
	39,000

In this case, there was a pre-acquisition profit of ₦20 million which was the opening retained earnings.

ELEVENTH PRINCIPLE:

UNWINDING OF DISCOUNT ON DEFERRED/CONTINGENT CONSIDERATION

ILLUSTRATION 21:

Arsenal acquired 80% interests in the equity of Chelsea as January 1, 2016. The Board of Arsenal strictly wants to comply with the requirement of IFRS regarding consolidation of the financial statements of the subsidiary with that of the parent as at December 31, 2016.

Income Statement for the year ended December 31, 2016

	Arsenal ₦'000	Chelsea ₦'000
Revenue	600,000	390,000
Cost of sales	(345,000)	(201,000)
Gross profit	**255,000**	**189,000**
Distribution costs	(75,000)	(45,000)
Administrative expenses	(105,000)	(90,000)
Profit on before tax	**75,000**	**54,000**
Income tax	(25,000)	(29,000)
Profit for the year	**50,000**	**25,000**

Consolidated Statement of Profit or Loss and Other Comprehensive Income; and Statement of Changes in Equity

Movement in Reserves:

Retained profits brought forward	120,000	20,000
Profit for the year	50,000	25,000
Retained profit carried forward	**170,000**	**45,000**

Required:

Prepare the consolidated of profit or loss and the consolidated statement of changes in equity, given that the share capital of Arsenal stood at ₦200 million and that of Chelsea amounted to ₦100 million, and the amount of non-controlling interest at acquisition as measured at fair value stood at ₦24 million. As an acquisition, the parent in addition to the shares consideration (shares exchange) offered to former shareholders of the subsidiary, a cash payment of ₦28.8 million is due to be paid on 31 December 2017 to the shareholders who sold their stakes to the parent. The hurdle rate (or cost of capital) of Arsenal is 20%.

In this context of this text, we will approach a step-by-step approach to explaining the requirement of **IFRS 10** with regards to consolidating the financial results of the parent and the subsidiary as depicted below.

Arsenal Group
Consolidated Statement of Profit or Loss for the year ended 31 December 2016

	₦'000
Revenue (600,000 + 390,000)	990,000
Cost of sales (345,000 + 201,000)	(546,000)
Gross profit	**444,000**
Distribution costs (75,000 + 45,000)	(120,000)
Administrative expenses (105,000 + 90,000)	(195,000)
Operating profit	**129,000**
Finance cost (unwound discount of deferred consideration – Note 4)	(4,000)
Profit on before tax	**125,000**
Income tax (25,000 + 29,000)	(54,000)
Profit for the year	**71,000**
Profit, attributable to:	
* Owners' of Arsenal (Note 1)	66,000
** Non-controlling interest (Note 1)	5,000
	71,000

Arsenal Group
Consolidated Statement of Changes in Equity for the year ended 31 December 2016

	Share Capital	Retained Earnings	Equity – of the Parent	Non-controlling Interest	Total Equity
	₦'000	₦'000	₦'000	₦'000	₦'000
As at 1 January 2016	200,000	120,000	320,000	24,000	344,000
		(Note 2)		(Note 3)	
Profit for the year		66,000	66,000	5,000	71,000
As at 31 December, 2016	200,000	186,000	386,000	29,000	415,000

Contemporaneous Accounting for Business Combinations and Group Accounts

Working Notes:

1. **Profit attributable to:**

	Arsenal ₦'000	Non-controlling interest ₦'000
Arsenal's profit after tax	50,000	-
Chelsea' profit after tax (80:20)	20,000	5,000
Less: Unwound discount	(4,000)	-
	66,000	**5,000**

Chelsea' profit after tax is shared between the parent and the non-controlling interest in the ratio of 80% to 20% in which profit or loss is required to be allocated based on the stake held in the ordinary shares of the subsidiary.

2. **Consolidated Retained Earnings as at 1 January 2016**

	₦'000
Arsenal's retained earnings as at 1 January 2016	120,000
80% of Chelsea's post acquisition retained earnings as at 1 January 2016	
{80% x (₦20 million – ₦20 million)}	-
	120,000

In this case, there was a pre-acquisition profit of ₦20 million which was the opening retained earnings. This is so because the subsidiary was acquired at the beginning of the year. There is no post-acquisition profit as depicted above.

3. **Non-controlling interest as at 1 January 2016**

	₦'000
Amount of NCI as at acquisition (1 January 2016)	24,000
20% of Chelsea's post acquisition retained earnings as at 1 January 2016	
{20% x (₦20 million – ₦20 million)}	-
	24,000

In this case, there was a pre-acquisition profit of ₦20 million which was the opening retained earnings. This is so because the subsidiary was acquired at the beginning of the year. There is no post-acquisition profit as depicted above.

4. **Unwinding of Discount on Deferred/Contingent Consideration (Finance Cost)**

The discount unwound represents the current period finance cost attributable to the unwinding of discount embedded in the present value of the deferred cash consideration made as at the acquisition date.

The amount of the deferred cash consideration at its (nominal) future value as at acquisition (i.e. as at 1 January 2016 was ₦28.8 million, and which is payable in 2 years' time (i.e. as at 31 December 2017.

The present value as at acquisition (in current money terms as at acquisition-date, 1 January 2016) would be ₦20 million (**i.e. present value of ₦28.8 million at 20% cost of capital, and discounted for 2 years; or ₦28.8 million x $(1.2)^{-2}$**).

The discount unwound for the first and current year is ₦4 million which is charged to parent's profit or loss (and which automatically charged to group profit, but only attributable to the parent). The basis of obtaining ₦4 million entails the multiplication of 20% cost of capital with the present value of ₦20 million as at the beginning of the year (which concurrently is the acquisition-date).

Consolidated Statement of Profit or Loss and Other Comprehensive Income; and Statement of Changes in Equity

ILLUSTRATION 22:

Arsenal acquired 80% interests in the equity of Chelsea as January 1, 2015, when the retained earnings stood at ₦20 million. The Board of Arsenal strictly wants to comply with the requirement of IFRS regarding consolidation of the financial statements of the subsidiary with that of the parent as at December 31, 2016.

Income Statement for the year ended December 31, 2016

	Arsenal ₦'000	Chelsea ₦'000
Revenue	600,000	390,000
Cost of sales	(345,000)	(201,000)
Gross profit	**255,000**	**189,000**
Distribution costs	(75,000)	(45,000)
Administrative expenses	(105,000)	(90,000)
Profit on before tax	**75,000**	**54,000**
Income tax	(25,000)	(29,000)
Profit for the year	**50,000**	**25,000**
Movement in Reserves:		
Retained profits brought forward	120,000	65,000
Profit for the year	50,000	25,000
Retained profit carried forward	**170,000**	**90,000**

Required:

Prepare the consolidated of profit or loss and the consolidated statement of changes in equity, given that the share capital of Arsenal stood at ₦200 million and that of Chelsea amounted to ₦100 million, and the amount of non-controlling interest at acquisition as measured at fair value stood at ₦24 million. As an acquisition, the parent in addition to the shares consideration (shares exchange) offered to former shareholders of the subsidiary, a cash payment of ₦28.8 million is due to be paid on 31 December 2016 to the shareholders who sold their stakes to the parent. The hurdle rate (or cost of capital) of Arsenal is 20%.

In this context of this text, we will approach a step-by-step approach to explaining the requirement of **IFRS 10** with regards to consolidating the financial results of the parent and the subsidiary as depicted below.

Arsenal Group
Consolidated Statement of Profit or Loss for the year ended 31 December 2016

	₦'000
Revenue (600,000 + 390,000)	990,000
Cost of sales (345,000 + 201,000)	(546,000)
Gross profit	**444,000**
Distribution costs (75,000 + 45,000)	(120,000)
Administrative expenses (105,000 + 90,000)	(195,000)
Operating profit	**129,000**
Finance cost (unwound discount of deferred consideration – Note 4)	(4,800)
Profit on before tax	**124,200**
Income tax (25,000 + 29,000)	(54,000)
Profit for the year	**70,200**

Profit, attributable to:

* Owners' of Arsenal (Note 1)	65,200
** Non-controlling interest (Note 1)	5,000
	70,200

Arsenal Group
Consolidated Statement of Changes in Equity for the year ended 31 December 2016

	Share Capital	Retained Earnings	Equity – of the Parent	Non-controlling Interest	Total Equity
	₦'000	₦'000	₦'000	₦'000	₦'000
As at 1 January 2016	200,000	152,000 (Note 2)	352,000	33,000 (Note 3)	385,000
Profit for the year		65,200	65,200	5,000	70,200
As at 31 December, 2016	200,000	217,200	417,200	38,000	455,200

Working Notes:

1. **Profit attributable to:**

	Arsenal ₦'000	Non-controlling interest ₦'000
Arsenal's profit after tax	50,000	
Chelsea' profit after tax (80:20)	20,000	5,000
Less: Unwound discount	(4,800)	–
	65,200	**5,000**

Chelsea' profit after tax is shared between the parent and the non-controlling interest in the ratio of 80% to 20% in which profit or loss is required to be allocated based on the stake held in the ordinary shares of the subsidiary.

2. **Consolidated Retained Earnings as at 1 January 2016**

	₦'000
Arsenal's retained earnings as at 1 January 2016	120,000
80% of Chelsea's post acquisition retained earnings as at 1 January 2016 {80% x (₦65 million – ₦20 million)}	36,000
Less: Unwound Discount in 2015 (20% x ₦20 million → Note 4)	(4,000)
	152,000

In this case, there was a pre-acquisition profit of ₦20 million which was the opening retained earnings.

3. **Non-controlling interest as at 1 January 2016**

	₦'000
Amount of NCI as at acquisition (1 January 2016)	24,000
20% of Chelsea's post acquisition retained earnings as at 1 January 2016 {20% x (₦65 million – ₦20 million)}	9,000
	33,000

In this case, there was a pre-acquisition profit of ₦20 million which was the opening retained earnings.

Consolidated Statement of Profit or Loss and Other Comprehensive Income; and Statement of Changes in Equity

4. **Unwinding of Discount on Deferred/Contingent Consideration (Finance Cost)**

    The discount unwound represents the current period finance cost attributable to the unwinding of discount embedded in the present value of the deferred cash consideration made as at the acquisition date.

    The amount of the deferred cash consideration at its (nominal) future value as at acquisition (i.e. as at 1 January 2015 was ₦28.8 million, and which is payable in 2 years' time (i.e. as at 31 December 2016.

    *The present value as at acquisition (in current money terms as at acquisition-date, 1 January 2015) would be ₦20 million (**i.e. present value of ₦28.8 million at 20% cost of capital, and discounted for 2 years; or ₦28.8 million x $(1.2)^{-2}$**).*

    The discount unwound for the first year (i.e. 2015) was ₦4 million which is considered to have been charged to parent's profit or loss in 2015 (and which automatically would have been reflected I its closing retained earnings as at 31 December 2015). The basis of obtaining ₦4 million entails the multiplication of 20% cost of capital with the present value of ₦20 million as at the beginning of the year (which was the acquisition-date).

    The discount unwound for the second and final year is ₦4.8 million which is charged to parent's profit or loss in 2016 (and which automatically charged to group profit, but only attributable to the parent). The basis of obtaining ₦4.8 million entails the multiplication of 20% cost of capital with the present value of ₦24 million as at the beginning of the year (which is the addition of the present value as at acquisition-date of ₦20 million and ₦4 million unwound discount for 2015 financial year).

TWELFTH PRINCIPLE:

TREATMENT OF PREFERENCE DIVIDEND

In this scenario, we will consider the basic treatment of preference dividend on preference shares recognised as an equity instrument in line with IAS 32, and its effect in the attribution of profit to non-controlling interest for the reporting period.

The share of **Non-controlling interest (NCI)** where there are no preference shares within the **Equity Capital Structure** of the subsidiary is determined as thus:

NCI's share =   % ordinary shares held x Profit for the year (i.e. PAT) of the subsidiary

The share of **Non-controlling interest (NCI)** where there is preference shares within the **Equity Capital Structure** of the subsidiary can be determined under the following scenario:

- **Where preference shares are held entirely by parent company**

NCI's share =   % ordinary shares held x (Profit for the year of the subsidiary – Preference Dividends)

- **Where preference shares are held entirely by the non-controlling interest**

NCI's share =	% ordinary shares held x (Profit for the year of the subsidiary – Preference Dividends)	XXX
	Plus: Preference Dividends	XX
		XXX

- **Where preference shares are held partly by the parent company and non-controlling interest**

NCI's share =	% ordinary shares held x (Profit for the year of the subsidiary – Preference Dividends)	XXX
	Plus: % preference shares held x Preference Dividends	XX
		XXX

Technical Note:
The preference dividend relevant for our calculation is only the post-acquisition dividend of the subsidiary.

ILLUSTRATION 23:

Arsenal acquired 80% interests in the equity of Chelsea as January 1, 2014, when the retained earnings stood at ₦20 million. The Board of Arsenal strictly wants to comply with the requirement of IFRS regarding consolidation of the financial statements of the subsidiary with that of the parent as at December 31, 2016.

Income Statement for the year ended December 31, 2016

	Arsenal ₦'000	Chelsea ₦'000
Revenue	600,000	390,000
Cost of sales	(345,000)	(201,000)
Gross profit	**255,000**	**189,000**
Distribution costs	(75,000)	(45,000)
Administrative expenses	(107,000)	(90,000)
Dividend Income	2,000	-
Profit on before tax	**75,000**	**54,000**
Income tax	(25,000)	(29,000)
Profit for the year	**50,000**	**25,000**
Movement in Reserves:		
Retained profits brought forward	120,000	67,000
Profit for the year	50,000	25,000
Dividend Paid – Ordinary	(10,000)	-
– Preference	-	(2,000)
Retained profit carried forward	**160,000**	**90,000**

Required:

Prepare the consolidated of profit or loss and the consolidated statement of changes in equity, given that the share capital of Arsenal stood at ₦200 million and that of Chelsea amounted to ₦100 million, and the amount of non-controlling interest at acquisition as measured at fair value stood at ₦24 million. Within the equity capital structure of the subsidiary, the parent held all of its preference shares as at the reporting date.

In this context of this text, we will approach a step-by-step approach to explaining the requirement of **IFRS 10** with regards to consolidating the financial results of the parent and the subsidiary as depicted

Arsenal Group
Consolidated Statement of Profit or Loss for the year ended 31 December 2016

	₦'000
Revenue (600,000 + 390,000)	990,000
Cost of sales (345,000 + 201,000)	(546,000)
Gross profit	**444,000**
Distribution costs (75,000 + 45,000)	(120,000)
Administrative expenses (107,000 + 90,000)	(197,000)
~~Dividend Income (2,000 + 0 – 2,000 Intercompany)~~	0
Profit on before tax	**127,000**

Consolidated Statement of Profit or Loss and Other Comprehensive Income; and Statement of Changes in Equity

Income tax (25,000 + 29,000)	(54,000)
Profit for the year	**73,000**
Profit, attributable to:	
* Owners' of Arsenal (Note 1)	68,000
** Non-controlling interest (Note 1)	5,000
	73,000

Arsenal Group
Consolidated Statement of Changes in Equity for the year ended 31 December 2016

	Share Capital	Retained Earnings	Equity – of the Parent	Non-controlling Interest	Total Equity
	₦'000	₦'000	₦'000	₦'000	₦'000
As at 1 January 2016	200,000	157,600 (Note 2)	357,600	33,400 (Note 3)	391,000
Profit for the year		68,400	68,400	4,600	73,000
Dividend		(10,000)	(10,000)	–	(10,000)
As at 31 December, 2016	200,000	216,000	416,000	38,000	454,000

Working Notes:

1. **Profit attributable to:**

	Arsenal	Non-controlling interest
	₦'000	₦'000
Arsenal's profit after tax	50,000	-
Chelsea' profit after tax	20,400	4,600
Less: Elimination of inter-company dividend income	(2,000)	-
	68,400	**4,600**

The amount of dividend income to be eliminated is the portion traceable to have been earned and received from other entities' within the group during the reporting period. In this context, the amount of dividend paid by the subsidiary to its preference shareholder (the parent) was ₦2 million. Hence, the amount reported in the parent's profit or loss also amounted to ₦2 million, which implies that that amount represents the dividend income solely received by the parent from the subsidiary in the reporting period.

The amount of subsidiary's profit attributable to the non-controlling interest is its 20% share in the subsidiary's profit after deducting the entire preference dividends solely due to the parent. That is ₦4.6 million which is based on 20% of (₦25 million – ₦2 million). While the sum of ₦20.4 million (made up of ₦18.4 million is attributable to the ordinary shares held by a parent and ₦2 million preference dividends due to the parent).

Also, Chelsea' profit after tax is shared between the parent and the non-controlling interest in the ratio of 80% to 20% in which profit or loss is required to be allocated based on the stake held in the ordinary shares of the subsidiary.

2. **Consolidated Retained Earnings as at 1 January 2016**

	₦'000
Arsenal's retained earnings as at 1 January 2016	120,000
80% of Chelsea's post acquisition retained earnings as at 1 January 2016 {80% x (₦67 million – ₦20 million)}	37,600
	157,600

Contemporaneous Accounting for Business Combinations and Group Accounts

In this case, there was a pre-acquisition profit of ₦20 million which was the opening retained earnings.

3. **Non-controlling interest as at 1 January 2016**

	₦'000
Amount of NCI as at acquisition (1 January 2014)	24,000
20% of Chelsea's post acquisition retained earnings as at 1 January 2016	
{20% x (₦67 million – ₦20 million)}	9,400
	33,400

In this case, there was a pre-acquisition profit of ₦20 million which was the opening retained earnings.

ILLUSTRATION 24:

Arsenal acquired 80% interests in the equity of Chelsea as January 1, 2014, when the retained earnings stood at ₦20 million. it

Income Statement for the year ended December 31, 2016

	Arsenal	Chelsea
	₦'000	₦'000
Revenue	600,000	390,000
Cost of sales	(345,000)	(201,000)
Gross profit	**255,000**	**189,000**
Distribution costs	(75,000)	(45,000)
Administrative expenses	(105,000)	(90,000)
Profit on before tax	**75,000**	**54,000**
Income tax	(25,000)	(29,000)
Profit for the year	**50,000**	**25,000**
Movement in Reserves:		
Retained profits brought forward	120,000	67,000
Profit for the year	50,000	25,000
Dividend Paid – Ordinary	(12,000)	-
– Preference	-	(2,000)
Retained profit carried forward	**158,000**	**90,000**

Required:

Prepare the consolidated of profit or loss and the consolidated statement of changes in equity, given that the share capital of Arsenal stood at ₦200 million and that of Chelsea amounted to ₦100 million, and the amount of non-controlling interest at acquisition as measured at fair value stood at ₦24 million. Within the equity capital structure of the subsidiary, its preference shares are all held by parties other than the parent as at the reporting date.

Consolidated Statement of Profit or Loss and Other Comprehensive Income; and Statement of Changes in Equity

In this context of this text, we will approach a step-by-step approach to explaining the requirement of **IFRS 10** with regards to consolidating the financial results of the parent and the subsidiary as depicted

Arsenal Group
Consolidated Statement of Profit or Loss for the year ended 31 December 2016

	₦'000
Revenue (600,000 + 390,000)	990,000
Cost of sales (345,000 + 201,000)	(546,000)
Gross profit	**444,000**
Distribution costs (75,000 + 45,000)	(120,000)
Administrative expenses (107,000 + 90,000)	(195,000)
Profit on before tax	**129,000**
Income tax (25,000 + 29,000)	(54,000)
Profit for the year	**75,000**
Profit, attributable to:	
* Owners' of Arsenal (Note 1)	68,400
** Non-controlling interest (Note 1)	6,600
	75,000

Arsenal Group
Consolidated Statement of Changes in Equity for the year ended 31 December 2016

	Share Capital	Retained Earnings	Equity – of the Parent	Non-controlling Interest	Total Equity
	₦'000	₦'000	₦'000	₦'000	₦'000
As at 1 January 2016	200,000	157,600 (Note 2)	357,600	33,400 (Note 3)	391,000
Profit for the year		68,400	68,400	6,600	75,000
Ordinary dividend		(12,000)	(12,000)	–	(12,000)
Preference dividend				(2,000)	(2,000)
As at 31 December, 2016	200,000	214,000	414,000	38,000	452,000

Working Notes:

1. Profit attributable to:

	Arsenal	Non-controlling interest
	₦'000	₦'000
Arsenal's profit after tax	50,000	–
Chelsea' profit after tax	18,400	6,600
	68,400	**6,600**

The amount of dividend income to be eliminated is the portion traceable to have been earned and received from other entities' within the group during the reporting period. In this context, the amount of dividend paid by the subsidiary to its preference shareholders (non-controlling interest) was ₦2 million.

The amount of subsidiary's profit attributable to the non-controlling interest is its 20% share in the subsidiary's profit after deducting the entire preference dividends solely due to its, plus ₦2 million preference dividends also due to it. That is ₦6.6 million which is based on 20% of (₦25 million – ₦2 million), plus ₦2 million preference dividends also due to it. While ₦18.4 million is attributable to the ordinary shares held by the parent as at the reporting date.

Also, Chelsea' profit after tax is shared between the parent and the non-controlling interest in the ratio of 80% to 20% in which profit or loss is required to be allocated based on the stake held in the ordinary shares of the subsidiary.

2. **Consolidated Retained Earnings as at 1 January 2016**

	₦'000
Arsenal's retained earnings as at 1 January 2016	120,000
80% of Chelsea's post acquisition retained earnings as at 1 January 2016 {80% x (₦67 million – ₦20 million)}	37,600
	157,600

In this case, there was a pre-acquisition profit of ₦20 million which was the opening retained earnings.

3. **Non-controlling interest as at 1 January 2016**

	₦'000
Amount of NCI as at acquisition (1 January 2014)	24,000
20% of Chelsea's post acquisition retained earnings as at 1 January 2016 {20% x (₦67 million – ₦20 million)}	9,400
	33,400

In this case, there was a pre-acquisition profit of ₦20 million which was the opening retained earnings.

ILLUSTRATION 25:

Arsenal acquired 80% interests in the equity of Chelsea as January 1, 2014, when the retained earnings stood at ₦20 million. The Board of Arsenal strictly wants to comply with the requirement of IFRS regarding consolidation of the financial statements of the subsidiary with that of the parent as at December 31, 2016.

Income Statement for the year ended December 31, 2016

	Arsenal ₦'000	Chelsea ₦'000
Revenue	600,000	390,000
Cost of sales	(345,000)	(201,000)
Gross profit	**255,000**	**189,000**
Distribution costs	(75,000)	(45,000)
Administrative expenses	(107,000)	(90,000)
Dividend Income	2,000	–
Profit on before tax	**75,000**	**54,000**
Income tax	(25,000)	(29,000)
Profit for the year	**50,000**	**25,000**
Movement in Reserves:		
Retained profits brought forward	120,000	67,000
Profit for the year	50,000	25,000
Dividend Paid – Ordinary	(10,000)	–
– Preference	–	(2,000)
Retained profit carried forward	**160,000**	**90,000**

Consolidated Statement of Profit or Loss and Other Comprehensive Income; and Statement of Changes in Equity

Required:

Prepare the consolidated of profit or loss and the consolidated statement of changes in equity, given that the share capital of Arsenal stood at ₦200 million and that of Chelsea amounted to ₦100 million, and the amount of non-controlling interest at acquisition as measured at fair value stood at ₦24 million. Within the equity capital structure of the subsidiary, the parent holds 40% stake in the preference shares capital, while the balance is held by parties other than the parent as at the reporting date.

In this context of this text, we will approach a step-by-step approach to explaining the requirement of **IFRS 10** with regards to consolidating the financial results of the parent and the subsidiary as depicted

Arsenal Group
Consolidated Statement of Profit or Loss for the year ended 31 December 2016

	₦'000
Revenue (600,000 + 390,000)	990,000
Cost of sales (345,000 + 201,000)	(546,000)
Gross profit	**444,000**
Distribution costs (75,000 + 45,000)	(120,000)
Administrative expenses (107,000 + 90,000)	(197,000)
Dividend Income (2,000 + 0 – *800 Intercompany*)	1,200
Profit on before tax	**128,200**
Income tax (25,000 + 29,000)	(54,000)
Profit for the year	**74,200**
Profit, attributable to:	
* Owners' of Arsenal (Note 1)	68,000
** Non-controlling interest (Note 1)	5,000
	74,200

Arsenal Group
Consolidated Statement of Changes in Equity for the year ended 31 December 2016

	Share Capital	Retained Earnings	Equity – of the Parent	Non-controlling Interest	Total Equity
	₦'000	₦'000	₦'000	₦'000	₦'000
As at 1 January 2016	200,000	157,600 (Note 2)	357,600	33,400 (Note 3)	391,000
Profit for the year		68,400	68,400	5,800	74,200
Ordinary dividend		(10,000)	(10,000)	–	(10,000)
Preference dividend				(1,200)	(1,200)
As at 31 December, 2016	200,000	216,000	416,000	38,000	454,000

Working Notes:

1. **Profit attributable to:**

	Arsenal	Non-controlling interest
	₦'000	₦'000
Arsenal's profit after tax	50,000	–
Chelsea' profit after tax	19,200	5,800
Less: Preference Dividend received by the parent	(800)	–
	68,400	**5,800**

370

The amount of dividend income to be eliminated is the portion traceable to have been earned and received from other entities' within the group during the reporting period. In this context, the amount of dividend paid by the subsidiary to its preference shareholders (parent and non-controlling interest) was ₦2 million. Hence, the amount reported in the parent's profit or loss of ₦1.2 million may have been attributable to other equity investment(s).

The amount of subsidiary's profit attributable to the non-controlling interest is its 20% share in the subsidiary's profit after deducting the entire preference dividends, plus its 60% share in ₦2 million preference dividends paid by the subsidiary. That is ₦5.8 million which is based on 20% of (₦25 million – ₦2 million), plus ₦1.2 million preference dividends also due to it. While the sum of ₦19.2 million (made up of ₦18.4 million is attributable to the ordinary shares held by a parent and ₦0.8 million being 40% preference dividends due to the parent).

Also, Chelsea' profit after tax is shared between the parent and the non-controlling interest in the ratio of 80% to 20% in which profit or loss is required to be allocated based on the stake held in the ordinary shares of the subsidiary.

2. **Consolidated Retained Earnings as at 1 January 2016**

	₦'000
Arsenal's retained earnings as at 1 January 2016	120,000
80% of Chelsea's post acquisition retained earnings as at 1 January 2016 {80% x (₦67 million – ₦20 million)}	37,600
	157,600

In this case, there was a pre-acquisition profit of ₦20 million which was the opening retained earnings.

3. **Non-controlling interest as at 1 January 2016**

	₦'000
Amount of NCI as at acquisition (1 January 2014)	24,000
20% of Chelsea's post acquisition retained earnings as at 1 January 2016 {20% x (₦67 million – ₦20 million)}	9,400
	33,400

In this case, there was a pre-acquisition profit of ₦20 million which was the opening retained earnings.

Consolidated Statement of Profit or Loss and Other Comprehensive Income; and Statement of Changes in Equity

SUMMARY OF CHAPTER

1. Consolidation of the profit or loss of the parent and its subsidiary entails the summation of the individual line items in the statement of profit or loss and other income of the parent and its subsidiary subject adjustment for unrealized profit, depreciation adjustment, elimination of inter-company transactions, elimination of dividend income earned by the parent from its subsidiary, and lots more.

2. The profit or loss and equally the total comprehensive income of the subsidiary should be attributed to the parent and the non-controlling interest in the proportion profit or loss of the subsidiary is shared between both, subject to relevant adjustments.

3. In ascertaining the opening consolidated retained earnings, the opening retained earnings of the parent and the share of the post-acquisition retained earnings brought forward is to be aggregated r combined.

4. Where the intercompany sale of goods occurs, the entire amount of revenue arising from such sales by the selling party should be eliminated from the combined revenue of the parent and the subsidiary, so as to obtain the true economic value of the group revenue earned from transactions with third parties.

5. Where the intercompany sale of goods occurs, the amount of unrealized profit (*if any*) should be ascertained and eliminated; and as such, it requires the elimination of inter-company cost of the sales. The amount of intercompany cost of sales to be adjusted is the difference between the inter-company revenue and the unrealised profit.

6. Where the intercompany sale of an asset (depreciable and/or non-depreciable) occur, the amount of unrealized profit (*if any*) should be ascertained and eliminated vis-à-vis the associated adjustment for depreciation for the depreciable assets (where necessary).

7. In a situation where the dividend is earned from the parent investment in the subsidiary, the amount of such dividend is eliminated.

8. When an inter-company loan(s) exist, the associated interest income to the lender and the interest expense to the borrower are to be eliminated.

9. In a situation where the subsidiary has preference shares (as an equity instrument in line with IAS 32) in its capital structure, necessary adjustment is required to ensure that separate consideration is availed the subsidiary profit attributable to ordinary shareholders and the preference shareholders on the premise the parent and non-controlling stake may not necessarily be the same in both situations (i.e. the ratio of investment by the parent and the non-controlling interest in the ordinary shares may not be the same with preference shares holdings).

10. Other comprehensive income should be consolidated in similar like with other items of income and expenses, and likewise, the attribution of total comprehensive income to the parent and non-controlling interest will exactly be the same as that of the profit or loss attribution.

11. Where goodwill has been impaired, the impairment loss in an integral part of the administrative (or operating) expenses of the group, but the attribution (or sharing) of the impairment loss(es) on the goodwill is a function of whether the goodwill so impaired is considered a partial or full goodwill.

12. Gain arising from bargain purchase transaction during a reporting period is considered an income to the parent and solely attributable to the acquisition initiated by the parent and should be reported as such in the group accounts.

END OF CHAPTER 10 EXERCISES

1. A parent sold goods worth ₦20 million to its subsidiary in a financial year. The profit on cost is approximately 25%. Of the goods purchased by the subsidiary from the parent, only ₦12 million has since been sold as at the reporting date. What are the amount of inter-company sales, the intercompany cost of sales and unrealized profit to be eliminated?

2. A subsidiary sold goods which cost it ₦20 million to its parent in a financial year. The profit-loaded is 20% margin. Of the goods purchased by the parent from the subsidiary, only ₦12 million has since been sold as at the reporting date. What are the amount of inter-company sales, the intercompany cost of sales and unrealized profit to be eliminated? And what treatment should be accorded the adjustment in the process of profit attribution to both the parent and non-controlling interest?

3. A parent transferred its motor vehicle with a carrying amount of ₦100 million to its subsidiary for a transfer price of ₦120 million as at 31 December 2016. What is the implication of this transaction in the course of preparing a consolidated statement of profit or loss for the year ended 31 December 2016?

4. A parent transferred its motor vehicle with a carrying amount of ₦100 million to its subsidiary for a transfer price of ₦120 million as at 1 January 2016, when the remaining useful life of the asset is 10 years. What is the implication of this transaction in the course of preparing a consolidated statement of profit or loss for the year ended 31 December 2016, assuming the group depreciation method is straight-line? What alternative treatment holds for the same transaction – if any?

5. A parent transferred its motor vehicle with a carrying amount of ₦100 million to its subsidiary for a transfer price of ₦90 million as at 31 December 2016. What is the implication of this transaction in the course of preparing a consolidated statement of profit or loss for the year ended 31 December 2016, assuming an event triggers possible impairment of the asset so transferred by the parent below its carrying amount?

6. A subsidiary appropriately declared and paid a dividend of ₦10 million in the financial year ended 31 December 2016. The parent holds 60% of the ordinary shares of the subsidiary. What treatment should be accorded this event as at the reporting date (31 December 2016) in the consolidated statement of profit or loss?

Chapter 11

Investment in Associates and Joint Ventures

INTRODUCTION

This chapter will focus on the principles for accounting for other forms of inter-corporate investment (other than investment in financial assets), and these principles differ from the acquisition method of accounting for a business combination and the dynamics of consolidation and its techniques.

The first phase of the chapter will focus on the aspect that tends to provide guidance to the readers in understanding what constitutes an investment in an associate and also on its initial accounting vis-à-vis its subsequent accounting.

In the second phase of the chapter, a similar approach will be adopted to explaining the dynamics of identifying and recognising investment in joint ventures and how such differs from a joint operations investment. A brief discussion of the requirement and propositions of IFRS 11 (Joint Arrangements) will be considered, so as to allow the readers understand the clear-cut differences between the two forms of joint arrangement.

Within the context of this chapter, it will be evident that the accounts of an associate and that of a joint venture cannot be consolidated, but rather a common accounting methodology called "*Equity Method*" will be adopted in line with the requirement of IAS 28 to account for both investments (i.e. investment in associates and joint ventures). The method equally accommodates necessary adjustments that may involve elimination of unrealized profits, impairment losses; and dividend received from investment in associates or joint ventures.

Investment in Associates and Joint Ventures

IAS 28 defines an *associate* as:

An entity, including an unincorporated entity such as partnership, over which an investor has significant influence and that, is neither a subsidiary nor an interest in joint venture.

The key concept in the definition is "*significant influence*". IAS 28 considers *significant influence* as "*the power to participate in the financial and operating policy decisions of the investee, but is not control over those policies*".

The existence of significant influence by an investor is usually evidenced by one or more of the following ways:

- Representation on the Board of Directors.
- Participation in policy-making processes.
- Material transactions between the investor and the entity.
- Interchange of managerial personnel.
- Provision of essential technical information.

Invariably, if an investor holds directly or indirectly, more than 20% of the voting rights of an entity (but less than or equal to 50%), IAS 28 states that there is a *presumption* the investor may have significant influence over the entity, unless it can be clearly demonstrated that this does not constitute significant influence.

Methods of Accounting for Associates in Consolidated Financial Statements

IAS 28 requires all investments in associates to be accounted for using the **equity method** unless the investments are classified as "*Held-for-Sale*" in accordance with **IFRS 5 (Non-current assets held for sale and discontinued operations)** in which case the provision or requirement of IFRS 5 applies.

Equity Method:

A method of accounting whereby the investment is initially recorded at cost and adjusted thereafter for the post-acquisition changes in the investor's share of the net assets of the investee. The profit or loss the investor will include the investor's share of the profit or loss of the investee.

An investor is exempted from applying the "*Equity Method*" if:

a) It is a parent exempted from preparing consolidated financial statements under IFRS 10 or

b) All of the followings apply:
   i. The investor is a wholly-owned subsidiary or it is a partially owned subsidiary of another entity and its owners, including those not otherwise entitled to vote, have been informed about, and do not object to, the investor not applying the equity method;
   ii. Its securities are not publicly traded;
   iii. It is not in the process of issuing securities in public securities markets; and
   iv. The ultimate or intermediate parent publishes Consolidated Financial Statements that comply with IFRSs.

The revised version of IAS 28 no longer allows an investment in an associate to be excluded from equity accounting when an investee operates under severe long-term restrictions that significantly impair its ability to transfer funds to the investor. Significant influence must be lost before the equity method ceases to be applicable (i.e. the use of equity method should be discontinued from the date that the investor ceases to have significant influence).

Therefore, from the date the investor ceases to have significant influence, the investor shall account for the investment in accordance with **IAS 39 (Financial Instruments: Recognition and measurement).** The carrying amount of the investment at the date that it ceases to be an associate shall be regarded as its cost on initial measurement of a financial asset under **IAS 39 (or IFRS 9, if early adopted)**.

The use of the equity method should be *discontinued* from the date that the investor ceases to have *significant influence*. From that date, the investor shall account for the investment in accordance with IAS 39/IFRS 9 Financial instruments. The carrying amount of the investment at the date that it ceases to be an associate shall be regarded as its cost on initial measurement as a financial asset under IAS 39/IFRS 9.

Recognition of Investment in Associates in the Separate Financial Statement of the Investor

If an investor issues consolidated financial statements (because it has subsidiaries), an investment in associate in its separate financial statements should be:

- *Accounted for at **cost**; or*
- *Accounted for at **fair value**, In accordance with IAS 39 (or IFRS 9 if early adopted); or*
- *Using the **equity method** (under IAS 28).*

If an investor does not issue consolidated financial statements (i.e. it has no subsidiaries) but has an investment in an associate; this should be included in the Financial Statements of the investor either *at fair value in accordance with IAS 39 (or IFRS 9 if early adopted) or adopt the equity method*.

Application of Equity Method in Consolidated Statement of Financial Position

The equity method should be accounted in the consolidated statement of financial position as thus;

❖ Investment in associate at cost	XXX
❖ *Plus* Group's share of post-acquisition profits/(losses)	XX
❖ *Less* Dividends received on investments from the associate to date	(X)
❖ *Less* any Impairment losses accumulated to date	(X)
	XXX

Application of Equity Method in Consolidated Statement of Profit or Loss and Other Comprehensive Income

The equity method should be accounted in the consolidated statement of profit or loss and comprehensive income as line items being a share of associate profit after taxes, subject to necessary adjustments.

Other Issues on Investments in the Associates

A. Uniform Reporting Date:

It is expected that the associate and investor have the same reporting date, but in the instance where the reporting is different, the investor can still go on consolidated the results of the associates by adjusting the results to effect necessary adjustments provided the difference in reporting dates is not more than Three (3) months.

B. Uniform Accounting Policies:

The investor and associate are expected to have the same accounting policies, and in the absence of uniform accounting policies, it is expected that upon consolidation the Financial Statements of the associates are adjusted appropriately to effect the accounting policies of the investor before consolidation.

C. Upstream and Downstream Transaction:

Downstream transactions involve transaction originated by the investor and directed to the associates, example involve the sale of assets or stocks from the investor to an associate, while an upstream transaction is, for example, the sale of assets or stocks from an associate to the investor.

Upon accounting for investments in associates in the financial statement of an investor, profit or losses resulting from 'upstream' and 'downstream' transactions between an investor (including its consolidated subsidiaries) and an associate are eliminated to the extent of the investor's interest in the associate. This is very similar to the procedure for eliminating intra-group transactions between a parent and a subsidiary.

Technical Note:
It is only the group share that will be eliminated.

Accounting Entries

1. Downstream Transaction

Elimination of unrealized profit on inventory/asset in profit or loss
- Debit: Cost of sale (or line items in profit or loss)
- Credit: Investment in associate

With the group's share of the unrealized profit.

Adjustments for excess depreciation on transfer/sale of depreciable assets
- Debit: Investments in Associates
- Credit: Cost of sale (or line items in profit or loss)

With the group's share of the excess depreciation.

2. Upstream Transaction

Elimination of unrealized profit on inventory/asset in profit or loss

- Debit: Cost of sale (or line items in profit or loss)
- Credit: Inventories (or class of assets)

With the group's share of the unrealized profit.

Adjustments for excess depreciation on transfer/sale of depreciable assets
- Debit: Group depreciable assets
- Credit: Cost of Sale/ Profit or Loss

With the group's share of the excess depreciation.

D. Associate's Losses

When the equity method is being used and the investor's share of losses of the associate equals or exceeds its interest in the associates, the investor should discontinue including its share of further losses. The investment is reported at *nil* value. The interest in the associate is normally the carrying amount of the investment in the associate, but it also includes any other long-term interests, for example, long-term receivables or loans.

After the investor's interest is reduced to *nil*, additional losses should only be recognised where the investor has assumed obligations or made payments on behalf of the associate (for example, if it has guaranteed amounts owed to third parties by the associate).

E. Impairment Losses in Associate

IAS 39 (Financial Instruments; Recognition and Measurement) or ***IFRS 9 (if early adopted)*** sets out a list of indications that a financial asset (including an associate) may have become impaired. An impairment loss is recognised in accordance with IAS 36 (Impairment of Assets) for investment held by an investor in an associate.

Upon accounting for investor's investments in the associate, any impairment loss will be deducted from the carrying value in the statement of financial position as thus:

	₦
Cost of Investment	XXX
Share of post-acquisition retained earnings (or losses)	X
	XXX
Less: Impairment loss	(X)
Carrying Amount of investment in associate	**XXX**

F. Dividend Received from Associates

Where dividends have been earned as income and equally received from the associate, in the process of equity accounting for such investments, the amount of dividends received by the investor will be deducted from the share of post-acquisition profit in arriving at the carrying amount investment in the associate, and likewise similar treatment is accorded the dividend income from associate in the profit or loss of the investor.

	₦
Cost of Investment	XXX
Share of post-acquisition retained earnings (or losses)	X
	XXX
Less: Dividend received from associate	(X)
Carrying Amount of investment in associate	**XXX**

ILLUSTRATION 1:

Faramola Plc with subsidiaries acquired 50 million shares of the 200 million shares in **Excellent Limited** for ₦55 million on January 1, 2016. In the year to 31 December 2016, Excel earns profits after tax of ₦20 million, from which it declares and paid a dividend of ₦10 million as at the reporting date.

How should Faramola Plc account for the investment in it's:

a) Separate financial statements as at 31 December 2016, and
b) Consolidated financial statements as at 31 December 2016?

Suggested Solutions:

Since the stake of Faramola Plc in Excellent approximate 25% (i.e. the ratio of 50 million shares acquired to 200 million shares issued by Excellent Limited), the investment is presumed to give "*significant influe*nce" to the investor.

a) In the separate financial statements; the investor (Faramola Plc) may elect to either account for its investment in Excellent Limited at *Cost* or at *Fair Value*. In this case, since the information about the fair value of its equity investment in Excellent Limited is not provided or obtainable through other means; the cost of ₦55 million will have to be recognised in the separate financial statements as at 31 December 2016.

b) In the consolidated financial statements; the investor (Faramola Plc) will have to account for its investment in Excellent Limited by adopting the "*Equity Method*". The carrying amount of the investment in associate is arrived at as thus:

	₦'000
Cost of Investment	55,000
Share of post-acquisition profit (25% of ₦20 million)	5,000
	60,000
Less: Dividend received from Excellent Limited (25% of ₦10 million)	(2,500)
Carrying Amount as @ 31 December 2016	**57,500**

ILLUSTRATION 2:

Lilly Plc, a company with a subsidiary acquires 50 million units of 200 million ₦1 ordinary shares in ZOE Limited for ₦120 million on 1 January 2016. In the year to 31 December 2016, ZOE Limited earns profits before tax of ₦60 million and income tax expense of ₦12 million. Of the dividend declared and paid by ZOE Limited in the financial year, the sum of ₦5 million represents what was received by Lilly as a return from investment in ZOE Limited.

Required: Advise on how ZOE Limited results should be accounted for in the "*Separate and Consolidated Financial Statements*" of Lilly Plc for the year ended 31 December 2016

Suggested Solutions:

Since the stake of Lilly Plc in ZOE Limited approximate 25% (i.e. the ratio of 50 million shares acquired to 200 million shares issued by ZOE Limited), the investment is presumed to give "*significant influe*nce" to the investor.

a) In the separate financial statements; the investor (Lilly Plc) may elect to either account for its investment in ZOE Limited at *Cost* or at *Fair Value*. In this case, since the information about the fair value of its equity investment in ZOE Limited is not provided or obtainable through other means; the cost of ₦120 million will have to be recognised in the separate financial statements as at 31 December 2016.

b) In the consolidated financial statements; the investor (Lilly Plc) will have to account for its investment in ZOE Limited by adopting the "*Equity Method*". The carrying amount of the investment in associate is arrived at as thus:

	₦'000
Cost of Investment	120,000
Share of post-acquisition profit (25% of {₦60 million – ₦12 million})	12,000
	132,000
Less: Dividend received from ZOE Limited	(5,000)
Carrying Amount as @ 31 December 2016	**127,000**

Investment in Associates and Joint Ventures

ILLUSTRATION 3:

Pally acquired 80% of the equity share capital of **Sussy** as at the reporting date 31 December 2013, when the retained earnings of **Sussy** was ₦40 million. Pally equally acquired 40% stake in **Mama** on 1 January 2015 for the sum of ₦20 million, when the retained earnings of the latter stood at ₦10 million. The statement of financial position of the three companies as at reporting date 31 December 2015 is as follows:

Statement of Financial Position as at 31st December 2015

	Pally ₦' million	Sussy ₦' million	Mama ₦' million
Property, plant and equipment	300	130	80
Investments	180	-	-
Current assets	100	70	40
Total Assets	**580**	**200**	**120**
Share Capital & Reserves:			
Equity share capital (@ ₦1 per share)	400	120	40
Reserves (Retained Earnings)	100	60	30
	500	180	70
Current liabilities	80	20	50
Total Equity and Liabilities	**580**	**200**	**120**

Suggested Solutions

First, we assumed that the parent at the point of acquisition (when control was obtained), measured the amount of non-controlling interests at the proportionate share of the subsidiary's identifiable net assets (assets and liabilities). In this case, the consolidation process will be as follows:

- ✓ **Step 1**: Determine the percentage holdings of investment of **Pally** in **Sussy** as at the acquisition date (31 December 2013), which represents the date of inclusion (first date of consolidation). In this case, the percentage holding is already determined and ascertained to be 80%.

- ✓ **Step 2**: Ascertain the form of group structure in this parent-subsidiary relationship. Since the subsidiary (**Sussy**) is *partly-owned* by the parent (**Pally**), the group structure is a simple structure as shown below:

```
        Pally
          \
           \ 80%
            \        20%
             Sussy ←——— Non-controlling interest
```

- ✓ **Step 3**: Determine the existence of goodwill or gain from a bargain purchase as at the date of acquisition based on the fair value of subsidiary's identifiable assets and liabilities. In this case, there exists goodwill as shown below.

To ascertain and determine the amount of goodwill or gain from a bargain purchase, the value of an investment of the parent (**Pally**) in the subsidiary (**Sussy**) will be compared with the parent's share of identifiable assets and liabilities of the subsidiary that were acquired.

PARTIAL METHODOLOGY

	₦' million	₦' million
Cost of investment of **Pally** in **Sussy** (i.e. ₦180 million – ₦20 million)		160
Less: **Pally**'s share of Identifiable net assets of **Sussy** acquired:		
• Share capital (80% of ₦120 million)	96	
• Pre-acquisition reserves (80% of ₦40 million)	32	(128)
Goodwill attributable to **Pally's** (a)		32
Amount of investments of non-controlling interest in **Sussy**		32
Less: Non-controlling interest share of the fair value of subsidiary's net assets:		
• Share capital (20% of ₦120 million)	24	
• Pre-acquisition reserves (20% of ₦40 million)	8	(32)
Goodwill attributable to **non-controlling interests** (b)		---
PARTIAL Goodwill (a + b)		**32**

Technical Note:

- *The amount of investment of Pally in Sussy of ₦160 million is ascertained after deducting the sum of ₦20 million, which represents the cost of investment of pally in Mama.*
- *The goodwill attributable to non-controlling should be zero since the investment to non-controlling interests is valued at the proportionate share of subsidiary's identifiable net assets as shown by the arrow.*

FULL METHODOLOGY

		₦' million
Cost of combination (i.e. cost of acquisition) to the parent		160
Amount of Investment in subsidiary to non-controlling interest*		32
Combined amount of interests in subsidiary to all investors		**192**
Less: Identifiable net assets of **Sussy** acquired (@ 31 December 2013):		
• Share capital	120	
• Pre-acquisition reserves	40	(160)
PARTIAL Goodwill - positive		**32**

✓ **Step 4:** Determine the amount of non-controlling interest as will be shown in the consolidated statement of financial position of the group. In this case, non-controlling interest will only be measured at the proportionate share of subsidiary's identifiable assets and liabilities, which could be depicted as thus:

Non-controlling interest's share of Identifiable net assets of **Sussy** upon acquisition: ₦' million

• Share capital (20% of ₦120 million)	24
• Pre-acquisition reserves (20% of ₦40 million)	8
NCI's investment on 31 December 2013 (*based on proportionate share of net assets*)	**32**
a) Post-acquisition reserves (20% of ₦20 million)	4
NCI's investment on 31 December 2013 (*based on proportionate share of net assets*)	**36**

✓ **Step 5:** Determine the amount to be included in the consolidated statement of financial position as consolidated reserves (otherwise known as consolidated retained earnings). The consolidated retained earnings to be included in the consolidated statement of financial position of **Pally-Group** are that of the parent and of the post-acquisition profits of the subsidiary. Invariably, it implies that the post-acquisition retained earnings (which is the sum of ₦20 million being the increase from ₦40 million profits upon acquisition to ₦60 million as at the reporting date 31 December 2015 - *2 years after*) of the subsidiary (**Sussy**) will now be combined with the retained

Investment in Associates and Joint Ventures

earnings (profits) of the parent (**Pally**) in ascertaining the group retained earnings. The consolidated retained earnings will be determined as follows:

	₦' million
Parent's (**Pally**) retained earnings	100
Share of subsidiary's (**Sussy**) post-acquisition profits (80% of ₦20 million)	16
Share of associate's (**Mama**) post-acquisition profits (40% of ₦20 million)	_8_
	124

✓ **Step 6:** The equity investment of Pally in Mama is considered to have resulted in the former having significant influence over the later. On this presumption, such equity investment is treated as an investment in associate, and the Equity Method is adopted, as thus:

Ascertaining the Carrying Amount of Pally Investment in Mama

	₦'m
Cost of Investment	20
Share of post-acquisition profit (40% of ₦20 million)	_8_
Carrying Amount as @ 31 December 2015	**28**

The post-acquisition retained earnings as at 31 December 2015 was ₦20 million (being the difference between ₦30 million retained earnings as at 31 December 2015 and ₦10 million retained earnings as at the date of the investment of Pally in Mama – i.e. 1 January 2015).

The share of the post-acquisition retained earnings attributable to Pally is ₦8 million (being 40% of ₦20 million post-acquisition retained earnings).

Accounting Entry:
  Debit: Investment in Mama
  Credit: Consolidated Retained Earnings
With the sum of ₦8 million share of post-acquisition retained earnings of Mama

✓ **Step 7:** Combine the assets and liabilities of the parent (**Pally**) and subsidiary (**Sussy**) on an item-by-item basis excluding the initial investment of **Pally** in **Sussy** as earlier shown in the separate financial statements of **Pally**, and also the exclusion of the equity share capital of **Sussy**, as it has already been considered alongside with the pre-acquisition retained earnings in ascertaining the amount of goodwill or gain from bargain purchase inherent/embedded in the acquisition. The consolidated statement of financial position of the group will now be shown as thus:

Pally Group
Consolidated Statement of Financial Position as at 31 December 2015

	₦' million
Assets:	
Non-current assets	
Property, plant and equipment (300 + 130)	430
Investment in Mama	28
Goodwill	32
Current assets (100 + 70)	170
Total Assets	**660**
Share Capital & Reserves:	
Equity share capital (@ ₦1 per share)	400
Reserves	124
Equity attributable to Pally's shareholders	**524**

Non-controlling interest	36
Total Equity	**560**
Current liabilities (80 + 20)	100
Total Equity and Liabilities	**660**

The consolidation schedule can equally be adopted for solving this group problem as scheduled below:

Consolidation Schedule

Subsidiary - Sussy		Cost of control (Pally in Sussy) as at 31 Dec. 2013 – 80%		Non-controlling Interests – 20%		Consolidated Reserves	
Equity Share Capital	120	(80% x 120)	96	(20% x 120)	24		
Reserves (Pre-acquisition)	40	(80% x 40)	32	(20% x 40)	8		
Reserves (Post-acquisition)	20		-	(20% x 20)	4	(80% x 20)	16
Net asset on acquisition			**128**				
Cost of combination (cost of investment)			(160)				
Goodwill (positive)			**(32)**				
Non-controlling interests					**36**		
Share of associate's post-acquisition profit							8
Pally Reserves							100
Consolidated Reserves							**124**

ILLUSTRATION 4:

Arsenal acquired 80% interests in the equity of Chelsea as January 1, 2014, when the retained earnings stood at ₦20 million. Arsenal also has an investment in Barcelona, which gave it a stake of 20% in the equity of the latter, and the retained earnings of Barcelona stood at ₦5 million upon acquiring the stake. The Board of Arsenal strictly wants to comply with the requirement of IFRS regarding consolidation of the financial statements of the subsidiary with that of the parent as at December 31, 2016.

Income Statement for the year ended December 31, 2016

	Arsenal	Chelsea	Barcelona
	₦'000	₦'000	₦'000
Revenue	600,000	390,000	100,000
Cost of sales	(345,000)	(201,000)	(80,000)
Gross profit	**255,000**	**189,000**	**20,000**
Distribution costs	(75,000)	(45,000)	(2,000)
Administrative expenses	(105,000)	(90,000)	(6,000)
Profit on before tax	**75,000**	**54,000**	**12,000**
Income tax	(25,000)	(29,000)	(4,000)
Profit for the year	**50,000**	**25,000**	**8,000**
Movement in Reserves:			
Retained profits brought forward	120,000	65,000	9,000
Profit for the year	50,000	25,000	8,000
Retained profit carried forward	**170,000**	**90,000**	**17,000**

Investment in Associates and Joint Ventures

Required:

Prepare the consolidated of profit or loss and the consolidated statement of changes in equity, given that the share capital of Arsenal stood at ₦200 million and that of Chelsea amounted to ₦100 million, and the amount of non-controlling interest at acquisition as measured at fair value stood at ₦24 million.

In this context of this text, we will approach a step-by-step approach to explaining the requirement of **IFRS 10** with regards to consolidating the financial results of the parent and the subsidiary as depicted below.

Arsenal Group
Consolidated Statement of Profit or Loss for the year ended 31 December 2016

	₦'000
Revenue (600,000 + 390,000)	990,000
Cost of sales (345,000 + 201,000)	(546,000)
Gross profit	**444,000**
Distribution costs (75,000 + 45,000)	(120,000)
Administrative expenses (105,000 + 90,000)	(195,000)
Operating profit	**129,000**
Share of associate's {Mama} profit (20% of ₦8,000)	1,600
Profit on before tax	**130,600**
Income tax (25,000 + 29,000)	(54,000)
Profit for the year	**76,600**
Profit, attributable to:	
* Owners' of Arsenal (Note 1)	71,600
** Non-controlling interest (Note 1)	5,000
	76,600

Arsenal Group
Consolidated Statement of Changes in Equity for the year ended 31 December 2016

	Share Capital	Retained Earnings	Equity – of the Parent	Non-controlling Interest	Total Equity
	₦'000	₦'000	₦'000	₦'000	₦'000
As at 1 January 2016	200,000	156,800 (Note 2)	356,800	33,000 (Note 3)	389,800
Profit for the year		71,600	71,600	5,000	76,600
As at 31 December, 2016	200,000	228,400	428,400	38,000	466,400

Working Notes:

1. **Profit attributable to:**

	Arsenal	Non-controlling interest
	₦'000	₦'000
Arsenal's profit after tax	50,000	-
Chelsea's profit after tax (80:20)	20,000	5,000
Share of Mama's profit after tax	1,600	
	71,600	**5,000**

385

Chelsea' profit after tax is shared between the parent and the non-controlling interest in the ratio of 80% to 20% in which profit or loss is required to be allocated based on the stake held in the ordinary shares of the subsidiary.

2. **Consolidated Retained Earnings as at 1 January 2016**

	₦'000
Arsenal's retained earnings as at 1 January 2016	120,000
80% of Chelsea's post acquisition retained earnings as at 1 January 2016	
{80% x (₦65 million – ₦20 million)}	36,000
Share of post-acquisition retained earnings of Mama (20% of ₦4 million)	800
	156,800

In this case, there was a pre-acquisition profit of ₦20 million which was the opening retained earnings.

The post-acquisition retained earnings of ₦4 million as at 1 January 2016 was ascertained based on the difference between the post-acquisition retained earnings of ₦9 million as at 31 December 2016 and the pre-acquisition reserves of ₦5 million as the acquisition of the 20% equity stake in Mama).

3. **Non-controlling interest as at 1 January 2016**

	₦'000
Amount of NCI as at acquisition (1 January 2014)	24,000
20% of Chelsea's post acquisition retained earnings as at 1 January 2016	
{20% x (₦65 million – ₦20 million)}	9,000
	33,000

In this case, there was a pre-acquisition profit of ₦20 million which was the opening retained earnings.

ILLUSTRATION 5:

The statement below represents the draft accounts of **Alpha** and its subsidiaries and of **Gamma**. Alpha acquired 30% of the equity capital of **Gamma** three (3) years ago when the latter's retained earnings stood at ₦10 million.

Statement of Financial Position as at 31 December 2016

	Alpha & its Subsidiaries ₦'m	Gamma ₦'m
Property, plant and equipment	200	120
Investment in **Gamma** (*at cost*)	50	
Loan to **Gamma**	30	
Current assets	120	30
Loan from **Alpha**	–	30
	400	**180**
Equity Capital (₦ 1 per Shares)	250	100
Retained Earnings	150	80
	400	**180**

Investment in Associates and Joint Ventures

Statement of Profit or Loss for the year ended 31 December 2016

	Alpha & its Subsidiaries ₦'m	Gamma ₦'m
Profit before tax	80	60
Income tax expense	(30)	(20)
Profit for the year	**50**	**40**

You are required to prepare a draft consolidated accounts of Arsenal FC as at 31 December 2015.

Notes:
- ✓ *Assume that the associate's assets and liabilities are stated at fair value.*
- ✓ *Assume that there are no non-controlling interests in the subsidiary companies.*

Suggested Solutions:

Since the stake of Alpha in Gamma 30%, the investment is presumed to give "*significant influence*" to the investor.

Alpha Group
Statement of Financial Position as at 31 December 2016

	₦'m	₦'m
Property, plant and equipment		200
Investment in **Gamma** – Equity (*Step 1*)	71	
– Loan to **Gamma**	30	101
Current assets		120
Total Assets		**421**
Equity Capital (₦ 1 per Shares)		250
Retained Earnings (Note 1)		171
Total Equity		**421**

Alpha Group
Statement of Profit or Loss for the year ended 31 December 2016

	₦'m
Operating profit	80
Share of Gamma profit after tax (30% of N40 million)	12
Profit before taxes	**92**
Income tax expense	(30)
Profit for the year	**62**
Profit attributed to:	
* Owners of Alpha	62
** Non-controlling interest	–
	62

Technical Note:

All profits within the group are solely attributable to the parent (Alpha) since there was no non-controlling interest.

Alpha Group
Consolidated Statement of Changes in Equity for the year ended 31 December 2016

	Share Capital	Retained Earnings	Equity – of the Parent	Non-controlling Interest	Total Equity
	₦'m	₦'m	₦'m	₦'m	₦'m
As at 1 January 2016	250	109 (Note 2)	359	-	359
Profit for the year		62	62	-	62
As at 31 December, 2016	250	171	421	-	421

Note 1: Ascertain the Carrying Amount of Alpha Investment in Gamma

	₦'m
Cost of Investment	50
Share of post-acquisition profit (30% of ₦70 million)	21
Carrying Amount as @ 31 December 2016	**71**

The post-acquisition retained earnings as at 31 December 2016 was ₦70 million (being the difference between ₦80 million retained earnings as at 31 December 2016 and ₦10 million retained earnings as at the date of the investment of Alpha in Gamma – i.e. 1 January 2014).

The share of the post-acquisition retained earnings attributable to Alpha is ₦21 million (being 30% of ₦70 million post-acquisition retained earnings).

Accounting Entry:
Debit: Investment in Gamma
Credit: Consolidated Retained Earnings
With the sum of ₦21 million share of post-acquisition retained earnings of Gamma

Note 2: Ascertain the [Adjusted] Opening Consolidated Retained Earnings as at 1 January 2017

	₦'m
Opening consolidated retained earnings (Alpha and its subsidiaries) @ 1 January 2016 (Working-back approach; ₦150 million Retained Earnings – ₦50 million Profit for the year)	100
Share of post-acquisition retained earnings of Gamma (30% of ₦30 million)	9
	109

The post-acquisition retained earnings of ₦30 million as at 1 January 2016 was ascertained based on the difference between the post-acquisition retained earnings of ₦70 million as at 31 December 2016 and the pre-acquisition reserves of ₦10 million as at 1 January 2014).

Joint Arrangements[33] – IFRS 11

Joint Arrangement is an arrangement of which two or more parties have joint control. The joint arrangement has the following characteristics:
- The parties are bound by a contractual arrangement, and
- The contractual arrangement gives two or more of those parties joint control of the arrangement.

A joint arrangement is either a *joint operation* or a *joint venture*.

Types of joint arrangements

Joint arrangements are either joint operations or joint ventures:
- A *joint operation* is a joint arrangement whereby the parties that have joint control of the arrangement have rights to the assets, and obligations for the liabilities, relating to the arrangement. Those parties are called joint operators.
- A *joint venture* is a joint arrangement whereby the parties that have joint control of the arrangement have rights to the net assets of the arrangement. Those parties are called joint venturers.

Classifying Joint Arrangements

The classification of a joint arrangement as a joint operation or a joint venture depends upon the rights and obligations of the parties to the arrangement. An entity determines the type of joint arrangement in which it is involved by considering the structure and form of the arrangement, the terms agreed by the parties in the contractual arrangement and other facts and circumstances.

Regardless of the purpose, structure or form of the arrangement, the classification of joint arrangements depends upon the parties' rights and obligations arising from the arrangement.

A joint arrangement in which the assets and liabilities relating to the arrangement are held in a separate vehicle can be either a joint venture or a joint operation.

A joint arrangement that is not structured through a separate vehicle is a joint operation. In such cases, the contractual arrangement establishes the parties' rights to the assets, and obligations for the liabilities, relating to the arrangement, and the parties' rights to the corresponding revenues and obligations for the corresponding expenses.

Accounting by parties to a Joint Arrangement

JOINT OPERATIONS

A joint operator recognises in relation to its interest in a joint operation:
- Its assets, including its share of any assets held jointly;
- Its liabilities, including its share of any liabilities incurred jointly;
- Its revenue from the sale of its share of the output of the joint operation;
- Its share of the revenue from the sale of the output by the joint operation; and
- Its expenses, including its share of any expenses incurred jointly.

---

[33] IASplus webpage... http://www.iasplus.com/en/standards/ifrs/ifrs11

A joint operator accounts for the assets, liabilities, revenues and expenses relating to its involvement in a joint operation in accordance with the relevant IFRSs.

The acquirer of an interest in a joint operation in which the activity constitutes a business (as defined in IFRS 3 *Business Combinations)*, is required to apply all of the principles on business combinations accounting in IFRS 3 and other IFRSs with the exception of those principles that conflict with the guidance in IFRS 11. These requirements apply both to the initial acquisition of an interest in a joint operation, and the acquisition of an additional interest in a joint operation (in the latter case, previously held interests are not re-measured).

Technical Note:
The requirements above were introduced by Accounting for Acquisitions of Interests in Joint Operations, which applies to annual periods beginning on or after 1 January 2016 on a prospective basis to acquisitions of interests in joint operations occurring from the beginning of the first period in which the amendments are applied.

A party that participates in, but does not have joint control of, a joint operation shall also account for its interest in the arrangement in accordance with the above if that party has rights to the assets, and obligations for the liabilities, relating to the joint operation.

JOINT VENTURES

A joint venturer recognises its interest in a joint venture as an investment and shall account for that investment using the ***equity method*** in accordance with IAS 28 (Investments in Associates and Joint Ventures) unless the entity is exempted from applying the equity method as specified in the standard. A party that participates in, but does not have joint control of, a joint venture accounts for its interest in the arrangement in accordance with IFRS 9 Financial Instruments (or IAS 39 – Financial Instruments, if it has not early adopted IFRS 9); unless it has *significant influence* over the joint venture, in which case it accounts for it in accordance with IAS 28 (as amended in 2011).

Separate Financial Statements

The accounting for joint arrangements in an entity's separate financial statements depends on the involvement of the entity in that joint arrangement and the type of the joint arrangement:

- If the entity is a joint operator or joint venturer it shall account for its interest in
    - A joint operation in accordance with IFRS 11 (Joint Arrangements)
    - A joint venture in accordance with IAS 27 Separate Financial Statements.
- If the entity is a party that participates in but does not have joint control of, a joint arrangement shall account for its interest in:
    - A joint operation in accordance with IFRS 11 (Joint Arrangements);
    - A joint venture in accordance with IFRS 9 (or IAS 39), unless the entity has significant influence over the joint venture, in which case it shall apply IAS 27 (as amended in 2011).

SUMMARY OF CHAPTER 11

1. Inter-corporate investment in which an investor owns between 20% and 50% of the equity instrument of the investee is presumed to give the investor a 'significant influence'.
2. The existence of significant influence in the investee connotes that the investee is an associate of the investor.
3. An associate is considered as an entity, including an unincorporated entity such as partnership, over which an investor has significant influence and that, is neither a subsidiary nor an interest in joint venture.
4. A mutual agreement with shared responsibilities and rights give rise to the existence of joint control.
5. A *joint venture* is a joint arrangement whereby the parties that have joint control of the arrangement have rights to the net assets of the arrangement. Those parties are called joint venturers.
6. A *joint operation* is a joint arrangement whereby the parties that have joint control of the arrangement have rights to the assets, and obligations for the liabilities, relating to the arrangement. Those parties are called joint operators.
7. Investment in associate and joint venture are required to be measured using 'equity method' of accounting.

END OF CHAPTER 11 EXERCISES

1. _____ is an entity, including an unincorporated entity such as partnership, over which an investor has significant influence and that, is neither a subsidiary nor an interest in joint venture.

2. _____ is a joint arrangement whereby the parties that have joint control of the arrangement have rights to the net assets of the arrangement. Those parties are called joint venturers.

3. How should associates be accounted for in the separate financial statements of the investor which prepares group accounts?

4. What is the effect of the equity method on the consolidated statement of profit or loss and statement of financial position?

5. Alpha Plc, a parent with subsidiaries, holds 40% of the equity shares in Beta Limited. During the year, Alpha Plc makes sales of ₦12,000,000 to Beta Limited at cost plus a 20% mark-up. At the year end, Beta Limited has all these goods still in inventories. What treatment should be accorded this transaction in the consolidated financial statements as at the reporting date?

6. Alpha Plc, a parent with subsidiaries, holds 40% of the equity shares in Beta Limited. During the year, Beta Limited makes sales of ₦12,000,000 to Alpha Plc at cost plus a 20% mark-up. At the year end, Alpha Plc has all these goods still in inventories. What treatment should be accorded this transaction in the consolidated financial statements as at the reporting date?

Chapter 12

Introduction to Accounting for Fellow Subsidiaries in a Group Structure

INTRODUCTION

This chapter will introduce the readers to the principle of consolidation of more than one subsidiary within a group. A parent entity can have two or more subsidiaries, in which none of the subsidiaries has interest in one another. The subsidiaries are then considered "fellow subsidiaries".

The principle of consolidation of fellow subsidiaries can be likened to the same principle of consolidating a single subsidiary, except for repeating the entire process for every one of the subsidiaries of which its financial statements are to be consolidated with the parent.

Also, the accounting policies of the parent in the measurement of non-controlling interest at the acquisition of each subsidiary need not be the same. It means, if a parent entity has two subsidiaries, it may adopt fair value model for the first business combination (i.e. when the first subsidiary was acquired), while it adopts the method of the proportionate share of the identifiable net assets for the second business combination (i.e. when the second subsidiary was acquired).

In summary, where the first and second business combinations produce goodwill, then the group goodwill will be the summation of both, even though the goodwill has to be tested for impairment on a separate basis and based on its allocation to cash-generating units in line with IAS 36. Same applies to where the two business combinations result in gains arising from a bargain purchase transaction. The gains will be recognised in the profit or loss of the group as they arise. But, where one of the business combinations gives rise to goodwill and the other give rise to gain on bargain purchase, the goodwill and gain on bargain purchase cannot be offset (or netted off) even when they both arose on the same date, rather the goodwill is accounted for and reported separately as an intangible asset (in line with IFRS 3 and IAS 38), while the gain on bargain purchase is credited to group profit or loss upon acquisition (in accordance with the requirement of IFRS 3).

Introduction to Accounting for Fellow Subsidiaries in a Group Structure

Fellow Subsidiaries

This involves a parent company and two (2) or more subsidiaries with direct control exerted by the former, and neither of the two subsidiaries have an equity stake in the other. In consolidating the subsidiaries financial statements, the same principles of consolidating a single subsidiary applies, except that two subsidiaries accounts are consolidated with the accounts of the parent.

Illustration 1:

Pally acquired 80% of the equity share capital of **Sussy** as at the reporting date 31 December 2013, when the retained earnings of **Sussy** was ₦40 million. Pally equally acquired 60% stake in **Mama** on 1 January 2015 for the sum of ₦30 million, when the retained earnings of the latter stood at ₦10 million. The statement of financial position of the three companies as at reporting date 31 December 2015 is as follows:

Statement of Financial Position as at 31st December 2015

	Pally ₦' million	Sussy ₦' million	Mama ₦' million
Property, plant and equipment	300	130	80
Investments	190	-	-
Current assets	80	70	40
Total Assets	**570**	**200**	**120**
Share Capital & Reserves:			
Equity share capital (@ ₦1 per share)	400	120	35
Reserves (Retained Earnings)	100	60	30
	500	180	65
Current liabilities	70	20	55
Total Equity and Liabilities	**570**	**200**	**120**

Suggested Solutions

- **FIRST SUBSIDIARY – Sussy**

First, we assumed that the parent at the point of acquisition (when control was obtained), measured the amount of non-controlling interests at the proportionate share of the subsidiary's identifiable net assets (assets and liabilities). In this case, the consolidation process will be as follows:

- ✓ **Step 1**: Determine the percentage holdings of investment of **Pally** in **Sussy** as at the acquisition date (31 December 2013), which represents the date of inclusion (first date of consolidation). In this case, the percentage holding is already determined and ascertained to be 80%.

- ✓ **Step 2**: Ascertain the form of group structure in this parent-subsidiary relationship. Since the subsidiary (**Sussy**) is *partly-owned* by the parent (**Pally**), the group structure is a simple structure as shown below:

```
        Pally
       /      
    80%      20%
     ↓        
   Sussy  ←——— Non-controlling interest
```

Introduction to Accounting for Fellow Subsidiaries in a Group Structure

✓ **Step 3:** *Determine the existence of goodwill or gain from a bargain purchase as at the date of acquisition based on the fair value of subsidiary's identifiable assets and liabilities.* In this case, there exists goodwill as shown below.

To ascertain and determine the amount of goodwill or gain from a bargain purchase, the value of an investment of the parent (**Pally**) in the subsidiary (**Sussy**) will be compared with the parent's share of identifiable assets and liabilities of the subsidiary that were acquired.

PARTIAL METHODOLOGY

	₦' million	₦' million
Cost of investment of **Pally** in **Sussy** (i.e. ₦180 million – ₦20 million)		160
Less: **Pally**'s share of Identifiable net assets of **Sussy** acquired:		
• Share capital (80% of ₦120 million)	96	
• Pre-acquisition reserves (80% of ₦40 million)	32	(128)
*Goodwill attributable to **Pally's** (a)*		32
Amount of investments of non-controlling interest in **Sussy**		32
Less: Non-controlling interest share of the fair value of subsidiary's net assets:		
• Share capital (20% of ₦120 million)	24	
• Pre-acquisition reserves (20% of ₦40 million)	8	(32)
*Goodwill attributable to **non-controlling interests** (b)*		---
PARTIAL Goodwill (a + b)		**32**

Technical Note:
- The amount of investment of Pally in Sussy of ₦160 million is ascertained after deducting the sum of ₦20 million, which represents the cost of investment of pally in Mama.
- The goodwill attributable to non-controlling should be zero since the investment to non-controlling interests is valued at the proportionate share of subsidiary's identifiable net assets as shown by the arrow.

FULL METHODOLOGY

		₦' million
Cost of combination (i.e. cost of acquisition) to the parent		160
Amount of Investment in subsidiary to non-controlling interest*		32
Combined amount of interests in subsidiary to all investors		**192**
Less: Identifiable net assets of **Sussy** acquired (@ 31 December 2013):		
• Share capital	120	
• Pre-acquisition reserves	40	(160)
PARTIAL Goodwill - positive		**32**

✓ **Step 4:** *Determine the amount of non-controlling interest as will be shown in the consolidated statement of financial position of the group.* In this case, non-controlling interest will only be measured at the proportionate share of subsidiary's identifiable assets and liabilities, which could be depicted as thus:

Non-controlling interest's share of Identifiable net assets of **Sussy** upon acquisition: ₦' million

- Share capital (20% of ₦120 million) — 24
- Pre-acquisition reserves (20% of ₦40 million) — 8
- NCI's investment on 31 December 2013 (*based on proportionate share of net assets*) — **32**
- Post-acquisition reserves (20% of ₦20 million) — 4
- NCI's investment on 31 December 2015 (*based on proportionate share of net assets*) — **36**

395

- **SECOND SUBSIDIARY – Mama**

First, we assumed that the parent at the point of acquisition (when control was obtained), measured the amount of non-controlling interests at the proportionate share of the subsidiary's identifiable net assets (assets and liabilities). In this case, the consolidation process will be as follows:

- ✓ **Step 1**: Determine the percentage holdings of investment of **Pally** in **Mama** as at the acquisition date (1 January 2015), which represents the date of inclusion (first date of consolidation). In this case, the percentage holding is already determined and ascertained to be 60%.

- ✓ **Step 2**: Ascertain the form of group structure in this parent-subsidiary relationship. Since the subsidiary (**Mama**) is *partly-owned* by the parent (**Pally**), the group structure is a simple structure as shown below:

    Pally
    60%   40%
    Mama ←——— **Non-controlling interest**

- ✓ **Step 3**: Determine the existence of goodwill or gain from a bargain purchase as at the date of acquisition based on the fair value of subsidiary's identifiable assets and liabilities. In this case, there exists goodwill as shown below.

To ascertain and determine the amount of goodwill or gain from a bargain purchase, the value of an investment of the parent (**Pally)** in the subsidiary (**Mama**) will be compared with the parent's share of identifiable assets and liabilities of the subsidiary that were acquired.

PARTIAL METHODOLOGY

	₦' million	₦' million
Cost of investment of **Pally** in **Mama**		30
Less: **Pally**'s share of Identifiable net assets of **Mama** acquired:		
• Share capital (60% of ₦35 million)	21	
• Pre-acquisition reserves (60% of ₦10 million)	6	(27)
*Goodwill attributable to **Pally's** (a)*		3
Amount of investments of non-controlling interest in **Mama**		18
Less: Non-controlling interest share of the fair value of subsidiary's net assets:		
• Share capital (40% of ₦35 million)	14	
• Pre-acquisition reserves (40% of ₦10 million)	4	(18)
*Goodwill attributable to **non-controlling interests** (b)*		---
PARTIAL Goodwill (a + b)		3

Technical Note:

- *The goodwill attributable to non-controlling should be zero since the investment to non-controlling interests is valued at the proportionate share of subsidiary's identifiable net assets as shown by the arrow.*

Introduction to Accounting for Fellow Subsidiaries in a Group Structure

FULL METHODOLOGY

	₦' million
Cost of combination (i.e. cost of acquisition) to the parent	30
Amount of Investment in subsidiary to non-controlling interest*	<u>18</u>
Combined amount of interests in subsidiary to all investors	**48**

Less: <u>Identifiable net assets of **Mama** acquired (@ 1 January 2015)</u>:

• Share capital	35	
• Pre-acquisition reserves	<u>10</u>	<u>(45)</u>
PARTIAL Goodwill - positive		<u>**3**</u>

✓ **Step 4:** *Determine the amount of non-controlling interest as will be shown in the consolidated statement of financial position of the group.* In this case, non-controlling interest will only be measured at the proportionate share of subsidiary's identifiable assets and liabilities, which could be depicted as thus:

<u>Non-controlling interest's share of Identifiable net assets of **Mama** upon acquisition</u>: ₦' million

• Share capital (40% of ₦35 million)	14
• Pre-acquisition reserves (40% of ₦10 million)	<u>4</u>
NCI's investment on 1 January 2015 (*based on proportionate share of net assets*)	**18**
• Post-acquisition reserves (40% of ₦20 million)	<u>8</u>
NCI's investment on 31 December 2015 (*based on proportionate share of net assets*)	**26**

✓ **Step 5:** *Determine the amount to be included in the consolidated statement of financial position as consolidated reserves (otherwise known as consolidated retained earnings).* The consolidated retained earnings to be included in the consolidated statement of financial position of **Pally-Group** are that of the parent and of the post-acquisition profits of the subsidiaries. Invariably, it implies that the post-acquisition retained earnings of **Sussy** (which is the sum of ₦20 million being the increase from ₦40 million profits upon acquisition to ₦60 million as at the reporting date 31 December 2015 - *2 years after*) and the post-acquisition retained earnings of **Mama** (which coincidentally is ₦20 million, being the increase from ₦10 million profits upon acquisition to ₦30 million as at the reporting date 31 December 2015 - *1 year after*); will now be combined with the retained earnings (profits) of the parent (**Pally**) in ascertaining the group retained earnings. The consolidated retained earnings will be determined as follows:

	₦' million
Parent's (**Pally**) retained earnings	100
Share of subsidiary's (**Sussy**) post-acquisition profits (80% of ₦20 million)	16
Share of subsidiary's (**Mama**) post-acquisition profits (60% of ₦20 million)	<u>12</u>
	<u>128</u>

✓ **Step 6:** Combine the assets and liabilities of the parent (**Pally**) and subsidiaries (**Sussy & Mama**) on an-item by item basis excluding the initial investment of **Pally** in **Sussy & Mama** as earlier shown in the separate financial statements of **Pally**, and also the exclusion of the equity share capital of **Sussy & Mama**, as it has already been considered alongside with the pre-acquisition retained earnings in ascertaining the amount of goodwill or gain from bargain purchase inherent/embedded in the acquisition. The consolidated statement of financial position of the group will now be shown as thus:

Pally Group
Consolidated Statement of Financial Position as at 31 December 2015

Assets:	₦' million
Non-current assets	
Property, plant and equipment (300 + 130 + 80)	510
Goodwill (32 + 3)	35
Current assets (80 + 70 + 40)	190
Total Assets	**735**
Share Capital & Reserves:	
Equity share capital (@ ₦1 per share)	400
Reserves	128
Equity attributable to Pally's shareholders	**528**
Non-controlling interest (36 + 26)	62
Total Equity	**590**
Current liabilities (70 + 20 + 55)	145
Total Equity and Liabilities	**735**

The consolidation schedule can equally be adopted for solving this group problem as scheduled below:

Consolidation Schedule

Subsidiaries – Sussy & Mama		Cost of control (Pally in Sussy) as at 31 Dec. 2013 – 80%	Cost of control (Pally in Mama) as at 1 Jan. 2015 – 60%	Non-controlling Interests – 20% & 40%	Consolidated Reserves
Equity Share Capital	120	(80% x 120) 96		(20% x 120) 24	
Reserves (Pre-acquisition)	40	(80% x 40) 32		(20% x 40) 8	
Reserves (Post-acquisition)	20	-		(20% x 20) 4	(80% x 20) 16
Net asset on acquisition		128			
Cost of combination (cost of investment)		(160)			
Goodwill (positive)		(32)			
Equity Share Capital	120		(60% x 35) 21	(40% x 35) 14	
Reserves (Pre-acquisition)	40		(60% x 10) 6	(40% x 10) 4	
Reserves (Post-acquisition)	20		-	(40% x 20) 8	(60% x 20) 12
Net asset on acquisition			27		
Cost of combination (cost of investment)			(30)		
Goodwill (positive)			(3)		
Transfer of Goodwill in Mama		(3)	3		
Combined Amount of Goodwill		(35)	-		
Non-controlling interests				62	
Pally Reserves					100
Consolidated Reserves					**128**

Introduction to Accounting for Fellow Subsidiaries in a Group Structure

Illustration 2:

Arsenal acquired 80% interests in the equity of Chelsea as January 1, 2014, when the retained earnings stood at ₦20 million. Arsenal also has an investment in Barcelona, which gave it a stake of 60% in the equity of the latter, and the retained earnings of Barcelona stood at ₦5 million upon acquiring the stake. The Board of Arsenal strictly wants to comply with the requirement of IFRS regarding consolidation of the financial statements of the subsidiary with that of the parent as at December 31, 2016.

Income Statement for the year ended December 31, 2016

	Arsenal ₦'000	Chelsea ₦'000	Barcelona ₦'000
Revenue	600,000	390,000	100,000
Cost of sales	(345,000)	(201,000)	(80,000)
Gross profit	**255,000**	**189,000**	**20,000**
Distribution costs	(75,000)	(45,000)	(2,000)
Administrative expenses	(105,000)	(90,000)	(6,000)
Profit on before tax	**75,000**	**54,000**	**12,000**
Income tax	(25,000)	(29,000)	(4,000)
Profit for the year	**50,000**	**25,000**	**8,000**
Movement in Reserves:			
Retained profits brought forward	120,000	65,000	9,000
Profit for the year	50,000	25,000	8,000
Retained profit carried forward	**170,000**	**90,000**	**17,000**

Required:

Prepare the consolidated of profit or loss and the consolidated statement of changes in equity, given that the share capital of Arsenal stood at ₦200 million and that of Chelsea and Barcelona amounted to ₦100 million and ₦60 million respectively, and the amount of non-controlling interest at acquisition of Chelsea and Barcelona as measured at fair value stood at ₦24 million and ₦7 million respectively.

In this context of this text, we will approach a step-by-step approach to explaining the requirement of **IFRS 10** with regards to consolidating the financial results of the parent and the subsidiary as depicted below.

Arsenal Group
Consolidated Statement of Profit or Loss for the year ended 31 December 2016

	₦'000
Revenue (600,000 + 390,000 + 100,000)	1,090,000
Cost of sales (345,000 + 201,000 + 80,000)	(626,000)
Gross profit	**464,000**
Distribution costs (75,000 + 45,000 + 2,000)	(122,000)
Administrative expenses (105,000 + 90,000 + 6,000)	(201,000)
Profit on before tax	**141,000**
Income tax (25,000 + 29,000 + 4,000)	(58,000)
Profit for the year	**83,000**
Profit, attributable to:	
* Owners' of Arsenal (Note 1)	74,800
** Non-controlling interest (Note 1)	8,200
	83,000

Arsenal Group
Consolidated Statement of Changes in Equity for the year ended 31 December 2016

	Share Capital	Retained Earnings	Equity – of the Parent	Non-controlling interest	Total Equity
	₦'000	₦'000	₦'000	₦'000	₦'000
As at 1 January 2016	200,000	158,400 (Note 2)	358,400	41,600 (Note 3)	400,000
Profit for the year		74,800	74,800	8,200	83,000
As at 31 December, 2016	200,000	234,000	433,200	49,800	483,000

Working Notes:

1. **Profit attributable to:**

	Arsenal ₦'000	Non-controlling interest ₦'000
Arsenal's profit after tax	50,000	–
Chelsea's profit after tax (80:20)	20,000	5,000
Barcelona's profit after tax (60:40)	4,800	3,200
	74,800	**8,200**

Chelsea' profit after tax is shared between the parent and the non-controlling interest in the ratio of 80% to 20% (with respect to investment in Chelsea) and ratio 60% to 40% (with respect to investment in Barcelona) in which profit or loss is required to be allocated based on the stake held in the ordinary shares of the subsidiaries.

2. **Consolidated Retained Earnings as at 1 January 2016**

	₦'000
Arsenal's retained earnings as at 1 January 2016	120,000
80% of Chelsea's post acquisition retained earnings as at 1 January 2016 {80% x (₦65 million – ₦20 million)}	36,000
60% of Barcelona's post acquisition retained earnings as at 1 January 2016 {60% x (₦9 million – ₦5 million)}	2,400
	158,400

3. **Non-controlling interest as at 1 January 2016**

	₦'000
Amount of NCI as at acquisition (1 January 2014) of Chelsea	24,000
Amount of NCI as at acquisition of Barcelona	7,000
20% of Chelsea's post acquisition retained earnings as at 1 January 2016 {20% x (₦65 million – ₦20 million)}	9,000
40% of Barcelona's post acquisition retained earnings as at 1 January 2016 {40% x (₦9 million – ₦5 million)}	1,600
	41,600

SUMMARY OF CHAPTER 12

1. Fellow subsidiaries involve a parent company and two (2) or more subsidiaries with direct control exerted by the former, and neither of the two subsidiaries has an equity stake in the other.

2. Every business combination is treated as a separate class of transaction, and the goodwill or gain on bargain purchase is obtained independently of one another. Where two business combinations result in goodwill, the combined amount is reported in the consolidated statement of financial position; and likewise for gain on bargain purchase. Whereas, if the first business combination resulted in a goodwill, while the second business combination resulted in a gain arising from a bargain purchase; they are to be treated in accordance with the fundamental principles of capitalising the goodwill, and the gain on bargain purchase credited to the parent profit or loss.

3. Accounting policy adopted for measuring non-controlling interest at acquisition may not necessarily be the same (i.e. in the first business combination, the fair value model may be adopted; while the second business combination may warrant the choice of proportionate share of the identifiable net assets of the subsidiary), since each business combination is considered a separate class of transactions.

Chapter 13

Disclosure of Interests in Other Entities

INTRODUCTION

This chapter will focus on the disclosure of interests in other entities applies to entities that have an interest in a subsidiary, a joint arrangement, an associate or an unconsolidated structured.

The chapter will provide the readers the opportunity to appreciate the requirement of IFRS 12 with respect to entities disclosing information that enables users of financial statements to evaluate: the nature of, and risks associated with, its interests in other entities; and the effects of those interests on its financial position, financial performance and cash flows.

Also, the chapter will allow readers understand the specific minimum disclosures that an entity must provide, and appreciate the standard as it permits entities to disclose whatever additional information necessary to meet the objective of providing information to aid decisions of users of the financial statements.

Disclosure of Interests in Other Entities

The objective of IFRS 12 (*Disclosure of Interests in Other Entities*) is to require an entity to disclose information that enables the use of its financial statements to evaluate:

- The nature of, and risks associated with, its interests in other entities; and
- The effects of those interests on its financial position, financial performance and cash flows.

To meet the objective of IFRS 12, an entity shall disclose:

1. The significant judgements and assumptions it has made in determining:
   - the nature of its interest in another entity or arrangement;
   - the type of joint arrangement in which it has an interest;
   - that it meets the definition of an investment entity, if applicable; and

2. Information about its interests in:
   - subsidiaries;
   - joint arrangements and associates; and
   - *structured entities* that are not controlled by the entity (unconsolidated structured entities).

If the disclosures required by IFRS 12, together with disclosures required by other IFRSs, do not meet the objective, an entity shall disclose whatever additional information is necessary to meet that objective.

An entity shall consider the level of detail necessary to satisfy the disclosure objective and how much emphasis to place on each of the requirements in IFRS 12. It shall aggregate or disaggregate disclosures so that useful information is not obscured by either the inclusion of a large amount of insignificant detail or the aggregation of items that have different characteristics.

The requirement of IFRS 12 shall be applied by an entity that has an interest in any of the following:

- a) Subsidiaries
- b) Joint arrangements (i.e. joint operations or joint ventures)
- c) Associates
- d) Unconsolidated structured entities

IFRS 12 does not apply to:

- a) Post-employment benefit plans or other long-term employee benefit plans to which IAS 19 Employee Benefits applies.

- b) An entity's separate financial statements to which IAS 27 Separate Financial Statements applies. However:
   - i. If an entity has interests in unconsolidated structured entities and prepares separate financial statements as its only financial statements, it shall apply the requirements of when preparing those separate financial statements.
   - ii. An investment entity that prepares financial statements in which all of its subsidiaries are measured at fair value through profit or loss in accordance with IFRS 10 shall present the disclosures relating to investment entities required by the standard.

Disclosure of Interests in Other Entities

c) An interest held by an entity that participates in, but does not have joint control of, a joint arrangement unless that interest results in significant influence over the arrangement or is an interest in a structured entity.

d) An interest in another entity that is accounted for in accordance with IFRS 9 Financial Instruments. However, an entity shall apply this IFRS:

   i. when that interest is an interest in an associate or a joint venture that, in accordance with IAS 28 Investments in Associates and Joint Ventures, is measured at fair value through profit or loss; or

   ii. When that interest is an interest in an unconsolidated structured entity.

Significant Judgements and Assumptions

An entity shall disclose information about significant judgements and assumptions it has made (and changes to those judgements and assumptions) in determining:

a) That it has control of another entity, i.e. an investee as described in IFRS 10 *Consolidated Financial Statements*;
b) That it has joint control of an arrangement or significant influence over another entity; and
c) The type of joint arrangement (i.e. joint operation or joint venture) when the arrangement has been structured through a separate vehicle.

The significant judgements and assumptions disclosed in accordance with the standard include those made by the entity when changes in facts and circumstances are such that the conclusion about whether it has control, joint control or significant influence changes during the reporting period.

Also, to comply with IFRS 12, an entity shall disclose, for example, significant judgements and assumptions made in determining that:

a) It does not control another entity even though it holds more than half of the voting rights of the other entity.
b) It controls another entity even though it holds less than half of the voting rights of the other entity.
c) It is an agent or a principal.
d) It does not have significant influence even though it holds 20 percent or more of the voting rights of another entity.
e) It has significant influence even though it holds less than 20 percent of the voting rights of another entity.

Investment entity status

When a parent determines that it is an investment entity in accordance with IFRS 10, the investment entity shall disclose information about significant judgements and assumptions it has made in determining that it is an investment entity. If the investment entity does not have one or more of the typical characteristics of an investment entity, it shall disclose its reasons for concluding that it is nevertheless an investment entity.

When an entity becomes, or ceases to be, an investment entity, it shall disclose the change of investment entity status and the reasons for the change. In addition, an entity that becomes an investment entity shall disclose the effect of the change of status on the financial statements for the period presented, including:

a) The total fair value, as of the date of change of status, of the subsidiaries that cease to be consolidated;
b) The total gain or loss, if any, calculated in accordance with IFRS 10; and
c) The line item(s) in profit or loss in which the gain or loss is recognised (if not presented separately).

Interests in subsidiaries

An entity shall disclose information that enables users of its consolidated financial statements to:

i. understand the composition of the group
ii. understand the interest that non-controlling interests have in the group's activities and cash flows
iii. evaluate the nature and extent of significant restrictions on its ability to access or use assets, and settle liabilities, of the group
iv. evaluate the nature of, and changes in, the risks associated with its interests in consolidated structured entities
v. evaluate the consequences of changes in its ownership interest in a subsidiary that do not result in a loss of control
vi. evaluate the consequences of losing control of a subsidiary during the reporting period.

Interests in unconsolidated subsidiaries

[*Technical Note: The investment entity consolidation exemption referred to in this section was introduced by Investment Entities, issued on 31 October 2012 and effective for annual periods beginning on or after 1 January 2014.*]

In accordance with IFRS 10 Consolidated Financial Statements, an investment entity is required to apply the exception to consolidation and instead account for its investment in a subsidiary at fair value through profit or loss.

Where an entity is an investment entity, IFRS 12 requires additional disclosure, including:

i. The fact the entity is an investment entity.
ii. Information about significant judgements and assumptions it has made in determining that it is an investment entity, and specifically where the entity does not have one or more of the 'typical characteristics' of an investment entity.
iii. Details of subsidiaries that have not been consolidated (name, place of business, ownership interests held).
iv. Details of the relationship and certain transactions between the investment entity and the subsidiary (e.g. restrictions on the transfer of funds, commitments, support arrangements, contractual arrangements).
v. Information where an entity becomes, or ceases to be, an investment entity]

An entity making these disclosures are not required to provide various other disclosures required by IFRS 12.

Interests in joint arrangements and associates

An entity shall disclose information that enables users of its financial statements to evaluate:

i. The nature, extent and financial effects of its interests in joint arrangements and associates, including the nature and effects of its contractual relationship with the other investors with joint control of, or significant influence over, joint arrangements and associates.

ii. The nature of, and changes in, the risks associated with its interests in joint ventures and associates.

Interests in unconsolidated structured entities

An entity shall disclose information that enables users of its financial statements to:

i. Understand the nature and extent of its interests in unconsolidated structured entities.

ii. Evaluate the nature of, and changes in, the risks associated with its interests in unconsolidated structured entities.

Chapter 14

Guidance on End-of-Chapter Exercises

Guidance on End-of-Chapter Exercises

Chapter 1:

1. Inter-corporate investment involves investment made by a corporate entity (i.e. an entity) in another entity via debt or equity. The equity investment can either give rise to control, significant influence, joint control or trade investment considered a financial asset.

2. The intercorporate investment represents an important component of management strategy, which involves a company investing in other companies to achieve diversification, growth, and competitive advantage, but the structure and scope of these investments create comparability challenges for the potential investors', analysts, and the investing public at large. While a business combination entails a transaction or other event in which an **acquirer** obtains control of one or more **businesses**. Invariably, a business combination arose from inter-corporate equity investment in which control of the investee is obtained by the investor.

3. The four categories of intercorporate investment are as thus:

    Minority Passive:
    A company's ownership interest of less than 20% in the equity of another company can be considered a passive investment.

    Minority Active:
    An ownership interest between 20% and 50% is technically regarded as a non-controlling investment for consolidation purposes. However, the investor is considered to have *significant influence* in the investee's business operations and decisions.

    Controlling Interest:
    An ownership interest of *more than 50%* in the voting rights of an entity (usually ascertained through shareholdings) is presumed to be a *controlling interest investment*.

    Joint Ventures/Entities:
    A *joint venture/entity* is an entity where control is *shared* by *two or more investors under mutual agreement*.

4. Debt investments in a corporate entity do not necessarily give investors right to a residual interest in the net assets of the investee; and invariably, will not result in the investor obtaining control of the investee. In this case, a business combination cannot arise; rather based on management philosophy or strategy of such investments, they could either be considered minority active or minority passive inter-corporate investments.

5. Inter-corporate investments

6. IFRS 3

7. IAS 27

8. The objective of IFRS 10 is to establish principles for the presentation and preparation of consolidated financial statements when an entity controls one or more other entities.

While, the objective of this IFRS is to improve the relevance, reliability and comparability of the information that a reporting entity provides in its financial statements about a business combination and its effects.

9. A business consists of inputs and processes applied to those inputs that have the ability to create outputs. Although businesses usually have outputs, outputs are not required for an integrated set to qualify as a business. The three elements of a business are input, process and output.

10. Controlling interest investment or business combination.

11. The strategy that begets the consideration for business combination may not be far-fetched from the synergy and potential unveiling of inherent values attributable to such consideration, but empirical evidences depict that more than half of business combinations (via mergers and acquisitions) may not met the desired expectation that preceded the consideration for business combination, which may be partially caused by cultural differences, economic regime changes, political instabilities, policies changes, legal and regulatory bottlenecks, lack of effective management, management of change, tax implications, etc.

12. Techniques for structuring business combination is not limited to the following:

    - One or more businesses become subsidiaries of the acquirer. As subsidiaries, they continue to operate as separate legal entities.
    - The net assets of one or more businesses are legally merged into that if the acquirer. In this case, the acquiree entity ceases to exist (in legal vernacular, this is referred to as a statutory merger and normally the transaction is subject to approval by a majority of the outstanding voting shares of the acquiree).
    - The owners of the acquiree transfer their equity interests to the acquirer entity or the owners of the acquirer entity in exchange for equity interests in the acquirer.
    - All of the combining entities transfer their net assets or their owners transfer their equity interests into a new entity formed for the purpose of the transaction. This is sometimes referred to as a roll-up or put-together transaction.
    - A former owner or group of former owners of one of the combining entities obtains control of the combined entities collectively.
    - An acquirer might hold a non-controlling equity interest in an entity and subsequently purchase additional equity interests sufficient to give it control over the investee. These transactions are referred to as a step acquisitions (otherwise known as piecemeal acquisitions) or business combinations achieved in stages.

Contemporaneous Accounting for Business Combinations and Group Accounts

Guidance on End-of-Chapter Exercises

Chapter 2:

1. Parent-Subsidiary Relationship

2. Group accounts represent the accounts of the parent and all its subsidiaries as if it is the accounts of a single economic entity.

3. A parent company with at least a subsidiary can be exempted from preparing group account only when all of these conditions are met:
   - It is a wholly-owned subsidiary or is a partially-owned subsidiary of another entity and all its other owners, including those not otherwise entitled to vote, have been informed about, and do not object to, the parent not presenting consolidated financial statements;
   - Its debt or equity instruments are not traded in a public market (a domestic or foreign stock exchange or an over-the-counter market, including local and regional markets);
   - It did not file, nor is it in the process of filing, its financial statements with a securities commission or other regulatory organisation for the purpose of issuing any class of instruments in a public market; and
   - Its ultimate or any intermediate parent produces consolidated financial statements that are available for public use and comply with IFRSs.

4. A subsidiary can only be excluded from consolidation when control of the subsidiary is lost by the parent entity.

5. Non-controlling interest represents an interest in the net worth (or net assets) of the subsidiary other than those of the parent entity.

6. IFRS 3 permits the adoption of either of the identified two options. The options are the fair value of the equity instrument and the proportionate share of the identifiable net assets of the subsidiary at acquisition. The standard did not recommend an option; neither does the standard rank each option by order of prominence.

7. Non-controlling interest can now be recognised as a negative equity value based on IFRS 10. This negative amount will still be reported within equity but as a deduction from the equity so attributable to the parent in order to obtain the total equity in group accounts.

8. The treatments of these acquisition-related costs are as thus:
   - The issue of shares: This transaction cost is accounted for within equity as a deducted from the proceeds of the shares issued or exchanged (in accordance with IAS 32) in a business combination.
   - The issue of debt instrument: This transaction cost should be deducted from the proceeds of raising the debt, as contained in IAS 39 or IFRS 9.
   - Those transaction costs (as related to accounting services, legal, professional fees, valuation fees, etc.) are to be expensed in profit or loss.

9. It is not compulsory that the accounting policies and the reporting date of the parent and the subsidiary to be the same, but it is the preferable stance and recommendation of the standard (IFRS 10). By at large, IFRS 10 clearly requires that upon preparation of consolidated financial statements,

the accounting policies and the reporting date of the parent and the subsidiary should be aligned (i.e. harmonised).

10. **Reverse Acquisitions:**

    IFRS 3 also addresses a certain type of acquisition, known as a *reverse acquisition or takeover*. This occurs when a company (*hypothetically called Dynamic Limited*) acquires ownership of another company (*hypothetically called Success Plc*) through a share exchange. (For example, a private entity may arrange to have itself 'acquired' by a smaller public entity as a means of obtaining a stock exchange listing). The number of shares issued by *Dynamic Limited* as consideration to the shareholders of *Success Plc* is so great that *control* of the combined entity after the transaction is with the shareholders of *Success Plc*.

    In legal terms, *Dynamic Limited* may be regarded as the parent or controlling entity, but *IFRS 3* states that, as it is *Success Plc* shareholders who control the combined entity, *Success Plc* should be treated as the acquirer. *Success Plc* should apply the acquisition (or full consolidation) method to the assets and liabilities of *Dynamic Limited*.

    Furthermore, reverse acquisitions sometimes occur when a private operating entity wants to become a public entity but do not want to register its equity shares. To accomplish that, the private entity will arrange for a public entity to acquire its equity interests in exchange for the equity interests of the public entity. In this example, the public entity is the *legal acquirer* because it issued its equity interests, and the private entity is the *legal acquiree* because its equity interests were acquired. However, application of the guidance in the standard (*IFRS 3*) results in identifying:

    c) The public entity as the acquiree for accounting purposes (the accounting acquiree); and
    d) The private entity as the acquirer for accounting purposes (the accounting acquirer).

Contemporaneous Accounting for Business Combinations and Group Accounts

Guidance on End-of-Chapter Exercises

Chapter 3:

1. Separate financial statements

2. The position of CAMA is not clearly spelt out on the requirement for separate financial statements; but by virtue of section 335 (paragraph 1 – 11), the detailed requirement on the need to prepare individual financial statements is contained.

3. The purchase consideration for the acquisition of a subsidiary should be measured at acquisition-date fair value.

4. **Deferred consideration** involves an agreement made that requires part of the consideration for the business combination be paid in the future without any condition being attached (*i.e. it is a consideration that will be made in the future with certainty*). While **Contingent consideration** is the future consideration which is based on the *occurrence or non-occurrence* of *future uncertain events* that possibly exist based on attainment of some level of performance or targets by the acquired company sometimes into the future.

5. The movements (or changes) in the present (or fair) value of deferred and contingent consideration should be reported in the profit or loss of the acquiring (or controlling) entity, which is the parent entity.

6. A liability originally arising from the recognition of contingent liability can be de-recognised where it is no longer probable that (all or in part) the settlement(s) is/(are) no longer required. But, it may be unlikely that de-recognition of a deferred liability may occur, other than in a rare situation.

7. The fair value of the purchase consideration by the acquirer in a business combination amounted to ₦96,529,000, as determined below:

	₦'000
Cash consideration	80,000
Deferred (cash) consideration {₦20m $(1.1)^{-2}$)}	16,529
	96,529

8. The fair value of the purchase consideration by the acquirer in a business combination amounted to ₦100 million, as determined below:

	₦'000
Cash consideration	80,000
Deferred (cash) consideration (10 million shares x ₦2)	20,000
	100,000

Discounting principle is not applicable to equity as the market price at the date of acquisition is a reflection of the present value worth of the deferred equity instrument. Furthermore, so subsequent adjustment is required based on the requirement of IAS 32 for the changes in the market price of the equity instrument of the acquired entity.

Guidance on End-of-Chapter Exercises

9. The fair value of the purchase consideration by the acquirer in a business combination amounted to ₦96,529,000 as at the acquisition date, as determined below:

	₦'000
Cash consideration	80,000
Deferred (cash) consideration {₦20m $(1.1)^{-2}$}	<u>16,529</u>
	<u>96,529</u>

As at the end of the first year since the acquisition, the present value would have risen to ₦18,182,000 on the deferred cash consideration.

	₦'000
Cash consideration	80,000
Deferred (cash) consideration {₦16,529,000 $(1.1)^{1}$}	<u>18,182</u>
	<u>98,182</u>

The changes in *fair value or the present value* of the deferred cash consideration to be a charge to acquirer's (or parents) profit or loss is ₦1,653,000 (i.e. 10% of ₦16,529,000 or ₦18,182,000 – ₦16,529,000).

Guidance on End-of-Chapter Exercises

Chapter 4:

1. Consolidation entails the mechanics (or process) of combining the accounts of the parent and the subsidiary in order to obtain the single accounts that depict the financial position, financial performance and cash flows of the group as a whole.

2. In a wholly-owned subsidiary, all of the interests in the subsidiary are attributable solely to the parent. Invariably, there is no non-controlling interest in a wholly-owned subsidiary.

3. A non-controlling interest represents the equity interest in a subsidiary other than those of the parent (or controlling interest) in the net assets of a subsidiary.

4. The requirement of consolidation to cancel-out the fair value of purchase consideration and the net assets acquired in a subsidiary as at acquisition-date is to reflect the concept of the single economic unit (or single economic entity) thereby giving rise to the recognition of goodwill or gain on bargain purchase.

5. Pre-acquisition reserves represent reserves of the subsidiary as at acquisition, which forms part of the subsidiary's net assets acquired in a business combination. Post-acquisition reserves are profits or losses arising from the involvement of the parent in both the financial and operating policies of the subsidiary since acquisition. Pre-acquisition reserves as a component of the net assets acquired in the subsidiary influence the amount of goodwill or gain on bargain purchase recognised on acquisition of a subsidiary. While, the post-acquisition reserves are consolidated in the group accounts, but attributable to both the parent and non-controlling interest in the proportion the subsidiary's profit or loss is shared.

6. The essence of the cancellation of the fair value consideration on the acquisition of a subsidiary as against the fair value of the subsidiary's identifiable net assets is to reflect the concept of the single economic unit (or single economic entity) thereby giving rise to the recognition of goodwill or gain on bargain purchase.

7. This argument is not valid as it is a rare occurrence. The cancellation of the fair value consideration on the acquisition of a subsidiary as against the fair value of the subsidiary's identifiable net assets at acquisition may also result in either of goodwill or gain on bargain purchase.

8. A parent in a business combination may elect to either account for non-controlling interest at the proportionate share of the identifiable assets and liabilities (including recognisable contingent liabilities), or fair value of the equity instrument of the subsidiary at acquisition-date.

9. Consolidation of the entire amount of subsidiary's assets and liabilities is as a result of the fact that control is 100% involvement in the financial and operating policies of the subsidiary, which is represented by the elements of financial position (i.e. assets and liabilities) of the subsidiary.

10. A partly-owned subsidiary is a subsidiary co-owned by the parent and other equity interest holders (known as non-controlling interest). Upon acquisition, the parent has a responsibility to measure the amount of non-controlling interest in the subsidiary and recognised same within equity but as a separate class.

Guidance on End-of-Chapter Exercises

Chapter 5:

1. Purchased goodwill is the difference between the value paid for an enterprise as a going concern and the sum of its assets less the sum of its liabilities, each item of which has been separately identified and valued.

2. Goodwill is measured as the excess of the fair value of consideration (i.e. acquisition-date fair value of the consideration transferred plus the amount of any non-controlling interest in the acquiree plus the acquisition-date fair value of the acquirer's previously held equity interest in the acquiree) above the acquisition-date fair value of the identifiable assets acquired and liabilities assumed.

3. The accounting policy choice on measuring the amount on non-controlling interest at acquisition will influence the amount of goodwill recognised in the business combination. Where non-controlling interest is measured at the acquisition-date fair value of the equity instrument held, the amount of goodwill recognised will be in full (i.e. parent and non-controlling interest portions of it been recognised).

4. Goodwill can be negative. This occurs when the fair value of the consideration offered by the parent and the amount of non-controlling interest is below the fair value of the identifiable net assets of the subsidiary acquired. In accordance with IFRS 3, such negative goodwill after re-assessment is recognised as a gain arising from a bargain purchase.

5. Impairment loss on a full goodwill cannot be shared between the parent and non-controlling interest in the proportion of their contribution to goodwill arising from acquisition of a subsidiary; rather, IFRS 3 requires the impairment loss to be attributed and charged to the parent and non-controlling interest at the proportion subsidiary's profit or loss is shared.

6. **FULL METHODOLOGY**

		₦ million
Cost of combination:		
Investment of the **Parent** in the **Subsidiary**		100
Amount of Non-controlling interest (20% of ₦120 million)		24
Combined amount of interests in subsidiary to all investors		124
Less: Identifiable net assets acquired as at acquisition-date		
Ordinary share capital	20	
Share premium	60	
Pre-acquisition reserves	40	(120)
Goodwill - positive		**4**

Alternative, PARTIAL METHODOLOGY

	₦ million	₦ million
Investment of the **Parent** in the **Subsidiary**		100
Less: **Parent**'s share of Identifiable net assets of **Subsidiary** acquired:		
• Share capital (80% of ₦20 million)	16	
• Share premium (80% of ₦60 million)	48	
• Pre-acquisition reserves (80% of ₦40 million)	32	(96)
Goodwill attributable to **Parent** *(a)*		4
Amount of investments of Non-controlling interest in **Subsidiary**		24

Contemporaneous Accounting for Business Combinations and Group Accounts

Less: Non-controlling interest share of the fair value of subsidiary's net assets:		
• Share capital (20% of ₦20 million)	4	
• Share premium (20% of ₦60 million)	12	
• Pre-acquisition reserves (20% of ₦40 million)	8	(24)
Goodwill attributable to **non-controlling interests** (b)		---
Goodwill (a + b)		**4**

7. FULL METHODOLOGY   ₦' million

Cost of combination:		
Investment of the **Parent** in the **Subsidiary**		100.0
Amount of Non-controlling interest (4 million shares x ₦6.40)		25.6
Combined amount of interests in subsidiary to all investors		125.6
Less: Identifiable net assets acquired as at acquisition-date		
Ordinary share capital	20	
Share premium	60	
Pre-acquisition reserves	40	(120)
Goodwill - positive		**5.6**

Alternative, PARTIAL METHODOLOGY   ₦' million   ₦' million

Investment of the **Parent** in the **Subsidiary**		100
Less: **Parent**'s share of Identifiable net assets of **Subsidiary** acquired:		
• Share capital (80% of ₦20 million)	16	
• Share premium (80% of ₦60 million)	48	
• Pre-acquisition reserves (80% of ₦40 million)	32	(96)
Goodwill attributable to **Parent** (a)		4
Amount of investments of Non-controlling interest in **Subsidiary**		25.6
Less: Non-controlling interest share of the fair value of subsidiary's net assets:		
• Share capital (20% of ₦20 million)	4	
• Share premium (20% of ₦60 million)	12	
• Pre-acquisition reserves (20% of ₦40 million)	8	(24.0)
Goodwill attributable to **non-controlling interests** (b)		1.6
Goodwill (a + b)		**5.6**

8. FULL METHODOLOGY   ₦' million

Cost of combination:		
Investment of the **Parent** in the **Subsidiary**		100
Amount of Non-controlling interest (20% of ₦120 million)		24
Combined amount of interests in subsidiary to all investors		124
Less: Identifiable net assets acquired as at acquisition-date		
Ordinary share capital	20	
Share premium	60	
Pre-acquisition reserves	40	(120)
Acquired Goodwill		4
Impairment loss		(1)
Consolidated Goodwill		**4**

Guidance on End-of-Chapter Exercises

Alternative, PARTIAL METHODOLOGY	₦' million	₦' million
Investment of the **Parent** in the **Subsidiary**		100
Less: Parent's share of Identifiable net assets of **Subsidiary** acquired:		
• Share capital (80% of ₦20 million)	16	
• Share premium (80% of ₦60 million)	48	
• Pre-acquisition reserves (80% of ₦40 million)	32	(96)
Goodwill attributable to **Parent** (a)		4
Amount of investments of Non-controlling interest in **Subsidiary**		24
Less: Non-controlling interest share of the fair value of subsidiary's net assets:		
• Share capital (20% of ₦20 million)	4	
• Share premium (20% of ₦60 million)	12	
• Pre-acquisition reserves (20% of ₦40 million)	8	(24)
Goodwill attributable to **non-controlling interests** (b)		---
Acquired Goodwill		**4**
Impairment loss		(1)
Consolidated Goodwill		**4**

The impairment loss of ₦1 million is solely attributable to the parent, as thus:

Debit: Consolidated reserves (80% of ₦1 million) - ₦1,000,000
Credit: Goodwill   - ₦1,000,000

9. **FULL METHODOLOGY** — ₦' million

Cost of combination:		
Investment of the **Parent** in the **Subsidiary**		100
Amount of Non-controlling interest (20% of ₦120 million)		24
Combined amount of interests in subsidiary to all investors		124
Less: Identifiable net assets acquired as at acquisition-date		
Ordinary share capital	20	
Share premium	60	
Pre-acquisition reserves	40	(120)
Acquired Goodwill		4
Impairment loss		(1)
Consolidated Goodwill		**3**

Alternative, PARTIAL METHODOLOGY	₦' million	₦' million
Investment of the **Parent** in the **Subsidiary**		100
Less: Parent's share of Identifiable net assets of **Subsidiary** acquired:		
• Share capital (80% of ₦20 million)	16	
• Share premium (80% of ₦60 million)	48	
• Pre-acquisition reserves (80% of ₦40 million)	32	(96)
Goodwill attributable to **Parent** (a)		4
Amount of investments of Non-controlling interest in **Subsidiary**		24
Less: Non-controlling interest share of the fair value of subsidiary's net assets:		
• Share capital (20% of ₦20 million)	4	
• Share premium (20% of ₦60 million)	12	
• Pre-acquisition reserves (20% of ₦40 million)	8	(24)
non-controlling interests (b)		---
Acquired Goodwill		**4**
Goodwill attributable to		
Impairment loss		(1)
Consolidated Goodwill		**3**

The impairment loss of ₦1 million is attributable to the parent and non-controlling interest in ratio 80%:20%, as thus:

Debit: Consolidated reserves (80% of ₦1 million) - ₦800,000
Debit: Non-controlling interest (20% of ₦1 million) - ₦200,000
Credit: Goodwill   - ₦1,000,000

10. FULL METHODOLOGY   ₦' million
Cost of combination:
Investment of the **Parent** in the **Subsidiary**   95
Amount of Non-controlling interest (20% of ₦120 million)   24
Combined amount of interests in subsidiary to all investors   119
Less: Identifiable net assets acquired as at acquisition-date
Ordinary share capital   20
Share premium   60
Pre-acquisition reserves   40   (120)
Negative Goodwill (Gain on Bargain Purchase)   **(1)**

Alternative, PARTIAL METHODOLOGY		₦' million	₦' million
Investment of the **Parent** in the **Subsidiary**			95
Less: Parent's share of Identifiable net assets of **Subsidiary** acquired:			
• Share capital (80% of ₦20 million)		16	
• Share premium (80% of ₦60 million)		48	
• Pre-acquisition reserves (80% of ₦40 million)		32	(96)
Negative Goodwill (Gain on Bargain Purchase) *attributable to Parent (a)*			**(1)**
Amount of investments of Non-controlling interest in **Subsidiary**			24
Less: Non-controlling interest share of the fair value of subsidiary's net assets:			
• Share capital (20% of ₦20 million)		4	
• Share premium (20% of ₦60 million)		12	
• Pre-acquisition reserves (20% of ₦40 million)		8	(24)
(b)			---
Negative Goodwill (Gain on Bargain Purchase)			**(1)**

Guidance on End-of-Chapter Exercises

Chapter 6:

1. A preference share is a class of shares other than those that give residual interest in the net assets of an entity. In assessing the existence of control or otherwise, the amount preference shares held in an investee cannot be adopted as a measure of obtaining control.

2. Preferences shares held by other parties other than the parent should be treated either as:
   - A component of non-controlling interest, if the preference share capital is classified as "*Equity Instrument*" in line IAS 32.
   - A component of non-current liabilities to third parties, if the preference share capital is classified as "*Financial Liability*" in line IAS 32.

3. Where preference share capital is classified as "*Financial Liability*" in line IAS 32, the component attributable to third parties (other than those held by the parent) is recognised as non-current liabilities to third parties.

4. The pre-acquisition and post-acquisition reserves for the mid-year acquisition is as thus:
   - Pre-acquisition reserves = ₦20 million + {3/12 months of (₦56 million – ₦20 million)}
     = **₦29 million**
   - Post-acquisition reserves = 9/12 months of (₦56 million – ₦20 million)
     = **₦27 million**

5. The pre-acquisition and post-acquisition reserves for the mid-year acquisition is as thus:
   - Pre-acquisition reserves = ₦20 million + ₦26 million
     = **₦46 million**
   - Post-acquisition reserves = ₦56 million – ₦46 million
     = **₦10 million**

6. The pre-acquisition and post-acquisition reserves for the mid-year acquisition is as thus:
   - Pre-acquisition reserves = **₦26 million**
   - Post-acquisition reserves = ₦56 million – ₦26 million
     = **₦30 million**

Contemporaneous Accounting for Business Combinations and Group Accounts

Guidance on End-of-Chapter Exercises

Chapter 7:

1. Fair value
2. IFRS 3 requires the consideration and the net assets of the subsidiary acquired to be measured at the acquisition-date fair value.
3. In accordance with IFRS 3, there are three levels of fair value measurement or metrics, namely:
    - Level 1 inputs are quoted prices (unadjusted) in active markets for identical assets or liabilities that the entity can access at the measurement date. A quoted price in an active market provides the most reliable evidence of fair value and shall be used without adjustment to measure fair value whenever available.
    - Level 2 inputs are inputs other than quoted prices included within Level 1 that are observable for the asset or liability, either directly or indirectly. If the asset or liability has a specified (contractual) term, a Level 2 input must be observable for substantially the full term of the asset or liability.
    - Level 3 inputs are unobservable inputs for the asset or liability. Unobservable inputs shall be used to measure fair value to the extent that relevant observable inputs are not available, thereby allowing for situations in which there is little if any, market activity for the asset or liability at the measurement date.
4. The recognition of identifiable net assets (including recognised contingent liabilities) will have an impact on the measurement of resulting goodwill or gain on bargain purchase arising from a business combination as it is a measured compared with the acquisition-date fair value of the consideration offered in the business combination.
5. The fair value adjustments (positive and/or negative) arising from the acquisition method of accounting in a business combination should be considered as a pre-acquisition-adjustments inherent in the value of the identifiable net assets of the subsidiary acquired as at the acquisition date.
6. Based on IFRS 3, the acquiring entity (in the case of a parent) upon acquisition is required to re-measure the subsidiary's net assets acquired at the acquisition-date fair value and of which the resulting fair value adjustment should be reflected, so as to obtain the amount of any goodwill or gain on bargain purchase as at the acquisition date. The fair value adjustment will only be incorporated directly into the books of the subsidiary if its adopted accounting policy is a fair value or its equivalent (such as Revaluation Model of IAS 16 and IAS 38).
7. **FULL METHODOLOGY** ₦' million

Cost of combination:		
Investment of the **Parent** in the **Subsidiary**		100
Amount of Non-controlling interest (20% of ₦130 million)		26
Combined amount of interests in subsidiary to all investors		126
Less: Fair value Identifiable net assets acquired as at acquisition-date		
Ordinary share capital	20	
Share premium	60	
Pre-acquisition reserves	40	
Carrying Amount (or Book Value) of Net Assets Acquired	120	
Fair value adjustment (N130 million – N120 million)	10	
Fair value of Net Assets Acquired		(130)
Negative Goodwill (Gain on Bargain Purchase)		**(4)**

Alternative, PARTIAL METHODOLOGY	₦' million	₦' million
Investment of the **Parent** in the **Subsidiary**		100
Less: **Parent**'s share of Identifiable net assets of **Subsidiary** acquired:		
• Share capital (80% of ₦20 million)	16	
• Share premium (80% of ₦60 million)	48	
• Pre-acquisition reserves (80% of ₦40 million)	32	
• Fair value adjustment (80% of ₦10 million)	8	(104)
Negative Goodwill (Gain on Bargain Purchase) *attributable to* **Parent** *(a)*		(4)
Amount of investments of Non-controlling interest in **Subsidiary**		26
Less: Non-controlling interest share of the fair value of subsidiary's net assets:		
• Share capital (20% of ₦20 million)	4	
• Share premium (20% of ₦60 million)	12	
• Pre-acquisition reserves (20% of ₦40 million)	8	
• Fair value adjustment (20% of ₦10 million)	2	(26)
(b)		---
Negative Goodwill (Gain on Bargain Purchase)		**(4)**

Guidance on End-of-Chapter Exercises

Chapter 8:

1. 3 months

2. IFRS 10 preferably requires the accounting policies of the parent and subsidiary to be uniform (or the same), rather in practice the accounting policies may be different but the standard requires that upon consolidation the subsidiary's accounting policies must be aligned with that of the parent in order to reflect the true financial and economic position and performance of the group as at the reporting date.

3. IFRS 3 requires that upon acquisition, the contingent liabilities that are considered of a present obligation and of which the fair value can be reliably measured should be recognised as at acquisition date.

4. IFRS 10 permits the consolidation of the parent and subsidiary accounts even though their reporting dates may be different but not more than a difference of 3 months, and upon consolidation, material adjustments to reflect the transactions and events within the 3 months are required. But, where the accounting dates are so far apart (or simply put at more than 3 months, a reconstruction of the accounts of the subsidiary for the overlap accounting periods may be required before consolidation can be effected, so as to reflect the financial performance and financial position of the group for the reporting period of the group (i.e. of the parent).

5. After their initial recognition, the acquirer should measure contingent liabilities that are recognised separately at the higher of:
   - The amount that would be recognised in accordance with IAS 37; and
   - The amount initially recognised.

Guidance on End-of-Chapter Exercises

Guidance on End-of-Chapter Exercises

Chapter 9:

1. Adjustment for unrealised profit on inventory is required only when there is an intercompany sales in which the price include an element of profit-loading and of which part or all of the goods remain unsold in the hands of the other entity within the group as at the reporting date.

2. An unrealised profit on inventory within the group should be eliminated against the profit of the selling party (in this case, the subsidiary) and adjust also the inventory value of the buying party (in this case, the parent). This is required in order to allow the group presents the inventory value at cost in line with the requirement of IAS 2 or net realisable value (as the case may be). Both the parent and the non-controlling interest bear the effect of the adjustment where the sales were initiated by the subsidiary.

3. An unrealised profit on the sale of a motor vehicle within the group should be eliminated against the profit of the selling party (in this case, the parent) and adjust also the carrying amount of the motor vehicle of the buying party (in this case, the subsidiary). This is required in order to allow the group presents the asset value at its original carrying amount (as if the sale was not initiated). Given that the sales were initiated by the parent the entire unrealized profit is adjusted against the parent's profit or loss.

4. *Conversion of Mark-up to Margin*

    Given: Mark-up = $\dfrac{\text{Profit}}{\text{Cost Price}} = \dfrac{25}{100}$

    And, Margin = $\dfrac{\text{Profit}}{\text{Selling Price}} = \dfrac{\text{Profit}}{\text{Cost Price + Profit}} = \dfrac{25}{100 + 25} = 20\%$

    Unrealised profit = Margin x Unsold Goods
    = 20% x (₦20 million – ₦12 million) = **₦1,600,000**

5. **Unrealised profit** = Margin x Unsold Goods
    = 20% x (₦20 million – ₦12 million) = **₦1,600,000**

    The unrealised profit of ₦1.6 million will be charged against the profit of the subsidiary and invariably its effect is to reduce the parent share of the group profit by its proportionate share of the unrealized profit based on the ratio to which it shares the subsidiary's profit or loss; while the non-controlling interest is charged with the remaining amount. Invariably, the entire amount representing the adjustment will be credited to reduce the group inventory value as at the reporting date.

6. Since the sale of the motor vehicle is within the group, such transaction should not give rise to increase in the amount of the group asset, therefore an adjustment to eliminate unrealized profit of ₦20 million arising from the transfer/sale of the motor vehicle is required as at the reporting date in which the transfer occurred.

7. As at 31 December 2016, it is evidenced that there exists a trail of group adjustments as regards the elimination of unrealized profit on transfer of motor vehicle sometime in 2014 vis-à-vis the subsequent adjustments regarding adjusting for excess depreciation in the books of the buyer

(in this case the subsidiary). As regards preparation of consolidated financial statements for 2016, the only adjustment required (on the premise of the aforesaid) will be the current period adjustment for excess depreciation which is to be reversed in the books of the subsidiary by adjusting its profit upward (or loss downward).

8. An adjustment for unrealized loss of ₦10 million (in similar like with that of unrealised profit) on transfer/sale of an asset may have been necessary only if the sale below its carrying amount is a not a trigger of an impairment loss that may have occurred.

9. The cognate adjustment required is to recognise a cash-in-transit and by so doing, debit the group cash and cash equivalent and credit the group receivables account; and thereafter eliminate the reconciled (or agreed) inter-company balance.

10. The accounting treatment is to eliminate the inter-company balance of ₦6 million (being the dividend payable within the group at 60% of the dividend payable of ₦10 million), while the remaining balance of ₦4 million is attributable to the non-controlling interest and should be reported as a component of the current liabilities of the group as at the reporting date.

Guidance on End-of-Chapter Exercises

Chapter 10:

1. The amount of inter-company sales to be eliminated is the entire transaction between the parent and the subsidiary termed as a sales transaction, which in this case is ₦20 million. The unrealised profit to be eliminated is ₦1,600,000 (being 20% after conversion from mark-up of 25% to margin, and multiplied by ₦8 million is the value of unsold goods {i.e. ₦20 million - ₦12 million}). The adjustment for cost of sales is ₦18.4 million (being the difference between ₦20 million and ₦1.6 million).

2. The amount of inter-company sales to be eliminated is the entire transaction between the parent and the subsidiary termed as a sales transaction, which in this case is ₦20 million. The unrealised profit to be eliminated is ₦1,600,000 (being 25% after conversion from the margin of 20% to mark-up and multiplied by ₦8 million is the value of unsold goods {i.e. ₦20 million - ₦12 million}). The adjustment for cost of sales is ₦18.4 million (being the difference between ₦20 million and ₦1.6 million). Since the sales transaction was made by the subsidiary, the effect of the adjustment will both impact the parent and non-controlling interest in the proportion the subsidiary's profit is shared between both.

3. The implication is to eliminate the deemed unrealised profit of ₦20 million (i.e. ₦120 million – ₦100 million) attributable to the inter-company transfer/sale of the motor vehicle during the reporting period.

4. The required adjustments include the elimination of unrealized profit of ₦20 million (i.e. ₦120 million – ₦100 million) on the transfer/sale of the motor vehicle during the year vis-à-vis adjustment for excess depreciation of ₦2 million (i.e. ₦20 million unrealised profit divided by 10 years remaining useful life).

5. An adjustment for unrealized loss of ₦10 million (in similar like with that of unrealised profit) on transfer/sale of an asset may have been necessary only if the sale below its carrying amount is a not a trigger of an impairment loss that may have occurred.

6. The accounting treatment is to eliminate the dividend income of ₦6 million earned by the parent (being the dividend earned within the group at 60% of the dividend declared of ₦10 million.

Guidance on End-of-Chapter Exercises

Chapter 11:

1. An associate.

2. Jointly Controlled Entity (or Joint Venture)

3. At cost (in accordance with IAS 27) or fair value in line with IAS 39 (or IFRS 9 if early adopted)

4. The share of associate post-acquisition profit or loss (subject to relevant adjustments) is what is recognised alongside the initial cost of investment in order to obtain the carrying amount of such equity investment that gives significant influence in the investee. The parent in its consolidated statement of profit or loss and other comprehensive income recognised as a line item, its share of associate profit vis-à-vis the share of associate's other comprehensive income. While with its consolidated statement of financial position the carrying amount of the investment in associate based on equity method is reported (or presented) as a single line item separate from other investment that qualified as a financial asset under IAS 39/IFRS 9.

5. *Conversion of Mark-up to Margin*

   Given: Mark-up = $\dfrac{\text{Profit}}{\text{Cost Price}}$ = $\dfrac{20}{100}$

   And, Margin = $\dfrac{\text{Profit}}{\text{Selling Price}}$ = $\dfrac{\text{Profit}}{\text{Cost Price + Profit}}$ = $\dfrac{2}{100 + 20}$ = 16.67% (or $1/6^{th}$)

   Unrealised profit = = Margin x Unsold Goods
   = 40% x ($1/6^{th}$ x ₦12 million) = ₦800,000

   The accounting entry (Downstream Sales Transaction) is as thus:

   Elimination of unrealized profit on inventory/asset in profit or loss
   Debit: Cost of sale (or line items in profit or loss)
   Credit: Investment in associate
   With the group's share of the unrealized profit, which is ₦800,000.

6. *Conversion of Mark-up to Margin*

   Given: Mark-up = $\dfrac{\text{Profit}}{\text{Cost Price}}$ = $\dfrac{20}{100}$

   And, Margin = $\dfrac{\text{Profit}}{\text{Selling Price}}$ = $\dfrac{\text{Profit}}{\text{Cost Price + Profit}}$ = $\dfrac{2}{100 + 20}$ = 16.67% (or $1/6^{th}$)

   Unrealised profit = = Margin x Unsold Goods
   = 40% x ($1/6^{th}$ x ₦12 million) = ₦800,000

   The accounting entry (Upstream Sales Transaction) is as thus:

   Elimination of unrealized profit on inventory/asset in profit or loss
   Debit: Cost of sale (or line items in profit or loss)
   Credit: Inventories (or class of assets)
   With the group's share of the unrealized profit, which is ₦800,000.

Chapter 15

Comprehensive Exercises

Contemporaneous Accounting for Business Combinations and Group Accounts

Comprehensive Exercises

Exercise 1

On 1 October 2012, Application acquired 75% of Knowledge's equity shares by means of a share exchange of two new shares in Application for every five acquired shares in Knowledge. In addition, Application issued to the shareholders of Knowledge ₦100 10% loan note for every 1,000 shares it acquired in Knowledge. Application has not recorded any of the purchase consideration, although it does have other 10% loan notes already in issue.

The market value of Application's shares at 1 October 2012 was ₦2 each.

The summarised statements of financial position of the two companies as at 31 March 2013 are:

Statement of Financial Position as at 31 March 2013

	Application	Knowledge
	₦' 000	₦' 000
Non-Current Assets:		
Property, plant and equipment (Note 1)	47,400	25,500
Investments (Note 1 & Note 4)	7,500	3,200
Current Assets:		
Inventories (Note 2)	20,400	8,400
Trade and other receivables (Note 3)	14,800	8,500
Cash and cash equivalents	2,100	500
Total Assets	**92,200**	**46,100**
Equity and Liabilities:		
Ordinary share capital (₦1 each)	40,000	20,000
Retained earnings – as @ 1 April 2012	19,200	(4,000)
- for year ended 31 March 2013	7,400	8,000
	66,600	24,000
Current Liabilities:		
10% Loan Notes	8,000	
Current Liabilities:		
Trade and other payables (Note 3)	17,600	13,000
Bank overdrafts	-	9,100
Total equity and liabilities	**92,200**	**46,100**

Note 1:

At the date of acquisition, Knowledge produced a draft statement of profit or loss which showed it had made a net loss after tax of ₦2 million at that date. Application accepted this figure as the basis for calculating the pre- and post-acquisition split of Knowledge's profit for the year ended 31 March 2013.

428

Also at the date of acquisition, Application conducted a fair value exercise on Knowledge's net assets which were equal to their carrying amounts (including Knowledge's financial asset equity investments) with the exception of the following items:

- The plant had a fair value of ₦3 million below its carrying amount. The plant had a remaining economic life of three years at 1 October 2012.
- The property had a fair value of ₦4 million (depreciable amount of ₦3 million) above its carrying amount. The building has 10 years remaining useful life since acquisition.

Application's policy is to value the non-controlling interest at fair value at the date of acquisition. For this purpose, a share price for Knowledge of ₦1·20 each is representative of the fair value of the shares held by the non-controlling interest.

Note 2:

Each month since the acquisition, Knowledge's sales to Application were consistently ₦4·6 million. Knowledge had marked these up by 15% on cost. Application had one month's supply (₦4·6 million) of these goods in inventory at 31 March 2013. Knowledge's normal mark-up (to third party customers) is 5%.

Note 3:

Application's current account balance with Knowledge at 31 March 2013 was ₦2·8 million, which did not agree with Knowledge's equivalent receivable due to a payment of ₦900,000 made by Application on 30 March 2013, which was not received by Knowledge until 2 April 2013.

Note 4:

The financial asset equity investments of Application and Knowledge are carried at their fair values as at 1 April 2012. As at 31 March 2013, these had fair values of ₦7·1 million and ₦3·9 million respectively.

Note 5:

The impairment loss on the goodwill as at 31 March 2013 amounted to ₦1·5 million.

Required:

(a) **Prepare the consolidated statement of financial position for Application as at 31 March 2013.**

(b) Application has a strategy of buying struggling businesses, reversing their decline and then selling them on at a profit within a short period of time. Application is hoping to do this with Knowledge.

As an adviser to a prospective purchaser of Knowledge, explain any concerns you would raise about basing an investment decision on the information available in Application's consolidated financial statements and Knowledge's entity financial statements.

Solution to Exercise 1

Application Group
Consolidated Statement of Financial Position as at 31 March 2013

ASSETS:		₦' 000
Non-current assets		
Property, plant and equipment (47,400 + 25,500 – 3,000 + 4,000 + 500 -150)		74,250
Investment:		
- Other financial assets (7,500 + 3,200 – 400 + 700)		11,000
Intangible assets – Goodwill		3,000
		88,250
Current assets		
Inventories (20,400 + 8,400 - 600)	28,200	
Trade and other receivables (14,000 + 8,500 – 900 – 2,800)	19,600	
Cash and cash equivalents (2,100 + 500 + 900)	3,500	51,300
Total Assets		**139,550**
EQUITY & LIABILITIES:		
Share Capital & Reserves		
Ordinary share capital (40,000 + 6,000)		46,000
Share premium		6,000
Retained earnings		32,913
Equity attributable to the shareholders' of **Application**		84,913
Non-controlling interest		8,238
Total Equity		93,150
Non-current liabilities		
10% Loan Notes (8,000 + 0 + 1,500)		9,500
Current liabilities		
Trade and other payables (17,000 + 13,000 – 2,800)	27,800	
Bank overdrafts (0 + 9,100)	9,100	36,900
Total Equity and Liabilities		**139,550**

Working Notes

1. **Purchase Consideration of Application acquisition of Knowledge** ₦'000
    Shares Exchange   12,000
    10% Loan Notes   1,500
                                                                       13,500

   a) **Shares Exchange (or Shares Consideration)**
      - Knowledge shares in issue amounted to 20 million (being share capital of ₦20 million divided by nominal price of ₦1.00 kobo per ordinary share)
      - Application acquired 15 million of Knowledge's ordinary shares (being 75% of 20 million shares)
      - 6 million shares of Arsenal is exchanged for 15 million shares of Chelsea (being 2 Application shares exchange for 5 Knowledge shares multiplied by 15 million shares of Knowledge acquired by Application {or 2/5 shares x 15 million shares})
      - Fair value of the shares consideration @ ₦2.00 per share of 6 million shares offered by Application amounted to ₦12 million

Comprehensive Exercises

Accounting Entry:
Debit:	Investment in Knowledge	- ₦12 million
Credit:	Ordinary share capital (with nominal value of ₦1.00 x 6 million shares)	- ₦6 million
Credit:	Share premium (with premium of ₦1.00 x 6 million shares)	- ₦6 million

b) 10% Loan Notes
- Loan notes issued was 15,000 units (being 15 million shares acquired divided 1,000 shares for every loan note {or 15 million shares/1,000 shares per loan note})
- Fair value of the loan notes amounted to ₦1.5 million (being the nominal value of ₦100 multiplied by 15,000 loan notes)

Accounting Entry:
Debit:	Investment in Knowledge	- ₦1,500,000
Credit:	10% Loan Notes	- ₦1,500,000

2. **Measurement of Non-Controlling Interest (NCI) as at Acquisition-Date (1 April 2011)**
   - Knowledge's ordinary shares held by NCI amounted to 5 million (being 25% of 20 million shares of Knowledge)
   - The acquisition-date fair value @ ₦1.20 per share of 5 million shares amounted to ₦6 million

3. **Fair Value Adjustment on Acquisition of Knowledge**

   a) **Fair value adjustment on plant:**
   Debit: Pre-acquisition reserve
   Credit: Group plant
   With ₦3 million

   b) **Fair value adjustment on property [made-up of Land & Building]:**
Debit:	Group property (Non-depreciable component – Land)	- ₦1 million
Debit:	Group property (Depreciable component – Building)	- ₦3 million
Credit:	Pre-acquisition reserve	- ₦4 million

   The separation of property into its significant components (being land and building) is because of the subsequent effect of depreciation charges in accordance with IAS 16. A land that is freehold is not subjected to depreciation since it is deemed to be an indefinite life (i.e. the useful life cannot be definitely and reliably estimated, rather than subject same to depreciation, only impairment charges can be effected. Rather, for the building component of the property, the useful life can easily be estimated and depreciation charges can be effected. In conclusion, as it relates to this question, adjustment for depreciation (being excess depreciation charges) will only be required for the 'Depreciable Component', which is the building component.

   c) **Adjustment for Excess (Over) Depreciation of Plant:**

   Additional depreciation for 6 months (since acquisition of the subsidiary till current reporting date) amounted to ₦500,000 (being 6 months of the 3 years remaining useful life of the plant since acquisition, and multiplied by ₦3 million or 6/36 months x ₦3 million})

Debit:	Group plant	- ₦500,000
Credit:	Consolidated retained earnings (75% of ₦500,00)	- ₦375,000
Credit:	Non-controlling interest (25% of ₦500,00)	- ₦125,000

d) Adjustment for Additional Depreciation of Property (Building Component):

Additional depreciation for 6 months (since acquisition of the subsidiary till current reporting date) amounted to ₦150,000 (being 6months of the 10 years remaining useful life of the plant since acquisition, and multiplied by ₦3 million {or 6/120 months x ₦3 million})

Debit:	Consolidated retained earnings (75% of ₦150,00)	- ₦112,500
Debit:	Non-controlling interest (25% of ₦150,00)	- ₦37,500
Credit:	Group property	- ₦150,000

4. Adjustment for Cash In-Transits and Elimination of Intercompany Balances:

a) Goods-In-Transit
Debit: Group cash
Credit: Trade and other payables - Knowledge
With ₦900,000

b) Elimination on Inter-Company Trade Receivable and Payable:
Debit: Trade payable – Application
Credit: Trade Receivable - Knowledge
With ₦2.8 million

5. Unrealised Profit on Goods In-Transit (Upstream Transaction):

- Mark-up = Profit/Cost Price   15.00%
- Margin = Profit 15/(Cost Price 100 + Profit 15)   13.04%
- Goods in-transit {GIT} value (₦'000)   4,600
- Unrealised profit – ₦'000 (Margin x GIT value)   600

Accounting Entry:

Debit:	Consolidated retained earnings (75% of ₦600,00)	- ₦450,000
Debit:	Non-controlling interest (25% of ₦600,00)	- ₦150,000
Credit:	Group inventory	- ₦600,000

6. Impairment of [Full] Goodwill

Debit:	Consolidated retained earnings (75% of ₦1.5 million)	- ₦1,125,000
Debit:	Non-controlling interest (25% of ₦1.5 million)	- ₦375,000
Credit:	Goodwill	- ₦1,500,000

The impairment loss on the goodwill is charged against the parent and non-controlling interest in proportion to which they share the profit or loss of the subsidiary, and this is as a result of non-controlling interest contributing to the amount of goodwill recognised on acquisition of Chelsea.

7. Fair Value Adjustment on Financial Assets:

a) *Application's investment in financial assets*
Debit: Consolidated retained earnings
Credit: Financial assets
With ₦400,000 being loss on fair value changes of the financial assets (₦7.5 million – ₦7.1 million)

b) _Knowledge's investment in financial assets_

Debit:	Financial assets	-₦700,000
Credit:	Consolidated retained earnings (75% of ₦700 million)	-₦525,000
Credit:	Non-controlling interest (25% of ₦700 million)	-₦175,000

With ₦700,000 being gain on fair value changes of the financial assets (₦3.9 million – ₦3.2 million).

8. Determination of Goodwill

FULL METHODOLOGY

		₦' 000	₦' 000
Cost of combination:			
• Cost of investment of **Application** in **Knwoledge**			13,500
• Non-controlling interest in **Knwoledge** (_At Acquisition-date fair value_)			6,000
			19,500
Less: Identifiable net assets of **Knowledge** acquired (@ 1 April 2011):			
• Ordinary share capital		20,000	
• Pre-acquisition Reserves:			
- Retained earnings {- 4,000 + (- 2,000)}	(6,000)		
- Fair value adjustment - Plant	(3,000)		
- Fair value adjustment – Property	4,000	(5,000)	(15,000)
FULL Goodwill - positive			**4,500**
Less: Impairment loss			_(1,500)_
Consolidated Goodwill (@ 31 March 2013)			**3,000**

	₦' 000	₦' 000
Alternatively, PARTIAL METHODOLOGY		
Cost of investment of **Application** in **Knowledge**		13,500
Less: **Application's** share of Identifiable net assets of **Knowledge** acquired:		
• Share capital (75% of ₦20 million)	15,000	
• Pre-acquisition reserves (75% of - ₦5 million)	(3,750)	(11,250)
Goodwill attributable to **FARA's** (a)		2,250
Amount of investments of non-controlling interest in **Knowledge**		6,000
Less: Non-controlling interest share of the fair value of subsidiary's net assets:		
• Share capital (25% of ₦20 million)	5,000	
• Pre-acquisition reserves (25% of - ₦5 million)	(1,250)	(3,750)
Negative Goodwill attributable to **non-controlling interests** (b)		2,250
Full Goodwill (a + b)		**4,500**
Less: Impairment loss		_(1,500)_
Consolidated Goodwill (@ 31 March 2013)		**3,000**

9. **Non-controlling Interest as @ 31 March 2013:**

	₦'000
Added on acquisition @ 1 October 2012	6,000.0
Share of post—acquisition reserves (25% of ₦10 million)	2,500.0
Adjustments:	
- Impairment loss on goodwill	(375.0)
- Unrealised profit on goods in-transits	(150.0)
- Excess (Over) depreciation adjustment	125.0
- Fair value gain on financial assets held by knowledge	175.0
- Additional depreciation on plant	(37.5)
	8,237.5

*The post-acquisition retained earnings of ₦10 million is the as the profit made since acquisition (dated 1 October 2012) till the reporting date 31 March 2013. This is determined as the difference between the retained earnings of ₦4 million as at 31 March 2013 (i.e. the sum of ₦8 million profit made during the year and the negative opening retained earnings of ₦4 million loss) and the pre-acquisition (negative) retained earnings of ₦6 million loss as at the acquisition-date (refer to **working note 8** above).*

10. **Consolidated Retained Earnings as @ 31 March 2013:**

	₦'000
Application's retained earnings (19,200 + 7,400)	26,600.0
Share of post—acquisition reserves (75% of ₦10 million)	7,500.0
Adjustments:	
- Impairment loss on goodwill	(1,125.0)
- Unrealised profit on goods in-transits	(450.0)
- Excess (Over) depreciation adjustment	375.0
- Fair value loss on financial assets held by Application	(400.0)
- Fair value gain on financial assets held by knowledge	525.0
- Additional depreciation on plant	(112.5)
	32,912.5

Comprehensive Exercises

Exercise 2

Arsenal acquired 80% interests in the equity of Chelsea as 1 April 2016. The Board of Arsenal strictly wants to comply with the requirement of IFRS regarding consolidation of the financial statements of the subsidiary with that of the parent as at December 31, 2016.

Income Statement for the year ended December 31, 2016

	Arsenal	Chelsea
	₦'000	₦'000
Revenue	600,000	390,000
Cost of sales	(345,000)	(201,000)
Gross profit	**255,000**	**189,000**
Distribution costs	(75,000)	(45,000)
Administrative expenses	(105,000)	(90,000)
Profit on before tax	**75,000**	**54,000**
Income tax	(25,000)	(29,000)
Profit for the year	**50,000**	**25,000**
Movement in Reserves:		
Retained profits brought forward	120,000	65,000
Profit for the year	50,000	25,000
Retained profit carried forward	**170,000**	**90,000**

Additional Information:

a) At acquisition, the parent in addition to the shares consideration (shares exchange) offered to former shareholders of the subsidiary, a cash payment of ₦22 million is due to be paid on 1 April 2017 to the shareholders who sold their stakes to the parent. The hurdle rate (or cost of capital) of Arsenal is 10%.

b) It was obtained that on 19 May 2016, Arsenal already sold goods to Chelsea for ₦50 million, when it actually cost Arsenal ₦40 million. As at the year-end, included in the inventory of Chelsea Plc is 40% of the goods sold by Arsenal Plc as of 19th May 2016.

c) As at the reporting date (31 December 2016), the goodwill has been impaired to the tune of ₦5 million, and of which all the ₦5 million represents the impairment loss attributable to 2016 financial year.

Required:

Prepare the consolidated of profit or loss and the consolidated statement of changes in equity, given that the share capital of Arsenal stood at ₦200 million and that of Chelsea amounted to ₦28.75 million; and the amount of non-controlling interest at acquisition measured at the proportionate share of the identifiable net assets of the subsidiary which stood at ₦20 million.

Solution to Exercise 2

In this context of this text, we will approach a step-by-step approach to explaining the requirement of **IFRS 10** with regards to consolidating the financial results of the parent and the subsidiary as depicted below.

Arsenal Group
Consolidated Statement of Profit or Loss for the year ended 31 December 2016

	₦'000
Revenue (600,000 + {9/12 x 390,000} – 50,000 {Note 1})	842,500
Cost of sales (345,000 + {9/12 x 201,000} – 46,000 {Note 1})	(449,750)
Gross profit	**392,750**
Distribution costs (75,000 + {9/12 x 45,000})	(108,750)
Administrative expenses (105,000 + {9/12 x 90,000} + 5,000 Impairment loss on goodwill)	(177,500)
Operating profit	**106,500**
Finance cost (unwound discount of deferred consideration – Note 4)	(1,500)
Profit on before tax	**105,000**
Income tax (25,000 + {9/12 x 29,000})	(46,750)
Profit for the year	**58,250**

Profit, attributable to:
* Owners' of Arsenal (Note 1)	54,500
** Non-controlling interest (Note 1)	3,750
	58,250

Arsenal Group
Consolidated Statement of Changes in Equity for the year ended 31 December 2016

	Share Capital	Retained Earnings	Equity – of the Parent	Non-controlling Interest	Total Equity
	₦'000	₦'000	₦'000	₦'000	₦'000
As at 1 January 2016	200,000	120,000 (Note 2)	320,000	–	320,000
Profit for the year		54,500	54,500	3,750	58,250
Transactions within Equity:					
Added on Acquisition				20,000 (Note 3)	20,000
As at 31 December, 2016	200,000	174,500	374,500	23,750	398,250

Working Notes:

1. **Profit attributable to: interest**

	Arsenal	Non-controlling
	₦'000	₦'000
Arsenal's profit after tax	50,000	–
Chelsea' profit after tax (80:20)	15,000	3,750
Less: Unwound discount	(1,500)	–
Less: Unrealised profit on inventories	(4,000)	–
Less: Impairment loss on goodwill	(5,000)	–
	54,500	**3,750**

Comprehensive Exercises

Adjustments regarding the elimination of intercompany sales, the intercompany cost of sales and invariably elimination of unrealized profit are required in this context. This is as a result that, as of 19th day of May 2016 when the sales transaction was initiated between Arsenal and Chelsea, a parent-subsidiary relationship has since been established, and such sales transaction can be termed an intercompany transaction that requires such an adjustment.

Only post-combination transactions between the parent and subsidiary are required to be accorded strict treatment of elimination, so as to depict the true economic and financial performance of the Group.

The intercompany sales of ₦50 million will have to be eliminated alongside the intra-group cost of sales (which is arrived at by deducting the amount of unrealised profit from the intercompany sales)

The unrealised profit is determined by multiply the percentage of unsold goods (which in this case is 40%) by the profit on sales as made from the intercompany sales of goods during the reporting period.

The profit on sales amounted to ₦10 million (being the difference between the proceeds of ₦50 million earned on the intercompany sales and cost price of ₦40 million to the seller, which in this case is the parent).

Hence, the amount of unrealised profit stood at ₦4 million (being 40% unsold inventories multiplied by ₦10 million profit on sales made during the reporting period).

Then, the amount of inter-company cost of sales will amount to ₦46 million (being amount of intercompany sales of ₦50 million less the ₦4 million unrealised profit as at the reporting date).

The unrealised profit being eliminated is solely attributable to the parent, as the sales transaction was made by the parent being a downstream transaction.

The income statement items are presumed to have accrued evenly, and on this premise, the individual items (expense and income) are apportioned into pre-acquisition and post-acquisition items on the basis of time proportion. In this scenario, since the acquisition took place sometimes during the year (specifically on 1st day of April 2016), then the portion of pre-acquisition was considered 3 months (i.e. between 1 January 2016 and 31 March 2016), while post-acquisition period stood at 9 months (1 April 2016 to 31 December 2016).

The portion to be consolidated alongside that of a full calendar year (of 12 months) of the parent is the post-combination period of 9 months. This is what gave rise the prorated amount of income and expense consolidated (as shown above).

The attribution of subsidiary's profit in this illustration was based on the 9 months post-acquisition results of Chelsea, which stood at ₦18,750,000 (i.e. 9/12 of ₦25 million profit after tax for the whole year).

Chelsea' profit after tax is shared between the parent and the non-controlling interest in the ratio of 80% to 20% in which profit or loss is required to be allocated based on the stake held in the ordinary shares of the subsidiary.

The effect of the impairment loss of ₦5 million will be charged to the parent only. This is so because the goodwill that has been impaired is considered a Partial Goodwill. That is, a partial goodwill is a goodwill that is attributable to only to the parent at the acquisition of the subsidiary, which only exists on the accounting policy choice of measuring non-controlling interest at the proportionate share of subsidiary's identifiable assets and liabilities at acquisition-date.

2. **Consolidated Retained Earnings as at 1 January 2016** ₦'000
   Arsenal's retained earnings as at 1 January 2016   120,000
   80% of Chelsea's post acquisition retained earnings as at 1 January 2016   - (Nil)
   120,000

   In this case, there is no post-acquisition profit as the subsidiary was acquired during the reporting year. Same can be said of a subsidiary acquired on the first date of the reporting period.

3. **Non-controlling Interest (Added on Acquisition) as at 1 April 2016**

   In this case, there is no opening balance for non-controlling interest as at 1 January 2016, as there was no Group and neither would a non-controlling interest in Chelsea would have been recognised as at 1 January 2016 (being the start of the reporting period of the presumed parent). Rather, the amount to be recognised with respect to non-controlling interest will be the amount added on the acquisition of Chelsea, which will be based on the accounting policy of the Group on the measurement of the amount of non-controlling interest upon acquisition. In this case, the amount of non-controlling interest is considered to have been measured at an acquisition-date fair value of ₦20 million, or 20% of ₦100 million (being Share Capital of ₦28.75 million plus Pre-Acquisition Reserve of ₦71.25 million obtained by adding ₦65 million as at 1 January 2016 to 3 months result of ₦6.25 million.

4. **Unwinding of Discount on Deferred/Contingent Consideration (Finance Cost)**

   The discount unwound represents the current period finance cost attributable to the unwinding of discount embedded in the present value of the deferred cash consideration made as at the acquisition date.

   The amount of the deferred cash consideration at its (nominal) future value as at acquisition (i.e. as at 1 April 2016 was ₦22 million, and which is payable in a year's time (i.e. as at 1 April 2017).

   *The present value as at acquisition (in current money terms as at acquisition-date, 1 April 2016) would be ₦20 million (**i.e. present value of ₦22 million at 10% cost of capital, and discounted for 1 year; or ₦22 million x $(1.1)^{-1}$**).*

   The discount unwound for the first and only period (i.e. 1 April 2016 – 1 April 2017) was ₦2 million, while only 9 months finance cost of ₦1.5 million (i.e. 1 April 2016 – 31 December 2016) is what is considered to have been charged to parent's profit or loss in 2016. The basis of obtaining ₦1.5 million entails the multiplication of 10% cost of capital with the present value of ₦20 million as at the beginning of the year (which was the acquisition-date) multiplied by 9/12 months.

Exercise 3

Arsenal acquired 80% interests in the equity of Chelsea as January 1, 2015, when the retained earnings stood at ₦20 million. The Board of Arsenal strictly wants to comply with the requirement of IFRS regarding consolidation of the financial statements of the subsidiary with that of the parent as at December 31, 2016.

Income Statement for the year ended December 31, 2016

	Arsenal ₦'000	Chelsea ₦'000
Revenue	600,000	390,000
Cost of sales	(345,000)	(201,000)
Gross profit	**255,000**	**189,000**
Distribution costs	(75,000)	(45,000)
Administrative expenses	(105,000)	(90,000)
Profit on before tax	**75,000**	**54,000**
Income tax	(25,000)	(29,000)
Profit for the year	**50,000**	**25,000**
Movement in Reserves:		
Retained profits brought forward	120,000	65,000
Profit for the year	50,000	25,000
Retained profit carried forward	**170,000**	**90,000**

Additional Information:

a) As an acquisition, the parent in addition to the shares consideration (shares exchange) offered to former shareholders of the subsidiary, a cash payment of ₦28.8 million is due to be paid on 31 December 2016 to the shareholders who sold their stakes to the parent. The hurdle rate (or cost of capital) of Arsenal is 20%.

b) Chelsea sold goods to Arsenal for ₦50 million, when it actually cost the parent company ₦40 million. As at the year-end, included in the inventory of Arsenal Plc is 40% of the inventory sold by Chelsea Plc.

c) As at the reporting date (31 December 2016), the goodwill has been impaired to the tune of ₦12 million, and of which only ₦5 million represents the impairment loss attributable to 2016 financial year.

Required:

Prepare the consolidated of profit or loss and the consolidated statement of changes in equity, given that the share capital of Arsenal stood at ₦200 million and that of Chelsea amounted to ₦100 million, and the amount of non-controlling interest at acquisition as measured at fair value stood at ₦24 million.

Solution to Exercise 3

In this context of this text, we will approach a step-by-step approach to explaining the requirement of **IFRS 10** with regards to consolidating the financial results of the parent and the subsidiary as depicted below.

Arsenal Group
Consolidated Statement of Profit or Loss for the year ended 31 December 2016

	₦'000
Revenue (600,000 + 390,000 – 50,000)	940,000
Cost of sales (345,000 + 201,000 – 46,000)	(546,000)
Gross profit	**440,000**
Distribution costs (75,000 + 45,000)	(120,000)
Administrative expenses (105,000 + 90,000 + 5,000 Impairment loss on goodwill)	(200,000)
Operating profit	**120,000**
Finance cost (unwound discount of deferred consideration – Note 4)	(4,800)
Profit on before tax	**125,200**
Income tax (25,000 + 29,000)	(54,000)
Profit for the year	**61,200**
Profit, attributable to:	
* Owners' of Arsenal (Note 1)	58,000
** Non-controlling interest (Note 1)	3,200
	61,200

Arsenal Group
Consolidated Statement of Changes in Equity for the year ended 31 December 2016

	Share Capital	Retained Earnings	Equity – of the Parent	Non-controlling Interest	Total Equity
	₦'000	₦'000	₦'000	₦'000	₦'000
As at 1 January 2016	200,000	146,400	346,400	31,600	378,000
		(Note 2)		(Note 3)	
Profit for the year		58,000	58,000	3,200	61,200
As at 31 December, 2016	200,000	204,400	404,400	34,800	439,200

Working Notes:

1. | Profit attributable to: | Arsenal | Non-controlling interest |
   |---|---|---|
   | | ₦'000 | ₦'000 |
   | Arsenal's profit after tax | 50,000 | - |
   | Chelsea' profit after tax (80:20) | 20,000 | 5,000 |
   | *Less:* Unwound discount | (4,800) | - |
   | *Less:* Unrealised profit on inventories (80:20) | (3,200) | (800) |
   | *Less:* Impairment loss on goodwill (80:20) | (4,000) | (1,000) |
   | | **58,000** | **3,200** |

Chelsea' profit after tax is shared between the parent and the non-controlling interest in the ratio of 80% to 20% in which profit or loss is required to be allocated based on the stake held in the ordinary shares of the subsidiary.

2. **Consolidated Retained Earnings as at 1 January 2016**

	₦'000
Arsenal's retained earnings as at 1 January 2016	120,000
80% of Chelsea's post acquisition retained earnings as at 1 January 2016 {80% x (₦65 million – ₦20 million - ₦7 million impairment loss on goodwill)}	30,400
Less: Unwound Discount in 2015 (20% of ₦20 million → Note 4)	(4,000)
	146,400

In this case, there was a pre-acquisition profit of ₦20 million which was the opening retained earnings.

3. **Non-controlling interest as at 1 January 2016**

	₦'000
Amount of NCI as at acquisition (1 January 2016)	24,000
20% of Chelsea's post acquisition retained earnings as at 1 January 2016 {20% x (₦65 million – ₦20 million - ₦7 million impairment loss on goodwill)}	7,600
	31,600

In this case, there was a pre-acquisition profit of ₦20 million which was the opening retained earnings.

4. **Unwinding of Discount on Deferred/Contingent Consideration (Finance Cost)**

The discount unwound represents the current period finance cost attributable to the unwinding of discount embedded in the present value of the deferred cash consideration made as at the acquisition date.

The amount of the deferred cash consideration at its (nominal) future value as at acquisition (i.e. as at 1 January 2015 was ₦28.8 million, and which is payable in 2 years' time (i.e. as at 31 December 2016.

*The present value as at acquisition (in current money terms as at acquisition-date, 1 January 2015) would be ₦20 million (**i.e. present value of ₦28.8 million at 20% cost of capital, and discounted for 2 years; or ₦28.8 million x $(1.2)^{-2}$**).*

The discount unwound for the first year (i.e. 2015) was ₦4 million which is considered to have been charged to parent's profit or loss in 2015 (and which automatically would have been reflected I its closing retained earnings as at 31 December 2015). The basis of obtaining ₦4 million entails the multiplication of 20% cost of capital with the present value of ₦20 million as at the beginning of the year (which was the acquisition-date).

The discount unwound for the second and final year is ₦4.8 million which is charged to parent's profit or loss in 2016 (and which automatically charged to group profit, but only attributable to the parent). The basis of obtaining ₦4.8 million entails the multiplication of 20% cost of capital with the present value of ₦24 million as at the beginning of the year (which is the addition of the present value as at acquisition-date of ₦20 million and ₦4 million unwound discount for 2015 financial year).

5. The intercompany sales of ₦50 million will have to be eliminated alongside the intra-group cost of sales (which is arrived at by deducting the amount of unrealised profit from the intercompany sales)

   The unrealised profit is determined by multiply the percentage of unsold goods (which in this case is 40%) by the profit on sales as made from the intercompany sales of goods during the reporting period.

   The profit on sales amounted to ₦10 million (being the difference between the proceeds of ₦50 million earned on the intercompany sales and cost price of ₦40 million to the seller, which in this case is the subsidiary).

   Hence, the amount of unrealized profit stood at ₦4 million (being 40% unsold inventories multiplied by ₦10 million profit on sales made during the reporting period).

   Then, the amount of inter-company cost of sales will amount to ₦46 million (being amount of intercompany sales of ₦50 million less the ₦4 million unrealised profit as at the reporting date).

   The unrealised profit being eliminated is attributable to the parent and the non-controlling interest in the proportion to which profit or loss is being shared. This treatment is required because the unrealised profit sits within the enlarge profit of the subsidiary as at the reporting date (as the sales transaction was made by the subsidiary being an upstream transaction).

   Chelsea' profit after tax is shared between the parent and the non-controlling interest in the ratio of 80% to 20% in which profit or loss is required to be allocated based on the stake held in the ordinary shares of the subsidiary.

6. The effect of the impairment loss of ₦5 million will be charged to the parent and the subsidiary in the ratio the subsidiary's profit is shared. This is so because the goodwill that has been impaired is considered a Full Goodwill.

Comprehensive Exercises

Exercise 4

On 1 April 2011, Arsenal acquired 80% of Chelsea's equity shares by means of an immediate 10 million share exchange (of its own shares) and a cash payment of 88 kobo per acquired share, deferred until 1 April 2012. The Share price of Arsenal as at 1 April 2011 was ₦2.40. Arsenal has neither recorded the share exchange nor the cash consideration. Arsenal's cost of capital (hurdle rate) is 10% per annum.

The summarised statements of financial position of three companies as at 31 March 2012 are:

Statement of Financial Position as at 31ˢᵗ March 2012

ASSETS:	Arsenal	Chelsea	Barca
Non-current assets	₦'000	₦'000	₦'000
Property, plant and equipment	38,100	28,500	12,000
Investments (Note 2)	10,500	-	-
	48,600	28,500	12,000
Current assets			
Inventories (Note 3)	13,900	10,400	7,100
Trade and other receivables (Note 3)	11,400	5,500	2,000
Cash and cash equivalents (Note 3)	900	600	400
Total Assets	**74,800**	**45,000**	**21,500**
EQUITY & LIABILITIES:			
Share Capital & Reserves:			
Ordinary share capital (@ ₦1 per share)	15,000	8,000	5,000
Share premium	3,600	2,000	-
Retained earnings – as @ 1 April 2011	16,200	18,000	6,000
– for the year ended 31 March 2012	14,000	8,000	4,000
	48,800	36,000	15,000
Non-current liabilities			
11% Bond (Note 2)	12,000	4,000	-
Deferred tax liability	4,500	-	2,000
Current liabilities			
Trade and other payables (Note 3)	9,500	5,000	4,500
Total Equity and Liabilities	**74,800**	**45,000**	**21,500**

The following information is relevant:

Note 1:
At the date of acquisition, Arsenal conducted a fair value exercise on Chelsea's net assets which were equal to their carrying amounts with the following exceptions:

– An item of the plant had a fair value of ₦3 million above its carrying amount. At the date of acquisition, it had a remaining life of five years. Ignore deferred tax relating to this fair value.
– Chelsea had an unrecorded deferred tax liability of ₦1 million, which was unchanged as at 31 March 2012.

Arsenal's policy is to value the non-controlling interest at fair value at the date of acquisition. For this purpose, a share price for Chelsea of ₦3·50 each is representative of the fair value of the shares held by the non-controlling interest.

443

Note 2:

The investments of Arsenal are made up of:
- Shares held in Chelsea
- Shares held in Barca
- Shares held in other entities
- Bonds held in Chelsea

Immediately after the acquisition, Chelsea issued ₦4 million of 11% Bonds, ₦2·5 million of which was bought by Arsenal. All interest due on the loan notes as at 31 March 2012 has been paid and received.

Arsenal bought 1·5 million shares in Barca on 1 October 2011 for the sum of ₦6 million; and as at 31 March 2012, Barca's retained profits had increased by ₦2 million over their value on 1 October 2011.

The other equity investments of Arsenal are carried at their fair values on 1 April 2011. At 31 March 2012, these had increased to ₦2·8 million.

Note 3:

Arsenal sells goods to Chelsea at cost plus 50%. Below is a summary of the recorded activities for the year ended 31 March 2012 and balances as at 31 March 2012:

	Arsenal ₦'000	Chelsea ₦'000
Sales to Chelsea	16,000	
Purchases from Arsenal		14,500
Included in Arsenal's receivables	4,400	
Included in Chelsea's payables		1,700

On 28 March 2012, Arsenal sold and despatched goods to Chelsea, which Chelsea did not record until they were received on 3 April 2012. Chelsea's inventory was counted on 31 March 2012 and does not include any goods purchased from Arsenal.

On 30 March 2012, Chelsea remitted to Arsenal a cash payment which was not received by Arsenal until 2 April 2012. This payment accounted for the remaining difference in the current accounts.

Arsenal sold goods valued at ₦4 million to Barca at a margin of 10% on 25 March 2012, and as at 31 March 2012 25% of the goods had been sold.

Note 4:

Impairment tests were carried out on 30 March 2012 which concluded that goodwill was impaired by ₦2·4 million.

Required:

Prepare the consolidated statement of financial position for Arsenal as at 31 March 2012.

Comprehensive Exercises

Solution to Exercise 4
Arsenal Group
Consolidated Statement of Financial Position as at 31 March 2012

		₦'000
ASSETS:		
Non-current assets		
Property, plant and equipment (38,100 + 28,500 + 3,000 - 600)		69,000
Investments:		
- Barca (Associate)	6,023	
- Other financial assets (2,000 + 800)	2,800	9,310
Intangible assets – Goodwill		2,320
		80,630
Current assets		
Inventories (13,900 + 10,400 + 1,500 - 500)	25,300	
Trade and other receivables (11,400 + 5,500 – 1,200 -3,200)	12,500	
Cash and cash equivalents (900 + 600 + 1,200)	2,700	40,500
Total Assets		**121,130**
EQUITY & LIABILITIES:		
Share Capital & Reserves		
Ordinary share capital (15,000 + 10,000)		25,000
Share premium		17,600
Retained earnings		34,498
Equity attributable to the shareholders' of **Arsenal**		**77,098**
Non-controlling interest		6,600
Total Equity		**148,072**
Non-current liabilities		
10% Bond (12,000 + 4,000 – 2,500)	13,500	
Deferred tax liability (4,500 + 1,000)	5,500	
		19,000
Current liabilities		
Trade and other payables (9,500 + 5,000 + 1,500 - 3,200)	12,800	
Deferred consideration (5,120 + 512)	5,632	18,432
Total Equity and Liabilities		**121,130**

Working Notes

1. **Breakdown (Analysis) of Arsenal's Investments in the Financial Statements**

	₦'000
Investment in Chelsea (Not Recorded in the Accounts)	-
Shares held in Barca	6,000
Bonds held in Chelsea	2,500
Shares held in other entities (*Balancing Figure*)	2,000*
	10,500

2. **Purchase Consideration of Arsenal acquisition of Chelsea**

	₦'000
Shares Exchange	24,000
Deferred [Cash] Consideration	5,120
	29,120

3. **Shares Exchange (or Shares Consideration)**
   - Chelsea shares in issue amounted to 8 million (being share capital of ₦8 million divided by nominal price of ₦1.00 kobo per ordinary share)
   - Arsenal acquired 6.4 million of Chelsea's ordinary shares (being 80% of 8 million shares)
   - 10 million shares of Arsenal is exchanged for 6.4 million shares of Chelsea
   - Fair value of the shares consideration @ ₦2.40 per share of 10 million shares offered amounted to ₦24 million

   Accounting Entry:
   Debit: Investment in Chelsea   - ₦24 million
   Credit: Ordinary share capital (with nominal value of ₦1.00 x 10 million shares) - ₦10 million
   Credit: Share premium (with premium of ₦1.40 x 10 million shares)   - ₦24 million

4. **Deferred [Cash] Consideration**
   - Additional cash consideration deferred till 1 April 2012 was ₦6,532,000 (being ₦0.88 x 6.4 million shares)
   - Time to settlement from acquisition is 1 year and cost of capital of 10%
   - Hence, the present value at acquisition date amounted to ₦5,120,000 (being ₦6,532,000 multiplied by the discounting factor of $(1.1)^{-1}$

   Accounting Entry:
   Debit: Investment in Chelsea   -   ₦5,120,000
   Credit: Provision for deferred consideration   -   ₦5,120,000

5. **Measurement of Non-Controlling Interest (NCI) as at Acquisition-Date (1 April 2011)**
   - Chelsea's ordinary shares held by NCI amounted to 1.6 million (being 20% of 8 million shares of Chelsea)
   - The acquisition-date fair value @ ₦3.50 per share of 1.6 million shares amounted to ₦5.6 million

6. **Fair Value Adjustment on Acquisition of Chelsea**

   a) **Fair value adjustment on plant:**
      Debit: Group plant
      Credit: Pre-acquisition reserve
      With ₦3 million

   b) **Adjustment for un-recognised deferred tax liability (now recognised on acquisition):**
      Debit: Pre-acquisition reserve
      Credit: Group deferred tax liability
      With ₦1 million

   c) **Adjustment for Goods and Cash In-Transits and Elimination Intercompany Balances:**
      i. **Goods-In-Transit**
         Debit: Group inventory
         Credit: Trade and other payables - Chelsea
         With ₦1.5 million (being the difference between ₦16 million and ₦14.5 million)

Comprehensive Exercises

Reconciliation of Inter-Company Balance	Arsenal Receivables	Chelsea Payables
	₦'000	₦'000
As at 31 March 2012	4,400	1,700
Less: Goods in-transit		1,500
	4,400	3,200
Less: Cash in-transit (Balancing figure)	(1,200)	-
	3,200	3,200

ii. Cash In-Transit
Debit: Group cash and cash equivalents
Credit: Trade Receivable - Arsenal
With ₦1.2 million (₦4.4 million – ₦1.7 million – ₦1.5 million)

iii. Elimination on Inter-Company Trade Receivable and Payable:
Debit: Trade payable – Chelsea
Credit: Trade Receivable - Arsenal
With ₦3.2 million (₦4.4 million – ₦1.2million or ₦1.7 million + ₦1.5 million)

7. Unrealised Profit on Goods In-Transit:
- Mark-up = Profit/Cost Price 50.00%
- Margin = Profit 50/(Cost Price 100 + Profit 50) 33.33%
- Goods in-transit {GIT} value (₦'000) 1,500
- Unrealised profit – ₦'000 (Margin x GIT value) 500

Accounting Entry:
Debit: Consolidated retained earnings
Credit: Group inventory
With ₦500,000 (since the sales was made by the Arsenal to Chelsea – Downstream Transaction)

8. Impairment of [Full] Goodwill
Debit:	Consolidated retained earnings (80% of ₦2.4 million)	- ₦1,920,000
Debit:	Non-controlling interest (20% of ₦2.4 million)	- ₦480,000
Credit:	Goodwill	- ₦2.4 million

The impairment loss on the goodwill is charged against the parent and non-controlling interest in proportion to which they share the profit or loss of the subsidiary, and this is as a result of non-controlling interest contributing to the amount of goodwill recognised on acquisition of Chelsea.

9. Additional Depreciation Adjustment
- Depreciation adjustment for 1 year since acquisition amounted to ₦600,000 (being 1/5 years of ₦3 million)

Accounting Entry:
Debit:	Consolidated retained earnings (80% of ₦600,000)	-	₦480,000
Debit:	Non-controlling interest (20% of ₦600,000)	-	₦120,000
Credit:	Group plant	-	₦600,000

10. Finance costs – Unwinding of Discount Embedded in Deferred Consideration:
- The unwound discount in 1 year amounted to ₦512,000 (being 10% of ₦5,120,000)

Accounting Entry:
Debit: Consolidated retained earnings
Credit: Deferred [Cash] consideration (Current liability)
With ₦512,000

11. Unrealised Profit on Inventory (Regarding Goods Sold by Arsenal to Barca):
- Margin = 10%
- Inventory value {75% x ₦4 million} (₦'000) 300
- % holdings of Arsenal in Barca 30%
- Unrealised profit – ₦'000 (Margin x Inventory value) 90

Accounting Entry:
Debit: Consolidated retained earnings
Credit: Investment in Barca
With ₦90,000 (since the sales was made by the Arsenal to Barca – Downstream Transaction)

12. Inter-company Bonds (Asset and Liability):
Debit: 11% Bond Liability - Chelsea
Credit: Investment in Chlesea's Bond – Arsenal
With ₦2.5 million

13. Fair Value Adjustment on Financial Assets
Debit: Financial Assets Investment
Credit: Consolidated retained earnings
With ₦800,000 (difference between ₦2.8 million and ₦2 million)

14. Determination of Goodwill
FULL METHODOLOGY

Cost of combination:		₦' 000	₦' 000
• Cost of investment of **Arsenal** in **Chelsea**			29,120
• Non-controlling interest in **Chelsea** (At Acquisition-date fair value)			5,600
			34,720
Less: *Identifiable net assets of **Chelsea** acquired (@ 1 April 2011):*			
• Ordinary share capital		8,000	
• Share premium		2,000	
• Pre-acquisition Reserves:			
- Retained earnings	18,000		
- Fair value adjustment - Plant	3,000		
- Recogniton of unrecognized deferred tax liability	(1,000)	20,000	(30,000)
FULL Goodwill - positive			**4,720**
Less: *Impairment loss*			*(2,400)*
Consolidated Goodwill (@ 31 March 2012)			**2,320**

Alternatively, PARTIAL METHODOLOGY

	₦' 000	₦' 000
Cost of investment of **Arsenal** in **Chelsea**		29,120
Less: Arsenal's share of Identifiable net assets of **Chelsea** acquired:		
• Share capital (80% of ₦8 million)	6,400	
• Share premium (80% of ₦2 million)	1,600	
• Pre-acquisition reserves (80% of ₦20 million)	16,000	(24,000)
Goodwill attributable to **FARA's** (a)		5,120
Amount of investments of non-controlling interest in **Chlesea**		5,600
Less: Non-controlling interest share of the fair value of subsidiary's net assets:		
• Share capital (20% of ₦8 million)	1,600	
• Share premium (20% of ₦2 million)	400	
Pre-acquisition reserves (20% of ₦20 million)	4,000	(6,000)
Negative Goodwill attributable to **non-controlling interests** (b)		(400)
Full Goodwill (a + b)		4,720
Less: Impairment loss		(2,400)
Consolidated Goodwill (@ 31 March 2012)		**2,320**

15. Investment in Barca (Associate)

Carrying Amount (Based on Equity Method of Accounting):	₦'000
Cost of investment in Batrca	6,000
Share of post—acquisition reserves (30% of ₦2 million)	600
Adjustments:	
- Unrealised profit of sale of goods by Arsenal to Barca	(480)
	6,510

16. Non-controlling Interest as @ 31 March 2012:

	₦'000
Added on acquisition @ 1 April 2011	5,600
Share of post—acquisition reserves (20% of ₦8 million)	1,600
Adjustments:	
- Impairment loss on goodwill	(480)
- Additional depreciation on plant	(120)
	6,600

17. Consolidated Retained Earnings as @ 31 March 2012:

	₦'000
Arsenal's retained earnings (16,200 + 14,000)	30,200
Share of post—acquisition reserves (80% of ₦8 million)	6,400
Adjustments:	
- Share of Barca's (Associate) post-acquisition profit	600
- Impairment loss on goodwill	(1,920)
- Additional depreciation on plant	(480)
- Unrealised profit on goods in-transit	(500)
- Unrealised profit on goods sold to Barca	(90)
- Fair value gains on financial assets	800
- Finance cost (unwound discount on deferred cash consideration	(512)
	34,498

Exercise 5

The Management of FARA Plc went on an investment spree (extravaganza) after a careful decision and investment analysis were completed by its BOARD. The investment included the following:

- On 1 January 2013, FARA acquired 40% of the equity capital of MADE. The purchase consideration comprised the following:
    - An issue of equity shares (Exchanged 2 shares of FARA for 5 shares of MADE, when the market price of FARA share was ₦1.50, and MADE was ₦0.75 as at 1 January 2013)
    - A deferred cash payment of ₦5 million due on 1 January 2017. On 1 January 2013, FARA's hurdle rate (i.e. cost of capital) was 10% per annum.
- No entry has yet been made in FARA's financial statements regarding the investment except for 10% Bond Investment of ₦8 million made by FARA in MADE sometimes in 2011 which constituted part of the investments reported in the financial statements.
- The other 60% of MADE's shares are held by a wide variety of investors, none of whom owns more than 0·5% individually. None of the other shareholders has any arrangements to consult any of the others or make collective decisions. Since 1 January 2013, FARA has actively participated in establishing the operating and financial policies of MADE.
- On 1 January 2013, FARA equally acquired 5 million shares in MOLA for the sum of ₦4 million which has since been recorded in the books of FARA as at acquisition date at fair value.

Statement of Financial Position as at 31st December 2014

ASSETS:	FARA	MADE	MOLA
Non-current assets	₦' 000	₦' 000	₦' 000
Property, plant and equipment (Note 2)	98,000	30,000	10,000
Investments (Note 1)	20,000	5,000	1,000
Intangible assets	2,000	1,500	5,000
	120,000	36,500	16,000
Current assets			
Inventories (Note 3)	25,000	18,000	10,000
Trade and other receivables (Note 4)	43,000	24,500	12,000
Cash and cash equivalents	12,000	5,000	2,000
Total Assets	**200,000**	**84,000**	**40,000**
EQUITY & LIABILITIES:			
Share Capital & Reserves:			
Ordinary share capital (@ ₦1 per share)	50,000	20,000	10,000
Retained earnings	42,000	15,000	9,000
Other component of equity	10,000	5,000	3,000
	102,000	40,000	22,000
Non-current liabilities			
10% Bond (Note 2)	50,000	10,000	-
Deferred tax liability	4,000	2,000	1,000
	54,000	12,000	1,000
Current liabilities			
Trade and other payables (Note 4)	31,000	28,000	15,000
Current tax payable	12,000	4,000	2,000
Provision	1,000	-	-
Total Equity and Liabilities	**200,000**	**84,000**	**40,000**

Comprehensive Exercises

Statement of Profit of Loss and Other Comprehensive Income
for the year ended December 31, 2014

	FARA	MADE	MOLA
	₦'000	₦'000	₦'000
Revenue	320,000	140,000	120,000
Cost of sales	(180,000)	(80,000)	(70,000)
Gross profit	**140,000**	**60,000**	**50,000**
Administrative expenses	(50,000)	(21,000)	(18,000)
Personnel costs	(60,000)	(24,000)	(22,000)
Depreciation, amortization and impairment charges	(11,000)	(2,500)	(1,000)
Operating profit	**19,000**	**12,500**	**9,000**
Other income	1,800	500	200
Finance cost	(5,000)	(1,000)	-
Profit on before tax	**15,800**	**12,000**	**9,200**
Income taxes	(3,800)	(3,000)	(2,200)
Profit for the year	**12,000**	**9,000**	**7,000**
Other comprehensive income:			
Gains on revaluation of property	4,000	-	400
Fair value gain/(loss) on Financial Assets	(3,000)	1,000	100
Total Comprehensive Income	**13,000**	**10,000**	**7,500**

Statement of Changes in Reserves for the year ended 31 December 2014

	FARA Retained Earnings	FARA Other Component of Equity	MADE Retained Earnings	MADE Other Component of Equity	MOLA Retained Earnings	MOLA Other Component of Equity
	₦'000	₦'000	₦'000	₦'000	₦'000	₦'000
As at 1 January 2014	30,000	9,000	6,000	4,000	2,000	2,500
Profit for the year	12,000		9,000		7,000	
Other comprehensive income:						
Gain on revaluation of property		4,000		-		400
Fair value gain/(loss) on financial assets		(3,000)		1,000		100
As at 31 December 2014	42,000	10,000	15,000	5,000	9,000	3,000

Notes:

1. The investment of FARA comprises 10% Bond investment in MADE, investment in ordinary shares of MOLA and others in Available-for-Sale Financial Assets. The Reserves as at 1 January 2013 (i.e. Retained Earnings and Other component of Equity) is as follows:

    MADE – Accumulated losses is ₦3 million and other component of equity of ₦1 million.
    MOLA – Retained earnings is ₦1 million and other component of equity of ₦2 million.
    ** Other component of equity comprises of Share Premium and other reserves.

2. As at I January 2013, the fair value of assets and liabilities equal the carrying amount except for Plant with a Fair Value of ₦10 million and a Carrying Amount of ₦8 million in the books of MADE which has a remaining useful life of 5 years as at that date.

3. FARA usually buy goods from its investee - MADE but sold to MOLA and as at the reporting date, included in the inventory of FARA are goods purchased from MADE for ₦20 million and included in the inventory of MOLA are goods purchased from FARA for ₦10 million respectively. The profits made on inter-company sales are pegged at 10% of Cost.

4. The Inter-company trade receivable and trade payable did not agree due to cash payment made by FARA to MADE on 31 December 2014 but was not credited to MADE until 3rd January 2015. The outstanding balances shown in the respective books are as thus:
   MADE – Trade Receivable of ₦4 million
   FARA – Trade Payable to MADE of ₦3 million

5. The accounting policy of FARA indicates that at any point when a subsidiary is acquired, its policy regarding accounting for any non-controlling interest would be at acquisition-date fair value.

Required:

a) Discuss the appropriateness of the directors' view that MADE became a subsidiary of FARA on 1 January 2013.

b) Prepare the consolidated statement of financial position, consolidated statement of profit or loss and other comprehensive income, and consolidated statement of changes in equity of FARA for the year ended 31 December 2014, assuming MADE is a subsidiary from 1 January 2013, and that the Goodwill (if any) has been impaired in the total of ₦2,215,000 (2013 – ₦ 1million and 2014 – ₦1,215,000).

Solution to Exercise 5

a) Discussion of status of investment in MADE

Under the principles of IFRS 10 – Consolidated Financial Statements – MADE became a subsidiary of FARA on 1 January 2013 if FARA obtained control of MADE on that date. IFRS 10 states that an investor controls an investee if and only if the investor has:
- o Power over the investee: Given the absolute size of its shareholding relative to the other shareholdings and the absence of any collective agreements between the other shareholders, it would appear that FARA does indeed have power over MADE.
- o Exposure to variable returns from its involvement with the investee: FARA's shareholding will entitle FARA to dividends which will vary with the level of MADE's profits.
- o Ability to use its power to affect those returns: Given its effective control of the board of directors, FARA is able to control the operating and financial policies of MADE which will affect its profits and in turn its dividends.

Therefore MADE would be regarded as a subsidiary of FARA from 1 January 2013.

b) **FARA Group**
Consolidated Statement of Financial Position as at 31st December 2014

		₦'000
ASSETS:		
Non-current assets		
Property, plant and equipment (98,000 + 30,000 + 2,000 – 800)		129,200
Investment in MOLA (associate)		6,023
Other investment in financial assets (20,000 + 5,000 – 4,000 – 8,000)		13,000
Intangible assets – Goodwill		8,800
Others (2,000 + 1,500)		3,500
		160,523
Current assets		
Inventories (25,000 + 18,000 – 1,818)		41,182
Trade and other receivables (43,000 + 24,500 – 1,000 + 3,000)		63,500
Cash and cash equivalents (12,000 + 5,000 + 1,000)		18,000
Total Assets		**283,205**
EQUITY & LIABILITIES:		
Share Capital & Reserves		
Ordinary share capital (50,000 + 3,200)		53,200
Retained earnings		48,322
Other component of equity		18,250
Equity attributable to the shareholders' of FARA		**119,772**
Non-controlling interest		28,300
Total Equity		**148,072**
Non-current liabilities		
10% Bond (50,000 + 10,000 – 8,000)	42,000	
Provision for deferred cash consideration	4,133	
Deferred tax liability (4,000 + 2,000)	8,000	
		62,133
Current liabilities		
Trade and other payables (31,000 + 28,000 – 3,000)	56,000	
Current tax payable (12,000 + 4,000)	16,000	
Provision (1,000 + 0)	1,000	73,000
Total Equity and Liabilities		**283,205**

FARA Group
Consolidated Statement of Profit of Loss and Other Comprehensive Income
for the year ended December 31, 2014

	₦'000
Revenue (320,000 + 140,000 - 20,000)	440,000
Cost of sales (180,000 + 80,000 – 18,182)	(241,818)
Gross profit	**198,182**
Administrative expenses (50,000 + 21,000 – 1,215)	(72,215)
Personnel costs (60,000 + 24,000)	(84,000)
Depreciation, amortization and impairment charges (11,000 + 2,500 - 400)	(13,900)
Share of MOLA's (associate) profit	1,523
Operating profit	**29,590**
Other income (1,800 + 500 - 800)	1,500
Finance cost (5,000 + 1,000 - 800 + 376)	(5,576)
Profit on before tax	**25,514**
Income taxes (3,800 + 3,000)	(6,800)
Profit for the year	**18,714**

Other comprehensive income:		
Gains on revaluation of property (4,000 + 100)	4,100	
Fair value gain/(loss) on Financial Assets (1,000 – 3,000 +25)	(1,975)	2,125
Total Comprehensive Income		**20,839**

Profit attributable to:	
Owners of FARA	15,374
Non-controlling interest	3,340
	18,714
Total Comprehensive Income attributable to:	
Owners of FARA	16,899
Non-controlling interest	3,940
	20,839

FARA Group
Consolidated Statement of Changes in Equity for the year ended 31 December 2014

	Share Capital	Retained Earnings	Other Component of Equity	Equity Attributable to FARA	Non-controlling Interest	Total Equity
	₦'000	₦'000	₦'000	₦'000	₦'000	₦'000
As at 1 January 2014	53,200	32,948	16,725	102,873	24,360	127,233
Profit for the year		15,374		15,374	3,340	18,714
Other comprehensive income:						
Gain on revaluation of property			4,100	4,100	-	4,100
Fair value gain/(loss) on financial assets			(2,575)	(2,575)	600	(1,975)
As at 31 December 2014	53,200	48,322	18,250	119,772	28,300	148,072

Comprehensive Exercises

Working Notes

1. **Purchase Consideration of FARA acquisition of MADE**

	₦'000
Shares Exchange	9,600
Deferred [Cash] Consideration	3,415
	13,015

2. **Shares Exchange (or Shares Consideration)**
    - 2 shares of FARA is exchanged for 5 shares of MADE
    - MADE shares in issue amounted to 40 million (being share capital of ₦20 million divided by nominal price of ₦0.50 kobo per ordinary share)
    - FARA acquired 16 million of MADE's ordinary shares (being 40% of 40 million shares)
    - Hence, FARA shares offered in exchange amounted to 6.4 million (being 2/5 of 16 million MADE's ordinary shares acquired).
    - Fair value of the shares consideration @ ₦1.50 per share of 6.4 million shares offered amounted to ₦9.6 million

    Accounting Entry:
Debit:	Investment in MADE	-	₦9.6 million
Credit:	Ordinary share capital	-	₦3.2 million
Credit:	Other component of equity (Share premium)	-	₦6.4 million

3. **Deferred [Cash] Consideration**
    - Additional cash consideration deferred till 1 January 2017 was ₦5 million
    - Time to settlement from acquisition is 4 years and cost of capital of 10%
    - Hence, the present value at acquisition date amounted to ₦3,415,067 (being ₦5 million multiplied by the discounting factor of $(1.1)^{-4}$

    Accounting Entry:
Debit:	Investment in MADE	-	₦3,415,067
Credit:	Provision for deferred consideration	-	₦3,415,067

4. **Measurement of Non-Controlling Interest (NCI) as at Acquisition-Date (1 January 2013)**
    - MADE's ordinary shares held by NCI amounted to 24 million (being 60% of 40 million shares of MADE)
    - The acquisition-date fair value @ ₦0.75 per share of 24 million shares amounted to ₦18 million.

5. **Fair Value Adjustment on Acquisition of MADE**

	₦'000
Fair value of plant	10,000
Carrying Amount	(8,000)
	2,000

    Accounting Entry:
Debit: Group plant	-	₦2 million
Credit: Pre - Acquisition Reserves	-	₦2 million

6. **Additional Depreciation**
    - Accumulated adjustment for depreciation (2 years) amounted to ₦800,000 (being 2/5 years of ₦2 million)

Accounting Entry:

Debit:	Consolidated retained earnings (40% of ₦800,000)	-	₦320,000
Debit:	Non-controlling interest (60% of ₦800,000)	-	₦480,000
Credit:	Group plant	-	₦800,000

Impacts further analyzed as thus:
- Prior year(s) – 2013 (1/5 years x ₦2 million) = ₦400,000
- Current year – 2014 (1/5 years x ₦2 million) = ₦400,000

7. **Unrealised profit on inventories with:**

	FARA	MOLA
Mark-up = Profit/Cost Price	10.00%	10.00%
Margin = Profit/(Cost Price + Profit)	9.09%	9.09%
Inventory value (₦'000)	20,000	10,000
Unrealised profit – ₦'000 (Margin x Inventory value)	1,818	909
Adjustment for 25% stake in Associate (25% x ₦909,000)		227

Accounting Entry:

Debit:	Consolidated retained earnings (40% of ₦1,818,182)	-	₦727,273
Debit:	Non-controlling interest (60% of ₦1,818,182)	-	₦1,090,909
Credit:	Group inventory	-	₦1,818,182

With ₦1,818,182 (since the sales was made by the MADE to FARA – Upstream Transaction, the adjustment is charged against FARA and Non-controlling Interest in ratio 40% to 60%)

Accounting Entry:

Debit:	Consolidated retained earnings (40% of ₦1,818,182)	-	₦227,273
Credit:	Investment in MOLA (Associate)	-	₦227,273

Group Profit Adjustments:
- Intercompany Sales (FARA and MADE) = ₦20 million
- Intercompany cost of sales (Intercompany sales of ₦20 million – Unrealised profit of ₦1,818,182) = ₦18,181,818

8. **Cash-In-Transit**

    The amount of reconciled difference between the inter-company payable and intercompany receivable between FARA and MADE amounted to ₦1 million (being ₦4 million – ₦3 million)

    Accounting Entry:

Debit:	Group cash and cash equivalents	-	₦1 million
Credit:	Trade Receivable - MADE	-	₦1 million

9. **Elimination of Inter-Company Balance**

	FARA Payable	MADE Receivable
	₦'000	₦'000
As at 31 December 2014	3,000	4,000
Less: Cash in-transit		(1,000)
	3,000	**3,000**

    Accounting Entry:

Debit:	Trade payable – FARA	-	₦3 million
Credit:	Trade Receivable - MADE	-	₦3 million

10. **Impairment on [Full] Goodwill**

    The accumulated impairment losses on goodwill as at the reporting date 31 December 2014 amounted to ₦2,215,000

Comprehensive Exercises

Accounting Entry:

Debit: Consolidated retained earnings (40% of ₦2,215,000)	- ₦886,000
Debit: Non-controlling interest (60% of ₦2,215,000)	- ₦1,329,000
Credit: Goodwill	- ₦2,215,000

The impairment loss on the goodwill is charged against the parent and non-controlling interest in proportion to which they share the profit or loss of the subsidiary, and this is as a result of non-controlling interest contributing to the amount of goodwill recognised on acquisition of MADE.

Impacts further analyzed as thus:
- Prior year(s) – 2013 = ₦1,000,000
- Current year – 2014 = ₦1,215,000

11. **Elimination of Inter-Company Loans**
    Accounting Entry:

Debit: 10% Bond Liability of MADE	₦8 million
Credit: Investment in Financial Assets by FARA	₦8 million

12. **Elimination of Inter-Company Interests on Loan**
    The annual interest expense to be eliminated amounted to ₦800,000 (i.e. 10% of ₦8 million)
    Accounting Entry:

Debit: Other income of FARA	₦800,000
Credit: Finance cost of MADE	₦800,000

13. **Adjustments on Unwinding of Discounts**

    Unwound discount: ₦'000

Present value (PV) @ 31 December 2014 = ₦5 million*$(1.1)^{-2}$	4,132
Present value (PV) @ 1 January 2013 = ₦5 million*$(1.1)^{-4}$	3,415
Finance costs for 2013 & 2014	**717**

    Accounting Entry:

Debit: Consolidated retained earnings	- ₦717,164
Credit: Provisions – Deferred consideration	- ₦717,164

    Impacts further analyzed as thus:
    - Prior year(s) – 2013   ₦'000

Present value (PV) @ 31 December 2013 = ₦5 million*$(1.1)^{-3}$	3,757
Present value (PV) @ 1 January 2013 = ₦5 million*$(1.1)^{-4}$	3,415
Finance costs for 2013	**342**

    - Prior year(s) – 2014   ₦'000

Present value (PV) @ 31 December 2014 = ₦5 million*$(1.1)^{-2}$	4,132
Present value (PV) @ 31 December 2013 = ₦5 million*$(1.1)^{-3}$	3,757
Finance costs for 2014	**376**

14. **Determination of Goodwill**
    FULL METHODOLOGY

	₦'000	₦'000
Cost of combination:		
• Cost of investment of **FARA** in **MADE**		13,015
• Non-controlling interest in **MADE** (*At Acquisition-date fair value*)		18,000
		31,015

457

Less: Identifiable net assets of MADE acquired (@ 1 January 2013):

• Ordinary share capital	20,000		
• Pre-acquisition Reserves:			
- Accumulated losses	(3,000)		
- Other component of equity	1,000		
- Fair value adjustment on plant	2,000	-	(20,000)

FULL Goodwill - positive   **11,015**
Less: Impairment loss   *(2,215)*
Consolidated Goodwill (@ 31 December 2014)   **8,800**

Alternatively, PARTIAL METHODOLOGY   ₦' 000   ₦' 000
Cost of investment of **FARA** in **MADE**   13,015
Less: **FARA's** share of Identifiable net assets of **MADE** acquired:
• Share capital (40% of ₦20 million)   8,000
• Pre-acquisition reserves (80% of NIL after adjustment)   -   (8,000)
Goodwill attributable to FARA's (a)   *5,015*
Amount of investments of non-controlling interest in **MADE**   18,000
Less: Non-controlling interest share of the fair value of subsidiary's net assets:
• Share capital (60% of ₦20 million)   12,000
• Pre-acquisition reserves (80% of NIL after adjustment)   -   (12,000)
Goodwill attributable to non-controlling interests (b)   *6,000*
Full Goodwill (a + b)   **11,015**
Less: Impairment loss   *(2,215)*
Consolidated Goodwill (@ 31 December 2014)   **8,800**

15. Consolidated Reserves and Non-Controlling Interest as @ 31 December 2014

Determining Consolidated Reserves and Non-controlling Interest as @ 31 December 2014	Retained Earnings (40%)	Other Component of Equity (40%)	Non-Controlling Interest (60%)
	₦' 000	₦' 000	₦' 000
FARA Reserves	42,000	10,000	
Post-acquisition reserves of MADE:			
- Retained earnings (₦15 million - - ₦3 million)	7,200		10,800
- Other component of equity (₦5 million – ₦1 million)		1,600	2,400
Additional depreciation on plant	(320)		(480)
Unrealised profit on inventory of FARA	(727)		(1,091)
Unrealised profit on inventory of MOLA	(227)		
Impairment charges on Goodwill	(886)		(1,329)
Share of associate's (MOLA) post-acquisition profit/(loss)	2,000	250	
Added on acquisition of MADE (NCI @ Fair Value)			18,000
Share premium on acquisition of MADE		6,400	
Finance cost (unwound discounts)	(717)		
Balances as @ 31 December 2014	**48,322**	**18,250**	**28,300**

Comprehensive Exercises

16. Investment in MOLA (Associate) - *Equity Method:*	₦' 000	₦' 000
• Cost of investment of *FARA* in *MOLA*		4,000
• 25% share of post-acquisition profit:		
- Retained earnings (25% of {₦9 million – ₦1 million})	2,000	
- Other component of equity (25% of {₦3 million – ₦1 million})	250	
- Unrealised profit on inventory	(227)	2,023
		6,023

17. Consolidated Reserves and Non-Controlling Interest as @ 31 December 2014

Determining Consolidated Reserves and Non-controlling Interest as @ 1 January 2014	Retained Earnings (40%)	Other Component of Equity (40%)	Non-Controlling Interest (60%)
	₦' 000	₦' 000	₦' 000
FARA Reserves	30,000	9,000	
Post-acquisition reserves of MADE:			
- Retained earnings (₦6 million - - ₦3 million)	3,600		5,400
- Other component of equity (₦5 million – ₦1 million)		1,200	1,800
Additional depreciation on plant	(160)		(240)
Impairment charges on Goodwill	(400)		(600)
Share of associate's (MOLA) post-acquisition profit/(loss):			
- Retained earnings (₦2 million - - ₦1 million) @ 25%	250		
- Other component of equity (₦2.5 million – ₦2 million) @ 25%		125	
Added on acquisition of MADE (NCI @ Fair Value)			18,000
Share premium on acquisition of MADE		6,400	
Finance cost (unwound discounts)	(342)		
Balances as @ 31 December 2014	**32,948**	**16,725**	**24,360**

18. Profit for the year, attributed as thus:	FARA	NCI
	₦'000	₦'000
FARA Profit for the year	12,000	
MADE profit for the year (40%:60%)	3,600	5,400
Adjustments:		
- Share of MOLA's (Associate) profit {(25% of ₦7 million) - ₦227,273}	1,523	
- Unrealised profit on inventory (40%:60%)	(727)	(1,091)
- Finance cost (unwound discount) for the current year	(376)	
- Elimination of inter-company interest expense on loan	800	
- Elimination on inter-company interest income on loan	(800)	
- Impairment of Goodwill for the year (40%:60% 0f N1,215,000)	(486)	(729)
- Additional depreciation on plant for 2014 (40%:60%)	(160)	(240)
Profit for the year	**15,374**	**3,340**
Other comprehensive income, attributed as thus:		
- Gain on revaluation of FARA property	4,000	
- Fair value loss on financial assets of FARA	(3,000)	
- Fair value gain on financial assets of MADE (40%:60%)	400	600
- Gain on revaluation of MOLA property (25% of ₦400,000)	100	
- Fair value gain on financial assets of MOLA (25% of ₦100,000)	25	
Total Comprehensive Income	**16,899**	**3,940**

Bibliography

Companies and Allied Matters Act (CAMA C20 LFN 2004 as amended). *Law of the Federation of Nigeria (LFN)*. Nigeria.

Astranti Financial Training. (2014). *CIMA F2 Course Notes*. Strategic Business Coaching Ltd. Retrieved from www.astranti.com

BPP Learning Media. (2015). *Corporate Reporting - P2 (Study Text & Revision Kit)* (8th Edition (International and United Kingdom) ed.). London: BPP Learning Media Ltd.

BPP Learning Media. (2015). *Financial Reporting - F7 (Study Text & Revision Kit)* (8th Edition ed.). London: BPP Learning Media Ltd.

CFA Institute. (2010; 2011; 2012). *Financial Reporting and Analysis* (5th Edition; 6th Edition and 7th Edition ed., Vol. Volume 2; Level 2). Pearson Learning Solutions.

Chartered Institute of Management Accountants (CIMA). (2014). *PAPER F1 – FINANCIAL OPERATIONS*.

Deloitte. (2016). *IFRSs*. Retrieved from IASplus: www.iasplus.com

Deloitte. (2016). *iGAAP* (Vols. A-D). Wolters Kluwer.

Elliot, B. E. (2009). *Financial Accounting and Reporting* (13th Edition ed.). Singapore: Pearson Education South Asia Pte Ltd.

EY. (2016). *A comprehensive guide on Business Combinations*. EY.

Finch, C. (2012). *A student's guide to International Financial Reporting Standards* (3rd Edition ed.). Berkshire: Kaplan Publishing UK.

IFRS Foundation. (2016). *Blue Book - International Financial Reporting Standards* (Vol. 1 & 2). London: IFRS Foundation.

IFRS Foundation. (2016). *Green Book - International Financial Reporting Standards* (Vol. 1 & 2). London: IFRS Foundation.

IFRS Foundation. (2016). *Red Book - International Financial Reporting Standards* (Vol. 1 & 2). London: IFRS Foundation.

PWC. (2015 & 2016). *Manual of Accounting* (Vol. 1 & 2). West Sussex: Bloomsbury Professional (Bloomsbury Publishing Plc).

University, B. M. (n.d.). Group Accounting.

WILEY. (2009, 2011). *Interpretation and Application of International Financial Reporting Standards*. New Jersey: JohnWiley & Sons. Inc.

INDEX

1
100% OWNERSHIP OF THE SUBSIDIARY BY THE PARENT ..*80*

A
A COMPLEX GROUP STRUCTURE *79*
A SIMPLE GROUP STRUCTURE *78*
ACCOUNTING FOR GAINS ON BARGAIN PURCHASE *121*
ACCOUNTING TREATMENT OF FAIR VALUE IN A BUSINESS COMBINATION *150*
ACCRUED INTRA GROUP SERVICE CHARGES AND INCOME *243*
ACQUIREE *43*
ACQUIRER *43*
ACQUISITION DURING THE YEAR *138, 343*
ACQUISITION METHOD *9, 19, 40, 59, 60, 376, 394, 420*
ACQUISITION METHOD *10, 40, 59*
ACQUISITION-RELATED COSTS *50*
ADJUSTMENTS TO GROUP ACCOUNTS *199*
APPLICATION OF EQUITY METHOD *378*
ASSOCIATE'S LOSSES *379*
ASSOCIATES *9, 10, 11, 52, 66, 78, 269, 376, 377, 378, 379, 393, 394, 404, 407*
ATTRIBUTION OF LOSSES *52*

B
BARGAIN PURCHASE *43*
BASIC CONSOLIDATION TECHNIQUES *307*
BASIC PRINCIPLES OF CONSOLIDATION AND CONSOLIDATION MECHANICS *78*
BILLS OF EXCHANGE *247*
BILLS OF EXCHANGE DISCOUNTED *251*
BONUS ISSUE *263*
BUSINESS COMBINATIONS *3, 7, 9, 10, 11, 19, 23, 34, 39, 41, 45, 48, 63, 66, 96, 391*
BUSINESS MODELS *9*

C
CAMA *7, 13, 18, 38, 75, 76, 412*
CANCELLATION OF INTRA-GROUP TRANSACTIONS *323*
CAP C20 .... *7, 13, 38*
CASH CONSIDERATION *66*
CASH IN-TRANSIT *235*
CASH-GENERATING UNITS *112*
CIRCULAR COMBINATION *23*
CLASSIFYING JOINT ARRANGEMENTS *390*
COMPANIES AND ALLIED MATTERS ACT *7, 13, 38*
CONSOLIDATED FINANCIAL STATEMENTS *9, 10, 12, 41, 42, 45, 47, 48, 200, 201, 320, 377, 381, 405, 406, 452*
CONSOLIDATION SUBSEQUENT TO ACQUISITION AND ACCOUNTING FOR PRE & POST ACQUISITION RESERVES IN GROUP ACCOUNTS *87*
CONTEMPORARY ISSUES ON GROUP ACCOUNTS *49*
CONTINGENT CONSIDERATION *43, 53, 54, 362, 365, 437, 440*
CONTINGENT LIABILITIES *58*
CONTROL .*8, 9, 10, 11, 12, 19, 21, 23, 34, 37, 39, 42, 43, 44, 46, 47, 48, 49, 50, 51, 52, 57, 58, 59, 62, 63, 66, 75, 76, 83, 86, 87, 90, 99, 100, 102, 103, 105, 106, 108, 109, 111, 114, 117, 120, 122, 124, 127, 132, 133, 134, 138, 139, 142, 145, 146, 147, 153, 155, 158, 159, 162, 165, 166, 170, 174, 179, 180, 183, 186, 187, 188, 191, 194, 207, 211, 217, 222, 226, 231, 235, 239, 243, 246, 250, 254, 256, 258, 259, 263, 269, 273, 278, 281, 282, 285, 287, 306, 312, 377, 382, 385, 390, 391, 392, 393, 395, 397, 399, 402, 405, 406, 407, 408, 409, 410, 411, 414, 419, 452*
CONTROL *307*
CONTROLLING INTEREST *8, 9, 87, 408, 430, 445, 454, 457, 458*
CONTROLLING INTEREST INVESTMENTS *8*
COST OF COMBINATION *43*

D
DATE OF INCLUSION *51, 132*
DEBT CONSIDERATION *69*
DEBT SECURITIES *8*
DEFERRED OR CONTINGENT CONSIDERATION *69*
DEFINITION OF A BUSINESS *19*
DIAGONAL COMBINATION *23*
DIFFERENT REPORTING DATES *51*
DIVIDEND ANALYSIS *274*
DIVIDEND RECEIVED FROM ASSOCIATES *380*
DOWNSTREAM TRANSACTION *324, 326, 331, 337, 379, 446, 447*

E
EFFECT OF ELIMINATION ON UNREALIZED PROFIT ON NON-CONTROLLING INTEREST *328*
EQUITY INSTRUMENTS *9, 10*
EQUITY INTEREST *43*
EQUITY METHOD *9, 10, 376, 377, 378, 381, 384, 394, 448, 457*
EQUITY SECURITIES *8*
EVENTS AFTER THE REPORTING PERIOD *274*
EXCLUSION OF A SUBSIDIARY FROM CONSOLIDATION *49*
EXEMPTION FROM PREPARING GROUP ACCOUNTS *48*
EXERCISES .*39, 64, 76, 93, 130, 147, 177, 197, 304, 375, 393*
EXIT PRICE *12*

FAIR VALUE *151*

F

FAIR VALUE *43*
FAIR VALUE *149*
FAIR VALUE THROUGH OTHER COMPREHENSIVE INCOME
   (FVOCI) *9*
FAIR VALUE THROUGH PROFIT OR LOSS (FVTPL) *9*
FELLOW SUBSIDIARIES *395*
FINANCIAL INSTRUMENTS: RECOGNITION AND
   MEASUREMENT *378*

G

GAIN FROM A BARGAIN PURCHASE TRANSACTION *121*
GAIN ON A BARGAIN PURCHASE *53*
GOODS IN-TRANSIT *239*
GOODWILL *95*
GOODWILL AND IMPAIRMENT *56*
GROUP *42*
GROUP ACCOUNTS *1, 41, 87, 199, 312, 315, 321*

H

HOLDING COMPANY *13, 14, 15, 16, 17*
HORIZONTAL COMBINATION *23*

I

IAS 1 .... *18, 41, 306*
IAS 10 .... *274*
IAS 12 .... *41, 48*
IAS 21 .... *41, 113*
IAS 24 .... *41*
IAS 27 *10, 41, 42, 46, 48, 49, 52, 66, 274, 286, 299, 320, 391, 404, 408, 426*
IAS 28 *9, 10, 11, 41, 52, 66, 75, 76, 376, 377, 378, 391, 394, 405*
IAS 31 .... *9, 10*
IAS 32 *10, 11, 41, 50, 53, 62, 133, 134, 146, 147, 255, 303, 365, 373, 410, 412, 419*
IAS 36 .... *41, 56, 94, 112, 113, 121, 213, 301, 380*
IAS 37 *41, 53, 54, 58, 63, 70, 72, 150, 151, 178, 187, 196, 274, 422*
IAS 39 *9, 10, 11, 41, 49, 50, 52, 53, 54, 58, 60, 62, 66, 67, 69, 70, 72, 75, 76, 378, 380, 391, 410, 426*
IAS 7 .... *41*
IAS 8 .... *41, 56, 62, 73*
IASB *10, 274*
IFRS *7, 9, 10, 11, 12, 18, 19, 20, 34, 37, 38, 39, 40, 41, 42, 43, 44, 45, 46, 47, 48, 49, 50, 51, 52, 53, 54, 55, 57, 58, 59, 60, 62, 63, 66, 67, 69, 70, 72, 75, 76, 83, 84, 93, 95, 96, 100, 121, 129, 148, 149, 150, 151, 176, 177, 178, 179, 180, 187, 190, 193, 196, 198, 222, 274, 301, 302, 308, 310, 311, 313, 315, 316, 317, 318, 321, 322, 324, 326, 327, 329, 331, 332, 334, 335, 337, 338, 340, 341, 343, 344, 345, 346, 348, 351, 353,* *354, 356, 357, 358, 359, 360, 361, 363, 366, 369, 370, 371, 376, 377, 378, 380, 385, 386, 390, 391, 394, 400, 403, 404, 405, 406, 408, 410, 411, 415, 420, 422, 426, 434, 435, 438, 439, 452*
IFRS 10 .... *9, 42, 49, 52, 178, 408, 410, 452*
IFRS 11 .... *391*
IFRS 13 .... *43*
IFRS 39 *, 10, 11, 19, 20, 39, 40, 41, 42, 43, 44, 45, 47, 48, 50, 52, 53, 54, 55, 57, 58, 59, 60, 63, 70, 72, 83, 93, 95, 96, 100, 121, 129, 148, 149, 150, 151, 176, 177, 178, 179, 187, 190, 193, 310, 353, 391, 408, 410, 411, 415, 420, 422*
IFRS 7 .... *11*
IFRS 9 *9, 10, 11, 41, 49, 50, 52, 53, 54, 58, 62, 66, 67, 69, 70, 72, 75, 76, 378, 380, 391, 405, 410, 426*
IMPAIRMENT LOSS ON GOODWILL *356*
IMPAIRMENT LOSSES IN ASSOCIATE *380*
IMPAIRMENT OF GOODWILL *112*
INDEMNIFICATION ASSETS *55*
INTER-COMPANY DIVIDENDS – ORDINARY SHARES *315*
INTER-CORPORATE INVESTMENT *392, 408*
INTER-CORPORATE INVESTMENTS *8, 37, 39, 408*
INTERESTS IN JOINT ARRANGEMENTS AND ASSOCIATES *407*
INTERESTS IN SUBSIDIARIES *406*
INTERESTS IN UNCONSOLIDATED STRUCTURED ENTITIES *407*
INTERESTS IN UNCONSOLIDATED SUBSIDIARIES *406*
INTERNATIONAL ACCOUNTING STANDARD BOARD *10, 18*
INTERNATIONAL FINANCIAL REPORTING *7, 10, 11, 18, 37, 41*
INTRA GROUP CURRENT ACCOUNTS *231*
INTRA GROUP LOANS *255*
INTRA-GROUP INTERESTS *321*
INTRA-GROUP SALES *324*
INTRA-GROUP TRANSFER/SALE OF PROPERTY, PLANT &
   EQUIPMENT *213*
INVESTMENT ENTITIES CONSOLIDATION EXEMPTION *48*

J

JOINT ARRANGEMENT *44, 390*
JOINT CONTROL *10, 44*
JOINT CONTROL *8, 44, 390, 392*
JOINT OPERATION *44, 390, 391, 392, 405*
JOINT OPERATION *44*
JOINT OPERATIONS *390*
JOINT VENTURE *10, 37, 42, 44, 54, 66, 199, 269, 273, 307, 376, 377, 390, 391, 392, 393, 394, 405, 408*
JOINT VENTURE *8, 9, 10, 426*
JOINT VENTURES *391*

L

LESS THAN 100% OWNERSHIP OF THE SUBSIDIARY BY THE PARENT *83*

M

MEASUREMENT PERIOD *56*
MECHANICS OF CONSOLIDATION *306*
MID-YEAR ACQUISITION *138*
MID-YEAR ACQUISITION AND RECOGNITION OF GAIN ON BARGAIN PURCHASE *351*
MINORITY ACTIVE *8, 9, 10, 408*
MINORITY PASSIVE *8, 9, 10, 408*

N

NEGATIVE GOODWILL *121*
NON-CONTROLLING INTEREST *42*
NON-CONTROLLING INTEREST *306*

O

OTHER COMPREHENSIVE INCOME *353*

P

PARENT *42*
PARENT-SUBSIDIARY RELATIONSHIP *41, 81, 84, 88, 98, 100, 103, 106, 109, 115, 117, 122, 125, 133, 134, 139, 143, 153, 156, 159, 162, 166, 170, 180, 183, 189, 192, 205, 209, 214, 219, 223, 228, 232, 236, 240, 244, 248, 252, 256, 259, 265, 270, 275, 279, 282, 287, 347, 349, 382, 395, 397, 436*
POST-ACQUISITION RESERVE *43*
POTENTIAL VOTING RIGHT *50*
POWER *42, 46, 47, 452*
PRE-ACQUISITION RESERVE *43*

R

RECOGNITION OF INVESTMENT IN ASSOCIATES IN THE SEPARATE FINANCIAL STATEMENT OF THE INVESTOR *378*
REGULATORY REQUIREMENTS *10*
RELATED PARTY TRANSACTION *199*
RESERVES BROUGHT FORWARD *306*
RESTRUCTURING AND FUTURE COSTS *54*
REVERSE ACQUISITIONS *57, 411*

Printed in Great Britain
by Amazon